FROM ANNE TO VICTORIA

FROM
ANNE TO VICTORIA

Essays by various hands

Edited by
Bonamy Dobrée

Essay Index Reprint Series

Originally published by:

CASSELL
and Company Limited

BOOKS FOR LIBRARIES PRESS, INC.
FREEPORT, NEW YORK

First published 1937
Reprinted 1967

Reprinted from a copy in the collections of
The New York Public Library
Astor, Lenox and Tilden Foundations

LIBRARY OF CONGRESS CATALOG CARD NUMBER:
67-30184

PRINTED IN THE UNITED STATES OF AMERICA

CONTENTS

v

CONTENTS

INTRODUCTION

WE begin in a dim and distant world of periwigs and Jacobite movements, of virulent religious feelings and the tittle-tattle of *The Spectator*, of a great war and the polished couplets of Pope: we end in an age when the clothes were not very different from our own and the rightness of Whiggery was largely accepted, in the age of evangelicalism and the Oxford Movement, of terrific Magazines (with a capital M) peremptorily laying down the law; we are well in the period of a great peace, and an age in which romantic poetry has conquered the rigour of Pope. At the beginning the landed interest was still supreme, though, as Swift noted, the moneyed interest had begun its inroads on the old structure; at the end society is at grips with the Industrial Revolution and the power of finance. In short we emerge from "history", from a time whose problems seem remote, into a period of which we are now living out the end, grappling with the problems that it in its turn hatched out.

Most of us were brought up with a picture of the eighteenth century as The Age of Reason; it has latterly, with more justice, been called the century of passion, or the century of uneasy romanticism. The truth is that, as Blake remarked: "All the ages are equal," compounded of much the same measure of common sense and irrationality. And if we look at the eighteenth century, who, among the people who rank as great, can really be described as reasonable? You can count them on the fingers of one hand. Addison, shall we say,

INTRODUCTION

Robert Walpole, Chesterfield, Hume, and—well, who? Jane Austen, if we can include her as belonging to the eighteenth century. Steele was certainly not reasonable, Pope and Swift were neurotics, the latter almost maniacal; Chatham's gloomy fits were probably due to manic depressive insanity, and the greatest poets were mad, Smart, Cowper, and, in a sense, Blake. Horace Walpole was a sensitive, and perhaps the first sur-realist writer; Wesley was one of the most passionate men that ever lived. The scientists and architects were no more and no less reasonable than scientists and architects are in any age. The mass of the people was far less reasonable than that of either the preceding or succeeding centuries; the mob rioted on every possible occasion, over the Gin Act, over a supposed threat to Protestantism—far more alarmingly and with much less cause than in the days of the Popish Plot, over employing foreigners in a theatre, over the activities of the Wesleys. Nor was the age an irreligious one; there was a proportion of sceptics such as Mandeville and Gibbon, but there had been atheists in Elizabeth's day, and the nine-teenth century hatched out a swarm of agnostics.

What one can really say about the eighteenth century is that it was a brutal age, and, like so many brutal ages it had its superficial garniture of exquisite refinement, its veneer, which in the arts shows itself in a love of finish, and in society as a determination of fops and beaux to the drawing- and pump-rooms—Beau Nash, Beau Brummell, the Prince Regent. In fact most people when they think of the eighteenth century conjure up their memory of the last revival they saw of a Sheridan play. Emotionally the veneer shows itself as sentimentality; the word itself was invented in the eighteenth century, by Sterne. Not that Sterne himself was sentimental in the bad sense, but others were; there was Mackenzie and *The Man of Feeling* school. But, as the basis of all this, the condition of the people was appalling, terribly indigent in the

country, animal and gin-sodden in the towns, while the most
trifling offences were punished with a revolting ferocity. With
all these contrasts it is not surprising that it was an extremely
interesting century in producing a series of fascinating
'characters'; it is interesting also in that it witnessed the
birth of much that was to be the hallmark of the nineteenth
century, as one would, of course, expect—if there is any
causality or sequence in history.

Politically it was the period of the second great struggle
between Parliament and Prerogative, or, to put it another
way, the Georges tried in vain to maintain the constitution
as it had been handed to them; they failed, owing largely to
the rise to power of the money interest, which, in its efforts
to make its foreign investments profitable, lost us the American
Colonies. In literature, the period was that in which the
foundations of the romantic movement were laid, by Aken-
side, Young, Collins, Percy and the ballads, Blake. We are
apt to forget that *Lyrical Ballads* was first published in 1798.
Music and the drama died, and remained dead in the next
century, but on the other hand the novel as we know it was
born and made great strides towards maturity, while the pioneer
work in Shakespeare criticism was being done. In architecture,
the century saw, alas, the beginnings of the Gothic revival.
Wesley and his helpers founded the evangelical movement,
and made evangelicalism the moral characteristic of the early
part of the nineteenth century; Wesley himself was a Puseyite
before Pusey. But perhaps the most significant thing is the
birth of the social conscience which made the England of
the nineteenth century the great reformist and 'meliorist'
country of the world. At the beginning of the eighteenth
century very few people cared about the poor, though there
were indeed Charity Schools; but later there was Howard
with his prison reforms, Shelburne with his model villages,
and Wilberforce agitating for the abolition of the slave trade.

INTRODUCTION

The naval mutineers of 1797 had a great many sympathisers in the country. One can say that during the century England became far more tolerant and humane; this spirit led to Catholic Emancipation in the first thirty years of the nineteenth century, and the Factory Acts of 1834. In fact we can say that in almost every department of life the period from the accession of Queen Anne to that of Queen Victoria witnessed a revolution.

It will be easy for every reader to compile a list twice as long as the one of persons included in this volume, consisting of men or women who ought on no account to have been left out. Among statesmen, where is Newcastle, or Shelburne? Among soldiers why are Stanhope and Cornwallis not here, both extremely interesting people?—among sailors why not Hood and Howe? Why is there no essay on Richardson or Jane Austen, on Hume or Hartley, on Goldsmith or Gibbon, on Cowper or Crabbe or Cobbett? Why are Cavendish, Jenner, and Watt omitted, and Reynolds, Gainsborough and Chambers? Why, all the most important figures have been omitted! That is true; but there are limits to the size of a book, and I have attempted to gather together for appreciation a number of men and women who will, between them, give a fairly representative picture of the age in all its variety. I have tried to include one at least of each kind of person, and though this is an impossible task since every individual is unique, I hope I have included the chief of those of each kind who had an influence on the succeeding age, throwing in one or two who had no influence at all, for the sake of giving greater verisimilitude to the picture. Very often it has been the mere toss of a coin that has decided whether one man or another should be represented. But if my own faults as editor are obvious, I am confident that they will be largely compensated by the virtues of the distinguished writers who have been kind enough to contribute, and whom I would here like to thank for their help.

BONAMY DOBRÉE.

JOHN CHURCHILL, DUKE OF MARLBOROUGH

(1650–1722)

by A. S. TURBERVILLE

BY universal consent John Churchill, Duke of Marlborough has only one possible rival among great English soldiers—the Duke of Wellington. Wellington had a complete singleness of character, integrity of purpose, and austere devotion to rigid canons of duty and loyalty beyond the reach of Churchill, even accepting the most favourable interpretation of the latter's character and conduct: on the other hand, Marlborough was Wellington's intellectual superior, was more nimble-witted, more imaginative, more gifted with those powers and intuitions which we are wont to describe as genius.

Let us consider both the man and the soldier. In his own day, when party antagonisms were fierce, the character of Marlborough was industriously painted in the blackest colours, and he was accused of vicious living in his youth, of meanness, avarice, and financial dishonesty, of the grossest perfidy, and of an egotism so overweening that he was prepared to protract a great war deliberately for the gratification of his selfish military ambitions. The rancour of his enemies knew no restraint, and he was unmercifully traduced, not only in the scurrilous lampoons of the Grub Street hack, and in the scandalous anecdotes of Mrs. Manley's abusive allegory, *The New Atlantis*, but also in the much more reputable pages of the political pamphlets and the self-styled histories of so great a writer as Swift. In later times a most damaging version of Marlborough's character has been popularized by Macaulay. Led astray as he so often was by his instinct for the dramatic, seeing everything in the hardest tones of black and white, Macaulay chose to exhibit in the career of Marlborough a glaring contrast between the most splendid talents and the most depraved instincts. Unfortunately Macaulay in his *History* deals with that period in which the crimes with which Churchill has been charged are alleged to have been committed; he did not live to relate the reign of Queen Anne in which Churchill's great triumphs were accomplished. Recently a complete vindication of Marlborough has been attempted by Mr. Winston Churchill in his brilliant biography of his great ancestor.* Unfortunately, while assailing the errors of his *bête-noire*, Macaulay, with an almost vindictive assiduity, Mr. Churchill reveals a quite remarkable likeness to him not only in the picturesqueness, animation and often rhetorical quality of his narrative, but also in the violence of his partisanship. Though it may be agreed that in the majority of instances he has proved his case, the adoption of a more judicial method would have done a greater service in the end to his hero's memory.

---

*Many books have been written about Marlborough, some of them of small worth, but the following are valuable in their different ways. The earliest, published in 1736, is by T. Lediard, who took part in several of the campaigns. Coxe's *Memoirs of Marlborough* is dull to read, but it is based upon the original authorities, accurate, and of balanced judgment. It cannot be regarded as wholly superseded even by Mr. Winston Churchill's infinitely more interesting work, which will undoubtedly become the standard biography. The unfinished study of the Duke's campaigns by the late Mr. F. Taylor was a purely military study, but one of high merit. Mr. C. T. Atkinson's book in the Heroes of the Nation Series is the best life within the compass of a single volume. There is a very brief outline life by the late Sir John Fortescue, but it is better to read the relevant portions of his *History of the British Army*, Vol. I.

JOHN CHURCHILL, DUKE OF MARLBOROUGH

John Churchill, one of the twelve children of Sir Winston Churchill, was born at Ashe near Axminster on June 6, 1650. He received some education at St. Paul's School, but early entered the household of James, Duke of York, Charles II's younger brother, as a page. His sister Arabella joined the same royal household, and became James's mistress, bearing him four children, one of whom, the Duke of Berwick, lived to be among the most distinguished soldiers of his day, fighting as a Jacobite exile in the French service, and being sometimes pitted against his still more illustrious relative. In 1666 the young Churchill received a commission in the Guards, and he saw active service at Tangier. Returning to England in 1671, now an extraordinarily handsome youth of twenty, he fell a victim to the charms of Barbara Villiers, Duchess of Cleveland, whom Burnet once crudely described as Charles II's "first and longest mistress". She was nine years Churchill's senior, but he became her lover, and was probably the father of her youngest child. When he was twenty-four the young and impecunious officer succeeded in investing £4,500 in an insurance scheme which gave him an annuity of £500. The money almost certainly came from the Duchess of Cleveland, who was said by the scandal-mongers of the day to have made him a gift of £5,000 for his adroitness in jumping out of her bedroom window when the King surprised them together. The story explaining why the royal mistress gave Churchill a large sum of money is almost certainly apocryphal; that he was the willing recipient of such a sum seems to be true. The Barbara Villiers episode has seemed to some writers odious; to others a mere peccadillo: it all depends whether the standards of Charles II's Whitehall are accepted or not. But let this be added: Churchill had only one other love affair in his life, and that was of a very different character. In 1677 he fell in love with that remarkable woman, Sarah Jennings, and against the wishes of his parents, who had hoped that he would make a much more lucrative match, this alleged monster of cupidity insisted upon marrying her despite her lack of dowry. This was the beginning of a married life of very tender and deep devotion.

Between 1672 and 1674 Churchill saw much active service both on sea and land, being present in the Duke of York's flagship at the great naval battle of Solebay against the Dutch, and in the English contingent which fought under the command of Turenne at the siege of Maastricht. On his return to England he was promoted lieutenant-colonel, and he became Master of the Robes in the Duke of York's household. He was in attendance on James in Scotland when the latter undertook the ruthless suppression of the Covenanters, following upon their defeat at Bothwell Brigg. When James came to the throne it was Churchill, who, though placed under the command of the much less able and less experienced Roman Catholic Earl of Feversham, was really responsible for the defeat of the unhappy supporters of Monmouth's rebellion at Sedgemoor.

In December, 1682, Churchill had received a Scottish peerage, and in 1685 he obtained the English title of Baron Churchill of Sandridge. Brought up in James's household since boyhood, he owed his whole advancement to the favour of his royal master. But a fortnight after the landing of William of Orange he, being now a lieutenant-general, left the royal forces at Salisbury, and joined the Prince. It is true that considerations of the public welfare must prevail over loyalties, and that Marlborough, whose staunch adherence to the Church of England is undoubted, had probably, like the great majority of his fellow-countrymen, grown more and more alarmed by the King's Catholicizing policy; but it is impossible to regard his conduct in the Revolution in the same light as that of Danby, Shrewsbury, and Compton, and the other ringleaders in the revolt who were under no private obligation to James. But Marlborough's attitude in this crisis was of particular importance, if only because it determined that of the Princess Anne, over whom he and his wife had acquired a dominating influence, and who abandoned the cause of her father for that of her sister Mary and William of Orange, Mary's husband.

Marlborough was rewarded for his adherence to William's cause by the grant of an earldom and by admission to the Privy Council, and the new reign seemed likely to bring him further advancement and prosperity. He achieved distinction in a small action in the war against France at Walcourt on the Sambre, in which he got the better of the French under d'Humières; in the war in Ireland, where the French were assisting the numerous partisans of James's cause in that country, he seized Cork and Kinsale in the autumn of 1690. With sure strategic insight he had perceived the great significance of these two posts on the southern coast of Ireland because of the excellent opportunities they afforded, so long as they remained in Jacobite hands, for the French to send reinforcements and supplies to the rebels. His proposals for their reduction did not find favour with the English Ministers, but were ultimately approved by the King, and Marlborough himself was entrusted with the task of carrying them into execution, thus obtaining his first independent command. The complete success of his enterprise brought him high praise from William. "No officer now living who has seen so little service," he declared, "is so fit for great commands."

Despite this encomium no high command was forthcoming, and the years 1691 and 1692 are the most regrettable in Marlborough's career. There can be no doubt that he was in correspondence with the exiled Jacobite Court, as were a good many others who had taken part in bringing about the Revolution; but this was probably no more than an easy form of insurance, betokening no desire whatever for a Jacobite restoration, but only a cautious anxiety to be on the safe side in case a restoration should perchance take place. However,

in 1692 Marlborough was consigned to the Tower, on a charge
of being party to a scheme for bringing back James to the
throne. His accuser was a worthless fellow, whose evidence
was shown to be wholly untrustworthy, and after some months
of incarceration Marlborough was released. More serious was
the disgrace that had befallen him the previous January, when
he was dismissed from the army and both he and his wife
forbidden the Court. The reasons for this proscription were a
mystery at the time and have not been fully cleared up since.
But we know that William had become greatly incensed at
Marlborough's recent behaviour; he remarked one day that
had he been a private individual he would have felt constrained to demand satisfaction of the Earl on the field of
honour. Marlborough seems to have been deeply chagrined
because the King gave so many important military appointments to his Dutch fellow-countrymen and other foreigners,
and to have been deliberately fomenting discontent and opposition both in the army and in Parliament. The situation
which he created was the more troublesome and possibly
even dangerous to William in that the Churchills exercised so
absolute an influence over the Princess Anne, who happened to
have a grievance of her own against the King, since she considered the financial arrangements which had been made for
her as quite inadequate. We may discard the wild story that
Marlborough was scheming to transfer the crown from
William to Anne, and yet realize, that the King regarded it as a
very serious and disloyal action on the Earl's part to endeavour
to make the Princess's Court a centre of disaffection against
himself. This episode constitutes the gravest blot upon Marlborough's good name.

It is not the worst crime with which he has been charged,
for it used to be confidently believed that he betrayed to the
Jacobites the intelligence of the expedition sent against Brest
in 1694, and Macaulay was so foolish as to make the malicious

suggestion that he did so in the hope of bringing disaster upon the general commanding the troops in the enterprise, his only rival among English generals, Talmash or Tollemache. It has for some time been appreciated that the French had knowledge of the intended attack and had made effective preparations to meet it well before the date upon which Marlborough is supposed to have made his communication, and it has been agreed that it was precisely because he realized that the news he was giving was really no news to the French Government that he hoped to gain some credit with the Jacobites without doing any harm to the English undertaking. But even so his conduct was infamous, and it is not surprising that in his efforts to rehabilitate his hero, Mr. Winston Churchill, following upon the lines of Colonel Parnell, has subjected the evidence for Marlborough's having given any information at all to the severest scrutiny. He has done so to such good effect that the most damaging verdict that can possibly now be presented on this count is one of Non Proven, while many may be prepared to say definitely Not Guilty.

Before the end of the reign of William III Marlborough had been restored to favour. In 1698 he was appointed Governor to Anne's sole surviving son, the Duke of Gloucester, and readmitted to the Privy Council; and in 1701, when a new war with France became imminent and William sought to recreate the Grand Alliance against Louis XIV, the King took him over to Holland with him, and as Ambassador Extraordinary to the United Provinces he was responsible for much of the important work of negotiation which followed. He was also placed in command of the English forces on the Continent. The King evidently intended that he should now take a prominent part in affairs, and on William's sudden death Marlborough at once stepped into his place as national leader, becoming commander-in-chief of the Dutch forces as well as of all English troops at home and abroad. With the accession of

Queen Anne, whose complete confidence he so thoroughly enjoyed, there dawned the brilliant days of Marlborough's career, which were not only an honour to himself but a permanent enrichment of our English heritage.

No attempt can be made in a brief sketch which aims only at being a summary appraisement of his character and capacity, to narrate the course of the great campaigns which Marlborough fought between 1702 and 1711. Nearly every one of them from the first to the last was marked by glorious exploits. In 1702 he not only saved Holland from the fear of invasion, but seized Venloo and Kaiserwerth and Liége, for which services he was granted a dukedom. In 1704 there took place the famous march from the Rhine to the Danube, followed by the battles of Schellenberg and Blenheim, the latter being the greatest feat of arms accomplished by English troops since the days of Crecy and Poitiers. Austria was saved from imminent danger and the French armies were driven helter-skelter back to French soil. In 1705 his own plans for an invasion of France by the valley of the Moselle having been thwarted by the failure of our allies to co-operate, Marlborough was occupied in endeavouring to break or turn the strong defensive position held by the skilful Marshal Villars, the ablest of the French generals, on the line of the river Dyle. Eventually he succeeded in turning the position, having completely mystified and out-generalled his adversary. He sought to give him battle on much the same ground on which the battle of Waterloo was fought 110 years later, and he anticipated a victory even more decisive than Blenheim, but the Dutch vetoed the engagement as too rash an undertaking. In 1706 there occurred the splendid triumph of Ramillies, which was followed by the speedy occupation of Brussels, Antwerp, Ghent, Ostend, and indeed of so much of the Belgian territory hitherto held by the French that Marlborough boasted that the Allies had done in four days what they might reasonably have thought themselves lucky to have done in four years. In 1708 Marshal Vendôme was so badly defeated at Oudenarde that Marlborough, with perhaps undue optimism, maintained that had he been given but one more hour of daylight the whole campaign would have been finished at a single blow. He himself desired to march straight into France, simply masking the great frontier fortress of Lille; but this was felt, even by Prince Eugene, to be too daring a policy, and the remainder of the year was occupied in the siege of Lille, which was eventually taken after such immense difficulties that contemporary expert opinion was inclined to rank this as the greatest of all Marlborough's exploits. In the following year there occurred the grim battle of Malplaquet, as the result of which the French under Villars were eventually driven out of a very strong position, but at exceedingly heavy cost. The victory in itself was quite a notable achievement, but hopes that had been entertained of finishing the long war by means of a single decisive stroke had now been disappointed; the British people were growing weary of military triumphs which seemed to bring peace no nearer, while the French were stiffened in their resistance by the preposterously severe and indeed insulting terms which the British Government had demanded in recent negotiations. In 1711 Marlborough was presented with the problem of piercing an elaborate defensive system which Villars had created, consisting of river frontages, inundations, and entrenchments, and which he described as his *non plus ultra* lines. By a masterpiece of strategic ingenuity Marlborough surprised the enemy, entered the lines without loss, and captured the fortress of Bouchain. Once again he contemplated an invasion of France. But a Ministerial crisis had taken place in England, and the new Government were intent upon making peace, not upon prosecuting war, and Marlborough was recalled. His military career was over.

In order to appreciate the greatness of Marlborough as a general it is necessary to bear in mind one or two of the conditions of warfare with which he was confronted. In the first place, most of his campaigning was done in the Low Countries, where the numerous rivers in the basins of the Scheldt and the Meuse and the ease with which the country could be flooded offered effective obstacles to attack. Roads upon which armies were dependent for their movements were dominated by powerful fortresses, and in Vauban the French possessed by far the greatest military engineer of the age. In the hands of the majority of its practitioners in Marlborough's day the art of war was little more than one of marching and countermarching, attacking and defending fortified towns. In such circumstances decisive engagements were few and far-between, and wars were apt to be protracted. Another factor which made for their prolongation was inability to carry on active operations in heavy weather, so that armies went into winterquarters, and there were two seasons, a campaigning season in the summer and a recruiting season in the inclement months. Thus it was often difficult to derive adequate advantage in a new campaign from successes gained in the last. It is important to note a third feature of Marlborough's campaigns. The forces he commanded were always composed of different nationalities, the English contingent forming sometimes quite a small minority, and he always had to accommodate his plans to the wishes of foreign colleagues. Happily at Blenheim, Lille, Malplaquet he was associated with a soldier of his own calibre, and with whom he acted in the closest harmony, in Prince Eugene of Savoy. But more often he had to work with Dutch commanders, who were apt to be jealous or sluggish, and who were in any case (quite naturally) intent mainly on the defence of their own country, so that they regarded Marlborough's far-reaching schemes as dangerously venturesome. He once complained of the mortification of finding more obstruction from his friends than from his enemies. Numerous as were his victories, they would have been still more numerous and more decisive had not his plans been so frequently thwarted by the obstacles placed in his way by reluctant and suspicious colleagues, or by the civilian field-deputies whom the Dutch States-General sent to accompany their armies and invested with a power to veto strategy.

Only when these inherent difficulties are remembered can Marlborough's greatness in war be fully realized. To begin with, while the conditions of the *terrain* in which most of his campaigns were fought and also the predilections of the Dutch generals favoured deliberate and procrastinating methods, he was always an aggressive commander, seeking to bring the enemy to action, aiming at battles, not sieges, in order to obtain swift decisions. This characteristic, which was due to his confidence in himself and in his men, was perhaps the feature that most distinguished him from the less adventurous spirits common in his day and generation, who preferred to wage war according to rules which were both precise and leisurely. It was a characteristic early and strikingly revealed. When in 1702 he was not allowed to bring Boufflers and Berwick to action, he took the extraordinary course of sending them a personal message to assure them that his failure to do so was due to no fault of his! He was also sharply differentiated from associates of normal mentality and short and narrow view by his strategic insight and his capacity of imaginative vision (such as is found only in the very greatest soldiers), which enabled him to envisage a European war as a whole. Thus it was that he perceived in 1704 that even from the point of view of London and Amsterdam his troops would be more effectively occupied in crossing the Continent to save Vienna than in defending the Netherlands. Thus, again, in the case of Cork and Kinsale and in many other instances he showed a capacity, rare among soldiers, to appreciate the military significance of naval operations. Being gifted with imagination, he was a master of stratagem, constantly mystifying the enemy as to his intentions and springing surprise attacks upon him.

Not all Marlborough's powers as a strategist would have brought his brilliant schemes to success had they not been accompanied by a zealous care for tactical and administrative detail. The English infantry were armed with a flint-lock musket which was superior to the French weapon, but its effectiveness was largely the result of Marlborough's efforts to secure the most efficient fire discipline training. In important engagements he was wont to supervise personally the siting of artillery positions. He gave indefatigable attention to matters of commissariat and supply, and his men had constant evidence of his care for their welfare and comfort. He was a severe disciplinarian; he had a most fastidious objection to brutality, roystering, and misconduct, and insisted on the strictest order in camp. He made at times very heavy demands upon the physical endurance of his men. Yet he was personally popular with the rank and file, as his nickname "Corporal John" indicates, and as Wellington never was. In those days a commander-in-chief did not direct operations in an office miles away from the firing line. The debonair handsome figure of Marlborough was familiar to every man in his army; his troops had frequent ocular proof of his bravery, for at crises in battle he would himself lead the cavalry and charge into the thick of the mêlée. Thus the force of his personality told directly in the field.

Marlborough was a strong man, but he had none of the characteristics of the bully and the *poseur*, which are nowadays too often associated with the term. He was a remarkable statesman as well as a great general; an adept in the arts of diplomacy and conciliation, winning people by his deftness, courtesy and tact, and the sheer fascination of his address. Twice when there were fears that the formidable and erratic Charles XII of Sweden might intervene in the war against the Allies—in 1701 and in 1707—the adroitness of Marlborough as a negotiator secured that adventurous monarch's neutrality. His great diplomatic skill was reinforced by a phenomenal capacity for patience and self-control. Even when physically exhausted and seeing his most cherished schemes and greatest opportunities ruined by timidity and obstinacy, even on occasions when he was assailed with violent abuse in the House of Lords, he showed an almost superhuman forbearance. Once or twice only was his temper frayed; when the normal man would have been exasperated beyond all bearing, he mildly expressed "uneasiness"!

There was plenty to disturb Marlborough's equanimity after his recall in 1711. In those days when politicians were intent upon destroying their foes they affected a lofty standard of public virtue just for the moment, of which they would not have been suspected at other times. Marlborough, whom Swift and other supporters of the Tory Government in their propaganda in favour of a peace were accusing of having deliberately prolonged the war for selfish reasons, found himself charged with extortion and embezzlement of public moneys amounting to about £350,000. He was able to show that if he had accepted £63,000 from army bread-contractors, this had been a recognized perquisite of previous English commanders on the Continent, and that all, and more than all, the sums alleged to have gone into his pockets had been utilized for the purpose of obtaining secret information regarding the enemy's movements, as there existed no regular intelligence service maintained out of national funds. Nevertheless Marlborough, pending an inquiry into his conduct (which was never followed up), was dismissed from all his employments. It is not surprising that he threw himself wholeheartedly into the schemes of the Whig Opposition and did all he could to embarrass the Government; and as he was *persona grata* with the Electoral Court at Hanover, his enmity was dangerous to Ministers, some of whom were suspected of Jacobite sympathies and intentions. But failing to frustrate the Government's peace policy, which he regarded as immoral in its methods and pusillanimous in its objects, weary of the ceaseless campaign of abuse and misrepresentation waged against him in the Tory press, in the autumn of 1712 the Duke left an ungrateful country and for the remainder of Anne's reign he lived abroad. On the day after the Queen's death he returned to England, and the new sovereign speedily reappointed him Commander-in-chief and Master-General of the Ordnance. But his public life was over, for his health broke down in 1716, when he had a slight stroke, and on June 16, 1722, he died. All that there was of greatness in the life of Marlborough had been accomplished within the compass of a dozen years; but his achievements in that period both in war and in diplomacy were so remarkable, that despite episodes in his earlier career that are at least unsatisfactory, if they do not deserve a less lenient epithet, his fame as one of the greatest of Englishmen rests upon secure foundations.

2

ADDISON AND STEELE

(1672-1719 : 1672-1729)

by WILLARD CONNELY

EARLY in the brief reign of James II, the year being 1686, two boys who met in the writing-school of old Charterhouse, Aldersgate, struck up acquaintance. Apart from their age, fourteen, Joseph Addison and Richard Steele seemed unlike enough: one an oppidan, the other a poor-scholar; a slim boy and a tubby boy; one pale as an angel, one brown as an elf; a subdued one and an excitable one; one good at hexameters, the other at games; an amused listener and a chatterbox. Of Addison's father, everyone knew. He was the learned Dean of Lichfield, who had so devotedly bred up his eldest son that the boy at fourteen was ready even for Oxford, and was only waiting at Charterhouse to grow a year older. But Steele was an unheralded orphan from Dublin, now in the school because his uncle by marriage happened to be secretary to one of its governors. For "Nephew Steele" the years of boyhood had been as troubled as for Addison they were serene. Dick had grown up fatherless and mother-less, with a feeble-minded sister for a playmate, and the boy was exposed to indifferent schooling—his uncle being con-stantly away from Dublin—in a neighbourhood in which squalor everywhere encroached upon respectability. The upbringing of Addison at home had on the other hand been a drill in taste and thoroughness, ultimately exprest in Latin verses, while from the age of three he knew only surroundings of grandeur, for he lived at the very threshold of the cathedrals of Salisbury and Lichfield.

Dick had been two years in Charterhouse when Addison arrived, and he had to stay as long again after his friend left. He seemed to be in need of flogging, and he got it, for bad spelling and worse construing. As Addison waited those two years in Oxford for his schoolmate to turn up he so far progressed in Latin poetry that he earned a demyship which provided for him to migrate from Queen's College to Magdalen. Then the two friends met again, but to renew greetings rather than intimacy. Steele went to Christ Church. Later he got a small scholarship at Merton, where he veered at once towards Whig politics and talk of war, while Addison studied on, wrote poems, misbehaved a little and was taken up by the proctors, but stayed in the shelter of Magdalen.* Dick Steele by fits of firmness managed to read his Horace and his Theocritus for two years, until soldiers came marching through Oxford from the Irish wars. Then he just fell in step with them and tramped off. Nothing could have driven Addison into such a venture; though he might celebrate in verse the doings of heroes, he preferred not to be one. He took pupils to tutor, cultivated Jacob Tonson the publisher, and began to correspond with Dryden. Cloistered years in Magdalen did not keep him stranger to London, nor to the uses of poetry to flatter those in power.

In this respect Steele again arrived on common ground with his friend. He joined the Horse Guards, known for their resplendent trappings and black horses, and for their colonel, who was his uncle's employer the young Duke of Ormond.

*See *Sir Richard Steele*, Willard Connely.

But if Dick on that account expected favour he was disappointed, for the duke was generally absent, fighting. Steele's chance came when Queen Mary died in 1695. He was ordered to mount guard, and the funeral inspired him to a memorial in verse, which he dedicated to Lord Cutts, colonel of another regiment, the Coldstream Guards. This arrow in the air struck home. Cutts made Steele his secretary, got him a commission as captain, and kept him on his personal staff for seven years. Meantime Addison had written a poem to King William, met Congreve through Dryden, and then met the Whig politicians. In 1699 he was by them sent abroad on a Crown allowance of £300 a year, to learn languages, and to fit himself to serve not the Church but the Whigs.

Addison was still abroad, a celibate in France, when Dick Steele at home was producing a love-child by the daughter of Jacob Tonson's brother Richard, a publisher lately dead. He repented of his mishap by writing *The Christian Hero*. Of that, Dick had to repent as well, in order to defeat the mockery of his fellow-soldiers; accordingly, he wrote *The Funeral*, a comedy with richly vulgar scenes from life in the army. It was noticed by the King. But no sooner had Steele pitched his hopes on it than William III died, Cutts dismissed his secretary, and the captain was transferred to Landguard Fort, a sand-dune in Suffolk. There he could only write more plays.

When Addison returned from the continent in 1703 he found Dick about to produce *The Lying Lover*, a comedy described newly as "sentimental". Addison himself had brought back a Roman tragedy which he called *Cato*. Colley Cibber and Steele read it. Cibber insisted on production; but the author lacked the courage. Still it was now plain that no matter what course war or politics might take, both Addison and Steele were going to write. They were elected to the Kit-Cat, a Whig society for poets and politicians; and as the Age of Anne unfolded, the two old Carthusians began to get their bearings. In the spring of 1704 the Town was startled by an anonymous satire called *A Tale of a Tub*. The author suspected was Jonathan Swift. This slashing pamphlet drew attention to the eccentric vicar, already remarked for his irruptions into St. James's Coffee-house. Addison and Steele, there together one day, met Swift, who to them seemed an absolute delight. All three talked Whig politics to exhaustion. But that Swift had to return to his miserable congregation in Ireland, and Steele to his wretched soldiers in Suffolk, Addison would not have been left unoccupied.

He did not wait long. The Whig leaders, desiring a poem to celebrate Blenheim, called upon him. In his Haymarket garret Addison whittled out 500 lines, now and again interrupted by Captain Dick, a little drunk, quite impassioned over Addison's verses, and loquacious about a further new comedy of his own. But the poem, *The Campaign*, made Addison. He could now pause and give an eye to his friend's play, for Steele had produced no piece which swept London like either *The Campaign* or *A Tale of a Tub*. Addison tinkered with *The Tender Husband*, and doubtless improved it, since the characters of Humphry Gubbin and Biddy Tipkin went far ahead of any previous creations by Dick. Still what here mattered was that the captain first noticed, in the writing of them both, a kinship which they ought to make use of.

As the theme of *The Tender Husband* was fortune-hunting, its author himself surprised no one by marrying the first lady he met who was capable of supporting him. She was one Margaret Stretch, a widow, owner of plantations in the West Indies, and she gave her hand to the captain just in time to appease an old school friend of his who was hounding poor Dick for a debt of £600. The bridegroom at once sold 500 acres of the Stretch domains. As for Addison, so acclaimed was his *Campaign* that a post under the Secretary of State came to him without asking; through Addison at least Steele might now hope for political patronage. But it was fully a year before the captain got an appointment, as gentleman-waiter to Prince George, a little connection with court which may have reconciled Mrs. Steele somewhat to her costly husband. Yet nothing very long mattered with her, for at Christmastide, 1706, she died, suddenly.

Perhaps the captain was less broken-hearted than embarrassed upon his early widowerhood. The residue of his wife's estate proved encumbered, while his services to the Prince turned no way remunerative. Addison, on the other hand, was getting on. He not only wrote a government pamphlet, *The Present State of the War*, but he tried lyric poetry in an opera, *Rosamund*, to the further eulogy of Marlborough, and if the opera failed, the pamphlet perfectly gave what was wanted. Then came the government at last to acknowledge Captain Steele; they made him editor of their newspaper, the *Gazette*, whereupon Dick set about a whirlwind courtship of Molly Scurlock of Carmarthen, a friend of his late wife. This time he was in love. After a month of the most rhapsodic wooing, she believed him.

When, in the next winter, the Tories were forced out and Swift came hastily back for pickings, Addison, Steele and the vicar dined, and tried to count the vacancies they might fill. Addison was made secretary to the Lord-Lieutenant of Ireland, Swift got nothing and left in a rage for Laracor, and Steele was refused even the place vacated by Addison. The captain, now with both wife and child, had to do something, and the hint as to what course he might take soon arose from the insipidity of his work for the *Gazette*. He had long thought that women would support a paper if it tickled their vanity. Knowing he could count on the coffee-houses for the men, Steele, with an eye to the tea-tables, decided to issue thrice-a-week a publication to be called the *Tatler*. Its very first number struck the tone: an anecdote of a flirtation and a spirited review of Congreve's *Love for Love*. Subsequently came characters of men and of women, and discourses upon manners, conversation, fashions.

All England bought the paper with delight. In Ireland happily Swift and Addison soon identified Isaac Bickerstaff, the editor, with Steele, and sent him contributions. Steele then started series against duelling and gamesters, on gentlemen and rakes, on rambles in town, on gallantry, on domesticity (life with his own "Prue"). By inviting readers to send in personal sketches he was often able to make up an issue with no exertion himself. "All the town are full of the *Tatler*," wrote one lady to another, "no visit . . . but Mr. Bickerstaff is mentioned." After fifteen years of trial Steele had hit upon that writing he could best do. He had found the middle classes. When Addison came to London on a visit, he and Steele collaborated, and for almost a year the *Tatler* continued its triumphant course. Then the trial of Dr. Sacheverell for denouncing the Whig government in the pulpit rather side-tracked the women readers. Steele wisely took a holiday. He turned over the paper to Addison, who at once proceeded to capture a new following, in a manner almost indistinguishable from Steele's, but with his matter developing classical themes, such as Homer, Virgil, or Cato. The importance of this relay in editorship was that by it Addison in turn discovered the kind of writing he was born for.

Yet neither Addison nor Steele relinquished politics. Addison was prudently saving his large salary and was expecting high office, while the captain, though his paper prospered, saved nothing, but hoped every day that the ministry would reward him for being a good Whig. As soon as Addison set out again for Ireland, Steele began to write politics into the *Tatler*. His friends begged him not to. But Steele objected to the dismissal of ministers consequent upon the Queen's quarrel with the Duchess of Marlborough, and insisted that he wrote in the cause of "public spirit". Robert Harley now crept to the head of the government. Recklessly Steele turned a *Tatler* into a stinging satire on Harley, in spite of a warning from Swift to "consider what a day might bring forth," while the Tories, goaded to action, started the *Examiner*, which insinuated that Steele was disloyal and announced that its burden would be the politics proper for England. In the thick of this fracas Addison turned up, to stand for Parliament, and saw Steele being escorted to a sponging-house for debt. Addison was always more circumspect than fervid. He filled the *Tatler* with non-political essays until Steele was released.

When, in September, Swift followed Addison into Town the triumvirate dined together rejoicing; though the vicar was savagely incensed at the Whigs, he believed politics nothing amongst friends, and he had ready new essays and humorous verse for the *Tatler*. But even as the trio were renewing cordialities three things happened: Swift paid an ingratiating visit to Harley, Addison was elected M.P. for Malmesbury, and Steele was dismissed as Gazetteer. Swift did not tell his friends he was about to contribute to the *Examiner*. Both Addison and Steele sensed this defection, with annoyance. By November, Swift was writing whatever Harley and St. John commanded him, was gloating over his revenge against Whigs who had ignored him, and was still trying to be convivial with his two companions. He made a great stir about arranging for Steele to see Harley, to help Steele retain a commissionership of stamps; but Steele chose to see Harley independently. It was a short interview with long consequences. Harley was a man who gave nothing unless he received: if he should spare Steele, what would Steele undertake for him? At the new year, 1711, the *Tatler* ceased publication.

There was possibly method in Steele's surrender. He was too sharp a publicist not to have discovered the profit for himself and Addison in the essay, and in March the two men planned a daily paper, which should keep strictly outside the business of Harley. To suggest this detachment they called it the *Spectator*, and to safeguard the limits of it Steele assigned all editing to Addison. But it was Steele who invented the catch: the character of Sir Roger de Coverley, bachelor, jilted by a widow, petted by the young women, sought after by the young men. This appeal to four sets of readers the captain broadened by putting Sir Roger at the head of half a dozen kindred characters, forming a club, which lent personality to a degree the *Tatler* had lacked. Soon the *Spectator* circulated 3,000 copies a day.

Success was due not alone to the superior talents of Addison, but to the freshness which he brought to his task, and if the bloom of Steele's powers had gone into the *Tatler*, Addison now set a mark which Steele extended himself to keep up to. They dealt with every sort of topic from a description of Steele's bun of a face to Westminster Abbey, from a lady's library to manners in servants. Addison developed the paper to win the scholars, with essays on French classicism, on an English academy of letters, on the old ballad of Chevy Chase. If these proved too strong for the less learned, Steele regained them by a letter from a footman, or by a tirade against debtors (such as himself). They next dwelt upon Sir Roger: the baronet in Worcestershire, and essays upon his staff, friends, dogs, pictures, and the widow. Demand for the *Spectator* became national. Addison then brought Sir Roger through everyday London, so vividly, so wittily, so urbanely that the de Coverley papers grew to be the literary craze. Not since Beaumont and Fletcher had two writers in English so luckily united their gifts. With the Whigs almost completely out of politics, the men behind the *Spectator* were able to devote themselves to literature only, to encourage living young poets like Pope, and to revive neglected ones like Milton.

Addison was growing ever more conscious that writers of the day deferred to him. This leadership he was not averse to preserving as good business, and to the end desired he set up his man Button in a coffee-house opposite Will's in Russell Street. If, as Swift said, Addison had wit enough to give reputation to an age, Addison at once showed that he had followers enough to give clientele to a coffee-house. Most of the known poets followed him: Ambrose Philips, Budgell, Tickell, Gay, Garth, and above all, Pope. It was well the move was made in the heyday of the *Spectator*. For in the summer thereafter, a Tory stamp-tax suddenly sheared off more than half its edition, and Addison, rather than revert to political essays or other attempts to equalize, decided to kill Sir Roger and the paper with him. Now Addison, neither burdened with a family nor endowed with Steele's prodigality, could afford to wait until the Whigs returned to office; but Steele knew that the essential of the moment, for him, was a third paper, which he again should control. As the *Spectator* went out the *Guardian* came in, with the assurance that Addison and others would contribute, although Steele in his first number threatened that the *Guardian's* politics could not be "neuter".

Since the Whigs were now badly in need of a demonstration, Steele undertook to convince Addison that a production of his *Cato* would instruct the public. Addison took fright at the thought, in spite of his ringing success with the de Coverley papers. But he could not resist Steele's importunity, and *Cato* was performed. With Barton Booth and Nance Oldfield, to say nothing of thunderous applause led by Steele from the pit, the tragedy became in a night the sensation of the season. However, so readily could its noble lines be applied to either party that the Tories claimed it as well as the Whigs. *Cato* ran for over a month. By any reckoning, Addison emerged so much the greater man, more prized by the Whigs, more respected by the government in office.

Soon afterward this government signed the unfavourable Peace of Utrecht, articles by Swift in the *Examiner* exasperated the Whigs all the more, and personal enmities became inevitable. When the *Examiner* printed a slur upon the daughter of a Whig peer, Steele could keep back his indignation no longer. In the *Guardian* he struck out with a rejoinder that someone who wrote for the *Examiner* was "a fawning miscreant". Swift, who for assistance to the Tories had just been made Dean of St. Patrick's and was feeling reasonably elevated, sent a furious letter to Addison. Addison quietly handed it to Steele. Then Steele and Swift began an exchange of bitterly recriminatory messages, which culminated in Steele's resigning as stamp commissioner and in the departure of Swift for Ireland, with this last word to Steele: "I may never see you again."

While Addison calmly kept up for the *Guardian* his amiable fantasies, Steele grew almost warlike as he saw the French trying to evade their obligations under the treaty. In August he boldly printed "The British nation expect the demolition of Dunkirk". The *Examiner* called him "contemptible wretch". By way of retort Steele took coach to Stockbridge and bought his election to Parliament. Returning, he published *The Importance of Dunkirk Considered*. Whereupon Addison, convinced that his old colleague was irrepressible, left London.

But the captain simply started a new paper, the *Englishman*, lest France impose the Pretender upon the British throne. Not satisfied with this alone, he projected separately a booklet on the Hanoverian cause, to be entitled *The Crisis*, and with such vehemence did he urge the need of this warning that he lured Addison back to revise it. Then Steele used his new periodical to advertise *The Crisis* with a thump. The Tories took fright and summoned Swift. Yet in spite of a highly abusive pamphlet from the Dean, "*The Importance of the Guardian Considered*," preparations for *The Crisis* went on, whilst Captain Dick deferred publication and lengthened his subscription list. By the time Addison had supplied his adroit finishing touches the edition called for 40,000 copies. On the great day of publication, in January, 1714, every reader heard its trumpet of alarm, "The Protestant Succession in the House of Hanover is in danger under Her Majesty's administration!"

Tory retribution quickly set in. Copies of *The Crisis* were distributed to the House of Commons, and as soon as the session reopened Oxford's brother and his nephew attacked Steele. The Kit-Cat ordered Addison to write Steele's defence. On the day of the trial Addison appeared at the side of the accused; whatever Steele did, he could do it better if Addison was close by. The captain spoke desperately for three hours, quoting in justification his own works. Then Walpole and other Whigs debated with eloquence on Steele's behalf. But the House was Tory by a full hundred, and Captain Richard Steele was expelled for "sedition".

There might have been cause for discouragement but that four months thereafter Queen Anne died, George I was proclaimed, and the fortunes of Addison and Steele like those of every other Whig changed in a twinkling. The regents chose Addison their secretary. He was only too ready. He had been occupying himself only with a diluted continuation of the *Spectator*. For Steele the initial appointment was as commissioner of the theatre. Then the two pamphleteers were selected for patronage by two Lords-Lieutenant, but with a difference: Addison was unhappily banished to Dublin as secretary, his old post, while Steele, appointed one of the three deputies to Lord Clare, Lord-Lieutenant of Middlesex, was by Clare backed at Boroughbridge for Parliament. Steele won the seat, and on the anniversary of his expulsion he re-entered the House of Commons unperturbed. Again, Clare, having to deliver a congratulatory address to the King, engaged Steele to write it. Accompanying Clare to St. James's in April for the reading of the speech, Steele and two other deputies were knighted for their services to the House of Hanover.

Addison had put in for a place on the Board of Trade, but in spite of his acidulous protests from Ireland had had to wait nearly a year for it. He returned to London to find Sir Richard rewarded still further, as commissioner for Scottish estates confiscated from rebels under the Pretender. Was nothing more in reserve for the secretary from Ireland? As if for consolation, recompense of quite unpolitical nature came to Joseph Addison. For eight years he had been wooing the wealthy Countess of Warwick; at last, his absence in Dublin had inclined her to his suit. They were married in August.

When Dick Steele's friend became Lady Warwick's husband the two great essayists drifted out of intimacy. It had not been so when Steele took Prue to wife. But Lady Warwick transported Addison far from Button's coffee-house, to a suburban home of her own, and perhaps to company of her own. Addison by his marriage lost nothing with Whigs both noble and mighty, and when, in the following spring, 1717, a new ministry came in, with a duke and two earls, the secretaries of state were Sunderland and Addison. Steele was disappointed that the fresh cabinet found no place for him. At dinner, Addison tried to explain that his friend's Scottish post made him ineligible, though what Addison might promise if Steele should resign it was not gone into.

The Rt. Hon. Joseph Addison, now in poor health, accepted the cushions of Holland House as often as he could escape Whitehall. He was asthmatic, and he drank brandy. Within a year he had to resign, though he continued to attend the House of Commons. When in March, 1719, a bill for creating peers came up, Steele believed that to foster ambition the King should continue to raise commoners to peerages, and this argument he published in *The Plebeian*, whereas Addison took the view that an overpopulated House of Lords would nullify both crown and ministry, and he so replied in *The Old Whig*. Steele refuted him, mentioning tyranny. As Addison kept silent Sir Richard in a third number rebuked him, whereupon Addison in another *Old Whig* became personal. This was more than Steele could bear; in his fourth and last he commented upon Addison's "insolence". There was no forgiving.

Addison went back to luxury and Lady Warwick, and grew absorbed in devotional writings, as if to repent for his bibulous years. Yet his asthma so taxed his heart that before the age of forty-seven he had become a chronic invalid. He had always drunk more than he could stand, because it seemed he could stand ever more than he drank. Dropsy set in. Addison collapsed. Within three months after his final break with Dick Steele he was dead. It was June, 1719.

Steele, whose wife had also died within the year, lived ten years longer, though his play *The Conscious Lovers*, which was his final triumph, was performed in 1722. Gout and debts then drove him into retirement in Wales. He settled in a farmhouse across the Towy from Carmarthen, his wife's house, as Addison at the end settled in the house of Lady Warwick. But the likeness in the last days of Addison and Steele ended there. Steele dwindled into an impoverished exile, neglected, gout-ridden, cut off from his friends, remote from all life that he loved, and at last stricken dumb by paralysis; Addison, dying in a suburban palace, had come to his end like the prince of letters that he was, his every want supplied, and about him all such friends as he desired. A moralist might have said they died like an ant and a sluggard, as if there were nothing to be said for the sluggard. With due pomp Addison had been taken to Westminster Abbey. Steele was buried in his village church. As it happened, the tomb of Steele was nearer to the altar.

3

JONATHAN SWIFT

(1667–1745)

by JOHN HAYWARD

ALMOST exactly two hundred years ago, George Faulkner—"the Prince of Dublin printers"—published in four volumes the first collection of Swift's writings in verse and prose. At the time of its publication, Swift's name and some part, at least, of his work must have been familiar to almost every literate man and woman in two kingdoms. And yet, while the author of *Gulliver's Travels* and *The Drapier's Letters* was known and loved by thousands of people of every age and rank, scarcely one of them could have said that he knew the man. It is doubtful if the few who had enjoyed his company in London and Dublin, or the many who had watched, with mingled affection and respect, his ordinary progress through the streets of the two capitals, had any conception of the character and personality of the man they knew so well by sight. Then, as now, the exact nature of them seems to have baffled the inquirer. Curiosity was, and in a large measure still remains, unsatisfied.

Swift has had his biographers—none more admirable than Sir Walter Scott—but they can tell us very little about the inner life of the man whose physical activities they record.

Our knowledge of these is more than ample. There is little we do not know about Swift's movements, from his childhood in Dublin onwards. We know where he lived and how; the extent and direction of his travels; the nature of his various activities and engagements over the best part of half a century. For certain periods of his life the wealth of detail is almost oppressive. We are told what food he ate, the clothes he wore, his personal whims and domestic habits, the history of minor ailments and much more besides. And yet all this information, all these everyday facts seem merely to emphasize our ignorance of the man they concern. Admittedly, no man's character is an open book, not even to his most intimate friends, but Swift's, when it is not incomprehensible, is consistently hard to read. After two centuries, our interpretation of it is still largely a matter of conjecture.

Apart from what we can learn from contemporary letters and biographies, our main source of information comes, of course, from Swift's own writings. These fall naturally into two classes, the one comprising his "Works" in prose and verse, the other his personal papers, the most revealing of which are the letters, collected and printed after his death under the title *The Journal to Stella*, in which daily for nearly three years he described every incident of his life in London for the entertainment of the young unmarried protégée, Esther Johnson, he had left behind in Dublin. All these books and papers, whether composed originally for public or private ends, tell us much. Yet they leave much unsaid. We are left wondering what kind of man it was that wrote them. It is not that we are troubled by obscurity either in style or subject-matter. No Englishman has written more simply or more clearly than Swift. Even the dry bones of forgotten controversies live again in his most ephemeral pamphlets. His meaning is always transparent and a child can understand it. Lemuel Gulliver, indeed, has always been better appreciated in the nursery than in the drawing-room, though that appreciation is more often than not misplaced. Even since they first took the world by storm, Gulliver's *Travels into several remote Nations of the World* have been enjoyed for the wrong reasons; for Swift's object, he tells us, was to vex his readers not to divert them. It is possible, in fact, to read a great deal, if not the bulk of his work without realizing either its purpose or the nature of the mood in which it was written. Directly we attempt to discover why Swift wrote as he did we are confronted by uncertainty.

It is easy to generalize from particular works and draw from them some conclusions about Swift's character and personality. His epitaph, for instance, which he composed himself, speaks of his savage indignation with mankind. Almost everything he wrote confirms that hatred of *la bêtise humaine* in all its horrible forms, which could turn his ink into gall and his pen into a formidable weapon of irony and satire. Even his wit, which he sometimes wasted upon the most absurd and laboured trifles, is seldom untouched by scorn; and his scorn is never more withering than when it is softened with pity. But none of these things explain Swift. They may go some way towards helping us to understand what kind of man he was; they do not, however, explain why. Anyone, after all, can read the numerous labels that have been attached to him. It is said, for example, that he was obstinate, dominating, selfish, independent, sensitive, egoistical, insolent, restless, proud, kind-hearted, amiable, high-humoured; and the evidence of his contemporaries alone is sufficient to justify these epithets. The question still remains, though, why his character and personality were expressed through these channels.

There is one answer that deserves consideration, and it is based on the contention that Swift was frustrated from within. Now there is nothing singular in this, for, in a sense, frustration, in one form or another, is a condition of civilized existence. Only, frustration for a man of Swift's intellectual calibre and with his highly organized nervous system, the sense that life is in some way thwarting his strongest instincts and desires, is bound to be greater and in its effects more terrible than for most men. It may lead, at times, to violence in words or even deeds, or to mental disturbance culminating in madness; or, worse than these, because it is an admission of the defeat of the spirit, it may lead to a sullen compromise. Living, we know, is largely an act of compromise, but the compromise to which Swift was forced to submit was enforced, it would appear, by a degree of frustration more acute than most people are aware of.

It is not simply that he was disappointed. There is a distinction here. Swift certainly suffered many rebuffs and disappointments. He was early excluded from high preferment in the Church on account of *A Tale of a Tub*; later he was to find himself brushed aside by the statesmen to whom he thought himself indispensable; and finally he was sent away, all but exiled, to Ireland, a country he abhorred. But he accepted and overcame them as matters beyond his control. His spirit was proud enough to endure the blows of worldly misfortune; he could bear disappointment. In what way, then, was he frustrated? To answer this it is necessary to explore, as far as possible, the nature of the inner conflict in which Swift was engaged.

Much has been written and many theories advanced to show that he was, in some way, frustrated in the strongest of human instincts. If the secret lies in his physical relations with the other sex, then the secret must remain there, since nothing is known beyond his own guarded statements about his intimacy with the two women he is said to have loved— Stella Johnson and Hester (Vanessa) Vanhomrigh. Speculation over the whole field of psychological and physiological probability has proved nothing. Some have supposed him to have been syphilitic; others have assumed he was impotent; some again speak darkly of undergraduate escapades; others affirm that he was Stella's husband and Vanessa's lover. There is no evidence one way or the other. Nevertheless, a possible solution of the whole problem of Swift's psychological frustration, not merely that of his supposedly thwarted sexual instincts, and one which goes some way towards elucidating his attitude to the world in general and his fellow-men in particular, may after all be found in a physiological cause.

When he was still a young man, Swift was overcome, without warning, by a sudden access of giddiness and deafness. Waterfalls thundered in his ears; the earth swam before his eyes. It was the first of a series of attacks which became progressively more frequent and severe as he grew older and which ultimately impaired his brain. Swift contended, somewhat whimsically, that his disability—it has been diagnosed as labyrinthine vertigo—was the unlucky consequence of a chill and a surfeit of apples in childhood. Whatever its origin, there can be no doubt that it must have haunted him like a perpetually recurring but never predictable nightmare. It is difficult for a normally healthy man or woman to imagine the nervous strain of such an affliction; and more especially difficult to imagine how profoundly it must have affected a man of Swift's great physical and mental powers. In his middle and later years he would sometimes complain fretfully to his friends of pain and misery, though, on the whole, he seems, as one would expect, to have suffered in silence until his mind gave way under pressure of dreadful torment and he was no longer able to control himself. Yet, very early on in life he must have seen that this imperfection differentiated him from other men and that he was, in consequence, predestined to abnormal frustration. He must have realized, also, the extent to which he would have to compromise with life if it were to be worth living.

It is a terrible thing when some disabling circumstance forces a man to regard his own body, not as an ally, but as his worst enemy, ready at any moment and without warning to interrupt his intellectual and emotional activities. Swift was such a man, a tiger confined within a cage of unruly flesh and blood, or, to adapt his own metaphor, a rat slowly stifling in its hole. Perhaps only those who have themselves been struck by an incurable disability, which still enables them to play a normal part in social life, can appreciate the apprehension which Swift expresses in one place where he speaks of his constant fear that giddiness might make him fall down in public. For a spirit as proud and sensitive as his, anticipation of helplessness and dependence must have been doubly fearful. And though, in a sense, an indomitable will and a powerful intellect were compensations for physical instability, they cannot have been sufficient to resolve a feeling of inner frustration, even if they helped him to conceal it from the world.

His treatment of the world, both in his actions and in his writings, may indeed have been prompted by some such physiological discord. His personality and character—his entire psychological make-up in fact—certainly seem in some degree to have been conditioned by it. One can understand why, if he despised and even hated his own body, he was fascinated and at the same time repelled by the functions in which the body is the chief actor. It is not without significance, in this connection, that Swift only mentions the organs of generation to draw attention to their excretory offices. The ruthless and repugnant passages in his poems where he reveals the secrets of a woman's toilet; his violent revulsion from such creatures as Maids of Honour and scatter-brained gossips; even his crushing unkindness to Vanessa, the only woman, one cannot help suspecting, with whom he went further than he intended, are no longer unaccountable if it is true that

Swift's awareness of a fatal constitutional flaw caused him to brood over his physical loneliness and prevented him from consummating his desires freely like other men. The same explanation holds for his horror of the Struldbruggs in the island of Luggnagg, whose bodies were senile but immortal, and of the Yahoos in the country of the Houyhnhnms, whose bodies were filthy and deformed. His contempt for the flesh is constantly expressed in his disgust of it, and in his pathological insistence on cleanliness. Time and again, he shatters the illusion that the human body is beautiful.

Psychological frustration with a physical origin provides a plausible explanation also of his mysterious relations with Miss Johnson, whom he adored, but never met, it is recorded, save in the company of a third person, as though fearing what might ensue from a too intimate contact; and it throws light as well on those killing words he wrote on the night of her funeral: "I am of opinion that there is not a greater folly than to contract too great and intimate friendship which must always leave the survivor miserable." What he is trying to convey, one feels, is that it was not the fear of actual bereavement or physical separation that appalled him, but the abnormal fear that ultimately his condition might leave him isolated and alone in the presence of those he loved without the intervention of death. It is possible that this neurosis was responsible for his delay in answering letters from friends in England as well as for his disinclination to visit them once he had established himself uneasily at the deanery of Saint Patrick's.

The secret conviction that he was doomed to frustration by a mechanical fault would account for many aspects of his life and writings, and explain the evolution of his personality and character. For, if he alone was conscious of a distinction between himself and the rest of mankind—and the conscious awareness of it can have been but a fraction of a suppressed, sub-conscious anxiety as to its possible repercussions—it is not unreasonable to conclude that his desire to dominate his fellow-men, his obstinacy, self-assertiveness, insolence and egotism were in the nature of compensations. The world, at least, should not be allowed to suspect any weakness. He would sublimate his own vexation by vexing it with an account of its follies and vices and damn it as "the most pernicious race of little odious vermin that Nature ever suffered to crawl upon the surface of the earth". And yet Swift was no misanthrope. He needed love, while dreading its consequences; and, as we know from the testimonies of many friends, he inspired it. He needed sympathy too, even though he frequently acknowledged it, knowing how easily and deeply he could be moved, by a kind of teasing playfulness. By contrast, there is nothing more pathetic or tender than the whimsical "baby-talk" in *The Journal to Stella*—the language of frustrated emotion in which he spoke to the one person to whom he ventured to open his heart and to that person alone, unaware that one day conscientious scholars would attempt to interpret it to the public. In it there is more than a hint of the verbal submissiveness and humility of the last years of his life when his mind was slowly parting company with his body.

An impending fear, such as Swift's, can hardly be put into words. A psychosis, in fact, cannot be formulated with any precision, and can be expressed only by implication. And even so, the implication may be distorted, through pride or vanity or unwillingness to admit defeat. There are, as we have seen, certain characteristics in Swift's work, which may possibly be related to a pathological condition inducing psychological frustration. But the process by which he passed from an intuition of it to implicit statement is nearly always elaborately disguised by his choice of subject matter. This is most apparent, as one would expect, in those essays and pamphlets where the subject was dictated by some special occasion or set of circumstances. It is significant, though, how much importance he attached to those two peculiarly original works *Polite Conversation* and *Directions to Servants*, and how long he took over their composition and revision. There is, however, among all his writings, one fragment in his own hand, found amongst his papers after his death and still extant, which in some ways suggests more directly than even his most intimate letters a sense of brooding frustration. This is the strange document, composed, presumably, for his eyes alone, in which he recorded certain resolutions to be followed *When I Come to be Old*. They are as follows:—

Not to marry a young woman.

Not to keep young company unless they really desire it.

Not to be peevish or morose, or suspicious.

Not to scorn present ways, or wits, or fashions, or men, or war, etc.

Not to be fond of children, or let them come near me hardly.

Not to tell the same story over and over to the same people.

Not to be covetous.

Not to neglect decency, or cleanliness, for fear of falling into nastiness.

Not to be over severe with young people, but give allowances for their youthful follies, and weaknesses.

Not to be influenced by, or give ear to knavish tattling servants, or others.

Not to be too free of advice nor trouble any but those that desire it.

To desire some good friends to inform me which of these Resolutions I break, or neglect, and wherein; and reform accordingly.

Not to talk much, nor of myself.

Not to boast of any former beauty, or strength, or favour with ladies, etc.

Not to hearken to flatteries, nor conceive I can be beloved
by a young woman, *et eos qui hereditatem captant odisse
ac vitare* [and to hate and shun legacy-hunters].

Not to be positive or opinionative.

Not to set up for observing all these Rules, for fear I
should observe none.

With certain reservations, this list is one that many men, in
a fit of self-analysis, might draw up in anticipation of old age,
though few, perhaps, would go so far as to put it down on
paper. Yet Swift did; and one cannot help suspecting that
he had reasons for his action which would not occur to those
who are not forced by some inner compulsion to take account
of the future. In 1699, when he noted down these resolutions,
he was no longer in his first youth. He was already in his
thirty-third year with only some forty years active life ahead
of him. He had written *A Tale of a Tub*. He was confident of
his powers. But the threat of progressive disability had already
been sounded and he must by then have recognized the first
symptoms of a nervous condition which later developed an
almost obsessional character. So, while it is clear that his
resolutions are based substantially on certain general principles by which any sensible man would wish to be guided in
his old age, they are undoubtedly influenced in places by
individual forebodings. The most striking evidence of this
occurs in the grim resolve "not to be fond of children, or let
them come near me hardly", a sentence so terrible that someone
has deleted the last seven words in the original manuscript.
It is scarcely credible that Swift's object here is simply to
anticipate and guard against the ridicule of doting senility.
The implication surely is that he dreaded an appeal to the
heart which could only be answered at the risk of indulging
feelings he had steeled himself to conceal from the world.
Children, in short, might remind him of pleasures from which

his condition had alienated him. Frustrated in his emotions, he was perhaps more easily moved by the feelings of others; his capacity for tenderness and affection, when he ventured to show it, is, indeed, singularly touching. With children, though, he dared not trust himself. There is something of the same mistrust, which made him resolve to forgo their company, in his attitude to young women.

For the rest, it is surprising and indeed perturbing how clearly he recognized the necessity for these rules of social behaviour in his own case. At the age of thirty-two, he seems to have foreseen with remarkable insight the potential weaknesses of a frustrated spirit—peevishness and moroseness, the shadows cast by despair; a tendency to scorn and contempt; the fear of physical dependence, implicit in the resolve not to be covetous or to neglect the body—the psychiatrist will not miss the significance of these juxtaposed resolutions; the temptation to rely upon the posthumous generosity of other men; the temptation, also, to establish self-confidence and exercise power by giving advice and holding forth in company; and above all the fear of emotional entanglement.

Our understanding of Swift, as I have said, is largely a matter of conjecture, but it is not unreasonable to suppose that his personality and character were profoundly modified and his actions conditioned by the effort, conscious or otherwise, to suppress or sublimate these apprehensions. That his efforts were never wholly successful can be deduced from his biography. As his physical infirmity became more burdensome through increasingly recurrent attacks of giddiness and deafness, so it became more difficult for him to control its psychological manifestations. The surprising thing is that he supported it so long and so bravely. In the end, he did give way to many of the weaknesses he had earlier resolved to avoid. The last third of his life was intermittently overcast by his inability to overcome frustration and resign himself completely to the endless compromise it involved. He was too proud and too ambitious. The picture is a tragic one, though not more so than that of any other fiery spirit fretted away by some inner conflict, and under a perpetual necessity to adjust itself to society. And yet there must surely have been for Swift, withdrawn by old age and sickness and loss or absence of former friends more and more deeply into himself, some consolation, if not satisfaction, in the thought that he had succeeded in imposing himself on the world, had stirred one nation, at least, out of its age-long apathy, and, though he had failed to rule mankind with scorpions, had commanded its respect and diverted it with an account of its own follies.

SARAH, DUCHESS OF MARLBOROUGH

(1660-1744)

by Beatrice Curtis Brown

AROUND the years 1676 and 1677 some amusement was caused at Whitehall by Colonel Churchill's courtship of Sarah Jennings. Churchill's charm, good manners, military reputation and integrity could easily have won him a rich and influential wife: Sarah was neither. She was a fairhaired little girl, with a high complexion, sharp eyes and a perfectly undisciplined tongue. Being observant and quick of speech she was good company; and in a court where hope of advancement depended largely on keeping on the right side of someone of consequence, very few unimportant people could afford to be amusing.

But Churchill was attracted by more than Sarah's wit or good looks; his wisdom and gentleness (for these, along with all the heroic virtues, he possessed) recognized a tenderness and a power of noble affection in her—qualities of which she herself must have been nearly unconscious and which would have been hidden from the world, had his love for her not testified to their existence. For two years the struggle went on between them. For all Sarah's shrewdness she knew no better than to treat the courtship of this chivalrous and heroic lover as the advances of the ordinary court philanderer. She was, as she always remained, a vulgar woman. Being vulgar she knew no other way to answer his vows of love but with contradictions, his patience with abuse. When he took her at her word and turned away, she said: "There you see!" She could have been forgiven some hesitation; it was a lax-mannered court, Churchill himself had been Lady Castlemaine's lover, the marriage was frowned upon by his family. But her disingenuousness (for she clearly loved him) was not pretty and her rudeness was intolerable.

"I have been so extreme ill with the headache all this morning that I have not had the courage to write to know how you do (Churchill writes, one time) but your being well is what I prefer much above my own health. Therefore pray send me word, for if you are not in pain I cannot then be much troubled, for were it not for the joy I take in the thought that you love me, I should not care how soon I died . . . if the Duchess sees company, I hope you will be there; but if she does not, I beg you will then let me see you in your chamber, if it be for one hour. . . ."

Says Sarah:

"At four o'clock I would see you, but that would hinder you from seeing the play, which I fear would be a great affliction to you and increase the pain in your head, which would then be out of anybody's power to ease until the next new play. Therefore pray consider, and without any compliment to me, send me word if you can come to me without any prejudice to your health."

For two years Sarah turned and twisted, fighting like a possessed body under the hands of the exorcist, and, like the exorcist, Churchill held on, his eyes fixed on that angry resentful face, in which he saw something which was worth more to him than peace of mind or even happiness. With a last twist, Sarah gave in ("As I have always shown more kindness for you than perhaps I ought," she wrote on the eve of their marriage). From that moment she accepted eagerly the love he offered, was overwhelmed and shamed by it and gave it back in her own strange, tempestuous, crazy fashion till the end of her life. For his sake she became ambitious and for his sake at last she ruined herself and him too. However much the world learned to praise him, she could outdo it; at the end of her life the sight of his name moved her to a tenderness she never showed at any other time, and in writing of him then she would tumble out the words, mixing praise and love and admiration all together; "I have read Lediard's History . . . everything I have yet read is so true of the late Duke of Marlborough that I could not read it without wetting the paper . . . He was naturally genteel, without the least affectation and handsome as an angel though ever so carelessly drest . . ."

Sarah's love for Churchill is the main factor of her life and the impulse behind nearly all her actions. As he had exorcised her wild demoniac spirit in girlhood, so his patient nobility tamed and quietened her during the next twenty years—though he was never able to curb her during her violent storms of temper. But at least, while he was more or less constantly beside her, she allowed herself to be guided by him in her general conduct. When his quietening presence was removed for the greater part of each year—as happened after 1702—her passions and prejudices, unchecked by him, led her to the ruin that was their inevitable consequence.

There was at this time one other person who felt a deep affection for Sarah, and that was the daughter of Churchill's master the Duke of York—the young princess Anne. Anne was also lively-minded and observant, though far less articulate than

Sarah—partly because her royal good manners imposed upon her speech bounds that Sarah never recognized, and partly because she had no quickness of tongue. She was, on the other hand, of a more reflective turn of mind than her friend and she possessed at least the glimmerings of imagination, which Sarah almost entirely lacked. Anne was wretchedly placed: she was a staunch Protestant, yet daughter of an unpopular Catholic. Her father was heir to the throne and she herself had to marry and comport herself as one who might some day be Queen—yet this prospect was uncomfortingly remote. In this position, she found Sarah's gay spirits, shrewdness and nonconforming mind the greatest refreshment, and to Sarah herself Anne was so sympathetic a companion that when the princess married she offered to leave her post in the Duchess's household and join Anne's. The offer was eagerly accepted. By this time they were far too intimate friends to allow any nonsense of rank to come between them. Anne suggested that they should call each other Mrs. Morley and Mrs. Freeman. Sarah agreed; "I shall be Mrs. Freeman because it suits my frank, open temper," she stipulated.

The friendship between them was intensified and extended by Anne's admiration of and trust in Churchill. When James came to the throne the three of them made a little knot of anxious but unwavering protestantism amid the retreats and apostasies of the rest of the King's servants. Sarah had few illusions about court life but these years of James's reign made an impression upon her which later became an obsession. Hereafter she saw a conspirator in every Catholic—eventually in every churchman—and a traitor in every favourite. She managed to hold her tongue in public—Churchill saw to that— but she said, no doubt, plenty to Anne in private. But Anne needed no telling. She had put herself in Churchill's hands and in the hands of her sister, Mary of Orange, who wrote her weekly letters of advice. It was an anxious time for them all, but there was nothing that the ladies could do but sew, play with their children, and gossip, while Churchill and the other patriots worked out a scheme with William of Orange. When the day came for action, Sarah carried out her small part without a hitch. She roused Anne from sleep, got her down the wooden ladder she had had made for the occasion, into the Bishop of London's coach and so safely out of London.

So far, Sarah's "frank, open temper" had not attracted any special attention. She was no more, if no less, than the wife of Baron Churchill (now Earl of Marlborough)—though she was known to be an intimate friend of the Princess Anne's. But now circumstances put her in a position where her personality could usefully be exploited by her opponents. For Marlborough's principles led him to support Anne in the disputes that broke out almost immediately William and Mary came to the throne. The root of these disputes lay in the reigning sovereigns' jealousy and fear of Anne as the heir; Marlborough, as Anne's friend and, moreover, as one who had already helped to turn out a previous monarch, was particularly suspect. Where he led, his wife followed: the three of them made a clique which must be broken up. This situation was bound to arise and actually Sarah did not have much responsibility for what followed. Had she been a different type of woman, however, Queen Mary could not so boldly have taken a step which split the country's loyalty and led to a lasting alienation from her sister—her command to Anne to dismiss Lady Marlborough. Mary, no doubt, believed, or pretended to believe, that Anne was entirely under Sarah's thumb. There is nothing to show that this was true; but Sarah's frank, open temper was there for all to see; she said what she thought (and she thought the court's treatment of Anne was scandalous—as it was) and she said it often. Anne, on the other hand, said little. Therefore (the fallacy is great but it persists) Anne must be doing what Sarah told her.

Courteously and with great dignity, Anne declined to dismiss her friend. Letters flew back and forth. Sarah immediately offered to resign. Anne brushed the offer aside. The Queen forbade Sarah to come to court: Anne's answer was to withdraw from court herself and retire into the country. The Queen then removed her guards and forbade officials to pay her honour. Broadsheets and letters were full of the quarrel; and out of it all, though she was only superficially responsible for what had happened, Sarah emerged as a national figure.

So now the friendship between Sarah and Anne, founded on the common interests of their youth and young womanhood, was deepened by the sacrifices they had made to maintain it. Either could have deserted the other and spent the next few years in glory at court rather than in disgrace in the country. What they had surrendered for the sake of their love, made that love the more valuable. Since they had always been victims of the same persecutions, moreover, their resentments —that is, their political opinions—appeared to be identical. The throne had ill-used them; therefore they were both opposed to the throne and its friends: the Papist peril had threatened them both. United in opposition, yet powerless to act, they did not need to distress themselves over minute differences in their general political point of view. If Sarah's anti-papistry impelled her to say "Down with all Churchmen", and Anne's resentment of William was filling her with a distrust of all Whigs and republicans, this was forgotten in their agreement about the outrageousness of everything. And from Anne's point of view, there was nothing to fear from Sarah's occasional intractability, because Marlborough was a loyal Tory and churchman. But they were chiefly drawn together now, as before, less by politics than by the joys and sorrows of their private lives. They each lost a son during these years, Marlborough was sent to the Tower for a short time, Prince George was insulted by William. Through all this Anne and Sarah solaced and comforted each other; neither was lacking in tenderness. For though no letters from Sarah to Anne survive of this period, the affection in Anne's letters is a testimony to the affection she had been shown. Even the softhearted Anne could not maintain a one-sided friendship for so long.

In 1694, the Queen died and all three were recalled from exile. Marlborough rose high in William's favour, Anne and Sarah took their rightful place in court life. These were Sarah's best years. She was making many friends; her children were a credit to her. She married her eldest daughter to the son of her husband's dearest friend, Godolphin, another to Sunderland's republican son, Lord Spencer. She herself, now nearly forty, was more beautiful than ever, her opinions were popular, her wit was no longer mistaken for insolence. She was clearly a woman intended for a conspicuous position and in March 1702 she succeeded to it, for Anne came to the throne.

For nearly twenty-five years, she had been the Queen's most intimate friend; no wonder the eyes of the world were fixed upon her now. But the world drew the same inferences that the court had drawn fourteen years before; Sarah was quick-witted and talkative, Anne was slow-thinking and silent; there fore Anne would wear the crown while Sarah reigned. The world could not read their letters nor hear their private conversations. It could not know that only six months after her accession Anne was writing:

"I cannot help being extremely concerned you are so partial to the Whigs, because I would not have you and your poor unfortunate faithful Morley differ in opinion in the least thing . . . and upon my word, my dear Mrs. Freeman, you are mightily mistaken in your notion of a true Whig. . . ."

Neither of the two women had realized that when Anne came to the throne, their political views must be translated into action, and the slight divergences in those views—mere differences of definition hitherto—would be revealed as a real cleft in their political philosophy. And Sarah never realized, till too late, that her friendship with Anne was, from Anne's point of view, a private and not a political affair; years of fireside gossip, of making quilts and bringing up children together had built up an affection in which public affairs played little part. On this plane, Anne was Morley to Sarah's Freeman, Sarah was encouraged to speak out and her advice was solicited. But reigning over England was Anne's own business; Sarah had no part in this—more particularly since her Whiggish, anti-church opinions were her one flaw. As soon as she came to the throne, Anne closed a door upon Sarah. Sarah saw the door, but the distinction Anne drew between Sarah private and Sarah political seemed so preposterous to her that she would not accept it. She spent the next ten years —the years which should have been the time of her greatest glory, the years for which she is famous—kicking angrily at the door.

The world, no more perceptive than Sarah, waited for her to play her part: to the Whigs she was to be an ally, to the Tories a dreaded enemy. So far as she played a part, she involuntarily reversed the roles. One thing no one could believe: that she affected the course of events hardly at all. So long as she was at court, statesmen came to thank her for their advancement and solicited her favour. She had all the glory of the position they imagined for her. But Sarah never cared for glory: she knew that she had failed and drew nothing but bitterness from the illusion of success.

There was really only one thing that was required of Sarah by those she wished to help—that she should remain the Queen's most delightful companion and ensure that the associations she evoked should always be pleasant ones. For in Anne's mind, Sarah was, of course identified with Marlborough, away directing the Allied armies on the Continent, and with Godolphin, the Lord Treasurer. These two were carrying on a war with the most unwilling co-operation of their Tory colleagues and under the suspicious eyes of their Whig opponents, who felt a proprietary interest in the war which they were prevented from putting into action by the Queen's distrust of their party. Godolphin and Marlborough were Tories as yet; Sarah was becoming daily more and more of a Whig.

Up to this time, Marlborough had been able to keep his wife in check; now, at the most important moment of his career, he had to leave her for six months of every year. She was to keep the Queen happy and act as liaison officer between the Queen and Godolphin. She was not called upon to have political opinions of her own or to put any pressure upon the Queen herself. Marlborough knew this was vain. "I have observed, when she thinks herself in the right, she need no advice," he wrote to Sarah some years later.

But Sarah failed to do any of these things; she did exactly the opposite, because she was, fundamentally, a stupid woman. She never showed that "masculine sagacity" with which she has been credited; she possessed only an impatient desire to "get things done". She was interested in ends—means never concerned her. Whigs were pro-war (war was all-important— it was Marlborough's war); why not put them in office at once? Tories were churchmen—churchmen were Jacobites— Jacobites were Papists: so suppress the Tories. While Godolphin and Marlborough were trying delicately to walk a tightrope between the parties, Sarah did her best to cut the rope down altogether. If the Queen had preferences, that was unreasonable; she must be talked out of them. She scolded the

Queen, harried Godolphin and bullied her husband. But Anne only replied:

> "I must own to you that I never cared to mention any-thing on this subject to you, because I knew you would not be of my mind . . . never let difference of opinion hinder us from living together as we used to do. . . ."

And Marlborough wrote wearily: "I can by no means allow that all the Tory party are for King James and con-sequently against the Queen, but the contrary."

Instead of seeking new tactics, Sarah merely pursued the attack more vigorously than before. Marlborough was made miserable by her letters, the Queen was reduced to tears Sarah was not happy herself—she did not possess Marl-borough's vision; "England will take care of herself," he wrote, "and will not be ruined because a few men are not pleased." To Sarah, every minor Tory triumph was a disaster because she saw her husband's downfall reflected in it. As she grew more frightened so she grew more reckless; there was no question now of her keeping the Queen happy—she must never be left in peace till she surrendered. But the Queen replied:

> "I have the same opinion of Whig and Tory that I ever had. I know both their principles very well and when I know myself to be in the right nothing can make me alter mine. It is certain there are good and ill people of both sorts. . . ."

If Sarah could only have been patient! For all this time events were slowly moving in the direction that she desired— it was inevitable that they should. Of her own free will, early in the reign, Anne dismissed her most die-hard Tory ministers. In 1705, she found she was obliged to take the Whig, Cowper, as her Lord Keeper—though she fought hard against the appointment. But this fight was nothing to the opposition she put up to Sunderland, Sarah's son-in-law, when he was proposed for Secretary of State in 1706. Sarah plunged furiously into the fight over these two appointments; while Godolphin pleaded and Marlborough reasoned with the Queen, Sarah used her own truculent measures. In vain did Marlborough write (during a temporary lull): "It is a pleasure to me . . . that you are easier with the Queen, I think for the good of everything you should make it your business to have it so"—to be "easy" was now almost a physical impossibility. She bombarded Anne with insulting letters when she was away from her, and when they were together the voice of the Duchess, raised in reproach, could be heard all over the palace. In the Sunderland dispute she went so far that the Queen was dangerously offended and the wretched Godolphin (for whom Sarah was to have made things easy) had to hurry to Windsor to patch up the quarrel. Eventually Sunderland was appointed and the Whigs triumphed, but Sarah had not contributed an iota to their success. Not one of her angry letters had moved the Queen; she had remained adamant till Marlborough returned from the front and reasoned her into compliance. "There is no reason to hope for the least assistance from Mrs. Freeman in this matter," Godolphin had written to Marlborough that summer.

There was still time to reclaim lost ground with Anne. "If you could see my heart, you would find it as sincere, as tender and passionately fond of you as ever . . . though we have the misfortune to differ in some things . . ." wrote Anne this year. But panic for Marlborough's career, Sunderland's flattery (he was her evil genius at this time) and political obsessions, made Sarah incapable of seeing Anne as a person at all: affection had been crowded out long ago. Anne might have written to a stone wall for all the response she got.

So the Queen naturally turned elsewhere. A young woman in the household, called Abigail Hill, was doing for the Tories exactly what Sarah should have done for the Whigs—that is to say, doing nothing but behave agreeably, slipping in a suggestion here and there and reporting back to Harley, the Tory leader, anything that might be of use to him. Sarah soon got wind of this new alliance—here was indeed a new peril for Marlborough, and here was a new stick with which to belabour the Queen. She set to, with a savagery as yet held in reserve, and gave Abigail more points in the game than that mild, uninspired woman could ever have won for herself. The Queen was past patience now; "I believe others that have been in her station in former times have been tattling and very impertinent, but she is not at all of that temper," she wrote when Sarah complained of her new intimacy. So Sarah sent her an account of her own faithful services for twenty-six years, of the Queen's appreciation of this in the past, of the loss of her favour "by the artifices of my enemies," and added to all this extracts from *The Whole Duty of Man*, the directions in the Common Prayer Book with regard to conciliation before Communion and the rules laid down by Bishop Taylor on this matter.

But the new alliance continued and in 1708 Sarah disgustedly retired from the court, attending on the Queen only when her presence was officially required. Almost at the same moment Harley was forced to resign by the Whigs who now took full control of the Cabinet.

Sarah and Anne met only once more as friends—over Prince George's dead body—and only then because Sarah was determined to prevent Abigail from being comforter-in-chief. But though she and Anne were scarcely on speaking terms, Sarah did not cease to pour forth angry letters; Anne was not allowed to forget her, or to remember her save with irritation. For though the Whigs were in power, everyone knew that Harley and Abigail had the Queen's heart—Marlborough, now at the height of his power was never less safe: Tory propaganda was preparing the way for his downfall. Two years after her retirement Sarah forced her way into Anne's presence and demanded an opportunity of justifying herself against her enemies' libels. But: "You shall have no answer," said Anne. "You shall have no answer." A few months later she was asked to resign all her offices; by then the Whigs had fallen, never to return during Anne's life. Only for one moment did Sarah realize how she had failed. When she received her dismissal, she wrote to the Queen begging for a second chance, "if I am still so unlucky as not to make use of any expression in this letter that can move your Majesty, it is purely for want of understanding; for I really am very sorry that I ever did anything that was uneasy to your Majesty . . . I do solemnly protest that . . . I will never mention either of those subjects to you or do any one thing that can give you uneasiness." But now it was too late. In 1711 Marlborough himself was dismissed.

There is little left to tell, though she lived for thirty-two years longer. Bitter and homesick she followed Marlborough into exile next year. Still bitter, if triumphant, she returned with him in glory when Anne died. Then followed six joyful years while Marlborough lived retired and honoured among his friends and children. But in 1720 Marlborough died and Sarah, sixty years old, a relic of King Charles's days, was left to the amused attention of Georgian London. Yet at this age she was most truly and magnificently herself. There was no one to check her now. The outrageous temper which had waxed in strength during Queen Anne's reign, was let loose on anyone at a moment's notice. Most of her remaining twenty-four years she spent in endless lawsuits against enemies, friends and kinsmen. She libelled everyone, including the now triumphant Whig statesmen (Walpole above all). She quarrelled with all her children and most of her grandchildren. She entered into barren political intrigues; she insulted the Crown. Her personal remarks were drier and wittier than ever; her political judgments as extreme and shortsighted as before; indeed her strictures on Walpole and his love of peace greatly resemble the manifestoes of a certain patriot-editress of to-day.

But absurd or not, she was at this time magnificent; in her pride, in her loneliness, in her courage and wit, in her moments of tenderness, in her loyalty to the memory of Marlborough. The young men could call her Old Marlborough and laugh at her—but they never failed to repeat her latest sayings to each other. Pope loved her and enjoyed her company; Mary Wortley Montagu was her intimate. Now, as an eccentric, angry, brave old woman she held her own, and none could overthrow her. So that even to-day Horace Walpole's words, "Old Marlborough is dying" call up a majestic and tragic image to our minds; we remember some picture of a noble and fabulous lion lying wounded and alone on a bare mountain.

Sarah's life is a paradox: she is famous for what she failed to do. She had an opportunity which no one but a fool could have missed; she was no fool, yet she mishandled it because she was insensitive and unimaginative—and because her love and anxiety for Marlborough crowded out her discretion. And yet if she had acted her part well she might never have become famous; the obstreperousness which caused her failure is also responsible for her fame. To-day it is clear that Sarah could have had no positive influence on the course of events; no Mistress of the Robes, however powerful, could swing the pendulum from war to peace, or Whig to Tory. But the distress of spirit borne by Anne, by Marlborough, Godolphin and Sarah herself, during those years might have been lightened; Anne's bitter cruelty to Marlborough at the end, and the peculiar brutality of the Tory attack upon him, might have been avoided, if Sarah had possessed the foresight and sagacity with which she has been credited. But even now, when Anne's letters and the political and social correspondence of the time are open to us, and we can tell how far Sarah failed, she remains a great figure, and always will. And this is because though insensitive and arrogant she was vital, dauntless and unashamed in a world which at all times must be composed mainly of the timid, the colourless and the defeated.

5

DANIEL DEFOE

(1660–1731)

by G. D. H. Cole

DANIEL DEFOE was known best during his own life as "the Author of *The True-born Englishman*" or "the Author of the *Review*". Posterity knows him best as "the Author of *Robinson Crusoe*". Among his contemporaries he had the distinction of being the most abused of all writers. Pope reviled him in *The Dunciad*, pretending to believe that he had lost his ears as well as stood in the pillory: Swift again and again referred to him contemptuously as an illiterate scribbler: Whig and Tory, Jacobite and Hanoverian, alike slung mud at him. He was accused of dishonesty in his business relations, of being a secret spy in Government pay, ready at all times to turn his coat in order to keep his place, of writing only for pay and caring not at all what he wrote. Even in his own day no one could say with certainty how much that was attributed to him was really his; and on this issue the critics are still disputing, and will dispute as long as he is remembered at all. He was twice imprisoned, and twice pilloried: he became a bankrupt, and was haunted by creditors most of his life. He made several fortunes and lost them; and, amid many mysteries that still attend his career, the last year of his life remains the greatest mystery of all. For Defoe died in hiding; but no endeavour of his biographers has availed to discover what or who pursued him. It may even be that he was flying only from his own too lively imagination.

Defoe was in his day a merchant, and he never ceased for long to meddle with commercial concerns, over and above his writing, which was for him very much a matter of business. But he was above all else a writer with an itch to write. He could not possibly have stopped writing, even if nobody would have paid him a penny for what he wrote. He was more than thirty when the first work we know to be his appeared in print, and he seems to have published little for six or seven years after that. But then the spate began; and when Defoe had once set up as an author it was quite impossible for him ever to stop. He began with political pamphlets, some in prose and some in verse that is near doggerel at its worst but has pungency and rises at its best into effective satire. He was in his forty-fourth year before he had written anything more extensive than an enlarged pamphlet. Then, in 1704, he made his bow as a journalist, with the famous *Review* which, published usually two or three times a week, he conducted practically single-handed for more than nine years. All this time he went on writing pamphlets and verses, in addition to his journalism; but when he was fifty-five he had published, apart from two collected volumes of his shorter writings, only two books of any account—*The Consolidator*, a satirical account of a journey to the moon which in some ways foreshadows *Gulliver*, and his elaborate *History of the Union of Great Britain*, dealing with the Union of the English and Scottish Parliaments, with which he had been throughout the negotiations very closely concerned. Even then, four years were still to pass before the opening of his great period of writing. *Robinson Crusoe*, the first of his novels, appeared in 1719, when he was nearly fifty-nine; and within the next six years he produced in swift succession *Memoirs of a Cavalier, Captain Singleton, Moll Flanders, A Journal of the Plague Year, Colonel Jacque, Roxana,* and *A New Voyage Round the World,* to say nothing of his *Tour through the Whole Island of Great Britain,* and the first volume of his *Complete English Tradesman,* or of a host of minor writings of any and every sort. Moreover, through these crowded years he was still the assiduous journalist. He conducted a daily newspaper, wrote regularly for more than one weekly, and had a finger in a host of other journalistic pies. His last years are hardly less crowded with writing: up to the moment of the illness which preceded his mysterious flight he went on scribbling hard. It is even difficult to believe that he did not die with a pen in his hand.

An author who wrote so much had no leisure to polish what he wrote. But Defoe would not have bettered his writing by being at greater pains. He wrote as the words came; without elegance, but with directness, force and simplicity. His best effects depend upon these qualities: he has a supreme naturalness, an ordinariness of phrasing that makes his fancy seem truth, and gets right home to his readers. With this he has an ordinary mind, so that, whatever extraordinary things his characters may do or suffer, they are all ordinary people, acting or reacting in ways that anyone can immediately understand. This is as true of Roxana, or of Moll Flanders, in their most disreputable adventures, as it is of Crusoe on his island, or of any of those real people whose lives Defoe translated into stories to amuse or instruct his public. There is no difference between Defoe the reporter and Defoe the novelist. His real and his fictitious characters are just the same. *The Apparition of Mrs. Veal* passed for a masterly flight of his imagination till, quite recently, some industrious delver found out that it was all true.

Defoe's contemporaries called him an illiterate scribbler because the wits of the age—Swift and Pope, Addison and

Prior—loved polish, and Defoe had none. The polite world of his day despised him, and resented his circulation among the vulgar. Their contempt riled Defoe, who liked to think himself a man of culture, and was proud of being a wit and scholar who knew how to be a "complete English tradesman" as well. He hated "fops" and aristocrats who looked down their noses at honest commercial gentlemen, and deemed the latter of far more use to the country because they lived not at its expense but to its gain as well as their own. But he wanted his claims to intellectual equality to be admitted. There were only two charges, among the many flung at him, that he really resented. One was that he was a mere hireling, writing only for bread. The other was that he was illiterate; and I think the second rankled the more.

Defoe wrote many people's lives, real or imaginary, but never his own, save to the extent to which *Robinson Crusoe* is to be regarded as an allegory of his own experience. But he wrote much about himself, not only in his *Appeal to Honour and Justice*, in which he defended himself against his critics, but also in his journalism, which he was constantly seasoning with personal allusion and anecdote. A good part of an autobiography could be pieced together out of his own words; but it would not tell the whole story. For one vital part of the story could not be fully told at the time, though even then much of it was half known. Defoe was for many years, first probably under William III and certainly later under Anne and George I, a political agent in the Government's pay; and estimates of him as a man, and of his honesty as a writer, turn largely on what is made of this aspect of his crowded career. Let me say at once one thing about what I make of it. After a fairly extensive study of his writings, I feel confident that he never wrote a word against his convictions, though he often edited for the press other men's writings with which he did not agree, and often kept out of his own writings things that he would have said if he had felt free to speak his whole mind. Few professional journalists, I think, can claim more than that.

But before we come to Defoe the journalist, something must be said of his earlier career. Daniel Foe—the "De" is of his own adding—was born in 1660, the son of a London butcher who was an active Dissenter. He was meant for the ministry, and educated at a Dissenting Academy in Newington, whither he returned later to live in a substantial house of his own building. But he felt himself unsuited for the ministry, though he remained a staunch Dissenter all his life; and instead he was apprenticed to a merchant who dealt in hosiery and wine, exporting the one and importing the other. His time out, he set up for himself as a hose-factor in 1685, became a City liveryman in 1688, and failed in business in 1692, partly by his own fault, but also partly because of losses due to the war. In 1694 he received a small Government post as accountant to the Commissioners of the Glass Duty, and kept it till the duty was abolished in 1699. Meanwhile, he had become secretary and manager to a company which set up a brick and pantile factory at Tilbury—a new branch of the manufacture designed to rival the Dutch. This lasted till 1703, when his imprisonment ruined his business—or so he explained his severance from it. Thereafter, although he engaged from time to time in commercial speculations, especially in his latter years, his business career was over. He lived by writing, and by serving the Government as a secret agent.

Defoe had achieved fame as an author two years before he published the pamphlet which brought him into conflict with the law. Until 1701 he was merely one of a host of pamphleteers on the Whig side, devoted to the "glorious Revolution" of 1688 and the cause of Protestantism, though he had already written one book which posterity ranks among the best of his secondary works. His *Essay on Projects*, published in 1698, foreshadows much of his later economic and social writing. It has often been praised for its anticipations of reforms which were long in coming, for its enlightened outlook on women's education, and for its plain common sense amid the darkness and confusion of the times. But it was not much noticed by his contemporaries. Nor did his vigorous controversial pamphlets against the practice of Occasional Conformity do more than embroil him with his own friends, the Dissenters; for even those who were not prepared, in Defoe's own phrase, "to play bo-peep with God Almighty," resented his action in writing openly against those who did, on the ground that what he said might strengthen the hands of the "High-flyers" (the High-Church Tories) in procuring more drastic penal laws against Dissent. Defoe found fame, not by solemn argument, but by satire, through *The True-born Englishman*, which is undoubtedly by far the best of his verse.

The True-born Englishman was a political squib, in defence of "Dutch William" and his foreign favourites at court. John Tutchin, in *The Foreigners*, and many others had sought to rouse their countrymen against the King's foreign friends. Defoe retorted with an effective exposure of the Englishman's own mongrel antecedents:—

> "A true-born Englishman's a contradiction,
> In speech an irony, in fact a fiction."

and

> "The silent nations undistinguished fall,
> And Englishman's the common name of all.
> Fate jumbled them together, God knows how;
> Whate'er they were, they're true-born English now."

At this, and much more like it, the true-born Englishman knew how to laugh. The satire brought Defoe King William's favour, so that, till the sovereign's death the following year, the poet had clearly some degree of the King's confidence, and was his adviser in more than one commercial and political scheme. Perhaps, indeed, the connection had begun earlier, while Defoe still held his minor official post. Whether or no, there is no reason to doubt his repeated assertions that he was on terms of trust and service with William III during the last years of his reign. But the King's death ended that, and ended too the immunity from prosecution which printers and authors had for the most part enjoyed under his rule.

It will be remembered that, when Royal Anne became our Queen, the Vicar of Bray hastened to turn Tory. The press was kept busy with "High-flying" pamphlets; and the Dissenters felt themselves in imminent danger of a renewal of severely repressive measures. Dr. Sacheverell preached his "Oxford" sermon against them; and Bills for suppressing Dissenting conventicles and academies and for the rigid exclusion of Dissenters from all forms of public office were everywhere in the air. Into the very midst of the prevailing excitement the "Author of *The True-born Englishman*" flung forth his pamphlet, *The Shortest Way with the Dissenters*.

The Shortest Way was anonymous—on the face of it, the work of the highest-flyer of all the Church of England covey. It advocated, in so many words, not repressing the Dissenters, but exterminating them—stamping them out till no such thing as a Dissenter should be left in the land. Defoe's aim was, by invoking the help of irony, to laugh the persecutors out of court. He carried their doctrine to a ridiculous extreme; but, instead of raising a laugh, as he had done with *The True-born Englishman*, he had the misfortune this time to be taken seriously. Tory High-flyers lauded his work from the pulpit— and then discovered that *The Shortest Way* was a hoax.

The true-born Englishman has a sense of humour; but it does not embrace irony. In England a man is ironical at his peril. What Butler met with when he published *The Fair*

Haven, Defoe had to encounter over *The Shortest Way.* For there are few things so infuriating as to be the victim of a joke one has not seen. Nearly everybody was rabid against Defoe; for his Dissenting friends could appreciate his irony as little as his Tory enemies. The Tories, however, had more immediate power to hurt him. He was prosecuted for a seditious libel, shut up in Newgate, and in due course sentenced to be fined and imprisoned, and to stand in the pillory, where it was hoped all parties would unite to pelt him with stones and rotten eggs.

But the ironist was not left wholly without friends. John Tutchin, known as *Observator,* from his newspaper, and a fellow-pamphleteer, did see the joke, and organized a Whig mob to protect him from the missiles of the Tories—his Dissenting critics, as sober citizens, not being addicted to the throwing of rotten eggs. Moreover, Defoe entered into the spirit of the occasion with his *Hymn to the Pillory,* written from Newgate and hawked as a broadside among the crowd that came to watch his exposure. His humiliation was turned into a popular triumph—for the moment. Nevertheless, haled back to prison with a prospect of prolonged confinement before him, ruined in business and still pursued by his creditors of ten years before, out of credit with the Dissenters and hated inveterately by the Tories, Defoe was in no position to glory overmuch in turning the tables on his adversaries. By his own testimony he was in despair; and out of his despair came the negotiations which procured him, within a few months, the Queen's pardon for his "offence" and a new role as the confidential agent of Harley and, through Harley, of the Government itself.

Defoe's relations with Harley, which long remained obscure, have been partly cleared up by the publication of his correspondence found by the Historical Manuscripts Commission among the Portland Papers. Defoe was enlisted in Harley's service, with Lord Godolphin's approval and the Queen's, to report on the state of opinion in the country, to build up a body of local correspondents who would inform him of currents of feeling in each area, and to influence opinion as well as to sound and record it. But he was not asked—that is plain from the correspondence—nor did he undertake to do anything against his own convictions. For a long time past Defoe, despite his capacity for embroiling himself, had been essentially a "moderate", deprecating violent quarrels between parties and seeking a tolerant pacification that would secure the Protestant succession on a foundation of "live, and let live". This suited Harley, who was himself a friend to the Dissenters, and Godolphin, who saw in political assuagement the best hope of retaining power for himself and Marlborough and the Whig-cum-Protestant interest. Defoe's post with the Government was as honourable as any post in the secret service can be. Indeed, his record over the next few years fully vindicates his honesty—for he freely criticized the Government in print on many matters, even while he was drawing its pay. He attacked its measures against the Dissenters, which Harley no doubt disliked as much as he. But he also freely criticized the terms of the Treaty of Utrecht, and ventured on other occasions to dissent publicly from the policy of his official paymaster.

What Defoe wanted from the Government was a regular office, such as he had enjoyed previously under William III. But, though the hope of this was again and again held out to him, he had to make the best of irregular subventions through Harley, either from that astute politician's own pocket or, more probably, from the secret service funds. Before long he went touring England on his mission of sounding and influencing opinion, especially among the provincial Dissenters, whom he sought to turn to moderate support of the Government for fear its fall might let in something worse. Already he was taking an interest in the affairs of Scotland, where the question of Union with England was being hotly discussed. In 1706 Harley sent him to Scotland as a secret agent, to mingle with the Scots without revealing his mission, to register and to mould opinion, and to lend a hand, out of his commercial knowledge, in drafting the economic terms of the Act of Union.

There can be no doubt that Defoe, posing usually as a merchant on the look-out for commercial openings, did his work in Scotland well. During the next few years, first as Harley's agent and later as Godolphin's after Harley's fall from office, he was in Scotland most of the time; and he did many things there besides his official work on behalf of the Government. All this while, despite the extreme badness of communication by road—of which we hear a great deal in his letters—he managed regularly to bring out his *Review* in London. He had established it in 1704, at the same time as he entered into the Government's service; and it was doubtless run with the aid of Government money, for Defoe is emphatic that it never paid its way. Part of the time he published it also in a special Scottish edition; and after he had dropped this he conducted for a time a Scottish newspaper of his own—the *Edinburgh Courant*. Beyond all this, he found time to pour out from the press a stream of pamphlets, to write *The Consolidator* and his elaborate *History of the Union*, and to make numerous journeys about the country and keep in touch with a host of correspondents upon political affairs. Of course he must have had "ghosts" to help him do all this—at the least a faithful "man Friday" to take charge of his affairs in London when he was away. But whatever hands helped him with his journalism, there is no reason to suppose that any hand but his wrote the numerous books and pamphlets that went out from him during these years, or that he failed to keep full control over any of his numerous affairs. He was assuredly sincere in his protest that he had never accepted dictation from any source about what he should write, or shown Harley any of his writings with a view to censorship before they were put into print.

Nevertheless, being a secret agent is an equivocal business, especially when the agency is only half a secret. Defoe's close relations with Harley were, almost from the beginning, pretty widely known, though their exact nature was not; and accordingly the worst construction was put upon them by Harley's political opponents—Whigs and High-flyers alike. Nor was Defoe himself immune from the effects of his employment. He developed a habit of mystification beyond the need; and this never left him afterwards. Indeed, it grew upon him in later life, till, in the words of his son-in-law, Henry Baker, he had become a man who loved "to hide himself in mists", and was quite incapable of giving a plain relation of his own affairs. This foible had, however, its literary compensations; for without it he would hardly have written with so astonishing a semblance of reality the histories of Moll Flanders, or Roxana, or Robinson Crusoe himself.

As long as Harley or Godolphin remained in office, Defoe's position was assured; for he was far too valuable an agent for them to lose, whatever liberties he might venture to take. His taste for irony did, indeed, threaten to get him again into serious trouble in 1713, when, despite his connection with the Government, he had a second short spell in gaol. This was over his "Hanover" pamphlets, of which the first, *Reasons against the Succession of the House of Hanover*, was seriously mistaken for a Jacobite tract, though it was in fact an ironical exposition of the absurdity of the Jacobite case, and it is very difficult to understand how anybody ever managed to mistake its real meaning. On this occasion Harley, suspect himself of coquetting with the Pretender, nevertheless speedily got his indiscreet employee the Queen's pardon, and his jest was forgiven, even if it was not appreciated. But in the next year

Harley fell from office; and the accession of the Whigs and George I landed him in the Tower, under a charge of treason. Defoe was let alone; but his irony, and his association with Harley, had offended the Whigs: his protector and his employment were gone.

The *Review* had ended before that, in 1713, killed by the newspaper stamp tax imposed in the previous year; and though for a time *Mercator* took its place, Defoe was only a regular contributor, and not the responsible proprietor of the new venture. *Mercator*, in which he strongly pressed the case for freer trade, ended in 1714, and left him without a regular journal, though he conducted for a time Hurt's *Flying Post*. To top his misfortunes, he fell seriously ill, in the midst of writing his *Appeal to Honour and Justice*, in which he set out to defend his political conduct and incidentally provided his biographers with a great deal of material to record and to quarrel over concerning his career. At one point, his life was despaired of; but he got better, and began to look about him for a new way of earning his living, on the assumption that his career as a Government agent was over and done with.

In all probability it is to this break in Defoe's career that we owe *Robinson Crusoe* and the rest of his romances. True, he began his new career as a writer apart from politics not with a story, but with a highly moral and instructive manual of conduct, after the pattern of many Puritan manuals of the previous century. It is difficult now, despite enlivening passages here and there, to recapture the quality that made Defoe's *Family Instructor*, for a century and more, close neighbour to the family Bible in the parlours of the devout. It is as dead as mutton now, save as an historical document. But that it was very much alive until well on in the nineteenth century is proved by its many editions and by its ubiquity in the second-hand bookshops even to-day.

The Family Instructor was probably written while Defoe was sick, and minded to be a saint. Many will reckon his next action as a sign of renewed health. In 1715 he became involved in another prosecution, for criminal libel against the Earl of Anglesey, a prominent leader of the "Hanoverian Tories", and an active mover in the proceedings against Harley. Defoe was released on bail: sure that he would be convicted, he first absconded, and then threw himself upon the Government's mercy, offering his services to it as a loyal Hanoverian, who had nevertheless friends in the opposite camp, and was well equipped for keeping the Government informed about what was toward. The sequel was the acceptance of his offer, and his re-enlistment, far more secretly than under Harley, in the public service. In 1716 we find him re-established as a journalist, writing regularly for a newspaper, *Mercurius Politicus*, over which he had, however, no absolute or exclusive control, and, presumably, drawing again a salary of some sort from the secret service funds.

It would not be fair to pass to this new phase of Defoe's career without recording that, both before and after his new appointment, he exerted himself energetically on behalf of his former patron. In *The Secret History of the White Staff* and in other pamphlets he did his best to defend Harley against the charge of treason, and to put his conduct in a favourable light. That Harley seems not to have appreciated his help does not alter the fact of Defoe's loyalty, when loyalty could not possibly pay.

The nature of the services expected from Defoe by the Government was not made fully plain until 1718, when he entered into a formal arrangement. As a secret agent, he was to connect himself with the Jacobite press, to write and edit for it, with the purpose of keeping its expressions of opinion within moderate limits. Apart from his connection with the openly moderate *Mercurius Politicus*, Defoe began to write for, and soon to edit, *Mist's Weekly Journal*, the leading Jacobite organ, and to contribute to other Tory and Jacobite papers, seeking to suppress contributions that were plainly seditious, to modify offensive expressions against the Government and the dynasty, and to guide the Jacobites towards reconciliation with the new order—always without betraying his purpose, or openly changing the character of the papers for which he wrote. From time to time, despite his endeavours, seditious articles would slip in; for Mist did not give his editor absolute control. But on these occasions Defoe was able more than once to save Mist from the consequences of prosecution, to exact guarantees of moderation, and to persuade the Government to let the case drop—still without betraying his position as a Government agent. The affair ended, as such things will, in a quarrel, when Mist discovered what Defoe had been about. But their connection lasted in all for seven years; and when it was over Defoe was able to go on playing the same role for two years more as editor of *Applebee's Weekly Journal*, another Tory organ of a complexion somewhat less pronouncedly Jacobite. Indeed, for four years, from 1720 to 1724, Defoe wrote for both *Mist's* and *Applebee's*, and at the same time conducted a succession of journals of his own. In 1718 he founded the *Whitehall Evening Post*, which he sold in 1720; but meanwhile he had founded, in 1719, the *Daily Post*, over which he kept his control till 1725. Then, in 1726, something happened—we do not know precisely what—to sever Defoe's connection with popular journalism for good and all. Possibly it was a full exposure of his relations with the Government: more probably a cessation of the Government payments that made such journalism worth his while. He seems to have come back to journalism, as contributor to and perhaps as editor of the Whig *Political State of Great Britain*, on Abel Boyer's death in 1729. But, apart from that doubtful exception and a few occasional articles, he wrote no more for the papers after 1726.

This record of Defoe's activities as journalist and secret agent has taken me on far beyond his "arrival" as a great teller of stories. From 1715 to 1718 he had been writing pamphlets with almost incredible activity—the list of works that are probably his runs to thirty-three in 1715, fourteen in 1716, twenty-six in 1717 and thirteen in 1718. But then, in 1719, appeared the two narrative volumes of *Robinson Crusoe*; and he was instantly established as pre-eminent in a new field. The publishing "pirates", from whom he had suffered before —over *The True-born Englishman*, for example—instantly attested his popularity with a flood of unauthorized and abridged editions. *Robinson Crusoe* became immediately a popular classic; and so it has remained ever since.

Having found the new vein, Defoe, despite all his journalistic preoccupations, was prompt to develop it. In addition to the *Serious Reflections of Robinson Crusoe*, which only quarriers in Defoe's biography can bear to read, 1720 gave the world *Captain Singleton*, with its romance of piracy and its delightful Quaker (Defoe had known William Penn well, and had several times assumed the character of a Quaker in his political writings), *Duncan Campbell*, forecasting his later preoccupation with magic and the supernatural, and, most important, *Memoirs of a Cavalier*. In 1721, apart from journalism, he was almost silent; but in 1722 came *Moll Flanders*, *Colonel Jacque*, and *A Journal of the Plague Year*. His publications in 1723 do not count; but then, in 1724, came *Roxana*, and the first volume of his *Tour*, and in 1725 the second volume of the *Tour*, *A New Voyage Round the World*, and the first volume of *The Complete English Tradesman*. 1726 completes the *Tour*, and adds *The Political History of the Devil* and *A System of Magic*. 1727 brings the rest of *The Complete English Tradesman*, *A General History of Discoveries in the Useful Arts*, and *The History and Reality of Apparitions*. 1728 adds *Augusta Triumphans* and *A Plan of the English Commerce*, and also *Captain Carleton*, if that be Defoe's, as Il ncline to think it is. Then at last the flood turns to a trickle, and there is nothing more of note till *The Compleat English Gentleman*, which was stopped in the press in 1730, and left unfinished at the author's death in 1731.

Apart from *The True-born Englishman*, and perhaps *The Shortest Way with the Dissenters*, most people nowadays know nothing of Defoe's that was written before *Robinson Crusoe*. His works, for most readers, mean *Robinson Crusoe* and the stories and narratives which followed it during the next few years. Defoe's great literary following and reputation rest on these products of his latter years. Nor is the verdict unjust, from the purely literary standpoint. Defoe was a great political journalist and a great occasional pamphleteer. But it is of the nature of most political journalism and of most pamphleteering not to outlive the occasion. Literary journalism can, witness *The Spectator*; and so can journalism in which politics is mingled inextricably with more durable and personal impressions—witness *Rural Rides*. But most of Addison, or of Swift, and most of Cobbett, is dead to the reader of to-day; and so is most of Defoe's journalism, even at its best. Arguments die: only personality, and the human story, go on living for ever.

Defoe, then, lives by his stories—by *Robinson Crusoe* most of all, and thereafter by *Roxana*, by *Moll Flanders*, by *Memoirs of a Cavalier*, and by the *Journal of the Plague Year*. *Robinson Crusoe* comes first; but what next? Opinions differ. To-day, the *Cavalier* and the *Plague Year* are for highbrows only, or at the most do not go beyond the middle-brows. *Moll Flanders* and *Roxana*, however—especially *Moll Flanders*—have also a second public. You can find them, in a dress that shamefully suggests obscenity, cheek by jowl with *Aristotle's Works* and other salacious morsels, in shops where "high-class rubber goods" rub cheeks with vigour-restorers to reinforce the energies of "weak men". Inevitably, this second blossoming

6

invites a doubt. Was Daniel Defoe, Dissenter and pious author of *The Family Instructor* and other elevating works of piety, also a conscious purveyor of pornographic delights? Did he moralize only with his tongue in his cheek, and write his *Lives* of Jack Sheppard, Jonathan Wild, Captain Avery, and other notorious malefactors, his fictions about *Moll Flanders* and *The Lady Roxana*, and the moral reflections of *Robinson Crusoe*, only to conceal his own immorality and screen his prurience behind a show of moralizing?

The answer, I am sure, is that he did not. *The Family Instructor* is writ serious; and when *Robinson Crusoe* moralizes, the reader is meant to take his pious reflections to heart. The repentance of *Moll Flanders* and of *The Fortunate Mistress* is meant seriously: there is no consciousness of hypocrisy in the author's mind. Other times, other manners; and what attracts by its exceptional frankness now was then only a serious representation of what was written in levity by a host of other writers. Defoe is no more "frank" than Congreve, or Wycherley, or Aphra Behn; but he meant to point the moral, where they were content merely to adorn the tale. He was, no doubt, fully conscious that it is more interesting to read about vice than about virtue, and quite ready to play on his readers' desire for sensation and the amorous *macabre*. But there was no insincerity about his giving his stories of crime and passion and mere mercenary pandering to lust a moral twist. The underworld, which he had met with in Newgate and in the Mint as prisoner, as fugitive from his creditors, and then as journalist, interested him and stirred his fancy. He knew it, and how to write about it; but he regarded it in all sincerity as evil, and meant to make it so appear. If *Moll Flanders* has become a *conte sale* to many of its modern readers, that is not Defoe's fault. He was as outspoken, and as reticent, as his contemporaries: his work outlives theirs in popular appeal, because of its abounding realism. His readers of to-day may skip his moralizings; but he meant them to be read and taken to heart.

It is true that Defoe had an illegitimate child, *plus* seven legitimate. Wordsworth had one too. It is true that you can read *Moll Flanders* as a "filthy book", and enjoy it so, if your taste runs that way. It is true that for many years Defoe played an equivocal part, acting the Government spy upon the Jacobites, and concealing his receipt of public money under the cloak of the honest journalist, deeply maligned by his inveterate enemies. It is true that a sensitive character could never have sustained such a part. But Defoe was not sensitive. He was coarse-grained—even, if you will, a little vulgar. He did enjoy, as well as reprehend, Moll Flanders; and, I am not ashamed to say, so do I. He did do things which, to-day, no decent man could do, and continue to deem himself honest. But it is ridiculous to judge men out of the standards of their time. After all, Defoe was no more a hired scribbler than Swift; and he stuck at least as close in his writings to what he really felt and believed.

This is not an exculpation, but plain justice. For Defoe has been dubbed "rogue", both in his own day and subsequently, far oftener than he deserves. He was, I feel sure, far less a rogue than St. John, or Harley, or Marlborough, or even Swift. As for his public life, it was of the times, dusty; but not dustier than the rest. At any rate, he stuck to two principles through all his troubles, and whoever paid him for what he wrote—to toleration and, what goes with it, the desire to appease violent political or religious passions. He was a Dissenter, without hostility to the Church; for he regarded the Church's security as an essential shield against Papists and Jacobites. He was a Whig, who was ready to steer a middle course with the moderate Tories—or a Tory, ready to join hands with the moderate Whigs. But he was a moderator and a conciliator only on the basis of preserving certain fundamentals in which he believed. As a young man, he joined Monmouth's rebellion, and was lucky enough to escape Jeffreys's vengeance. He joined the Prince of Orange in 1688. All his moderation was based on preserving the Revolution settlement intact. On that point he never compromised. If Harley had dealings with the Pretender, Defoe did not.

Yet, about all this, who really cares? What matters is that Defoe wrote *Robinson Crusoe* and, much less, that he wrote *Moll Flanders* and the *Journal of the Plague Year*. Having largely created English journalism, he went on to create the English novel. For, in truth, there were no novels before Defoe's— no naturalism in story-telling, no attempts to create in fiction the sense of reality in the reader's mind. Defoe achieved at one blow this realism—so thoroughly that even to-day no one can quite tell what in his books is based on real happenings and what is sheer invention. That does not matter: nor does it matter whether this achievement was the outcome of supreme literary art, or craftsmanship, or of the lack of it—as Boswell's faults made his *Life of Johnson* the best biography ever written. The accomplishment is Defoe's, whatever lies behind it; and the inheritance is ours. We can afford to be grateful for it, highbrows and lowbrows together; for Defoe appeals to both.

6

BISHOP BERKELEY

(1685–1753)

by GEORGE SANTAYANA

YOUTH and genius, piety and radicalism conspired to make of Berkeley the most amiable of philosophers. Even if he was not always young or always radical— for he became a bishop—the genius of youth and of radicalism never forsook him. His intuition remained ardent and simple, even when his piety was clothed in ampler and more learned robes. His maturest projects were chimerical: to found a college at Bermuda from which to christianize North America, and to cure all minor human ills by the virtues of tar-water. It was in youth that his philosophy had come to him, as if by inspiration: and whilst he recognized afterwards its affinity to Platonic speculations, he never explored or analysed its affinity with any technical diligence. It sufficed him to have shattered the illusion that we are living in an obdurate material world, and to feel instead that this world was nothing but a beautiful picture-book, a book of fables, in which God was teaching our childish minds his admirable ways.

It is usual to regard Berkeley, in the history of philosophy, as a stepping-stone between Locke and Hume; but this seems to me a grave injustice, convenient for compiling text-books, but born of the mania for seeing evolution everywhere and, what is worse, evolution in single file. Undoubtedly Hume had read Berkeley, and Berkeley had read Locke: and there are points in which each carried the arguments of his predecessor one step further, or applied them to a further problem; but Berkeley had speculative genius; his thought was radical, single and complete; whereas Locke had only miscellaneous intelligence and Hume analytic malice. These two critics of human opinion really carried on the same work, and progressively dissolved traditional philosophy into something else, they knew not what; for they hardly asked themselves whether it was logic passing for psychology, or psychology becoming metaphysics. But Berkeley, like Descartes, though more simply, saw suddenly what seemed to him a new and safer way of defining Christian philosophy and purifying it, as well as all human science, of useless accretions. To call Berkeley a stepping-stone between Locke and Hume is like calling an upright obelisk a stepping-stone between two sphinxes that may be crouching to the right and to the left of it. No doubt the three are in perfect alignment along one particular path, and this may be the most interesting fact about them to a person hurrying by them towards something else. Yet even that subjective analysis of ideas which was begun by Locke and completed in Hume, figured in Berkeley only as a cathartic, or an argument *ad hominem*, calculated to clear the mind of proud scientific illusions and bring it in all humility face to face with God. His intuition pointed steadily, like an obelisk, to the zenith; whilst his more contorted and pregnant neighbours, like sphinxes, digested their inward contradictions.

Youthful genius is essentially lyrical rather than cognitive: in Berkeley, as afterwards in Shelley, it was blinded by too much light. Like Shelley, Berkeley felt how horribly unnecessary everything was that contradicted the convictions that came to him irresistibly when he first looked upon and challenged the world. Such assurance is not always immature; it may be radical and ultimate in one direction. In Berkeley it brought a fresh intuition of the nature of experience, a true, if partial, intuition never to be cancelled; had it been otherwise, there would be no occasion to speak of genius, but only of one more academic extravagance. Young courage may embrace any illusion; but only young genius, justifying courage, can clear away vast accumulations of prejudice and convention, and discover the obvious. Berkeley gloriously detached the "idea", the pure phenomenon, from the irrelevant strains of presumption and idolatry with which animal life originally encumbers it. The stupid world calls this an act of abstraction; but Berkeley, who hated abstractions, knew it to be an act of realization. Realization, indeed, simply of the obvious, and of the ideality and unsubstantiality of the obvious. He rose at once to a radical insight which it had taken all the experience and discipline of Indian gymnosophists to reach, the insight that perception, if taken for truth, is illusion: the very insight that the aged Malebranche was then propounding critically, basing it on the lamentable incapacity and deceptiveness of the human senses. But this discovery, in the ear of youth, may have a pleasant sound; it may bring not so much renunciation as enfranchisement. The instinct to look for the sake of looking, to play for the sake of playing, to enjoy making-believe, and to find the highest vitality in enacting a great show known not to be real, is no incapacity in a child; and for a poet the power of imagination is not deceptive, but on the contrary the one free, beautiful, appointed way of celebrating the truth. When Berkeley denied the existence of matter, he felt not the unreality but the intense reality of experience, enjoying it as a vast web of heavenly music, perfectly composed and performed, with its recurrent phrases coming in at the right places: and he felt no base craving to hug the words or hold on to the notes, but passed over everything buoyantly at the due pace, as it was meant to be passed over. This exercise, which we call life, is difficult enough, and we get sadly out of time and tune; yet it is essentially a festive ritual and a rare spectacle for the eye, the very tragedy of it being a fable. This world would have been horrible, had it been more real than that. The gladness of it came of its vividness as an experience and its unreality as a power.

Nevertheless such an intuition, by its lyrical truth and sufficiency, cuts off the young enthusiast from the complexity of mundane things, and even from other forms of intuition. His inspiration seems to him adequate only because it mono-polizes his attention, and arrests him, as it were, at a sort of spiritual adolescence. The mark of his genius may remain in the world indelibly, but only like the portrait of a noble child, consecrating an innocence that we are both glad and sorry he never should have lost.

For anyone with a speculative turn of mind this simplicity and depth in Berkeley render him an approachable and exciting writer. He stimulates attention at once by a tremendous para-dox, telling us that we are bodiless spirits, and that material things are nothing but images in our minds. At the same time he partly reassures us, in what might seem our sudden visionary solitude, by a religious revelation. These images—including that image of our own bodies to which we seem so mercilessly tied—though unsubstantial in themselves are full of signifi-cance. They are visible or tangible words, in which God is continually speaking to us with an overwhelming eloquence, marshalling them in irresistible cohorts, in order to manifest his power, guide our affections, and prove his love.

Piety thus steps in opportunely to correct the bottomless scepticism that might otherwise have invaded us. I am a bodiless spirit, certainly; but I am a *created* spirit. This second perception, or this reversion to an underlying unquestioned belief, if less intuitive than the first perception, is far wiser.

It might be justified by the cumulative evidence of all history and practical art; yet the intuitive first principle of Berkeley, or of Descartes, if it had stood alone, could never have justified this correction. A conventional unchallenged piety was requisite to convince the idealist that the ideas visiting him had their source beyond his own spirit. It was religion, not critical acumen or worldly wisdom, that introduced this element of sanity into Berkeley's system. He felt from the beginning to the end that he was dependent on a sustaining power at work behind the scenes, a divine musician that kept the variegated notes of this sensuous symphony in their due places and order. No substance or power whatever lay *within* our "inert ideas" to lend them an efficacious existence on their own account; yet a power and a substance did most emphatically lie *behind* the fact of their occurrence, lending the most precise moral and practical import to their quality and sequence, as to the metrical words of an oracle. The plot of life retained all its seriousness and dangers, although it was only the plot of a poetic drama.

Youth, genius, and piety could thus accept with alacrity a view of the world which might easily have proved morose and paralysing or, as afterwards in Schopenhauer, mephistophelian. Were we not wisps of consciousness floating in vacancy? Who could tell what would become of us next? So a heathen poet might have cried, overcome by the visionary self-dissolving mockery of life; but Berkeley felt religiously so secure, that he rejoiced rather that his limpid direct intuitions should have no substance and no inside. It became absurd to burrow into them or to fear them. He was happy to connect surface with surface. Was not the glory of God visible in the Bay of Naples? Why prowl about the unsavoury town or hurl oneself into the crater of Vesuvius? Empedocles had been doubly a madman, first in his mechanical philosophy and then in his blasphemous suicide. Berkeley hated "minute philo-

sophers" even more than "scholastic triflers". Not that he
despised argument when carried on with the courtly elegance
of that age. A part of his perennial youthfulness was to be
keen and brilliant in controversy, composing capital debating
dialogues and noble sermons; but in theology as in metaphysics
he kept to large edifying views and ignored difficulties.

Moreover, this idealist was no hermit. His ardent temperament and staunch Protestantism drew him into the vortex
of contemporary society, then most confident of its lights and
superior powers. Even his piety was not too secret or mystical,
but public and sober, like that of a good Churchman; and he
was always a diligent student, a man of many projects, a
controversialist, and as a recent commentator has said, "a
fighting Irishman; and when he saw a head to hit, he hit it."*
His metaphysics never disturbed his moral sanity and heartiness, never induced in him any reversal of values or radical
challenge to Church or State. Unworldly he was eminently,
as an unspoiled child is unworldly; yet he was a man of the
world; and this conjunction in him of convention with intuition and of culture with fervour lent a singular felicity and
charm to his words. A golden light suffused all things in his
mind, without distorting them; and in his philosophizing he
avoided both too much analysis and too much elaboration.
There was no construction in his science, as there was no
criticism in his theology; a good Englishman in race and type
of allegiance, even if Irish by birth and somewhat Irish in
imagination. He knew how a gentleman should live and feel;
and this moral sureness removed all undue urgency from the
speculative radicalism of his views. There was, unfortunately,
the mystery of evil; but this mystery could only quicken one's
missionary zeal in the cure of souls. A hopeful cure, since
the most degraded of spirits was still by nature an angel and
a native of heaven.

* A. B. Luce: *Berkeley and Malebranche*, p. 131.

BISHOP BERKELEY

Living as Berkeley did in this atmosphere of convention electrified by intuition, it is intelligible that the technical developments of his philosophy should not have been thorough or solid. His first impetuous desire was to denounce occult entities and abstractions, of which matter was the worst. Yet wasn't the idea of spirit at least as abstract and unimaginable as that of matter? To this objection Berkeley replied that we had indeed no *idea* of spirit, but we had a *notion* of it; we knew what it meant. This notion, in his case, could not have been any primitive animistic semi-material notion of spirit, but was doubtless that of Descartes, who had said that the essence of the soul was to think: so that if it ceased to think it would cease to be. From this Descartes had drawn the inference that the soul, being immortal, can never stop thinking. But an opposite and less edifying inference could have been drawn just as well: namely, that since thought as a matter of fact is often interrupted, the soul too only exists intermittently; or rather that no soul or spirit exists at all, but only discrete and scattered perceptions, each thinking or feeling itself. This was the conclusion adopted by Hume and by all later British empiricists; and it might seem only inadvertence or prejudice in Berkeley that kept him from anticipating it. Or perhaps we should rather say that if his genius had been as patient as it was brilliant and as subtle as it was clear, he might have discerned the nature of spirit in almost any intuition. For in surveying any complex image we are aware of contrasting and comparing its parts, thereby distinguishing apprehension from its subject-matter; so that evidence of thinking, or of the presence of spirit, is continually at hand. Attention, inspection, analysis, and synthesis, not to speak of expectation and memory, are spiritual lights flooding ideas, which but for this intellectual dominion over them would compose no cumulative experience and would appear to nobody. Even a dream includes a witness that is engrossed in the dream.

It was another consideration, however, less intuitive and more traditional, that probably would have had most weight with Berkeley in confirming the reality of spirit. Spirit, he took for granted, was a power; and matter being removed, and ideas being passive and merely spectacular, there remained no other power except spirit to carry on the world. Unfortunately the will, or spirit exerting power, was open to the same dissolving psychological analysis as spirit merely thinking. Dissected retrospectively, wishing, deciding, and commanding are sheer phenomena. They may be conjoined with other phenomena, if there is a synthetic memory to conjoin them. But phenomena cannot be derived from one another inwardly by a material generation, since by definition there is no substance in them and no power. The alleged regularity or law of their sequence is a scientific fiction, based on a few recorded instances roughly similar, with no insight into any real continuity or necessity in the original events.

This psychological analysis, reducing power to a superstition, was instantly obvious to Hume: why did it escape Berkeley? Because his piety and simplicity transported him initially into a moral world; and in a moral sense there is more than juxtaposition between the will to do a thing and the performance, between the desire for a thing and the possession of it, or between a prayer and the answer to that prayer. Nor are these things connected by a scientific law. They go together, when they do (which is not always) because it is fit and beautiful that they should do so. The only power morally perspicuous is the power of God, or of the good; for as the Scholastics said the will acts always *sub specie boni*, attracted by something that seems a good. Love of the good moves the spirit which moves the world.

Moral sentiment carried Berkeley smoothly over these serious difficulties; and, strange as it may seem, intellectual prejudice carried him no less smoothly over others. His early confident radicalism and nominalism were not based on intuition, but rather on verbal arguments, reinforced by sympathy with the spirit of the times and a semi-political hostility to scholastic tradition. Loving warmth and immediacy as he did, and hating the chill of distance, he was not content with the lightning vivacity that sensuous images actually have—since every landscape shows, at each instant, precisely the degree of clearness or confusion which it shows—but he impetuously ascribed to these treacherous images a kind of precision only to be found in conceptual objects or material things. Yet as any impressionist painter will tell us, our conventional physical and mathematical standards of reality are irrelevant to the proper lucidity of vision. The vaguest thing intellectually may be æsthetically the most obvious. That a three-cornered hat has three corners, or triangularity, may be perceived as directly as its precise shade of colour; and this mere three-corneredness is far more easily ascertained and remembered and may be more expressively indicated in a bold sketch, than the total image cast upon the retina, or the total shape and exact size of the material hat. Evidently Berkeley, when he argued about ideas, was thinking and not looking. He supposed them to be definite physically, and sometimes called them things. The idea of the triangular hat had to be equilateral or non-equilateral; and every image had to choose between conceptual alternatives which in actual intuition are not broached at all.

Even in the religious or spiritual direction Berkeley hardly reached the heights or the depths to which his primary intuition seemed to open the way. This intuition was mystical, in the sense of vaulting over and discarding all intermediaries between spirit and spirit, between the heart and God. The world was nothing and could be nothing but the language in which God, for the moment, was speaking to the soul. In this intercourse we might be dull and sullen, like a dog disobeying his master, or we might be quick to follow or even to anticipate the thought that conducted us. Evidently a most difficult and heroic spiritual discipline lay before any human being really possessed by such an inspiration: for how should the least wilfulness, the least impurity, subsist in us, when there exists no machinery at all for our ingenuity or our strength to work upon, and no source for our own darkness or suffering except our perverse wishes, or the beneficent chastening of a fatherly hand? All care, all concern about the future, should instantly vanish; and an indomitable faith, accepting all things with equal thanks, should fill the dark night of our worst trials with an unearthly joy. This joy would be that of a perpetual martyrdom, since every natural preference or hope, for another life no less than for this life, would first have to be extirpated. All our interests must have ceased to be ours, before we can unfeignedly accept every turn of fortune. No labours or dangers would any longer seem terrible to us. The greatest mystics may be prodigious fighters or missionaries or controversialists: not for a moment that these tasks represent any ambition or hope of their own—for they have renounced all hope and ambition—but because, the tasks being imposed or inspired by the manifest will of God, to labour at them becomes as easy and as indifferent as to suffer martyrdom in any other form. Yet it is always martyrdom: because these saints are men living in the body; and a complete exaltation above all human instincts and affections can be obtained only by continually fresh self-abdication: above which the rapture of spiritual freedom and divine love floats like a sunset cloud over the silent earth.

Was this the spirit of Berkeley's life? Was he a martyr? Where are the tears, the fasts in the desert, the Job-like trials, the heart-searchings and temptations, the agonized soul abandoning all things that have betrayed it, and dying, happy to die, upon the cross?

Berkeley was a Low-Church bishop of the eighteenth

century. He could be blameless, he could be benevolent: it would have been unseemly in him to be a saint. Neither his heart nor his station called him to austerity of life. Experience was indeed to him a conversation with God, but not with God alone. There were other well-known spirits, like Dean Swift and Dr. Johnson, taking part on equal terms in the dialogue. No sane man, no hearty kindly Christian could doubt it. Yet how did this matter stand on Berkeley's principles? In each of us the notion of human society is evidently a dramatic reading of men's actions and speech. But if men's bodies are only ideas in my mind, the notion of their minds, suggested by those ideas, must be doubly native to my fancy. The case is like that of the characters in a novel. The only actual spirit concerned, beyond that of the reader, is that of the author. Certainly the divine Poet who is speaking to me in all my perceptions may be speaking also to countless other spirits: but that is not my affair. The persons that laugh and suffer in my painted world are figures in a fable that God is inventing for my instruction. They come, as does the rest of my experience, to test and develop my character and to enlarge my knowledge of God's mind, as do these lovely vistas of earth and sky, and this menagerie of curious animals, which are also theophanies. Morally the most decisive and transforming part of my fate is precisely the character of the people I live with and love, and who perhaps love or do not love me. If this part of experience be subtracted from my contact with God, the importance of that contact will be singularly diminished. Life would be a conversation with God only for an hour on Sundays, or when I walked expressly alone among the mountains, hoping to be inspired, or perhaps in the presence of death or of an earthquake. But that is the religion of the worldling: nature and society might get on, he thinks, perfectly well by themselves, and the divine presence and power in all things seems to him an empty word. The whole spiritual elevation of Berkeley's philosophy comes with the opposite intuition, that sees God in all things and all things in God. People will be masks and voices in a divine revelation, as they are in Dante's *Divine Comedy*. If they become powers collateral with God's power, and spirits collateral with the spirit in us that finds or imagines them, then we have lapsed altogether from our idealistic insight and reverted to the assumptions of common sense and of vulgar naturalism.

Perhaps Berkeley should be congratulated on having halted half-way in his idealism, assigning only material phenomena to God, and social phenomena to the dubious devices of the human heart. In this he may have been true to a certain positivistic and moral instinct latent in his blood. Where trade prevails over agriculture, debate over handicrafts, politics over war, and morality over religion, it is intelligible that society and social intercourse should seem the first and surest of realities. Philosophers may then be prone to intercept their criticism of knowledge, and to reason as if men's moral personalities could exist in a physical vacuum, like so many angels, remaining distinct and communicating magically, without any bodies or any books. Society, which is a development of animal life, may then seem to subsist undisturbed, after we have spirited away, in theory, the animal life that supported it. Berkeley lived under the spell of this social convention, as we see also in his philanthropic endeavours. A Buddha or a Saint Francis would have been more impartial in scepticism or in faith; and charity in either of them would have been all the more religious and tender for being without political illusions.

Even in politics, however, the immaterialism of Berkeley might have suggested utopias more visionary than any that he actually entertained. When meditating on the future of America he composed some verses, of which the last stanza is well known:

BISHOP BERKELEY

Westward the course of empire takes its way:
  The first four acts already past,
A fifth shall close the drama with the day;
  Time's noblest offspring is the last.

Here, if there be any illusion, it is the illusion of simplicity.
We have Ockham's razor applied to history, leaving it shorn
of all sad tangles and gross hybrid endless extensions. Only
Babylon, Greece, Rome, and England, with America to
follow; and then nothing. The five clear episodes of a classical
tragedy would end with a pleasant hush of exaltation, like an
eloquent sermon: an enthralling composition, and not too
long. America, flatteringly expected to be the noblest of
empires, was also to be the last: the force of nature, or of
divine intervention, could no further go either in time or in
sublimity; and just as physical objects had no inside, and as
events had no causes save the moral fitness that they should
come as they do, so when once the general edifying function
of existence had been fulfilled, any further events would have
lost their excuse for being.

In fine, Berkeley never transferred his life to the world
revealed by his philosophy. Like other idealists, he had been
bred in the atmosphere of homely materialism and traditional
religion, and he loved them both: it was only scientific
materialism, incompatible with religion, that he hated. His
mystical paradox, if taken to heart, would have dissolved these
conventions; but he used it only argumentatively, as a technical device for defending them. The simplification, when once
familiar, made all things easy. It was a private product of
critical wit, like the answer to a riddle; a happy thought
that seemed suddenly to clarify and to explain everything. It
was a *trouvaille*. And Berkeley kept it, certainly not hidden,
yet lovingly held somewhat in reserve, as many an Englishman, half humorously, half proudly keeps his dearest hobby,

87

to be bravely defended in public when occasion demands, but not to be suffered in the meantime to derange at home the rational course of his existence. Yet neither the homely materialism nor the historical Christianity by which Berkeley lived could ever have arisen if mankind had been possessed from the beginning by his new intuition of a universal miraculous intercourse between disembodied spirits. This intuition had to remain somewhat intermittent and esoteric.

Perhaps a humorous logician, convinced by the same arguments, might have allowed his common sense and his traditional religion to subsist in an ironical form; and having become secretly aware that life is a dream, he might have continued talking to his friends, eating, and travelling: all with a not unpleasant sense of acting a harmless comedy and fooling himself to the top of his bent. But this was not at all the mood in which Berkeley took his philosophy. He was not humorous. His logic had made a scenic illusion of the world, but he was not by nature histrionic. If ever he mocked fashionable infidels or cast ridicule on glib philosophers, he did so in profound earnest, and for the triumph of truth. He was all noble charity, luminous conviction, and untroubled faith. If his thought never rose into devout ecstasy, as his speculative system seemed to demand, it was never narrowed to the logical dilemmas which that system presented. His manhood kept the balance. He remained a humanist, with religious faith strained through the triple sieve of good breeding, simpleness, and high speculation: a Quixote of the Schools, conventional at heart, in spite of his mysticism, and tenderly loving mankind, whilst demonstrating, with proofs strong as Holy Writ, that they had all been arrant fools from the first dawn of creation.

POPE

(1688–1744)

by W. H. AUDEN

ABOUT 1705 Wycherly's visitors began to "meet a little Aesopic sort of animal in his own cropt hair, and dress agreeable to the forest he came from —probably some tenant's son of Wycherly's making court for continuance in his lease on the decease of his rustic parent— and were surprised to learn that he was poetically inclined and writ tolerably smooth verses." As is so often the case, just as Proust was a Jew, and Hitler is an Austrian, the man who was to epitomise Augustan culture was not of it by birth. The invalid self-educated son of a Roman Catholic linen merchant, it was not a very promising beginning for the man who was to become the friend of dukes, the gardener and gourmet, the poet to whom a mayor was to offer £4,000 for a single couplet.

If Pope's social advantages were few his physical charms were even less. Only four feet six in height, he was already a sufferer from Pott's disease, "the little Alexander whom the women laugh at", and in middle age was to become really repulsive. ". . . so weak as to stand in perpetual need of female attendance; extremely sensible of cold, so that he wore a kind of fur doublet, under a short of a very coarse warm linen with fine sleeves. When he rose, he was invested in a bodice made of stiff canvas, being scarce able to hold himself erect till they were laced, and he then put on a flannel waistcoat. One side was contracted. His legs were so slender, that he enlarged their bulk with three pairs of stockings, which were drawn on and off by the maid; for he was not able to dress or undress himself, and neither went to bed nor rose without help. His weakness made it very difficult for him to be clean. His hair had fallen almost all away. . . ."

Nor, it must be admitted, even if not as sublimely odious as Addison, was he a prepossessing character. He was a snob and a social climber, who lied about his ancestry and cooked his correspondence; he was fretful and demanded constant attention, he was sly, he was mean, he was greedy, he was vain, touchy, and worldly while posing as being indifferent to the world and to criticism; he was not even a good conversationalist.

As a poet, he was limited to a single verse form, the endstopped couplet; his rare attempts at other forms were failures. To limitation of form was added limitation of interest. He had no interest in nature as we understand the term, no interest in love, no interest in abstract ideas, and none in Tom, Dick and Harry. Yet his recognition was immediate, and his reputation never wavered during his lifetime.

If we are to understand his contemporary success, if we are to appreciate the nature of his poetry and its value, we must understand the age in which he lived.

At the beginning of the eighteenth century, although one quarter of the population was in receipt of occasional parish relief, England was the most prosperous country in Europe. According to Gregory King, out of a population of about five million, the two largest classes were cottagers and paupers, and the labouring people and outservants, both of which the

Act of Settlement of the Poor prevented from leaving the parishes in which they were born; about a quarter were tenant farmers or freeholders; an eighty-seventh small landed gentry with an income of from £250-450 a year; and the remainder the large landowners. One tenth of the population lived in London which was more than fifteen times larger than her nearest rival, Bristol. The relative prosperity of the country was due, partly to colonies and Britain's favourable position on the Atlantic seaboard, partly to her export of cloth to Europe partly to her free internal trade and partly to the comparative lack of friction, compared, for example, with France, between the landed aristocracy and business. Though the former professed to look down on the latter, they were ready to profit from them; the younger sons of the poorer gentry were frequently apprentices to business houses, and successful business men could and did become landed gentry. The Act of Toleration prevented religious difference from interfering with trade; and the establishment of the Bank of England and the National Debt drew financial and political interests close together.

The dependence on air and water for motive power preserved the balance between town and country; indeed, through the wish to escape obsolete borough restrictions, industry was less urban than in earlier times. There was therefore no emotional demand for "nature" poetry.

If a large number of the population were illiterate; if, by our modern liberal standards, their amusements of drinking, gambling, and cock-fighting were crude, their sanitation primitive, their politics virulent and corrupt, there had nevertheless been an improvement. There were more educated people than ever before, a greater interest in education—charity schools were being built everywhere—and England's increasing importance in, and ties with, Europe, gave her culture a breadth and balance hitherto unknown. The arts have hitherto flourished best where cultured society was large enough to provide variety and small enough to be homogeneous in taste. The eighteenth century in England fulfilled both these conditions. There was a growing consciousness of the value of refinement and good manners—a society for the Reformation of Manners is a symptom of a social rather than a puritan conscience—and the age saw the development of these typical modern amusements—smoking—tea- and coffee-drinking—shooting birds on the wing instead of sitting—horse-racing—and cricket. Whether intentional or not, the wearing of wigs helped to delouse the upper classes, and in politics bribery may not be desirable but it is an improvement upon imprisonment and political murder.

You have, then, a society which, in spite of very wide variations in income and culture varying from the cottager with his bible and peddler's ballads, through the small squire with his *Hudibras* and Foxe's *Book of Martyrs*, through the Squire Westerns and the Sir Roger de Coverleys, up to the Duke with his classical library, his panelled room, his landscape garden, his china and mahogany furniture, and his round of London, Bath, and his country estate, was at no point fundamentally divided in outlook and feeling. Owing to the fusing of landed and trade interests, owing to the fact that England was still rural, was a genuine economic unit, and rising in power, there was little clash between politics and economics, no apparent class conflict.

In studying the ideas and art of this period, therefore, we are studying firstly those of any rising class which has recently won power and security for itself—(perhaps the surest sign of victory in a political struggle is the removal of the Censorship; this happened in 1695)—and secondly those of a particular example of such a class in a small European island shortly before the Industrial Revolution. In consequence we may find certain characteristics which seem likely to recur through history, and others which are peculiar to the particular circumstance of the time, and can never happen again.

To take the more universal characteristics first; what should we expect to find? Those who have risen from a subordinate to a dominant position are, firstly, pleased with themselves, and, secondly, anxious to preserve the status quo. No one is so ready to cry Pax and All's well as he who has just got what he wants. They are optimistic, full of vitality, pacific, within their circle, and conservative.

> All Nature is but Art, unknown to thee;
> All Chance, Direction, which thou canst not see;
> All Discord, Harmony not understood;
> All partial evil, universal Good;
> And, spite of Pride, in erring Reason's spite,
> One truth is clear, WHATEVER IS, IS RIGHT.

Secondly, they bring with them a sense of social inferiority; they are anxious to possess and develop the culture and social refinements of the class they have replaced. Contempt for art and manners is a symptom of a rising class that has not yet won power. When they have, they will welcome and reward handsomely art which teaches them refinement, and proves them refined. Because they have been successful, they are interested in themselves. The art of their choice will celebrate their activities, flatter their virtues, and poke fun at their fables.

Certain qualities of Augustan poetry, then, its air of well being, its gusto, its social reference,

> Correct with spirit, eloquent with ease.

are those which might occur after any social revolution. Others are more unique.

The Reformation split the conception of a God who was both immanent and transcendental, a God of faith and works, into two, into the Inner light to be approached only through the private conscience, and the Divine Architect and Engineer of the Physical Universe and the laws of Economics, whose operations could be understood but not interfered with. The religious life tended to become individualized, and the social life secularized. The evil effects of what a Catholic writer has described as

> "Sundering the believer from his laicised body
> Sundering heaven from an earth evermore hireling,
>   secularised, enslaved,
> tied down to the manufacture of the useful".

are more apparent now than then, but of the importance of such an attitude to nature and historical law in the development of the physical sciences, there can be no doubt, and the secularization of education hastened the growth of culture among others than those in orders, and the creation of a general reading public.

At first the emphasis was all on the liberty of the individual conscience, and the Renaissance glorification of the individual, on anti-authoritarianism and anti-popery. But when those who believed in private illumination gained political and public power, they became, as they were bound to become, tyrants. After the Restoration, therefore, there was a swing over to the other pole, to a belief, equally one-sided, in reason against inspiration, in the laws of nature against enthusiastic private illumination, in society against the individual fanatic.

> For Forms of Government let fools contest
> Whate'er is best administered is best:
> For Modes of Faith let graceless zealots fight;

His can't be wrong whose life is in the right:
In Faith and Hope the world will disagree,
But All Mankind's concern is Charity:
All must be false that thwart this one great end;
And all of God, that bless Mankind or mend.

Anti-popery remained, reinforced by the events of 1688, Louis XIV's power in Europe, and his persecution of the Huguenots, but to it was added Anti-Dissent. Neither were violent enough to lead to real persecution or to prevent social intercourse; they were the natural distrust that people who are doing very nicely as they are, have for those who might interfere with them, with their social order, their pleasures, and their cash, but are in point of fact powerless.

The appreciation of law extended itself naturally enough to literature, and literary criticism became for the first time a serious study. Suspicious of enthusiasm and inspiration, Dryden and his successors based their psychology of creative work on Hobbes.

"Time and education beget experience.
Experience begets Memory.
Memory begets Judgement and fancy.
Memory is the world in which the Judgement, the severer sister, busieth herself in a grave and rigid examination of all the parts of Nature, and in registering by letters their order, causes, uses, differences, and resemblances; whereby the Fancy, when any work of Art is to be performed, finding her materials at hand and prepared for her use, needs no more than a swift motion over them.
Imagination is nothing else but sense decaying or weakened by the absence of the object."

Such a theory reduces imagination to a recording device,

and makes creative work a purely conscious activity. It has no place for the solar plexus or the Unconscious of modern writers, nor for the divine inspiration of the Ancients. Poetry becomes a matter of word-painting of the objective world.

The difference is apparent if we compare Pope's invocation at the beginning of his philosophical poem with those of a Catholic like Dante, or a puritan like Milton.

> O good Apollo. . . .
> Into my bosom enter thou, and so breathe as when
>   thou drewest
> Marsyas from out what sheathed his limbs.

> And chiefly thou, O spirit, that dost prefer
> Before all temples the upright heart and pure,
> Instruct me, for thou knowest . . .
>   . . . What in me is dark
> Illumine; what is low, raise and support.

> Awake, my St. John! leave all meaner things
> To low ambition and the pride of Kings.
> Let us (since life can little more supply
> Than just to look about us and to die)
> Expatiate free o'er all this scene of Man;
> A mighty maze! but not without a plan.

But it would be a mistake to say that the best poetry of Dryden or Pope or any of the Augustans was deliberately written to their theories. The writing of poetry is always a more complex thing than any theory we may have about it. We write first and use the theory afterwards to justify the particular kind of poetry we like and the particular things about poetry in general which we think we like. Further, like most theories, it has its points. We, who have been brought up in the Romantic tradition, are inclined to think that whenever the Augustans wrote bad poetry, they were using their own recipe, and whenever they wrote good poetry they were using the Romantic recipe by mistake. This is false. Without their ideas on nature and the Heroic poem, we should miss *The Rape of the Lock* and the *Dunciad* just as much as we should be spared *Eloisa to Abelard* or Darwin's *Loves of the Plants*. The gusto, objectivity, and perfection of texture of the one, owe quite as much to their theories, as does the bogus classicism of the other.

All theories are one-sided generalizations; and are replaced by their opposite half-truths. When society has become too big to manage, when there is a class of persons whose incomes are drawn from investments without the responsibilities of landowners or employers, when the towns are congested, we shall hear other voices. Instead of Hobbes's psychology, we shall have Blake's "Natural objects deaden and weaken imagination in me". Instead of Pope's modest intention to please, the poets will proclaim themselves, and be believed in so far as they are listened to at all, as the Divine legislators of the world.

We, again, fancy we know better now; that the writing of poetry is a matter of neither a purely unconscious inspiration, nor purely conscious application, but a mixture of the two, in proportions which vary with different kinds of verse; that it is rarely the tortured madness which some of the Romantics pretended it was, and certainly never the effortless and thoughtless excitement the cinema public imagines it to be.

If the Augustans had the defects of their qualities, so did the Romantics. If the former sometimes came down, according to the late Professor Housman, to "singing hymns in the prison chapel", the latter sometimes went off into extempore prayers in the county asylum.

And on the whole, yes, on the whole, I think we agree with Byron "Thou shalt believe in Milton, Dryden and Pope.

Thou shalt not set up Wordsworth, Coleridge and Southey".
But then we know better now.

During the two centuries preceding Pope, the literary
language had undergone considerable change. We cannot
tell how far Shakespeare's conversations in *The Merry Wives
of Windsor* is a realistic transcript, but it is remote from us
in a way that the dialogue of the Restoration dramatists is not.
In Dryden's essay on *The Dramatic Poesy of The Last Age*
he gives as the reason, "the greatest advantage of our century,
which proceeds from *conversation*. In the age wherein these
poets lived, there was less of gallantry than in ours; neither
did they keep the best company of theirs."

The change in social status is important. It is doubtful if
the Elizabethan dramatists would have been received in the
best drawing-rooms. The poets of a later age certainly were,
and if poetry lost that complete unity of language and sensation which the Elizabethans at their best achieved,

in her strong toil of grace

the rise of the writer into society was at least partly responsible.
A classical education and the company of ladies and gentlemen
may have advantages, but they make an instinctive vocabulary
very difficult.

But it is the mark of a great writer to know his limitations.
Had Dryden attempted to continue the Elizabethan traditions,
he would have been no greater than Massinger. Instead, he
did what Nature has usually done in evolutionary changes,
he turned to a form which, though it had once been important,
during the last age had played second fiddle to blank verse.

The couplet had nevertheless had a continuous history,
parallel to and influenced by blank verse. The couplet of
Chaucer's time degenerated with the dropping of the final
"e", and with the exception of Dunbar's *Freiris of Berwik*,

is hardly seen, till it turns up again in Spenser's *Mother Hubbard's Tale*.

> To such delight the noble wits he led
> Which him relieved as their vain humours fed
> With fruitless follies and unsound delights.

Its principal use was for narrative, as in Marlowe and Chapman's *Hero and Leander*, with enjambement and spreading of sentences over several couplets, a feature which developed in Donne and Cowley to a point where the feeling of the couplet is almost lost.

> Seek true religion, O where? Mirreus,
> Thinking her unhoused here and fled from us,
> Seeks her at Rome, there, because he doth know
> That she was there a thousand years ago;
> And loves the rags so, as we here obey
> The state-cloth where the prince sate yesterday,
> Crants to such brave loves will not be enthrall'd,
> But loves her only who at Geneva's call'd
> Religion, plain, simple, sullen, young,
> Contemptuous yet unhandsome; as among
> Lecherous humours, there is one that judges
> No wenches wholesome, but coarse country drudges,
> Graius stays still at home here, and because
> Some preachers, vile ambitious bawds, and laws,
> Still new, like fashions, bid him think that she
> Which dwells with us, is only perfect, he
> Embraceth her, whom his godfathers will
> Tender to him, being tender; as wards still
> Take such wives as their guardians offer, or
> Pay values. Careless Phrygius doth abhor
> All, because all cannot be good; as one,
> Knowing some women whores, dares marry none.

But side by side with this, through the use of rhyming tags to round off dramatic scenes, through the conclusions of the sonnets, and occasional addresses, there is a development of the end-stopped epigrammatical couplet. Lytton Strachey in his essay on Pope has drawn attention to a series of couplets in *Othello*, ending,

> She was a wight if ever such wight were
> To suckle fools and chronicle small beer.

And there are plenty of other instances. Fairfax's Tasso and Sandys's Metamorphoses are no sudden new developments.

The evolution of the end-stopped couplet from Spenser through Drayton to them and Waller and Denham, and on to Dryden and Pope is continuous. It is only the pace of the development that alters.

The choice of a verse form is only half conscious. No form will express everything, as each form is particularly good at expressing something. Forms are chosen by poets because the most important part of what they have to say seems to go better with that form than any other; there is generally a margin which remains unsaid, and then, in its turn, the form develops and shapes the poet's imagination so that he says things which he did not know he was capable of saying, and at the same time those parts of his imagination which once had other things to say, dry up from lack of use.

The couplet was not Dryden's only instrument—the *Ode on St. Cecilia's Day*, *Annus Mirabilis*, the *Threnodia Augustalis* succeed in expressing things that the couplet could not have expressed—but it was Pope's.

Nor is the heroic couplet the only tune of the eighteenth century. There are the octosyllabics of Swift, the blank verse of Thomson, the odes of Gray and Collins. There is Prior:

POPE

Now let us look for Louis' feather
That used to shine so bright a star
The general's could not get together
Wanting that influence great in war.

There is Gay, forestalling Byron.

See generous Burlington with Goodly Bruce
  (But Bruce comes wafted in a soft sedan)
Dan Prior next, beloved by every Muse;
  And friendly Congreve, unreproachful man!
(Oxford by Cunningham hath sent excuse;)
  See hearty Watkins come with cap and can,
And Lewis who has never friend forsaken;
  And Laughton whispering asks "Is Troytown Taken?"

or Dr. Johnson, forestalling Housman,

All that prey on vice and folly
  Joy to see their quarry fly;
There the gamester light and jolly
  There the lender grave and sly.

and a host of popular songs and hymns.

Come cheer up, my lads, 'tis to glory we steer
To add something more to this wonderful year.

No, the poetry of the eighteenth century is at least as varied
as that of any other, but Pope is labelled as the representative
Augustan poet, and as he confined himself to the couplet, the
couplet is labelled as the medium of Augustan poetry. As far
as Pope personally was concerned, his limitation of form—he
even denied himself the variety of an occasional Alexandrine—
had its advantages. "Of this uniformity the certain con-

101

sequence was readiness and dexterity. By perpetual practice, language had in his mind a systematical arrangement, having always the same use for words, he had words so selected and combined as to be ready at his call."

With this limit of form went a limit of interest. Pope was interested in three things, himself and what other people thought of him, his art, and the manners and characters of society. Not even Flaubert or Mallarmé was more devoted to his craft. "What his nature was unfitted to do, circumstance excused him from doing"; and he was never compelled to write to order, or to hurry over his work. He missed nothing. If he thought of something in the midst of the night, he rang for the servant to bring paper; if something struck him during a conversation, he would immediately write it down for future use. He constantly altered and rewrote, and always for the better. The introduction of sylphs and gnomes into the *Rape of the Lock*, and the conclusion of the *Dunciad* were not first thoughts.

> Let there be Darkness (the dread power shall say)
> All shall be Darkness, as it ne'er were day:
> To their first chaos Wit's vain works shall fall
> And universal Dullness cover all.
> No more the Monarch could such raptures bear;
> He waked, and all the Vision mixed with air.
>
> (1728)
>
> Lo! the great Anarch's ancient reign restored
> Light dies before her uncreating word. . . .
> Thy hand, great Dullness! lets the curtain fall
> And universal Darkness covers all.
> Enough! enough! the raptured Monarch cries;
> And through the ivory gate the Vision flies.
>
> (1729)

and finally,

POPE

Lo! thy Dread Empire, Chaos! is restored
Light dies before thy uncreating word.
Thy hand, great Anarch! lets the curtain fall
And universal darkness buries all.

The beauties and variety of his verse have been so brilliantly displayed by others, notably Miss Sitwell, that I shall
confine myself to considering two popular ideas about Pope.
That his language is either falsely poetic, or "a classic of our
prose" and that his poetry is cold and unemotional. The
question of poetic diction was the gravamen of the Romantic's
charge. The answer is that Pope and his contemporaries
were interested in different fields of experience, in a different
"nature". If their descriptions of cows and cottages and birds
are vague, it is because their focus of interest is sharp elsewhere,
and equal definition over the whole picture would spoil its
proportion and obscure its design. They are conventional,
not because the poets thought that "the waterpudge, the
pilewort, the petty chap, and the pooty" were unpoetic in
their naked nature and must be suitably dressed, but because
they are intended to be conventional, a backcloth to the more
important human stage figures. When Pope writes in his
preface to the *Odyssey*, "There is a real beauty in an easy, pure,
perspicuous description even of a low action," he is saying
something which he both believes and practises.

To compass this, his building is a Town,
His pond an Ocean, his parterre a Down:
Who but must laugh, the Master when he sees,
A puny insect, shivering at a breeze!
Lo! what huge heaps of littleness around!
The whole, a laboured Quarry above ground;
Two Cupids squirt before; a Lake behind
Improves the keenness of the Northern wind.
His Gardens next your admiration call,

103

8

FROM ANNE TO VICTORIA

On every side you look, behold the Wall!
No pleasing Intricacies intervene,
No artful wildness to perplex the scene;
Grove nods at grove, each Alley has a brother,
And half the platform just reflects the other.
The suff'ring eye inverted Nature sees,
Trees cut to Statues, Statues thick as trees;
With here a Fountain, never to be played;
And there a Summer-house, that knows no shade;
Here Amphitrite sails through myrtle bowers;
There Gladiators fight, or die in flowers;
Un-watered see the drooping sea-horse mourn,
And swallows roost in Nilus dusty Urn.

Now lap-dogs give themselves the rousing shake,
And sleepless lovers, just at twelve, awake:
Thrice rung the bell, the slipper knocked the ground,
And the pressed watch returned a silver sound.

There is no vagueness here. There are the images of contemporary life. This poetry, not Wordsworth's, is the ancestor
of "the patient etherized on the table", of Beaudelaire's,

On entend ça et là les cuisines siffler,
les théâtres glapir, les orchestres ronfler;
les tables d'hôte, dont le jeu fait les délices,
s'emplissent de catins et d'escrocs, leur complices,
Et les voleurs, qui n'ont ni trève ni merci
Vont bientôt commencer leur travail, eux aussi,
Et forcer doucement les portes et les caisses
Pour vivre quelques jours et vêtir leurs maîtresses.

Those who complain of Pope's use of periphrasis, of his
refusal to call a spade a spade, cannot have read him carefully.
When he chooses he is as direct as you please.

POPE

So morning insects that in muck begun
Shine, buzz, and flyblow in the setting sun.

And when he does use a periphrasis, in his best work at least,
it is because an effect is to be gained by doing so.

While China's earth receives the smoking tide.

To say that Pope was afraid to write, as Wordsworth might
have written,

While boiling water on the tea was poured

is nonsense. To the microscopic image of tea-making is added
the macroscopic image of a flood, a favourite device of Pope's,
and the opposite kind of synthesis to Dante's, "A single
moment maketh a deeper lethargy for use than twenty and
five centuries have wrought on the emprise that erst threw
Neptune in amaze at Argo's shadow."

There are places in Pope, as in all poets, where his imagination is forced, where one feels a division between the object
and the word, but at his best there are few poets who can rival
his fusion of vision and language.

Chicane in furs, and casuistry in lawn

Bare the mean heart that lurks beneath a star.

How hints, like spawn, scarce quick in embryo lie,
How new-born nonsense first is taught to cry,
Maggots half-formed in rhyme exactly meet,
And learn to crawl upon poetic feet.
Here one poor word an hundred clenches makes,
And ductile Dulness new maeanders takes;
There motley images her fancy strike,
Figures ill paired, and Similes unlike.

She sees a Mob of Metaphors advance,
Pleased with the madness of the mazy dance;
How Tragedy and Comedy embrace;
How farce and Epic get a jumbled race;
How Time himself stands still at her command,
Realms shift their place, and Ocean turns to land.
Here gay Description Egypt glads with showers,
Or gives to Zembla fruits, to Barca flowers;
Glitt'ring with ice here hoary hills are seen,
There painted valleys of eternal green;
In cold December fragrant chaplets blow,
And heavy harvests nod beneath the snow.

You will call this Fancy and Judgment if you are an Augustan, and the Imagination if you are a Romantic, but there is no doubt about it.

Like Dante, Pope had a passionate and quite undonnish interest in classical literature. The transformation of the heroic epic into *The Rape of the Lock* and the *Dunciad*, is not cheap parody; it is the vision of a man who can see in Homer, in eighteenth century society, in Grub Street, similarities of motive, character, and conduct whereby an understanding of all is deepened. Rams and young bullocks are changed to folios and Birthday odes, and

> Could all our care elude the gloomy grave
> Which claims no less the fearful than the brave
> For lust of fame I should not vainly dare
> In fighting fields, nor urge thy soul to war

becomes

> O if to dance all night and dress all day,
> Charmed the small pox, or chased old age away;
> Who would not scorn what housewife cares produce,
> Or who would learn an earthly thing of use?

POPE

Literature and life are once more happily married. We laugh and we love. Unlike Dryden, Pope is not a dramatic poet. He is at his best only when he is writing directly out of his own experience. I cannot feel that his Homer is anything but a set task, honourably executed: the diction gives it away. But show him the drawing-rooms where he longed to be received as a real gentleman, let him hear a disparaging remark about himself, and his poetry is beyond praise. The *Essay on Man* is smug and jaunty to a degree, until we come to Happiness and Fame

> All that we feel of it begins and ends
> In the small circle of our foes and friends.
> To all beside as much an empty shade
> An England living, as a Cæsar dead.

Pope knew what it was to be flattered and libelled, to be ambitious, to be snubbed, to have enemies, to be short, and ugly, and ill, and unhappy, and out of his knowledge he made his poetry, succeeded, as Rilke puts it, in

> transmuting himself into the words.
> Doggedly, as the carver of a cathedral
> Transfers himself to the stone's constancy.

and won his reward as he perceived

> . . . . how fate may enter into a verse
> And not come back, how, once in, it turns image
> And nothing but image, nothing but ancestor,
> Who sometimes, when you look at him in his frame
> Seems to be like you and again not like you.

SIR ROBERT WALPOLE

(1676–1745)

by Sir Richard Lodge

SIR ROBERT WALPOLE'S name is one of the most familiar in English history. Every well-trained undergraduate will tell his examiners that Walpole was the first Prime Minister, though he repudiated the title; that he held that position for a record period of twenty years; that he was in the habit of saying: "Every man has his price" (a perversion of his actual words) and "Let sleeping dogs lie"; that he read the reports of his gamekeeper before turning to state papers; that he once boasted to Queen Caroline that in a great European war, "50,000 men have been killed in Europe this year and not one Englishman": and that, when the populace greeted with enthusiasm the outbreak of war with Spain, he uttered the gloomy forecast: "They are now ringing their bells, they will soon be wringing their hands." He will probably add that Walpole proved himself to be an able financier after the bursting of the South Sea Bubble, that he was a master of the art of political corruption, though he did not invent it, and that his resolute adhesion to a policy of peace gave much-needed security to the Hanoverian dynasty, stimulated English prosperity, and so enabled the country to bear the burden of the wars in which it was involved after his downfall. To these glib answers of the examinee may be added the significant facts that John Morley included Walpole in his select team of "Twelve English Statesmen", that he reserved him for his own pen, and that the late Mr. F. S. Oliver chose his career as the most appropriate peg on which to hang the notable analysis of political method and achievement to which he gave the title of *The Endless Adventure*.

The outline of Walpole's career is fairly simple. He was born in 1676, the third son and the fifth child of a large family. The death of two elder brothers made him his father's heir, and in 1700 he succeeded to the family estates, which brought in what was then the more than comfortable income of about £2,000. He succeeded also to his father's constituency, being returned for Castle Rising in the two elections of 1701. In the following year, Anne's accession having necessitated yet another election, he transferred himself to the larger but equally manageable constituency of King's Lynn, which he represented until, in 1742, his active political career came to an end and he went to the House of Lords with a title taken from the charming Suffolk town of Orford. Meanwhile, the vacant seat of Castle Rising was transferred to his younger brother Horatio (later Baron Walpole). The two brothers were destined in later years to be closely associated in the conduct of foreign policy.

From the outset Robert Walpole joined the ranks of the Whig party and became an active and keenly interested politician. By constant practice he made himself an efficient speaker, though he was never an orator like his contemporary and rival, the later Viscount Bolingbroke. He had other assets, a mastery of finance, a cool judgment, and a growing power of influencing his associates. These qualities raised him gradually into favour with the Whig leaders, with one of whom,

Charles Townshend, he was already intimate as a neighbour in Norfolk. The result was that, when Marlborough and Godolphin were forced by the growing Tory opposition to the continental war into alliance with the Whigs, Robert Walpole was appointed to succeed Henry St. John as Secretary at War (1708) and later he added the lucrative post of Treasurer of the Navy (1710). Against his will he was forced to be one of the managers of the ill-judged impeachment of Dr. Sacheverell, which completely alienated the Queen from her Whig ministers. At the end of 1710 he was dismissed from office, and a year later was formally accused of venality and malversation. Having been found guilty by a party majority, he was expelled from the House and, when King's Lynn again loyally returned him, was declared incapable of sitting. This persecution, which curiously anticipates some features of the later treatment of John Wilkes, elevated him to the rank of a martyr in the Whig cause, and increased his prominence in the party. When the accession of George I gave the Whigs an undisputed ascendancy for nearly half a century, Walpole had good cause to expect compensatory preferment, especially as Charles Townshend, now his brother-in-law, was Secretary of State and one of the leading men in the new ministry. But Walpole was not yet a *persona grata* to the King and his Hanoverian followers, and he was only made Paymaster of the Forces without a seat in the Cabinet. From this comparative obscurity he suddenly emerged in October, 1715, when he was promoted to be First Lord of the Treasury and Chancellor of the Exchequer. This marks his final entry into the forefront of political life.

Walpole's first occupancy of high office was of brief duration. The Whigs were securely in the saddle, while the Tories were unfairly and impudently discredited by the convenient label of Jacobites. But, as so often happens, excessive security was fatal to the unity of the dominant party. By 1716 a distinct fissure was visible among the Whig leaders. The main dividing force, apart from personal jealousy, is to be found in the tangles of foreign politics. The Whig tradition, inherited from William III, was based upon hostility to France, and prescribed close co-operation with those powers, notably Austria and Holland, whose interests were also in the main anti-French. The Whig denunciations of the Treaty of Utrecht and its Tory authors were directed against the desertion of old allies and the dangerous concessions made to the enemy, notably the leaving of the crown of Spain on the head of the Bourbon claimant. France was not only the natural enemy but also the impenitent patron of the exiled Stuarts. As long as Louis XIV lived the Whigs clung to their "old system". So far there was no discord. The tangle began when the death of the old King gave the Regency in France to the Duke of Orleans, who had no reason to love the Bourbon King of Spain, his rival for the French succession, and who was prepared to throw over the Stuarts provided the Hanoverian ruler of England would guarantee his claim to be the legal heir, if the sickly Louis XV should die without issue. It became clear to many Whigs, and notably to Stanhope, that in these altered conditions a bigoted adherence to the letter of Whig traditions would be impolitic, and that the Protestant succession, which was the immediately imperative Whig aim, could be more securely buttressed by co-operation with France than by the continuance of the former hostility. Hence arose the curious Anglo-French alliance or *entente*, which was Stanhope's great contribution to contemporary history, which is one of the most notable features of the next two decades, and which has a vital bearing on the later career of Walpole.

The Anglo-French alliance, which grew into a Triple and later into a Quadruple Alliance, was not the only disturbing force. The Accession to the British throne of a German Elector brought this country into new and close relations with German and Baltic problems, and these relations inevitably influenced general policy. The ramifications and limits of Hanoverian influence under the first two Georges have never been thoroughly explored, even by Mr. J. F. Chance, and are not likely to be explored by anybody else. The charge of pandering to the Crown and of using British power and prestige for alien ends was an easy and obvious whip for the trouncing of ministers, and it was unscrupulously wielded by the rhetoric of Chesterfield and Pitt, but it is incontestable that Hanover did in many ways count in the European actions of Britain, and it was inevitable that it should do so at a time when ministers were still primarily the servants of the Crown, and when the control of foreign affairs was regarded as being peculiarly within the province of prerogative.

It would have been unnatural if all the Whig ministers had equally and simultaneously grasped and accepted all that was involved in the novel method of co-operation with France and in the need of securing the maximum of coincidence between British and Hanoverian interests in the disputes of the Baltic states. Stanhope was the most agile in assimilation, and Sunderland followed him. Townshend, a slower, duller and more obstinate man, was inclined to be hesitating and critical. There is no evidence that Walpole, absorbed in the work of his own department, took any active part in what became a ministerial quarrel. The issue was decided by the King in favour of Stanhope and Sunderland, while Townshend had to go, first to Ireland, and then into retirement. Both George I and the triumphant ministers wished to keep Walpole, but he insisted upon following his brother-in-law, to whose support his own advancement hitherto had been largely due.

For the next three years Walpole was a hostile and persistent critic of his former colleagues, and set an example which was readily followed by those Whig politicians whom in subsequent years he excluded or drove from the ministry.

He joined the Tories in approving the repeal of the Schism
Act, which was loathed by all orthodox Whigs. He vehemently
denounced the Quadruple Alliance, the masterpiece of Stanhope's policy, although it was based upon principles to which
in later years he himself obstinately adhered. Chance, however,
enabled him to render at this time what some critics have
deemed to be his greatest service to the country. In their
dread of the probable action of the Prince of Wales, when he
should come to the throne, Sunderland and Stanhope brought
in their Peerage Bill which imposed narrow limits on the royal
power to create new peerages. To this short-sighted measure,
which would have altered the whole balance of the constitution, Walpole offered an opposition which was not only
astute but also completely successful. This triumph had its
desired result. It was necessary to muzzle so dangerous an
opponent. So, in 1720, Townshend resumed office as Secretary
of State, and Walpole accepted the humbler bribe of the Pay-
mastership of the Forces, but without a seat in the Cabinet.
Promotion came, however, with startling rapidity. The
complete collapse of their South Sea scheme discredited
the ministers who had promoted it, and Walpole, who had
opposed it, was called in to set matters straight. In April,
1721, he was once more First Lord of the Treasury and Chancellor of the Exchequer, and he held these offices for twenty
years.

It is customary to consider that Walpole was virtual Prime
Minister during the whole of this period. But his ascendancy
was by no means complete as long as Townshend was his
colleague. For a decade the main interest of England was in
foreign affairs, and these were guided in a large measure
of independence by the King and the dominant Secretary of
State. The result was a virtual dyarchy. Walpole had a free
hand in domestic administration, which was comparatively
uneventful, except for Atterbury's plot, in 1722, and the later

disturbances in Ireland over Wood's halfpence and in Scotland over the malt tax. The only critical moment in the general tranquillity of England was the accession of George II, in 1727. His first impulse was to get rid of his father's ministers, and Walpole was only saved from dismissal by his own astuteness and competence, and by the favour of Queen Caroline, which was his chief buttress at the court for the next ten years.

Meanwhile continental affairs were more tangled than ever. The alliance which Stanhope had made with France had never been an easy one, and its chief foundation was removed by the death of the Duke of Orleans, in 1723. But it was suddenly galvanized into new life by the startling conclusion, in 1725, of an alliance between the Bourbon King of Spain and the Hapsburg Emperor in Austria, who had hitherto been engaged in what appeared to be irreconcilable antagonism to each other. As this unnatural and alarming alliance had been provoked by the reckless conduct of the French First Minister, Bourbon, France was again, as in 1716, a suppliant for English support, and Townshend eagerly seized the chance to recover the upper hand which England had lost since the death of Stanhope. The counter-treaty of Hanover, which was peculiarly the work of Townshend, seemed likely at one moment to lead to a general European war. This, however, was averted by the Treaty of Seville, in 1729, which was successful so far as it detached Spain from her unnatural alliance with Austria, but had also the unfortunate result of ranging England with the two Bourbon states for the avowed purpose of coercing Austria into the acceptance of terms dictated by the latter two powers. If this policy were adhered to, as Townshend's obstinacy prescribed, and if England went to war with her former ally, the Whig tradition would be completely abandoned and the whole balance of power would be endangered by the establishment of a Bourbon ascendancy comparable to that once achieved by Louis XIV. It was at this critical juncture that Walpole made up his mind to take the conduct of foreign affairs out of the hands of his brother-in-law. His sister, Lady Townshend, had died in 1726 so that the family relationship had been weakened, and the political tie was broken when Townshend was forced into retirement in 1730. In defiance of the Treaty of Seville, which had forbidden separate negotiations, Walpole instituted overtures to the Court of Vienna without consulting or considering France, and Austrian opposition to the Seville terms was bought off by the undertaking that England and Holland would guarantee Charles VI's Pragmatic Sanction, which assured the succession of his daughter Maria Theresa to the undivided aggregate of the Austrian dominions. As France had hitherto obstinately refused to accept this settlement, the Treaty of Vienna, in 1731, which embodied these terms, was not only a repudiation of French ascendancy, but a virtual severance of the Anglo-French alliance.

The retirement of Townshend, who magnanimously refused to join the Opposition, left Walpole without any rival in the ministry. For the next ten years he was more like a French *Premier Ministre* than an English Prime Minister. Foreign policy as well as domestic administration was under his control. The two Secretaries of State, Newcastle and Harrington, were little more than clerks who wrote their despatches at his dictation. His position was extraordinarily strong. As long as he could control royal patronage and could count on the loyalty of expert wire-pullers like Newcastle, he had little to fear from parliamentary opposition, however venomous. There was one moment, in 1737, when the death of the Queen seemed likely to weaken his hold upon George II. But the opposition leaders played into Walpole's hands by their intrigues with the Prince of Wales, and habit soon induced the King to continue his attachment to his proved adviser. This calls attention to another contributory cause of Walpole's prolonged domination. His opponents, Pulteney, Carteret, Chesterfield, Marchmont, Windham, Pitt and others, were individually both able and eloquent. But the industrious coaching of Bolingbroke, excluded by Walpole's astuteness from active intervention in parliamentary debate, failed to give to these men the industry and cohesion which were needed for a successful assault on the well-guarded ministerial fortress. But for an extraneous addition to the attacking forces and for a weakening of the internal garrison, Walpole could have defied his inept opponents to the end.

The immense strength of Walpole's position is conclusively demonstrated by two events in 1733. In that year he brought forward his most celebrated legislative proposal, the Excise Bill. Economic historians have agreed that it was a very moderate and a very wise instalment of financial reform. But it was damned by its title. In the popular mind the word excise was associated with the inquisitorial inspection of private premises, and it was generally believed that the appointment of excisemen would give to the Government an excessive and unwholesome influence over elections. The opposition made the most unscrupulous use of these prejudices, and succeeded in raising a stormy protest against the Bill. Walpole, who could probably have carried the measure through both Houses in spite of the protest, thought it wiser to give way and calmly withdrew it from the parliamentary programme. In modern times such an action would be interpreted as a confession of weakness and would fatally discredit a ministry. But, in the eighteenth century, when legislation had not come to be regarded as a primary ministerial duty, Walpole's deferences to public opinion left him still so securely dominant that he could venture to punish those opponents of the Excise Bill who were within reach of his displeasure. There is a savour of dictatorship about this conduct.

The other notable event of 1733 was the outbreak of the

so-called War of the Polish Succession. The title is wholly misleading. Succession in Poland was a matter with which Britain was not connected, and it was settled by a war in which there was never any suggestion that Britain should take part. But linked in a very astute way with this succession dispute was a quite distinct war which did affect both British obligations and British interests. The French Foreign Minister, Chauvelin, had for some time formed the project of overthrowing a fundamental part of the Utrecht settlement by ousting the Hapsburgs from their Italian gains and by substituting Bourbon ascendancy in the peninsula. In this scheme he was assured of the passionate support of Spain. For the commencement of the necessary war a pretext was needed, and this was supplied by the fact that Austria was opposed to the candidature of Louis XV's father-in-law for the Polish throne, and that the Emperor had collected forces on the frontier of Poland, though their use was rendered unnecessary by the successful intervention of Russia. To punish Austria for this conduct or attitude with regard to Poland, France and Spain formed a close family alliance, and Austria was attacked both in Italy and in Germany with overwhelming forces. Fleury's consent to this militant policy was purchased by the assurance that everything should be done to secure the neutrality of the two maritime powers, England and Holland, and for that reason there must be no invasion of the Austrian Netherlands. What Fleury dreaded was a revival of the Grand Alliance against France.

The Emperor, thus wantonly attacked, as he very naturally thought, promptly appealed to Britain for the support which had been promised by the Treaty of Vienna in 1731. The appeal was, no doubt, indiscreetly worded and pressed with too dictatorial assurance. But it had great force. We had guaranteed the Pragmatic Sanction, which stipulated for the integrity of the Austrian dominions. These dominions were now threatened with partition. British policy for the last twenty years had consistently aimed at the maintenance of the main lines of the Utrecht Settlement in Europe. If Chauvelin's scheme were carried out, a vital part of that settlement would be overthrown. The Whigs had always prophesied that a family compact would result from leaving a Bourbon king in Spain, and that such a family compact would be fatal to the balance of power, to the retention of Gibraltar and Minorca, and to the security of British trade both in the Mediterranean and in the western seas. Such a family compact had been concluded at Fontainebleau in October, 1733. Although its terms were secret, and although it was primarily directed against Austria, there was more than a suspicion that it contained anti-British clauses, as it actually did. It was all very well for France to promise to respect the neutrality of the Netherlands, but those provinces had been given to Austria in order that they might be defended against France. To conduct such a defence Austria must be strong, and if Austria were fatally weakened the Netherlands would be at the mercy of their powerful neighbour.

The argument for intervention was strong on the ground of obligation: it was far stronger on the ground of interest. The King, guided no doubt mainly by his German traditions and his electoral obligations, was strongly in favour of supporting the imperial head of Germany. The Queen, also a German by birth and early training, was on the same side. The Whig party, so far as it adhered to its own traditions, could not refuse to support the chief continental rival of France and to oppose the dreaded combination of the two Bourbon states. Public opinion, though not yet fully alive to the danger of the situation, would have welcomed a war against the revived ascendancy of France. The two Secretaries of State, New-castle and Harrington, who had to conduct the correspondence with the courts of France and Austria, were inclined to war.

Walpole, backed up by his brother Horatio, who believed in the pacific professions of Fleury, stood out resolutely for the maintenance of peace. Whether it was wise or prudent to stand aside, whether it was quite honest to take advantage of the treaty of Vienna in 1731 and to evade its obligations in 1733-4, are matters which may be disputed for all time. But, whatever one's opinions may be on matters of obligation or policy, it is impossible not to admire the rock-like obstinacy with which Walpole held his own against what appeared to be an overwhelming combination of forces against him. His strongest argument was that a war with France would lead to a renewal of foreign encouragement and support to the Jacobites, and that the dynasty would be endangered. He may not have been as completely bamboozled by Fleury's hypocritical professions of disinterestedness as appears at first sight, and he may have merely used them to buttress his position. In the end fate was kind to him, because Chauvelin was not allowed to carry out his scheme in full, and Fleury, in 1735, granted to Austria more moderate terms than might have been exacted if France and Spain had pressed their military superiority. It is true that the Spanish Bourbons gained Naples and Sicily, and that France obtained the reversion of Lorraine; but Austria recovered Lombardy and got compensation for the loss of southern Italy by the acquisition of Parma and the virtual acquisition of Tuscany. The peace was not in any direct way due to British action or British mediation, but it could be plausibly contended that its moderation was due to the dread that more extreme demands might force Britain to intervene. Hence, in its immediate consequences, the war did nothing to weaken Walpole's ascendancy, and many historians award to him the posthumous justification of his policy in the fact that the subsequent European war did give occasion for a Jacobite rising which for a moment seemed really formidable.

So far Walpole's peace policy, in spite of denunciations on

the part of his opponents, was condoned and from the domestic point of view was not indefensible. But its repercussions on the Continent were not quite so fortunate. It lowered the prestige of England, and created the impression that the settled policy of its ministers was peace at any price. This gave fatal encouragement to the bellicose forces in France and Spain. Of the two powers Spain, which had been compelled, in 1713, to cede Gibraltar and Minorca and to make humiliating concessions with regard to trade with her colonies, had the most obvious grievances against England; but France had also humiliations to avenge, notably the compulsory dismantling of Dunkirk. So it was pretty certain that Spain could count upon eventual support from France. In 1726, when for a time hostilities had actually broken out, the first action of Spain had been to lay siege to Gibraltar. The quarrel had then been postponed for a time because the Spanish Queen, Elizabeth Farnese, had put the dynastic interests of her family in Italy before the national ambitions of her subjects. Now that Italian problems were for the moment settled, in 1738, when Spain acceded to Fleury's terms for the closing of the Polish succession war, Spain was free to resume its anti-English attitude and to offer active resistance to English encroachments upon trade in Spanish waters. The story of how Captain Jenkins lost his ear in an attempt to resist the search of his ship by Spanish coastguards is only a sample of the stories of Spanish brutality which stirred public opinion to its depths. The opposition eagerly welcomed a wave of opinion, which proved even stronger than that which had defeated the Excise Bill, in that it undermined the loyalty or submissiveness of Walpole's colleagues and so weakened his control of parliament.

It is to Walpole's credit that he did not give way to pressure without a struggle. He did his utmost to settle by diplomacy a quarrel in which England was quite as much at fault as Spain, and he was so far successful as to conclude a Convention which was to be the basis on which a final settlement was to be negotiated. The Convention was extremely unpopular in England, and whatever chance Walpole had of maintaining peace was swept away when it appeared that public opinion in Spain was equally hostile to any compromise. War became inevitable and Walpole entered it with a premonition of disaster which unfitted him for its guidance. It has often been suggested that he should have resigned rather than carry out a policy which was forced upon him. On this point it can only be said that the idea of voluntary resignation was contrary to all contemporary tradition and little likely to commend itself to a man of Walpole's obstinate self-confidence.

The naval war with Spain was wholly devoid of glory, but this might not in itself have sufficed to bring about Walpole's downfall. Within a year it was thrust into the background by major happenings on the Continent. In 1740 the death of the Emperor Charles VI opened the question of the Austrian succession. If paper assurances were of any value, the accession of Maria Theresa seemed to be threatened by nothing more formidable than a very questionable claim on the part of the Elector of Bavaria. The election of a new Emperor was a more open matter, but it was less vitally important and it concerned Hanover rather than England. The storm, which the late Emperor had striven to avert by his Pragmatic Sanction, began in a wholly unexpected quarter. The young Frederick of Prussia, of whose character and talents little was known, invaded Silesia and impudently offered to support Maria Theresa's claim to her other provinces and to give his vote to her husband if she would buy off his quite preposterous claims. The offer was promptly rejected and Walpole was for the second time called upon to fulfil the promises made in the Vienna treaty of 1731. This time there seemed no reason to refuse. The attack by Prussia was wholly unprovoked and

George II, as Elector of Hanover, was eager to prevent the aggrandisement of his inconvenient neighbour and nephew. English obligation and Hanoverian interest equally urged the support of Maria Theresa. The sending of auxiliaries to help Austria to chastise a rash and unprincipled invader seemed a comparatively trifling matter. But Walpole's luck was by this time completely out. The early Prussian successes, and especially the startling victory of Mollwitz, encouraged all the would-be despoilers to come forward. Even Fleury, who had bought the reversion of Lorraine by a promise to maintain the Pragmatic Sanction, and who genuinely desired to limit French intervention to securing the election of a non-Hapsburg Emperor, found it impossible to resist the wave of bellicose opinion, and France undertook to support not only the Bavarian candidature for the imperial title but also the Bavarian claims to Hapsburg provinces. The Queen of Spain, not satisfied with the Italian kingdom which she had obtained for her eldest son, eagerly grasped the opportunity to gain a principality for his younger brother. Hence arose a formidable coalition between France, Spain and Bavaria for the partition of Maria Theresa's inheritance, and the coalition assumed almost irresistible proportions when it was joined by the King of Prussia and the Elector of Saxony. Neither England nor Walpole was prepared to face such a sudden and unexpected storm, and an additional humiliation was added when George II, alarmed for Hanover, purchased an ignominious security by promising to remain neutral in his electoral capacity and to give his vote in the Empire for the Bavarian candidate. Maria Theresa had now no hope of securing the imperial crown for her husband, and little hope of retaining more than a fragment of her father's dominions for herself. It was, perhaps, fortunate for her that Walpole fell at the beginning of 1742. Public opinion was inflamed by the ill-success of the Spanish war and by the disasters of Maria Theresa, for whose cause there was a good deal of enthusiasm in England. The docile House of Commons, elected in 1734, came to an end in 1741, and the general election, though not disastrous, diminished the security of the Government. It was inevitable that opinion should demand a scapegoat, and Walpole's isolated ascendancy exposed him to personal attack. His colleagues did not hesitate to intrigue behind his back, in order to secure their own safety and their own places. Diminished majorities on vital questions and an actual defeat on an election petition convinced Walpole that it was necessary to resign his office, and in 1742 he went to the House of Lords as Earl of Orford.

Walpole fell, as he had ruled, practically alone. His principal colleagues, the Pelham brothers and Lord Hardwicke, survived. The only intruder to the ministry of vital importance was Carteret. Sir Spencer Compton, who had been on the verge of superseding Walpole in 1727, now took his place as First Lord of the Treasury, with the title of Lord Wilmington, but he was only a dummy Premier. Pulteney committed political suicide by refusing to take office and by quitting the House of Commons, where he had been hitherto a real force. In these circumstances all attempts to bring Walpole to trial on the charges fulminated against him were doomed to farcical failure. His former colleagues had no desire for disclosures which might incriminate themselves, and the newcomers could not condemn methods which they intended to employ. Hence Walpole, with his vast experience, remained for his last three years a sort of oracle in the background, consulted alike by King and by ministers. It was a not undignified end to a great career.

From his retirement Walpole watched with keen interest the ill-assorted coalition which had been formed on his overthrow. Carteret, who had some real aptitude for diplomacy, set himself with temporary success to redeem what he regarded as the blunders of the last decade. He persuaded the King, whose personal favour he gained, to repudiate the ignominious neutrality of Hanover and to lend or sell Hanoverian troops for the service of Austria. With greater difficulty he induced Maria Theresa to consent to the sacrifices necessary to buy off her non-Bourbon opponents, and he hoped with the help of a powerful anti-Bourbon coalition to wrest from France and Spain the gains which English neutrality in the previous war had allowed them to appropriate. Engaged in these lofty enterprises, he treated his ministerial colleagues with a contemptuous neglect which they resented even more than the masterful control which Walpole had exercised. Just as this ill-feeling was at its height, the death of Lord Wilmington made it necessary to appoint a new First Lord of the Treasury. This brought the situation to a head. Carteret had pledged himself to back the claims of Pulteney, now Lord Bath, who had apparently repented of his self-denying ordinance. The other aspirant was Henry Pelham, Newcastle's brother, the pupil and professed disciple of Walpole. For some weeks politicians were on tenterhooks, and the final choice of Pelham was universally attributed to Walpole's influence with the King. But Carteret accepted the decision with such cheerfulness that it is difficult to believe that he pressed his candidate with all his force. At the moment when this apparently adverse decision was given, he was at the height of his influence on the Continent, and he was the sole minister in attendance on George II.

In 1744 there was another and more serious crisis, and again Walpole played a part in its issue. The confident hopes excited by the early success of Carteret's anti-Bourbon alliances had been shattered when Frederick of Prussia, alarmed by the prospect of a complete revival of Austria, suddenly abandoned the neutrality which had been purchased by the cession of Silesia, concluded a new treaty with France, and without any provocation threw his army into Bohemia. The consequent abandonment of the invasion of Alsace from Italy dislocated all the hopeful plans of the allies, and the English ministers had to face a renewed storm of hostile criticism in Parliament. Carteret was denounced as bitterly as Walpole had ever been, and his jealous colleagues determined to appease the House of Commons by discarding the minister who had claimed the direction of foreign affairs. In order to secure the necessary majority the Pelhams undertook to form a wider coalition, known in contemporary jargon as the Broad Bottom, and the King, again guided by Walpole, was forced to abandon the minister whom he liked and trusted rather than risk a contest with Parliament at a critical stage of the war.

The removal of Carteret and his few personal adherents was Walpole's last political service or disservice to the country. He died in March, 1745, and he left the dominant voice in the Government to men who had been trained under his guidance. Henry Pelham has been called a miniature Walpole, and in many ways, especially in his handling of finance, he showed himself an apt pupil of his master. But in some notable respects he reversed Walpole's precedents. The unity of control which had been so conspicuous from 1730 to 1742 was replaced by a dyarchy not dissimilar from that which Walpole had terminated in 1729. The Duke of Newcastle gradually asserted a dominant voice in the control of foreign policy, much as Stanhope and Townshend had done in the past. Pelham acquiesced in the claim, so long as his restless brother did not make excessive financial demands, and the cohesion of the ministry which Walpole had drastically enforced by the exclusion of dissidents was destroyed under Pelham by their admission to the ministry. The Broad Bottom lasted till 1754. It was not a very efficient or successful administration, except perhaps in finance, but it did succeed for ten years in reducing parliamentary opposition to a minimum. This was something which Walpole never achieved or attempted.

On few politicians in any country has the historical verdict been so unanimous and on the whole so favourable as on Walpole. Nobody has attributed to him any high ideals other than a love of peace, or any desire for constitutional or social reform. Everybody is agreed that he was a supreme realist, who took men and circumstances as he found them, without any strong desire to make them better. Everybody is agreed that he was a patriot, and that, if he loved power, he exerted it for what he considered to be his country's good. He was coarse in fibre, but not flagrantly immoral. He used rogues for his own ends, but he was not himself a rogue. The wealth which he expended on re-building Houghton was not dishonestly gained. If he procured endowment for the members of his family and his loyal supporters, he only did what all men in his station were expected to do. The charges brought against him by his opponents broke down at the time, and no serious attempt has since been made to revive them.

Rather curiously, Walpole's eulogists have singled out for special commendation his foreign policy, a department for which he had neither training nor aptitude. And in their view his greatest achievement was his resolute refusal to take part in the mis-called War of the Polish Succession. John Morley says of this that "his ends were wise, his diplomatic management was penetrating and skilful, and his union of tact and patience with immovable determination is a standing lesson in political action". Mr. F. S. Oliver summed up the arguments for and against neutrality in the war with judicial calm and decided on every count in Walpole's favour. And Walpole's most recent biographer is almost lyrical in his laudation. "His further triumph was in keeping the nation out of the war of the Polish succession, when the Emperor expected Britain to fight by his side against the French. It was a brilliant piece of work. When it came to diplomacy the country squire was the master of the most intriguing foreign secretaries in

Europe". It is difficult for one who has soaked himself in the diplomatic records of the period to accept these complacent verdicts. The actual contemporary documents supply convincing proof that the dominant diplomatist in these years was not either of the Walpole brothers but Cardinal Fleury, a statesman whose ability has hardly received due appreciation from either French or English historians. With consummate skill he professed complete disinterestedness, and in the end induced the baffled English ministers to approve a treaty which broke through the bounds imposed by the Utrecht settlement on the Bourbon powers, gave substantial gains to both France and Spain, and, in the words of Frederick the Great, left France the arbiter of Europe. Walpole's apologists plead that this was a small price to pay for the avoidance of war. But was war really avoided? It is a reasonable contention that war was only postponed, and that England paid the penalty for Walpole's ill-timed pacifism when Spain rigidly enforced her right of search against English traders, and when Fleury before his death repudiated that guarantee of the Pragmatic Sanction which had been the sweetmeat to soften the nauseous dose of Bourbon aggrandisement. The Duke of Newcastle was not a great minister, but he had been a Secretary of State for twenty-eight years and he had an intimate familiarity with the courts of Europe when he declared, in 1752, that if England had taken part in the war of 1733-5, either there would have been no subsequent war or it would have taken a wholly different course.

The weakness of Walpole's foreign policy lay in the fact that he concentrated his attention upon the immediate problem without any adequate consideration of future consequences. His first notable act was the conclusion of the Treaty of Vienna, in 1731, and this was his one great triumph in diplomacy. But he failed to see how this inevitably shattered the Anglo-French alliance, which had for fifteen years averted any serious

European war, and how equally inevitably it drove France into closer alliance with Spain and thus led to the conclusion of the Family Compact which the Whigs had always regarded as a certain danger both to the Hanoverian dynasty and to the interests of British Commerce. Nor did he realize clearly that his master-stroke, in 1731, imposed upon England obligations which he might find burdensome in the future. He successfully evaded these obligations in 1733, only to find them still confronting him in 1741, when they had the deplorable result of placing England and France upon opposite sides in a great European war. At the outset the two powers were merely auxiliaries, but in 1744 they became the principal belligerents, and England was confronted with the two dangers which Walpole had set himself to avert, a French invasion of the Netherlands, and a Jacobite rising with foreign encouragement, and probably foreign aid.

It is this lack of prescience which excludes Walpole from the ranks of supremely great statesmen. But no criticism can deprive him of his claim to be regarded as perhaps the most successful of English politicians. He was for ten years the nearest approach to a dictator that England has seen since the days of Oliver Cromwell, and, unlike Cromwell, he had no army at his back. He owed his unique authority to the adroit way in which he mastered the Crown and the House of Commons, the two rivals for the selection and control of ministers. No precedent had yet fixed the boundary between the King's right to choose and dismiss men who professed to be his servants and the claim of the Commons to censure and in extreme cases to impeach those servants of the Crown who had incurred their distrust or displeasure. Walpole set himself to avoid any testing dispute, and thus secured his long tenure of office. His successors were less adroit, and in 1744 and again in 1746 George II was compelled by the need of gaining parliamentary support to dismiss ministers whom he desired to retain, and to retain ministers whom he desired to dismiss.

With all his skill and experience Walpole had to reckon with one force he could not control. Public opinion was rarely roused in those days of slow and scanty communication, but once roused it was irresistible. Walpole was as powerless in 1739 to avert a war with Spain as Mr. Baldwin, with his parliamentary majority, was unable in 1935 to obtain approval of the Hoare-Laval treaty. Public opinion may have been wrong on both occasions, but that does not detract from its omnipotence. And Walpole realized that when ill-success in war had inflamed opinion against him he had no alternative but to surrender his power.

Walpole's eminence is perhaps best measured by comparison with his contemporaries. Most of them have been forgotten or have become mere names. Bolingbroke is the most famous, but he lacked character and consistency. Carteret was a more brilliant foreign minister, and might have achieved no inconsiderable success if he had had sufficient tact and skill to secure the support of his colleagues and of parliament. Pulteney proved to be little better than a windbag. Chesterfield has a place in literary history and some claim to distinction as a diplomatist, but as a Secretary of State he was a failure. The only great man among Walpole's opponents was William Pitt, and he was as yet too young and too irresponsible to be regarded as a possible rival. The simple fact is that Walpole bestrode his generation like a Colossus, and the two decades from 1720 to 1740 will always be known as the Age of Walpole.

9

HANDEL

(1685-1759)

by NEWMAN FLOWER

§ 1. *The Beginning*

THE Saxon youth of twenty-five who, in the autumn of 1710, wandered off the Holland boat into London, was in many ways a lost and lonely person. He had no friends in this city, and his knowledge of the English language was as scant as his friends. He was endeavouring to find his way through the badly-marked London of his time to the Queen's Theatre in the Haymarket. With only his native German tongue, some colloquial Italian and a smattering of French, the task was not easy in an age when other people's languages did not matter to the citizens of London.

After some perambulation this young Handel found the Queen's Theatre, and found also another youth—one Aaron Hill—who controlled the theatre's fortunes. True, those fortunes were not in the ascendant when Handel walked through the theatre doors for the first time. But the meeting was historic. It led to the partnership between the heart of a man and the heart of a nation. Handel was to live in London forty-nine years after that eventful day, and to give all his greatest music to London.

Handel's activities were often mysterious in origin, and one may wonder why he came to London at all. He had a certain reputation on the Continent which he was content to throw away for adventure in an unknown city. He had left his Saxon birth-city of Halle at the age of eighteen for Hamburg, then the centre of opera in northern Europe. He was content to start as a fiddler in the orchestra there. What chance had a fiddler? But he found his chance. He persuaded the management to produce his first opera *Almira*, a poor, amateurish thing with a few sparks of promise in it.

It failed. But the management had courage enough to speculate again. When Handel was twenty, the Hamburg Opera House suddenly billed *Nero; Or Love Obtained Through Blood and Murder*. There must have been some mad speculators in those days to have passed even the title. Another failure. All the music of this ill-starred work is lost, and the only souvenir that remains of it is a book of the words sold in the theatre on the night it was produced in 1705, which lies on my table as I write.

Neither Germany nor England discovered Handel. All the argument between the two nations as to which parented his genius is so much "poppy-cock". Italy discovered Handel. After the Hamburg failures, Handel set out for Rome, and reached the capital in January, 1707, when he was barely twenty-two.

He arrived at a happy moment. Cardinal Ottoboni—the rich nephew of a Pope—was the established head of the Arts in the City. He poured out money on music. He discovered youthful genius in the gutter, and gave it foundation. He spent a fortune on hidden charity. He had a secret bakery which made bread for all the poor of Rome, and he gave the bread away anonymously. Through unknown sources some knowledge came to him of the musical brilliance which lay waiting in Handel. He drew him into the *musicales* held at his palace every Monday evening. Corelli, the composer, head of the

Cardinal's music, was always present; Alessandro Scarlatti was there.

The "production" of Handel had begun. He composed his first religious work, *La Resurezzione* for Rome. Was it not a forerunner of *Messiah*? He passed from Rome to Naples, to Venice. At the end of December, 1709, his opera *Agrippina* was produced in Venice. It was the first night of the season, and Handel had given the best fruiting of his youth. The audience poured out of the theatre into the winter night exclaiming: "Long live the dear Saxon!" But the triumph was worth no money to him. With true Italian nonchalance, they forgot that he had to pay his bills. Nevertheless, he had put his first foot on the ladder; a long ladder with many weights to bear as he climbed.

He left Italy and went to Hanover to be Kapellmeister to the Elector (afterwards George I of England) at a salary of £300 a year. It was a bad move. It was a stalemate. Handel realized, before many months had passed, that all the moods stirring in him would depart, and leave him mouldering under the pomp of a silly Court.

He cast his eyes towards England. Purcell had been dead fifteen years. The London theatres were struggling on with bad Italian singers who had left Italy for London because they were bad. These singers had short engagements in London and departed as rapidly into the murk from which they had emerged. Music in London was moribund. The "quality", for lack of intelligent concerts, kept to their *salons* and gambled. When they did go out to a theatre, their chairs were overturned as often as not by footpads in the muddy lanes, and milady robbed of her jewels. Theatres were floundering. Such as kept open were financed by the rich for the face of a mistress rather than for her art.

That is why Handel walked up the Haymarket in 1710. He saw his chance in London. It was fortunate for England that

Aaron Hill, in spite of his bunch of failures at the Queen's Theatre, had heard of this young man's success in Italy. Hill was a gambler. He was out for the last throw because his "till" had become scarcely worth collecting. He decided at that first meeting to employ Handel. He told him to go away and write an opera. In a fortnight—mark the time as evidence of what young genius can do when it is pressed—Handel returned with the full score of *Rinaldo*.

On February 24th, 1711, the opera was produced. The *libretto* by Rossi would have destroyed most operas on the first night owing to its imbecility. But the music was fresh with life; glowing and glorious in its greater moments. It is true that Addison, bitter with the three nights' failure of his *Rosamund*, slaughtered the work with a pen more vile than its common habit. It is true that the caged sparrows, let loose for dramatic effect during the first performance, made havoc of the ladies' dresses. But *Rinaldo* was new with a freshness in every bar. The "quality" forgot their cards, and a congestion of carriages lay at the theatre doors—those doors which of late had been so scarcely sought.

Now, so great were the crowds that many ticket-holders could only gain their seats when each performance had well advanced. People fought at the entrances. Dresses were ripped to pieces whilst laughing pedlars—who enjoyed the discomfiture of those better off than they—offered to sell the exasperated ladies oranges.

Handel had come to London.

§ 2. *The Operas*

Handel's work in London may be divided into three epochs. The first covered the range of the operas which he produced with unbroken sequence from 1711 to 1732. Even after that date an occasional opera came from him, the last being *Berenice*, with its lovely minuet, in 1737.

The second epoch—the period mainly devoted to oratorio—began with *Esther* in 1732, and continued until complete blindness fell upon him in 1751 when he was sixty-six.

The third epoch was the "patchwork period"—those eight years of blindness (1751-1759) when he resuscitated old works, and dictated new numbers for them to his amanuensis, Christopher Smith. He made London crowd to hear old works which it had spurned when they were newly given. So it came about that from the state of penury in which he existed when he became blind, he made enough during those years in the dark to leave a fortune of £20,000—a large sum for those days.

To return to *Rinaldo*. After its success in 1711, Aaron Hill left the Queen's Theatre. He was ever a bird of passage, and he sought new fields. In his place came a man named Mac-Swiney. The fellow had no knowledge of music, even if he had some ability as a producer. Into his hands fell the new Handel opera, *Teseo*, a work of considerable strength and passion, a work as rich in melody as *Rinaldo*. It was produced on January 10th, 1713. The "Town" acclaimed it. Here was a brilliant successor to *Rinaldo*. But after the second performance MacSwiney disappeared with the entire box-office receipts, leaving the singers unpaid, and the cost of the production as a legacy for his successor. All that Handel received from *Teseo* was the proceeds of the last performance given for his benefit.

Nevertheless, the incident was to be important in its effect. The theatre was left in a state of chaos. Handel, at the moment when it seemed that Fortune was within reach, was left without a supporter. But not for long. The theatre was suddenly taken over by Jakob Heidegger, and thereby the most important partnership of the operatic world in the eighteenth century was begun.

This Heidegger figured so prominently in the life of Handel that some details of him are necessary. He came from an old Nuremberg family which had settled in Zurich. He was grim and ugly, and, having been discarded as a lover in Zurich, he travelled about Europe as a valet. In 1707 he had come to England on some secret mission to the English Government, but the Government would have none of him. He enlisted as a private in the Guards. He was hideous to look upon, and was known as the ugliest man in London. Nevertheless, his personality was extraordinary, and he was assisted by an outstanding cleverness.

He left the Guards and suddenly appeared at the tables of Society. No one knew how or why. He gambled and won money; he borrowed with the utmost ease by sheer plausibility. Then he produced an opera out of which he made £500. He put on masquerades of a free and licentious order, and made £400-£500 out of each of them.

Such was the man with whom Handel cast in his lot during the run of *Teseo*. Heidegger himself wrote the *libretto* for Handel's next opera, *Amadigi*; he produced the work in sumptuous fashion and carried it to success. Not that the partners were entirely responsible for this success, for Anastasia Robinson—one of the finest contraltos of her age—drew the Town as Oriana. No one was aware that she was secretly married to an irascible old peer with one leg in the grave. It was not until some of the young "bloods", who crowded the stage door during the run of *Amadigi*, began to make love to her that Lord Peterborough emerged from his seclusion, and publicly thrashed one of them. Then he called all the relatives and friends of Anastasia together at the house in Fulham which he had given the singer, and announced to the gathering that he was her husband and scandalized the Town.

The Handel-Heidegger partnership had become well established when, in 1719, the Royal Academy of Music was founded. King George I, now settled down to comfort on the English throne, gave a thousand guineas, and Society opened its purse accordingly. Handel hurried abroad to secure singers. He visited Hamburg, Dresden, Halle. Hearing that he was in Halle, Bach walked the twenty-one miles from Leipzig to meet him. But, on the day he reached Halle, Handel left for London. Only two hours forbade a meeting of the giants which was destined never to take place.

The Royal Academy started with a star of Fortune ablaze in the sky. Handel had composed *Radamisto*, one of the most striking operas of his early years. Long before the *première* every seat was sold. People offered £2 for a place in the gallery, and were turned away. The new opera, with its wonderful arias, its tenderness, its martial effects, played to crowded houses till the end of the season.

The Directors of the Academy laid their plans accordingly. Handel should continue to compose and Heidegger produce. In November, 1721, the new Handel opera *Floridante* was ready for production. It was well cast. Anastasia Robinson was back again. Also Senesino—the greatest *castrato* of the Handel epoch—had been brought over from Italy. Senesino was new to London. Although a vile little cad, he instantly became a demi-god in Society. He was smothered with presents by the wives of the rich, who were entranced by his voice. Peeresses, whose pattern of life had been above reproach, waited in the queues at the theatre door to kiss his hand.

Floridante failed. It was poor work, and perhaps Senesino had some grounds for his charge that Handel had let him down. The opera ran but a few nights. Handel for the first time had made a bad break.

Things were changing for him. There was an anti-German movement secretly abroad in certain sections of Society. The King was not popular; he had never been. He had lost all interest in the Academy, and cared not a jot if it smashed and all the distinguished shareholders lost their money. He had given his thousand guineas anyway. All that amused him now were the bawdy French farces which filled certain theatres. He loved to lie in the Royal box, shaking with laughter at the blatant indecencies, whilst his ladies giggled behind their fans.

Handel, aware of a waning popularity, went on with his work undisturbed. He began to compose *Tamerlane* on July 3rd, 1724, and completed the entire opera in twenty days. It was great work; an opera built on superb lines and rising to a majestic climax. Why this opera and *Radamisto* and *Rodelinda*— the next opera he was to compose—have been neglected since the middle of the eighteenth century, it is difficult for any student of Handel to understand.

On the night of February 13th, 1725, the curtain went up on *Rodelinda*. Only three weeks previously Handel had put its last bars to paper. He was well aware that, unless he gave the Town something to talk about, the Academy was doomed. Whether the beauty of his composing, or the brown silk dress trimmed with silver worn by the singer Cuzzoni, made the greater sensation, it is difficult to say. Contemporary criticism gave the triumph to Cuzzoni, for, with this brown and silver dress, she not only carried the opera to success, but started a fashion which swept through Society. All the *élite* appeared dressed in brown and silver. The opera was made. It ran the length of the season and filled the box-office.

Throughout the rest of the year Handel waited. Then in March, 1726, he produced *Scipio* which, except for the one clattering march which has survived the years, was a *fiasco*. It ran thirteen nights and was forgotten as a Handel failure.

But Handel remained faithful to London. In February, 1727, he appealed to the House of Lords for naturalization as an English subject. He had lived in London for sixteen years, he belonged to it. Six days later the King signed the bill which made this native of Halle an Englishman.

Handel had now reached a stage in his operatic life when the circumstances about him became the governing factors in the success or failure of his work. In a measure he had ceased to control his own fate. He was jostled here and there; he was a sort of "toss-ball" between the King and his arrogant and unprodigal son. The rivalry between singers became an encroaching nuisance to him. Heidegger—his partner—was becoming more interested in his licentious masquerades, because the takings were greater than those of the best opera.

The trouble began with *Alessandro*, which Handel produced at the Academy in May, 1726. Already he had brought over Cuzzoni, that Italian lumpish figure of fat who came on the stage like a sack of corn and made the audience laugh at the farce till her singing held it to silence. Her career had been full of drama. She had poisoned her husband, but her voice, so wonderful and uplifting, saved her from execution for a new career. Handel was paying her £2,000 a year. True, he had threatened to throw her out of his window in a fit of temper, because she refused to sing one of his songs, but he could forgive the owner of a lovely voice anything.

Then for *Alessandro* he engaged another singer to run in double harness with Cuzzoni, a mezzo-soprano, Faustina Bordoni-Hasse. He stole her from the Court Theatre at Vienna, and, oddly enough, both Faustina and Cuzzoni had each made her *debut* the same night at Venice in 1719. Handel, aware of the jealousy of professional women, gave her the same fee as Cuzzoni—£2,000 a year which meant, with presents, anything over £3,000.

The two women were as unlike as the Poles, save that their voices were the finest in Europe. Cuzzoni was plain, fattening rapidly, coarse. Faustina was elegant and beautiful, lovely to look upon. Her beauty was sought after in the operatic circles of Europe, but she remained faithful to her husband. She was the true Venetian lady of the quality.

The pair sang together in *Alessandro* and the two voices in the Handel duets were so wonderful in their blending that even the rich and gouty crawled from their beds to attend the theatre. It might have been one of the greatest partnerships in musical history had not feminine jealousy destroyed it on factional prejudice.

Society began to split into two factions after the success of *Alessandro*. The admirers of Cuzzoni attacked those who believed Faustina to be the greatest singer of the Handelian epoch. Participants gave parties for this singer or that. They acclaimed this singer and booed the other. And yet, with all these signs of storm before him, Handel went on unperturbed.

The crisis arrived when *Admeto* (1727) was assuming the character of a great success. The fighting between the two factions became more bitter. In the street heads were cracked, carriages overturned and dowager duchesses thrown into the filth.

The fight waxed fast and furious until one night—shortly before the close of the season—the storm broke over auditorium and stage alike. The two famous singers fought on the stage like a pair of viragos in a fair booth. They tore out each other's hair and ripped their clothes to ribbons. Then the audience joined in, until the theatre became a battleground. Many were felled with loosened seats and were trampled underfoot. Law and order had fled; the house became a churning mass of maddened humanity.

Eight days after the great fight, news reached London that King George I had died in his coach at Osnaburg. The funeral obsequies and the Coronation of the new King kept London clear of other amusement till November, when Handel produced his hastily-written opera *Richard I*. It failed and was succeeded in February, 1728, by an equally loose piece of work, *Siroe*, and then by *Tolemeo*, which played but seven nights. These three succeeding failures settled the fate of the Academy.

At the end of April it closed down, and the £50,000 subscribed to it by its aristocratic shareholders was entirely lost.

At this stage the future of Handel seemed obscure. He appeared to have lost his hold on the public, even if he retained to the full his confidence in his powers. But a few months later he made a partnership with Heidegger to take the King's Theatre; each of the partners putting in £10,000. To Handel this represented almost the whole of his savings. He was gambling on his powers.

It was not until the end of 1729 that they rang up the curtain at the King's with Handel's *Lothario*, and the opera failed from the first night. Handel was not yet aware, as he did become aware when his next opera *Parthenope* followed *Lothario* into failure, that a change was coming over the musical taste of London. The *Beggar's Opera* had "hit" the Town, and some of its music had been stolen from Handel's earlier operas.

Two more Handel operas were produced and as quickly failed. *Poro* and *Sosarmes* are forgotten names in opera now, save for single excerpts one hears occasionally on the world's radio. Moreover, the Prince of Wales, in order to flaunt his father George II in his patronage of Handel, had started the "Opera of the Nobility". He raised the money from his rich friends in Mayfair, bought off Handel's singers and the theatre over his head, and set up a campaign of hate against him. The end was not long in doubt. The Handel-Heidegger partnership was smashed and both partners lost £10,000. True, the "Opera of the Nobility" at a later stage broke up like a ship battered on the rocks of importunity, and lost £12,000 for the Prince's friends who could well afford it. But its gay adventure of bad music with its singers and actresses—most of them mistresses of some of the wealthy shareholders—drove Handel into penury. He departed from London, and the Town declared that some bright comet had disappeared from its sky.

A differing mood was stirring in Handel; he was turning to

oratorio. The religious fervour, so strong in him from his earliest years when he first set his *Passion of St. John* at Hamburg, and his *La Resurezzione* in Rome, was working through his mind and into his composing. He would leave opera for good. But not yet. He had still to give London *Alcina* and *Berenice*. He had still to taste again the sweets of operatic success, and hear the clink of coin in a full till.

But the mind of the man was working slowly and gradually away from opera. What he earned in opera now he poured out again in losses over *L'Allegro, Deidamia* and *Imeneo* in 1739 and 1740. Not his fault, perhaps, for winter held London in a grip of iron. The Thames became a frozen field, and the poor died like flies in their ramshackle hovels. He warmed his theatre, screened the auditorium with thick curtains, and advertised the fact in the Press. But London would not stir beyond its doors on such nights, so he was compelled to watch his small store of capital wither away.

The winter destroyed him. He crept out of London with a flat purse and his body torn with the pains of gout, created by mental worry and inattention to diet.

Again London said that he was finished.

§ 3. *The Oratorios*

Few people ever pause to think why a Handel Oratorio is always performed by a choir without costume or scenery. The story is an interesting one.

During his residence at Cannons near Edgware, as *Kapellmeister* to the Duke of Chandos (1718), Handel composed the music to Pope's *libretto Haman*. At the beginning of 1732 he resolved to produce the work at a London theatre, employing the choristers of the Chapel Royal therein, with full costume and scenery.

The idea scandalized the Church. That a religious story should be given on the stage was the height of sacrilege! So declared Dr. Gibson, Bishop of London. Moreover, he made it known that, as he was Dean of the Chapel Royal, the choristers should not be employed. Furthermore, he forbade the performance with scenery and costume at all within the diocese.

Handel was fired to temper. He persuaded a *librettist*, Samuel Humphreys, to add to the *libretto* until it became a full length work for which he composed new numbers and renamed it *Esther*. Because the Bishop had forbidden him to put on a religious story with costume and scenery, Handel had the work sung by singers in ordinary dress. Owing to this bigoted Bishop, Handel's oratorios have been performed in this manner ever since.

Esther was the first oratorio. If you go into the church at Whitchurch, near Edgware, you will see an inscription on the organ which declares that Handel composed *Esther* on that organ. This is pure fabrication. Handel never composed on any instrument. He composed sitting at a table, just as if he were writing a letter, and he often talked as he composed. This was his habit throughout his life.

The success of *Esther* impressed him. It set him thinking. Here, at a time when his operas were doing badly, was a purely musical work from his brain that needed no scenery nor costume to carry it to success. And all the while he and Heidegger were spending thousands of pounds on elaborate settings to the operas. The *Esther* venture had been good. He would try again.

So a year later he put on *Deborah*. He began the composition of the work in February. Samuel Humphreys, who had succeeded so well with the additions to *Esther*, made him the *libretto* from the Biblical story, and he produced the work in March.

Deborah was a Handel bantling that was never destined for life because of a mistake on the part of its begetter. He put up the charges at the theatre, and this at a time when London was smarting under new taxation—the revival of the Salt Tax, a new tobacco tax, and two shillings on wine and spirits. A very deluge of taxation. A letter was circulated through the Press warning the public against his oratorio, since he had introduced the habits of Sir Robert Walpole into his theatre! The result was that only 120 people paid to see the first performance, and *Deborah* was dead.

Hardly had he closed the doors upon *Deborah* than Oxford University offered him the honorary degree of Doctor of Music. The idea pleased him; he would accept it. Then he discovered that he would have to pay £100 in fees for the patent. He was furious with anger. They were making him buy an honour! He refused it, and resolved to go to Oxford and perform there his new oratorio *Athaliah*, as if to show Oxford what he could do. He took no count of the fact that, at this very time when he was pacing his room in Brook Street in wild spleen against Oxford and its "tricks", the Prince of Wales and the "Opera of the Nobility" had its forces gathered for war against him. He was well informed of their manœuvres. His singers were departing like leaves from an old tree in autumn, but with the dignity and storm that was Handel he would go to Oxford and make it listen, with its ears well open, to *Athaliah*.

It was fine work, and as finely received. A new Handel was arising. He listened to the appraise of *Athaliah* but said nothing. For nearly two years he produced no other oratorio. He was waiting. The "Opera of the Nobility" broke down. Then, in 1735, he came out of seclusion with *Alexander's Feast*, the greatest work of his middle years. It was this work which decided Handel. He had found his own again.

Three years passed before any new religious expression occurred in his music. He seemed to be a traveller lost on a long road during this period—a traveller uncertain of his path. *Saul* came from him in 1738. He produced it entirely on his own money, for Heidegger had now left him, and it was but a moderate success. He had begun the composition on July 23rd, and finished it on September 27th.

Four days after the completion of *Saul*, he began the composition of *Israel in Egypt* (which he called *Exodus*), and he composed the second act before the first. This work, with its glorious "Hailstone Chorus", "The Horse and its Rider", and the great alto aria "Thou Shalt Bring Them In", ran but nine nights. Handel did not live to see what *Israel in Egypt* was to become in the coming years. Nor did this failure destroy his faith in oratorio.

Messiah. In any life of great adventure there is always an experience so outstanding that it does not seem to belong to the ordered happenings of that life. *Messiah* was the most remarkable experience in Handel's composing, and the mystery which brought forth this masterpiece has never been explained and never will be.

Between February and November, 1741, Handel was a dead figure to London. He had left the Town, a broken man, comparatively penniless, after the failure of his three operas due to the intense winter. He had gone to Tunbridge Wells. He wrote to no one and lived a life of extreme solitude.

He was back in his house in Brook Street in the summer of 1741, and had been there for many weeks before London was aware of it. He seldom left the house. This seclusion, and the mental state produced in him by his failures, and the parlous position of his finances, may have been contributory to, and part of, the great work which was arising in him.

All that we know is this: at the end of August, 1741, Handel produced from a drawer some biblical excerpts which had been sent to him many months previously by Charles Jennens—a pompous gentleman of the Midlands—as a theme for an oratorio.

With these excerpts from the Bible before him, Handel composed the whole of *Messiah* in twenty-four days. It is the most stupendous feat ever known in the long history of music. He remained in one room in Brook Street the whole time—the room on the first floor overlooking the street in the building which still stands. He worked there, slept there, ate—what little he did eat—through these twenty-four days and nights of tempestuous emotion. What happened to him during that period no man can say. His servant, Jan de Bourke, brought his food at certain hours, and, when he called later for the platter, often found the food untouched. Throughout those twenty-four days Handel belonged to another world.

He completed *Messiah* on September 14th, 1741, and put it in a drawer. Aware of its quality as he must have been, why did he not seek production? He seems to have been so disinterested in it after its completion that he began the composition of *Samson* fifteen days later. Had he become so distressed, so embittered by London's attitude towards his later composing that he worked on, caring nothing about production? His behaviour almost suggests that he did.

That he was fully aware of the merit of *Messiah* is made plain by the fact that, when Dublin wrote to him a few months later (1742), and invited him to go over and give some charity concerts for the inmates of its prison who starved unless money was forthcoming from without to feed them, Handel decided to leave for Dublin. He put *Messiah* in his bag. He took Mrs. Cibber, the greatest singer of her epoch. He occupied some poor lodgings in Abbey Street, Dublin, and, on April 13th, produced *Messiah* for the first time to the world at Neal's Music Hall. He gave the performance again in June in weather so tropical that he had one pane of glass removed from a narrow window!

The performances created all the *furore* of the old Handel nights, and, having raised £400 for the prisoners thereby, he returned to London. But not to produce *Messiah*. News of his success in Dublin was the talk of the Town, but Handel made no attempt to take advantage of this publicity. Possibly he believed that the attitude of the Church towards his religious work would raise fresh storm, and, as time was to prove, such surmise was correct.

For the moment he gave no further thought to *Messiah*. Instead he produced *Samson* at Covent Garden on February 18th, 1743, with Mrs. Cibber carrying one of the chief parts, together with John Beard—the best tenor he ever discovered—who had first appeared in *Alexander's Feast*. The oratorio had no fortune at its beginning, for a gang of thieves secretly entered the auditorium and proceeded to rob the ladies of quality of their jewels whilst the performance continued. The King and his ladies were present, and one of the robbers was even discovered hiding in the Royal Box.

But *Samson* was played to success. The season was doubled in extent, and Handel resolved to put on *Messiah* for three performances. He had taken the precaution of announcing the work as *A Sacred Oratorio*, in order to allay the possible uprising of Church antagonism.

Messiah, which fills every hall, every church at which it is performed to-day, left London unmoved when it was produced. Horace Walpole openly laughed at it. "Handel has set up an oratorio against the opera and succeeds," he wrote. "He has hired all the goddesses from the farces, and the singers of roast beef from between the Acts at both theatres, with a man with one note in his voice, and a girl without ever an one, and so they sing and make brave hallelujahs." So little was thought of *Messiah* at the time that twenty-four years had to pass before the complete work was put into print.

Again the storm of the Church rolled over the head of Handel. He was called a heretic, a blasphemer for producing such a work, a fellow with no feeling of real religion in him. Never was a charge further from the truth. When Lord Kinnoul congratulated Handel on *Messiah* as being excellent entertainment, he replied: "My lord, I should be sorry if I only entertained them: I wished to make them better."

Handel had now definitely chosen oratorio as his means of musical expression. During the next seven years he produced eight oratorios with varying success, and, no doubt, would have continued to produce as many more, had not his eyesight deserted him in 1751. Then, practically in the dark, he completed and produced his last oratorio, *Jephtha*.

He drew more closely into himself as these years moved past him. He made little money and lived in a state amounting nearly to poverty. The Town thought *Judas Maccabaeus* (1746) fine work, but it was about the Jews, and the Town disliked Jews. It was the Jewish audiences that kept him going.

Susanna and *Solomon* which followed were of Jewish character, and the Jews remained faithful to his box-office. But, when he produced an oratorio that had no bearing on the Jews, the Jewish fraternity kept away, and the Gentiles would have none of it because he had dared to lend his talents to acclaiming in music "these accursed people".

The outlook then appeared as forbidding for Handel as it had been when he discovered that opera was wearing to unwanted shreds. He began then to juggle with these oratorios, shifting a piece from one into another. The famous chorus, "See the Conquering Hero Comes," which Handel declared with truth would be remembered long after his death, was taken from *Joshua*, in which it had first appeared, and was now given in a revival of *Judas Maccabaeus*. Again, some years were to pass before the chorus which he composed when his eyes were dimming with blindness—"Zion now her Head shall Raise"—was included in *Judas*.

The revival of one oratorio after another brought a new favour to Handel. He was regarded as a composer who had given himself over entirely to religious composition. He was now drawing towards himself a new and better public. A thinking public. The materialists had left him. True, they still strummed the melodies from his operas and sang his love songs according to their fashion. But, for them, this man who had given them merriment and love and life had passed on, and in his place was an ageing, hulking figure, setting prayers to music. So they said. But whilst the public that had followed his operas—up and down—through the years was laughing at the "corpse", a circle was growing about him, and widening. A circle that wished to listen. For the first time in his life there were people in London who spoke of him as a genius.

In 1749 he put on his last oratorio (save one) *Theodora*, the *libretto* of which came from Dr. Morell, a small and fussy replica of Jennens. Incidentally, the Morell manuscript which Handel set is beside me as I write, with Handel's inscription on the fly-leaf:—"I intend to perform this Oratorio at the Theatre Royal in Covent Garden.

George Frideric Handel."

He carried out his intention. *Theodora* is remembered now only by a single number "Angels Ever Bright and Fair". Handel declared—even a few months before his death—that "He Saw the Lovely Youth" in *Theodora* was the greatest chorus he ever composed. Handelians usually agree, but has London heard it publicly this century?

Theodora was made for success. The *libretto* was trivial as were most of the *libretti* Handel set. Nevertheless, it had all the makings of a success. But just as the oratorio was launched, an earthquake shook London. Handel, who had seen his works killed by storm and heat, by intense winter, was to suffer once more.

Houses toppled in London and killed the occupants in their beds. Society left in an endless stream for Bath, Tunbridge Wells, Oxford and the North. All places of public entertainment were closed down, and the curtain fell on *Theodora*. No form of amusement could survive the public panic. A destroying winter had forced Handel into bankruptcy before: now an earthquake brought him face to face with ruin, and, at a time when his eyes, in their last struggle to function, were beginning to trouble him. But he kept his faith. "God will never destroy his servant!" he declared with more truth than he knew.

His last oratorio, *Jephtha* was the fierce fight of a giant against the oncoming dark. He began it, laid it aside owing to the increasing pain in his eyes. In May, 1751, the greatest oculist of the day, William Bramfield, surgeon to the Princess of Wales, warned him that the dark was approaching, that it could not be staved off. But Handel struggled on, stopping at times, lying inert and steeped in gloom in his house at Brook Street. Then he would go to his table and work a little.

He went to Cheltenham to take the waters. It was all wasted effort. He could not stem the oncoming enemy. He completed *Jephtha* in August when only a speck of light was visible to one eye.

He produced the oratorio at Covent Garden in February, 1752. He was now completely blind.

§ 4. *The Years of Blindness*

The blind man sat in his front room on the first floor of his house in Brook Street, week by week, month by month, receiving no one save a few close intimates. Occasionally his servant, de Bourke, would lead him out to Marylebone Gardens, so that he could sit in the sun and listen to the band. Or the same faithful servitor would guide him carefully to his pew in St. George's, Hanover Square, on Sundays.

Handel was living in extreme simplicity, but he was not idle. He recast his works by dictation to his amanuensis, Christopher Smith, and had them performed in one series of concerts after another. He dictated new numbers to Smith, he re-furbished and elaborated by dictation the works composed in those years when his eyes were strong and his pen was free. In 1757 he entirely revised *The Triumph of Time* which he had composed at the age of twenty-three, and gave it out afresh as a new and glorious work which the public flocked to hear. He altered *Solomon, Susanna, Samson, Judas,* and now behold! London crowded and fought for admission to his concerts. *Messiah!* The *Messiah* which the Church had sought to destroy was the same *Messiah* that crowded every performance now.

He was seventy-four. On February 23rd, 1759, his birthday came. His concerts were never given to better houses. On April 6th, he decided to perform *Messiah* at Covent Garden. Bent and ill, but with the old fires in him burning to full measure, he determined to be present, in spite of the warnings of Dr. Warren. On that evening they saw the ageing figure sitting beside the organ, staring sightless over the audience. Christopher Smith carried out the concert. Just as the vast audience was pouring from the theatre into the night, Handel fainted in his chair. No one was aware of it, save those immediately beside him. Mr. Handel had fainted; how often had the Doctor told him that he would die on his stairs!

He was hurried home to Brook Street. Dr. Warren was sent for again. Handel was most certainly dying. The Doctor had no false ideas about it, nor had Handel, who declared that he wished to die on the same day as his Saviour, Good Friday, which was April 13th.

He lay during that week alone, seeming to wait for Good Friday. An occasional friend came to see him. Dr. Warren daily. James Smyth, the Bond Street chemist. On April 13th Handel said he had done with the world, and bade farewell to his friends one by one. He said he wished now to be left alone. . . . The day sped and darkness came in through an unlit window.

It was in this state of loneliness that he passed over during the night of April 13-14th. At what hour no one knew.

10

CLIVE

(1725–1774)

by Maurice Collis

C LIVE was the man who took India. That is what he stands for in popular estimation and it is correct enough. He was not ordered to take India; the English had no desire whatever to take a yard of the place. All they wanted was to be able to buy there in security cotton goods for sale in England. But while they were thinking of dividends, Clive presented them with a continent.

It was a considerable shock, and we have never got over it. At first we pretended that we had not acquired the property. We posed as lessees and confined ourselves to trade. But as there was no owner but ourselves, the country went to ruin and we were obliged to devise means of putting it in order. To do this we had to assume ownership, but the idea that we had adjusted a title, without giving the other party an option, continued to haunt us, until recently we invented the theory that we held India in trust for the inhabitants until their majority. That majority is now said to be approaching and we look forward to a near future when we can prove to the world that we never took India. In that way we will be disentangled from the legal briar bush into which Clive led us.

CLIVE

But how did Clive do it? If no one wanted India, thought of a dominion over an eastern kingdom, how was it that we were landed with the thing? That is the mystery of action. There are schools of thought which deplore action—by non-action, say the Taoists, you can accomplish everything. But action taken by a man of genius is like the non-action of the Taoists. It is not an intellectual process; something incalculable flows through and out. There is nothing so startling to decent people as action of this kind. A man of genius may be operating in circumstances where an ordinary result is attended. Michael Angelo is asked to paint the ceiling of the Sistine, a few biblical scenes, a landscape, views of heaven. He gets up on the scaffolding and strikes the plaster with his brush. Something unforeseen happens and for ever, as we look, we puzzle at a mystery. Clive was instructed to get the Company merchants of Calcutta back into the factory from which they had been driven, so that the Directors in London might be able to pay their usual dividends. He arrives with a few men at Plassey Grove and, without calculation, strikes. When the English look again, they find he has taken India.

In the lives of men of genius there is often but one thunderous act, like a focal point. For Clive that act, that point was Plassey. At Plassey something enormous came out of him. The rest was explaining Plassey. We are still explaining Plassey. But it is not more explicable than the ceiling of the Sistine. A great event took place, but its essence escapes us.

However, one can trace outwardly how Clive became master of that event.

He entered Madras road at 7 p.m. on Friday the 1st of June, 1744, aged eighteen, to take up his duties as writer or clerk in the East India Company. His salary was five pounds per annum, but under his indenture he was allowed after a probationary period of some years to engage in private trade. Writing bills of lading, copying letters—that was his day's work. It was sufficiently dull. The company was a large commercial enterprise of a hundred and fifty years' standing. Madras was one of its trading posts, whence for a hundred years clerks and merchants had consigned home cotton goods. There was nothing more in it than that.

So Clive was a clerk, and a miserable clerk. Besides being very poor, he was bored with his work, desperately homesick and subject to fits. These fits were epileptic and led to periods of despair. To his companions he appeared gloomy and intractable. It is said that at this time he attempted suicide. Claustromania gave him a horrible sensation of restriction, he would fly out at a word, and when angered he could not be appeased. Something violent, uncompromising, extreme burned in him. There was the duel, for instance, when he missed and his opponent walked up, calling on him to apologize as he covered him point blank. Clive was not intimidated, refused the smallest satisfaction, invited death and appalled his adversary by the glimpse of some bleak power. The man dropped his pistol, as if he had looked into an abyss.

For two years Clive lived in this manner of tension, high pressure within, something formidable that could not get out. The Company's policy was, as it had been in the past, trade and security, nothing further. Trade was excellent, but security was less sure. The empire of the Mogul, under the patronage of which the English merchants had flourished, was beginning to crumble. Its official governors were becoming princes over whom the Emperor exercised no control. The settled administration essential to trade was undermined. In the vast hinterland anarchy threatened.

Before the Company had decided how to protect itself and its dividends, the French, who had a similar company, had made up their minds. At the head of their factory was a man very different from the English merchants. Dupleix was an adventurer and he jumped into the brawl. If security to trade was the primal necessity, he would obtain it, not merely by strengthening his fortifications as was the policy at Madras, but by going into the Indian continent, selecting a pretender to the local throne and backing him to win. Thereafter the French would bask in his smile and monopolize the concessions they had shared with the English.

Thus it was that during 1746 a new situation arose. The English Company was obliged to copy the French and start out on adventures much against its will. For ten years the French, the English, and a variety of contending princes became elements in the general confusion of a dissolving empire.

When this period began Clive was twenty years of age. He transferred from the commercial to the military side. With no knowledge of military affairs, he found that in the field he possessed a natural intuition of what to do. This was noticed at once. He was made Ensign in 1747. Then commenced for him a long series of marches, sieges, knockabout battles, danger of death. The forces involved were small. The Company seldom had available more than a thousand Europeans and two thousand native soldiers. It was a campaign in miniature. Considering his age, Clive began to acquire an exceptional reputation. In '49 he was Lieutenant. He became noted for coolness in action and for that perception of the critical moment in a battle which has always been the mark of a great military leader. By '52, aged twenty-six, he was Captain, frequently in command of important detachments. It was very largely thanks to this young man that the Company worsted the French and secured for the throne of the Carnatic (that area of the coast in which they traded) a prince favourable to their interests.

Now this first period in Clive's career affords some clue to what is coming. The epileptic clerk grows to be a good soldier, brave and resourceful. His commanding officers think highly of him. The rank and file admire him immensely, as they always do a mysterious character. He still has fits, is sombre, inscrutable. Knowing the rest of the story, we can see further. A great spirit was there. A force of soul competent to overwhelm a continent was fiddling with halfpenny battles. But for onlookers in India, he was just a gallant young man and no fool either, for during the intervals of fighting he made a fortune of £50,000, equal to a quarter of a million nowadays, in partnership with Orme, his future historian.

In 1753, he married for love an ancestress of the famous illusionist, Maskelyne, and sailed for London. There the Company presented him with a jewelled sword worth £500; he was very liberal to his indiscreet father, helping him with money to keep up the old place at Styche; and he made friends with distinguished people, one of whom, Lord Sandwich, brought him into the House of Commons. But party intrigues unseated him and he was left with the bill of a contested election. When the Directors of the Company offered him a colonelcy with a seat in Council at Madras, he accepted and left for India in April, 1755. Aged twenty-nine, he had done pretty well, but there was as yet nothing to show that he was destined to bestride history.

He had been in India six months when news reached Madras that Calcutta, the headquarters of the Company in Bengal, had suddenly been sacked by Suraj-ud-Daula, called the Nawab or Viceroy, but who was in fact King of Bengal, as he was independent of the Emperor. The story brought to Madras was that this man, frightened by the rising power of the English in the south, had decided to anticipate anything of the kind in the north. After his sack of the factory, one hundred and forty-four of his European prisoners were shut up one June night of 1756 in a barrack cell, eighteen by fourteen feet, where most of them suffocated. The President and others, who had deserted their comrades before the assault was pressed home, took refuge in a poor village further down the river. A disagreeable point was that the French who had an estate at Chandernagore, near Calcutta, laughed heartily over the affair, finding it amusing that 600 English troops, provided with all sorts of munitions and sheltered in a regular fort, should have fled before the Nawab with scarcely a shot fired. So they put it, exaggerating of course.

The Council at Madras, after long confabulations, decided to send an expedition to restore the situation. In September, 1756, Clive was appointed to command it. On October 5th, writing to his father, he said: "This expedition, if attended with success, may enable me to do great things. It is by far the grandest of my undertakings. I go with great forces and with great authority." And next day he wrote with sombre fire to the chairman in London: "Be the event what it will, there is no Hardship or Risque I will not undergo to obtain Success." And five days later, as if he had seen a vision, he declared to the London Committee: "I flatter myself that this Expedition will not end with the retaking of Calcutta only," adding in a kind of ecstasy: "Success on this Occasion will fill the Measure of my Joy."

The "great forces" consisted of some 600 white troops and a thousand sepoys, conveyed by five men-of-war. But Clive was right, they were great forces, for he was in command. His genius had descended upon him; he was irresistible and he knew it.

On arrival, he occupied the ruins of Calcutta without difficulty, as Suraj-ud-Daula was not there. When the Nawab advanced with 40,000 foot, 20,000 cavalry and with artillery, Clive penetrated his camp in a morning mist and frightened him into retirement. A temporary accommodation was signed, restoring the English to what they had lost. To pay out the French for their merriment and to prevent their junction with the murderous Nawab, Clive suddenly took Chandernagore, the seat of their factory, where they had a palace with frescoes and Ionic pillars. This done, he was face to face with Suraj-ud-Daula, misnamed Lamp of the State, who foolishly had boasted: "I will destroy him and his nation." For that, for everything, Clive was going to settle him.

Before an enchantment there is always a palaver. March '57 having sufficed for the French, it was to be April and May for the performance of this rite. It took the form of a correspondence between the Nawab and Clive. The former sometimes wrote him as many as ten letters a day, each contradicting the last, "which the Colonel answered punctually with all the calmness and complacence imaginable." Below this correspondence was another strata of letter-writing, between Clive and Meer Jaffier, the Nawab's paymaster, whom, following Dupleix's model for a policy, he proposed to enthrone as his man-of-all-work. Clive's assistants, such as the Admiral in charge of the men-of-war and the restored President and Council of Calcutta, knew something extraordinary was developing, but having no faith in miracles heartily wished they were out of it. But all these letters were like the patter of a prestidigitator. The event was coming along by itself.

When Clive knew that the hour had arrived, he left Chandernagore, his headquarters during the correspondence, and with 613 European foot, ninety-one half-caste soldiers, ten field pieces served by 171 men, and 2,100 sepoys, he headed by road and river for Plassey, eighty miles north, where lay the Nawab, surrounded by his power. To that prince he had sent a last letter in which appeared the phrase: "it is necessary for me to wait on you immediately."

Shortly before they reached Plassey, there was a moment when the disintegrating light of reason was turned upon the fantasy of their promenade. A tiny force, they were a hundred miles from Calcutta, marching against an entrenched position held by a huge army. Meer Jaffier, for all the letters, had not declared himself definitively. The smallest reverse and they were dead men, for succour from their base was without possibility. It was lunacy to go on, or so thought most of the assembled officers. Moreover, to advance further meant to cross the river, and a river in the rear is an alarming tactical situation. Even Clive agreed to pause. But as he agreed, something within him protested the contrary. He retired alone into a neighbouring grove. There he remained an hour taking council with his soul. When he left the grove, the inner certainty, which he had lost for a moment, possessed him again. Without giving reasons, he ordered an advance. He could not give reasons, for none were valid. It is noteworthy that the common soldiers were not assailed by doubts. With no intellectual handicaps they felt the approach of the grand event.

Meanwhile Suraj-ud-Daula was waiting in his camp; 15,000 horse, 35,000 foot, and fifty-three guns of large calibre were his numbers. But he was not as confident as when he had boasted. Meer Jaffier might or might not stand; and other noblemen had been spat upon unfortunately. Clive's letter too had been received; the intimidating phrase "it is necessary for me to wait on you immediately" had reverberated like a voice from the edge of the world. As he sat in his magnificent tent an ominous event occurred. Scenting a waft of death, like rats his servants slipped away imperceptibly. When he looked up, he was alone; the gold knob of his hookah had already been looted. In terror he cried aloud: "surely they see me dead!" He had, in fact, exactly ten days more of life.

The next morning the battle joined. Of that battle it stands out that the Nawab's troops in general fought for him. Meer Jaffier did not go over; he waited on the event. Clive's three thousand attacked and beat fifty thousand, his ten light guns fifty heavy guns. Many pages have been written to explain it, but we can never know how it was done. It is argued that

Clive by getting his men to lie down behind a bank in a mango
tope saved them from being cut to pieces by the Nawab's
horse, pounded to pulp by his cannon balls. That may be so,
but what were the 35,000 foot doing? Why did they not
enfilade or mount the bank? Others have said that a heavy
shower which fell before mid-day saved the situation, damping
the enemy's powder, when our own was kept dry by tar-
paulins. Do we then owe our possession of India to a shower?
That our fire killed some of the Nawab's staunchest commanders is also given as an explanation. But does not that
show that the Indians were led steadfastly? We almost incline
to believe Orme, when he says that Clive was asleep during
part of the action. Such a battle as Plassey belongs to the
realm of dreams.

If the exact reasons for Clive's victory at Plassey are esoteric,
the significance of the battle, though now plain, was at the
time no less obscure. He himself knew it no more precisely
than that he was master of an event "scarcely to be paralleled
in History." When he had accomplished his tremendous act,
he descended from the region where he had talked with his
genius and never did anything of importance again. But he
did much that was interesting. For instance the bill he sent in
to Meer Jaffier for services rendered was prodigious. He
received £160,000 down, but that sum was multiplied many
times, for on arrival in England three years later he had an
income of £40,000 a year, equal to £200,000 a year nowadays.
Besides that he obtained jewels worth a million pounds in
modern values. Professing to be amazed at how little he had
taken, he called his fortune "a genteel competence". It was
the biggest competence that had ever been made overseas.

A curious drama was the sequel of these events. When the
news of Plassey reached England it was taken to mean little
more than that the Company had been restored to the enjoyment of their trading rights. Accordingly Clive on his arrival

was given an Irish peerage and a seat in the Commons. Rich though he was, he had little political influence. Even in Indian affairs he could not make himself felt. He tried, but failed, to dominate the Court of Directors. If he understood incomparably how to resolve the tension called a battle, in London he afforded a striking instance of a man of genius divorced from his medium of expression.

As time went on, the meaning of what had happened in India began to be clearer. There was an uneasy feeling that Plassey had given the country to England because it had established there the English as the dominant military power. But it was firmly decided to do nothing about it. We had destroyed the existing government, but we were not going to be responsible for setting up a new one. An era of loot accordingly developed, an interregnum of lawlessness which in the East always lies between two dynasties. The oppression which supervened exceeded anything of the kind under the Mogul. As Clive wrote afterwards: "Never was such a scene of Anarchy and Confusion, Bribery, Corruption and Extortion." It was organized robbery. The Company itself abandoned normal trade. An aforetime respectable merchant would now fit out an armed boat, and coming to an up-country market, would forcibly buy at his own rate, say fifty per cent below current prices. There was nothing to prevent him. In consequence production was discouraged and this began to show in the Company's dividends.

The news of these events was a profound shock to the English public. In 1764, seven years after Plassey, Clive was asked to go out to Bengal as President of the Council of Calcutta, and restore normal trading. There was to be no question of shouldering the responsibilities which the act of Plassey had laid upon us. All was to be as before; the Company was a commercial body; Clive was to reform abuses; dividends not government, were to be the object.

That Clive accepted such an appointment shows that he himself but vaguely understood the meaning of his own masterpiece. But notoriously artists cannot explain their work. It further shows that like all men of genius he was simple. What he had done was known to the world; it never occurred to him that his position was equivocal, that as he had made an enormous fortune, he was the wrong man to prevent others doing the same. When he declared his resolution to refuse further presents, he expected applause for his disinterestedness. His position resembles England's to-day at Geneva.

As soon as he tried to put his instructions into effect in Bengal, there was an uproar. It was brutally pointed out to him by the merchants there that he was the last person who could talk of clean hands. When he protested that what he had taken was not by oppression but in the ordinary course after a battle, he was laughed down. In the circumstances he failed to eradicate abuses, but incurred great odium for making the attempt.

Always a neurotic, except in battle when he was the most collected of men, his nervous system rapidly deteriorated. In England after Plassey he had sometimes been pretty bad, but now a worse agitation seemed to shake him. He fell to long weeping. "It grieved me beyond measure" wrote at this time his friend Carnac to Lady Clive, "to see a Person endued with such extraordinary firmness oppressed in his spirits as to exceed any degree of hysterics I was ever witness to." In this state he returned to England in 1767.

Then followed the culmination of the act of Plassey. The House of Commons, painfully flustered at the notion that India had passed into their possession, shamed by the abominable oppressions which had supervened upon that event, decided to salve the national conscience by turning upon the prime author of these disturbing events. They thought that if Clive's money was confiscated, their rape of India would not look so bad. This course was suggested to them by Clive's enemies, baulked looters from Bengal, and members of the directorate in London whom he had irritated, and who feared that if he was not made a scapegoat the national conscience might seek satisfaction at their expense.

For two years Clive was subjected to an inquisition by a Select Committee. In retrospect the affair appears pure comedy. All Clive had done was to win Plassey. That he had accepted presents after the battle had been known and winked at for fifteen years. But it was obscurely felt that if a moral line was adopted now about the presents, Plassey and all that prodigious stroke implied of wholesale appropriation, of contingent pillage, could be swallowed without discomfort.

Two years of high falutin gave the Commons such a stomach that they felt able to be generous. The sentiments of Burke were so grand that it seemed hardly necessary to mulct Clive as well. He was allowed to keep his money.

But if the inquiry into Clive's conduct is a comedy in retrospect, it was no fun for him. His system was totally unsuited to stand anything of the kind. Six months after its termination, he cut his throat. Dr. Johnson, keeping up the comedy, said it was his conscience. Friends buried him secretly at midnight under one of the pews of his parish church near Styche. He was only forty-nine.

11

ELIZABETH MONTAGU

(1720-1800)

by REBECCA WEST

IN every age there are certain women who, because they are feminine without being womanly, because they conform completely to the masculine notion of what a woman should be and disregard all instructions from their own nature, enjoy great material success yet leave no sense of triumph. This class was conspicuously represented in eighteenth-century England by Mrs. Elizabeth Montagu, the Queen of the Blue Stockings. The world put itself out to go her way. She was extremely rich; when she built the great house which still stands across the north-west corner of Portman Square, she paid for it out of income. All her life long, and she lived for eighty years, she never lacked the company of amusing acquaintances and affectionate friends, and because an international reputation rewarded her extravagantly for her intellectual gifts, which were, in fact, negligible, she could know whomsoever she chose out of all Europe. It is a life that knew only once the touch of defeat, yet it radiates a low degree of light and heat. It dispenses through the ages hardly more warmth than chandeliers blazing away behind the closed windows of a great house; and even in its own day it could not relieve Mrs. Montagu herself from a sensation of debilitating chill. For what saves her record from being intolerable is that she was the first to think it so.

From the first her circumstances were favourable. She was born in 1720, fourth of the twelve children, nine of whom lived to grow up, born to a country gentleman named Matthew Robinson by his wife, an heiress named Elizabeth Drake, whom he had married when he was eighteen. They were both advantageously connected. One of Elizabeth's brothers inherited the Barony of Rokeby from Richard Robinson, Archbishop of Armagh and Primate of Ireland; and her father was close kin to "Long" Sir Thomas Robinson, of whom Chesterfield wrote:

> Unlike my subject will I make my song,
> It shall be witty, and it shan't be long,

and of whom Walpole maliciously suggested that he was appointed to the Governorship of Barbadoes because a member of the Government wanted to rent his house. Elizabeth's mother belonged to an established Kentish family from which she inherited Mount Morris, near Hythe, a pleasant seat where the Robinsons spent most of their time, though her husband had three other estates, two in Yorkshire and one in Cambridgeshire.

Though Elizabeth was brought up in the country there was nothing bumpkinish about her upbringing. Her father made no secret that he would have lived in London had it not been that he needed to manage his lands and consider the interests of his young family, and that he regarded this as the natural preference of any sensible man. He was, moreover, something of a dilettante, being one of the innumerable members of the English governing classes who have been said by their relatives to have "acquired so great a proficiency as to excel most of the professed artists of his day in landscape", and he was considered a wit, with a turn for sarcasm and a languid inclination towards free thought. His children were not brought up to be very pious, though they received an excellent education. The brothers were taught enough to put them on the road to being sound scholars at Cambridge, and their sisters shared in their studies sufficiently to make them what would have counted in any age as very well-read women. Elizabeth's interest in things of the mind was still further stimulated by her grandmother's second husband, Dr. Conyers Middleton, fellow of Trinity College, Cambridge, and University Librarian. He believed the child a genius and tried to train her intellect from the tenderest age by making her listen attentively to the conversation of his learned friends. This is represented by those relatives of Mrs. Montagu who have been her chief biographers as a bland baptism in the Pierian spring; but it must be remembered that this is the same Dr. Middleton who wrote a famous pamphlet: *A true account of the Present State of Trinity College, Cambridge, under the Oppressive Government of their Master, Richard Bentley, D.D.*, with the aim "to give a better Light into the *general Character of the Man*, which cannot be perfectly drawn in short, than in what was said of him the other Day, *by a Gentleman in Conversation*, that he is one of the *greatest Savages these latter Ages have produced*." He also was inclined to free thought, being more of a deist than most people thought a clergyman should be.

Elizabeth grew up, therefore, with a full knowledge of what strands in life were worth taking hold of, if one wanted permanent dignity and interest. From her earliest years she had the intention of distinguishing herself socially and intellectually. She had to help her, as well as her family connections, a certain amount of prettiness, as much as comes from a combination of dark hair, blue eyes, and a brilliant complexion.

We are forbidden to credit her with more by the testimony of her nephew, who, aching and straining with domestic piety, can only declare, "she was of middle stature, and stooped a little, which gave an air of modesty to her countenance, in which the features were otherwise so strongly marked as to express an elevation of sentiment befitting the most exalted condition." She was also gifted with great mental and physical vitality, which made her able to read books and write letters all day and dance all night. But she owed most of her advancement to that irrational disposition of humanity to feel coldness and impatience towards people who betray possession of the power to love, and to welcome warmly those whose most salient characteristic is indifference to their·fellow-creatures. From first to last her writings show an inherent lack of geniality. She was not without deep founts of feeling, but for all practical purposes they were sealed. Her attitude to people whom she met casually was gibing and incurious, and though in later life she was slowly and ponderously to build up a number of friendships, she was apt to imply that her friends had earned their position by successfully discharging an onus of proving themselves free from certain vices and fully inoculated with certain virtues. But all her life long the world denied her nothing that was in its power to give her.

She entered social life at the very early age that was then permitted; she was at Canterbury Races and Assembly before she was twelve, and at Tunbridge Wells a year later. If she suffered any defeats such as awkward youth usually experiences, she would have recorded them, for she was not insensitive and was strictly honest. But nobody seems to have done other than admire her, and very early she made a useful friendship with Lady Margaret Cavendish Harley, Lord Oxford's daughter, a girl just six years her senior, who at twenty married the Duke of Portland. Both the young Duchess and her husband were deeply fond of their dear "Fidget" and were of great service to her. "You know," Elizabeth wrote to her father when she was seventeen, "this year I am to be introduced by the Duchess to the best company in the town, and when she lies in, am both to receive in form with her all her visits as Lady Bell used to do on that occasion, all the people of quality of both sexes that are in London, and I must be in full dress, and shall go about with her all the winter, therefore a suit of cloathes will be necessary for me, the value of which I submit to give you." After moving happily between London, the spas, her father's country estates, and the Duchess's seat, Bulstrode, until she was twenty-two, she resolved to marry. It is certain that she had several suitors to choose from, and that some among these were deeply and passionately in love with her. She decided on a very wealthy Member of Parliament, named Mr. Edward Montagu, grandson of the great Earl of Sandwich who was Lord High Admiral of the Fleet to Charles II, and cousin to the Earl of Halifax and the Duke of Montagu. He was twenty-nine years older than she was, but he was a man of great good will and considerable intellectual gifts, and she felt as warmly towards him as she ever did towards any man; for she records that she never fell in love. Until senility fell upon him he never failed in generosity towards her.

A year after Mrs. Montagu's marriage she gave birth to a son. It is possible that had he not died in his second year she might have made a very different figure in the world. Though she objected to child-birth with a definiteness rare in women of that time, she adored the boy and wrote of him with a self-less joy which nothing else evoked in her. She who could write copiously on any subject under the sun could write hardly a word about his death; and in a will made over thirty years afterwards she ordered that when she came to be buried he should be taken from his little grave and laid beside her. It is probable that the world never saw a mature Mrs. Montagu, and that at the period when she should have left her immaturity behind her she was confirmed in it for ever, because the mainspring of her character had been broken by shock. After her loss she went back and continued to carry out the programme of advancement in the social and literary worlds which she had conceived when a child. Her letters to the Duchess of Portland became longer and more portentous than ever, young sermons, embryo contributions to an encyclopædia; and they were but a portion of her fertility. She cast a network of correspondence over Great Britain, and by the time she had reached middle life she was regularly exchanging voluminous letters with the "good" Lord Lyttelton; with the first Earl of Bath, that delightful old man who had been first the friend and then the foe of Walpole; with the Reverend Gilbert West, the translator of Pindar and imitator of Spenser; with Mrs. Vesey, the Irish hostess known as the Sylph, whom the world and Laurence Sterne loved none the less because her mind was slightly deranged; with Dr. Messenger Mounsey, the eccentric physician who was licensed buffoon to a group of great ladies; and with Mrs. Elizabeth Carter, the hearty old soul who translated Epictetus and wrote the ode to wisdom used by Richardson in *Clarissa*. These were only her chief correspondents, grandees of an extensive society. There were scores more, and all alike rejoiced in their privileges. Gilbert West showed a copy of her letter on Warburton's attack on Bolingbroke to the Archbishop of Canterbury, who was deeply impressed and desired a copy; Lord Bath and Lord Lyttelton urged her to publish her letters; Mrs. Carter filled page after page during three decades recommending her qualities to the posthumous daughter of the second son of the Bishop of Durham. Thus was built up a reputation as solid as her fortune.

Yet Mrs. Montagu was not one of the world's great letter-writers. She was for the most part, indeed, not a tolerable letter-writer at all. Only when something had pricked her down to the level of original sin did she write really well and wittily. Occasion vouchsafed her the strength to describe the sweetness of Mrs. Vesey in these acid terms, "Even Samuel Johnson was seldom brutally rude in her society," and to coin an unforgettable image of indecorum in the perfectly decorous phrase, written regarding Miss Chudleigh's appearance at a masquerade, "She was Iphigenia for the sacrifice, but was so naked, the High Priest might easily inspect the entrails of the victim;" and under the stress of family feeling she could rise to an eloquence that recalls King Lear. But at all other times she wrote a prolix, colourless and empty style, which can interest us to-day only as it illustrates the calamitous change that befell our language at the beginning of the eighteenth century. In earlier ages people seemed to be beating out English as they felt the need of it to express their ideas and desires, but now the leisured classes were so excessively literate that the common consciousness bore a burden of phrases far beyond what they could possibly require for the purposes of communication. Writers had no longer the air of seeking for words. Rather it was as if words had found them out and were threatening smotheration if they were not guided down the conduit of some recognized literary form. Readers were in the position of people who have the radio turned on all day, and so are miserable if they find themselves in silence and must whistle or sing. Mrs. Montagu was something of a writer and very much of a reader, so when Mr. Gilbert West stocked his garden with evergreens, it was a relief for her to write:

"You introduce me to a known world when you carry me into a garden planted with firs and laurel, and you offer them to me for subjects of moral reflections, for which, as you rightly judge, I have by nature and circumstances, all the leisure and dulness from whence they usually proceed. You seem so satisfied in your choice of plants, it would be barbarous to say anything against so well-weighted an opinion, and perhaps, considering how small a part of time they share, 'That are both wonderous sweet and fair,' you may do best to prefer the lasting to the delicate beauties of nature: however, I am far from thinking, as you seem to do, that you have triumphed over the power of Time. You have deferred to him as men do to a tyrant in a rigorous government, where the penalty of sumptuary laws imposes an involuntary temperance in luxury and ornament, and they can escape the fine only by homely plainness and rigid simplicity. There are animals and vegetables whose existence . . ."

And so on, and so on, for pages. Nor did she write more tolerably when she was dealing with more learned matters. Though she was extremely well-read in history and philosophy her mind never grasped the subject-matter of these sciences, though she could at times pass a shrewd enough judgment on the temper and dialectics of a particular work. Her intellectual limitations are curiously exposed by a letter she wrote to "the good" Lord Lyttelton's son, Tom, when he went up to Oxford, attempting, vainly, since the lad was soon to earn the name of "the bad" Lord Lyttelton, to indicate the proper lines of his moral and intellectual development. On such a challenging occasion she had nothing to produce except a string of platitudes.

Mrs. Montagu made only two incursions into other literary forms than the letter. One of these, her contributions to "the good" Lord Lyttelton's *Dialogues of the Dead*, is on the same level as her letters. The other, an essay on Shakespeare, is a much better piece of work. It was an intervention in that amazing controversy which convulsed literary France and England for a generation, did a great deal of harm by starting off the debate between classicism and romanticism at a time when the debaters were in a state of confusion regarding their terms, and did no good whatsoever except to demonstrate what an odd fish a great man can be. Voltaire had furnished a supreme proof of his genius by effectively plagiarizing the works of Shakespeare from an understanding and knowledge of them so elementary that he believed Falstaff to have been a Lord Chief Justice. At the same time he conceived against Shakespeare one of those long, bickering, unscrupulous hatreds which were as hobbies to him; and just as when he attacked Pascal he became at every turn of the argument more recognizably the Pascalian man, so when he attacked Shakespeare he appeared every minute more like an amalgam of Shakespearian character, a pedant run mad, a winking snapper-up of unconsidered trifles, a fantastical duke of dark corners. It was a strange performance, and when Dr. Johnson, after long delays, brought out his edition of Shakespeare he rebuked Voltaire in the preface, and Voltaire took vengeance on him in his essay on Dramatic Art in his Dictionary. Dr. Johnson never replied, but Mrs. Montagu took the matter in hand by publishing anonymously *An Essay on the Writings and Genius of Shakespeare, compared with the Greek and French dramatic poets, with some remarks upon the misrepresentations of Monsieur de Voltaire.*

Though this is not as good a book as it was said to be at the time of its publication, it is much better than a great many people have pretended since. It is important to note that it was not a mere desire to stand on the side of accepted opinion which made her take up the challenge for Shakespeare. She was less swayed by such considerations than one might suppose. For example, the piety which she constantly expresses in her letters sounds conventional, but it is actually proof of an independent spirit; for her husband, like her father and her stepfather, was inclined to free thought. She was as hardy in her defence of Shakespeare, since a great many of the writers with whom she would have liked to rank as an equal, such as Shaftesbury, Bolingbroke, Chesterfield, and David Hume, regarded him as either unimportant or as an inspired barbarian. Had she joined them in their shuddering rejection, it might have given her a pleasantly eclectic reputation. But she owned to her real opinions and made a very creditable show in justifying them. It is true that she makes some concessions to the legend of Shakespeare's barbarism, but it must be remembered that the Georgians were genuinely shocked by the Elizabethans, though they were certainly under a misapprehension regarding the reason for their emotions. It cannot really have been Shakespeare's lack of the classical spirit which distressed Mr. Aaron Hill, whose drama, *Hengist and Horsa*, ends in a scene laid in a Druidical grove, where Merlin shows Hengist and Vortigern a vision of the future glories of English History, culminating in the "whole present Royal Family, surrounded above with angels, smiling and pointing thro' clouds; from the midst of which a beam of light shoots down, over the head of the King." Yet Mr. Hill was really distressed by something in Shakespeare, and so too, probably, was Mrs. Montagu.

But she soon got over that emotion, and settled down to a treatment of her subject which, even when compared with Dr. Johnson's Preface, is not at all contemptible. It is, of course, pompously and diffusely written, and the examination of Corneille is hardly fair, since it dwells too much on his least important works. But it contains a very workmanlike exposure of Voltaire's inaccuracies and mistranslations. In the exegetical passages there are hardly any fatuities to match Dr. Johnson's opinion that in Shakespeare's "tragick scenes there is always something wanting", or that Catherine of Aragon's last speech is "above any other part of Shakespeare's tragedies", and his blindness to the poetic value of Ariel's songs and

Antony and Cleopatra. Her discussion of *Macbeth* is very much more intelligent than his, and in her chapter on "Preternatural Beings" she actually begins to discuss what Herder was discussing in Germany, on such an infinitely higher critical level than herself and her friends that it seems extraordinary they were contemporaries: the place of myth in poetry. She is not to be despised when she points out the immense advantage enjoyed by poets who write of myths in which they and their hearers believe, and the diminution in poetic intensity caused by the change from fable to allegory which is bound to accompany an advance towards rationalism. Dr. Johnson said the worst about her book when he said that it was nearly impossible to get through it. There is certainly a nucleus of critical thought in it which makes it regrettable that Mrs. Montagu did not write on behalf of Shakespeare as lucidly and tersely as when she spoke for him. For she scored an indisputable point when, on a visit to Paris, she was shown the letter to d'Argental in which Voltaire alluded to Shakespeare as *"un énorme fumier"*, and she observed that *"ce malheureux fumier avait engraissé une terre ingrate"*.

But neither Mrs. Montagu's spoken wit nor her written ponderousness accounted for her authority over society. The basis of that was her great wealth. Mr. Montagu had been a rich man when she married him, and shortly afterwards Chancery made him the guardian and trustee of his cousin, John Rogers, a lunatic with immense estates in Northumberland that included several collieries. These estates, which had for years been derelict, were restored to order by Mr. Montagu's able management; and when John Rogers died, fifteen years later, Mr. Montagu acquired "half the estate by descent, a share by testamentary disposition, and a part by purchase". On hearing the news Mrs. Montagu wrote to him, with an air of exclusively moral satisfaction which is not quite decent: "It gives me pleasure to think I shall see you with unblemished integrity and unsoiled with unjust gain, enjoying that affluence many purchase with the loss of honesty and honour." When he died in 1775 all that affluence, save for bequests amounting to a few thousand pounds, came to his widow. Such wealth would by itself command the respect of any community; and Mrs. Montagu laid hers out in ways that impressed both the worldly and the serious.

A few years after her marriage she moved from her husband's old house in Dover Street to a fine newly-built house in Hill Street, Berkeley Square, which was decorated in the Chinese taste while that was the fashion, and was then repainted with amoretti by the brothers Adam. "Mrs. Montagu received me with the most encouraging kindness," wrote Hannah More. "She is not only the finest genius, but the finest lady I ever saw; she lives in the highest style of magnificence; her apartments are in the most splendid taste; but what baubles are these when speaking of a Montagu!" In those days she gave receptions that lasted from eleven in the morning till eleven at night, and called together more than a hundred guests at a time, and in her widowhood her hospitality became still more sumptuous. Stuart built her her great house in Portman Square, famous for its pillared hall and its room hung with birds' feathers, and there the guests came by the five hundred, and the Queen and six princesses sat down to one o'clock breakfast. All this dazzled the worldly; and at the same time she pleased the serious by her respect for them, and her determination to incorporate them into her social life. If she had to have her Queen and her princesses, she also had to have her Dr. Johnson and her Sir Joshua Reynolds. Even she had to have her Mrs. Carter and her Hannah More, for she was never more obstinate than in her flouting of the English tradition that intellectual distinction is an asset to a man and a handicap to a woman. She filled her rooms with wits of both sexes, forbade them to follow the custom of separating into two groups on opposite sides of the room, banished cards, and made them talk. These parties, and those like them which were given by Mrs. Vesey and other of her close friends, were called the meetings of the Blue Stockings' Club. It is said that they received that title when the naturalist, Benjamin Stillingfleet, a delightful being who had struggled against all forms of misery without losing his sweetness, pleaded the lack of evening clothes as a reason for not accepting one of Mrs. Vesey's invitations; for she answered him, drawing out of her tumbled mind a seventeenth century phrase alluding to puritanical homeliness of attire, "Pho, pho! Don't mind dress! Come in your blue stockings!" Whether the story be true or not, it aptly illustrates the character of these gatherings, which was easy and cheerfully contemptuous of materialistic standards. By this characteristic dualism of routs and Blue Stocking parties, of conformity and unconventionality, Mrs. Montagu built up an influence unique in breadth of scope, and made an honourable impress on social tradition.

But she hoped that the intellectual value of these gatherings would be high; and that it was not can be seen by a glance at those which were taking place at the same time in Paris under like female dominance. A sensible contemporary observer, Sir Nathaniel Wraxall, who had opportunities of comparing Mrs. Montagu with Madame du Deffand, Madame Geoffrin, and Mademoiselle de Lespinasse, formed the opinion that, "neither in the period of its duration, nor in the number, merit, or intellectual eminence of the principal members, could the English society be held up on any parity with that of France." The time and place were against the Blue Stocking parties, working on the guests and on the hostess alike. Even the ablest Englishmen loved inordinately to gamble and to drink; for that they would run from any party to their clubs. Also, the art of general conversation was cultivated and enjoyed in

France, and a band of friends could arrange to meet one or two days a week in confidence that sufficiently serious and amusing topics would be thrashed out in concert; while in London a party was a matter of jostling contacts and fortuitous groups, and a regular succession of them could not be trusted to provide a continuous, developing interest. But even more important, a factor of differentiation lay in the personalities of the hostesses. Madame du Deffand and Madame Geoffrin and Julie de Lespinasse were women; they were of unequal moral value, and one of them was horrible, but they were all women. Mrs. Montagu and Mrs. Vesey and Hannah More and Elizabeth Carter and Fanny Burney were not. There is hardly a line written by Madame du Deffand or a phrase uttered by Madame Geoffrin, and not a twist or turn in the untrue lover's knot of Julie de Lespinasse's life, which could possibly be ascribed to a man. But in all their works and ways the Englishwomen might have been youths seeking to please parents and tutors by fidelity to the programme laid down for them. The poor Blue Stockings had created themselves according to the image of the female presented to them as a pattern by male opinion, and they can have been hardly more inspiring companions than a pile of neat copy-books. The Frenchwomen had not unsexed themselves, and they could meet their visitors with the strength and attraction that proceeds from the reality of womanhood.

The time and the place were very powerful enemies of Mrs. Montagu. Had she lived elsewhere and in another age, it might well have been that her finest attribute would not have so closely resembled a vice that all her judges, and possibly herself, were thrown into confusion. She expressed this essential part of her character in a phrase she used when she wrote to Mrs. Vesey about Mrs. Thrale's marriage to Piozzi: "She has very uncommon parts, but certainly never appeared a Person of sound understanding; who ever possesses that blessing never is guilty of absurd conduct, or does anything which the world calls strange." At first sight this looks simply a case of adherence to the system of prudential morality, so much more prudent than moral, which was enjoined on women of that time with a cynicism more disagreeable than much which has excited the utmost wrath of the historians. Countless moralists have reproached Lord Chesterfield for informing his son that a love-affair with a woman of the world would improve his manners; but few have denounced his grandfather, Lord Halifax, for laying down laws in his "Advice to a daughter", which would deny the well-bred woman none of the experiences of a prostitute save those which might possibly humanize her. Mrs. Montagu had been brought up in an atmosphere poisoned by such prescriptions, and she was deeply tainted by them. If she did not believe that a woman should live wholly without principle and think no ruse illegitimate if it gained her public reputation, she did believe that a woman should never utter what she found in her heart if it was critical of existing institutions or altered the *status quo* of art and thought as men had made them. But in her objection to "anything which the World calls strange" she was writing not only as a cringing woman, but also as a sane and energetic human being who was determined to be sensible in an age which was pitifully lacking in sense. It was that determination which reinforced the authority of her wealth, and which makes her character profoundly respectable.

The eighteenth century deserved to be called the Age of Reason only when it had its head in its books, for in its domestic relationships and its economic affairs it practised the purest folly. As we turn over the pages of letters and memoirs belonging to that time, we find that, although the persons involved incessantly utter the most prudent and practical maxims, their model of conduct appears to have been the goose. If we take an example at hazard, and look into the life of Mrs. Delany, one of Mrs. Montagu's most charming friends, we must be appalled by the wild silliness of the actions which conditioned her life. When she was a girl of fifteen, so exquisite that she could have had half the world as her suitors, her uncle, Lord Lansdowne, who was apparently very fond of her, married her off for no ascertainable reason to a drunken and eccentric country squire of sixty, and took no precautions to see that the old man left her his money; and when she married Swift's friend, Dr. Delany, they became involved in interminable legal difficulties because from sheer ineptitude he had destroyed the marriage settlement of his first wife. This is the age of monstrous and causeless family quarrels; of elopements so frivolous that the lovers separated in a few weeks and so catastrophic that they brought historic houses to misery; and, above all, of vast and imbecile financial recklessness. Great men and little alike lost immense fortunes at the gaming tables: Charles James Fox incurred a debt of £140,000, Chesterfield had to recoup himself for his ill-luck by his undelectable marriage, countless lordlings lost ten and fifteen thousand pounds in an evening. Because of these and other improvidences families that had been famous and that were to be so again, lay in sluttish ruin; and Mrs. Montagu, who wanted the world to be proud and glittering, perceived the horror of it. In 1767 she writes of a visit to Hatfield:

". . . The fate of the Cecil family affects one disagreeably as their Seat, one feels for it a pity mixed with contempt and loathing. To see the heir of that Burleigh who so long held the reins of government now proud to drive a pair of coach horses is horrible. In this great Seat there are only two or three inhabitants. I observed a guitar lying in a window, and the maid who shews the house, told me it was played on by the *young Lady* who was Housekeeper, and I observed a dumb waiter with three bottles of wine, or gin perhaps, proposed for the same *young Lady's dinner*. Horses and Strumpets are the noble Earl's noble delight. The Park is the only spot in all Hertfordshire that is not green, it betrays the carelessness and poverty of the owner. Thus, alas, terminates Burleighs wisdom, Elizabeths power, the pilfering of the Treasury, and the extortions of the Star Chamber."

But Mrs. Montagu was even more powerfully affected by a certain manifestation of the irresponsibility of the privileged classes in that age which frequently brought misery on old and helpless people. Her letters contain repeated references to the shamefully careless wills left by her wealthy contemporaries. The Duchess of Portland, who had been her friend from girlhood, muddled her fortune to the edge of bankruptcy and left no legacy to her dependent, the charming Mrs. Delany, then eighty-five years old. Lord Bath, with an estate consisting of over twelve hundred thousand pounds in land and money, and four hundred thousand pounds in cash, stocks and mortgage, left nothing to his many needy relations and friends and handed it almost intact to his aged brother. "The legacies he left were trifling, for in truth he cared for nobody;" wrote Lord Chesterfield, "the words *give* and *bequeath* were too shocking for him to repeat and so he left all, in one word, to his brother." But Lord Chesterfield's own will was remarkable for its tasteless and illegal treatment of his wife and its crazily inadequate provision for servants of whom he was sincerely fond. This testamentary dementia operated even in Mrs. Montagu's own very united family. When her cousin, the Primate of Ireland, died he disinherited the young man who was to inherit from him the Barony of Rokeby, for the unprimatical reason that he had advised the lad "to go to White's Coffee House, as he wd there meet young men of fashion," and the young man had refused on the ground that "they were Cardplayers, it made it so dull he could not do it". The Primate's brother, Long Sir Thomas Robinson, did his heirs an even worse mischief by dissipating his fortune till he was obliged to sell the Yorkshire estate which had been in the family two hundred and fifty years.

Mrs. Montagu was, therefore, not bending before the wind of fashion when she professed the gospel of good sense and moderation, but breasting a running tide; and she practised what she preached with greater success than is usual. She wrote once that her letters were ever "fond to spread friendships and to cover heats", and she could have made the same claim for her social and intimate relationships. In an age which was as coarse as it was fine, which was as boisterous in its brawling as it was delicate in its courtesy, she sustained the peace of drawing-rooms. In spite of a superb equipment for conducting feuds, the nearest she ever came to one was her excessive, but not lasting or envenomed, resentment against Dr. Samuel Johnson, for his patronizing remarks about Lord Lyttelton in his *Lives of the Poets*. Her marriage was an unremitting attempt to guarantee two people tranquillity and comfort, good fame and a sense of honourable achievement, by excluding from their lives all emotions but sage benevolence towards each other and the outer world. There exist the letters in which she and Mr. Montagu discussed whether she should pay her respects at Court or sacrifice this social advantage out of regard for his career as a Whig member of Parliament; and these show with what patience and delicacy these people considered how to safeguard their relationship from rage and reproach.

But even more patient and delicate was Mrs. Montagu's repudiation of the financial recklessness common in her kind. She had always been a model housewife, and at her country house, Sandleford, describes herself as being "deep in accounts" and "travelling from tubs of soap to firkins of butter, and from thence to chaldrons of coal"; and that this was not meanness but a way of handsomeness is proved by the happiness her guests found in staying with her. When her husband inherited the Rogers estate she helped him in the heavy task of bringing it back to order, and after his death she managed it alone with the greatest possible wisdom, facing and solving both agricultural and industrial problems. Then, as always, she kept faith in her disposal of it with her conviction that "it is the duty of the rich to *justify the ways of God to Man* by imparting to unendow'd merit some of their abundance". It is true that she showed an ineffective regret that boys of seven were working in the collieries from which she drew her fortune, but nobody can be blamed for not being in advance of the social ideas of their time. One of her first acts after she became a widow was to give allowances to Dr. Johnson's blind friend, Miss Anna Williams, and to Mrs. Carter, for whom she had not been able to provide before because Mr. Montagu, with a solitary gesture of preference for the orthodox conception of muliebrity, had always disliked the worthy female scholar. This was but a trifle in that steady munificence which made Dr. Johnson reply, when Boswell jeered at it as a means of self-advertisement: "I have seen no beings who do so much good from benevolence as she does from whatever motive." It took a charming form in her annual May Day feast for the little chimneysweeps, who could come to the "Palace in Portman Square" any time from one o'clock to four and sit at tables in the garden eating beef and pudding; but it often took less spectacular and more thoughtful and enduring form in housing schemes and works for the unemployed. Indeed, she built her fortune into a solid edifice which could repel criticism from both the economic and moral points of view; and she saw that it should not fall to ruins after her death by adopting one of her nephews and training him to continue her administration on the same lines. She deserved the respect of contemporary society because she was as fine a justification for its capitalist system as the time provided, and not to remember her as that to-day is to withhold justice.

But Mrs. Montagu had her failures. "Of what use," she once asked peevishly concerning an explorer, "is the discovery of the source of the Nile? I have a due respect for this River of old and long established fame and power, but it derives little of its consequence from its source; it owes its greatness to other causes. I may be interested to know by what means a great Man, son of a mean one, acquired wealth and importance, but I don't wish to see his mean Parents' picture." It is a point of view that has its drawbacks. Sometimes from far-off sources, mean parents of a great river, there come floods which engulf its banks and bridges and turn it into a straggling swamp. When she was sixty-three a frenzy swept her from some such unexamined sources. She had a quarrel with her beautiful young companion which is like a tinkling echo of the quarrel between Madame du Deffand and Julie de Lespinasse. Miss Dora Gregory did nothing worse than go home to Scotland on holiday and become engaged to the Reverend Archibald Alison, who was later to write a popular *Essay on Taste*; but the painful howl went up in Portman Square, as it had in the Convent St. Joseph, of a passion so fundamentally unreasonable that it must shelter in such a corner of the mind as is most inaccessible to reason, and therefore must bear its frustration unconsoled. It was the more baffling in England because it never forgot to use the terms of prudence, and spoke of the disadvantages of marriage on inadequate means when it wanted to complain that it had lost the light of its eyes.

And there were the Sternes. Laurence Sterne had married Mrs. Montagu's needy cousin, Elizabeth Lumley, and the pair was a thorn in her side. They were indigent, for one thing, and it was not spiritually easy for her to relieve them, because of *Tristram Shandy*. She found a good phrase for Laurence, "he is full of the milk of human kindness, harmless as a child, but often a naughty boy, and a little apt to dirty his *frock;*" and she believed she had once moved him to "penetent tears". But "I can assure you," she explained after his death, "his witt never atoned with me for the indecency of his writings;" and she felt no special tenderness for his widow and his daughter Lydia, of whom she wrote to her sister:

"I had a letter from Miss A. Morett of York on Sunday telling me she had collected upwards of £700 for Miss Sterne, that she had promised the subscribers it should be converted into an annuity for the girl for she added Mrs. Sterne was so little loved or esteemed there would not have been a single guinea given if that condition had not been made. I had heard Miss Morett extremely well spoken of, and by her manner of acting by the Sternes and from her letters I imagine she has an uncommon share of goodness and of sense. She begs me to advise Miss Sterne not to affect witt, a desire of being distinguished that way she says has ruined the whole family."

This bracing advice she transmitted to Miss Sterne, who humbly answered:

"As to inheriting my father's witt I have not the least grain in my composition, we both thought it an unhappy turn in my father. I look on satire with detestation and I must own when we returned from France we were much hurt with the satirical things we hear in every company we went into, having lived for six years amongst people who know not what it is to be satirical—and instead of attacking anybody endeavour to make everyone in the company happy and *never speak ill of the absent*. I am so far from being a diseuse of bon mots I think I never made one in my life. I am when in company extremely diffident, seldom give my opinion but upon the most trivial things."

If she had gone on long enough she would surely have proved that as a matter of fact, owing to some oversight of her parents, she had never learned to speak. Perhaps because of this and other overtones in the letter Mrs. Montagu allowed her and her mother but twenty pounds a year. It is true that we know Lydia to have been something of a slut, from her dealings with her father's posthumous publications; but one should temper the wind to the shorn sluts. That Mrs. Montagu was never able to do in this particular case. Lydia, some years later, wrote from France to ask her to pay to Mrs. Sterne alone the allowance she had been paying to both, since she herself was going to marry a Frenchman, whose father insisted on her mother giving her whole estate as part of the dowry; and Mrs. Montagu replied:

"I cannot hesitate a moment to transfer entirely to your Mamma during her life the little I used to send for your mutual service so that the article of your letter which relates to this point is most easily answered, and with as much pleasure on my side as it can be received on yours. The more momentous affair your marriage I cannot assent to with the same good will. What I shall say on this subject is not meant to offend the gentleman who you have a desire to marry. I am a perfect stranger to his character, his fortune and even his name. You do not say anything of them, all you give your friends is that you are going to marry a man of a different Religion, and to reduce your Mother to almost beggary, both these things you confess. You seem at the same time to declare steadfastness in Religion and Filial piety to your parent. My dear cousin, the actions not the words are what shall decide the judgment of God and man.

If your husband has any zeal or regard for his religion he will be earnest to make you embrace it from regard to you and reverence to God, if he is void of religion he will think such a mark of your complaisance a trifle, and the authority of the husband will interpose where Faith stands Neuter. Your children must of necessity be——"

Here the copy Mrs. Montagu took of her letter ends abruptly. She was probably herself distressed by the violence of the flood that had swept down on her from the "mean Parents" of her nature. Perhaps a part of her rage was due to that sudden sick panic at the thought of indigence which is one of the occupational risks of wealth; but its ultimate cause was the difference between the children of Mary and the children of Martha, and that unjust and divine judgment regarding the better part. An honest part of her mind had to recognize that the shiftless, leering parson who wrote *Tristram Shandy* was to the impartial stars less valuable and yet more precious than herself; and that must have been torture to her whose passion was order, since it proved that the universe was framed on a principle which seemed clearly disorderly to her intellect, remarkable as that had been certified to be by Lord Bath and the good Lord Lyttelton, by Dr. Beattie and Gilbert West. It must have tortured her when the order of her own character broke down, for then there was disorder within and without. And such moments came, particularly as Mr. Montagu drew near his end. There is a letter in which she complains of him in his eighty-second year; at its beginning comes the superb phrase, "his temper is less violent than in health, and perfect churlishness spreads over the whole character," and at its end there whistles through it a full blast of Goneril-like loathing for senility. So ended a marriage which had begun with the intention not "to enlist entirely under the banners of Cupid or Pluto, but take prudent consideration and decent inclination for my advisers", and which had been carried on handsomely and reasonably for over thirty years. But nobody could be more aware of these things than Mrs. Montagu herself. Her letters are given a form and coherence not to be ascribed to her ideas, by the unremitting pressure of merciless self-criticism, which owned handsomely that though everywhere there was much to be censured it found most censurable what was within her nature. Perhaps that is why her personality chills the spectator through the ages. It hints at the futility of all human effort that a moral force so intense, and so patiently aided by the intellect, should be unable to remove the causes of her despondency. But that cause lay in an irreconcilable difference between what she was and what she chose to be, which was contrived by her time. She had elected to live the classical life by the calm application of wisdom; her century informed her that it was proper to do so. But she was a romantic by temperament. The ardour with which she proclaims her own coldness, the passion with which she professes moderation, betray her type. For this reason she is uneasy as she is distinguished; and though her gifts were clear cut, the fuzzy outlines of a pretentious thinker and pedant blur the image of a woman of action which she should have stamped on the page of history, profoundly respectable in power and generosity.

12

WILLIAM PITT, EARL OF CHATHAM

(1708–1778)

by BASIL WILLIAMS, F.B.A.

WILLIAM PITT, Earl of Chatham, was our greatest orator and our greatest war-minister, but never, perhaps, so great as when, in the evening of his days, he failed, by his exertions, to save America for England. His achievements as well as his one failure are writ large in the history of his country, so it will be needless, in this brief biographical sketch, to do more than glance at them. While, too, it is rather the historian's part to indicate the effect of a man's action or inaction on the destinies of his country, the biographer's particularly is to trace the influences which helped to form his character and to discover the secret springs of his activities. In some ways the biographer's is the harder task, for, whereas the historian deals chiefly with a man's achievements in action, art or literature, achievements notorious and open to the world, the formative years of a man's life, when his future greatness is still unforeseen, are apt to be dim from want of contemporary records, nor are the motives that impelled his actions always easily discernible even in the years of his achievements. Of Chatham's early life we have but scanty records; and rarely does he give us an inkling of his inmost thoughts. Most of his involved and stilted letters are a despair to the biographer; but fortunately a few, to his wife, give us a glimpse into the man's soul, while his public despatches during his great ministry, make clear his methods of administration. For the rest, if he had any real confidant in the days before he married,—in mature middle age,—it was the people of England, whom he loved and served so well. Addressing them through the House of Commons, where he throned supreme, he occasionally broke off into self-revealing asides in which he explained his motives or admitted his past mistakes. "For when I am on my feet," he once said, "I speak everything that is in my mind!"

With these slight helps some attempt may perhaps be made to explain how the Great Commoner became what he was, and what were the main ideas at the back of his mind.

§ 1. *Education*

What elements went to the formation of Pitt's character? He came of good Dorsetshire stock whose members had for centuries been worthies in and about their native Blandford as parsons, doctors, mayors, some even rising to greater eminence at the courts of Elizabeth and James I. The family gradually amassed lands in Hampshire as well as their native Dorsetshire, and according to their means were notable for benefactions to their poorer neighbours. Pitt's grandfather broke out into a new line by a life of adventure in India, first as an interloper on the East India Company's preserves, later, a poacher turned gamekeeper, as the Company's forceful governor of Madras. By his trading ventures he had already amassed great wealth and on his return from Madras made a further profit of over £100,000 by the sale of his famous diamond to the French Regent; most of this wealth he invested in lands and pocket boroughs in the western counties and soon made clear his intention of supporting the Protestant succession with uncompromising vigour. A rough, forceful man, who owed his success to his own will and courage and to some extent to his ruthless methods, he set up good business standards for himself and his offspring. "Give good example to your family by your life and conversation; avoid lending money or being surety for others; be cautious what company you keep and do not misspend your time . . . show yourself on all occasions a good Englishman, and a faithful servant to your country"; such was the advice, couched in almost Shakespearian language, he gave to his eldest son Robert, who proved a sad disappointment, but the last clause at any rate bore fruit with his favourite grandson William. He, being already eighteen when Governor Thomas died, was formed to the true Whig principles growled out to him by the old man and must have heard endless stories of his adventures in the East and how by unceasing vigilance and resolute methods he had preserved from foes within and without the great Company's first settlement at Madras: in fact in later days Chatham confessed that in India "I had garnered up my heart, where our strength lay, and our happiest resources presented themselves". From this grandfather he must have inherited some of that fiery power of command which awed and silenced those who ventured to oppose him; from the long line of solid Dorsetshire squires and parsons that instinctive gift of sympathy with the common folk of this green and pleasant land of England, who came to look on him as their great Commoner.

Nor must be forgotten the influence of his uncle Stanhope, the great warrior-statesman, who loved the boy and called him "the little marshal".

Besides these favourable influences derived from his family, others were less fortunate. The aloofness and the streak of arrogance in him which estranged many who might have been useful allies came, it is not fanciful to suppose, partly from his grandmother, descended from James V of Scotland, and from his mother, a Villiers, one of the proudest houses in England. His father was a man of little account, cowed possibly for life by the autocratic Governor, while his mother retired to Paris before he was of age and appears to have taken little interest in him. His elder brother Thomas was as futile as his father, while of his five sisters, two showed traces of madness, one of them being his favourite sister Ann, whose subsequent estrangement from him "had embittered", he wrote, "much of my life and will always be an affliction to me." From the Governor he inherited, besides his capacity and power of command, that inability to work with colleagues not definitely subordinate to him which often proved a serious handicap in his career, and also a tendency to gout, which appeared first when he was a boy at Eton and during his last ministry brought him for a time to a state hardly distinguishable from madness.

His education at Eton, Trinity, Oxford and Utrecht seems at any rate to have developed in him his native faculty for hard and thorough work and capacity for getting to the root of the matter, and brought him many of the friends, Lyttelton, Fox, the Grenvilles, Hanbury Williams, Pratt, Murray, Fielding, who made easy his entry into political life and the world of letters and fashion; nevertheless he disliked both Eton and Oxford and took care that none of his sons should go to either. Through the Grenvilles he obtained his cornetcy in their uncle Lord Cobham's regiment of horse, and during his brief period in the army, by his diligence in mastering all the tactical and strategical instruction to be obtained from books, he gave promise of justifying his uncle Stanhope's nickname for him, and at any rate proved himself, twenty-five years later, the greatest war-minister we have ever had. At twenty-seven he was provided with a seat in Parliament; and when, a year later, Walpole tried to "muzzle this terrible cornet of horse" by depriving him of his commission, he was already regarded as the rising hope of the Boy Patriots who attached themselves to the formidable band of statesmen whom Walpole had disobliged or otherwise antagonized:— Carteret, Pulteney, Marchmont, Windham, Chesterfield, Bolingbroke, with the great Mr. Pope as their poet laureate.

But if we would best understand the beauty of Pitt's nature and the influence which proved the most abiding support for this otherwise solitary man, this understanding will be found in his happy marriage and fatherhood. He found real love only when he was already forty-six, at a time too when his fortunes and his hopes seemed at their lowest. His discovery of his love for Hester Grenville was sudden as a thunder-clap and caught him in a rapture which seemed to bring out the highest powers of his nature. Fortunately we can get some inkling of this intense joy from the letters these two lovers exchanged. There are still, maybe, some phrases in them which seem to us stilted, but the pride and joy of mutual love pierce through in such sentences of his as: "I have the glory to be yours and the happy permission to call you mine. I press your sweet letter to my heart, run over every word, kiss every letter of it with transports of love and gratitude . . . You speak of my letters as a 'healing blessing'; the end of yours is 'a healing blessing' like the evening sun in Milton after clouds *with farewell sweet*, as he calls it, to cheer drooping nature," or her—"No joy can equal mine in having reason to believe your happiness depends upon me, because the highest ambition and the fondest wish I can form is to bestow it upon you, who are worthy of more than all I could bestow, had I all that the world could give . . . My Fame, my Pride, my Glory is centred in you . . . Yes, and yet I have but one short thing to say—you speak. That is the only way of praising what I would praise to the highest."

And throughout their married life this love remained un-dimmed, all the more radiant for the fine children with whom they were blessed. In the days of his great ministry he loved above all things to hear from his wife at Hayes "a thousand particulars of all those *little-great* things which, to those who are blessed as we, so far surpass in excellence and exceeding attraction, all the *great-little* things of the restless world"; and when he could himself snatch a few days' rest at Hayes his letters are full of "Hetty drunk with spring and joy" or Hetty's chase of a butterfly, "but the sport was growing too hot, and we wisely agreed to whip off to renew the hunt another day."

What care and thought, what abounding love he lavished on the up-bringing of these children is well-known. That this care was not wasted is seen by their careers. The daughters Hester and Harriet were famed for their capacity, wit and sweet natures; even John, the second Lord Chatham, though poor as an administrator is said to have been wise in council; James Charles the youngest was a gallant sailor, while "eager Mr. William", "William the orator", "the hope and comfort of my life", as Chatham called him, lives in our history only second to his father.

§ 2. *Speeches*

"I am not fond of making speeches (though some may think I am). I never cultivated the talent but as an instrument of action in a country like ours." So wrote Pitt to his friend Lyttelton at a moment of deep depression. It may seem para-doxical of one of our supreme orators; but it is evidently true. He was almost silent in Parliament when he had business to conduct for the country, during his ten years as Paymaster, still more so during his glorious ministry: and during these periods such few speeches as he made would never have brought him his fame as an orator. He rose to the height of his eloquence only when he was trying to get rid of a minister or a policy he thought a danger or a disgrace to the country. Thus for his great speeches we look to the last days of Walpole's rule, during Carteret's administration, during the opening period of the Seven Years War, when the country was being led to the edge of a precipice under Newcastle's fumbling rule, and above all in his final years, when his speeches reached their utmost magnificence in his vain effort to prevent the loss of America.

With Walpole, in regard to the chief service he rendered the country in his wise economic and financial system, Pitt in later days admitted with engaging frankness that he had no just cause for quarrel. But apart from his belief that Walpole was sacrificing the rights of "the despairing merchants" of England and neglecting "the two millions of people in our American colonies" by his Spanish convention of 1738, he had a deeper cause of resentment against him for his government based on corruption and narrow class interests. He and the Boy Patriots he led remind one of those vigorous young "bacheliers d'Angleterre" under Simon de Montfort's leadership, who suddenly took action in Henry III's reign not only against the King but also against his baronial opponents concerned only with their own particular interests. "I shall," said Pitt in one of his philippics against the ministry, "without scruple trample upon all those forms with which wealth and dignity entrench themselves . . . With regard to those whom I have offended . . . the heat that offended them is the ardour of conviction, and that zeal for the service of my country which neither hope nor fear shall influence me to suppress." So it was that, when Walpole, thrust from office but still powerful in the House, silenced his most eminent opponents, Carteret, Sandys, Pulteney, even the Prince of

Wales, by securing for them places or advantages under the new ministry reconstructed by his influence, Pitt refused offers and was one of the most forward in clamouring for an inquiry into the abuses of patronage and bribery which had formed the basis of Walpole's system of government.

In later days, again, Chatham paid a noble tribute to the schooling he had had from Carteret "in the upper departments of government. To his patronage," he said, "to his friendship and instruction I owe whatever I am." But that was true only of the days when Pitt and Carteret were comrades in opposition. During the three years, 1742-4, when Carteret was conducting the country's foreign policy and the war on the continent, Pitt attacked him with a bitter and unceasing vehemence. In his view Carteret entirely misapprehended the true policy for England, which was to direct all our energies against the Bourbon powers, always in Pitt's eyes the implacable foes of this country, instead of wasting all our substance on futile armies sent to wander round Germany for nobody's advantage except that of the Elector of Hanover. Moreover, though nobody could accuse Carteret of basing his power on the corruption of Parliament, in his case it was, thought Pitt, upheld by base servility to the King and pandering to his love of "a despicable electorate, whereof," as he put it, "this great, this powerful, this formidable kingdom is considered only a province." Even then Pitt saw what was amply proved during his own ministry, that Frederic of Prussia was our most natural as well as most useful ally, and with some justice accused Carteret of missing his opportunities of securing him and exciting his suspicions about George's beloved Pragmatic army. In those days Carteret appeared to Pitt nothing but "a Hanover troop minister, a flagitious taskmaster, whose only party are the 16,000 Hanoverians, the placemen by whose means he had conquered the Cabinet . . . an execrable, a sole minister, who has renounced the British nation and seemed to have drunk of the potion described in poetic fictions, which made men forget their country"; and he called on the House to save the King, "now situated upon the brink of a precipice. At such a time at least it little becomes his faithful Commons to be strewing flowers of flattery and panegyric under his feet. They should rather, with a rough but friendly hand, snatch him from the abyss he is ready to fall into, and with their timely aid place him again upon the secure basis of the affections of his people."

Largely owing to these attacks Carteret fell; but it is hardly surprising that Pitt himself earned the lasting aversion of the King whose favourite minister he had pilloried, whose Electorate he had turned into ridicule, and whose personal courage he had unjustly called in question. Nevertheless, two years after Carteret's fall, the King was forced by the Pelhams to admit Pitt into the ministry, though only in the subordinate post of Paymaster. By his conduct during the '45, when he was almost the only man in the House who kept his head, refusing to countenance factious opposition, and concentrating on the need of saving the country by its own exertions instead of through foreign mercenaries, he had made himself indispensable. Until Pelham died, in 1754, Pitt confined himself almost entirely to the work of his office, earning the gratitude and admiration of the country by refusing to make the usual private profit out of its funds; and his only effective intervention in general policies was to insist on the upkeep of the navy—England, he said, must, like Athens, "put herself on board her fleet."

But when with the death of Pelham the chief power fell into Newcastle's nerveless hands, once more came the need for great speeches to expose the imbecility of the Duke's foreign policy. Pitt rose to the occasion, showing up with merciless vehemence and ridicule and with thundering eloquence the futility of his measures and blasting the men of straw put up in the House of Commons to support them. To this period belongs one of his most famous speeches in which, by a sudden inspiration, he compared the duke to the Saône, "a gentle, feeble, languid stream, and though languid of no depth," and Fox, the Duke's temporary henchman, to the Rhône, "a boisterous and overbearing torrent," where it joins the Saône below Lyons; "they meet at last," he concluded, "and long may they continue united, to the comfort of each other, and to the glory, honour and happiness of this nation." In turn Robinson, Murray, Fox wilted and faded away before the blast of his eloquence; and at last Newcastle himself had to give place to "the private gentleman of a slender fortune to whom the eyes of an afflicted despairing nation were now lifted up", the man who said: "I know that I can save this country, and that no one else can."

§ 3. *The Organizer of Victory*

Of Pitt's thoughts and methods during his great ministry it is easier to speak than of any other period of his life, for the evidence is all before us in his appeals to the country, in the despatches elaborating his plans of campaign, in the recorded interviews with his trusted commanders and agents and finally in the results. Almost his first step was to compose a King's speech "captivating the people", and bringing home to them the life struggle in which they were engaged with France and the part each man must take in it. The response was instant from "a willing, giving people". He dismissed the foreign mercenaries, called over by Newcastle in a panic to defend the country, and taught his countrymen to take that defence into their own hands by organizing themselves into county-militias: he helped England "to put herself on board her fleet" by strengthening and encouraging the navy:

for foreign service he "looked for merit in the mountains of the north. I called it forth and drew it into your service, a hardy and intrepid race of men; men who . . . had gone nigh to have overturned the state in the War before the last," the former Highland rebels in fact who, within a dozen years of the '45, helped us to win Canada: regardless of apparent, though not real, inconsistency with his attack on Carteret's policy, he supported Frederic the Great with subsidies and an auxiliary force of English and German troops to distract the French from overseas and thereby in his own phrase, "to conquer America in Germany": lastly by his tact in removing grievances and his eloquent appeals to their own interests, he was the first minister to soothe the American colonists' susceptibilities and to win their loyal co-operation.

During the winter months, when the armies were quiescent, he was wont to survey the whole theatre of operations, India, West Africa, the West Indies, America, Germany and the coast of France, to form his plans of operation on broad lines, incorporated in despatches to his commanders, and then to leave them to work out the details without niggling interference. He gradually superseded the old incompetent generals and admirals and sought out or encouraged younger or more vigorous leaders, Boscawen, Saunders, Hawke, Keppel, Watson, Pocock, Steevens, Hughes, Amherst, Clive, Forde, Granby, Prince Ferdinand and Wolfe. He had them up before him to give them parting words of cheer; and, as one of them said: "No man ever entered his closet who did not feel himself, if possible, braver at his return than when he went in." He supplied them with all their needs even to the smallest details, such as spruce beer and fishing nets to provide fresh, anti-scurvy nourishment for the men; and when some ordnance officer told him that it was impossible to provide certain equipments in time, he held out his two gouty crutches saying: "Sir, I walk upon impossibilities," and saw to it that his orders were punctually obeyed. As a result, by 1759 Horace Walpole was complaining that "our bells are worn threadbare with ringing for victories"; and by the end of the war Pitt had secured Canada, Guadaloupe, Martinique, Belleisle off France itself, Goree and Port Louis in Senegal, and the mastery of India.

§ 4. *Eclipse*

With all his vital power of impressing his personality on his subordinates Pitt never had the faculty of dealing with those who fancied themselves his equals. Had he used more conciliatory methods with his colleagues in the cabinet of October, 1761, when he resigned, he might well have persuaded them to declare war on Spain at once, as they were forced to do in less favourable conditions barely three months later. But soon George III, who had seen him go with pleasure, found that the men who replaced him, Bute, Grenville, Rockingham were poor substitutes, and began to think that with Pitt he could find a basis for co-operation. One of Pitt's constant watch-words was "Measures not Men"; in other words to him the essential was to get the right things done, not to aim merely at satisfying the rapacity of place hunters from the various parliamentary groups: George III likewise, bent on being a Patriot King, had no use for the claims of particular men for office but wished to choose his ministers, solely for their capacity to carry out his own behests: nor did he see that, though equally averse to party connections, Pitt had a very different conception to his own of Measures. At any rate the King, though largely responsible for Pitt's resignation in 1761, only two years later began angling for him to form a new ministry. He realized especially during the feeble Rockingham ministry of 1766 what immense influence

Pitt still wielded in the House of Commons, for he it was, and not the ministry, who by his eloquent pertinacity had persuaded Parliament to repeal the ill-omened Stamp Act for America. Nevertheless Pitt was already a tired and sick man, suspicious too of so sudden a change, and it was not till the Rockingham ministry had fallen in 1766 that he at last consented. The ministry then formed was almost bound to fail, composed as it was like a tessellated pavement brought together from the leavings of every party; its failure was made certain, first when Pitt deserted the Commons, where he ruled supreme, to enter the Lords as Earl of Chatham, and a few months later when he succumbed to a bout of complicated gouty disorders lasting over two years, which for the time entirely unhinged his mind. During one of his brief intervals of lucidity in 1768 he discovered that every aim he had and every measure he cared for had been jettisoned during his absence, and sent in his resignation; and, fully recovered in July, 1769, he went to make his last majestic obeisance to the King and inform him of his entire disapprobation of the measures, largely prompted by George himself, that had been carried out during his illness. He has been accused of malingering during these two years and more of retirement, because he found himself unable to carry out the policy he had planned. Nothing could be more unjust, for during most of that time he was a physical and mental wreck. Nevertheless it is very doubtful, even had he been still the Great Commoner of his glorious days, whether he could have accomplished much with his fantastic ministry, all at odds with one another; for it was not then the case, as in war-time, of carrying out a formed plan of his own, but of persuading an obstinate King and discordant ministers to elaborate policies for dealing with complicated questions in India, in America, in foreign policy and at home—a form of patient diplomacy in which he was never an adept.

WILLIAM PITT, EARL OF CHATHAM

§ 5.   *The Glorious Failure*

When Chatham returned to the Lords in 1770 he found "this venerable, this lovely constitution" of England being undermined by those who should have been its staunchest guardians. The House of Commons, at the King's behest, had declared to be duly elected a man returned by a small minority of the Middlesex electors in order to keep out the King's enemy, Wilkes, who was at the head of the poll: Townshend, his own chancellor of the exchequer, had re-imposed taxes on America: the ministry had been re-constituted by the elimination of all his Whig friends: and the Whig opposition was too timid or too indifferent to fight for the liberty they professed. Chatham soon announced that he would be "a scarecrow of violence to the gentle warblers of the grove, the moderate Whigs and timid statesmen", and a scarecrow he became with a vengeance. Fighting almost single-handed, in 1770, the first year of his return to active life, he spoke in fifteen debates, mostly initiated by himself. It was no new thing for him to be alone:

> "Be of good cheer, noble love."

(he quoted to his wife)

> "Yes, I am proud, I must be proud to
> See Men not afraid of God afraid of me."

In electoral reform he was almost a pioneer. The Wilkes case had taught him that the Commons as constituted no longer represented the people, the boroughs, corrupt and often in the hands of a few or even one borough-monger, being notably "the rotten parts of the constitution"; and he anticipated his son in proposing to correct this corruption by adding a third member to the country-membership chosen on a more popular basis. He attacked his old antagonist Lord Mansfield's doctrine that the judge alone and not the jury could decide on the criminality of a libel, thereby anticipating the reform carried by Fox in 1792. He persisted in motions to reverse the Commons' unconstitutional decision on the Middlesex election and twice proposed to address the King for a dissolution owing to the dangerous state of the kingdom and the incompetence of his ministers in the Falkland Islands business. On one occasion he even aimed at the King himself and hoped that his eyes might, ere it was too late, be opened to the state of his kingdom by some figure such as that which

> Drew Priam's curtain in the dead of night,
> And would have told him half his Troy was burned:
> But Priam found the fire ere he his tongue.

But he is best remembered in these his last years for his glorious struggle against the policy which lost us America. Some of his great phrases have become embedded in our history, and though they made little impression on "Xerxes and the multitudes at his heels", as he once described the serried ranks of ministerialists, they have become the Magna Carta of relations with our colonies. Already in one of his great speeches for the repeal of the Stamp Act he had electrified the Commons by his phrase "I rejoice that America has resisted": now, when methods of repression were being resorted to, he repeated to the Lords that "This country has no right under Heaven to tax America"; the only way of dealing with her was "to proceed like a kind and affectionate parent over a child whom he tenderly loves" and that "It is not repealing this Act of Parliament, it is not repealing a piece of parchment, that can restore America to your bosom: you must repeal her fears and her resentments: and you may then hope for her love and gratitude." As for "your talk of your powerful forces, to disperse their army . . . I might as well talk of driving them before me with this crutch! . . . If you conquer them, what then? You cannot make them respect you, you cannot make them wear your cloth . . . coming from the stock they do they can never respect you." And with the prophet's eye to the future of our great colonies he already spoke of America as a *nation* and looked forward to "the period not far distant", when "England, whose welfare has always been my greatest and most pleasing consolation, will want the assistance of her most distant friends" such as this new "nation", not yet separated from her when he spoke.

But when it was a question of granting independence to America at the behest of France, the old warrior came to make his dying speech in the Lords. "Shall a people," he exclaimed, "that fifteen years ago was the terror of the world now stoop so low as to tell its ancient inveterate enemy: 'Take all we have, only give us peace'? " Such was the last expiring utterance of the man who, before his time, had a Pisgah-like vision of what the British Empire has become to-day, a voluntary union of free and self-governing nations, though maimed by the absence of that great republic overseas which he, beyond all others, had made secure from the enemy on her borders.

13

JOHN WESLEY

(1703-1791)

by JOHN BERESFORD

IN summing up the life of the Venerable Bede, St. Boniface used a striking phrase—"the candle of the Church which the Holy Spirit had lighted." The words can be applied with equal sincerity and truth to the life of John Wesley.

We are not accustomed to think of the eighteenth century as one of the heroic periods of English History. Despite the great and growing interest in that age our minds are still too prone to think of it mainly in terms of an amiable and even tranquillity, of a rational and philosophic outlook, of a background of calm thought, religion and morality, of disciplined, academic and rounded expression. In politics we remember particularly the long peace of Walpole and the powerful combination of the Pelhams; in literature the figures of Addison, Pope, Gray, Dr. Johnson, Horace Walpole and Gibbon; in art the canvases of Gainsborough, Reynolds and old Crome; in religion Law of *The Serious Call*, Bishop Berkeley, Bishop Butler and Parson Woodforde.

But in the political sphere the eighteenth century witnessed also the most romantic and the most forlorn adventure of any age—the Jacobite rebellion of 1745, the great destiny of the

Pitts, the foundation of the British Empire by heroic struggle and pioneering in Canada, in India, in Australia and South Africa; in literature it produced the dynamic force of Swift, the haunting originality of Sterne, the pure inspiration of Blake and of the youthful Coleridge and Wordsworth; in art, the powerful and grotesque humour of Hogarth; in religion, the burning light of Whitfield, of John Wesley and of his brother Charles.

These events and these personalities are all cast in the mould of genius, the mould of the unexpected, of the creative and of the most high in human endeavour and imagination. Neither the age of Elizabeth, nor of Charles I and of Cromwell can surpass the age of Anne and of the Georges in the breadth of achievement, and in the power of spiritual regeneration. We do well, therefore, to approach that period in the mood of the ancient and beautiful invocation:

"Let us now praise famous men, and our fathers that begat us."

The supreme evangelists of medieval, renaissance and modern times—Francis of Assisi, Ignatius Loyola and John Wesley came, not from the ranks of the poor and the ignorant, but from the educated classes of society. St. Francis was the son of a rich merchant, St. Ignatius was of noble birth, John Wesley was the son of a clergyman of the Church of England, himself sprung of an old West Country family. The sense of discipline and of obedience was thus not acquired but was inborn, and it was, perhaps, partly, if not mainly, due to this fact that these three men were enabled to build upon secure foundations the great movements forever associated with their names. The Methodist Church to-day numbers, it is believed, some 50,000,000 adherents in all parts of the world—mainly, of course, in the United States of America, in this country and in the Dominions. Its strength is largely due to its organization, and it owes its organization to the administrative genius of John Wesley. It was not for nothing that John Wesley was descended on both sides—for his mother was an Annesley—from families with fine traditions, that he and his ancestors had been educated in the university of Oxford, and that he was brought up in a home supremely ruled by two influences—the spirit of love and the spirit of obedience.

To the objection that John Wesley himself was not obedient to the Church of England of which he was ordained a priest, there is sufficient answer: in the first place the Methodist movement never separated from the Church during Wesley's life-time, and Wesley passionately declined to contemplate separation to his dying day; in the second place separation need never have taken place if the Anglican Church had, at the time, been faithful to that principle of comprehension which is, perhaps, its supreme glory and characteristic; in the third place, the period of a century and a half is but as yesterday in spiritual history, and the tide of re-union, now flowing so strongly in many places, may, in due time, carry Methodism back into the mild and magnanimous arms of the Church of England.

We must now take a rapid glance at Wesley's early life and the circumstances surrounding it, in order to obtain a just perspective of what he accomplished, and of how he accomplished it.

It will surprise no one who is at all acquainted with the genealogies of earlier times to learn that John Wesley was the fifteenth child of a family of nineteen; indeed, his mother, Susanna Wesley, was the twenty-fifth child of Dr. Samuel Annesley, a nephew of the first Earl of Anglesea. He was born on June 17th, 1703, and his early childhood was spent at Epworth in Lincolnshire, a village or township of some 2,000 inhabitants of which his father, Samuel Wesley was the Rector. The inhabitants of Epworth, or a number of them, were barbaric to an almost incredible degree and it was many years before Samuel's devoted ministry—assisted by his brave and noble wife—was able to civilize them. They showed their objection to their Rector by maiming his cattle, and by two if not three attempts to burn down the Rectory. Southey, in his memorable though critical life of Wesley, says definitely that it was the third attempt which succeeded in its object on the night of February 9th, 1709, for the Rectory was destroyed, and John Wesley, then a child of five and a half years of age was only saved by a miracle. He awoke to find his room brilliantly lighted; he tried to get into the passage but it was ablaze, and his father was unable to reach him by the stairs; the child climbed on to a box by the window; he was seen from the yard, and one man climbing upon the shoulders of another managed to reach and to rescue him; immediately afterwards the roof fell in. In Wesley's *Journal*—one of the most remarkable documents of the eighteenth century—the following entry occurs under the date February 9th, 1750: "We had a comfortable watch-night at the Chapel. About eleven o'clock it came into my mind, that this was the very day and hour in which, forty years ago, I was taken out of the flames. I stopped, and gave a short account of that wonderful providence."

Throughout his long life Wesley had many experiences of extraordinary preservation from sudden death, but this early experience at Epworth Rectory particularly affected his mind. It is noteworthy how often he employs metaphors associated with fire. At the end of his great sermon on the death of Whitfield in 1770 he exclaims: "Let his spirit rest upon these thy servants! Show thou art the God that answerest by fire! Let the fire of thy love fall on every heart!" Fire, says Dr. Eayrs in his work on *Wesley as Christian Philosopher and Church Founder* was "his favourite metaphor to represent his Christian experience".

Frequently in his great missionary journeys Wesley returned to the place of his birth and preached to great and attentive congregations, standing upon his father's tombstone; the village ferocity of earlier days had submitted to humanizing influence and to love. To those who are familiar with the bye-paths of the eighteenth century, and with the character of the mobs—their beast-like manifestations and dreadful fury—the civilizing force of John Wesley must always appear as a factor of outstanding social significance. As we follow that wonderful life, and watch the gradual transformation of the most ruffianly elements in the population all over the country into orderly beings, and frequently into men and women of great goodness and holiness, it is impossible not to recognize, with Hamlet, that there are more things in heaven and earth than are dreamed of in our philosophy.

After an austere period of schooling at the Charterhouse, John Wesley entered Christ Church, Oxford, as a scholar in June, 1720. The Oxford period of Wesley's life lasted fifteen years, for after he had taken his degree, he was made a fellow and subsequently tutor of Lincoln College. At intervals after his ordination he helped his father in his two parishes of Epworth and Wroot, but Oxford was his main headquarters and home. There he lectured in logic, philosophy and Greek—he was an extremely accurate scholar—and there he began that life of asceticism for himself, and of loving kindness for his fellow men which, with other gifts and qualities, has made him so renowned a figure in the history of humanity.

It is said that a poor servant, the college porter, of Christ Church, Oxford, was responsible for the first impulse which turned the mind of John Wesley, in the year 1725, the year of his ordination, towards that dedicated life which he was henceforth to lead. The servant had but one coat and was half starved: yet he was happy and grateful. "You thank God," said the astonished Wesley, "when you have nothing to wear, nothing to eat, and no bed to lie upon. What else do you thank Him for?" "I thank Him," the servant replied in words of beautiful simplicity, "that He has given me my life and being, and a heart to love Him, and a desire to serve Him." These words are memorable, for they lie at the root of Methodism, and illustrate the Gospel of the Redeemer in the great saying— "the Kingdom of Heaven is within you."

It has been suggested by a distinguished French historian, Professor Halévy, and his view is endorsed by English historians, that this country was saved from internal convulsion at the time of the French Revolution, and in the earlier part of the nineteenth century, by the great religious movement set on foot by John Wesley: "it directed into other channels," says Mr. George Trevelyan in his *History of England*, "the first rebellion of the uncared-for millions, for it gave them other interests and ideals besides the material, it fostered in them self-respect as citizens of another world whose franchise was not confined to the well-to-do, and it provided them with a democratic religious and educational organization of their own."

I have here connected the episode of the college porter, in the year 1725, with the eventual influences of Methodism on the history of England, and therefore on the history of the world, a century or so later, because it is desirable to apprehend at the outset the ultimate meaning of great movements.

But though that early conversation was of importance in John Wesley's life, it is essential to realize that thirteen years elapsed before he himself fully understood what was expected of him as a great Evangelist. We must pass rapidly through these years. Between 1725 and 1729 we are to think of him as living an ordinary Christian life partly as a don at Oxford, and partly as his father's curate in Lincolnshire. Then, in 1729, he is called back to Oxford as Tutor of Lincoln College, and in Oxford he found that his younger brother Charles who was at Christ Church, had gathered round him a few young men who were leading an exemplary life of religious devotion. John at once became the leader of this group—George Whitfield subsequently became a member of it—which now received the scornful nick-name of "Methodists", on account of the regularity of their behaviour. They were constant in worship, they visited the prisoners, they ministered to the sick, they gave away their money to the poor.

"This," said Wesley, in speaking of charity, "was the practice of all the young men at Oxford who were called Methodists. For example: one of them had thirty pounds a year; he lived upon twenty-eight, and gave away forty shillings. The next year, receiving sixty pounds, he still lived on twenty-eight, and gave away two and thirty. The third year he received ninety pounds, and gave away sixty-two. The fourth year he received an hundred and twenty pounds; still he lived as before on twenty-eight, and gave to the poor ninety-two." Southey and other biographers say that Wesley was here speaking of himself, and we certainly know that he consistently practised this principle throughout the rest of his life, in the course of which he gave away the tens of thousands of pounds which he earned by his writings.

Most people, if they were capable of only a tithe of Wesley's self-abnegation at Oxford, would be regarded as very good Christians. But Wesley did not so regard himself, nor did his period of missionary work in Georgia, between October, 1735, and the beginning of 1738, bring him any satisfaction. That episode in his life, indeed, taught him how far he still was from understanding the ultimate meaning of Christianity. His High Church formalism in religious observances, and his almost arrogant austerity antagonized the colonists, and he returned to England in February, 1738, in a state of spiritual depression. At Oxford, on March 5th, he enters in his *Journal* that he was clearly convinced by Peter Böhler, the good Moravian, "of the want of that faith whereby alone we are saved." He now understood that good works were not enough, and it was on these, he saw, that he had hitherto really grounded his hope of salvation. He was in great agony of spirit till, on Wednesday, May 24th, 1738, occurred the central experience of his life.

On that day, at five o'clock in the morning he opened his Greek Testament at the words: "There are given unto us exceeding great and precious promises, even that ye should be partakers of the divine nature." A little later he opened the Testament and read: "Thou art not far from the Kingdom of God." In the afternoon he went to St. Paul's Cathedral and listened to the magnificent anthem: "Out of the deep have I called unto Thee, O Lord; Lord, hear my voice . . . for with the Lord there is mercy, and with Him is plenteous redemption." In the evening he went, "very unwillingly," as he says in his *Journal*, "to a society in Aldersgate Street, where one was reading Luther's preface to the Epistle to the Romans. About a quarter before nine, while he was describing the change which God works in the heart through faith in Christ, I felt my heart strangely warmed. I felt I did trust in Christ, Christ alone for salvation; and an assurance was given me, that he had taken away *my* sins, even *mine*, and saved *me* from the law of sin and death."

The brief passage just quoted from Wesley's *Journal* can convey but a slight and inadequate idea of that poignant event in his life, and if the reader wishes to form his own impression of Wesley's experience on that twenty-fourth of May, two centuries ago, he must turn to the *Journal* itself and read the whole account. He will then quickly realize that he has been brought into vivid contact with a man of singular purity of heart, and of profound sincerity and truthfulness. And he will realize, too, that the style is the man, that the lucidity and simplicity of the language interpret a character and mind which have nothing to conceal, and that there emerges—endowed with a unique dignity—the portrait of one of the greatest of men.

"It is scarcely an exaggeration to say," observes Lecky in his *England in the Eighteenth Century*, "that the scene which took place at that humble meeting in Aldersgate Street forms an epoch in English history. The conviction which then flashed upon one of the most powerful and most active intellects in England is the true source of English Methodism."

After a brief interval in Germany, where he visited the Moravian settlement at Herrnhut, Wesley returned to London and "began again," as he says, "to declare in my own country the glad tidings of salvation." He seems to have contemplated remaining in London, but in March, 1739, he received a pressing call from Whitfield, who was in Bristol and about to go to America, to come there without delay. Whitfield had already begun the innovation of open-air preaching, partly because— though he was a clergyman of the Church of England—he was not welcomed in the parish Churches, and partly because his extraordinary gift of oratory attracted enormous audiences which no building could hold. Wesley went to Bristol, and after a little hesitation, preached his first sermon in the open air to some three thousand people on April 2nd, 1739. He preached from the text "The Spirit of the Lord is upon me, because He hath anointed me to preach the Gospel to the poor." From this date to within ten days of his death, in his eighty-eighth year, Wesley conducted without pause his great evangelizing mission throughout the length and breadth of England and Wales; he made also frequent visits to Ireland and Scotland.

What was the spiritual and moral background of the nation at the time when Wesley began his great mission? Sweeping generalizations are usually unsound. Nevertheless no competent historian of the eighteenth century would question Wesley's own description of the spiritual world as being, at that time, "drowsy." Hogarth's admirable caricature entitled *The Sleeping Congregation*—in which he depicts almost everyone in Church soundly snoring except the Parson and the clerk— may not be absolutely true to life, but it is certainly true as a parable. The eighteenth century Church was terrified of what was called "enthusiasm", remembering too well the internecine conflicts of the preceding century. Hence her teaching emphasized morality, and tended to forget the pure flame of the Gospel and the living faith which has transformed the morals of men, in waves of evangelical preaching, ever since the Sermon on the Mount.

Consequently on the side of morality itself the state of things was in many respects deplorable. Drunkenness was widespread, and the curse of spirit-drinking with its awful consequences—Hogarth's engraving *Gin Lane* shows them in graphic form—compelled Parliament to pass drastic restrictive legislation in 1751. Blasphemy and cursing, profligacy, sports of great cruelty, widespread smuggling, robbery on the highway and off it—these were largely prevalent when Methodism began, and almost from the first preaching of the new Gospel Wesley was able to claim that "not a few whose sins were of the most flagrant kind, drunkards, swearers, thieves, whoremongers, adulterers, have been brought from darkness unto light, and from the power of Satan unto God."

It is impossible here to follow the remarkable story of Methodism. It must suffice to say that by 1756 a great transformation had taken place, the fury of the mobs, to which some reference has already been made, had been very largely curbed, and the organization of Methodism—the "class" system, the institution of itinerant lay preachers, and the annual Conference (the keystone of the edifice) had been fairly established.

So far we have represented everything as being Wesley's work. In a sense that is just, since his was the master spirit, the intellectual and the organizing force. But Wesley could not have accomplished his work without the help of two great men, his brother Charles, and George Whitfield. We have already mentioned Whitfield, and here we have only space to emphasize that the power of his preaching and the essential goodness of his character can hardly be exaggerated. Of Charles Wesley who like his brother John was a clergyman of the Church of England, something more must be said. The enduring power of Methodism is largely due to its Hymnody, and Charles Wesley's Hymns by their lyrical beauty, their simplicity and their sincerity have become famous in the Protestant communities in all parts of the English speaking world. Thirty of them are included in *Hymns Ancient and Modern*, and represent one of Methodism's best legacies to the Church of England. Such a Hymn as "Come, O Thou Traveller unknown" deserves to rank with the highest religious poetry, whether of George Herbert, Henry Vaughan or Christina Rossetti. Charles Wesley was himself a great itinerant preacher till 1756. Like his more famous brother he, too, kept a Journal which is too little known: it contains some admirable writing.

Before John Wesley died the adherents of Methodism numbered well over a hundred thousand in this country and America, and in the nineteenth century the numbers swelled into tens of millions. In the last years of his life he had become one of the outstanding figures in the country, universally respected and honoured. On December 27th, 1789, he proudly notes in his *Journal*: "So are the tables turned, that I have more invitations to preach in Churches than I can accept of." In justice to the Church of England, however, it must be remembered that Wesley was never without help and sympathy from some of the clergy: such notable men as Grimshaw, Berridge, Romaine, Venn and the saintly Fletcher of Madeley were his good friends. The later evangelical movement within the Church, which began about 1780, owed much of its impulse to Methodism.

In that great work of literature, the *Journal*, the true Wesley throughout his long Mission must be sought, and also in his admirable *Letters* which have recently been edited in eight volumes by the Rev. John Telford, one of his best biographers. He retained his intellectual, and a great measure of his physical vigour right up to his death. He himself explained the human means of his good health as due to his constantly rising at four in the morning, generally preaching at five in the morning, and never travelling less than 4,500 miles a year by sea or land. Until 1773 he rode on horseback; afterwards he took to a chaise or carriage. His range of reading was very wide, as a mere glance at the index to his *Journal* will show, and his publications run into scores of volumes.

All his immense energies were dedicated solely to the welfare of his fellow men. John Wesley's amazing love for humanity expressed itself in the last letter he ever wrote—on February 24th, 1791, a week before his death. The letter is addressed to the youthful Wilberforce and encourages him in his crusade against the slave-trade, and indeed against slavery itself. "Go on," says the old man, "in the name of God and in the power of His might, till even American slavery (the vilest that ever saw the sun) shall vanish away before it. . . . That He who has guided you from youth up may continue to strengthen you in this and all things is the prayer of, dear sir, your affectionate servant."

On March 2nd, 1791, in his eighty-eighth year John Wesley died at City Road, London.

In thinking over that marvellous life we recall one of the *Logia* of Jesus:

"Jesus saith, Let not him who seeks cease until he finds, and when he finds he shall be astonished; astonished he shall reach the Kingdom, and having reached the Kingdom he shall rest."

14

SAMUEL JOHNSON

(1709-1784)

by HUGH KINGSMILL

JOHNSON has come to be looked upon as a typical Englishman, although he was no more a typical Englishman than the Pacific Ocean is a typical pond. He was tender-hearted and unsentimental; generous to private distress and not associated with schemes of public benefaction; witty and imaginative in his speech, not inarticulate or rhetorical. He respected intellect in others and cultivated it in himself.

Johnson's life was largely shaped by his disabilities, physical and emotional. From his father he inherited a melancholia which clouded his imagination with the fear of death and a causeless sense of guilt. Through the carelessness of his mother he was handed over, when a few weeks old, to a wet-nurse whose own baby was scrofulous and short-sighted. "In a few weeks," Johnson wrote in an autobiographical fragment, "I was taken home, a poor diseased infant, almost blind." His sight and hearing were permanently impaired, the lower part of his face disfigured, and a nervous irritation set up which showed itself throughout his life in what his step-daughter called "convulsive starts and odd gesticulations which tended to one's surprise and ridicule".

As these disabilities were combined with extraordinary strength of body and mind, and a dominating nature, Johnson might have revenged his misfortunes on the world by becoming a buccaneer of the Mirabeau kind. "Ah, sir," he said to Boswell, of his time at Oxford, "I was mad and violent. It was bitterness which they mistook for frolick. I was miserably poor, and I thought to fight my way by my literature and my wit." But this escape from his wretchedness was closed to him by his innate virtue. From his earliest years he was, partly because of his melancholia and physical disadvantages, preoccupied with moral questions. He might, therefore, have taken the opposite way of escape, and become a religious leader, but while he had too much virtue to be a Mirabeau he was too human and poetic to be a Loyola or a Calvin. In *Rasselas* he speaks of "that hunger of imagination which preys incessantly upon life", and his imagination, although half suffocated by his melancholia, was the deepest and strongest element in his nature. As a boy his happiest hours were spent in day-dreaming and in the reading of romances, his passion for which, he once said, had unsettled him so much as to prevent him from taking up a profession. In later life he had the poet's love of remembering the past, not for its triumphs but as a landscape shining with hope and freed by distance from the pain of experience. "The friends which merit or usefulness can procure us," he once wrote to Boswell, "are not able to supply the place of old acquaintance, with whom the days of youth may be retraced, and those images revived which gave the earliest delight; " and to Mrs. Thrale he wrote from Lichfield: "I took a walk in quest of juvenile images," and on another occasion told her that everything in Lichfield recalled to his remembrance years in which he had proposed what he had not done, and promised himself pleasure which he had not found.

When, in 1737, at the age of twenty-seven, Johnson went to

London "to try his fate with a tragedy", he was accompanied by David Garrick, one of the three pupils in the school he had opened after his marriage. Within a few years Garrick was wealthy and famous. Apart from his genius as an actor he had all the arts by which success is achieved, and could get round everyone except Johnson, who used to treat the universally popular actor with a brusquerie which caused Garrick endless mortification. There was a great deal of resentment in Johnson, which neither his pride nor his piety could extirpate, and he never reconciled himself to the ease with which Garrick attained the goal to which he himself had struggled through years of difficulties and disappointments. "The first appearance of excellence," he wrote in the *Rambler*, "unites multitudes against it; unexpected opposition rises up on every side. . . . The strength and unanimity of this alliance is not easily conceived." By "excellence" Johnson clearly does not mean talent of any kind, for he had not to look further than Garrick to learn that some kinds of talent are rewarded almost as soon as they show themselves. He meant the talent of an original and sincere mind, working outside the currents of thought and feeling of the moment. In *London*, a satirical poem composed shortly after he reached the metropolis, he wrote:

> How, when competitors like these contend,
> Can surly virtue hope to fix a friend?

In these lines he forecast the struggle ahead of him, and epitomized the rebuffs he had already met with. In the whole course of his career he never hit the public taste except when he was reporting the Parliamentary debates for the *Gentleman's Magazine*, four or five years after he arrived in London. These reports, which were based on hearsay, were accepted by the public as genuine. They raised the circulation of the magazine from ten thousand a month to fifteen thousand, and would have placed Johnson permanently beyond the need to worry about money had he gone on with them. But when he realized that he was misleading the public he threw the job up, clearly to the disgust of the proprietor of the magazine, from whom Johnson subsequently obtained very little work.

A year after abandoning these reports Johnson published his *Life of Savage*, one of the finest short biographies in the language. It was praised in Fielding's magazine in the highest terms: "A more engaging or more improving treatise, on all the excellencies and defects of human nature, is scarce to be found in our own, or, perhaps, any other language." But it did not sell, the extreme poverty in which Johnson was living was not mitigated, and three years later he agreed in desperation to compile a dictionary of the English language for a group of booksellers.

Johnson's indolence is a legend firmly rooted in the public mind, and it is true that his melancholia produced a lethargy which paralysed him during long periods. But his energy, when he shook off his lethargy, was stupendous, and there is no single achievement in letters which surpasses for range of effort and minuteness of application the production of this dictionary, the first of any merit in our language. Yet it was a melancholy task for a man of genius to grapple with, and the reflections with which he tried to console himself reveal how he shrank from it. Though not a splendid employment, he wrote in the preliminary prospectus, it was a useful one. Though it could not make his life envied, it would keep it innocent; it would awaken no passion, engage him in no quarrels (a rash forecast), and expose him to no temptation from flattery.

Had he not been hampered both by his constitutional melancholy and by the indifference with which the public had received his *London* and his *Life of Savage*, he would have filled the seven years occupied by the *Dictionary* with original work. At the risk of prejudicing the esteem in which the English hold Johnson, it is necessary to point out that he valued literary fame. In his talk he was sometimes cynical, in order to hide his disappointments, and everyone knows his remark that no man ever wrote except for money. But in his writings he was always sincere. A nation's authors, he says in the Preface to the *Dictionary*, are its chief glory, and he continues: "Whether I shall add anything by my own writings to the reputation of English literature must be left to time."

While he was at work on the *Dictionary*, he wrote the essays of the *Rambler* and *The Vanity of Human Wishes*. If Johnson's talk had not been allowed to overshadow his writings, the genius in these two productions would be more widely recognized. There is no verse between Milton and Wordsworth with such weight and depth as Johnson's in *The Vanity of Human Wishes*, and there are no essays in English, except Bacon's, comparable for wisdom with the best in the *Rambler*. As Johnson's popularity largely derives from the belief that he was an extraordinary specimen of an ordinary man, a John Bull with a voice which enabled him to roar down the opinions of those who did not share the prejudices of the herd, it will be of interest to quote his view of the barbarous penal code of his time, as he expressed it in the *Rambler*: "Since experience of past times gives us little reason to hope that any reformation will be effected by a periodical havock of our fellow beings, perhaps it will not be useless to consider what consequences might arise from relaxations of the law, and a more rational and equitable adaptation of penalties to offences. . . . And whatever epithets of reproach or contempt this compassion may incur from those who confound cruelty with firmness, I know not if any wise man would wish it less powerful, or less extensive."

Except in the heat of talk, or when some nerve inflamed by his secret suffering was touched, Johnson was wise, human and tolerant in his judgments. This bulwark of social institutions, as he has generally been represented, wrote as follows to Dr. Taylor, a clergyman who had quarrelled with his wife: "Any incident that makes a man the talk and spectacle of the world without any addition to his honour is naturally vexatious, but talks and looks are all the evils which this domestic revolution has brought upon you. I knew that you and your wife lived unquietly together, I find that the provocations were greater than I had known, and do not see what you have to regret but that you did not separate in a very short time after you were united." His views on filial obligations were equally unconventional. Parents, he said, were not entitled, merely as parents, to the respect and gratitude of their children. The parent's moral right over his child could arise only from his kindness, and his civil right only from his money.

The popular conception of Johnson as a cantankerous though amusing old bigot derives partly from Boswell, but chiefly from Macaulay. It was Boswell's habit to prod Johnson until he gave out an angry roar, which was duly noted down by Boswell, to be subsequently conned by posterity as a deliberate pronouncement on some complex question of social or sexual ethics. Macaulay took Boswell's subtle and delightful caricature and reproduced it with all its subtlety and charm wiped out. His famous essay, written in the flood-tide of Whig optimism over a world rapidly being transformed into paradise by steam and the merchants of Manchester, was intended to illustrate the obscurantism of an eighteenth century Tory, but is now interesting only as a revelation of what a fashionable philosophy looks like when it has ceased to be fashionable. Macaulay could not understand a man who believed not in the progress of a nation but in the virtue of the individual. Macaulay, in short, was what Johnson is generally believed to be, the spokesman of the herd, and in this capacity he resented Johnson's realistic view of mankind. Johnson, he said, judged everyone from a narrow insular standpoint, and held that civilization ceased outside a radius of ten miles from Fleet Street. What Johnson really held was that there is more intelligence concentrated in a great capital than diffused over the countryside. He was not a fanatical Londoner, and would have travelled widely, had he not been prevented by his poverty. The first use he made of his pension was to go to Devonshire with Reynolds, and during the remaining twenty-two years of his life he allowed no year to pass without some expedition out of London. He went with Boswell to the Hebrides, and with the Thrales to North Wales and Paris. When he was nearly seventy he tried to persuade Boswell to accompany him up the Baltic, and he planned to visit Italy with the Thrales, and even considered "taking a ramble" to India on his own. He was interested in everything that concerned humanity, though he did not delude himself with the hope of finding, whether in London or at the furthest extremes of the earth, any evidence that wise and good men were plentiful. His saying that for anything he could see most foreigners were fools has often been quoted against him. But it was only an ungrudging extension to the inhabitants of other lands of a conclusion he had already come to about the inhabitants of his own.

Johnson's wife died when he was halfway through the Dictionary. She was twenty years his senior, and perhaps one of his inducements to marry her was the fact that she was past child-bearing. He had suffered so much from his inherited and acquired disabilities that he may have resolved not to hand them on. It is significant that while he ignored attacks on his writings, he flared up when he heard that Foote proposed to mimic his personal peculiarities on the stage, and wrote to the comedian to say that, as the theatre was intended for the reformation of vice, he would be present at Foote's performance with a stick, and would correct him before the audience—a collaboration in which Foote was not public-spirited enough to assist.

After the death of his wife, who had shielded him from the terrors which afflicted him in solitude, Johnson took Miss Anna Williams, a crotchety spinster, into his house, and in later years added other inmates, partly out of charity and partly for the sake of their company. He was forty-two when his wife died and fifty-three when he was granted the pension which put an end to his struggles for money and gave him the opportunities for talk to which he owes the greater part of his fame. It is often said that, but for Boswell, he would be forgotten, for, it is urged, no one reads him nowadays. This argument seems to imply that a great many people read his contemporaries and immediate predecessors. It is a cheering notion, for which one would like some evidence. In default of such evidence one may assume that, if there had been no Boswell, Johnson would be read as much or as little as Dryden or Pope or Swift, apart from *Gulliver's Travels*, which has become a nursery book. If Boswell has made any difference to the numbers of persons who read Johnson, he has diminished them, by putting Johnson's talk into competition with his writings. Had Boswell not existed, Johnson would still be known as the greatest literary figure between Swift and Carlyle, and his *Rasselas*, his *Lives of the Poets*, his poems and his essays would still have their place among the classics of the language.

One may go further and say that even without Boswell Johnson would be the most famous of English talkers. In the *Life* and the *Tour to the Hebrides*, Johnson and Boswell form a pair unrivalled for humour and richness in all literature, except perhaps in the first part of *Don Quixote*. The marvellous charm of this dramatization has eclipsed all the other reports of Johnson's talk. Had Boswell never lived, someone would have compiled from Mrs. Thrale, Fanny Burney, Hawkins, Miss Reynolds, Hannah More, Anna Seward and half a dozen others a volume which in detail, though not in its total impression, would have equalled Boswell. Mrs. Thrale, in especial, caught the peculiar character of Johnson's talk almost as skilfully as Boswell. One day, she narrates, Johnson was advising a youth on his education, and "there arose some talk about animals, and their divisions into oviparous and viviparous; 'And the cat here, sir,' said the youth who wished for instruction; 'pray in which class is she?' Our Doctor's patience and desire of doing good began now to give way to the natural roughness of his temper. 'You would do well (said he) to look for some person to be always about you, sir, who is capable of explaining such matters, and not come to us (there were some literary friends present as I recollect) to know whether the cat lays eggs or not: get a discreet man to keep you company, there are many who would be glad of your table and fifty pounds a year.' "

In the ease and fame of his later years Johnson regarded the world more complacently than when he was struggling for money and recognition. No one, however sincere, can judge life without being influenced by his circumstances, and the respect for the world which Johnson often expressed in his talk was the inevitable echo of the respect which the world paid to him after a Scotch opportunist had, for political reasons, picked him out for official recognition as a man of letters. But his inner life, his loneliness, his fears and his struggle to perfect himself, remained almost untouched till his death. In spite of his travels, and his visits to the Thrales and Dr. Taylor, he still passed most of his time with his poor dependents and in the exercise of his charity among the destitute. Within a few years of his death, he wrote a letter to Mrs. Thrale which brings us nearer to him than any record of his talk. The subject was a poor man who had worked with

him on the *Dictionary* twenty years earlier, and whom he had
continued to befriend in the intervening years. "Poor Peyton
expired this morning. He probably during many years, for
which he sat starving by the bed of his wife, not only useless
but almost motionless, condemned by poverty to personal
attendance, and by the necessity of such attendance chained
down to poverty—he probably thought often how lightly he
should tread the path of life without his burthen. Of this
thought the admission was unavoidable, and the indulgence
might be forgiven to frailty and distress. His wife died at last,
and before she was buried he was seized by a fever, and is now
going to the grave." The art with which Johnson reconciled
his wealthy friends to the pain of parting with a guinea or
two for some struggling writer appears in Mrs. Thrale's:
"When he raised contributions for some distressed author, or
wit in want, he often made us more than amends by diverting
descriptions of the lives they were then passing in corners
unseen by anybody but himself." Of the "wits in want" helped
by Johnson, the most famous is Goldsmith. Johnson sold
The Vicar of Wakefield for him, supported his election as one
of the nine original members of the Literary Club, and in the
following year revised and added to *The Traveller*, the poem
which gave Goldsmith his first success with the public. Goldsmith owed a great deal to Johnson's thought. The Vicar of
Wakefield's speech on the severity of the penal code, for
example, is simply an expansion of Johnson's essay in the
Rambler. But his genius for expression was so delicate and
varied that he probably accepted Johnson's assistance with *The
Traveller* only because he did not dare to reject it. Johnson
overpowered him with his self-confidence and readiness in
talk. "Goldsmith," Miss Reynolds records, "always seemed
to be overawed by him, particularly when in company with
people of any consequence, as if impressed with fear of disgrace." But although Johnson was ruffled by what he called

Goldsmith's "malice towards him", and Goldsmith resented Johnson's domineering manner, each in his calmer moments had the highest appreciation of the other. Goldsmith, Johnson said, was a man who, whatever he wrote, wrote it better than any other man could do; and Goldsmith said: "Johnson, to be sure, has a roughness of manner; but no man alive has a more tender heart. He has nothing of the bear but his skin."

The chief difference which the freedom bestowed by his pension made to him may be seen by comparing his two principal works, *Rasselas* and *The Lives of the Poets*. *Rasselas* was written in his fiftieth year, shortly before the pension, the *Lives* when he was seventy. *Rasselas* has far less ease and variety than the *Lives*, though the subject admitted of as much invention and picturesqueness as Voltaire's *Candide* or *Gulliver's Travels*. But its reflections on life have a wisdom and balance not to be found in Voltaire or Swift, and there is a solemn music in its finest passages which reveals the poetry embedded beneath Johnson's melancholy. There is no nobler passage in our prose than Imlac's valediction to the desires and ambitions of the world: "Praise is to an old man an empty sound. I have neither mother to be delighted with the reputation of her son, nor wife to partake the honours of her husband. . . . My retrospect of life recalls to my view many opportunities of good neglected, much time squandered upon trifles, and more lost in idleness and vacancy. I leave many great designs unattempted, and many great attempts unfinished. My mind is burdened with no heavy crime, and therefore I compose myself to tranquillity; endeavour to abstract my thoughts from hopes and cares which, though reason knows them to be vain, still try to keep their old possession of the heart, expect, with serene humility, that hour which nature cannot long delay, and hope to possess in a better state that happiness which here I could not find, and that virtue which here I have not attained."

SAMUEL JOHNSON

In *The Lives of the Poets*, which incidentally were not written for money, Johnson's interest in the varieties of human character, overlaid during his long struggle, reveals itself. At a distance of one hundred and fifty years the justice and sympathy with which he treated his subjects are apparent, though less than due credit has as yet been paid him as the first English biographer to substitute truth for eulogy. But at the time his sincerity caused extreme resentment in literary circles, where it has always been the practice to balance malice towards the living with magnanimity towards the indifferent dead. Anna Seward cried out against "the turbulent fierceness and jealousy of his unbridled passions". Cowper, when he read the essay on Milton, exclaimed that he would thrash Johnson's old jacket till his pension jingled—a threat which it would have been alarming to see Cowper trying to put into execution. At the Thrales a Mr. Pepys remonstrated with Johnson over his innocuous sketch of Lyttelton, and Mrs. Montagu also rushed to Lyttelton's aid. Johnson's defence is recorded by Hawkins. It was, he said, the business of a biographer to give a complete account of his subject, and to discriminate him from all other persons by his peculiarities of character and sentiment.

The close of Johnson's life was embittered by Mrs. Thrale's marriage with Piozzi, but he died tranquilly. What a friend said on hearing of his death has been said of many others in the first shock of loss, but its peculiar applicability to Johnson will be more and more realized as time passes. "Johnson is dead. Let us go to the next best: there is nobody; no man can be said to put you in mind of Johnson."

15

WILKES

(1727–1797)

by Douglas West

ALIKE in his good and his bad qualities, John Wilkes was a smaller man than most of those equally prominent in the eighteenth century. His faults sprang from lack of character; his virtues were commonplace, and his talents those of a clever, witty writer and talker with few settled convictions and little power of original thought. He was not a man of blameless or edifying private life; but it suited the book of many of his contemporaries and most later historians to exaggerate his frailties. Wilkes never tried to excuse his private life, and he deserves to be judged by his public career, about which it is harder to be censorious.

For ten years he fought bravely and with good humour against formidable odds, and at every stage the issues in dispute were of the liveliest concern to every man and woman in the kingdom. A victim of extravagant injustice, he naturally demanded first of all specific redress. But he represented, however shyly, a cause, that of civil liberty, upon which Englishmen of all classes felt deeply. The persecution of Wilkes by a resentful king and a pliant House of Commons was trivial compared with the terrible retribution visited upon champions of freedom in several European countries in our own day. But the sensitiveness of the public conscience to abuse of power and acts of violence has always been dependent upon time and place. A majority of George the Third's subjects were shocked by their ruler's treatment of Wilkes; by most current twentieth century standards, they were unduly shocked.

Wilkes was lucky enough not to live in an age of blunted sensibilities, and of communities incurably fickle towards either a man or a cause. He never came up against a blank wall of indifference; those who were not his foes became for the most part his energetic allies, however strong their dislike of him or their disapprobation of his conduct in general.

The long and heated conflict of which he bore the brunt aroused a storm of popular indignation, lowered the prestige of Parliament, made every second Englishman a rebel at heart, and gave George the Third reason to fear for the safety of his throne. None of these results was inevitable when in April, 1763, the two secretaries of state, with the full approval of the King, sent their officers, armed with a general warrant, to arrest John Wilkes, search his house, and seize his private papers.

That was a blunder. General warrants, in which the names of persons to be apprehended were not specified, were anathema in England. They vested in Government agents a discretionary power to pry wherever suspicion or malice might lead them, and to strike at political opponents in the dark. No judgment has ever been more warmly applauded in this country than that of Lord Camden declaring general warrants illegal, and denouncing them as "rods of iron for the chastisement of the people of Britain". The crowd's cheers for Camden were even louder than those it gave Wilkes, who came out of court with £1,000 damages in his pocket.

Camden deserved those cheers. He was the most honest and respected judge on the Bench, and the only one at that time with an international reputation. Distinguished foreigners who had listened to Pitt at Westminster, and Garrick at Drury-lane, were taken to hear Camden as the third wonder of London. He had ruled earlier that Wilkes's privilege as an M.P. forbade his arrest on a libel charge, and had refused to commit himself on the subject of general warrants. There were, in fact, bad precedents, and Camden, an ambitious man, must have been tempted to shelter behind them. By giving a verdict for Wilkes he made an enemy of George the Third, the fount of office and honour. Not even royal displeasure could keep a man of Camden's force and prestige from reaching the Woolsack. But at the height of the dispute over the Middlesex Election six years later he resigned from the Cabinet rather than appear to be even a passively consenting party to the continued persecution of Wilkes; and largely as a result of this gesture he remained out of office for twelve years.

A curious perversity of fate linked the utterly dissimilar careers of the two men—the proud, uncorrupt judge and the notorious *guerrilist* of politics. Camden strongly disapproved of Wilkes, and cut him dead when they met as private citizens. But at Westminster not even Burke fought for the cause of Wilkes and the Middlesex freeholders with more vehemence, or a loftier appeal to principle. Camden was the greatest lawyer-statesman of the eighteenth century, and held high office long after Wilkes was an extinct volcano.

The grounds upon which Wilkes was arrested under that infamous general warrant have been dismissed by most historians as altogether trumpery. In a large part of Europe to-day physical and not verbal lashes are the accepted weapons of political controversy, and even in this country the lampooner has been forced out of business for lack of an audience attuned to invective, and by a well justified fear of the law of libel. No daily or weekly newspaper in England would to-day print paragraphs of much milder tenor than those to which George

the Third and his ministers took exception in No. 45 of the
North Briton. Wilkes, after a violent attack on Cabinet policy,
went on to accuse the King, by implication, of countenancing
an "infamous fallacy" in the Speech from the Throne, and
added, parenthetically, that the honour of the Crown was
"sunk even to prostitution".

This followed a number of articles in which Wilkes, with
elaborate innuendo, had hinted at a liaison between the King's
mother and the then Prime Minister, Lord Bute. Such scur-
rilities had naturally wounded George the Third, always the
most filial of sons; and any astute modern lawyer could find a
criminal libel in almost every line. But the eighteenth century
had a less squeamish attitude towards political journalism. The
London apprentices and shopkeepers who cheered Wilkes
as he drove through the streets of the capital regarded him as
a man who was being unfairly punished for writing what
most people were thinking.

Wilkes, when he became a popular hero overnight, was in
danger of being sunk by his debts and profligate habits. He
was thirty-six. He had for six years represented Aylesbury
in the House of Commons as a Chathamite Whig, but he was a
lightweight in political life. Socially, he had made more mark.
He had, as Dr. Johnson testified later, "great variety of talk,
and the manners of a gentleman." His flow of wit and pleasan-
tries, and repertoire of highly-spiced anecdotes, made him
acceptable in any company except the most censorious. It is
noteworthy perhaps that, though he might keep their husbands
up half the night, he was on the dinner list of very few leading
London hostesses.

But Wilkes was attractive to women, despite a pronounced
squint and features irregular to the point of ugliness. He
could always, he said, talk away his face in half an hour. His
amours were notorious. He never attempted either to excuse
or conceal them, but he appears to have conducted them with

rather more scruple than most men of his generation. His marriage to a lethargic heiress ten years his senior had ended in a legal separation, after he had played the open-handed country squire on his wife's money, become a colonel of militia, and found his feet in a society of rakes. He was known as a boon companion of some of the most dissolute men of the day, and as a frequent guest at the orgies in Medmenham Abbey (which, we may be sure, lost nothing in hearsay). He was as lax in his personal finance as he was afterwards puncti- lious in the handling of public moneys.

A distiller's son, and by birth and early upbringing a Dissen- ter, he had little hope of ever climbing into the charmed circle of hereditary legislators, though Pitt and the Grenville con- nection had smoothed his entry into politics, and encouraged him to believe that a place of profit would soon be within his grasp. He had acquired a reputation for never being quite serious about anything, which then and later did him much harm. He could never resist a jest, however ill-timed, and he invariably ascribed the worst possible motives to his own actions. He possessed neither the arts nor the humbug of a demagogue. Wilkes was, throughout his career, a very modest man, who neither courted nor overvalued the frenzied adula- tion he received.

He was no iconoclast. The twelve Wilkite M.P.'s who later sat in the House of Commons went, like their constituents, far beyond the ideas of their titular leader in their advocacy of parliamentary reform, and in their tirades against corruption in high places. Wilkes, as he told his king, when at last the two were on speaking terms, was never a Wilkite; never, that is to say, in favour of drastic reforms, or in genuine sympathy with men who regarded him as a chosen instrument for humb- ling the Crown and Parliament. Probably the truest thing he ever said about himself was that accident made him a patriot, or ostentatious "friend to liberty". He had no quarrel with either the social or political system as such, provided he received a fair share of the good things going. Failure to obtain the embassy or governorship which he believed to be his due was his main reason for founding the *North Briton*. It is pleasant to reflect that he found, after the years of stress, just the sort of snug sinecure upon which his heart had always been set. As City Chamberlain, making neat little harangues in honour of the eminent warriors and pro-consuls who came to the Mansion House to receive the City's freedom, he was more at his ease than he ever was as a tribune of the people.

But in 1763 there was no question of snug sinecures for Wilkes. Instead of wisely staying their hands, and allowing the alarm they had caused to subside, George the Third and his parliamentary friends proceeded to deal blow after blow against him. They struck at Wilkes through his moral character, admittedly his weakest spot, as a means of discrediting him with his middle-class supporters. Government agents had obtained from one of Wilkes's printers a copy of a grossly indecent parody, the "Essay on Woman"; thirteen copies had been struck off on Wilkes's press, but none had been offered for sale. It is doubtful whether Wilkes was the author, though he probably had a hand in the notes, ascribed very imprudently to Bishop Warburton, the irascible editor of Pope. His opponents gave him no opportunity of denying or admitting authorship.

The Government discharged both its barrels at him in one day. While the Commons by resolution denounced No. 45 of the *North Briton* (which Wilkes had indiscreetly reprinted) as a seditious libel, the Lords condemned the parody as an impious libel; some of their lordships had, however, relished its salacity well enough in the past, over supper-tables graced by Wilkes. He was now prosecuted and convicted in the Court of King's Bench; whereupon the House of Commons, ruling that he had forfeited his privilege, expelled him by a large majority of votes. Wilkes had already fled to Paris, where his daughter Polly, then and for the rest of his life the one person he really cared for, was at school.

Flight was imperative if he was not to be overwhelmed by catastrophe, and cannot be imputed to any want of moral or physical courage. In recent months Wilkes had twice faced a duellist's pistols, and at no time in his career were his stamina and fortitude ever in question. But as he did not return from Paris to receive sentence, he was declared an outlaw. That seemed to ruling-class England to complete his ruin; but he was only at the beginning of his fame.

During the next decade his name was seldom off English lips, and in the role of a champion of freedom he played everyone else off the stage. Chatham, little given to that kind of rant, might describe him as "a libeller of his King and a blasphemer of his God", and a timid Opposition refuse to come out boldly for his cause. But the King and Parliament did not represent the nation. Innumerable partisans, drawn from all classes, with a preponderance of homespun, kept Wilkes's name alive throughout his four years of exile. They realized that more was at stake than the vindication of a wronged man. There had been an arbitrary assault on personal liberty; isolated no doubt, and aimed at a man of ill repute, but a forerunner, if not checked, of more serious encroachments.

The impression that Wilkes had gained a moral victory was not confined to his own countrymen. In France profound thinkers like Diderot and d'Alembert welcomed him almost as a brother in arms; and from the American colonies future signatories of the Declaration of Independence wrote to him in the manner of diffident disciples to a venerated master. Carolina voted him £1,500 to pay his debts. Wilkes lived as a man of fashion in France and Italy on funds supplied by his English and American sympathisers. But he disliked exile, and he was always insolvent. Having failed to make his peace with his oppressors, he decided that he "must raise a dust or starve", and early in 1768 he landed at Dover.

He had chosen his moment well. A General Election was pending at a time of widespread discontent, at least as much economic as political in origin. The nation was in a mood for sweeping change, under any leader who could show the way and supply arguments and battle cries. When royal and ministerial folly silhouetted Wilkes in a new and dazzling light, all the malcontents in the kingdom rallied to him. The only genuine popular movement in the whole of the eighteenth century was thus, from the first, hopelessly sidetracked. It achieved, however, important results.

A sure instinct led Wilkes to London. The capital in that day was still democratic in spirit, and enjoyed more than nominal self-government; it was a much truer barometer than the House of Commons of the state of national feeling. As alderman, sheriff, and later Lord Mayor, Wilkes fought his battles during the next few years with the formidable backing of a commercial community stronger, in the last resort, than any ministry composed of the King's friends. Having failed to carry a City seat, he offered himself as an independent candidate to the freeholders of Middlesex. No modern politician could teach Wilkes much that he did not know about electioneering. He was returned at the head of the poll, and that night there were demonstrations in London. Exuberant partisans broke thousands of windows, shouted "Wilkes and Liberty" until they were hoarse, and chalked a symbolic No. 45 on every door.

Now began a conflict unsought by Wilkes, and unique in English constitutional history. He appealed against his outlawry; it was reversed on a technical point, but on the five-year-old conviction for libel he was sentenced to twenty-two months' imprisonment, and ordered to pay a fine of £1,000. Outside the court a crowd several thousands strong carried off

Wilkes in triumph to a tavern in Bishopsgate; he escaped in disguise, made his way to the prison, and knocked up the gaoler at midnight. From prison, in the incredibly lax conditions prevailing, Wilkes was able to circulate inflammatory appeals to his supporters, and to expose in print the Government's secret instructions to magistrates to suppress riots by gunfire. He thereby provided his opponents with a new weapon against him. The House of Commons, when it met, had before it a plain statement from George the Third that "the expulsion of Wilkes appears to be very essential, and must be effected". The Cabinet wavered, but obedient placemen carried by a substantial majority a motion to expel Wilkes which lumped together all his crimes, past and present, in one accumulated indictment.

The Middlesex freeholders immediately re-elected Wilkes; the House of Commons expelled him again, and passed a resolution declaring him incapable of being elected as a member of parliament. These unconstitutional proceedings aroused alarm and resentment throughout the country. The injustice done to Wilkes was so blatant, and the royal animus which inspired it so marked, that men of spirit and conscience in all classes became perforce his partisans. There was scarcely a day during his two years' imprisonment in which a modern editor could have kept Wilkes's name off the front page. His constituents were determined to return him as often as the House of Commons rejected him. When a third election had been annulled, and the writ issued for a fourth, the ministry put up a candidate, an adventurer named Luttrell. He polled one vote for every four given to Wilkes; but, by yet another resolution in defiance of the law and of freedom, he was declared the duly elected member for Middlesex.

For the next year or two English political life revolved round Wilkes. He was the most popular and cherished man in the country. The mob which shouted "Wilkes and no King" meant business. So did the deputations from the City wards and liveries which made their vigorous protests to George the Third under his own roof. Remonstrances against a policy known to be his, though attributed by custom to his ministers, poured in from half the towns and counties in the kingdom. Chatham emerged from retirement to loose his thunder in vindication of Wilkes and his constituents. The Whig opposition embraced the cause with alacrity, but would gladly have repudiated the man whose grievances were the talk of every tavern, workshop and counting-house in England. Wilkes, however, was the only name to conjure with. Burke was the first of the Whigs to realize that no party capital could be made out of the Middlesex Election except in close alliance with the national hero; tardy overtures were made to Wilkes in prison.

Those who held that the patriot was a deeply wronged man quite rightly refused to regard as a mitigating circumstance the astonishing indulgence shown to him as a captive. He was free to write what he liked, and see whom he liked; to give agreeable little dinner parties in the comfortable rooms set aside for his use, or entertain a woman friend at supper. Presents of wine, game, fruit and tobacco were lavished upon him by admirers on both sides of the Atlantic. The Supporters of the Bill of Rights raised £18,000 for him in as many months, and then dissolved, too bankrupt in funds and energy to support anything or anyone else. Wilkes came out of prison solvent for almost the first time in his life.

The leadership of a great popular movement was his for the taking. He was far and away the most popular man in the country. His effigy decorated trinkets and swung before inn doors. Apprentices got drunk in his honour, and the pious thanked God in their prayers for so sturdy a champion of liberty. He could rely, too, on the formidable support of the City of London and of the greatest orators in Parliament.

But he viewed with distaste the course marked out for him.

He was resolved to be member for Middlesex before he died, and to place high among constitutional axioms the principle that the nation's representatives should be chosen at the polling booth, and not in the House of Commons. But he meant to pursue his aims in his own way and his own time. "I have not," he wrote to his daughter soon after his release from prison, "been at either House, to avoid every pretence of a riot, or influencing their debates by a mob." Seven years fighting had taught him circumspection. He was unfitted by temperament to be a tribune of the people, and he was far too intelligent to assume a role he could not sustain. A career was open to him in municipal politics; and though he found civic dignities flat and the company of his colleagues tedious, he discharged with energy and public spirit his duties, first as Sheriff and then as Lord Mayor of London.

He played a congenial part in the City's campaign for the removal of the ban on newspaper reports of parliamentary proceedings; he committed to prison officers of the House of Commons who had invaded the jurisdiction of the City in their search for offending editors, and had the satisfaction not only of extending the liberties of the nation, but also of covering his oppressors with ridicule. In 1774 the Commons, preoccupied with war in America, tacitly allowed Wilkes to take his seat for Middlesex. His constituents continued to elect him for as long as he wished; but it was another eight years before he secured formal redress through an almost unanimous vote of the House condemning its former conduct as "subversive of the rights of the whole body of electors in this kingdom".

The main object of Wilkes's life was achieved. He remained for a decade or more a fairly prominent politician; in debates on the American war and on tolerance for Dissenters he spoke as wisely and magnanimously as Burke, though with far less force and grace. He never completely overcame the distrust which the House of Commons has always felt for any reputation acquired outside its own walls. He introduced a Bill for a redistribution of seats which anticipated parliamentary reform by a generation, but only his Wilkite followers, his "twelve apostles", gave it support. In the Gordon Riots of 1780, which threw London into confusion, Wilkes displayed conspicuous zeal for law and order, and defended the Bank of England at the head of an armed band of citizens from his ward. But the spectacle of Wilkes parading in the cocked hat, scarlet coat, and jack boots of a colonel of militia was distasteful to his humble adherents of earlier days; and they regarded his conduct, for which he was publicly thanked by the City authorities, as a betrayal of the democratic cause. He lost all vestige of popular sympathy when, a few years later, he gave his support to the Younger Pitt.

Wilkes was incapable of bearing rancour. He lived to be reconciled to all his chief opponents. Even George the Third had to admit that he had never met "so well bred a Lord Mayor". Respectable Wilkes could never be; a succession of indiscreet love affairs and a few scandals gave his detractors a weapon against him which they were not slow to use. But Wilkes sat tight in his post as City Chamberlain; he had a house in Grosvenor Square and a "villakin" in the Isle of Wight, friends among the great, and the status of a man of fashion. His last official act was to welcome Admiral Nelson as a freeman of the City. He died in 1797, not quite solvent, and chose the words for his epitaph: "a friend to liberty."

Most of the causes espoused or resisted by our forefathers appear to-day immeasurably more remote than that of which Wilkes was the foremost and persistent champion. The liberties which his long ordeal preserved from extinction are among our indispensable democratic safeguards. But at a time when freedom has more secret enemies than whole-hearted defenders, these liberties are not so secure that we can afford to take them for granted. Lord Camden's judgment condemning general warrants was quoted with distinctly opposite effect in the course of a quite recent controversy; the rapid encroachment of the executive, and the power of the modern caucus, have made serious inroads on the rights of electors to return whom they choose to the House of Commons. Many an obscure Wilkes has been in need of championship in recent years in England.

Wilkes was never left to fight his battles alone. At every stage of his persecution by the most powerful bodies in the kingdom he could count on the support of great numbers of his countrymen who strongly disapproved of his conduct, disliked him as a man, and were well aware that he had brought many of his troubles on himself. Freedom cannot survive in a community which discriminates between victims of injustice, and withholds its sympathy and succour from unorthodox, or positively discreditable martyrs. Wilkes was fortunate to live in an age sensitive to every infraction of liberty, and honest enough to put a cause before prejudice.

16

LORD CHESTERFIELD

(1694-1773)

by Bonamy Dobrée

IT is easy to understand why people either like Lord Chesterfield extremely well or detest him. The reason is that he possessed a very definite character, and stands for something distinct, a philosophy, an attitude towards life, which you either agree with or don't. It is almost impossible to be indifferent about him, very difficult to be fair one way or the other. Most people have disliked him intensely. There is, indeed, something repellent to the majority about the Horatian attitude of being equal to life, taking with singular calm the joys chance may bring, and the buffets fate may deal out. There is nothing, on the surface at least, romantic about it. For them Chesterfield's famous wit is chilly; they remember that he thought laughter vulgar, that he taught his son "the morals of a whore and the manners of a dancing master"; that he was not even perturbed by his own death. For them he epitomizes all that is repugnant in the eighteenth century outlook. One may think, however, that this is a rather shallow judgment, and it is to be noticed that those who for one reason or another have paid close attention to his letters, and followed the vagaries of his life, usually end by a feeling of affection for him, however cool they felt towards him at the beginning. It was so with Lord Carnarvon when he edited the *Letters to his Godson.* "I can honestly say," he wrote, "that I began my task with little interest, perhaps with prejudice; I have ended it with strong interest, sympathy, and appreciation." If one delves below the surface to get at the real Philip Dormer Stanhope, fourth Earl of Chesterfield, one finds that he is not so easily dismissed.

He was born in 1694, a seven-months' child, maybe as a consequence weakly, which would account for his having passed his early years in London, under the care of his grandmother, Lady Halifax, and not at his family house, Bretby, in Derbyshire. Perhaps it was just as well, for though he never knew the care of a mother—she died in 1708—he would have gained nothing from his father, a deaf, crotchety Jacobite, who from the first felt an aversion towards his son. Instead, he flourished as a precocious infant in what was left of the brilliant Whig society his grandfather, George Savile, the Marquis of Halifax, had so splendidly adorned. Besides being rendered altogether urban, he acquired the Savile outlook, the Whiggism, the scepticism, the love of wit and of grace, and the integrity: he also acquired a delight in all things French, and an ineradicable feeling that London was necessarily a trifle provincial. He was a violently ambitious child, already at an early age in alarming control of his passions: one would almost say that he had been born with the idea in his mind of what he wanted to become.

At first blush, stated crudely, it sounds a callow, a ridiculous ambition: he wanted to be a fine gentleman. But what he meant by this was something complicated and difficult, involving stern discipline and long years of consciously directed training. It was a queer mixture of the fine gentleman of Restoration Comedy and the Roman patrician that he wanted to achieve, and saw that he might achieve. From the first he had a great

deal in his hand: he would in due course be an Earl, and be
tolerably rich. But there were physical defects which stood in
the way of his being a splendid figure. He was squat, of "the
ridiculous Stanhope size", he was able to say in his later years:
he was once called "a stunted giant", and George II referred
to him as a "dwarf baboon"—for if his body was small, his
head was enormous, and he was by no means so handsome as
the portrait painters made him appear. His eyes and head
were fine, certainly, but his eyebrows were too thick, his
teeth were discoloured—he used to draw his upper lip over
them to hide them—and his voice was raucous, rising sometimes to a scream. In the brilliant social world which he wanted
to dazzle, these were defects which would have to be overcome.

All in good time, however: first he had to acquire positive
qualities. At Cambridge, where he did not stay the whole
course, besides enjoying the usual amusements of the *jeunesse
dorée*, and acquiring a certain knowledge of law together
with a fair grounding in the Classics varied by dabbling in
anatomy, he laboured at the art of oratory, modelling himself
on the best patterns, learning by heart, translating, enunciating.
Then, in 1714, he set out for the Grand Tour, beginning with
the Hague, where he ingratiated himself with the Duke and
Duchess of Marlborough, then in virtual exile; but he curtailed
his tour on account of the death of Queen Anne, and made
for the town which was throughout life his Mecca—Paris.

Paris is important in connection with Chesterfield: he was
a born Parisian: a graceful society, where beauty moved and
wit delighted, and proofs of kindness were not too difficult
to obtain, was his idea of Paradise—at least of an earthly one.
If only he could make himself worthy of it! Success there
would repay infinite care and trouble. Luckily he already
knew French, could speak and write it fluently and correctly,
even if there was always a trace of Norman accent in his

speech: it only remained for him to overcome his physical disabilities by acquiring perfect manners—the Graces as he came afterwards to call them. He was very shy when he began, reduced almost to tears when a charming accomplished lady unbent to guide him in the right path: he stammered and stuttered, moved awkwardly, was painfully conscious of his defects. But soon his ambition conquered his timidity, and before long he was admitted to be a shining member of Parisian society. He had polished himself till he shone.

A little later, thanks to his birth, and the good offices of his cousin, General, afterwards Earl, Stanhope, he was returned to Parliament, obtained the place of Gentleman of the Bed-chamber to the Prince of Wales, and rapidly became a figure in society. Yet society did not wholly accept him, could not quite take for granted this strange, too well-mannered little figure, so conscious of itself, without being self-conscious. He was no great conqueror, but did not mind conquests being imputed to him: he gambled wildly; he would occasionally desert society for the company of Addison, Arbuthnot, Pope, or Swift; and wherever he went he achieved a resounding reputation for wit. He was, indeed, too fond of his wit: it did him irreparable harm in some quarters, for it was apt to be pungent; and he foolishly antagonized the Princess of Wales, afterwards Queen Caroline, who, even when he meant to conciliate her, was never quite sure that he wasn't bantering her. He also antagonized Walpole: but what did Walpole matter? He would go as soon as George I died, and then his own master, George II, would come to the throne.

Thus everything seemed to be shaping very well for him in 1726 when his father died, and he succeeded to the Earldom and the estates. But when in the next year George I died, it turned out that Walpole did not go, and that it had been a sad mistake to antagonize him. So instead of being at once made a Privy Councillor, given the Garter and an important political post, months were allowed to elapse before the first event took place, the second was never mentioned at all, and the post he was offered and accepted in 1728 was only that of Ambassador to the Hague. That, however, was the most important capital in Europe after London and Paris.

For a political career was the other part of Chesterfield's plan for himself: it was part of his ideal to become a great figure in the State, one of unblemished honesty, great oratorical skill, and undubitable power. The first two parts of this ideal he attained, not absolutely perhaps, but to the extent that only genius could better: in the third part he failed—not absolutely here either, but enough to fall obviously short of the prepared plan. The opening experience, however, was extremely promising: Chesterfield was an excellent ambassador; he carried through some difficult and very tiresome negotiations, and half-way through his time, during a visit home, he was given the Garter and made Lord Steward. He had temporarily made his peace with Walpole.

In 1732 he left the Hague, returning to the life he proposed to lead so brilliantly in London, and to oratorical triumphs in the House of Lords. But he could not work in harness under Walpole, and, moreover, disapproved of certain measures, so it can be no surprise to us, though it made some stir at the time, that in 1733 he was dismissed his court post. He then joined the opposition—with Pulteney, Carteret and others of the same sort, while Bolingbroke, whom he extravagantly admired, hovered in the background. But when at length, in 1742, Walpole fell, Chesterfield remained in opposition: in his view too many of the old gang were left. He was virtually leader of the anti-court party, and when, in 1744, Carteret was forced to resign, it was impossible to exclude him from the Broad-Bottomed ministry, though he had by this time made himself violently obnoxious to the King. He therefore accepted the viceroyalty of Ireland, preceded by an especial mission to the Hague which he accomplished successfully.

Ireland was a triumph for him. He is perhaps, the most successful viceroy in history, possibly for the reason implied by his preference for being called "the Irish Lord Lieutenant" rather than "Lord Lieutenant of Ireland". At all events, by a mixture of understanding, tolerance, humanity, with a threat of severity, he managed to keep Ireland quiet during the Jacobite rebellion of '45: he improved its condition, and when he left, was lamented by the whole population.

He was only there for a year, however, and soon after his return, somewhat against his better judgment, he accepted the seals of Secretary of State, becoming one of the Big Four of the cabinet responsible for England during the War of the Austrian Succession. But he was no match for the fussy, cunning Duke of Newcastle, past-master in political management: nor for that brilliant lawyer, Lord Hardwicke, nor for Pelham, Prime Minister and Newcastle's brother, slow, and averse to taking risks. Chesterfield was no politician: he could not work with other people. Given a free hand as ambassador or viceroy, he surpassed expectation: so though he was right upon the issue wherein he disagreed with his colleagues—namely on what the Dutch would or could do—he could not persuade them to his views: and in 1748, in disgust and weariness, not without a hint of petulance, he resigned the Seals, and retired from political life. Except, on request, as an adviser, he never took a hand in the game again.

Yet now his real life-work was beginning in earnest. But before we look at that, let us see to what extent, so far, he had created the personage of his imagination. That he was a famous figure was certain: socially he was known as a man of perfect manners, of great if dangerous wit, with a neat hand at occasional articles in the press, and for fabricating *vers de société*: as a politician he had achieved fame as a great orator, and a deserved reputation for incorruptibility: but if his hands were clean he cannot be absolved of factious behaviour during his period of opposition, and many had doubted the wisdom of his accepting the Seals. He had had *voix au chapitre*, as he used to say, but it had dwindled to a futile whisper. "As his going in produced no good effects," Lady Westmorland wrote on his resignation, "his going out can produce no bad ones." The truth was that there was a certain lack of robust vitality in him: he was always sceptical, dubious of the value of political effort, and no doubt applauded one of his grandfather Halifax's maxims which queried whether "business", as politics was called, was a fitting occupation for a man of sense. "I lack the two great springs of ambition, vanity and avarice," he once told Lord Marchmont, and by the time he had reached middle age, this was true. Yet if his stature was not universally recognized at home, abroad he was considered the greatest English genius of the age, by such people as Montesquieu, Fontenelle, Voltaire, and— Frederick the Great! and whatever vanity he had left must have been flattered, when, in 1755, he was made a foreign member of a French learned society, the Académie des Inscriptions et Belles Lettres.

It was at this stage of his life that he settled down to become so splendid an example of a certain outlook on life, an example of a type which always persists, but could only come to recognized perfection in the eighteenth century, permeated as it was with a neo-classical ideal:—a kind of stoicism, tempered by Renaissance ideas, coloured by scepticism, based on the remains of the aristocratic idea. In conformity with the Renaissance idea he built himself Chesterfield House, patronized the arts, himself wrote a few elegant articles: he had accomplished a part of his Roman idea by serving the State honourably and without personal gain: his aristocracy was shown by his active sentiment of *noblesse oblige*. As to his stoicism, that was shown in cheerfully bearing his deafness and giddiness, and, since he was largely deprived of the society of his fellows, in compensating himself as best he could by cultivating that of his "fellow vegetables", the melons he raised so assiduously in his country house at Blackheath.

It sounds as unromantic as his marriage in 1733 had been, when he allied himself—the expression is deliberate—with Melusina de Schulemberg, Countess of Yarmouth, a natural daughter of George I. She was much of his age, he can have had small hope of children from her: but, as he put it, she looked after his battered body and repaired his battered fortunes: it was quite honestly and openly, a marriage of convenience, and there is no reason to suppose that either he or his wife regretted it.

But romance, which he had so carefully eschewed all his life, had its revenge. When in Holland in 1731 or so, he had found a mistress, a governess called Du Bouchet, who in 1732 bore him a son, Philip. It was not the lady, but the son, who was the instrument of revenge selected by romance. All his suppressed feelings, all his emotions, all his frustrated ambitions and desires (for he felt these, even if he conquered them), his natural affection, the love of which he had been starved, concentrated themselves upon the youth. And the curious romance took a curious, though quite logical form. Young Philip was to be the perfectly constructed person: education could do all: had not Locke proved it? Never mind if the small boy was squat, lumpish, rather heavy-minded, even dull: these things could be conquered; the Corinthian pillar, in Chesterfield's own phrases, would rise upon the Tuscan base; the clod would be endowed with the Titian colouring, the Guido graces would animate it.

To us it seems pitiable, and absurd, especially when we think of the vast spate of letters that poured out from the father, from the time the child was five. As a free man, as

Viceroy, as Secretary of State, the Earl's spare time was wholly given to inditing tremendous educational epistles, now exhorting, now cajoling, again threatening or appealing. The boy was sent to Westminster, then, very young, on an extended Grand Tour in the hands of a pedantic parson. He acquired languages, living and dead, legal and historical learning—but when it came to politeness, manners, *le liant*, the graces, "decorum", he was woefully lacking. Even Paris did little good—for not all the father's wheedling could induce the son to have an affair with a clever married woman who would teach him all. It was a disappointment. And then other shocks occurred. There were disagreeable incidents in various ways on account of the young man's illegitimate birth, both at a foreign court, and at home, where this was considered a bar to a good appointment abroad. There was still Parliament, of course. Chesterfield paid handsomely for a seat, but Philip's attempt at oratory was a miserable failure, and he could never be induced to try again.

Chesterfield bore up, even when the youth was appointed to a poor position at Hamburg, which Chesterfield had once held up as derisory. Nevertheless, Chesterfield thought, there was still much left: he could get at his son's inner self, and he implored him, as a lover might implore his mistress, to let him into his mind. But the young man was strangely reserved, and small wonder; for when, a couple of years later, he died, it was found that he was secretly married and had two sons. Chesterfield gave no sign of the terrible wound this news inflicted on him: he wrote charmingly to the widow, and took the two children under his care.

Luckily, before this, he had had another charge on whom he could now lavish his affection, to whom he could generously give the wisdom his years had accumulated. This was his godson and heir, a cousin, also Philip Stanhope; and another bulky volume of letters tells the tale of the watchful affection.

These epistles are wholly delightful. There is less strain, less passionate hankering about them than in the letters to the son: worldly wisdom, stoic duty, are tempered by a wider kindliness and sympathy: the writer is more humane, and every youth would be the better for reading them.

Indeed, it is really in his old age that Chesterfield shows at his best: the work of creating a perfect figure had been accomplished; and the deaf, aged, half-crippled Earl stands now for the eighteenth century at its best. He is still brilliant and witty on occasion: but there is no longer anything puerile about him, or harsh. He never complained: he went on genially, almost gaily. The stoic attitude has been softened down, harmonized, impregnated with the ideals of Christianity as far as a professed Deist may hold them. Chesterfield had become the perfect humanist, wise, tolerant, self-controlled, regarding himself primarily as a member of society, and thinking the creation of a humane, civilized community as the ultimate endeavour of every sensible human being. Old friends loved to come and talk with him, old enemies, such as Horace Walpole, became his friends, the young were not ashamed to be instructed by him: he was easy, he was charitable: in fact his characteristic at this period is kindliness.

It was easy enough to laugh at him, yet he was universally respected, for in an age which was shamelessly corrupt (though not to the extent that is sometimes supposed), he was a shining example of honesty and intellectual integrity. There was not an atom of cant about him. He never pretended to believe what he did not believe, nor to feel what he did not feel. He hated the vices of his age, debauchery, drunkenness, and gambling, though the last vice he could not himself resist; yet he conquered it, and eschewed playing while he was a Minister of State. He was never a prig, nor a snob: the aristocracy he admired was one of taste, feeling, behaviour, not that of birth, for which he had an honest contempt. His ideal of a gentleman is almost that of Newman: there is nothing silly nor ungenerous about it.

His aloofness was irritating to his less balanced contemporaries. It was amusing, no doubt, for him to joke about himself, to say: "Tyrawley and I have been dead these two years, but we don't care to have it known;" or, excusing himself to a foreign ambassador when he was about to take his afternoon drive, to say he had to attend a rehearsal of his funeral. But surely, they thought, there is something wrong about being so detached—so dreadfully to lack the feeling of awe. So when he died, when his books and the letters to his son were published, his survivors, especially the ladies, tore him to pieces. It was the last revenge romance took upon him: but if, according to his somewhat vague expectation, his personality survived to know about it, he will have smiled a little, perhaps cracked a joke, and advised his son to notice that that was how the world behaved.

17

LORD MANSFIELD

(1705-1793)

by JOHN SPARROW

§ 1

THERE was a time when engravings and casts representing Lord Mansfield were to be found "almost in every cottage in Great Britain". To-day it is doubtful whether, except to lawyers and political historians, his name evokes a picture or recalls a fact. Yet for more than thirty years he was the most serious rival, in both Houses, of the elder Pitt; he showed himself to be, in the opinion of a critic both severe and well-informed, one of the greatest judges who have ever appeared in England; and he contributed as much as any single man to the development of the Common Law. Nor was Mansfield only a considerable figure in the public life of the eighteenth century, he was a link between that age and the age which succeeded it. "Most of all," says Lord Campbell (by far his best biographer*), writing in the

---

*The present account inevitably owes a very great deal to Campbell's *Lives of the Chief Justices*. I have studied also the accounts in Welsby's *Eminent Judges* (written by E. P. Burke), Foss's *Judges*, Brougham's *Historical Sketches*, Seward's *Anecdotes* (written by Charles Butler; see his *Reminiscences*), and Wynne's *Strictures on Eminent Lawyers* (1790), besides Holliday's biography (which deserves all the bad things that subsequent writers have said about it) and the contemporary Law Reports. References will be found in Walpole's *Memoirs* and his Correspondence, in Boswell, and of course in Junius. At the date of writing, Mr. Fifoot's study of Mansfield is announced for publication by the Oxford Press.

middle of the nineteenth century, "I look upon him with interest as a connecting link between the reign of Queen Anne and our own times. Having been the familiar friend of Pope, he was the familiar friend of my familiar friends. Occupying the stage of political life almost for a century, he brings to-gether systems as well as men that seem many generations asunder."

William Murray, the eleventh child of an impoverished Scottish lord, the fifth Viscount Stormont, was born on March 2nd, 1705, and received his first education in the Grammar School at Perth. Fourteen years later he set out alone on his pony to ride to London, to go to school at West-minster. At Westminster he worked (as always) with diligence and success, and left with the senior scholarship to Christ Church. While at Oxford he became a member of Lincoln's Inn, and in 1727 he moved to London and for three years applied himself, with a thoroughness which was always his leading characteristic, to preparation for the practice of the law. He took a small set of chambers in No. 1, Old Square, where he devoted himself to reading, and he has left appalling records of the historical knowledge which he then acquired.

But he was not wholly absorbed in study. "The marvellous circumstance is," says Campbell, "that, in the midst of these multifarious and severe studies, Mr. Murray was 'drinking champagne with the wits'. I am almost afraid to record it, lest it should seduce some heedless youths into the false and deceitful notion that dissipation is compatible with success in our profession. But let them remember, that before he went to *Will's* or *Button's* he had been eight or ten hours busily employed in professional studies; and that, when he associated with gay companions he never so indulged as to be prevented from rising to light his own fire next morning, or from sitting down to his books with a sound stomach and a clear head."

He had for his friend the leading man of letters of the day:

Pope was a frequent visitor at "Number Five", the chambers in King's Bench Walk where Murray fixed his residence after his call to the Bar in 1732, and from Pope we learn that Murray himself wrote verses ("How sweet an Ovid, Murray, was our boast") and that he was a frequenter of drawing-rooms as well as of coffee-houses, and a figure in society as well as in Court.

Nature, indeed, had formed Murray, in Pope's compendious if ungrammatical phrase, "not to admire, but be admired," and those who knew him unite in praising his elegant person, his pleasing manners, and, above all, the beauty of his voice. "In all he said or did, there was a happy mixture of good-nature, elegance, ease and dignity. . . . His voice was perhaps unrivalled in the sweetness and mellifluous variety of its tones."

Certainly he had all the qualities needed for success at the Bar, and though for two years he had little or no practice, when work came it came fast and was of the highest quality. After 1738, he says, "business poured in upon me from all quarters, and from a few hundred pounds a year, I fortunately found myself in receipt of thousands." Any literary ambitions that he may have formed were given up, and he turned his feet into the beaten path of marriage and professional advancement. In the apt words of Campbell, "since his altered fortunes, he could enter on a matrimonial negotiation with entire confidence," and in 1738 he married a daughter of the Earl of Winchelsea. His married life was characterized by the featureless and apparently effortless success which blessed all his undertakings: "Lady Mansfield, by the exemplary discharge of every domestic, social, and religious duty, made his home delightful till the 10th of April, 1784, when he resigned her in the hope of being speedily re-united to her in a better world." They had no children.

Thenceforward Murray's career was one of unbroken advancement: in 1742 he became Solicitor-General, and simultaneously took silk and a seat in Parliament, and became a Bencher of his Inn. Already the acknowledged leader of the Chancery Bar, he now achieved a corresponding success in the House of Commons.

Till his appointment as a Law Officer he had carefully abstained from forming any party ties; he had no antecedent political allegiance, and it would be folly, he thought, to forfeit the good will of any one section by joining any other. After the fall of Walpole, however, he consented to take office under his successor, and for fourteen years he supported the Government in the Lower House, first under Pelham, and then (as Attorney-General) under Newcastle.

Though he was not a member of the Cabinet, he was in the counsels of the Prime Minister, and was the chief bulwark of the Ministry against the attacks of Pitt. Such specimens of his Parliamentary oratory as survive are, in their suavity and reasonableness, the reverse of those of his great rival; but "the mellifluous tones, the conciliatory manner, the elegant action, the lucid reasoning, the varied stores of knowledge, the polished diction, the alternate appeals to the understanding and the affections, and, above all, the constant self-control", drew admiration even from Horace Walpole, his bitterest detractor.

Politics, however, was not the sphere in which Murray was destined, or desired, to shine. He had no personal ambition— more than once he refused the Chancellorship—and the death of Lord Chief Justice Ryder, in May, 1756, afforded him the opportunity of leaving an arena of which he was weary and entering on what he regarded as his life's real work, the improvement of the English common law. Newcastle, realizing how great a loss to the Government he would be, was reluctant to grant him promotion, but Murray was determined, and in November he was sworn in Chief Justice of the King's Bench and created Baron Mansfield.

The remainder of his career was uneventful; he was made an Earl in 1776; in 1788 he resigned his office, and retired to indulge in planting and landscape gardening on his estate at Kenwood, where he died, just as a new era was opening in Europe, in 1793.

His support of the Government throughout the American war, and in particular his hostility to Wilkes, earned him great unpopularity and the reputation of an uncompromising Tory, and he died deploring the French Revolution. But Burke summed up his political career by pronouncing him the father of modern Toryism—Toryism adapted to a system of representative government.

§ 2

A survey of Mansfield's life naturally falls into two halves, divided by his appointment to the Chief Justiceship in 1756. It is characteristic of the man that that appointment, which most would have regarded as the crown of their career, was to him no more than a beginning: "On the day of his inauguration as Chief Justice, instead of thinking that he had won the prize of life, he considered himself as only starting in the race."

The worthiest monument to Mansfield is to be found in the pages of Atkyns, Burrow, Douglas, Cowper, and Lofft, who reported the cases in which he appeared as counsel and which he decided as judge. The reader will be content to find the most important of these abstracted in Campbell's Life, and it will be sufficient here to mention one or two episodes of his career at the Bar and on the Bench which reveal the character of the man.

Most striking of such episodes was the trial of the rebel lords in 1746. Murray, "caught young" though he was, never shook off the reproach of his Scottish origin. Indeed, he was by many believed to be a clandestine Jacobite. His brother was for many years chief confidential adviser to the Young Pretender, and his mother is said actually to have assisted the rebels when they passed through Perth in 1745. Not many years later, an inquiry was held by the Privy Council to investigate the charge that, as late as 1732, Murray and his intimates had been used to drink the health of the Pretender; and though the charge was proved baseless, the stigma on Murray's name remained. Pitt taunted him with it in the House of Commons, and Junius raked it up against him twenty years later.

It might be thought that Murray, in 1746, would have declined to take an active part in prosecuting those who had espoused a cause to which his family was devoted and to which he himself must, before he entered public life, have been attached; or that, having embarked on the prosecution, he would have conducted it with enough severity to preclude his critics from ever again questioning his loyalty to the House of Brunswick. But he took neither of these courses: he spoke for the prosecution, and spoke with such firmness, such fairness, such moderation, that neither Jacobite nor Hanoverian could find any ground for criticism. The same qualities marked his prosecution of Lord Lovat, in 1747, when the prisoner himself acknowledged with warmth Murray's fairness and his eloquence.

Impeccable though his conduct was on occasions such as these, there is something almost soulless about the satisfaction with which Murray seems to have suppressed personal feeling when he was called upon to do (in his own words) something "required of a faithful representative of the people". One recalls the scene in the Lords when Chatham was carried dying from the Chamber, and when, among the bustle, the confusion, and the sympathy of his fellow-peers, his old rival sat with an unmoved countenance, exhibiting no trace either of satisfaction or of concern. If on such occasions he had displayed some common human failing he would have been then a more lovable, and to-day a more living, figure.

If there was one situation, however, where such immobile impartiality was in place, it was the Bench; and there that very lack of personal bias or passion contributed largely to his greatness as a judge. No better example of his enlightenment and his impartiality can be found than his judicial treatment of Catholics and Dissenters.

Mansfield never shrank from stretching the law so as to protect those against whom charges had been made or from whom penalties were sought to be exacted on the ground of their religion. A speech to a jury in 1780, practically directing them to acquit a Roman Catholic priest charged with the crime of saying Mass, gave rise to the rumour that he was a Jesuit in disguise. 1780 was a bad year in which to have such a rumour attaching to one's name, and not the least shocking episode in the Gordon riots was the burning of Mansfield's house in Bloomsbury Square, and with it the valuable library which he had been collecting since his youth.

In the ensuing debate in Parliament Mansfield, who himself barely escaped with his life from the clutches of the mob, made a noble profession of his tolerating principles—"My desire to disturb no man for conscience sake is pretty well known and, I hope, will be had in remembrance"—and conveyed by expressions at once mild and lofty—"I have not consulted books; indeed, I have no books to consult"—the detachment with which he viewed his personal loss. Nor did he lack an opportunity of proving in practice the truth of these professions. At Lord George Gordon's trial, at which he presided, "Lord Mansfield showed himself free from the slightest tinge of resentment or prejudice; but, at the same time, he made no parade of generosity of feeling"; and when applied to by the Treasury for an estimate of his loss with a view to compensation, he replied: "How great soever that loss may be, I think it does not become me to claim or expect reparation from the State. I have made up my mind to bear my misfortune as I ought."

It was the same spirit that prevented him from taking action against the publishers of Junius, who assailed him, as a supporter of the Government, with abuse the unfairness of which was equalled only by its virulence.

It was the same spirit that dictated his famous judgment reversing Wilkes's outlawry, at a time when he was a mainstay of the Government which Wilkes was seeking to undermine. While Westminster Hall was filled and surrounded with a mob clamouring for the reversal of the outlawry of their favourite, Mansfield soberly went through all the points that had been urged in Wilkes's favour and dismissed each as ill-founded. Then he paused, and, after a reference to the threatening letters that had been addressed to him, thus proceeded:

The lies of calumny carry no terror to me. I trust that my temper of mind, and the colour and conduct of my life, have given me a suit of armour against these arrows. If, during this King's reign, I have ever supported his government, and assisted his measures, I have done it without any other reward than the consciousness of doing what I thought right. If I have ever opposed, I have done it upon the points themselves; without mixing in party or faction, and without any collateral views. I honour the King, and respect the people; but many things acquired by the favour of either, are, in my account, objects not worth ambition. I wish popularity; but it is that popularity which follows, not that which is run after; it is that popularity which, sooner or later, never fails to do justice to the pursuit of noble ends by noble means. I will not do that which my conscience tells me is wrong upon this occasion, to gain the huzzas of thousands, or the daily praise of all the papers which come from the press: I will not avoid doing what I think is right, though it should draw on me the whole artillery of libels; all that falsehood and malice can invent, or the credulity of a deluded populace can swallow. I can say, with a great magistrate, upon an occasion and under circumstances not unlike, Ego hoc animo semper fui, ut invidiam virtute partam, gloriam, non invidiam putarem.

This, for Mansfield, is eloquent; his judgments as a rule were delivered in that level judicial prose which seems to have changed in diction little, and in tone not at all, from the eighteenth to the twentieth century.

After thus setting the passions of the mob at defiance, Mansfield proceeded to gratify them by declaring Wilkes's outlawry void on a technical point, discovered by himself.

One other example of Mansfield's judicial eloquence must not be omitted: his judgment in Somersett's case at once showed him superior to the prejudices of his day, and enabled him to introduce, in its concluding words, perhaps the happiest Virgilian quotation ever made:

The air of England has long been too pure for a slave, and every man is free who breathes it. Every man who comes into England is entitled to the protection of English law, whatever oppression he may heretofore have suffered, and whatever may be the colour of his skin:

Quamvis ille niger, quamvis tu candidus esses.
Let the negro be discharged.

Mansfield, however, was more than a just judge. He was a great law reformer. In the words of Burke, he sought to effect "the amelioration of the law, by making its liberality keep pace with justice and the actual concerns of the world; . . . conforming principles to the growth of our commerce and our empire". "Precedent and Principle often had a hard struggle which should lay hold of Lord Mansfield; and he used to say that he ought to be drawn placed between them, like Garrick between Tragedy and Comedy." There was no doubt, however, which of the two more often carried the day: Mansfield's enemies in the profession, who regarded the common law as the Ark of the Covenant, never on any pretext to be interfered with, and those in politics, who were ready to find in any decision which could not be justified by precedent an infringement of the rights of the people, united in the charge that he set the common law at naught and introduced into the King's Bench, by a sort of illicit Prætorian jurisdiction, unheard of equitable doctrines which enabled him to put the Crown above the Law. From these charges Mansfield has been fully exculpated by Campbell and by Wynne. If there is any substance in them, they amount only to this, that in some things he was in advance of his day. His view of contract, exalting moral obligation at the expense of the strict doctrine of consideration, has not found favour, and his attempt to relax some of the stricter doctrines of the law of real property was premature. The correctness of his oft-repeated doctrine concerning libel— that "libel or no libel" was a question not for the jury but for the judge—is still debated: it involved him in great unpopularity, and Fox's Libel Act settled the law against him. But his whole aim was to rationalize the law by breathing into its dead letter the spirit of equity and reason, and in particular to adapt a system fitted to a nation whose wealth consisted of land to the needs of a rapidly developing commercial empire. In the words of Baron Parke, Mansfield was the founder of our commercial law.

The jealousy of Pratt and the dislike of Eldon combined to cast a shadow over his name in the half century after his death: but he was soon restored to his full lustre, and, in the words of Campbell, "may now be compared to the unclouded majesty of Mont Blanc when the mists which for a time obscured his summit have passed away." The period that elapsed between Queen Anne and Queen Victoria saw a complete change in the economic and mercantile conditions of the English people: to Mansfield and to Stowell belongs the credit of having adapted the English legal system in accordance with those changes. In the words of a high authority, "No student of the legal history of the eighteenth century would deny that, in this century of great lawyers, Lord Mansfield is by far the greatest. From the time when he became Chief Justice . . . we can trace his influence upon all parts of the English legal system. It was an influence directed to the work of rationalizing, simplifying, and adapting to modern conditions, the medley of rules, from all periods of English history, which made up the fabric of the law."*

There is, moreover, a practical answer to Mansfield's detractors: during the more than thirty years that he presided in the King's Bench, there were only two occasions on which his opinion was not unanimously adopted by his brother judges, and only two occasions on which it was reversed on appeal. The public confidence in his judgment, and the fact that he introduced reforms which "speeded up" the trial of actions (he rarely reserved his judgment, and rigorously curtailed the then redundant arguments of counsel), induced a mass of litigation in his Court, and led to the practice of law-reporting in its modern sense. When it is added that he was a model of politeness to those who appeared before him, the picture is complete of a judge as nearly perfect as it is possible for a judge to be.

§ 3

The figure that emerges from an account of Mansfield's professional career is that of a man selflessly, even soullessly,

*See Sir W. Holdsworth in *Harvard Law Review* xliii-1-6.

efficient. His character in private life accords with this: bland, engaging, courteous, cultivated, correct, with no misgiving and with no redeeming weakness. He had to make his own success in life, but he made it early, and he never looked back.

It may be taken as symbolical that never, since the day when he rode South to go to school, did he retrace the path to Scotland.* Altogether, he was well contented with his lot: when Johnson observed that "Every man thinks meanly of himself for not having been a soldier, or not having been at sea" the contrary instance that immediately leaped to Boswell's mind was Mansfield: "Lord Mansfield does not". Mansfield had found his métier, and was happy in it. He gave up literature either because he had no talent for composition, or simply for lack of time; but he did not cease to show interest in the arts and in the Society of the cultured. He held formal Sunday evening conversations ("strangely" says Boswell "called levées"); he patronized the brothers Adam; and his favourite toast, "Young Friends and Old Books", testified his appreciation of the two pleasantest ornaments of a cultured life.

His appearance is best perpetuated in the portrait by Copley that hangs in the National Portrait Gallery; a handsome, genial, intelligent face that tells you nothing; an apt illustration of his whole career, a career in which Campbell could find evidence of but one defect, "his want of heart." For while no base motive (except it may be, on occasion, timidity) ever actuated him in public or in private life, still, "all that he did might have been done from a refined calculating selfishness." One turns to the man himself for a refutation of the judgment— but in vain: discreet and self-controlled, he moves about the

*His biographers, however, do him an injustice in saying that he never again met his parents after he left Scotland as a boy; there is a passage in the Gilpin correspondence printed in Richard Gilpin's *Memoirs* (Quaritch 1879) pp. 100-101 in which it is mentioned that his mother attended Carlisle Assizes in about 1740, and was "highly delighted" at hearing him plead with "applause on all sides."

background of the Memoirs, the Recollections, the correspondence of the period, scarcely doing or saying a single thing that proves him a human being. He made no close friends (unless intimacy with the cold-blooded Hurd deserves the name), nor did his enemies bestow on him that kind of personal immortality which Eldon (for instance) owes to his attackers; neither the invective of Junius nor the venom of Horace Walpole succeeded in creating a living image of him. He has, however, the immortality which would have meant most to him: he lives in his work.

HORACE WALPOLE

(1717–1797)

by ROMNEY SEDGWICK

IN a dim but indisputable way Horace Walpole (pronounced Warpool) is generally admitted to have left his mark on British literature and architecture. Out of his Gothic story, the *Castle of Otranto*, came the school of fiction which was satirized by Jane Austen in *Northanger Abbey*. Out of his Gothic villa, Strawberry Hill, came the style of architecture which was selected for the housing of the legislature and the judiciary, and was nearly selected for that of the executive as well. By a curious coincidence one of the products of the Strawberry Hill style now forms an addition to the original of the Castle of Otranto. Trinity College, Cambridge, whose Great Court was unconsciously adopted by Horace Walpole as the model for his imaginary castle, has returned the compliment by allowing his imitation castle to determine the architecture of Whewell's Court.*

If Horace Walpole had produced nothing but the works by which he was known in his lifetime it is unlikely that these claims to the attention of posterity would have been

---

*See Mr. Warren Hunting Smith's letter in *The Times Literary Supplement* of the 23rd May, 1936, for the grounds for identifying the Castle of Otranto with Trinity Great Court.

admitted. He belongs to the class of men whose reputation depends on writings which they knew could not be published till after their death. Like the Hervey and the Greville memoirs, to take other conspicuous examples in the same field, these writings served as a compensation to their author for his own thwarted political ambition by giving him a sense of power over contemporaries far more important than himself. His posthumous career has been all that he could have wished. Over a hundred years ago historical writers began to use him as the chief authority on his period. Since then a great many of them appear to have used no other.

Horace Walpole's chief contribution to the history of his own times are his letters and his memoirs. Nearly a quarter of his letters are addressed to Horace Mann, the British minister at Florence, with whom he had stayed during his grand tour. As Horace Mann never came on leave and Horace Walpole never returned to Italy, no contacts occurred to interrupt a correspondence which continued till Mann's death forty-five years later. Mann thus provided the principal, though of course not the only, outlet for one of nature's journalists. Horace Walpole's best and most characteristic letters are news-letters, written in his own style of conversation, as described by Fanny Burney:

"In the evening came Mr. Walpole, gay though caustic, polite though sneering, and entertainingly epigrammatic."

Their staples are accounts of Parliament and society by a well-placed and assiduous observer. "The true definition of me," Horace Walpole wrote when he was thirty-eight, "is that I am a dancing senator. Not that I do dance, or do anything by being a senator, but I go to balls, and to the House of Commons—to look on." The dancing senator has become posterity's London correspondent for the eighteenth century.

Horace Walpole's letters to Mann were periodically returned

to him at his own request and destroyed after they had been copied out, subject to such alterations as he thought desirable. The transcript, annotated by Horace Walpole, therefore represents the final text of letters which he had revised and preserved with a view to their eventual publication. Nevertheless they have never been published in an uncensored form. As late as 1919, when Lytton Strachey questioned the necessity for the omission of a number of passages on account of their "improprieties", Dr. Paget Toynbee, the editor of the latest edition, replied:

"Improprieties is far too mild a term for the passages in question. I can only compare them to the grossest avowals contained in the unexpurgated editions of Rousseau's *Confessions*, or to the filth which Dante likens to 'sterco che dagli uman privati parea mosso'."*

As Lytton Strachey did not fail to point out, the conclusion to be drawn from these observations was that Horace Walpole's letters, like Rousseau's *Confessions*, ought to be published in an unexpurgated edition. Apart from this point, it is entertaining to note that Horace Walpole, who regarded the Restoration writers as impolite because of their passion for calling everything by its proper name, should have been subjected by his own editor to language which would have been strong if applied to Rochester. In fact the omitted passages consist of current mots and stories, including a high percentage of wisecracks by Lady Townshend, the mother of Charles Townshend, which are of interest as contributing to the picture given by the letters of the *esprit de Guermantes* of the time, and to which no exception would be taken by any reasonable person to-day if they were published in their context. Since a properly edited text of Horace Walpole's letters is in course of preparation, it will be sufficient to quote the first of the omitted passages, partly as an example of Dr. Paget Toynbee's idea of

* *The Athenæum*, 15th and 29th August, and 5th September, 1919.

unspeakable filth, and partly as an illustration of the consequence of leaving gaps in the text to act as booby-traps for
other writers to fall into.

Horace Walpole's first letter to Mann was written during a
break in his journey to London from Dover on returning to
England after his grand tour. After describing his impressions of England, and in particular of Canterbury, in the spirit
of a tourist visiting a foreign country, he adds: "I write to-
night because I have time; to-morrow I get to London just
as the post goes. Sir R. is at Houghton." Then follows a
string of dots to which there is appended the note "passage
omitted". According to Mr. Stephen Gwynn, in his life of
Horace Walpole, these dots "make it possible to affirm that
Horace Walpole, on his return to England, but before he met
Sir Robert, used some expressions in regard to him which it is
thought better to withhold"; or, in other words, that Horace
Walpole used unprintable language about his father. This
Mr. Gwynn regards as important, because it confirms his view
that Horace Walpole's relations with Sir Robert were "not
exactly filial" in every sense of the expression. In point of
fact the omitted passage is as follows:

> "I have nothing to tell you yet, but of a woman who
> was prayed for lately at Canterbury, on the point of marriage.
> She was devout and timorous, wanted a blessing on her
> design, which she thought hazardous; so the Minister prayed
> for a gentlewoman who was *going to take a great affair in
> hand.*"

It is perhaps worth while pointing out the probable explanation of the familiar story that Horace Walpole was the son
not of Sir Robert but of the elder brother of Lord Hervey, the
author of the memoirs. The authority for this story is Lady
Louisa Stuart, writing in 1836, of what she remembered
reading forty or fifty years earlier in the journals of her grand-

mother, Lady Mary Wortley Montagu, before they were destroyed by her mother, Lady Bute. Though according to Lady Louisa Stuart the story was common gossip during Horace Walpole's boyhood, no reference is made to it by any-one writing at that time, and it appears to be merely but a ver-sion, progressively garbled as it was passed on from one lady to another, of the following piece of scandal which was current in the thirties and was known to Lady Mary Wortley Montagu. Both the Hervey memoirs and the Egmont diary mention that Sir Robert Walpole's grandson, afterwards the third Earl of Orford, was generally supposed to be the son of Sir George Oxenden. Hervey adds:

"This intrigue with Lady Walpole, and her having but one son, which the world gave to Sir George Oxenden, is alluded to in these two lines, in a copy of verses written by Lady Mary Wortley, wherein she supposes Sir Robert Walpole speaking of Sir George Oxenden:

"Triumph enough for that enchanting face,
That my damnation must enrich his race."

But supposing it were so, I do not imagine, since this boy would, as well as any other, transmit the name of Walpole to posterity, with the title Sir Robert had got for his son, that Sir Robert cared very much who had begot him; and I have the more reason for being of this opinion, as Sir Robert Wal-pole more than once, in speaking of this child to me, has, with all the sang-froid imaginable, called him that boy, got by nobody knows who, as if he had been speaking of a foundling. But had Sir Robert been more solicitous about the father of this boy, he would not have been without comfort; for though the public, from the little propensity it has to err, had always rather give a child to any father than the man whose name it bears, and did pretty currently impute this to Sir George

Oxenden, yet from the extreme aversion my Lady Walpole showed to this poor little animal from the very hour of its birth, all judicious, candid, and unprejudiced commentators sagaciously and naturally concluded that she, at least, who must be the ablest judge, entertained no doubt of its being her husband's."

If a similar misfortune had been generally supposed to have befallen Sir Robert, it is most improbable that both Hervey and Egmont would have failed to comment on the coincidence, and quite incredible that Hervey, when earlier in his memoirs he mentions an attempt of Sir Robert to seduce Lady Hervey, would have refrained from pointing out that the Herveys had got in first.

Though Horace Walpole was fully aware of the historical interest of his letters to Mann, he probably attached more importance to his memoirs. These consist of two separate works, covering the last ten years of the reign of George II and the first eleven years of the reign of George III respectively. Each of them was written more or less contemporaneously with the events which it describes, evidently from a journal similar to that to which Horace Walpole decided to confine himself after 1772, when he finished writing his second memoirs. They both relate to periods during which Horace Walpole took an active part, though from behind the scenes, in many of the political intrigues which he describes. A better idea of their contents would be given if instead of their respective titles of *Memoirs of the Reign of George II* and *Memoirs of the Reign of George III*, they were called *Memoirs of Horace Walpole during the years* 1751-1760 *and* 1760-1771.

The memoirs of 1751-1760 were first published in 1822. They were edited, or rather censored, by Lord Holland, who in his preface explained that he had replaced by asterisks a number of "coarse expressions", some passages "affecting the

private lives of people and nowise connected with any
political event, or illustrative of any great public character",
"sarcasms on mere bodily infirmity, in which the author was
too apt to indulge," and usually, "where private amours were
mentioned, the name of the lady." The following passage,
in which the words in italics are omitted in the existing edition,
is a typical example of editorial activities for which it is
interesting to learn that Lord Holland was paid by John
Murray no less than £2,000:

"It had already been whispered that the assiduity of Lord
Bute at Leicester House, and his still more frequent attendance
in the gardens at Kew and Carlton House, were less addressed
to the Prince of Wales than to his mother. The eagerness of
the pages of the back-stairs to let her know whenever Lord
Bute arrived *and a mellowness in her German accent as she spoke
to him, and that was often and long, and a more than usual swimming-
ness in her eyes** contributed to dispel the ideas that had been
conceived of the rigour of her widowhood. On the other
hand, the favoured personage, naturally ostentatious of his
person, and of haughty carriage, seemed by no means desirous
of concealing his conquest. His bow grew more theatric, his
graces contracted some meaning, and the beauty of his leg
was constantly displayed in the eyes of the poor captivated
Princess. Indeed, the nice observers of the Court-thermometer,
who often foresee a change of weather before it actually
happens, had long thought that her Royal Highness was
likely to choose younger Ministers than that formal piece of
empty mystery, Cresset; or the matron-like decorum of Sir
George Lee. *Her eyes had often twinkled intelligibly enough at her
countryman, Prince Lobkowitz, yet she perhaps had never passed the
critical barrier if* her simple husband, when he took up the
character of the Regent's gallantry, had *not* forced an air of
intrigue even upon his wife. When he affected to retire into

*For those words Lord Holland substituted, "[and some other symptoms]".

gloomy allées with Lady Middlesex, he used to bid the Princess walk with Lord Bute. As soon as the Prince was dead, they walked more and more, in honour of his memory" (pp. 204-5 of vol. II, 1847 edition).

All Lord Holland's excisions stand condemned by the sound principle laid down by Macaulay, who had collated his copy of the memoirs with the original manuscript, in the following marginal note on another omitted passage:

"The words omitted [viz. 'his body was more uniform, for that was throughout burlesque and uncouth,' which occur in a description of Horace Walpole's uncle on p. 141 of vol. I] might as well have been published. The asterisks led Croker to suspect, not altogether without reason, that something very gross had been left out. See the *Quarterly Review*. Except in very rare cases a hiatus is more injurious to all parties than the whole text would be".*

Lord Holland mentioned in his preface that before the manuscript was handed over to him for editing, "one gross, indelicate, and ill-authenticated story had been cut out by Lord Waldegrave," to whom Horace Walpole had bequeathed the memoirs. The story in question is told by Horace Walpole in a letter to Mann which by some oversight has escaped the attention of his editors. It relates to the attacks on Lord George Sackville and Dr. George Stone, the Primate of Ireland, during the Duke of Dorset's vice-royalty. Since there is no prospect of a further edition of the memoirs, the opportunity may as well be taken to repair Lord Waldegrave's excisions, which are more interesting than Lord Holland's:

"The indiscretion of the rulers presented a colour to the keenest invectives that a faction could wish to employ, especially as it was sure to engage that formidable voice of clamour, the fair sex, on the side of the opposition. The Irish are not further removed from the Italians in their situation

* Kindly communicated by Professor G. M. Trevelyan.

and climate, than in the manner and the integrity of their amours. The clergy, nay the very Bishops of Ireland, are buxom husbands, boon companions; the laity are too cele-brated disciples of such jovial priests to make it necessary to particularize their complexion. Yet in so Cyprian an isle was the Metropolitan himself accused of wayward passions, more consonant to the life of a Cardinal than to the supremacy of so orthodox a flock. His friend Lord George was suspected of the same heresy, for certainly in both it was mere matter of sus-picion, and had brought over a young Scotch officer, who being preferred to be Aide de Camp to the Primate, was pointed out as the centre at which all the arrows of satire were discharged. The Scotch and the Irish Protestants differ too widely in their principles not to be implacable; and the youth above-mentioned being after brought into Parliament by the same interest gave immeasurable offence, though he certainly ought to have had his birth overlooked by his warmest enemies, in consideration of the loyalty of his family, which was so obnoxious to the Jacobites of Scotland that during the Rebellion he had been seized by the Pretender's forces and had the halter round his neck, when the onset of the battle of Prestonpans interrupted his execution and gave him an opportunity to make his escape." (p. 281 of vol. I of the 1847 edition.)

"The Speaker was adored by the mob; they worshipped him under the name of Roger. Whatever that devout term implied, it was certainly meant as the reverse of the epithets they bestowed on the Primate. They made bonfires of reproach before the door of the Primate; they stopped coaches, and made them declare for England or Ireland. The Hackney Chairmen distinguished their patriotism by refusing to carry any fare to the Castle, and the ladies, that is such as neither go in coaches nor chaises, exposed the most opprobrious parts of their children in derision to the Primate as he passed along the streets." (*ibid*, p. 367.)

The omission of occasional passages is the least of the defects of the existing edition. The exasperation of the professional historian at the way in which the memoirs have been produced is expressed by Carlyle in a note in his *Frederick the Great*, where he describes them as "almost the one original English book yet written" on times which, "but for Walpole, burning like a small steady light there . . . would be for ever unintelligible." Yet for all practical purposes, Carlyle continues, the memoirs "may be characterized as still wanting an Editor; a book *un*edited; little but long ignorances of a very hopeless type; thick contented darkness . . .; no attempt at . . . any of the natural helps to a reader now at such a distance from it." Neither Carlyle's praise nor his blame is too strong. Horace Walpole's memoirs are a conspicuous example of the rule that an editor who censors his author is unfit for his job.

The affair of "the pretended memorial", as Horace Walpole calls it, illustrates the consequences of throwing the memoirs at the reader without any serious attempt to edit them. Horace Walpole devotes some thirty pages of his first volume to describing how an anonymous memorial was circulated at the end of 1752 accusing an eminent civil servant, Andrew Stone, then sub-governor to the Prince of Wales and formerly under-secretary of state to the Duke of Newcastle, and William Murray, then solicitor-general and afterwards Lord Mansfield, of being Jacobites and pupils of Lord Bolingbroke and of using their positions and the trust placed in them by the Pelhams to instil their arbitrary principles into the heir-apparent and to bring about a counter-revolution; how one of the recipients of the memorial brought formal charges of Jacobitism against Stone and Murray; how a lengthy inquiry conducted by the Cabinet showed that there was no foundation for such charges; and how the affair culminated and collapsed in a full dress debate in the House of Lords for which ministers were given special leave by the King to answer questons as to what had taken place in the Cabinet investigation. In a footnote Horace Walpole states, what would otherwise never have been known, that he was the author of the memorial, but neither in his note or in his text does he explain the motives or the grounds of his action or even whether he believed that his accusations were true. So senseless is the whole affair, as it appears in his narrative, that Macaulay compares it to the practical joke of a malicious boy who enjoys the embarrassment of the misdirected traveller. There can, however, be no doubt that the memorial was part of what Horace Walpole describes as his efforts "to blow up an opposition underhand" to the Pelhams and that his motive was largely resentment of Henry Pelham's refusal to grant his repeated application that the proceeds of a lucrative sinecure, which he drew for the life-time of an elder brother, should be secured to him for his own life. This fake Jacobite plot closely resembles the attempts made by politicians in the previous century to involve Pepys in the Popish plot for the purpose of bringing down Pepys's principal, the Duke of York. Its importance lies in its effects on Horace Walpole himself and through him on the histories of the period. In time he came to believe that his own fictions were facts and based on them his theory that the key to the history of the reign of George III was that the King as a child had imbibed from Stone and Murray the arbitrary and reactionary political principles of Lord Bolingbroke. From Horace Walpole this theory has percolated into historical text-books. It is as if the history of the reign of Charles II had been written on the basis of the narrative of Titus Oates.

Horace Walpole's second memoirs, covering the years 1760 to 1771, were also entrusted to Lord Holland, who kept the manuscript till his death in 1840, when it was discovered that he had not done a stroke of work on it. They were published in 1845 under the editorship of Sir Denis le Marchant, who followed Lord Holland's principles of censorship, except in not showing his omissions by asterisks. The only omitted passage worth quoting relates to the question of the precise nature of the relations between the Princess Dowager of Wales and Lord Bute:

"Not to return to this Atalantis-kind of anecdote again (tho' too much agitated and productive of too many consequences not to make it an essential part in the history of this reign), it remained an insoluble problem, what was the real secret of the interior of the Princess Dowager's Court. There was a Miss Vansittart, of a Jacobite family, who had suddenly been promoted by Lord Bute to be maid of honour. She had been pretty, but was past her bloom before the public ever heard her name. The Earl for several years visited her regularly every evening at seven for at least two hours. His wife, a very prudent and sensible woman, not apt to come to an eclat, had given some marks of jealousy on this connection. But what surprised much more, was that this young woman grew the sole female intimate of the Princess, and passed as many hours alone with her Royal Highness in the morning, as she did with the Earl in the evening. The Princess often went to her house herself. They who justified her from any improper correspondence with Lord Bute, affirmed that the Princess, who was infinitely distempered, saw her surgeons at Miss Vansittart's apartment. But her chair and servants standing in the street was an affair of much less secrecy than seeing them at her own uninhabited Palace. If too Miss Vansittart was the Favourite's mistress, it did not seem to recommend her to the favour of a greater mistress; nor did the Earl's age, turned of fifty, promise to be able to keep the peace between the two rivals. The junction of Lord Talbot to this singular trio did not make the mystery more explicable.

Of one use it is pretty certain Miss Vansittart was to the Princess; of being her agent for the sale of honours. Sir John Gibbon confessed that he had purchased a red ribbon thro that channel." (p. 36 of vol. I of the 1894 edition.)

This confused and somewhat ludicrous passage is extremely characteristic. Taking for granted that Lord Bute was the Princess's lover, Horace Walpole points out that, in spite of all appearances, it was difficult to believe that Lord Bute was also Miss Vansittart's. It never occurs to him to consider that, on the facts available, the obvious solution of the "insoluble problem" was that the Princess was not Lord Bute's mistress. It is equally characteristic that his editor should not have had the sense to perceive that the passage which he was suppressing in the interests of the reputation of the Princess of Wales pointed to the conclusion that her relations with Lord Bute were perfectly respectable.

The memoirs of 1760 to 1771 are even more valuable, if properly used, than their predecessors. In the interval Horace Walpole's technique had improved. Conway, whom he used as his stalking horse, was much better adapted for his peculiar political methods than the two tough professional politicians, Henry Fox and Richard Rigby, with whom he had been connected in the previous decade. His value as an authority on the intrigues of 1764 to 1767 is shown by the Duke of Grafton's tribute to his practical efficiency as an intelligence officer. There was no one, Grafton writes in his autobiography, referring to a time when he was acting Prime Minister, from whom he recovered such just accounts of the schemes of the various factions, and no one who had such good means of getting to know what was passing, as Horace Walpole. The weakness of the memoirs lies in their author's psychological and intellectual limitations. His opinions are almost invariably examples of the process of rationalization, by which some elaborate justification, based on general principles, is found for actions or views really based on different and less presentable grounds. In the absence of any attempt by his editors or his biographers at an analysis of his real motives, of which he himself was quite unconscious, a safe working rule to proceed on is that his facts are first-class and his generalizations worthless.

From the point of view of the general reader the memoirs cannot be recommended. They are much inferior in readability to the Hervey memoirs, to which they have often been compared. Their speciality, political intrigue, lacks the interest of Hervey's close-ups of the interior of the Palace and of the domestic life of the royal family. The relative merits of the two authors as writers may be judged from the extracts already cited from Hervey about Lady Walpole and from Horace Walpole's second memoirs about the Princess of Wales, which handle in characteristically different ways very much the same sort of theme. The warmest admirer could hardly claim that either of them keeps a good length, but it must be admitted that Hervey manages to put a good deal more spin on the ball. Horace Walpole could command plenty of spin but he reserves it entirely for his letters. In fact the more seriously he takes himself, the less sensible he becomes. When the dancing senator becomes historian he loses his wit without improving his judgment.

FIELDING AND STERNE

(1707-1754 : 1713-1768)

by GRAHAM GREENE

All, all, of a piece throughout:
  Thy Chase had a Beast in View;
Thy Wars brought nothing about;
  Thy Lovers were all untrue.
'Tis well an Old Age is out,
  And time to begin a New.

SO Dryden, looking back from the turn of the century on
the muddle of hopes and disappointments, revolution
and counter-revolution and revolution again. The age
had been kept busily spinning, but to the poet in 1700 it
seemed to have amounted to little: what Cromwell had overthrown, Charles had rebuilt; what James would have established, William had destroyed. But literature may thrive on
political disturbance, if the disturbance goes deep enough and
arouses a sufficiently passionate agreement or denial. One
remembers Trotsky's account of the first meeting of the Soviet
after the October days of 1917: "Among their number were
completely grey soldiers, shell-shocked as it were by the in-
surrection, and still hardly in control of their tongues. But
they were just the ones who found the words which no orator
could find. That was one of the most moving scenes of the

revolution, now first feeling its power, feeling the unnumbered masses it has aroused, the colossal tasks, the pride in success, the joyful failing of the heart at the thought of the morrow which is to be still more beautiful than to-day."

These terms can be transposed to fit the seventeenth century as they cannot to fit the eighteenth, the century to which Fielding was born in 1707 and Sterne six years later. Bunyan, Fox, the Quakers and Levellers, those were the grey, the shell-shocked soldiers who found the words which no official orator of the Established Church could find, and one cannot question among some of the poets who welcomed the return of Charles a genuine thankfulness for a morrow which they believed was to be still more beautiful. The great figure of Dryden comprises the whole of the late seventeenth century scene: like some infinitely subtle meteorological instrument, he was open to every wind: he registered the triumph of Cromwell, the hopes of the Restoration, the Catholicism of James, the final disillusionment. When he died, in 1700, he left the new age, the quieter, more rational age, curiously empty. Not until the romantics at the end of the century was politics again to be of importance to the creative, the recording mind, not until Newman and Hopkins orthodox religion. All that was left was the personal sensibility or the superficial social panorama from the highwayman in the cart and the debtor in gaol to the lascivious lord at Vauxhall and the virtuous heroine bent over the admirable, unenthusiastic, politic works of Bishop Burnet.

One cannot separate literature and life. If an age appears creatively, poetically, empty, it is fair to assume that life too had its emptiness, was carried on at a lower, less passionate level. I use the word poetry in the widest sense, in the sense that Henry James was a poet and Defoe was not. When Fielding published his first novel, *Joseph Andrewes*, in 1742, Swift was on the verge of death and Pope as well, Cowper was ten years old and Blake unborn. Dramatic poetry, which had survived Dryden's death only in such feeble hands as Addison's and Rowe's, was to all intents a finished form.

But fiction is one of the prime needs of human nature, and someone in that empty world had got to begin building again. One cannot in such a period expect the greatest literature: the old forms are seen to be old when the fine excitement is over, and all that the best minds can do is to construct new forms in which the poetic imagination may eventually find itself at home. Something in the eighteenth century had got to take the place of dramatic poetry (perhaps it is not too fanciful to see in the innumerable translations of Homer, Virgil, Lucan a popular hunger for the lost poetic fiction), and it was Fielding who for the first time since the Elizabethan age directed the poetic imagination into prose fiction. That he began as a parodist of Richardson may indicate that he recognized the inadequacy of *Pamela*, of the epistolary novel, to satisfy the hunger of the age.

In the previous century the distinction between prose fiction and poetic fiction had been a very simple one: one might almost say that prose fiction had been pornographic fiction, in the sense that it had been confined to a more or less flippant study of sexual relations (whether you take the plays of Wycherley, the prose comedies of Dryden, the novels of Aphra Behn, the huge picaresque novel of Richard Head and Francis Kirkman, the generalization remains true almost without exception), while poetic fiction had meant heroic drama, a distinction underlined in plays like *Marriage à la Mode* which contained both poetry and prose. Nowhere during the Restoration period, except perhaps in Cowley's superb comedy, does one find prose used in fiction as Webster and other Jacobean playwrights used it, as a medium of equal dignity and intensity to poetry, indeed as poetry with the rhythm of ordinary speech. It was from the traditional idea

of prose fiction that Defoe's novels were derived: *Moll
Flanders* is only a more concise *English Rogue*, and it was
left to Fielding, who had not himself the poetic mind (he
declared roundly: "I should have honoured and loved Homer
more had he written a true history of his own times in
humble prose"), to construct a fictional form which could
attract the poetic imagination. *Tom Jones* was to prove the
archetype not only of the picaresque novelists. James and
Joyce owe as much to it as Dickens.

To-day when we have seen in the novels of Henry James the
metaphysical poet working in the medium of prose fiction, in
Lawrence's and Conrad's novels the romantic, we cannot
easily realize the revolutionary nature of *Tom Jones* and *Amelia*.
Sterne who came later—the first volumes of *Tristram Shandy*
were published five years after Fielding's death—bears so
much more the obvious marks of a revolutionary, simply
because he remains, in essentials, a revolutionary still. Even
to-day he continues magnificently to upset all our notions of
what a novel's form should be; it is his least valuable qualities
which have been passed on. His sensibility founded a whole
school of Bages and Bancrofts and Blowers (I cannot remember who it was who wrote: "Great G—d, unless I have
greatly offended Thee, grant me the luxury, sometimes to slip
a bit of silver, though no bigger than a shilling, into the
clammy-cold hand of the decayed wife of a baronet," but it
was to the author of *The Sentimental Journey* that he owed his
sensibility), while his whimsicality was inherited by the
essayists, by Lamb in particular. But his form no one has ever
tried to imitate, for what would be the good? An imitation
could do nothing but recall the original. *Tristram Shandy*
exists, a lovely sterile eccentricity, the last word in literary
egotism. Even the fact that Sterne was—sometimes—a poet
is less important to practitioners of his art than that Fielding
—sometimes—tried to be one.

FIELDING AND STERNE

Sterne, the sly, uneasy, unhappily married cleric, the son of an elderly ensign who never had the means or the influence to buy promotion, had suffered so many humiliations from the world that he had to erect defences of sentiment and of small indecencies between him and it (he admired Rabelais, but how timidly, how "naughtily", his chapter on Noses reflects the author of *The Heroic Deeds of Gargantua and Pantagruel*) so that he has nothing to offer us on our side of the barrier but his genius, his genius for expressing the personal emotions of the sly, the uneasy, the unhappily married. The appalling conceit of this genius, one protests, who claimed Posterity for his book without troubling himself a hang over the value of its contents: "for what has this book done more than the Legation of Moses, or *The Tale of a Tub*, that it may not swim down the gutter of Time along with them?" The nearest that this shrinking sentimental man came to the ordinary run of life was Hall-Stevenson's pornographic circle, the nearest to passion his journals to Eliza who was safely separated from him by the Indian Ocean as well as by the difference in their years. There is nothing he can tell us about anyone, we feel, but himself, and that self has been so tidied and idealized that it would be unrecognizable, one imagines, to his wife.

Compare his position in the life of his time with that of Fielding, Fielding the rake, Fielding the country gentleman, Fielding the hack dramatist, and finally Fielding, the Westminster magistrate who knew all the outcast side of life, from the thief and the cut-throat to the seedy genteel and the half-pay officer in the debtor's court, as no other man of his time. Compare the careful architecture of *Tom Jones*: the introductory essays which enable the author to put his point of view and to leave the characters to go their way untainted by the uncharacteristic moralizing of Defoe's; the introduction of parody in the same way and for the same purpose as Joyce's in

Ulysses; the innumerable sub-plots which give the book the proportions of life, the personal story of Jones taking its place in the general orchestration; the movement back and forth in time as the characters meet each other and recount the past in much the same way as Conrad's, a craftsman's bluff by which we seem to get a glimpse of that "dark backward and abysm" that challenges the ingenuity of every novelist. Compare all this careful architecture with the schoolboy squibs—the blank, the blackened and the marbled leaves, the asterisks—of *Tristram Shandy*. We cannot help a feeling of ingratitude when we think of the work that Fielding put into his books, the importance of his technical innovations, and realize that Sterne, who contributed nothing, can still give more pleasure because of what we call his genius, his skill at self-portraiture (even Uncle Toby is only another example of his colossal egotism: the only outside character he ever really drew—and all the time we are aware of the author preening himself at the tender insight of his admiration).

The man Sterne is unbearable, even the emotions he displayed with such amazing mastery were cheap emotions. Dryden is dead: the great days are over: Cavaliers and Roundheads have become Whigs and Tories: Cumberland has slaughtered the Stuart hopes at Culloden: the whole age cannot produce a respectable passion. So anyone must feel to whom the change, say, from the essays of Bacon and his true descendant Cowley to the essays of Lamb is a change for the worse in human dignity: a change from "Revenge is a kind of wild justice" or "It was the Funeral day of the late man who made himself to be called Protector" to "I have no ear—Mistake me not, reader—nor imagine that I am by nature destitute of those exterior twin appendages or hanging ornaments . . ." or to the latest little weekly essay on "Rising Early" or on "Losing a Collar Stud". The personal emotion, personal sensibility, the whim, in Sterne's day crept into our literature.

FIELDING AND STERNE

It is impossible not to feel a faint disgust at this man, officially a man of God, who in *The Sentimental Journey* found in his own tearful reaction to the mad girl of Moulines the satisfactory conclusion: "I am positive I have a soul; nor can all the books with which materialists have pester'd the world ever convince me of the contrary."

It is a little galling to find the conceit of such a man justified. However much we hate the man—or hate rather his coy whimsical defences, he is more "readable" than Fielding by virtue of that most musical style, the day-dream conversation of a man with a stutter in a world of his imagination where tongue and teeth have no problems to overcome, where no syllables are harsh, where mind speaks softly to mind with infinite subtlety of tone. "The various accidents which befell a very worthy couple, after their uniting in the state of matrimony, will be the subject of the following history. The distresses which they waded through were some of them so exquisite, and the incidents which produced them so extraordinary, that they seem to require not only the utmost malice, but the utmost invention which superstition hath ever attributed to Fortune." So Fielding begins his most mature—if not his greatest—novel. How this book, one wants to protest, should appeal to the craftsman: the *tour de force* with which for half the long novel he unfolds the story of Booth and Amelia without abandoning the absolute unity of his scene, the prison where Booth is confined. It is quite as remarkable as the designed confusion of *Tristram Shandy*, but there is no answer to a reader who replies: "I read to be entertained and how heavily this style of Fielding's weighs beside Sterne's impudent opening: 'I wish either my father or my mother, or indeed both of them, as they were in duty both equally bound to it, had minded what they were about when they begot me. . . .' "

No, one must surrender to Sterne most of the graces.

What Fielding possessed, and Sterne did not, what was quite as new to the novel as Sterne's lightness and sensibility, was moral seriousness. He was not a poet—and Sterne was at any rate a minor one—but this moral seriousness enabled him to construct a form which would later satisfy the requirements of major poets as Defoe's plain narrative could not. When we admire Tom Jones as being the first portrait of "a whole man", (a description which perhaps fits only Bloom in later fiction) it is Fielding's seriousness to which we are paying tribute, his power of discriminating between immorality and vice. He had no high opinion of human nature: the small sensualities of Tom Jones, the incorrigible gambling propensities of Booth, his own direct statement, when he heard his poor dying body ugly with the dropsy mocked by the watermen at Rotherhithe ("it was a lively picture of that cruelty and inhumanity in the nature of men which I have often contemplated with concern, and which leads the mind into a train of very uncomfortable and melancholy thoughts"), prove it no more certainly than his quite incredible pictures of virtue, the rectitude of Mr. Allworthy, the heroic nature of the patient Amelia. Experience had supplied him with many a Booth and Tom Jones (indeed one of the latter name appeared before him at Bow Street), but for examples of virtue he had to call on his imagination, and one cannot agree with Saintsbury who remarked quaintly and uncritically of his heroines: "There is no more touching portrait in the whole of fiction than this heroic and immortal one of feminine goodness and forbearance."

It is impossible to use these immoderate terms of Fielding without absurdity: to compare the kept woman, Miss Mathews, in *Amelia*, as Dobson did, with a character of Balzac's. He belonged to the wrong century for this kind of greatness. His heroic characters are derived from Dryden—unsuccessfully (the relation between Amelia and a character like Almeyda is obvious). But what puts us so supremely in his debt is this: that he had gathered up in his novels the two divided strands of Restoration fiction: he had combined on his own lower level the flippant prose fictions of the dramatists and the heroic drama of the poets.

On the lower, the unreligious level. His virtues are natural virtues, his despair a natural despair, endured with as much courage as Dryden's but without the supernatural reason.

> Brutus and Cato might discharge their Souls,
> And give them Furlo's for another World:
> But we like Centries, are oblig'd to stand
> In Starless Nights, and wait th'appointed Hour.

So Dryden, and here more lovably perhaps, with purely natural virtue, Fielding faces death—death in the shape of a last hard piece of work for public order, undertaken in his final sickness with the intention of winning from government some pension for his wife and children: "And though I disclaim all pretence to that Spartan or Roman patriotism which loved the public so well that it was always ready to become a voluntary sacrifice to the public good I do solemnly declare I have that love for my family."

He hated iniquity and he certainly died in exile: his books do represent a moral struggle, but they completely lack the sense of supernatural evil or supernatural good. Mr. Eliot has suggested that "with the disappearance of the idea of Original Sin, with the disappearance of the idea of intense moral struggle, the human beings presented to us both in poetry and in prose fiction . . . tend to become less and less real", and it is the intensity of the struggle which is lacking in Fielding. Evil is always a purely sexual matter: the struggle seems invariably to take the form of whether or not the "noble lord" or Colonel James will succeed in raping or seducing

287

Amelia, and the characters in this superficial struggle, carried out with quite as much ingenuity as Uncle Toby employed on his fortifications, do tend to become less and less real. How can one take seriously Mrs. Heartfree's five escapes from ravishment in twenty pages? One can only say in favour of this conception that it is at least expressed with more dignity than in *The Sentimental Journey* where Sterne himself has stolen the part of Pamela, of Amelia and Mrs. Heartfree, and asks us to be breathlessly concerned for *his* virtue ("The foot of the bed was within a yard and a half of the place where we were standing—I had still hold of her hands—and how it happened I can give no account, but I neither ask'd her—nor drew her—nor did I think of the bed——"). But the moral life in Fielding is apt to resemble one of those pictorial games of Snakes and Ladders. If the player's counter should happen to fall on a Masquerade or a ticket to Vauxhall Gardens, down it slides by way of the longest snake.

But it would be ungrateful to end on this carping note. There had been picaresque novels before Fielding—from the days of Nashe to the days of Defoe—but the picaresque had not before in English been raised to an art, given the form, the arrangement, which separates art from mere realistic reporting, however vivid. Fielding lifted life out of its setting and arranged it for the delight of all who love symmetry. He can afford to leave Sterne his graceful play with the emotions, his amusing little indecencies: the man who created Partridge had a distant kinship to the creator of Falstaff. "Nothing," Jones remarks, "can be more likely to happen than death to men who go into battle. Perhaps we shall both fall in it—and what then?" "What then?" replied Partridge; "why then there is an end of us, is there not? When I am gone, all is over with me. What matters the cause to me, or who gets the victory, if I am killed? I shall never enjoy any advantage from it. What are all the ringing of bells, and bonfires, to one that is six foot under ground? there will be an end of poor Partridge."

Fielding had tried to make the novel poetic, even though he himself had not the poetic mind, only a fair, a generous and a courageous mind, and the conventions which he established for the novel enabled it in a more passionate age to become a poetic art, to fill the gap in literature left when Dryden died and the seventeenth century was over. He was the best product of his age, the post-revolutionary age when politics for the first time ceased to represent any deep issues and religion excited only the shallowest feeling. His material was underpaid officers, highwaymen, debtors, noblemen who had nothing better to do than pursue sexual adventures, clergymen like Parson Adams whose virtues are as much pagan as Christian. "At the moment when one writes," to quote Mr. Eliot again, "one is what one is, and the damage of a lifetime . . . cannot be repaired at the moment of composition." We should not complain; rather we should be amazed at what so unpoetic a mind accomplished in such an age.

20

CAPTAIN COOK

(1728–1779)

by WILLIAM PLOMER

"I HAVE explored more of the Great South Sea than all that have gone before me; in so much, that little remains to be done, to have a thorough knowledge of that part of the globe." In those few simple words Cook told of the best part of his life's work, conveying a natural pride in the great additions he was able to make to science, and also in his having been able to fit himself to make them, for he was born without any hereditary privileges but the best one a man can have, natural ability. "Cook did more," says Admiral Wharton, who edited the journal of his first great voyage, "incomparably more than any other navigator to discover new lands," and yet to the ordinary Englishman to-day he is little more than a name. Although he made it possible for his King to rule over a new continent and untouched islands, fertile and temperate, and for traders, missionaries, administrators, convicts, and other immigrants to extend the activities of Western civilization in those remote places; although, in fact, he "sought his country's glory in his own", yet the glamour that attaches to his memory is not the somewhat theatrical limelight which shines upon certain empire-builders of a later age. It is noteworthy that in recent years, when biography has been so much in fashion, so perfect and out-standing an exemplar of the active Englishman should have seldom been chosen as a subject. The story of his life does not lend itself to exploitation by cheap biographers. He was not a "great lover", he was a great worker; there was nothing scandalous or equivocal or cheaply sensational in his career; and nobody ever made fewer mistakes.

The first forty years of his life (1728-1769) were remarkable for steady application which resulted in solid achievement, and the last ten for the three great voyages of discovery that made his name. The son of a Yorkshire farm-hand, he served as a boy in a grocer's shop in a village near Whitby, but the sea was at the door, and the sea, as they say, called him, so at the age of eighteen he was bound apprentice to a local coal-shipper engaged in the coastal trade. In the intervals between voyages, while other boys were out doing the things boys do, he sat up reading by candlelight, teaching himself, it is sup-posed, the elements of navigation. After serving his appren-ticeship he went on working for the same employers, and when he was twenty-seven they offered him the command of one of their vessels, but he had other plans, and left them to join the navy as an able-bodied seaman. His reason for this was that he had "a mind to try his fortune that way". No further explanation need be sought: he had reason to believe in his ability to better himself. His confidence was not misplaced. His previous experience was valuable to him, he began as master's mate, was soon promoted, saw some varied service, and was entrusted with the task of surveying parts of the coasts of Canada and Newfoundland. In 1766 he made some observa-tions of an eclipse of the sun, and thought them of sufficient importance to be sent to the Royal Society, by whom they were published.

In the following year the Royal Society were beginning to make preparations for an expedition to the South Pacific in order that qualified persons might observe the Transit of Venus which was due in June, 1769. Their funds were not great enough to finance it, so they turned to the Admiralty for help, and the Admiralty, who had already sent more than one ship to explore in the South Seas, were perfectly ready to oblige: the Transit of Venus was to see Science and Colonization in conjunction, and Cook was chosen as the most suitable man to command the expedition. A sturdy tub of a boat, the *Endeavour*, was bought for the purpose, and Cook was given his commission in May, 1768. In August he sailed, "having on board 94 persons," including Joseph Banks (afterwards Sir Joseph Banks, P.R.S.), a botanist, a naturalist, and three artists, besides "near 18 Months' Provisions". His orders (quoted by Commander Gould in his excellent little life of Cook) instructed him to observe the Transit; it was then remarked that "the making of discoveries of countries hitherto unknown" would be of advantage to his own country, and he was to look for the continent which it was thought might exist in the Southern Pacific, and take possession of it in the King's name. It is really astonishing to think that it was possible only one hundred and seventy years ago to order a man to go and look for a continent.

And what kind of a man was this, entrusted with such responsibilities? In stature he was tall, and in appearance stern, with a broad forehead set in the contours of concentration, with a large and one may say a commanding nose, and the firm mouth and jaw of a man who sticks to his purpose. He had a strong constitution and was moderate in his habits, and not only did the languorous allurements of the South Seas fail to allure him, but it is said that even intervals of recreation were "submitted to by him with a certain impatience". His mind was naturally active, and he had all those qualities one would expect—he was energetic, just, cool, generally patient, and "fertile in expedients". Like many men of great achievement, he was modest; and even, on occasions, bashful. There can be no surer proof of his magnanimity than that he did not profit by his advancement to tyrannize over those who had formerly been his social equals. He never suffered from a swollen head, and almost the only fault he seems to have had was an impatience with those who were slow to fall in with his plans, an impatience that amounted at times to a hastiness of temper. Not only had he the power to lead and control others, but he had the extraordinary sense to realize that people are both more efficient and more docile when they are treated like human beings and made as contented as circumstances will allow. Thus he paid attention to the minutiæ of hygiene, and in an age when a commanding officer on a long voyage expected to lose a good number of his men from scurvy, Cook set himself to prevent it. This he did by ensuring that at times when fresh meat and vegetables were unobtainable the men should partake of "portable soup" and "the Sour Kroutt", a commodity they did not fancy until the officers set them an example by eating it every day at their own table. This was not his only hygienic rule. Having served for years before the mast he knew the wretched conditions of a seaman's life, and made sure that where they had been used to damp and dirty clothes and quarters they should as far as possible devote themselves to keeping dry and clean. He had his reward, for on his first voyage he did not lose a single man from scurvy. This care for the health of his men went with a humanity towards them which was exceptional, for the punishments he ordered them when he thought punishment was needed were more moderate than was common at the time. "His men suffered less," says Wharton, "than in any other ships, British or foreign, on similar expeditions. Though his tracks were in new and unknown waters, we never hear of starvation; he always manages to have an abundant supply of water." And as regards food, besides being a hygienist, he was a good manager:

it was his practice to economize on the ship's stores by eating local food wherever it could be obtained, except, we are assured, "when he was amongst the cannibals of New Zealand."

Early in 1769 the *Endeavour* rounded the Horn, and in April Cook cast anchor at Tahiti, where Wallis and Bougainville had been before him. He had several weeks to spare before the Transit, and spent the time in preparing a fortified observatory, in case the natives should turn aggressive. But their only aggression was a talent for thieving that amounted to virtuosity, and objects made of metal they found irresistible. Otherwise they were amenable. "After their meals," wrote George Forster pompously, "they resume their domestic amusements, during which the flame of mutual affection spreads in every heart." Venereal disease spread with equal rapidity, and after Cook had been three months at Tahiti his men were in a low state of health, so having finished his business, which included the making of a chart, he moved on to the Society Islands and then bore south to New Zealand. In a little over six months he managed to sail right round its entire coastline (which he charted with extraordinary exactness) and then ran westward until he came in sight of the south-eastern coast of Australia, up which he proceeded, threading and mapping his way through the unknown dangers of the Great Barrier Reef and having more than one narrow escape from disaster. He took formal possession of the land he had found, and called it New Wales. In October he reached Batavia, and arranged for the *Endeavour* to be refitted for the homeward voyage. His men were weakened by hardship and disease, and now dysentery spread amongst them. Between his arrival at Batavia and his arrival at the Cape he had thirty deaths to record, and at the Cape he had to land nearly another thirty sick. But in spite of everything, when he arrived home in July, 1771, he could feel a justifiable pride in having made a voyage "as compleat as any before made to the So. Seas on the same account", even though he had "failed in discovering the so much talked of Southern Continent (which perhaps do not exist)."

The Admiralty did not wait long before employing him on a new expedition, and he sailed from Plymouth in July, 1772.* It was still believed that a vast Southern Continent *might* exist, fertile and thickly populated, and his new instructions told him to sail round the world as far south as possible and see what he could find, beginning at the Cape and returning there. This time he was to have two ships, the *Resolution* and the *Adventure*. By November he had left the Cape, and soon afterwards ran into icebergs, fog, gales, and sleet. In January he entered the Antarctic Circle. Icefields prevented him discovering land, and he had to bear away again, and made for New Zealand. In June he was off again, called at Tahiti (where his men, according to Forster, indulged in "incredible excesses" on board with local girls of nine and ten), cruised about till November, and then sailed south-east and south and again crossed the Antarctic Circle. In the New Year he visited Easter Island and the Marquesas, returned again to Tahiti, and late in 1774 left New Zealand for home, rounded the Horn, stopped at South Georgia, and explored the extreme South Atlantic, reaching the Cape in March, 1775, and England in July. He had come home, says Commander Gould, "from one of the longest and most dangerous voyages ever made, with a total loss of four men in three years . . . Cook's second voyage is actually the greatest of the three—and, taking it all round, not far from being the greatest voyage ever made. . . . The ages-old conception of a temperate southern continent vanished like the dream it was; and for the first time, the true limits of the habitable world were determined."

On his return Cook was presented to the King, promoted, and given a house and salary, but already a new voyage of

*On this voyage also sailed Captain (afterwards Admiral) James Burney (1750-1821), Charles Lamb's friend.

discovery was being planned. This time it was thought desirable to find out whether a north-west passage did not perhaps lead from the Northern Pacific to Hudson Bay. Knowledge of the region where the extremities of Asia and America adjoin one another was hazy, and Cook was deputed to disperse the haze. He again sailed in the *Resolution*, and was accompanied by the *Discovery*. Among those with him on board were Bligh, the afterwards notorious bully, and Omai, a native of the South Seas who had been brought to England in the *Adventure* and was now to return home, taking with him —in order perhaps to show his compatriots that European civilization could charm, shock, or make one invulnerable— "a portable organ, an electrical machine, and a suit of armour". Cook sailed on this third and last voyage in July, 1776. Travelling via the Cape, Kerguelen, New Zealand, and the Friendly Islands, he arrived at Tahiti in August of the following year, visited the Society Islands, discovered the Hawaiian group, and early in 1778 made for the west coast of North America. In the face of considerable difficulties he managed to reach the Bering Strait, and pushed northward until he was stopped by pack-ice. He then turned back and charted the northern approaches to the strait, touched at the Aleutian islands, where he met some Russian traders, and returned to Hawaii in order to winter and refit. The natives were more than friendly and generous, they made it plain that they adored him. He left his anchorage to complete a survey, but bad weather forced him back to Kealakekua Bay, and the temper of the natives seemed also to have changed for the worse. They stole the *Discovery's* cutter, and Cook decided to land and seize either the king or one of the chiefs as a hostage, in order to get it back. He was unsuccessful, some of his men fired on the natives, a fight broke out, and Cook, standing on the beach, was stabbed in the back, fell into the water, and was hacked to pieces.

Cook's accomplishments were so great and his merits are

so obvious that it is almost surprising to find that things have been said against him. He has been blamed for treating the natives of the South Seas harshly, for allowing his men to introduce venereal disease amongst them, and for allowing the Hawaiians to pay him divine honours. Certainly the islanders were mostly friendly, but they were often incorrigible thieves: not having been brought up on the Ten Commandments or with English ideas of the sacredness of private property, they may be to some extent excused, especially as they seem to have been quite open in helping themselves to what they fancied—Cook's stockings were taken from under his pillow while his head was lying on it, wide awake. On the whole it is a wonder, considering the vast difference between the world Cook came from and the world he entered, that so little friction resulted. He cannot be called uniformly merciful, but not many people are made merciful by being robbed. During the first voyage a thief was shot at Tahiti, and a number of Maoris in a boat were fired at and killed because they did not choose to parley. During the second voyage, on the other hand, some Maoris ate a boatload of men from the *Adventure*. During the last voyage a number of Friendly Island natives were flogged for stealing, a Society Islander who stole a sextant had his ears cut off (an act Cook later regretted), and a Hawaiian was shot at the time of the *Resolution's* arrival at Kaui. Cook brought with him the standards of an alien world, but he was, as men go, a very just man, and his few asperities may be put down partly to the barbarous customs of the age and partly to the hastiness of his temper when his purpose was thwarted by others: his character was in accord with those of the more capable types of empire-builder, who make it their business to win the confidence of primitive peoples because they find it expedient to do so.

With regard to the "venereal distemper", Cook complained that most of his men were afflicted with it after the Tahitian women had shown themselves "so very liberal with their favours". George Hamilton, on the other hand, who sailed later as surgeon on the frigate *Pandora* (which was sent after the *Bounty* mutineers) said that the Tahitians spoke of it as "the British disease", and added: "Happy would it have been for those people, had they never been visited by Europeans: for to our shame be it spoken that disease and gunpowder are the only benefits they have ever received from us, in return for their hospitality and kindness." If the disease was not endemic (and little is proved in the matter) it was bound to be introduced sooner or later: it would be absurd to hold Cook personally responsible for the disadvantages of the civilization of which he was a representative.

As for his allowing the Hawaiians to worship him, there is reason to believe that they regarded him as one of their own deities returning after an absence. This was a certain pig-god named Lono, who had killed his wife, gone mad (his madness had taken the form of an addiction to all-in wrestling) and sailed away, saying he would come back "on an island bearing trees, pigs, and dogs". What could be more natural than that Cook's ship should be taken for the island, and Cook for the god? And whether or not he fully realized the import of the honour that was done to him, why should he have resisted such a novel experience or refused to accept such an unusual compliment? He was amply justified by necessity. "We must conclude," said Sir Walter Besant, "that Cook's attitude showed a readiness to accept any honours provided only that they [the natives] assisted in victualling his ships and promoting the success of his expedition. If they chose to worship him, they might." The chief danger was that they were bound to discover sooner or later that he was only human after all, and to this discovery, to their "strong revulsion of feeling", his death has been attributed. It was a false god who fell, with a spear in his back, face forward into the surf.

Bligh of the *Bounty* was to write that the charms of Tahiti were so great that it was no wonder if the sailors "imagined it in their power to fix themselves in the midst of plenty, on one of the finest islands in the world, where they need not labour, and where the allurements of dissipation are beyond anything that can be conceived". Even some of Cook's men tried, in such surroundings, to desert: they had perceived the difference between the happy life of the Tahitians and, in Forster's words, "the constant agitation, the nauseous food, and the coarse awkward garments of a set of seafaring Europeans." There is a terrible pathos in the longing of the sailors to live in the happy places which their successors were so soon to spoil: it is as if they knew instinctively that the Tahitian life was too beautiful to last. If Cook's incursions into what he called "those Terrestrial Paradises" were a prelude to Imperial expansion, he was also, since his objects and pursuits were largely scientific, a forerunner of those later voyagers, Darwin and Huxley, and in certain of his notes, in which he refers to the habits of primitive people in somewhat Biblical terms, it is perhaps not too fanciful to detect the first stirrings of the scientific revolution of the nineteenth century. "Scarce can it be said," he wrote of the natives of the South Seas, "that they earn their bread by the sweat of their brows. Benevolent nature hath not only provided them with necessaries, but many of the luxuries of life. Loaves of bread . . . grow here in a manner upon trees; besides a great many other fruits and roots, and the sea coasts are well stored with a vast variety of excellent fish." And the aboriginals of Australia caused him to observe that although "it is said of our first parents that, after they had eaten the forbidden fruit, they saw themselves naked and were ashamed, these people are naked and not ashamed." Missionaries, of course, had not yet arrived to correct them.

Cook's memory remains as that of an austere man and in a sense a lonely one, for there is no evidence that he ever entered into any relationship with anyone that could be called intimacy, or that he ever endeared himself by little peculiarities. "Cook had no friends," said Besant bluntly, and "for so distinguished a man," says another of his biographers, "there is a most curious dearth of personal anecdote, even from those who were in close companionship with him on his voyages." He was one of nature's commanding officers, and it is not easy to think of him with any sentiment softer than profound admiration. His business was with facts. Like many of the great, he moved unfalteringly along a special orbit, and was too busy, too single-minded, to indulge himself like other men. He was a little above the rest of mankind, and they have therefore always been obliged to look up to him. Even in his lifetime, his fame was as good as universal. France and the United States, at war with England, gave orders to their ships to treat him with deference and generosity, a circumstance of a kind that would be almost impossible to-day. He was trusted by those above and below him, his men obeyed him willingly, and the Hawaiians, for a time at least, received him like a god. Even his wife (who lived to be a nonagenarian, long surviving him and all their children) seems to have regarded "Mr. Cook" as a kind of superior being. As a widow, dressed always in black satin, her hair done in an ancient mode, and on her finger a ring containing the circumnavigator's hair, she was in the habit of giving dinner parties on Thursdays at three in her house at Clapham, and seated on such occasions among the curios he had brought back from the South Seas—necklaces, one may suppose, of sharks' teeth, ceremonial objects of tattooed wood, and hula-hula accessories—she used proudly to exhibit to her guests the gold medal struck by the Royal Society in honour of the husband with whom she had spent so little time, and who had been so much occupied, whenever he was at home, with his maps, charts, journals, and preparations for new expeditions.

21

WILLIAM HOGARTH

(1697-1764)

by HERBERT READ

IN England Hogarth is still perhaps the most familiar of
English artists. Since his time the whole range of European
painting has been made available by various processes of
reproduction, and public galleries have given us the basis for
a wide eclectic taste. But in spite of the competition of
thousands of gaudy lithographs and all the sentimental *Kitsch*
of the Victorian age, you may still find, in country inns and
farmhouse kitchens, some more or less debased print from the
"Harlot's Progress" or "Marriage à la Mode". Hogarth was
the first artist I myself was ever aware of, and I think my
experience is to some extent typical. Prints of the "Rake's
Progress" and of "Industry and Idleness" were the only works
of art to be found in my school, and for five years Hogarth's
pictures were not only the first, but perhaps the only works of
art I knew—I remember no others. If what I have to say in
this essay should give an impression of asperity or disillusion,
the effect is not wilful nor the effort pretentious. It is due to
no lack of an affectionate predisposition, but rather to the all
too natural triumph of critical faculties. Hogarth has not
wanted praise; Lamb's and Hazlitt's essays have, indeed,

established his reputation beyond any serious question. I am only concerned to point out what is not always recognized as an obvious truth: that the qualities for which Hogarth is rightly praised have little or nothing to do with the art of painting. There is hardly a phrase in either of those famous essays which might not be about a fellow writer. Hazlitt, indeed, included the painter in a series of lectures on the English Comic Writers. More significantly still, Hogarth himself in some of his advertisements speaks of himself as the "author"; and quite explicitly, in a much-quoted passage, confesses that he has "endeavoured to treat my subject as a dramatic writer; my picture is my stage, and men and women my players, who by means of certain actions and gestures, are to exhibit a dumb show."

I shall return presently to this aspect of Hogarth. First let us note a few details of his life. He was born in London in 1697, the son of parents who had migrated from Westmorland and who belonged to that same sturdy yeomanry which was later to produce Wordsworth. His stock is worth noting, for Hogarth possessed something of that shorthorn stolidity and staying-power which characterizes men of that region. His lack of education has often been held against him, but his father was a schoolmaster and there is no reason to suppose that he was any less cultured than Gainsborough or Turner, or for that matter, than Shakespeare. In the note-books of his contemporary, the connoisseur George Vertue, whose manuscripts have only recently been transcribed and published, there occurs a brief account of Hogarth which must be quoted as an illustration of this attitude, and as a lively summary of the essential features of the painter's career:

As all things have their spring from nature, time and cultivation—so Arts have their bloom & fruite, & as well in other places in this Kingdom. On this observation at present a true English Genius in the Art of Painting has sprung and by natural strength of himself chiefly, begun with little & low-shrubb instructions, rose to a surprizing hight in the publick esteem & opinion. As this remarkable circumstance is of Mr. Hogarth whose first practice was as an aprentice to a mean sort of Engraver of coats of arms, wch he left & applying to painting & study drew and painted humorous conversations, in time with wonderful succes—& small also portraits & family-peces &c. From thence to portrait painting at large, & attempted History, thro' all which with strong and powerfull pursuits & studyes by the boldness of his Genious, in opposition to all other professors of Painting, got into great Reputation & esteem of the Lovers of Art, Nobles of the greatest consideration in the Nation, & by his undaunted spirit, dispisd under-valud all other present & precedent painters, such as Kneller, Lilly, Vandyke—those English painters of the highest Reputation. Such reasonings or envious detractions he not only often or at all times made the subject of his con-versations & observations to Gentlemen and Lovers of Art, but such like invidious reflections he woud argue & maintain with all sorts of Artists, painters, sculptors, &c. . . .

Admitt the Temper of the people loves humorous, spritely, diverting subjects in painting, yet surely *the Foxes tale* was of great use to him. As Hudibrass expresseth:

> yet He! that hath but Impudence,
> to all things has a Fair pretence.*

That was written in 1745, but already in 1730 Vertue had noted that "the daily success of Mr. Hogarth in painting small family peices & Conversations with so much Air & agreeable-ness causes him to be much followd & esteemed, whereby he

Transactions of the Walpole Society. Vol. XXII (1933-4), pp. 123-4.

has much imployment & like to be a master of great reputation in that way." At his own instigation Hogarth had left school at an early age to become apprenticed to a silver-plate engraver, having discovered in himself a natural ability for drawing. "My exercises when at school were more remarkable for the ornaments which adorned them, than for the exercise itself." But long before the end of his apprenticeship he was looking farther afield. "Engraving on copper was, at twenty years of age, my utmost ambition." That meant, in effect, engraving plates for illustrated books, and this was work requiring a high degree of skill in draughtsmanship. The way in which Hogarth set about securing this skill is very characteristic of the man, and shows that from the beginning he was possessed of that independence of spirit which gives us the clue to his whole career. In the normal course he should have attended an academy, drawing from the life and from the antique, thus undergoing several years of arduous training. Hogarth had neither the temperament nor the time for such a procedure. He therefore invented his own "method", "laying it first down as an axiom, that he who could by any means acquire and retain in his memory, perfect ideas of the subjects he meant to draw, would have as clear a knowledge of the figure as a man who can write freely hath of the twenty-four letters of the alphabet and their infinite combinations . . . and would consequently be an accurate designer." Whether by virtue of practising such exercises, or from some innate talent, there is no doubt that Hogarth possessed a visual memory of exceptional acuteness and retentiveness. At first he put it to humble uses: coats of arms and shop-bills, plates for booksellers and caricatures. In 1724 he issued his first independent engraving, a satirical design entitled "Masquerades and Operas". In 1726 he engraved the illustrations for an edition of *Hudibras* and gained some fame, but little fortune. Meanwhile he was getting "some little insight & instructions in Oyl Colours, without copying other paintings or masters immediatly", as Vertue puts it, and finding this technique more agreeable to his mind, he "took up the pincill & applyd his studyes to painting in small conversations or fancyes". These pictures, "from twelve to fifteen inches high," proved to be very popular, and for a time procured him a living. But not a living on the scale he contemplated. In 1729 he had run away with the daughter of Sir James Thornhill, one of the most distinguished and successful painters of the day; and we may assume that he was anxious to win the approval of his outraged father-in-law. He was soon to succeed in this ambition, and in the process to effect something like a revolution in the history of English painting.

To understand the significance of what follows, we must realize the condition of English art at this period. During the Middle Ages this country had been famous all over Europe for its artists: English manuscripts, English embroideries, English alabasters were all much sought after, and there is a growing belief that even English painting had far more influence on Continental schools than has hitherto been recognized. But by 1530 at the latest we had lost this reputation, and for two centuries the people at large seem to have maintained a puritanical indifference or even hostility towards all native art. Such art as the court required for its dignity was imported from abroad—Holbein, Vandyck, Lely, Kneller, were all of foreign origin, and what English painters attained contemporary fame were comparatively feeble exponents of a foreign style. It is to Hogarth's eternal credit that he revolted against this enervate condition of our native art, and fought with all his lustiness against the snobbery and cant on which it subsisted. We are lucky to possess a letter, written to the *St. James's Evening Post* in 1737, in which he gives forceful expression to his point of view:

There is another set of gentry more noxious to the art than these [certain critics], and those are your picture-jobbers from abroad, who are always ready to raise a great cry in the prints whenever they think their craft is in danger; and indeed it is their interest to depreciate every English work, as hurtful to their trade, of continually importing shiploads of dead Christs, Holy Families, Madona's, and other dismal dark subjects, neither entertaining nor ornamental; on which they scrawl the terrible cramp names of some Italian masters, and fix on us poor Englishmen the character of *universal dupes*. If a man, naturally a judge of painting, not bigoted to those empirics, should cast his eye on one of their sham virtuoso-pieces, he would be very apt to say, 'Mr. Bubbleman, that grand Venus (as you are pleased to call it) has not beauty enough for the character of an English cook-maid.' Upon which the quack answers with a confident air, 'O Sir, I find that you are no connoisseur—that picture, I assure you, is in Alesso Baldovinetto's second and best manner, boldly painted, and truely sublime; the contour gracious; the air of the head in the high Greek taste, and a most divine idea it is.' Then spitting on an obscure place and rubbing it with a dirty handkerchief, takes a skip to the other end of the room, and screams out in raptures, 'There is an amazing touch! a man should have this picture a twelve-month in his collection before he can discover half its beauties.' The gentleman (though naturally a judge of what is beautiful, yet ashamed to be out of the fashion in judging for himself) with this cant is struck dumb, gives a vast sum for the picture, very modestly confesses he is quite ignorant of painting, and bestows a frame worth fifty pounds on a frightful thing, without the hard name on it not worth as many farthings.

All of which shows, not only an admirable sense of humour,

but a healthy attitude towards the art of painting. But it did not mean, unfortunately, that Hogarth was altogether disabused of the ambition to rank as a painter in "the Great Style". It is quite impossible, as we shall presently see, to rank Hogarth as a great original genius of the type of Giotto or Cézanne; he did not seek to transform or redirect a tradition. He merely sought to re-establish a native school, and if the method he was to adopt might fairly be described as a stroke of genius, the genius must then be qualified as commercial rather than artistic.

Let me, for the last time, quote Vertue's quaint account of the matter:

Amongst other designs of his in painting he began a small picture of a common harlot, supposed to dwell in drewry lane, just riseing about noon out of bed and at breakfast, a bunter waiting on her—this whore's desabillé careless and a pretty Countenance & air. This thought pleasd many; some advisd him to make another to it as a pair, which he did. Then other thoughts encreas'd & multiplyd by his fruitfull invention, till he made six different subjects which he painted so naturally the thoughts & strikeing the expressions that it drew every body to see them. Which he proposing to engrave in six plates to print at one guinea each sett, he had daily Subscriptions came in, in fifty or a hundred pounds in a Week—there being no day but persons of fashion and Artists came to see these pictures, the story of them being related, how this Girl came to Town, how Mother Needham and Col. Charters first deluded her, how a Jew kept her, how she livd in Drury lane, when she was sent to Bridewell by Sr. John Gonson, Justice, and her salivation & death.

Before a twelve month came about whilst these plates were engraving he had in his Subscription between 14 *or fifteen* hundred (*by the printer* I have been assured 1240 setts were printed) Subscribers that he publickly advertiz'd that those that did not come in before a certain day shoud be excluded. . . .

Such was the origin of "A Harlot's Progress", the first of that series of "moral subjects" by which Hogarth made his fame and his modest fortune. What in effect Hogarth had done was to open up a completely new market. He had devised a means by which the artist's invention could be broadcast. The technical means, it is true, existed before; but he had hit upon an idea for exploiting that means, and this he had done quite shrewdly and deliberately. "This I found was most likely to answer my purpose," he confesses, "provided I could strike the passions, and by small sums from many, by the sale of prints which I could engrave from my pictures, thus secure my property to myself." From the engravings we may reckon he secured £1,300; the originals he sold thirteen years later for only £88 4s. But when the present value of these sums is computed, it will be realized that Hogarth was at last a man of substance. And in effect Sir James Thornhill no longer delayed to recognize him as his son-in-law.

The only fault in the scheme was due to the lack of any legal protection for such an original kind of traffic; no sooner were his engravings issued than they were extensively pirated. So before continuing in this career, Hogarth set about to get the law amended, and as a result of his activities a bill was introduced into Parliament and duly passed which gave to designers and engravers an exclusive right to their own works and enabled them to control the multiplication of copies. With this security Hogarth then launched another series, "A Rake's Progress," which was equally successful. Piracy continued in spite of the Act, so Hogarth himself issued small copies of the series at 2s. 6d. the set, at which price the pirates presumably could not compete. At every stage, indeed, Hogarth pursued the commercial possibilities of his engravings; incited all the more because he soon discovered that the broadcasting of the engravings deprived the original paintings of their proper value "as (according to the Standard of Judgment, so righteously and laudably establish'd by Picture-Dealers, Picture-Cleaners, Picture-Frame-Makers, and other Connoisseurs) the Works of a Painter are to be esteem'd more or less valuable, as they are more or less scarce. . . ." He resorted to ingenious methods of auctioning these original paintings, but without much success. The eight paintings of "A Rake's Progress", for example, only fetched twenty-two guineas each.

There is no point in recounting the rest of the engravings issued by Hogarth; he continued to issue them throughout his life and on them he depended for his livelihood. We must, however, examine their general character, for they offer perhaps the best possible opportunity for considering one of the central problems of art—a problem which seems to divide critics into two irreconcilable camps. It must be clearly realized that two distinct factors were involved in Hogarth's scheme; one financial (obtaining, instead of a large sum from one purchaser, small sums from many) the other psychological ("provided I could strike the passions"). It is to this psychological factor that we should now give our attention. It was the factor on which the whole success of the scheme depended, for though any artist could engrave his paintings and sell the prints for a few shillings apiece, only a rare genius like Hogarth could devise subjects which would so "strike the passions" that the public would flock to buy them.

It is the distinction of Hogarth that more than any other artist he has been responsible for the habit, inveterate with the English, of judging a work of art by its subject-matter, to the almost complete neglect of its form. The fact that his own paintings are not without fine qualities, both of composition and handling, does not alter the fact that he appealed beyond these, and laid his full stress on the picture's moral theme.

"I . . . wished to compose pictures on canvas, similar to representations on the stage; and farther hope, that they will be tried by the same test, and criticized by the same criterion. Let it be observed, that I mean to speak only of those scenes where the human species are actors, and these I think have not often been delineated in a way of which they are worthy and capable. In these compositions, those subjects that will both entertain and improve the mind, bid fair to be of the greatest public utility, and must therefore be entitled to rank in the highest class." In this manner Hogarth described his aims, and his reference to the drama is no idle analogy. To understand its force we must consider for a moment the place occupied by the stage at the time we are speaking of. Ever since Jeremy Collier's famous attack on the excesses of Restoration comedy (1698), the English stage had shown a definite tendency to reform itself. The sincerity of these good intentions may perhaps be doubted; often enough it amounted to romping through four acts with all the old gaiety and licence, and pulling up suddenly in the fifth act to dole out the rewards and punishments demanded by the new moral consciousness of the age. Such was the sentimental comedy of Steele and Colley Cibber, of Sotherne and Rowe; and it was exactly contemporaneous with Hogarth's youth. At the precise moment at which Hogarth was looking round for some new device to strike the passions, this comic spirit, which had reached its highest point in *The Beggar's Opera* (1728) was given a tragic twist. In June, 1731, George Lillo's "domestic tragedy" *The London Merchant, or the History of George Barnwell*, was produced and was one of those wild popular successes which though of no lasting importance, at the time seemed to transform the whole course of life. In theme this play was based on "an excellent ballad of George Barnwell, an apprentice of

London who . . . thrice robbed his master, and murdered his uncle in Ludlow", and Lillo did not fail to squeeze every drop of moral unction out of his gloomy career. But the success of the play was due, not merely to its generous cathartic effect on the maudlin emotions of that generation, but also to the fact that Lillo had deserted the Aristotelian canon which requires that the characters of a tragedy must be persons of rank and fortune, and had written about the humble folk of everyday life. He had struck the petty bourgeois note, just as in our day authors are endeavouring to strike the proletarian note. It was a note that rang so clearly in Hogarth's ear that he set about converting it into the terms of his own art.

Hogarth completed the plates of "A Harlot's Progress" in September, 1731, four months after the successful production of *The London Merchant*, and this series of engravings, like the others which were to follow it, was in effect a "domestic tragedy" in the manner of Lillo's play, and appealed to the same emotions. Hogarth had struck well. His upbringing, his temperament and his manner of life, had supplied him with a rich and varied knowledge of "the human species"; he had trained himself to store in his mind visual images of human types, actions, expressions, gestures. He needed only the inspiration of Lillo's tragedy to precipitate this wealth of material in a vendable form.

He struck the passions of his contemporaries, and though Lillo's work is dead and forgotten, Hogarth still survives, and in every age his genius has evoked the eulogies of responsible critics. I have already remarked that these critics treat Hogarth as an author. Lamb compares him to Shakespeare, and though Hazlitt demurs against such "a staggering paradox", he admits that Hogarth had the advantage over Fielding, "and other of our comic writers, who excelled only in the light and ludicrous." "There is a general distinction," Hazlitt points out, "almost an impassable one, between the power of embody-

ing the serious and the ludicrous; but these contradictory
faculties were reconciled in Hogarth, as they were in Shakespeare, in Chaucer; and as it is said that they were in another
extraordinary and later instance, Garrick's acting."

If, in spite of these comparisons, which we may be prepared
to admit, we still deny that Hogarth was a great painter, we
must make the grounds of our objection very clear. There
are two possible lines of criticism, both decisive in Hogarth's
case. The first might be called formal, because it concerns his
ability in composition and in the handling of his medium.
This may be presented very briefly. "My picture is my stage,"
said Hogarth, "and men and women my players, who by means
of certain actions and gestures, are to exhibit *a dumb show*."
That statement, in actual fact, is more than a metaphor.
Hogarth's compositions are in a certain sense artless; they are
action arrested, but not the action of daily life (as later an
impressionist painter like Degas or Manet would arrest it).
It is the arrested action of a mechanical play, of figures crowded
into the unnatural space between a backcloth and the foot-
lights. The realization of absolute space, such as we get in
Raphael; the imponderability of light such as Rembrandt suggested; the organization of colour and mass such as Poussin
achieved—these are the major effects of the art of painting,
and they are altogether foreign to the homely efforts of
Hogarth. Let us admit that he had natural talents of a high
order—a lively line, a vigorous, at times a lyrical, brushstroke
and a happy instinct for colour. But these gifts were not
developed by that passion for the formal qualities of their art
which characterizes all great painters. At a certain stage in his
career Hogarth must have felt that he had enough for his
purpose; but enough, in art, is a confession of defeat.

It may be suggested that these remarks apply only to the
art of oil painting, and that Hogarth's chief claim to distinction lies in his engraving. But some of these deficiencies, as in

composition, are carried over into the prints, and to match the others there is a certain coarseness in the engraved line which cannot be ignored, and which is obvious enough if we compare his work with that of the great masters of the art, Schongauer and Dürer, or with artists more of his character who worked in a similar technique, such as Goya and Daumier.

Apart from such formal criticism, there is a limitation to Hogarth's genius of a more serious kind, and Hazlitt has already defined it. "There is a mighty world of sense, of custom, of every-day action, of accidents and objects coming home to us, and interesting because they do so; the gross, material, stirring, noisy world of common life and selfish passion, of which Hogarth was absolute lord and master: there is another mightier world, that which exists only in conception and in power, the universe of thought and sentiment, that surrounds and is raised above the ordinary world of reality, as the empyrean surrounds the nether globe, into which few are privileged to soar with mighty wings outspread, and in which, as power is given them to embody their aspiring fancies, to 'give to airy nothing a local habitation and a name', to fill with imaginary shapes of beauty or sublimity, and make the dark abyss pregnant . . . this is the ideal in art, in poetry, and in painting." Of that ideal Hogarth was not capable; it was not for him to paint "faces imbued with unalterable sentiment, and figures, that stand in the eternal silence of thought". Not to put too fine a point on the distinction, we may affirm that Hogarth had neither the sensibility nor the imagination of a great painter.

Hogarth himself was unwilling to admit his limitations. Throughout his life he "entertained some hopes of succeeding in what the puffers in books call *the great style of history painting*". The very words in which he refers to his ambition betray the self-satisfied impudence with which he approached that task;

and some of the paintings themselves unfortunately survive to bear witness to his ignominious failure.

And yet, when all is said and done, Hogarth lives! We have, we may feel, reduced to naught his claim to be taken seriously as a painter, and yet, as a genius of some kind, he survives. "Other pictures we see, Hogarth's we read." There is some truth in that statement which escapes the narrow categories of criticism. We are faced with a dilemma which Hazlitt stated but did not solve in uttering this sentiment: "I do not know whether, if the port-folio were opened, I would not as soon look over the prints of Hogarth as those of Raphael; but, assuredly, if the question were put to me, I would sooner never have seen the prints of Hogarth than never have seen those of Raphael." It is not sufficient to say that it is merely the literary interest which holds us. It is no longer the case of an art

> Whose pictur'd Morals charm the Mind,
> And through the Eye correct the Heart.

It is one of my strongest convictions that no work of art survives its age which is not justified by some strength of form or grace of execution—that possessing these, even a dictionary may survive. So when we have discounted all that is false in Hogarth's reputation, when we have waited for the echoes of his contemporary fame to die away in our minds, and then look at his paintings dispassionately, we have to admit that somewhere under the dead skin of varnish there always throbs the life which on a few rare occasions, and supremely in "The Shrimp Girl", blazed forth in sensuous splendour.

22

RODNEY

(1719-1792)

by G. E. MANWARING

THE passage of time has tended rather to obscure the name and fame of Rodney, yet he undoubtedly ranks as one of our greatest naval commanders. Had his great victory over the French fleet in 1782 gone down in history as the "Battle of Dominica", instead of the "Battle of the Saints", it would have provided his countrymen with a name more readily associated with that of Rodney. The label was wrong, and in consequence the victory, which deserves to be as well known as that of Trafalgar, has never caught the public fancy.

George Brydges Rodney came of a distinguished West country stock, and was baptized at St. Giles in the Fields on the 13th of February, 1719. On the recommendation of his relative, the Duke of Chandos, he was sent to Harrow School, and although his immediate ancestors adopted the military profession, young Rodney was destined for the Navy. After a short period at Harrow, he was sent to sea in July, 1732, as a "King's letter boy", or in official language as "a volunteer per order". His promotion was rapid; in 1739 he became lieutenant of the *Dolphin* frigate, and three years later he was made a post-captain.

In the great victory off Finisterre, in 1747, Rodney played a prominent part, and his ship the *Eagle* succeeded in capturing one of the French. On surrendering his sword the Frenchman is reported to have said "that he would rather have met the Eagle in the shape of a dove", to which Rodney instantly replied "Eagles do not beget doves"; an incident sufficiently vivid to be remembered years afterwards when Rodney chose the words as the motto for his arms. On his return to England Anson presented him to the King, who expressed surprise that he had so young a captain in his service, to which Anson very gallantly replied: "I most heartily wish your Majesty had one hundred more such captains, to the terror of your Majesty's enemies." If this story is true Rodney's debt to Anson is immense. Always anxious to be in the limelight; eager for his own advancement; and above all to be praised by his fellow men, Rodney was the aristocrat among sea officers. He was equally at home in a London drawing-room as on his own quarter-deck. Lionized by hostesses, he was a very lion in action. In person he was rather above the ordinary stature. His dress and bearing, according to a contemporary "was more elegant than seemed to become his rough profession". His striking personality, and fascinating manners —always polite, courteous and dignified—coupled with an agreeable and enlightened conversation, led to his society being courted by the fashionable and fastidious. His slender figure and delicately chiselled features are vividly portrayed for us in the National Portrait Gallery. There is there that "something that approached to delicacy and effeminacy", which his friend Wraxall drew attention to.

On shore his life was dominated by two outstanding passions—a love of gambling and the company of the fair sex. It was said that his youth had been distinguished by the personal attachment of the Princess Amelia, daughter of George the Second, and gossip even went so far as to say that he was the father of the mysterious "little Miss Ashe", a pretty, vivacious creature, the "Pollard Ashe" of Horace Walpole, who flits across the pages of the letter-writers of the day. Whether this is true or not, it was the gambling-table that ultimately proved more disastrous to Rodney.

It was at this period, 1748, that he became a member of White's Club, the great Tory stronghold and gambling centre in the West End of London. Walpole, writing in 1748, described him then as "a young seaman who has made a fortune by very gallant behaviour during the war", and relates the following amusing incident. Meeting the notorious Sir William Burdett in the neighbourhood of St. James's, Rodney and a young Irish peer were invited to Burdett's house. There, in company with a bogus Princess, and an equally bogus Count, Burdett succeeded in fleecing the two young bucks of one hundred and fifty pounds a piece, the debt being paid at Ranelagh the next morning. After all, it was perhaps fitting that men of action should celebrate the peace of Aix-la-Chapelle in this manner!

Peace time appointments were few and far between, and in May, 1749, when Rodney was appointed to the *Rainbow*, he was fortunate to secure the important post of "Governor and Commander-in-Chief in and over the Island of Newfoundland". His principal duty was the protection of the fisheries, and he was to keep constantly cruising to "effectually keep the pirates from those parts, and protect the trade and His Majesty's subjects". After the usual term of office, the *Rainbow* was paid off in 1752, and for the next five years Rodney had to be content with the command of various guardships.

During his absence he had been elected member of Parliament for Saltash, a Government borough, and being stationed at Portsmouth his vote was available whenever required. It was his first taste of Parliamentary life but not his last, and he continued to represent various constituencies until he was called to the Upper House in 1782. "A man," he wrote, "is nothing without being in Parliament; at all events I must have a seat."

Having satisfied this ambition, in conjunction with a shore appointment, it became imperative that Rodney should find a wife to do the honours of the occasion. He now moved in the highest circles; a great future was predicted for him; and many hostesses must have thought him a desirable son-in-law. His choice finally fell on the beautiful twenty-three year old Jane Compton, a niece of the Earl of Northampton, and Rodney's marriage to her on the 31st of January, 1753, at the fashionable Oxford Chapel (now St. Peter's), Vere Street, London, provided his fellow clubmen at White's with an excuse for exercising their inveterate gambling habits. Within a week of the ceremony, wagers of fifty guineas were freely laid that Mrs. Rodney would have a child born alive before Lady Abergavenny, who became a bride a few days after Jane.

Soon after his marriage Rodney settled in a house in Hill Street, Berkeley Square—near another great sailor—the unfortunate Admiral Byng. There is a tragic interest attaching to the two friends at this time. In 1756 Rodney was in command of the *Monarque* at Portsmouth, and in December of that year, while on sick leave in London, he was ordered to Portsmouth to take part in Byng's court martial. He excused himself on the ground of ill-health, and stated that he was being "constantly attended by a physician". In this respect there seems little doubt that Rodney was speaking the truth, but it is equally certain that he was anxious to avoid, if possible, such an unpleasant duty. Fortune once again favoured him in the dilemma. In February, 1757, he was moved into the *Dublin*, and a few weeks later Byng was executed on the *Monarque's* quarter deck.

Two years later, in 1759, Rodney obtained his flag as Rear-Admiral of the Blue. It was the "wonderful year" in our naval annals. Saunders and Wolfe were preparing to take Quebec; Boscawen was keeping watch over Toulon; Hawke was blockading Brest; and Rodney with his flag in the *Achilles*, in command of a small squadron, bombarded Havre for fifty-two hours, and also destroyed the flat-bottomed boats prepared for the invasion of England. His reputation was now firmly established; no task was too arduous for him, and no enterprise too dangerous. His one desire was to keep "the foreigner from fooling us", as he himself expressed it. Therefore, when it was decided to carry on a more vigorous offensive against the French in the West Indies, it was Rodney to whom the Government entrusted the policy, and he was given the important post of Commander-in-Chief on the Leeward Islands station. He sailed in October, 1761, with his flag in the *Marlborough*, in command of a squadron to capture Martinique. The fleet arrived off Martinique early in January, 1762, and under cover of the guns the troops were landed without loss. Within a short time the island was in British hands, and the surrender of St. Lucia, Granada, and St. Vincent followed. In October Rodney was advanced to the rank of Vice-Admiral of the Blue, and in the August following he returned to England.

His financial position was always causing him anxiety. He had many influential friends, and he not unnaturally turned to them whenever the occasion offered. Soon after his return in November, 1763, it seemed probable that the post of Governor of Greenwich Hospital might become vacant owing to the serious illness of the occupant. He immediately dashed off a very polite letter to Grenville, then Chancellor of the Exchequer, in which he reminded Grenville that he "always regarded" his friendship "as one of the happiest incidents of my life; and as I have always found you ready to promote my welfare, I shall, without further preface, acquaint you that in all probability a vacancy will soon happen in the sea department, which I aspire to . . . I have at this moment received a letter from Greenwich, acquainting me that Admiral Townshend has been struck with a palsy . . . Should he die, permit me to depend upon your friendship to succeed him." However, the fruit was not yet ready to fall from the tree, and it was not until two years later that Rodney succeeded to the desired post. His financial difficulties did not become less acute, however, and in this year, 1764, he married as his second wife, Henrietta, daughter of John Clies of Lisbon, who bore him several children but does not appear to have brought him any other riches than domestic happiness.

Rodney remained at Greenwich for some five years, and there is a story told of him at this period to prove that he was always "the seaman's friend". During his first winter at Greenwich, Rodney ordered greatcoats for all the pensioners, whereas formerly they had only been issued to the infirm. His deputy, William Boys, vigorously protested, and Rodney, eyeing him with indignation and contempt, replied: "I have the greatest respect for you as a man, who, by the greatest merit, has raised himself from the station of a foremast man to the rank of an Admiral . . . Let me warn you against two things. First, in future not to interfere between me and my duty as Governor; and the second is, not to object to these brave men having greatcoats, whilst you are so fond of one as to wear it by the side of as good a fire as you are sitting by at present." The story has been frequently repeated and accepted as true, but there is evidence to discredit this theatrical display. Boys was never a foremast man, and the gods had retired him with the rank of Captain.

It was during this period that Rodney incurred the load of debt which ultimately drove him from England. He courted society, and its consequent card playing; he was also determined to remain in Parliament. Since 1751 he had retained a seat as a nominee of the Government, but it was not so in the general election of 1768. He plunged into the contest; fought it presumably on borrowed money, and was returned as one of the two candidates for the Borough of Northampton. The election was notorious for its unblushing corruption, and Chesterfield records that it was carried "to a degree of frenzy hitherto unheard of; that for the town of Northampton has cost the contending parties at least £30,000 a side".

Service afloat now became a necessity. Luckily there was a prospect of war with Spain, and early in 1771, when he was offered the command of the Jamaica station, he jumped at the golden opportunity. This and the Governorship of Greenwich would surely restore the family fortunes. But fate had ordained otherwise, and much to his disgust Rodney was forced, in spite of protestation, to relinquish his shore appointment. He sailed from Plymouth on the 3rd of June, and arrived at Jamaica on the 7th of August. From the financial point of view the command was unsatisfactory. The difference with Spain was peacefully settled, and with the exception of a little contretemps with the Governor of Cartagena, nothing happened. Still, he was not altogether unhappy. In a letter of the 27th March, 1772, Sandwich had informed him privately that he did "not think that there is any of our Commanders-in-Chief, who stand at present upon a better footing than yourself". This was indeed encouraging. He would write to Sandwich to recommend him for the Governship of Jamaica. It was true there was no vacancy at the moment, but the Governor, Sir William Trelawny was old, and with luck—perhaps before the expiration of his naval command—might die. Sandwich, however, sent a reply which was very vague and chilling. He informed Rodney, that, so far as he knew, there was "at present, no competitor; but after all," he added, "what reason have you to expect a vacancy? for we have no intelligence here that it is likely to happen." But it did happen; Sir William died in December, 1772, and Rodney was passed over. He returned to England in the summer of 1774, disgusted with the ministry and his treatment generally.

In order to escape his creditors he was now forced to take refuge in Paris, and "from this period", according to his son-in-law, "the sunshine which had hitherto cheered his existence became obscured, and for the space of four years the oppressive gloom of want, disappointments and inaction hung over him like a mist." Although Lady Rodney failed in her efforts to secure a subscription among the members of White's, the mist was soon to clear, and the old Maréchal Biron gallantly advanced 1,000 louis in order to relieve Rodney from his awkward and intolerable position.

When Rodney returned to England it was with a heart full of bitterness against Sandwich. The latter showed equal resentment against the Admiral, and it was not until the close of 1779, that he was again offered the command of the Leeward Islands station, which seems to have been due to the King's initiative. A very important service had to be performed. Gibraltar had been besieged for six months by a Spanish army, while a large Franco-Spanish fleet closely blockaded it, and Rodney was instructed to relieve the fortress on his way to the West Indies.

The expedition was fortunate from the first, and not far from Finisterre Rodney chased and captured a valuable Spanish convoy laden with stores for the Spanish fleet at Cadiz and Cartagena. A week later, when off Cape St. Vincent, the Spanish Gibraltar squadron under the command of Don Juan de Langara, consisting of eleven ships of the line, was sighted making for Cadiz. Although very ill, and crippled with gout, Rodney at once ordered a general chase, and in the running fight, which did not cease until 2 a.m. on the following day, only two of the Spanish ships escaped. As soon as the news reached England Rodney was the hero of the hour, and the King is reported to have said, "that he knew when

Rodney was out everything would be well," but Sandwich was equally anxious to assume credit for the action. His letter to Rodney after the victory is probably unmatched in official circles for what has been aptly described as "sublime impudence". "The worst of my enemies," he wrote, "now allow that I have pitched upon a man who knows his duty, and is a brave, honest and able officer."

The relief of Gibraltar followed as a matter of course, and leaving the bulk of his fleet to return to England, Rodney sailed for St. Lucia to take over the command of the West Indies fleet. He reached Barbadoes in March, and a few days later joined Sir Hyde Parker at St. Lucia, having a total of seventeen ships of the line. The French were at Martinique under the command of the Comte de Guichen, and the English at St. Lucia. In numbers and position there was little to choose. The French immediately decided to attack Barbadoes, and during the night of the 13th of April they put to sea with that intention. The English fleet followed, and on the 16th Rodney sighted them between Dominica and Martinique. Throughout that afternoon a general chase ensued, and under cover of night Rodney formed his fleet in a line of battle ahead. The enemy's manœuvres indicated a desire to avoid battle, but he was determined to bring them to action. Soon after day-break on the 17th the French were discerned beginning to form the line ahead, and Rodney signalled his intention of attacking the enemy's rear with his whole fleet. Unfortunately his intention of bringing the whole of the fleet against part of the French line was doomed to disappointment. The English captains in the van instead of bearing down instantly upon the ships opposite to them at the moment, and in disregard of Rodney's order to keep a close formation, pressed on to the far distant head of the French line, and so shattered the Admiral's scheme.

The failure to achieve a decisive victory was one of the

bitterest disappointments of Rodney's life. He thundered at his captains for not obeying orders, and wrote to Sandwich that "the bareface disobedience to orders and signals, acknowledged by every ship, was such as calls aloud for a strict inquiry". Though Rodney laid the blame freely on his captains, it has been suggested that the cause of the failure rested mainly with himself in proposing an entirely novel mode of attack, which differed from the official fighting instructions. It was also asserted that in such a startling innovation he had not sufficiently taken his officers into his confidence. No real advantage was gained by either side in this battle, and although the fleets met twice afterwards, de Guichen never again gave Rodney an opportunity of the windward position. Two months later the French Admiral returned to Europe, but Rodney sailed for New York in the belief that de Guichen was going to North America. Finding that his services were not required on that station, he returned to more arduous duties in the West Indies, where he arrived in December, 1780. A few weeks later he received news of the declaration of war with Holland and a suggestion that he should attack St. Eustatius, whose inhabitants during the whole course of war had driven a thriving trade in war-like stores. He captured the island without difficulty, and the value of the accumulated merchandise was calculated at three million pounds, all of which Rodney seized. A certain proportion of it belonged to English merchants, but Rodney refused to listen to their pleas. His fury knew no bounds. They were traitors, he said, a very "nest of villains", who "deserve scourging and they shall be scourged". Unfortunately he did not take into consideration that the "villains" claimed to be Englishmen, and that the scourging must be a legal and not a private one. In consequence, the vexatious lawsuits which followed remained a crippling financial burden till the end of his days.

Ill-health now forced him to return to England, and he was absent from his command for six months. It was a critical time for England. The French under de Grasse had been heavily reinforced in the West Indies; St. Kitts had been captured, and an attack on Jamaica was imminent. The crisis had indeed come, and the country turned to Rodney in its hour of supreme need. His health was restored and he was confident of victory. "The fate of this empire is in your hands, and I have no reason to wish that it should be in any other," wrote Sandwich to him on the eve of sailing. He rejoined Hood at Barbadoes on the 19th February, 1782, and when he took up his old position at St. Lucia his fleet amounted to thirty-six sail of the line. De Grasse was at Fort Royal, and the Spaniards at San Domingo. It was essential that he should crush one or the other before they could combine. On April 8th de Grasse put to sea; within two hours the English fleet was under way and in pursuit. Before they reached Dominica he was close upon them, but the calms and baffling winds under that island nearly proved disastrous to the English fleet, for sixteen ships of the rear squadron lay helpless miles astern.

Had de Grasse seized this opportunity and fallen on our van it was Rodney's opinion that "half his fleet would have suffered extremely". Fortunately they kept "an awful distance", and although the heavy cannonade did considerable damage disaster was averted by the unwillingness of de Grasse to come to close quarters. At day-break on the 12th of April the English were once more in possession of the wind, and the signal to attack was instantly made. The battle, one of the most furious since the Dutch wars, began soon after seven in the morning. The French moved in one long line ahead; the English were parallel to them and passed at very close quarters. For some five hours it was a ding-dong struggle as ship after ship engaged its opponent. Then the wind failed. The smoke of the guns hung like a pall over the scene, and the ships were indistinguishable. Soon after noon a breeze sprang up, and as the smoke blew away it was seen that the French line was disordered. Rodney seized the golden opportunity. He would attempt the bold manœuvre of breaking the line, the inception of which has been credited to Rodney, but was really as old as the Dutch wars. His own ship the *Formidable* led the way and "surged through the middle of the French line". The action finds a prominent place in all naval histories, and it is only possible to devote a short space to it here.

An eye-witness thus describes the scene as the *Formidable* broke through. "In the act of doing so we passed within pistol shot of the *Glorieux* of seventy-four guns, which was so roughly handled that she was shorn of all her masts, bow-sprit, and ensign-staff, but with the white flag nailed to the stump of one of her masts, and breathing defiance as it were in her last moments." Almost at the same time Commodore Affleck in the *Bedford*, the leading ship of the rear division passed through a similar gap. The French now thrown into confusion ran to leeward in the hope of reforming their line, but the English pursuit was relentless. Before night-fall five of their ships had been captured, including the *Ville de Paris*, de Grasse's flagship, which surrendered to Hood in the *Barfleur*. Hood implored Rodney to pursue the flying enemy. He even offered to do so himself, but Rodney turned a deaf ear to all entreaties. "Come, we have done very handsomely as it is," was all the consolation that Hood received from his chief. His patience was exhausted, and to a friend he even expressed an opinion that twenty ships might have been taken but for Rodney's obstinacy. The truth is that Rodney was very tired and very ill, and had remained seated in a chair on the quarter-deck during part of the battle. One instance of his curious vanity in the heat of the action remains to be recorded. He had instructed a midshipman to make him a lemon squash. In the absence of a spoon the middy commenced to stir the mixture with the hilt of his dirk. Rodney sharply remonstrated with him for such a procedure. "That may do for the midshipmen's mess," he roared. "Drink it yourself, and send my steward here."

The importance of the victory was immense. It saved Jamaica and our West Indian islands, and prevented the great Franco-Spanish fleet from seizing what remained to England on the American continent, besides giving us the command of the Atlantic in one of the most critical periods of our history. Its influence on the naval tactics of the time was equally valuable and important. As such it was surely an irony of fate that before the news of the victory reached England, the ministry had fallen, and Rodney was recalled. Perhaps the greatest tragedy of his long sea service was that fate had denied him a spectacular end like Blake and Nelson, for in a letter to a friend he expressed "a serious and melancholy regret" that during the action with de Grasse, "a cannon ball had not struck off his head." As it was, he returned to England in September to receive a peerage and a pension of £2,000, but died, a very lonely and disconsolate old man, nearly ten years later at the residence of his son in Hanover Square on the 23rd of May, 1792.

23

COKE OF NORFOLK

(1754–1842)

by R. H. Mottram

FEW reputations can have been better earned or more pleasant to examine than that of Thomas William Coke, Earl of Leicester, Squire of Holkham in Norfolk and Longford in Derbyshire, Member of Parliament, widely known for his entirely voluntary services to agriculture, but best remembered as a great eighteenth century figure.

Unlike that of so many great clerics or generals, Coke's achievement did not consist in subordinating the spirit or mutilating the bodies of the fellow-creatures over whom he had so many advantages. Without complacency we may claim him as a man typical of his country, and of the best life of his time.

While he inherited an historic name, and along with it a fortune so solid that many a modern millionaire might envy him, he relied on none of these adventitious privileges to assume a leadership which he justified by an exceptionally long life of unremitting public service. No administrator chosen to advance the methods of agriculture could have done more than he did to increase the production of the necessities of life of the humblest. He did it all with an altruism so odd that it was

328

almost accidental, and we may despair of explaining his motives to the most sympathetic observers of other nationality. He was, in fact, a great amateur. No need constrained him to devote his time to the improvement of farming—to call it "agriculture" is at once to misrepresent his particular genius. For while he was a well-read and travelled man and acquainted with the scientific knowledge of his day, he was eminently practical. That which he discovered and taught was the actual planting of a grain of wheat, the preparing of the conditions in which it was to grow, or the selection, breeding and rearing of new strains of beasts. He might have relied on his power and prestige as a great landlord. Actually, he excited admiration by the fact that, tall, strong and hardy as any of the stalwart race who hired his land, he could use a billhook and a spade better than any of his hedgers and ditchers, and on occasion, did so.

Why? To answer the natural question is to reveal some of the national characteristics of which we may be legitimately proud. I never understood Coke until the day on which, engaged in a dispute with a group of those peerless cultivators, the peasants of French Flanders, I invoked the aid of the departmental agricultural authority, and shall never forget the grim laughter of men who spent their lives in the age-long struggle to make the earth yield up her fruits, at the notion of consulting, by appointment, one, however worthy and devoted, who spent his days in an office. How I longed for some descendant of Coke—the breed is not extinct—who could have said not merely: "I tell you to do thus and thus!" but: "This is how I do it!"

Coke—and it is significant that he is always alluded to by his family name, not his title, and always associated with Norfolk—was not a Norfolk man by birth or tradition. A series of unforeseen accidents brought him, a member of a very junior branch of the family, dwelling on one of its remote estates, to inhabit the neo-Grecian palace his distant relative, the previous Earl, had built of local brick, amid the half reclaimed semi-cultivation of North Norfolk. He did not invent land reclamation and improvement. His connections had begun to practise both long before he was born. No stronger defence of the principles of individual privilege could be made than the improbable fitness of an education that consisted in early rising, sport, Eton, the Grand Tour, and the corrupt political life of that day. For Coke came through it all with an innate sense of responsibility, unaccountable manual dexterity, and a passionate honesty. Never needing to boast, the one thing he seems to have said to his own credit was: "I have never touched a penny of public money."

He may be said, therefore, to have been neither born nor trained to be the man he became. Why did he feel that he must make those estates that he might have gambled away, as his relatives had tried to do, or retained for sport alone, as many of his associates did, the most productive land in England, perhaps in the world?

Therein lies not only the history of his class and his period, but something that cannot be omitted from the story of his country. There is no discoverable reason why he was what he was, save perhaps his descent, through his mother, from the sixth son of that sturdy lawyer who preferred his professional integrity to the favour of James I. If then we must have a reason for the character of Thomas William Coke, who was born in 1754, we may seek it in that of his great-great-grandfather, Lord Chief Justice of England, who died in 1633. Or perhaps, we may more reasonably feel that, among the ever-living growth of English society, never sterilized by too rigid a settlement of class distinction, the able and dependable professional sort, constantly mounting into the ranks of landed proprietorship, was bound to produce, when the need was greatest, the kind of man that England required. Thus

Thomas William Coke appeared just when it was necessary to supersede the old indiscriminate Manor cultivation by something more intensive, in order to provide food for a population which was just about, for the first time, to show an increase in the number of mouths to be fed.

All this seemed improbable enough when Thomas William Coke was born in 1754. His father's name had been Roberts until, in 1750, the death of the last of the sons of Clement Coke (sixth son of the Lord Chief Justice) threw the possession of the Longford estate upon him, as the son of Anne Coke. For yet nine years longer it was not certain that he would succeed to Holkham. But when the elder branch of the family died out, and instead of being a Roberts, Squire of Longford, the boy became heir to Coke of Holkham, the matter so impressed his parents that they had him painted by Reynolds as "Young Hannibal" complete with sword, a bad guess at the future of a boy who was to concern himself almost exclusively with ploughshares.

He seems to have spent much time with his grandfather Roberts, who told him: "Never trust a Tory!" the term then having a Jacobite flavour and an association with incompetent administration. For his father prophesied that he would see mischief accrue from the association of Lord Bute with the then Prince of Wales, afterwards George III. He lived to see the loss of the North American Colonies. But more impressive to the out-of-door, sport-loving boy was the sight of a pack of hounds that killed a fox in front of his father's house in Hanover Square. He shot snipe where stands Berkeley Square, and at Eton, where his career contrasted strongly with that of Charles James Fox, destined to be his friend, he added to the meagre resources of the school larder by his deadly accuracy with his gun, and was whopped for killing a pheasant in Windsor Park.

At the end of his unremarkable school years we can discern

some presage of the future. The proud, tragic, we may think almost demented old Lady Leicester—who survived, amid the immensities of the marble-lined palace of Holkham, the husband she can hardly have loved and the son she may have mourned but whose miserable wasted existence her influence may have helped to end so early—sent for the obvious inheritor of her unhappy splendour. She could not make him comfortable—she received him with a retinue, and in an environment many a prince might have considered adequate—but she may have brought him face to face with his responsibilities.

"I will live as long as I can!" she cried, shaking her fist in his face.

One other thing she did for him:

"I understand you have left Eton and probably intend to go to one of those schools of Vice, the Universities. If however, you choose to travel I will give you £500 per annum!"

This, with the £200 his father added, sent him off, insufficiently provided as it turned out, for his Grand Tour which did at least three things for him. It gave him some inkling of what continuity and authority, descending from Greece via Rome have meant to civilization, and how all three can be endangered by lack of restraint and responsibility. It introduced him to a frivolous, cosmopolitan world, in which the Princess of Charles Edward Stuart made love to him; he met his other, and even madder relative, Lady Mary, widow of the dead heir of Holkham he had succeeded, and morganatic relict of the Duke of York; and it saved him from the entanglement into which his dead cousin had been involved at a University where young landowners were then not encouraged to study and were left to gamble. All and each of these influences seem to have clarified and hardened his intention to be the man he, in fact, became. He turned his back on the silly parade and degrading time-wasting that obsessed so many of his kind.

The end of his Grand Tour was decided by the approaching marriage of his sister to one of the Duttons, a family which, of Irish origin, had succeeded to estates in Gloucestershire. Here Coke met his happy fate, for he fell in love with the sister of his new brother-in-law, much to the concern of his father who desired a more ambitious match. But Coke's instinct—one dare hardly use the word judgment in such a matter—was sound as the rest of him. Jane Dutton was devoted as she was beautiful, and their married life was simple, united and happy. Before his marriage could be brought about against his father's wishes, he became involved in the only gambling scrape of his life, being induced to join in a card party at Newmarket, with the result that to meet his debts he had to sell the fine horse he was riding. He vowed never to go near Newmarket again, and, in fact, during his many journeys, that could not always avoid the main road between Holkham and London, he drew down the blinds of his carriage as he passed the town.

But the decisive call to become what we now call him, came to him in the natural course of events. In 1776 his father died, he found himself the owner of Holkham, and was promptly called upon to take up the representation of the county in Parliament. He became immediately and permanently involved in that group of county families that then controlled Norfolk politics, the Harbords, Astleys, Wodehouses, Townshends, Orfords and Wyndhams. He seems to have told the freeholders that he was a Whig, an adherent of the principles of the Revolution of 1688, and that he intended to "Fear God, Help Man and hate the Tories". He did not fancy himself as an orator, and was if anything too blunt and plain spoken, too independent and unbribable. Then began the first of his many journeys to the hustings erected next the old Shirehouse, long burnt down and replaced by buildings which, designed and used as a gaol, became in 1894 Norwich Castle

Museum. There, on the ancient mound above the biggest cattle market in England, were held the corrupt and violent political contests of the time. Once he was knocked senseless, and often he must have watched mimic battles on the bridge (said to be Saxon and certainly Norman) that was the only approach to the polling booth. There, local grandees, with scores of mounted tenants armed with bludgeons, would seize and hold the narrow way, letting in two voters (of their own colours of course) per hour, which obliged the presiding officer, under legislation then governing elections, to keep the poll open.

There stands to-day in the eight-hundred-year-old Norman Keep which is now the principal hall of the Museum, a cumbrous elaborate chair, or rather throne, upholstered in crimson, with curious gilt emblems, the whole set upon an odd-looking platform. This is the chair in which parliamentary candidates, Coke among them, were "chaired" round Norwich market-place, four-and-twenty supporters carrying the chair shoulder-high, and tossing it and the occupant as high as they could, while the rival crowds fought with showers of kidney-shaped cobbles across a great steel chain that, in theory only, kept them apart.

However, Coke represented Norfolk or Derby from the age of twenty-two, through thirteen parliaments, over a period of fifty-six years. He found himself attached to the group led by Fox, and immediately incurred the hatred of local opponents, the Government, and King George III. Even this lofty opposition did not turn him from his opinion so much as to lead him to be cautious in his expressions. He openly entered hostile country, as when he dined with Yarmouth Corporation against the wishes of local notables. He upset the dignity of rival orators by exclaiming audibly amid their speeches:

"Lay it on thick
Some of it will stick!"

But above all, he opposed the American War. A meeting was summoned at the Maid's Head which still stands at the northern end of Tombland, in Norwich, to obtain support for that struggle. Coke attended the rival meeting at the Swan, shortly to be demolished, next St. Peter's Church, and led the latter meeting to encounter the former. He even refused the bribe of a peerage. It is wonderful that he did not suffer the fate that overtook many a lesser man. But Coke was strong. It was not easy to attack a popular figure whose rent roll, owing to his insistence on better methods, and his liberality in granting twenty-one-year leases, soon increased to £20,000 a year, who was a dead shot, hunted from Holkham to Epping, and whose life was blameless as his integrity was incorruptible. Behind him were massed, if not always politically mobilized, the solid ranks of East Anglian tenant farmers. They might find him autocratic, and he belonged to the central type of his time, regarding preserved game as a privilege given by God to a select number of persons (not necessarily aristocrats) as a reward for special responsibilities. But they knew well enough, those hard-fisted men who worked eighteen hours a day on the land and amid the beasts that belonged to it, what a difference he had made to their prospects, and in 1804 they gave him a piece of plate, three feet high, costing seven hundred guineas, lest there might be any doubt about their feelings. It was embellished with moulded panels showing cultivation by the drill (one of his innovations that completely superseded the old broadcast sowing), a Southdown Sheep, a Devon cow, and other matters. It might have recorded, but did not, his opposition to a tax on home-brewed beer, and his novel terms in farm leases. The inscription stated that they meant to testify to his "liberality as a landlord, his example as a practical farmer, and a valuable member of Society."

Such is the record of his deeds. But Coke passed into what can only be described as local folk lore. There is a story widely current of one of the great annual audit dinners, the kind of festival which can be read of in Parson Woodforde's Diary, multiplied by the difference between Woodforde's glebe, and Coke's estate. The old chief tenant, laboriously mopping his forehead, stood up, raising his mug in one hand with these words:

"Here's to Mr. Cewke, and his tenan's. And if they du, as he du, they 'ont du as they du du!"

The terse economical idiom of tongue-tied Norfolk stamps the story with truth, and preserves the pungency of contemporary feeling.

It is time, however, to preserve Coke from becoming that stock figure of biographical error, the one-dimensional man. He was an extremely human creature. Wealth and public esteem were his, and may have been sufficient substitutes for royal favour and political success. But common fate overtook him in his private life. Death struck at the infant who should have grown up to be heir of Holkham, and then at the mother, the dearly loved object of the youthful devotion that had never withered. The happily married elder daughter was widowed by one of those inexplicable gun accidents which in this case caused the death of Lord Andover, his well-liked son-in-law. Also, the solid character of the man, tested and clarified, by practical occupations and realistic projects, outlived many early attachments. He could no more keep up with the pyrotechnic career of Fox, than he could share his pastimes. The two drifted apart. An opponent of the American War and a sympathizer with so many advanced ideas, he hastened to rally to the aid of an England menaced from all quarters as she was increasingly in the early years of the nineteenth century. He took command of the West Norfolk Yeomanry. The rumour that Fox intended to join Pitt's government, however, nearly caused an irreparable breach between the old friends. Fortunately Fox denied the canard, and the friendship remained, strong enough for Coke to ask and obtain an Act granting Norwich Castle, then still a royal demesne, to the County of Norfolk, one of the last kindnesses that passed between them before Fox's death. Dr. Parr, the learned master of Norwich Grammar School, wrote the life of the dead statesman and Coke accepted the dedication with the words: "The mastering passion of Fox's life was the love of Liberty . . . which gave him moral power and makes his faults forgotten and his memory sweet."

Such were the words of a great landlord, who infinitely preferred to have his shot-gun or the reins of his favourite hunter in his hands, to any pen. And now, past middle life, the widowed, bereaved man, whose too-frankly expressed opinions had ruined his political career, set himself to what we now call "stage a come-back". It is from 1806 that we find him called by his adversaries, "The Dictator," as he flung himself into the muddy turbulence of Norfolk politics, or defended Burdett. The escape of the Prince Regent from attempted assassination was the occasion of a loyal address from Norfolk Whigs, which it was proposed Coke should present. It demanded, among more habitual phrases, a change in the Royal advisers. The Regent, knowing the Norfolk Dictator's passionate desire to remain a commoner, cried: "If Coke enters my presence, by God, I'll knight him!" This was repeated to Coke.

"If he dares, I'll break his sword!" was his remark.

We have only to look at any reproduction of Lawrence's portrait, or of Barber's, or best of all, Garrard's engraving, to feel that he could have done so, and undoubtedly would. He was in the thick of the Peterloo agitation, called the six Acts "Bills of Blood" and presided at a great banquet at St. Andrew's Hall, Norwich, at which some of the urgent reforms, trial by jury and redistribution of Parliamentary seats, which subsequently became part of the Reform Bill, were hotly

advocated. But this was only one side of his life. His friendships, correspondence and visits, embraced British Royalty
and admiring citizens of North America, the learned, such as
Dr. Parr and Roscoe, the gifted, such as Westmacott, Chantry
(who killed two woodcock with a single shot at Holkham)
and others. Cobbett, much to Coke's disgust, burst into one of
his meetings and fathered upon it, by methods Coke would
never have employed, a wild resolution, amid scenes that Mr.
Gurney, the Quaker banker, described as warranting: "the
overthrow of the legislature and the spoliation of the Church."
But Coke steadily held on his way. He refused to countenance
the continual demands for more Protective legislation to cure
the ills under which agriculture still suffered, and which he
attributed to mal-administration. He became drawn into the
manœuvres of Brougham, and antagonized by what he considered the autocratic temper of the Duke of Wellington.

His physical vigour was prodigious. He went among his
workpeople, disguised in a smock, and showed them how to
use their tools. He opposed military expenditure and grants to
the less deserving members of George III's family. Reinagle's
portrait shows us a bronzed and hearty veteran standing bare-
headed and upright, between his favourite dog and a tree that
had grown to maturity since he had planted it, at Holkham.

Everyone knows the story of how he and Lord Albemarle,
attacked by a riotous crowd on Norwich Cattle Market, were
rescued by a friendly butcher turning loose a fierce bull. Coke
was then sixty. It is not so well known that at seventy-seven
he rode up to a mob, seized the ringleaders, hurled them into
his coach and drove them to gaol. This was the man who, at
sixty-eight, married the eighteen-year-old daughter of Lord
Albemarle and started family life again, and amid so many
activities became the father of an heir, three other sons and
a daughter in ten years.

At last, the Reform Bill passed amid disturbances which

had caused him to consider seriously if Holkham could be placed in a state of defence, he accepted a peerage, and at the coronation of Queen Victoria (whom, as Princess he had received in his Norfolk palace) he took his place among the peers. Congratulations now showered upon him, even Amelia Opie, whose husband he had befriended forty years before, wrote in Quaker style to tell him: "We men and women of Norfolk loved and honoured thee as The Squire, and that was enough for us. But I give ample credit to the Queen and Ministers for having made such an Earl of Leicester and think this a promising beginning of a new reign."

Creevey, in his memoirs, described him as "King Tom" and Edwards drew a silhouette of him in his eightieth year, inscribed "The Queen's Best Subject and the People's Friend".

But, inevitably, the time for retirement had come. He left public life and visited Longford, where he had wandered as a boy. He could still kill twenty-four head of game with twenty-five shots. The great Annual Sheep Shearing had been discontinued, but when his Norwich admirers celebrated his eighty-seventh birthday he sent a pugnacious message:

"Tell the Tories there is no hope for them in the state of my health!"

His last act was to superintend the erection of two bridges at Longford, when his tenants took the horses out of his carriage and dragged it in triumph. Next day he was taken ill and in a week he was dead. His coffin was three days making the journey to Tittleshall Church, and the old family tomb. On the route, towns such as Derby closed their shops, the gentry rode hundreds strong behind the hearse, the country people lined the roads.

After him there was something like an anti-climax. No one could fill his place though his descendants were plentiful, his friends legion, his enemies long dead, or won over to admiration. It was not until 1850 that the obelisk with its pictorial panels commemorating his activities was set up at Holkham. Many minor efforts to write down his life and achievements only laid the foundation of the main biography of him by his great granddaughter, Mrs. Stirling, which appeared in 1908. He had long outlived his time. "Live and let live" was his motto. We may almost fancy that there was a kind of poetic justice in his being allowed to exceed the average span and the average use of it by so much. Not Wren himself left a monument more worthy or more vital. There, by the sea, at Holkham, lie the broad acres which he loved and made and which in turn, made him and keep his memory. Some may envy him the title he only bore six years, some his monument in the park. But he himself would have chosen the very fate that is his, to be remembered as "Coke of Norfolk".

24

DAVID GARRICK

(1717–1779)

by JAMES LAVER

IT used to be the mode to bewail the fate of actors and
to lament the fact that their art perished with them. Once
their work was done they sank into oblivion, and a few
years after their death their very names were forgotten except
by professed specialists in theatrical history. Authors, painters
and musicians seemed, by comparison, to have a better share
of what, for want of a better name, is called Immortality.

Every artist after his death goes through a period of eclipse.
The Valley of the Shadow is for him a real valley and the
shadow is sometimes dark. But even minor writers, lesser
painters and unimportant musicians emerge again, if only as
curiosities. Their works remain, and a revival of interest is
always possible. He must be a dull writer indeed whom no
critic of the future will make it his business to discover; he
must be an intolerably bad artist whom no dealer thinks it
worth while to corner and exploit. The art of the actor is
irrecoverable.

Yet certain actors survive, their reputation still lives, and
in this they are doubly fortunate. For if their art is beyond
revival it is also beyond criticism, and the fact that they are

remembered at all is a proof of greatness there is no gainsaying.
We are compelled, as in no other art, to accept the judgment
of the artist's contemporaries, and if that judgment was
unanimous there is no more to be said.

The unanimity of Garrick's contemporaries is extraordinary.
Even Irving, in some ways comparable, is not without his
critics. And those of us who never saw the great Victorian
actor have an uncomfortable suspicion that if he could return
to the stage to-day we should find his methods old-fashioned
and his mannerisms insupportable. Even the glamour of his
name did not prevent such criticisms in Irving's lifetime, but
with Garrick it is different. He seems to have convinced
everyone who saw him that he was a great actor—one of the
greatest actors that have ever lived. People might think him
better in one part than in another; they might dispute whether
he was not, after all, a greater comedian than a tragedian;
but the general verdict was unanimous, and the strange thing
is that it seems to have been unanimous from the start. Certain
members of the old guard no doubt raised objections. For
Garrick, like nearly all great artists, burst upon the world as
the apostle of a new naturalism.

Nothing seems more odd to us than what passed for
naturalism in the days of our fathers. The comedies of Tom
Robertson appeared to those who saw them first to be the
merest transcript from life and so, by comparison with the
ranting, roaring melodrama which had gone before, they were.
But to us they seem essentially artificial, and if we could see
Garrick on the stage to-day we should no doubt find his
manner highly stylized by comparison with the naturalistic
acting of to-day. To himself and to his contemporaries, he
seemed to be inaugurating a new reign of nature.

We should remember that James Quin, who dominated
the stage until Garrick's arrival, intoned tragedy as a kind of
plainsong and played Coriolanus in a ballet skirt. Quin's

reported remark, "We are all wrong if this is right," sums up the contemporary view, and the very form of the remark shows that even Quin was beginning to have his doubts.

There was jealousy, no doubt, among Garrick's fellow-actors. The professional has never loved the amateur, and Garrick was, in one sense, an amateur. How often it has fallen to the amateur to renew the best traditions of the stage! But amateur or not, Garrick certainly had acting in his blood. As a mere schoolboy he had acted in the Bishop's Palace at Lichfield; and wisely, before venturing to appear on the boards in London, he had played for a while with Gifford's Company Ipswich. He had acted as an amateur with Hogarth, and what leisure he could spare from his wine merchant's business had been spent in the theatre, or at the Bedford Coffee House in the Covent Garden piazza. In this tavern, frequented by actors, he had struck up a friendship with Macklin, an Irish actor older than himself, whose views on stage naturalism were substantially the same as his own. He had even written a play, *Lethe*, and had managed to get it included in the repertory at Ipswich. He tried to join the company at Drury Lane and at Covent Garden, but both managers refused him; and he was compelled to make his first London professional appearance at the little theatre in Goodman's Fields, situated in the heart of the City, near Aldersgate.

Here, on October 19th, 1741, he played Richard III. During the first few weeks he was anonymous, appearing on the bills as "A Gentleman who never appeared on any Stage", but the secret could not long be hid. Indeed, Garrick had no desire to hide it, once his success was assured. And assured it was. The news of the wonderful new actor spread like lightning among the coffee-houses. The West End realized that here was a new sensation, and very soon a string of glass coaches choked the way from Temple Bar to Goodman's Fields. There had been nothing like it since the Cock Lane Ghost.

We get a vivid picture of Garrick's triumph from the letters which he wrote to his angry brother in Lichfield to try and persuade him that he really *was* a success and that it was not mere folly which was leading him to abandon the safer paths of respectable commerce.

Garrick's reputation as an actor was established, and established for ever. His success at Goodman's Fields was followed by an even greater triumph at the Smock Alley Theatre in Dublin. When he returned, Drury Lane opened its doors to him, and here he remained, with a brief interval of one year at Covent Garden, from 1742 until his retirement from the stage in 1776. During the greater part of this time he was, as Manager, solely responsible for the plays put on. Like other managers, he had his failures. He had his quarrels with certain sections of the public. Once or twice his theatre was wrecked. But the quality of his acting seems throughout that period to have been above criticism, or, rather, if he had critics, they had singularly little to say.

Churchill, the satirist, may fairly represent, in *The Rosciad*, the tenor of their attack:

> Last Garrick came. Behind him throng a train
> Of snarling critics, ignorant as vain.
> One finds out—He's of stature somewhat low—
> Your hero always should be tall you know—
> True natural greatness all consists in height . . .

This does not seem very profound criticism, but the satirist goes on:

> Another can't forgive the paltry arts
> By which he makes his way to shallow hearts;
> Mere pieces of finesse, traps for applause—
> Avaunt! unnatural start, affected pause. . . .
> But when, from Nature's pure and genuine source,
> These strokes of acting flow with generous force,

DAVID GARRICK

When in the features all the soul's portray'd,
And passions, such as Garrick's, are display'd,
To me, they seem from quickest feelings caught,
Each start is nature, and each pause is thought. . . .
Let wits, like spiders, from the tortured brain
Fine-draw the critic-web with curious pain;
The gods—a kindness I with thanks must pay—
Have form'd me of a coarser kind of clay,
Nor stung with envy, nor with spleen diseased,
A poor dull creature, still with Nature pleased:
Hence to thy praises, Garrick, I agree,
And, pleased with Nature, must be pleased with thee.

In his next satire, Churchill, who had quarrelled with Garrick in the interval, represents him as a mean tyrant, but he says nothing of his acting to spoil the effect of these complimentary lines. In fact, all criticism of Garrick seems to divide itself under two heads, one concerning the person of the man and one his nature. He was said to be short and he was said to be mean.

Short, Garrick certainly was. When Foote was asked if the figures in his puppet-show were to be as large as life he replied: "Oh, no, not much larger than Garrick." Garrick himself was extremely sensitive concerning his lack of inches. He felt that he could only with difficulty compete in heroic parts with the tall handsome actor, such as Spranger Barry. His Hotspur was generally considered a failure from the mere lack of physical means to fill out the part; but in general, he had no need of inches. Barry played Lear at Covent Garden at the same time as Garrick was playing it at Drury Lane, and the epigram went round the town:

> "A king—nay, every inch a king,
> Such Barry doth appear.
> But Garrick's quite a different thing,
> He's every inch King Lear."

The charge of meanness, of a certain pettiness of character, needs a more elaborate defence or a deeper analysis. Some allowance must be made for the fact that Garrick was the manager of Drury Lane, as well as an actor. That is to say, he was brought into contact with his fellow-actors in both a personal and financial way. He had to measure their vanity against the claims of his own pocket. He could not hope to satisfy everyone in the distribution of roles; and, as an actor himself, as well as a manager, he was bound to be accused of monopolizing the best parts. He could not support every improvident fellow who had once acted for him in his theatre. He might, in the first warmth of friendship, or with the *fausse bonhomie* of the profession, promise services which, as a business man in charge of a theatre, he was unable to perform. All this goes a long way to explain the charges against Garrick, but not quite far enough. Even his friends on this point show a curious reluctance to praise him, as if there really were something a little mean and underhanded in his nature. We must examine this charge, if we are to understand the character of Garrick.

He had been trained in a hard school. Although the Garricks were genteel, they were singularly "low in the purse". For the greater part of the future actor's childhood, his father was a half-pay officer, and we have Johnson's word for it that he was "bred in a family whose study was to make fourpence do as much as others make fourpence halfpenny do". The letters which David wrote to his father, while the Captain was on five-years' duty at Gibraltar are full of little revealing details of the straits to which they were put to keep up appearances. They managed. The family was on visiting terms with the best society in Lichfield. But it must often have been a tight squeeze.

A stone's throw away from the Garricks' house was a bookseller's shop, and in this bookseller's shop an uncouth, myopic, growing lad whose name was Samuel Johnson. And when Johnson set up his famous, if short-lived academy at Edial, two and a half miles from Lichfield, David and George Garrick, the former eight years Johnson's junior, were sent to him as his first pupils. Much of Johnson's rather patronizing attitude to Garrick in later life can be explained by this circumstance; and Garrick, on his part, never shook off a certain awe of his former schoolmaster.

When Garrick was twenty and Johnson twenty-eight, they came up to London together, Garrick to study for the law and Johnson to work for the booksellers. The fortunes of the two men were very different, and this, too, may help to explain Johnson's occasional asperity. Garrick, having inherited a thousand pounds from an uncle, gave up the law and set up in business as a wine merchant. His brother, George, was to run the business in Lichfield, and David was to be in charge of the London office. As we have seen, he was speedily seduced from this worthy and profitable undertaking to more dangerous and, as it turned out, even more lucrative fields. Johnson, unfortunately, did not succeed so quickly, and this fact was scarcely calculated to make him look with more indulgence on the player's faults.

Garrick's chief friend in the early time of his success was Macklin, but he had also made the acquaintance of the famous Peg Woffington, the vivacious Irish actress whose successes in Dublin had been followed by even more striking successes in London. Garrick was, at this time, twenty-five years old and Peg Woffington was one year his junior. She became his mistress and, rather oddly as it seems to us, set up house with him and Macklin at 6 Bow Street. Later Macklin fell out and Garrick and Peg lived together at another address for a further two years.

Even as early as the house in Bow Street, we begin to hear the legend of Garrick's meanness; but a moment's reflection is enough to show that it could hardly have been otherwise. Macklin and Peg Woffington were both Irish, with the generosity and carelessness of their race. Garrick had a little Irish blood in his veins, but he was not Irish by nature. In fact, we can only understand Garrick if we realize that he was, and always remained, a Frenchman. His Huguenot grandfather had been compelled to fly from France at the time of the Revocation of the Edict of Nantes, and all the economy and order dear to the French soul remained Garrick's most striking characteristic throughout his life. It was fatal to arrange that he and Peg should pay the housekeeping accounts in alternate months. Few men, and certainly no Frenchman, could have emerged from such a test with a reputation for generosity.

There is a story in Boswell which shows which way the wind blew. Mrs. Woffington, during one of Garrick's months for meeting the bills, was entertaining Dr. Johnson to tea and, in honour of his company, was about to put an extra spoonful into the pot. Tea was thirteen shillings a pound, and Garrick was at the end of his patience. "The tea, madam," he cried, "is as red as blood," and brushed the spoon aside. If Garrick had realized that this little incident was to be enshrined forever in the pages of Johnson's biographer, he might well have stayed his hand.

His association with Peg Woffington lasted about three years. There is every reason to think that he intended to marry her, but Peg belonged to the eighteenth century tradition of actresses, and in 1745 we find Garrick setting up house by himself. He was, as Mrs. Clement Parsons says, in her admirable monograph, "an essentially decorous person." He liked order in his life and if that order brought him also the consideration of the world, so much the better. He did not like to think of actors as rogues and vagabonds. He wished them to take their place in the community as respectable citizens, able to mingle at ease with "the Best in Town".

DAVID GARRICK

Even from the first, from the days of Goodman's Fields, Garrick was a social success. We hear much in the letters to Lichfield of the titled nobility who flocked to the theatre to see him play. He was soon taken up by the aristocracy and became what we should call "a diner-out", but only in so far as it did not interfere with the claims of his profession. Indeed, he regarded it as part of his profession, as the most potent means of publicity available and the surest manner of keeping himself on good terms with the public that mattered. He was well able to conduct himself in elegant society, but he never aped the familiarity of a man like Foote, who made it a point of honour to call peers by their surname. If Garrick's attitude to "the great" seems to us to contain an element of sycophancy, we should make allowance for the very different conditions in the eighteenth century, when peers still went about in the daytime with their orders pinned on their coats and were, for every eye to see, of a different race of men than the common herd.

Garrick had no thought of equality. He regarded his appearances in society as a kind of subsidiary performance in which he never for a moment stopped acting. His powers as a mimic made him excellent company, and he was welcomed everywhere. Yet his eagerness to be received among the Best in Town was not wholly calculation: he genuinely liked it and was honest enough to admit that he did so.

Garrick was wise to do his best to make a good impression on all classes of Society, but it must be admitted that there was, in his very natural desire to stand well with the world, more than a hint of an almost morbid anxiety. His relations with Churchill, the satirist, which have already been referred to, bring this out very clearly. Churchill had praised him highly in the *Rosciad*, so highly that Garrick found himself in his Green Room in a position of some embarrassment. The actors all came to him with their complaints of Churchill's hard usage, and it was impossible for a man of Garrick's temperament not at least to pretend to sympathize. He laughed off the praise by which he had himself been bespattered by remarking that the fellow probably wanted the freedom of the playhouse and thought that servile flattery was the best way to obtain it. Of course, the remark was repeated and came to Churchill's ears. Churchill, in his next satire, showed quite plainly that, when he praised Garrick, he thought he was conferring a favour, not asking for one, and Garrick saw with horror that a well-wisher had been transformed into a potential and powerful enemy. He was most distressed.

He was on friendly terms with Lloyd, a friend of Churchill, who had himself written a satire about the theatre, and Garrick sat down and wrote what can only be described as a very careful letter to Lloyd, expressing himself Churchill's great admirer, and asking to be allowed to meet him. There is nothing undignified in the tone of the letter, but it is difficult not to feel that a greater man would not have written it, would have been content to rely on his own talent and let the Churchill storm blow over. But Garrick was not that kind of man. He took care to make Churchill his friend, even to the extent of doling out guineas when the improvident poet was hard pressed for money.

All went well henceforward, so far as Garrick was concerned, although he was thrown into great anxiety by hearing that Churchill intended to attack his old friend, Hogarth. On this occasion he wrote a letter to Churchill, which is so revealing that it must be quoted in full.

"Dear Churchill,

"I sent to you last night but could not hear of you—I cannot conveniently this week obey your commands but I will the latter End of the Next—I have made a purchase that has beggar'd Me, however should you be greatly press'd I'll strain a point before that time, tho I suppose it is the same thing to you. . . .

"I must entreat of you by the Regard you profess for Me, that You don't tilt at my Friend Hogarth before you see Me . . . He is a great and original Genius: I love him as a Man and reverence him as an Artist—I would not for all the Politicks and Politicians in the Universe, that you two should have the least Cause of Illwill to Each other. I am sure you will not publish against him if you think twice —I am very unhappy at the thought of it, pray make Me quiet as soon as possible by writing to me at Hampton or seeing Me here."

This would seem a very manly and even noble letter if it were not for the unlucky existence of the earlier epistle; and it is difficult to escape from the suspicion that even here there was an element of policy in Garrick's desire to make peace. Yet although Garrick desired peace, in order, quite naturally, that he might exercise his profession, there was nothing pusillanimous in his attitude, and when driven into a corner he could behave with exemplary courage.

For his Chinese festival in 1755, Garrick had imported a number of Swiss and Italian dancers. The patriotic mob in the pit, knowing that their country was on the eve of war with France, and considering, in the traditional manner, that all foreigners were more or less the same, would not suffer these performers to appear. For five nights they rioted, broke up the furniture of the theatre, smashed the lamps, assaulted the boxes, and even went in a body to Southampton Street where Garrick then lived, and broke the windows of his house. Garrick bowed to the storm and withdrew the unpopular entertainment, and a few nights later presented himself to the public in one of his most popular parts. As soon as he appeared on the stage, there were loud cries of "Pardon! Pardon!"

The hooligans in the pit expected him to go down on his knees and ask their pardon for having had his theatre smashed up. Garrick managed to impose sufficient silence to make a speech. He came forward to the front of the stage and, in a firm voice, told the audience that he was "above want, superior to insult", and that unless they allowed him to perform on that evening he would never appear on the stage again. He carried his audience with him, and the speech was greeted with tumultuous applause by the very people who had done so much damage three or four nights before.

Even in 1755, Garrick could have retired from the stage with a fortune and a high reputation. Actually he was to remain the chief ornament of the English theatre for more than twenty years still. But his fame was soon to be no longer confined only to one country. The Seven Years War ended, many distinguished foreigners were able to come to England. In spite of the War, the relations between the English and French aristocracies had remained very close, and it was quite natural that the English should wish to show their French friends one of the chief sights of London, Garrick's acting. Garrick received so many flattering attentions from these visitors that he decided to go on a foreign tour, not a tour of acting, but a holiday; and it is typical of the man that he should choose to go abroad at so precisely the right moment. He felt he had deserved a rest: the season of 1762 and 1763 had been disturbed by the Fizzgiggo Riots* and he thought that the British public would appreciate him more if he relieved them of his presence for a short time. Then, too, there was the call of his Continental friends; and in the autumn of 1763 he set out on an extended tour.

*The so-called Fizzgiggo Riots were promoted by one Fitzpatrick, at first Garrick's supporter but, on some fancied slight, his bitter critic. Garrick satirized him as Fizzgigg in *The Fribbleriad*, and Fitzpatrick's revenge was to create a riot at Drury Lane Theatre in 1763, ostensibly as a protest against the abolition of admission at half-price after the end of the third act. The disturbances lasted for two nights and Garrick was compelled to submit.

DAVID GARRICK

Although he did not act in public theatres, he exploited his talent for mimicry at private parties and was everywhere received with enthusiasm, especially in Paris. He seemed to the cultivated French, as he had seemed a generation before to the English, the exponent of a new kind of naturalism, and naturalism in Paris in the early 1760's was beginning to be the mode. He met Grimm and Holbach and Diderot and indeed every prominent Parisian figure of the time. Voltaire invited him to Ferney, and the foreign journey, continued through Lyons, Turin, Rome, Naples, Venice, Munich and back to Paris, was one continued social triumph.

On his return to Drury Lane in September, 1765, after an absence of two years, he was received with the utmost enthusiasm. His fame continued to grow until his retirement in 1776, and when he died, three years later, he was buried with enormous pomp in Westminster Abbey, the first actor to whom so signal an honour had been vouchsafed. Molière, little more than a century before, had been refused burial even in consecrated ground, and his widow could only console herself with the splendid epigram: "The man to whom Greece would have raised an altar France refuses a grave." Mrs. Garrick could have no such complaint against England. England gave her husband not only a grave, but a grave among the most glorious of her sons, and when she herself died, nearly half a century later, at the prodigious age of ninety-seven, she was buried in Westminster Abbey beside her husband.

It is sometimes urged against Garrick that during his long tenancy of Drury Lane, he should have done so little, not for the theatre, but for the drama. It is a complaint often brought against actor-managers, and indeed is almost inevitable from the nature of their double function. The man who is primarily an actor must necessarily think in terms of parts for himself. Those parts he is able to fill and animate with the breath of his own genius, but when that genius has been withdrawn, how flat and dull they seem! One is left with the impression that both Garrick and, later, Henry Irving, produced rubbish almost in preference to good work. But we must admit in justice that the period of Garrick's management of Drury Lane was one singularly devoid of original genius in the English drama. Even so, it is unfortunate that Garrick gave so little encouragement to the rising school, headed by Goldsmith. One of the most definite of his actions at Drury Lane was his refusal to put on *The Goodnatured Man*.

But if Garrick did little for the drama, he did much for the actor. He raised the standard of a debased and Bohemian profession to respectability and affluence. We are often told that Henry Irving did the same. So that perhaps it is continually necessary to raise the acting profession to respectability: perhaps that is the most healthy thing about the profession of acting. Great actors may be also great gentlemen, but the ideal of gentility is not one the acting profession can aspire to with any safety. For gentility is essentially a control of emotion, a determination to show no outward sign of passion, a deadening of exuberance, an elimination of gesture; and acting is, or should be, the reverse of all these things. Garrick was saved by his French blood, and no doubt also by the fire of genius which we, who come so long after him in time, can only accept on the evidence, the unanimous and overwhelming evidence, of all who saw him play.

25

WARREN HASTINGS

(1732–1818)

by Malcolm Muggeridge

THE British occupation of India is as strange a thing as ever happened. It began with greed. There was a chance to get rich, fabulously rich, quickly, and adventurers of all classes seized upon it. The conditions under which they had to live were terrible, the risk of dying before returning home to play the Nabob was great. They lived riotously, a little group of younger sons of gentry, down-and-outs who, as a last desperate gamble, had enlisted in the East India Company's service, ambitious persons who for one reason or another had failed to climb into importance, recipients of morsels of remote patronage contemptuously tossed to them by some politician they had managed to serve in a small way. In Calcutta when the monsoon broke after the hot weather they used to assemble to reckon up their numbers and see who had survived, a macabre roll-call that was followed by bacchanalia of thankfulness.

Even so, they represented almost the only stable element in a ramshackle, disintegrating Empire. Their very greed was a source of strength, something real amidst the decay of Mogul rule. It stood when all else was shadowy, crumbling, and provided the nucleus of a new administration which has only lately taken on the same quality of unreality as the one out of which it sprang.

Warren Hastings came to India just at the period of transition, when the East India Company was being forced, against its own inclination, to accept more and more administrative responsibility for the territory it had acquired only to exploit. He was exactly fitted to deal with such a situation, not brilliant and reckless and unscrupulous like Clive, but conscientious, intelligent, with a passion for orderliness, patient and determined, and aware, when few others were, of how trading settlements might become an empire. His ambitions were too subtle to be satisfied with the quick acquisition of a fortune. He was interested in India and its inhabitants, and saw in it a field for the exercise of his administrative talent. At the same time he was romantic. It showed in his marriage to Mrs. Imhoff, in the lavishness of his expenditure and general carelessness in money matters, in the duel he fought with Philip Francis, in the despair he sometimes noted down, in his occasional self-dramatization and self-consciousness. As with so many great administrators, the two strains, prudence and romanticism, were equally balanced in his nature, so that his minutes had a kind of glow about them, and his literary productions a painstaking dullness without any sparkle of inspiration. He set himself specific objectives only just near enough to be realizable, and was able with a wry, half cynical smile to suffer public ingratitude without bursting out into righteous indignation, sat patiently through a trial far longer and more laboured than the Meerut one without registering any dramatic protest, and, when it was over and his reputation cleared, did not unduly exult. When Sheridan, one of his foremost and most effective accusers, admitted in private conversation that he was convinced of the injustice of the charges preferred against him, Hastings merely asked him to put the recantation in writing. Just spoken it had no particular interest or significance in his eyes.

His first years in India revealed his capacities. Like any other servant of the Company, he combined private trading with his official duties, married while a fugitive at Fulta from the wrath of the Nawab Suraj-ud-Daula only to become a widower three years later, and returned to England in 1764, after fourteen years service, with £30,000. There he interested himself in Oriental scholarship, met and made a favourable impression on Dr. Johnson, and ran through his money more through generosity than extravagance. He felt rather lost in England. India has provided a refuge for many misfits, and an opportunity for much inordinate ambition to express itself. The streets of Calcutta are full of statues of obscure Englishmen who played at being important there in their day, and clubs still resound with fantastic egotism which, frustrated at home, grows luxuriantly in that peculiar environment. Hastings had left England at seventeen to become a clerk. He had mastered the technique of Oriental politics, and was ill-fitted to join in the cynical and cultivated demagogy which was necessary then for a political career at home, while his pride and quiet but intense determination to rehabilitate his family's fortunes prevented him from being content with comfortable obscurity. Thus it was with relief that he accepted the post of second Member of Council at Madras, and sailed for India in 1769. In 1771 he was appointed Governor of Bengal, and, under the Regulating Act of 1773, Governor-General of all the Company's territory.

On the way out to Madras he fell in love with Mrs. Imhoff, who, accompanied by her husband, an unsuccessful artist, was also on her way to India. A more reckless man would have broken his career in similar circumstances, a more prudent one have renounced so difficult a passion. Hastings, characteristically, did neither. His passion was too patient to become extravagant, and too intense to be denied. Like so much else in his life, he subdued it into commonplaceness without cooling its ardour, waited three years for a divorce, which he arranged and paid for, during all that time seeing Mrs. Imhoff constantly and yet providing no justification for serious scandal, and then, when it was legitimate, became and remained to the end of his life an ardent lover. Imhoff did well out of the transaction, Mrs. Imhoff never had cause to regret it, and Hastings always saw his wife, actually rather a vulgar but kindly woman, as the bride he had waited for and at last rapturously won. Macaulay, with his sure journalistic instinct, fastened on "the luxurious manner in which Hastings fitted up the roundhouse of an Indiaman for his wife's accommodation, the profusion of sandal wood and carved ivory which adorned her cabin, and the thousands of rupees which he had expended to procure for her the society of an agreeable female companion" during her last voyage to England. He failed to see, however, that this was not mere ostentation, nor even uxoriousness, but a belated fulfilment of Hastings's nature, like the bottle of champagne with which a third-class season-ticket holder celebrates the maturing of his endowment policy. Hastings was kind and generous to Mrs. Imhoff's children by her first husband, but she bore him none of his own.

Every one of Hastings's qualities was calculated to infuriate Philip Francis, reputed to have been Junius, and for many years his close colleague in Bengal. Francis hated him bitterly, pursued him bitterly with his hate, spent himself in hating Hastings. The two men were entirely antipathetic, Francis as characteristic a product of his age as Hastings uncharacteristic, words and ideas and political manipulations his medium, action unrelated to general principles abhorrent to him. He was an idealogue and Hastings an administrator. Savage because his great talents remained unrecognized and unrewarded in England, out of favour and out of sympathy with even the political factions he had served, he went to India hoping that there at least he would be able to taste the power he thirsted for, only to find the same obstacle—as he thought, mediocrity entrenched, commonplace pomposity untroubled by his attacks, visionless efficiency against which his brilliance broke hopelessly, like waves against a rock. Hastings came to personify all he hated, all that had stood in his way and prevented him from making himself felt. His pressed lips, and cool uneloquent efficiency; his capacity for dealing with problems as they arose and on their merits; the regard in which he was held by his undistinguished subordinates, and the stony routine of his days; his unimaginative endurance, and decision, and quiet obstinacy, maddened Francis. The governor of a great province with unlimited opportunities to extend his influence, and concerned only to remit dividends to his employers, and preserve order and administer justice from day to day as best he might; unaware of the splendour of his position, unconcerned with juristic and political abstractions, a clerk who had inherited the power of the Moguls, and exercised it in the same mood that he balanced a ledger! Francis, in his place, would have dazzled the world with the brilliance of his Governor-Generalship, or at least with the brilliance of his exposition of the principles that underlay it. He would have translated a commercial enterprise into an imperial relationship, and become, instead of a pettyfogging intriguer playing off one degenerate princeling against another and so ruining them all, a viceroy who revived the greatness of fallen dynasties in order to make them worthy and profitable vassals of the British Crown.

For the first years, when he commanded a majority on the Governor-General's Council, he pursued a policy of persistent obstruction, hoping thereby to force Hastings's resignation, and, if not succeed him in name, at least in fact through the succession of Clavering. Hastings was not so easily disposed of.

He watched the achievements of his careful administration being undone by Francis and his two allies, suffered rebukes from his directors, saw his friends dismissed and their places taken by Francis's creatures, without yielding. Through the breathless damp heat of Bengal the two men wrestled together, Hastings imperturbable, Francis sometimes possessed with frenzied energy, sometimes despairing, sometimes abandoning himself to the unfastidious pleasures of the English colony, washing away his melancholy in draughts of heavy unsuitable claret and wasting his cultivated amorousness on uncomprehending native mistresses. In 1780 they fought a duel, turning out at daybreak to fire at one another, their forms enveloped in mist, and moisture oozing from the ground where they stood. Francis was wounded.

At last he went. He had had enough, and, leaving his rival in possession, returned with a tolerable fortune to England, there to exercise his hate in an outpouring of venomous pamphlets, and tireless intrigues all aimed at discrediting Hastings. Burke became infected with his hate, and between them they managed to mobilize powerful political influences on their side in preparation for an ultimate revenge, their enemy's impeachment.

Hastings's administration saw the final destruction of French power in India, a steady extension of British influence and the shaping of future British rule. The clamour of his directors for money forced him often to be unscrupulous; the inevitable orientalizing of his own outlook, and his proneness to compromise, made him do many things which horrified Macaulay, and which would have more than horrified a League of Nations if one had existed then. At the same time, any other sort of man, whether more concerned with abstract justice or more cynically indifferent to the welfare of the territory he had to mulct, would have lost India as surely as the American colonies were lost. Patiently and laboriously he cleared away the debris of a moribund administration and provided the basis for another which, with all its deficiencies, has allowed an immense and diverse population to live in security, even if at the cost of being devitalized, for more than a century and a half.

In her admirable study, *Warren Hastings and Philip Francis*, Miss Weitzman shows that the quarrel between Hastings and Francis was more than a conflict of incompatible personalities. It was, as well, a conflict of policies. Francis wanted to "make the possession of Bengal beneficial and permanent by reverting to the ancient institutions of the country, as far as we are acquainted with them and present circumstances will permit", the Company taking no hand in its actual administration, and the "receipt of a fixed tribute from the native princes being the only bond of union between England and Bengal". Hastings, on the other hand, believed that existing institutions of government were irretrievably decayed, and that the only practicable policy was for the Company to accept administrative responsibility, and establish a government which would "reconcile native prejudices and customs with the exercise of an alien domination". It is easy to understand how a man like Francis arrived at his conclusions. Indeed, in view of subsequent developments, it is by no means as certain as Miss Weitzman suggests that he was entirely mistaken. Yet it is doubtful if his policy would have been practicable even on a short view, and certain that it would not have resulted in a British-Indian Empire. Hastings's policy was practicable, and did result in a British-Indian Empire.

He, far more than anyone else, is the originator of that Empire. It is his creation. His spirit lives in India still, in the administrative routine, in the breasts of innumerable English-educated clerks who protest shrilly against British domination and yet are themselves its very essence, in the lecture halls of colleges where fragments of alien learning are droned forth and absorbed with listless determination, in legislatures where unfelt hopes and unintended purposes tumultuously echo, in the suspenders which lurk within even swadeshi *dhoties* and in leading articles which rattle out bitterness and incoherent discontent as ponderously and pathetically as galley slaves rattling their manacles. Hastings might not like or approve of contemporary Anglo-India, but it is none the less his kingdom, the fabulous fruit his life has borne—fabulous and at the same time barren, like his marriage.

In Calcutta, as far as was possible, he lived the life of a country gentleman, abstemious in his ways, rising and retiring early, his hospitality lavish but formal, fond of his horses (he had two at great expense brought to England), interested in his houses, especially the one at Alipore, universally respected, even liked, but with few intimates. Considering the climate, his health was excellent, though in Francis's time he suffered from headaches. Their conflict had that effect on him— devastating headaches which kept him, full of melancholy, in a darkened room. In 1785, after hearing the details of Pitt's India Bill, he resigned, and sailed for England. In the course of a parting speech he said that he had managed to sustain hope in circumstances which would have broken down the persever- ance of an "abler mind". His only consolation, he said, was the conscious knowledge "of what I could have effected, had my destiny ordained that I should attain the situation to which I aspired, and that I have left no allowable means untried by which I might have attained it."* He took with him a fortune of £80,000, which, considering his salary had been £25,000 a year, and his unlimited opportunities for enriching himself, was surprisingly small. Even Macaulay acquits him of rapaciousness where his private fortune was concerned.

The impeachment that he went home to was one of the great spectacles of the time. Macaulay unctuously describes how:

* Quoted in *Warren Hastings* by Mervyn Davies.

There were gathered together from all parts of a great, free, enlightened and prosperous empire, grace and female loveliness, wit and learning, the representatives of every science and every art. There were seated round the Queen the fair-haired young daughters of the house of Brunswick. There the Ambassadors of great Kings and Commonwealths gazed with admiration on a spectacle which no other country in the world could present. There Siddons, in the prime of her majestic beauty, looked with emotion on a scene surpassing all the imitations of the stage. . . . There appeared the voluptuous charms of her to whom the heir to the throne had in secret plighted his faith. There too was she, the beautiful mother of a beautiful race, the Saint Cecilia, whose delicate featues, lighted up by love and music, art has rescued from the common decay.

It dragged on from February, 1788, to April, 1795, the French Revolution intervening. The minutest details of all Hastings's activities in India were subjected to a searching and persistent examination. Burke, constantly prompted by Francis, worked himself into a crescendo of fury. Where others lost interest, his venom intensified. He kept up a constant flow of abuse, which, at the end, became fantastic, even pathetic, in its incoherence and irrelevancy. He gnashed and frothed against Hastings—"He never dines without creating a famine. . . . He is like the ravenous vulture who feeds on the dead and the enfeebled. . . . A Man whose origin was low, obscure and vulgar, and bred in vulgar and ignoble habits; more proud than persons born under canopies of state and swaddled in purple. . . . A captain-general of iniquity, a fraudulent bullock contractor, thief, tyrant, cheat, swindler, sharper." The unbridled fury of a man disappointed in his own life, and out of sympathy with contemporary tendencies, lashed itself against the mild, inoffensive, ordinary

Hastings. He knew his impotence to hold back the tide which, with prophetic insight, he saw advancing to submerge his world, but Hastings was within his reach, and so he set upon him. He could no longer fulminate in general against oppressors of the poor and lowly when the Paris mob was slaughtering them; in Hastings he had a particular oppressor against whom he could fulminate, and did so hysterically, almost to the point of madness. Three years after the end of the impeachment he died, protesting on his deathbed that he was as convinced as ever of Hastings's guilt, and that in attacking him he had acted solely from a sense of duty.

The other accusers had a lighter and more fancifully rhetorical touch. For four days Sheridan ventilated the wrongs of the Begums of Oude. Ladies were led sobbing from Westminster Hall, and the orator himself, at the end of his oration, fainted into Burke's arms. Gibbon, a careful spectator, though he was far from considering Sheridan "a perfect orator", noted down that "there were many beautiful passages in his speech on justice, filial love, etc." The next day, however, to test the authenticity of his collapse, he visited him, and, finding him in excellent health and spirits, added to his original note: "A good actor!"

By the time Hastings was finally acquitted he was penniless, though not entirely because of his impeachment. He had bought Daylesford, his family's former country seat, and spent a lot of money on altering and repairing it. The Company voted him, in spite of serious opposition from Pitt, a series of grants and an annuity of £4,000 a year, and he lived on quietly and comfortably until 1818. Two years before he died he gave evidence before a Select Committee of the House of Commons which was considering the renewal of the Company's charter. When he had finished his evidence he received an ovation. Francis had the belated satisfaction of outliving him.

WARREN HASTINGS

Hastings's reputation has undergone many vicissitudes. The recent tendency has been to idolize him as much as, in his own time, and after, he was depreciated. Mr. Mervyn Davies, in the latest biography, is an earnest and erudite champion; Messrs. Thompson and Garratt, in *The Rise and Fulfilment of British Rule in India*, are more measured in their approval of the methods and character of his administration. Few would now suggest that his impeachment was justified, though even Mr. Davies fails to make the Nuncomar affair altogether creditable. If Nuncomar was treacherous and a scoundrel, it still remains true that, with Hastings's approval, Sir Elijah Impey sentenced him to death for a crime—forgery—that was only a minor offence in Hindu law. The impeachment, indeed, was such a monstrous piece of ingratitude that it is difficult not to exaggerate the qualities of its victim. In saner circumstances Hastings would have returned to England with a well earned peerage, and have gone down to history as a great administrator who, in his own words, "gave shape and consistency to the dominion which the valour of others acquired." As it was, he became a pawn in the political game; without even realizing what was happening, he brought down one Government and lent his name to another, and all unwittingly provided a focus for political conflicts in which he had no personal part. Behind the extravagance of Burke's denunciations and the extravagance of subsequent vindictors of his reputation lies the quiet and attractive personality of a man who filled a difficult post in difficult circumstances with notable success, whose ambitions were moderate and impulses generous and enlightened, aware of his own qualities and abilities and not prone to exaggerate them, an administrative genius, the peculiar founder of a peculiar empire.

26

JOSEPH PRIESTLEY

(1733–1804)

by GERALD HEARD

"THERE were giants in those days"! It is not merely our timid wish to underrate ourselves that prompts the exclamation. It is clear, the eighteenth century had to produce giants or nobodies. Scholasticism which quoted authority for every word, and so was essentially anonymous—or pseudepigraphous—was dead: team-work with *its* anonymity had yet to be born. The balance which had rested so long and so firmly in favour of the Ancients was now rapidly shifting: a single man might tip the beam. He might still master all the old conserved knowledge and make new, revolutionary finds. He had to be a big man, intellectually and emotionally, to do it. But if he were big enough, then, "nicking the minute with a happy tact," he found in the eighteenth century an upheaval of knowledge which could give him a worthy pedestal. So mounted, his shadow would be cast far down the generations, as moon mountains, which at the full look nothing, seen on the terminator-line of the lunar sunrise, each appears almost itself a star.

Joseph Priestley had the mind for the time. He was fortunate in being born with a first-rate brain, in 1733. He needed, however, one more condition if he was to gigantise to his full stature. He must be born on the middle-left. Should he find himself in an abject home, revolt or collapse alone would be possible—a Cobbett or a Chatterton. Born even in an "Established" parsonage, the sleepy Charybdis of College, Close, Palace; Don, Dean, Bishop, could hardly have failed to engulph him. True, a Bishop of Llandaff was to show the "sensible century" how by life-long absenteeism and a whole-hearted devotion to explosives a churchman might pass for a Natural Philosopher. Not, however a very good one— rather a rochetted minnow of the mind only not forgotten because of the oddity that one of the mitred crests of an extinct religion should have been peculiarly interested in blasting.

So Priestley undoubtedly owed much to being born a Nonconformist just when to be so was neither dangerous nor comfortable. He appears in that narrow fissure between frustrated revolt and futile order, where alone original knowledge can grow. Tolerated and despised, the Nonconformists were under that optimum pressure which gives the greatest stimulus to the lively mind. Austere in life, they had a fund of repressed energy. Denied the Establishment's easier task of making society's case for it, they had to exercise their minds in criticism. Nevertheless, influenced by their own tradition, that criticism had to be constructive and, influenced by the spirit of the age, intellectual. In the middle of that century it was all very well for Wesley of Lincoln College and University Lecturer in Greek to determine to show that Conformists could feel. The Nonconformists, for their part, had to show that, denied college as well as church, they could think.

The home into which Joseph Priestley was born might nevertheless have been too restrictive had his intelligence been of a more moderate dimension. The boy of good talents here might well have ended a man of large means, developing to the threshold of millionaire-hood his father's business of woollen-cloth dressing in the Yorkshire West Riding. In his home-county unprecedented fortunes were about to be made through the weaving industry in the generations through which he was to live. He was on the spot, in time, place and lineage if he desired a quantitative not a qualitative success—if Joseph Priestley was to be content simply to enlarge, with the first forces of the Industrial Revolution, the beginnings made by Jonas Priestley. The son, however, never had any hesitation himself nor gave any doubts to his father. Here it was clear, beyond any vocational mistake, was a mind which would never be content with making means but would always be seeking ends. He must make discovery, not exploit invention.

The eighteenth century, however, held no scholarships for pure, specialized research. The man who would discover must discover not microscopic fragments—leaving it to another to assimilate them into systems—but wholes, life-size wholes, obvious to the naked eye of the generally educated man. He must therefore be a Natural Philosopher. Indeed, this century has no Scientists—any more than the Carboniferous Era has warm-blooded animals. Well on in the nineteenth century *The Times* was still to raise its thick eye-brows at this vulgar term "scientist". Cultivated people knew no such term because there had been till then no such thing. There had been only the scientist's precursor, the natural philosopher. Therefore, Priestley, standing as he does between two epochs, must first learn the old knowledge and then himself lay bare the new, making for himself a complete theory of understanding. His life cannot be understood if he is thought of as a Scientist and not as a Natural Philosopher. Cavendish, the recluse of a ducal house, can shut himself away with his riches, his rank and his right to his humour; can complete work which Priestley failed to finish and be—because of his aristocratic isolation and irresponsibility—the first Scientist, the first of that typical nineteenth century frame of mind which discovers regardless of consequences, indifferent to application or uses or even to meaning. Priestley works all through his life with clear purpose. Philosophy in its three aspects, divine, natural and human, is proportionately represented in his theological, scientific and political writings.

As a philosopher he must, then, start at the beginning. At twelve he is at a neighbouring grammar school. Then a minister sees the boy's capacities and wisely devotes himself to equipping such a mind. Ordinary classical knowledge is not sufficiently fundamental. From sixteen to twenty, when most of the intelligent are content to master Latin and Greek, he must add Syriac, Chaldee and Arabic: while to open his way to the new learning he adds French, German and Italian. So much for a basis of "Rhetoric", the equipment for presentation. "Logic," the other aspect of the Humane Education, was mastered by standard text-books, to which were added not only metaphysics but also—significant addition—Gravesande's *Natural Philosophy*. The rules of expression and thought, the standard theories of the Universe, the new outlook on the physical world and nine languages with which to sift past knowledge and keep in touch with new—so equipped Priestley at nineteen goes to Daventry Nonconformist Academy. There this extraordinary mind is trained for the Ministry: he is given those peculiar and precarious definitions with which the uninformed enthusiasm of the seventeenth century had tried to convey in terms of the intelligence its subconscious dissatisfaction with the Anglican settlement. After three years he is certified as charged and is sent off to a tiny congregation in the Suffolk townlet of Needham Market.

Professor Toynbee believes that all great minds must suffer a banishment in early age—be "driven of the spirit into the wilderness" after the first realization of their powers. Certainly Needham Market was adequate as Priestley's wilderness.

Even his amazingly stable and fertile mind felt his isolation. That, however, did not last long. Three years after he can move to Nantwich. There he can express his need to be expressive, for he founds a small but successful school. Teach he must, for he was certainly an extrovert and presentation was to him almost as keen a pleasure, and indeed a need, as discovery itself. He himself remarked when he was explaining optics to a correspondent that he could tell her all about perspective now but should she come in a month's time asking for that knowledge he might not be able to give it. This, of course is the mind of that master of presentation—the lawyer. Should he not then have found his real outlet in the pulpit? It was, however, almost useless to him owing to the one abnormality in a nature which was singularly complete—that was a stammer. The school, then, gives him his real opportunity and, after another three years, it is clear that his pastoral vocation is to teach. He is consequently given a post at Warrington Academy and there enters on what is probably the happiest period of his life. Happiness, though, is only a relative term with Priestley. Well endowed as he was mentally and physically, perhaps his most fortunate gift was one of temperament—an outstanding equilibrium of mind. He was to suffer reverses which might be called disasters but none ever seriously threatened his peculiar equanimity. Nevertheless Warrington was undoubtedly as congenial as Needham Market was alien. He was now one of a number of men of really fine intelligence and they could boast without exaggeration that their Academy could compare favourably with the drowsing scholarship that chewed the cud in the reserves of Oxford and Cambridge. One result of this mental activity in the eighteenth century among clergymen was that these "scholar divines" all became, first Arians and then, as their scholarship pursued its way (for Arius held a Demiurgic theory even more repugnant to Reason than that of Athanasius), Socinians. To us that seems a queer outcome of Nonconformity. So to think is to fail to realize the gulf which separates us from the eighteenth century—whether it was being "sensible" or "enthusiastic". Nonconformity then was not merely protesting against all authoritative ritual: it was still also claiming the right to think against all authoritative dogma: while Priestley himself, though throughout his life he is a Socinian, finds nothing more shocking than "unbelief". Paris, with all its brilliant fellow savants, appears to him, because of this defect, to be a sorry place. The Christ whom he reverenced he believed to have supernatural powers and a divine mission. Nor did he stop there. He always claimed that: "The only prospect of immortality is from the Christian doctrine of the Resurrection."

It is necessary to keep the distinctiveness of Priestley's religious views continually in mind—otherwise we tend to conclude that he was only that favourite abstraction from eighteenth century reading, the parson who wears a black coat for his living but whose heart is wholly engrossed in interests which are alien from or hostile to theology. The Warrington Academy, however, not only kept him a practised and keen theologian and a polished scholar, it also gave him the first full opportunity for fame. Dr. Turner of Liverpool lectured there on Chemistry. Priestley recognizes his own strong experimental bent. He turns with his native energy to study electricity. Such is this energy and his fertility that in 1766, when he is only thirty-three years old, he is elected to the Royal Society, for electrical research.

Now fully developed and indeed set we can form a picture of the man, a picture which age will only engrave somewhat more deeply. The main features of body and mind will change little, for though gentle, stable, kind and good, the character was unmistakably one of steel. He always liked company but never showed vivid predilections or attachments. His curious equanimity has been noted. It showed in the body also. He stood firmly placed on the mean in everything and however wide the span of his mind and interests everything was balanced. Moderate in height (four inches under six feet), moderately athletic (a strong walker and seldom ill), often smiling, seldom heard to laugh, always friendly, never enthusiastic—this balanced temper informs his face. Grey-blue shrewd eyes, which would never dilate and seldom narrow—gleam rather than flash—that longish nose which so often points to inquiry, a capable mouth which obviously smiles at most things but could never gaffaw. The stammer is the one hint that such sanity and such intelligence may, far below the level of consciousness, have been locked by a grip which sometimes led to strain and even to distortion.

Certainly he could "dissociate" to a peculiar degree, for he was never disturbed by talk and could compose in his fluent, clear, unpretentious style on any subject, whatever that might be going on around him.

By 1767 he has accepted another "living": this time his chapel is in the growing town of Leeds. There, as his house is near a brewery, he can carry on his experiments with "fixed air", and thenceforward Airs or as we prefer to say "gases" become his chief scientific interest. This was natural and right. There was more to be done by the practical researcher in the study of gases than such could hope to do at that date in the study of electricity. So Priestley shortly after brings to light Carbonic Acid Gas and as he is always practical he begins to see how it might be possible to "impregnate water with fixed air". By 1772 he has achieved this triumph and a year after he receives the Copley Medal of the Royal Society for making Soda Water. Such an award has a faintly humorous effervescence in our ears to-day—the Royal Society's highest honour for a very common commercial invention. Our amusement is due, however, to this discovery becoming one of such popular value.

Priestley's fame by then is secure and, in consequence, for a time it seems as though he is after all going to follow eighteenth century precedent. Lord Shelburne offers him a "retaining income". He is to have a noble patron. A house in the country and £250 a year did not in any wise abate his energy. Indeed, it is while in receipt of this sinecure that Priestley makes the discovery which most assured his fame and confused his thought—Oxygen. "Dephlogisted Air" he insisted on calling it, so involving himself with this his greatest scientific discovery in his most persistent and traditional error. Four months after its discovery he is taken by his patron to Paris and there, in the November of 1774, he tells the savants, Lavoisier among them, of his achievement—Lavoisier who was to realize the true nature of what Priestley had found.

On his part, Lord Shelburne seems to have realized to the full the importance of his remarkable "client". Both sides behaved perfectly—so rare an event in the century when Europe was illuminated by the flashes from the Frederick-Voltaire thunderstorm that it should be placed on record as part of the achievement of this remarkable life. Nevertheless, after seven years and much travel and intercourse which was undoubtedly of the highest value to Priestley, they parted and Priestley once again goes into active life as a Minister. The alliance could not have been sustained, for Shelburne was a great politician working in parties over which the Throne was increasingly attempting to win decisive control; Priestley was an outspoken, un-franchised radical. The association was as dangerous for the one as for the other. Shelburne closed it with a fine generosity by persuading Priestley to accept a pension of £150 for life.

From the quiet of Calne, Priestley therefore moves to the site of his tragedy, Birmingham. He had never ceased to live the triple life in which alone he felt fully justified: as a writer on Theology, Politics and Science. While at Leeds he had

published tracts against the Government's American policy—
which of course was the King's. Now with incessant energy—
his output was enormous—he pursued his attacks on ignorance,
prejudice, and superstition. In this respect he suffered, of
course, from the limitation of his powers and age—he thought
he had only clearly, courteously but trenchantly to point out
to any other his mistakes for that other to own himself convinced, to yield and to reform. The Age of Reason could not
reason otherwise, but Nature, expelled with such a flimsy
fork as argument, only came back with redoubled violence.
Priestley was prosecuting his chemical researches but he was
also pouring out tracts against the Crown's policy and learned
but much read works against the Church's dogma. Either of
these two latter activities if not restrained we can see must
have led to trouble. Quite apart from the oncoming terrors
and reactions which the French Revolution would cause, long
before that storm appeared on the horizon the eighteenth
century belief that everything was open to the inspection and
modification of Reason was undergoing a change. Hume
could remark that the atmosphere in which during the earlier
part of the century "enthusiasm" could not live, was changing.
Priestley should have noted this. On the contrary, he was
completely innocent of any apprehension. He was happy and
assured as perhaps the most positive member of that remarkable provincial "Royal Society", the Birmingham Lunar
Society, which met on moonlit evenings to discuss natural
philosophy and which had Erasmus Darwin as one of its
members. Shortly before the outrage Priestley wrote of his
delight in living in a place and in an age when a man may
state: "Whatever appears to him to be truth without giving
the least offence!" It seems that even the most enlightened
can never apprehend the contemporary atmosphere but live
almost as much in the past, as Conservatives.

Priestley might however have escaped the blow, or at least

its full force, had not circumstances suddenly become acute. The French Revolution had frightened profoundly the comfortable. Priestley had supported the Revolution's initial reforms. Indeed he went so far as to use in one of his pamphlets in defence of its unsettling new social policy, the simile of gunpowder's use in the clearing away of ancient ruins. Such a metaphor, considering the long memory of the English for Guy Fawkes, could not have been more unhappy. Still, Priestley was a widely-honoured man and he was also a devout parson—of a sort. It would be hard to attack him openly— at least otherwise than in counter-pamphlets and here he was more than a match for his opponents. They could not turn the Law upon him—yet. But what if the comfortable could persuade the poor that he was destroying their religious hope —the spiritual comfort which Marx was later to call savagely the opium of the people. Then there would be a real explosion. Between mob fanaticism and suspicious gentility Priestley was in real danger. The engineered storm broke. His house was wrecked, his writings and plant destroyed and he himself only escaped by flight. Still, eighteenth century England was more ashamed of this scandalous outburst—however much it disliked the victim—than any twentieth century tyrant state. Some of the tools—the poor rioters—were brutally punished, and some compensation (half he had claimed) was without too much delay provided by the State. Priestley however, and no doubt he was right, felt he was not safe even when he had moved to London. The mob, of course, feared him and would therefore attack him. What however he failed to realize was that the governing classes really felt him to be a danger in such times. He tried to resume preaching, in Hackney, but it dawned on him that he had become an outsider. The Age of Reason, that opening of ranks which were willing to accept a man because he thought clearly and wisely, was closing. He felt he had no place. He resigned

375

from the Royal Society, his resignation was accepted, and in 1794 he spent the three months of late Spring in voyaging to New York to settle among "rebels" and "a new free Nation".

There he remained, a noble exile, for, though he was invited to do so by some of the Fathers of the country, he never renounced his British nationality, nor accepted United States citizenship. After ten years' residence he died in 1804, even in the tale of his years showing himself a "man of the perfect mean", for he had lived no more and no less than the appointed three score years and ten. The nineteenth century, the Romantic age, the generations when Revivals, both in religion and in art were popular, would have had little place for such a type. Indeed, few lives can illustrate so perfectly the particular ideal which the eighteenth century on the whole had striven to express, an ideal, which with no suspicion of irony, is engraved on the tomb of John Churchill, first Duke of Marlborough, the greatest captain of its age:—"In religion he was as removed from enthusiasm as from indifference." The seventeenth century was vaporous with enthusiasms. The nineteenth was to crystallize out into innumerable specializations over the hard discontinuous facets of which shimmered the rainbows of the Romantics. The eighteenth century attempted to be limpid, lucid, a clear and universal solvent of all man's conflicts and problems. Though then this liquid state, between the pervasive gaseous and the discrete solid, could not last, we can view it as an essential stage and, incidentally, as a happy one. In spite of his early narrow circumstances and his later cruel accidents Priestley was unmistakably a happy man, outstandingly happy in the possession of that equanimity of temper and that completeness of outlook which no doubt were inter-related and which, equally undoubtedly, a less balanced and checked genius could not have enjoyed. About the natural reasonableness of men he might have a disappointing, a wounding shock. About his own reasonableness and that of Nature and of God, about the complete sufficiency of such an outlook he never had a moment's doubt or hesitation. The bridge of such a sublime natural assurance spanned unshaken the human stream even when that swelled for an hour into a mob torrent.

He was as happy in his term of living as in the use he made of his full but not excessive years. Neither in Theology nor in Science could the future have been his and as a politician he would not have been any less bewildered at the power of survival and indeed revival shown by traditions he had disproved and dismissed. As a Scientist he was always discovering new things and yet failing to understand them. In Theology he was with equal frequency discarding old things, again without understanding their true nature. The way in which he clung to his beloved idea Phlogiston—a theory worthy of the Dark Ages—when in fact he had proved it to be wholly unnecessary vividly illustrates this. (He had in reality discovered Oxygen without realizing it; he was to repeat this queer uncomprehending find with Chlorine.) Likewise the manner in which he completely overlooked and dismissed the psychological problems inherent in the phraseology of Theology, show the same mind limited by its own definiteness. Indeed, these two conducts of his mind, give illuminating examples of the way his intellect worked—its power within its range and its complete unawareness of anything outside that range. It is clear that both the power and clarity of such an understanding lay in its native inability to examine its assumptions or to see in any problem elements which could not be stated with perfect definition in the language of its own time. Above the threshold of its consciousness such an intellect was extraordinarily keen, swift and ingenious. Below—a complete blank. Like a tropic day this typical eighteenth century mind had no twilight. It saw and, without a moment's hesitation, settled what it saw and never doubted it saw all. It was a singularly unsuspicious mind. It was the mind of an age and not of all time, for though it could not doubt Reason, had it continued it could not have failed in the end having to face the "painful antinomy" that "every reasonable man", in spite of being informed and logical was not arriving at the same conclusion. Priestley himself, though he had written a very respectable history of the Christian Church to the Fall of the Empire, is shocked by Gibbon. Even then it was clear that Reason was not going to make reasonable men able to agree, or even able to agree to differ without much pain and bewilderment. What then? Priestley had not solved that problem. He stood and stands, first and last, for perhaps our most characteristic Natural Philosopher, a man who believed that our experience contains and is completely expressed by three irreducible but reconcilable units:—A Humanity which is reasonable, a Nature which is reasonable and a God who is reasonable. The Natural Philosopher was a product of that century, son of the Pure Philosopher. In his turn he has been succeeded by his heir the Scientist. In our day the Scientist is already aged and his successor is even at the door. Whether the Scientist is better than the Natural Philosopher is not a problem that we can settle. Probably the elder man was not less useful and pretty certainly he was more happy. Certainly Priestley, by putting the above construction on all his experience, lived happily and beneficially. Some may think that such a figure lacks warmth but none can doubt that it shines in its setting and century, a clear lamp on civilization's roadway.

27

RICHARD BRINSLEY SHERIDAN

(1751–1816)

by W. A. DARLINGTON

O F all our great literary men, Richard Brinsley Sheridan has had most difficulty in securing the respect of posterity. Contemporary opinion seems to have entered into a tacit conspiracy to cry him down, and has succeeded in influencing against him the opinion of later generations.

Hardly any writer of his own time or of the half-century following his death mentions him without finding in him something deeply deplorable. The usual tone is affectionate regret in those who knew him and contempt in those who did not. Nobody denied his talents, whether as writer or as politician. Yet nobody would admit that he had made adequate use of them.

Arthur Murphy, in a biography of Garrick which was published in 1801, mentions Garrick's admiration of *The School for Scandal*, and goes on:

He augured the best from a genius that began in so auspicious a manner. It is to be regretted that his prediction has not been fulfilled. A few more such productions would, with propriety, have fixed on Mr. Sheridan the title of our modern Congreve.

It should be emphasized that though Sheridan was only fifty years old when these words were written, he had long since finished his career as a playwright. *The Critic*, which was the last of his original plays, was staged in 1779. Murphy's lament over promise unfulfilled was therefore based on exactly the same evidence as our own estimate of Sheridan—which puts him, as a dramatist, far ahead of Congreve.

Lady Holland, in her Journal, said of Sheridan: "His defenders (and their number is but slender) say that all his bad conduct has proceeded from his struggling against the meanness of his origin and the littleness of his means. "

There is no reason to suppose that the lady was writing anything but the truth as she saw it. But it must be taken into account that in her eyes the worst of Sheridan's "bad conduct" was his political split with her kinsman Fox; for she was a good party politician, and Sheridan, to the detriment of his career as a Whig, was a born independent.

However that may be, the portrait she here draws of Sheridan will hardly pass muster even as caricature. Sheridan, though his father was an actor, came of a good family of the mixed English-Irish blood which has given Ireland so many great men, and was a rich man by any ordinary standard.

That these, and other judgments equally wide of the mark, were made of him by his contemporaries is not very surprising. It is surprising, however, that such errors of judgment should have been placidly accepted as fact by the two generations immediately succeeding Sheridan's death. There is in existence a whole mass of anecdotes in which Sheridan figures as an idle, drunken profligate, a plagiarist, a dishonest wastrel, an altogether disgraceful person with (more's the pity!) a quick wit on which he could rely to get him out of scrapes. Some

of these stories are true, some have a nodding acquaintance
with the truth, some are wholly and wildly false. Most of his
earlier biographers, however, were so ready to believe anything against him that they often lent their authority to the
merest calumny.

Not until Sheridan had been dead eighty years, in fact, did
it occur to anybody that he was not a person who needed to
be apologized for and explained away. Then at last the real
Sheridan began to emerge from the mists, and it was seen that
his very obvious faults were balanced, or even outweighed,
by his less obvious but quite undeniable virtues. It was seen
that his swift success as a dramatist was due neither to happy
accident nor to cunning theft, but to natural ability backed by
knowledge of his job. It was seen that his failure to reach the
highest positions as a politician was due as much to his virtues
as to his shortcomings.

Georgiana, Duchess of Devonshire, writing in 1802 a
preface to her diary of 1788–89, gives unconscious testimony
to this. "Sheridan," she says, "not only gave convincing
evidence of his talents but at the same time evinc'd the danger
of his character. I do not mean to accuse him of any duplicity;
in fact he has stood the test of even poverty and I feel con-
vinc'd of the honour of his political sentiments—but he cannot resist playing a sly game; he cannot resist the pleasure of
acting alone, and this, added to his natural want of judgement
and dislike of consultation, frequently has made him commit
his friends and himself."

When the Duchess said this, the warm friendship which
had existed for years between herself and Sheridan had cooled.
Her respect for his integrity is therefore a dispassionate tribute.
But her irritation against a man in politics who presumed to
think for himself, and refused on occasion to vote just as his
leaders told him to, is not dispassionate at all. It is Whig
prejudice made vocal, and it gives the key to the whole of

Sheridan's parliamentary career. He was honest with himself, and therefore nobody trusted him.

It was an unhappy—even a tragic—moment for Sheridan when he set his heart, very early in life, on a political career. There were two other fields of activity at least—the theatre and the bar—in which he could have been pre-eminent without difficulty, by sheer force of talent. He actually proved himself the best playwright and the best forensic orator of his day. He chose instead the political field, in which talent could take him only part of his way.

The fatal fact was that Sheridan's deepest ambitions were social. He felt himself to be a great man, and he determined to make himself a big figure. Success in the theatre or at the bar could not put him where he wished to be. Either the one or the other might bring him wealth, and therefore was not lightly to be cast aside; but such success could be only a means to an end, never an end in itself. To be a big political figure, a man must have riches and be on easy terms with the elect. By means of the theatre Sheridan fulfilled the first condition, and in spite of the theatre ("the meanness of his origin") he achieved the second—only to find that neither was enough. No wealth that he could earn, either as dramatist or as manager of Drury Lane Theatre, could enable him to live at the rate of these new associates for whom money only existed as a thing which other people could be despised for not having. And though he was admitted to their friendship, he was never quite one of them. They laughed at his sallies, made use of his oratory, admitted him to the Privy Council, and kept the responsible Cabinet posts to themselves.

Consequently, he was at a continual disadvantage. The necessity to live always at the extreme pitch of his means was made more difficult by the necessity to insist and give constant proof that a man of the theatre could also be a gentleman. The best contemporary summing-up of this aspect of Sheridan's character comes from George IV, who, as Prince Regent, had befriended Sheridan, used him, and finally left him in the lurch. The passage, which comes from the Croker Papers, runs as follows:

> Sheridan was a great man, but in the simplicity of his nature he never knew his own greatness. His heart was too much enlarged to be governed by his head. He had an abounding confidence in every man; and although his pen indicated a knowledge of human nature, yet that knowledge was confined to his pen alone, for in all his acts he rendered himself the dupe of the fool and designing knave. He was a proud man, sir, a very proud man, with certain conscientious scruples always operating against his own interests. He was a firm and sound adviser; but he was so systematically jealous of his own honour, that he was always willing to grant what he was not willing to accept in return—favours, which might be interpreted as affecting his own independence.

It is interesting to compare with this the summing-up of Sheridan's grandfather, made by his friend Dean Swift many years before:

> Doctor Thomas Sheridan died at Rathfarnham the 10th October 1738. . . . He was doubtless the best instructor of youth in the three kingdoms, and as great a master of the Greek and Latin languages. He had a very fruitful invention and a talent for poetry. . . . He was, as is frequently the case in men of wit and learning, what the French call "a dupe", and in a very high degree. The greatest dunce of a tradesman could impose on him, for he was altogether ignorant in worldly management. . . . Instead of bringing up his daughters to housewifery and plain clothes, he got them at great expense to be clad like ladies who had plentiful fortunes; made them learn to sing and dance, gave them rich

silks and other fopperies; and his two eldest were married without his consent to young lads who had nothing to settle on them.

Here, plainly, is the foundation on which the younger Sheridan's character is built. It is remarkable how these two shrewd observers, of widely different times, temperaments and stations, seize on the same points. There is the same outstanding ability, the same social ambition, the same large extravagance and grand air of casualness about money, the same gullibility (leading to the use of the same word "dupe") with the same large-hearted trust behind it; and, it may be added, the same personal charm.

But tougher and more durable material than this had also gone to the making of Richard, and brought him to notable success where his grandfather had achieved only failure. Dr. Sheridan's wife was a formidable lady of whom Swift spoke as "Xantippe". His son, the younger Thomas, inherited her intractable temper, which showed in him at its best as unshakable courage and at its worst as obstinate self-righteousness.

Thomas the younger at first intended to be a teacher, but when his father died leaving him no money with which to complete his education, he took the decision, curious in one so pedantic, to go on the stage. His preoccupation was with oratory rather than with histrionics, and he must have been by our standards, as he was by his son's, a very dull actor indeed. He was very successful on the whole, however, and when he had a part that suited his declamatory methods was capable of meeting even Garrick on terms of equality. He was Sheridan enough to be extremely good company on occasion; but he developed, as time went on, into a typical heavy father and a portentous bore.

His wife, Frances Sheridan, was very different, She was quick-witted, charming, full of personality, the best woman novelist of her day, and author of a play in which Garrick had one of his best parts. Her chief beauty lay in a remarkable pair of eyes, which her son Richard inherited. She died when he was only fifteen. Indirectly, however, she shaped his career, for it was out of kindness to her memory that Garrick first interested himself in Richard, and it was through his friendship with Garrick that Richard was able to make himself, at the age of twenty-five, part owner and sole manager of Drury Lane. Also, he almost certainly got the idea of Mrs. Malaprop from a character in an unfinished comedy of his mother's which he found among her papers.

When she died, he was at Harrow, where he had to endure unpleasantness at first both from boys and masters, because he was an actor's son and because his bills were very irregularly paid—for Thomas the younger was just as grand and as hopeful about money as Thomas the elder had been. Richard lived this down, however, and ended as a popular and influential figure with a reputation for brilliance combined with indolence —much the same reputation, in fact, as he was destined to bear through life, and just as ill or well deserved. He could work ferociously when he liked. Lewis Ker, the tutor who had charge of him when he left Harrow, once said to him in a letter: "How it comes to pass that you are ever in appearance indolent without really being so, I cannot conjecture."

In 1770, Thomas Sheridan moved his family to Bath, where he lectured to fashionable audiences on elocution. Young Dick, now nineteen and with Harrow left behind him, seemed to his indignant parent to be developing into an idle waster. A little juvenile scribbling in collaboration with a school friend named Halhed, a few squibs contributed to the pyrotechnical display of wit always proceeding at Bath, and a political essay or two, might have shown a less prejudiced judge that all hope for him was not yet lost, but Thomas never from first to last understood his younger son. He concentrated his affection and approval on the elder, Charles Francis, a capable but priggish and calculating young man.

For two years this state of things continued. Then Dick brought himself into the public eye by eloping to France with Elizabeth Ann Linley, eldest daughter of Thomas Linley, chief music-maker of Bath.

This, which turned out the wisest act of Dick Sheridan's whole life, was the first example of the astonishing opportunism which raised him to fame and fortune. Elizabeth Linley, though she was only eighteen, was already a famous singer and a famous beauty. In 1770 she had been forced by a greedy mother into an engagement with a Mr. Long, a rich but elderly country gentleman, who later backed out of his bargain and paid the girl a handsome indemnity; and Foote had turned the incident into a comedy called *The Maid of Bath*. Yet her purity and modesty had never been called in question, and to be in love with her was now the fashion.

Charles Sheridan and Dick's young collaborator Halhed (who met her at Oxford) were her avowed adorers; Dick seems not to have been thought of at all in this connection. The Sheridans and the Linleys were intimate, and Dick, like his two sisters, was a family friend. Consequently, when one of her admirers, a strange being calling himself "Captain" Mathews, became violently importunate, it was to Alicia and Dick Sheridan that she turned for help and advice. Alicia suggested flight to France, Dick offered his services as escort; and the pair escaped in a post-chaise, respectably chaperoned as far as London, on March 18th, 1772.

From Alicia Sheridan's account of the whole affair, and a letter written some time afterwards from Elizabeth to Dick, it is clear that he was in love with her before they started, and that it was his devotion and chivalry during the journey that won her heart. He declared himself when they landed at Dunkirk, after a shocking crossing during which Elizabeth was so ill that he feared she would die; and they went through a form of marriage at Calais. Dick, however, regarded this simply as a means of safeguarding her reputation. The "marriage" remained a secret between them; meanwhile he found her quarters in a convent at Lille.

There Thomas Linley came up with them. A short conversation satisfied him that his daughter's honour had not been tarnished; but she was his bound apprentice, and though he made some vague promises for the future, he insisted now on taking her back to fulfil her professional engagements.

All three returned to England next day. Dick fought two duels with Mathews, was badly hurt in the second, and found himself a public hero. Thomas Sheridan utterly forbade the marriage, and pronounced an awful ban against the whole tribe of Linleys; and Thomas Linley, who was making a large income (at least £1,000 a year) from Elizabeth's singing, made her promise to give up all thoughts of Dick. She promised— and thought of nothing else. Dick went to Waltham to study law, and spent most of his time writing letters of romantic despair. After nine months of this, Linley relented. Dick and his Eliza were married at Marylebone Church on April 13th, 1773. Linley was present. Thomas Sheridan was not. He solemnly disowned his son, and forbade his daughters to communicate with him.

How profoundly he was mistaken, time soon showed. Elizabeth grew from a charming and talented girl to a wise, understanding and loyal woman. Though they moved in a society where infidelity in marriage was considered no very great crime, the Sheridans remained friends and lovers to the end of their married life, except for one brief and bitter time of estrangement. She was in his life the steadying influence which above all things he needed. Till the time of her early death, the curve of his fortunes led upward. After he had lost her, it dipped irrevocably down. Every significant achievement of his life was brought off during the nineteen years when he had her at his side. In the twenty-four years which followed, he was still an important figure, but he did nothing of real note.

But thoughts of an eventual decline had no place in the mind of the confident youth who, after a long and rapturous honeymoon at East Burnham, set out to conquer London in 1774. Means he had none, except half the money settled on Elizabeth by old Mr. Long (the other half having vanished into Linley's pockets). His wife's talent and position as a singer might have kept them in comfort, but he calmly refused to allow her to perform any more in public. Her singing was in future to be a social, not a commercial, asset.

Once more the opportunist, he took a house in Orchard Street, far beyond his means, and entertained lavishly. Society flocked to hear Eliza's singing and Dick's wit. Meanwhile, he must get money somehow, and various pamphlets and political essays which he wrote brought him nothing. There was nothing for it but the theatre; and towards the end of the year he wrote to Linley to say that a comedy of his would soon be in rehearsal at Covent Garden, and that he expected to make £600 out of it.

On January 17th, 1775, *The Rivals* was produced; and it was a dead failure. After two nights it was withdrawn.

Then Sheridan showed the real quality of his mettle. Refusing the offers of concert engagements for his wife which poured in, he revised his play in the light of practical experience. Nine days later it was produced again, and was instantly successful. In November he followed this up with *The Duenna* (for which Linley had written the music). This had the then enormous run of seventy-five nights. Dick Sheridan was established— and his father consented to own him again.

In 1776, he brought off yet another bold stroke, which finally consolidated his position. This was the purchase of

Garrick's half-share of Drury Lane Theatre for £35,000. Linley found £10,000 of the money, and a Dr. Ford £15,000. Sheridan's share was £10,000, which he borrowed on the security of the theatre; and he was to be sole manager.

For a time the new management put on nothing new; but early in 1777 Sheridan staged his own retouched version of Vanbrugh's *The Relapse* under the title of *A Trip to Scarborough*. Its success gave him time to complete *The School for Scandal*; and on May 8th of the same year his masterpiece was produced, and was acclaimed the finest comedy of manners in the language.

The theatre had now served its turn in his career, and he could afford to think seriously of politics. In 1779 he took a brilliant and untimely farewell to dramatic writing with *The Critic*, and in 1780 he entered the House of Commons as one of the two members for Stafford.

He soon proved himself an interesting speaker and a quick and witty debater, and the Whigs opened their arms wide to him. When Lord North was driven out of office by the unpopularity of the American War, Rockingham gave Sheridan an Under-Secretaryship; and he was one of the two Secretaries to the Treasury in the Coalition Government of 1783.

Fox brought in his India Bill, which broke up the Coalition. George III installed Pitt as Prime Minister, and the Whigs began a long period in opposition. The Prince of Wales, also out of favour, showed a political partiality for the Whigs and a personal one for Sheridan; and this doubled Sheridan's importance to his colleagues.

In 1787 the question of the Prince's secret marriage to Mrs. Fitzherbert was brought up in Parliament. Mrs. Fitzherbert, as a virtuous and devout Catholic, would not live with the Prince except as his wife. He could not be openly married to a Catholic. The position was only possible so long as a conspiracy of silence was maintained towards it. A blunt question by a country member and a tactless answer by Fox endangered that conspiracy, and only the ready diplomacy and personal charm of Sheridan steered the House past the awkward place and saved Mrs. Fitzherbert from public disgrace. After this, Sheridan naturally stood higher than ever in the Prince's favour.

Meanwhile, the public conscience had been growing steadily more uneasy about India, and the result was the first attack on Warren Hastings in this same year, 1787. In this, and in Hastings's trial in the following year, Sheridan took a most spectacular part. His speech in Parliament demanding the impeachment of Hastings took six hours to deliver, and moved the House to such a pitch of emotion that it agreed to defer the division till next day, for fear that under Sheridan's spell it might allow justice to miscarry.

The speech at the trial, delivered at Westminster Hall before a coruscating audience (some of whom had paid £50 for a seat) and spread over four days, raised his fame to the highest pinnacle. Mrs. Siddons was carried out in a faint, overwrought by the power of his eloquence. His wife, writing to her sister-in-law, referred to this speech as "a display of genius, eloquence and goodness which no one with anything like a heart about them could have listened to without being the wiser and the better for the rest of their lives."

This moment does, in fact, mark the peak of Sheridan's career. Till now, he had enjoyed unbroken success in the world and unbroken happiness at home. The glimpses we get of his life with Elizabeth up to this time make an enchanting picture. The letters between Elizabeth and her favourite sister Mary, Mrs. Tickell, are specially charming.

But Mary died of consumption in 1787. Elizabeth gave herself up to long and bitter grief, and Dick—flattered and sought after—found consolation elsewhere. He had an affair with Lady Duncannon (not, as was once thought, with her sister the Duchess of Devonshire) which nearly came to an open scandal. Elizabeth, shocked and resentful, allowed herself to listen to the love-making of the young Duke of Clarence, afterwards William IV, and probably did become the mistress of Lord Edward Fitzgerald. She bore a child, which may have been Fitzgerald's, in 1792. By that time she and Dick were completely reconciled, and Dick had taken upon himself all the blame for her lapse whatever it was; but by that time she too was dying of consumption. She died on June 27th, 1792, leaving her husband almost distracted with grief.

Since this account of Sheridan is a character-sketch rather than a record of events, it fitly closes here. From the time of Elizabeth's death he achieved nothing new, and soon began to find it difficult to maintain ground already won. He grew increasingly irrational and eccentric in his private behaviour; and though he managed to keep his head in politics it did him little good. He gradually became the subject for anecdote and calumny which his early biographers knew.

Three years after Elizabeth's death he tried to fill the gap in his life by marrying a young girl, Esther Jane Ogle, who admired him, infuriated him, spent money even faster than he did and never really understood him, but stuck to him loyally. She was with him at his death which, in its unnecessary futility and misery, was a fitting end to his long, slow decline. He died on July 17th, 1816, with duns and bailiffs about his door; yet when his affairs were straightened out his debts proved to be such that they were easily paid out of his estate without embarrassment to his family.

When he was safely dead the political world paid him lip-service as a great statesman, and followed him to the Abbey in a procession whose pomp moved passers-by to admiration and Sheridan's true friends to deaf contempt. But it buried him near Garrick, among the artists. It was a comment on his career which Sheridan would have resented; but posterity has endorsed it.

28

BURKE AND FOX

(1729-1797 : 1749-1806)

by CHRISTOPHER HOBHOUSE

L ET us suppose they met in February of 1769. Burke would then be just forty, and Fox just twenty: yet they would meet upon equal terms. Both were members of Parliament, each enjoyed a widespread reputation of a highly equivocal kind. But they had arrived by very different roads.

Burke's road had been uphill; and more of a corkscrew road, at that, than a Roman causeway. He was the son of a middling Dublin lawyer, had been to Trinity College, had come to England to read for the bar, but had been seduced into hack-writing. Many mysterious and difficult years he had spent in the obscurer regions of Johnson's London, filling his mind more successfully than his belly. He had married; he had published some estimable works; yet at thirty we find him angling unsuccessfully for a consular appointment. He had been secretary to Single-Speech Hamilton, but his Irish pride had cost him the post and its pension. He had become a close friend of Johnson and of Johnson's friends: and in the intimacy of the Club he had revealed the genius that lay beneath the adventurer. But he was hampered by other associations less illustrious and less disinterested. In the eyes of the world he was merely one of "the Burkes", a trio that comprised himself, his brother Richard and his cousin William: and the world thought pretty poorly of "the Burkes". In association with Lord Verney and various minor co-adventurers, they were in on every speculation that was going: but though their operations were neither small nor scrupulous, they had been as yet successful. Part of the stock-in-trade of "the Burkes" was inside information, and in 1765 William Burke procured for Edmund the post of secretary to the Prime Minister, Lord Rockingham, while Lord Verney fitted him out with a seat in Parliament.

This was a startling rise. Most men shook their heads over the promotion of one who was known to be an adventurer, and even suspected of being a Jesuit (for his mother, sister, and wife were Catholics): but "we who know Mr. Burke", said Johnson, "know that he will be one of the first men in the country." And so it proved. Burke had already shown the power of his pen, and his marvellous conversation was known to a few: but, once in Parliament, he revealed a vein of oratory so beautiful and so profound that although Rockingham's government fell within six months, the upstart secretary had already by that time made himself felt as a political force. As time went on, the whole of Rockingham's following of indolent and overbred Whigs came to rely on Burke as both the inspiration of their policy and the drudge of their party: while Burke, who loved a lord even more than he despised a fool, gladly took their pay and "to party gave up what was meant for mankind". But among the excitements of Whig high life he still remembered his kinsmen, and partook in their precarious good fortune. In 1768 this man, who three years earlier had been an underpaid literary hack, became the owner of a large house and large estate at Beaconsfield, where he continued to his dying day to farm, improve, extend, and to entertain lavishly. "Casting a little root in this country," he called it: but an envious world continued to marvel at such unheard-of prosperity, until the next year a panic that overtook East India stocks wiped out Burke's associates and caused his brother and cousin to leave the country. How Burke saved his own skin is one of the many mysteries that surround his financial past—mysteries that he showed no eagerness whatever to elucidate. What matters is less how he made his money than how he spent it; and he spent it royally. In his early days he had given his last few shillings to an Armenian whom he met in St. James's Park: and all his later life he kept his house, his purse, and his heart open for all who were poor and needy. No wonder he was loved by all who knew him: but no wonder he was mistrusted and envied by the world at large.

Charles James Fox was quite another proposition. His father had been Pitt's great rival in the politics of George II's reign: and while Pitt had found fame and glory in the victories of the Seven Years' War, Fox had found enormous wealth in a long tenure of the Paymaster's Office. Being as generous and soft-hearted at home as he was grasping and ruthless in public life, he had educated his darling Charles on a system of boundless indulgence to his slightest lust or whim. And Charles, whose mother was descended from the union of Charles II and Louise de Keroualles, responded readily and fully to this treatment. The *enfant terrible* of Holland House became the terror of Eton, a gambler and a rake at sixteen. A short spell of assiduity at Oxford was followed by a protracted tour in France and Italy, where his prodigality both financial and physical created a scandal that heralded his return to London. In February, 1769, soon after he was back, Fox had already been six months in Parliament, though he had not yet spoken; he was already known as one of the deepest gamblers in London, in an age of prodigious gambling; he was already deep in debt, already notorious as a dandy and an outrageous wit; but of his political capabilities nothing was known.

He was not long in making his mark, and upon Burke in particular. Within a few weeks we find him answering Burke "with great quickness and parts, but with confidence equally premature". The question upon which he spoke and which thus divided him from Burke was the perennial question of John Wilkes. Ever since 1763 that indomitable little man had been exploiting the Whigs and scoring off the Tories: until it seemed as if the question whether Wilkes was to be imprisoned or expelled or reprimanded or outlawed was the fundamental issue of the century. And indeed there was a great deal at stake: for to the nation the disreputable figure of Wilkes embodied a principle. George III knew that the triumph of Wilkes meant the beginning of the end of close boroughs and corrupt jobs; and the London mob knew that the defeat of Wilkes meant that Parliament was still a close sanctuary for wealth and birth, where a well-turned speech or a well-placed bribe outweighed the wishes of a nation of men. It was Wilkes inevitably who won: and in winning he made possible much of what Fox was later to achieve. But what was more natural than that Charles Fox, got by corruption out of privilege, should fling himself into the breach against this horde of ignorant invaders? Or that Burke, for all his loathing of democracy, should inveigle his unwilling lords and masters to make what capital they could out of the popular excitement?

For five years Burke and Fox were in opposition to one another. Fox, as the spoilt darling of the Tories, exercised his wits in boyish but alarming invectives against the populace and their leaders; he won two small ministerial jobs; but for the most part he was engaged in wasting his substance at Newmarket, in Paris, and among the great gaming-clubs of St. James's Street. Burke wrote his *Thoughts on the Causes of the Present Discontents*; with his pen and his tongue he laboured to arouse the Whigs to an enthusiasm that he did not really feel: for though he disapproved sincerely enough of some of the high-handed methods of the Tories, he still shuddered at parliamentary reform, which was the only rational outcome of Wilkes's agitation.

It was a period when men were Whig or Tory only by the accidents of heredity. Rockingham was a Whig because his family were Whig, and Burke was a Whig because he was Rockingham's secretary. But as between him and Fox, it was Burke who loved the monarchy and the old forms of the constitution, while Fox was a republican at heart, and cared for the laws and liberties of England only in so far as they might assist his own return to power.

It was another twenty years before Burke turned Tory: but Fox turned Whig in 1774, for many reasons. One was the death of his father; another was his debts. Lord Holland had already paid them off to the tune of £140,000, but still they mounted. Since his rapacity was only equalled by his rudeness, he began, in spite of his amazing personal charm, to lose his friends: and he hoped like many others to find in radicalism a salve for social wounds. Moreover, his unpopularity in society was nothing to his unpopularity at Court. George III, who still dreamed of a moral Britain governed by moral ministers, had made it clear that he would not have Charles Fox at any price; so that for Fox the Tory party could hold out none of its usually rich rewards.

Yet the fundamental cause of his conversion was deeper than any of these. The year 1774 saw the parting of the ways on the question of America. In April of that year, Burke made his speech on American taxation, the first of those stupendous orations that raised the secretary and the drudge to the rank of a statesman and a classic. Burke, it is true, was drawing much-needed pay as Agent for the State of New York, a fact which was enough to make Johnson, his cordial admirer, declare that he was acting from interest. But in his American speeches there is a note that rings true—a true wisdom, a true passion. Burke had found himself at last, and as his genius rang itself out in these noble phrases, it struck some echo in Fox's mind, some vein of altruism and sincerity that lay beneath all the coating of pride and indulgence that he showed to the world. What could he not do, what could he not say, in such a cause? Under such a banner he would become a great orator possibly, certainly a great nuisance.

Such was the beginning of Fox's partnership with Burke. At first Fox was the disciple, learning his politics all anew from the despised middle-class Irishman. It was always Burke's part to enunciate principles and policies: it was Fox's task to put them across the House of Commons with his matchless powers of persuasion. Burke was the orator, Fox the debater. So, as the American war progressed, it was Fox who came to predominate. He became a superlative House of Commons man: having nothing to lose, he stuck at nothing to harass the majority. The King and Lord North were bound together by many links of mutual loyalty and stolid virtue, and between them they could either command or persuade a large majority of the House to support the prosecution of the war. But Fox was undismayed. His heart was in his work: and he believed that the majority of his opponents were secretly on his side. There was no sort of trick or threat he did not use. There were setbacks, scandals, duels. But slowly year by year the temperature of the country and of its elected representatives rose against a war which had at first been popular, but which became more senseless with each campaign. It was six years before Fox secured his first majority, on Dunning's motion that the influence of the Crown had increased, was increasing, and ought to be diminished. But after 1780 the end came rapidly, both in America and at

Westminster. Six months after Yorktown, North resigned, and Lord Rockingham formed a government in which Fox was foreign secretary and Burke paymaster-general.

Unfortunately, Lord Rockingham's following was not so much a party as a little clique of Whig peers, incapable of forming or supporting a ministry by themselves. Another group of Whigs was led by the able and mysterious Earl of Shelburne: and the two rival bodies had to go into partnership. Now Shelburne, though he had been even more bitterly opposed to the war than Rockingham, was much better trusted by the King: and from this preference arose the most furious and fatal jealousy. Fox and Burke and Rockingham were all one in their detestation of Shelburne: and the negotiation of the peace treaty took place among perpetual recrimination. After three months, Rockingham died, and Shelburne was sent for to succeed him. Fox, left in a minority in a cabinet presided over by his hated rival, saw no other course open to him but to resign.

It was a pitiful anti-climax. Eight years of glorious struggle ended in a hundred days of discordant and fruitless power. And now he was in the wilderness again, in opposition to a rival Whig. Burke, though disappointed by his exclusion from Rockingham's cabinet, followed Fox in resigning: but Shelburne made good the loss by taking into his cabinet the great name and the great abilities of the younger Pitt, then twenty-three years old. So it was Shelburne who negotiated the treaty after all: and Shelburne could have braved Fox's opposition for years to come, if Fox had not resorted to a wicked and disastrous revenge. In order to defeat Shelburne—a Whig, a friend to the Americans, an able and upright minister—he formed an alliance with North, whom for the past eight years he had been execrating as the arch-villain of the war, the corruptor of Parliament, and the instrument of the King's arbitrary will. Nor did Burke disdain to support this outrageous coalition. Against Shelburne all methods were considered fair. Fox and North had no single thing in common, but between them they had a majority. Shelburne was duly defeated and ousted: but Fox's new coalition government (in which Burke was again excluded from the cabinet) found no easy task before it. The King was openly and irreconcilably opposed to them: the country was shocked and angry at their betrayal: and Pitt was gaining in stature every day. After an inglorious career of nine months, the King dismissed them. Pitt stepped into their place, with a minority in the House, but confident of a huge majority in the country. It was three months before he dissolved, but during those three month, the coalition melted away. Pitt went to the country in Marchs 1784, and came back with a majority that lasted him till 1801.

Fox's coalition with North was never forgiven or forgotten by the public: but little Fox cared for the opinion of the public. He saved his seat at Westminster, but that was all. For the next few years he virtually retired to a small domain at Chertsey, where he farmed and read and entertained in the delicious company of Mrs. Armistead, a lady who united easy virtue to sterling worth, and whom he married later on. Burke also retired unhappily to Beaconsfield, but only to undertake fresh labours and anxieties. Ever since the collapse of the American war he had been obsessed with the question of India, and particularly of Warren Hastings's administration. Hastings returned in 1785; but Sir Philip Francis had returned in 1781, and had four years' advantage of his adversary, in which to prepare his revenge. For four years Francis filled the sympathetic ear of Burke with tales of cruelty, extortion, and injustice. The fertile and spiteful imagination of the author of the *Letters of Junius* provided the material: Burke's loathing of injustice and despotism did the rest. Between them they concocted a legend that was enough to feed both Francis's rancour and Burke's rhetoric. As the phrases of his great speech formed themselves in his mind, Burke became intoxicated by his subject: reason fled before so violent an emotion. The actual impeachment of Hastings took 142 days, but was spread over eight years. Fox and Sheridan contributed of their best: but long before the ultimate acquittal the trial had lost all interest as well as all reason. Burke had ceased to be on speaking terms with his fellow prosecutors: he blundered on alone to the ridiculous end, still blinded with rage and emotion.

Great events had supervened: and first of all, the question of the Regency. Late in 1788 the King, who by now had won the affection of every class of his people, took leave of his senses, apparently for good. The Prince of Wales was now twenty-six, and had become (to the King's disgust) the bosom companion of Fox in all his pursuits, whether reputable or otherwise. If the Prince took over the Regency, he would certainly dismiss Pitt, and might contrive to keep Fox in power for some little time: Pitt's only hope lay in the Queen. Fox emerged from his philosophic retirement with a startling alacrity, and proceeded to uphold the Prince's claims in a series of violent, foolish, and disgusting speeches. Pitt played for time: and the King's unexpected recovery a few months later found Pitt still clinging to office, and the whole Whig faction routed and discredited. Fox, for all his Whiggism, had shown an extraordinary eagerness to come into power by royal favour, at a time when the whole country was against him. The Prince had given earnest of that flabby deceitfulness which was to make him an object of loathing to his contemporaries and of contempt to all posterity. And the seed had been sown of a quarrel that was to kill the Whig party: for among the shadow cabinet that Fox had assembled and was ready at any moment to instal, the name of Burke, the elder statesman of the party, was still not included.

The King returned to sanity in February, 1789: in July, the Bastille fell. Fox, living in his happy Surrey retreat a little out of touch with the happenings of the great world, was agreeably thrilled by this event. It was a whack at the *ancien régime*, and as a good liberal he gave three cheers for the Paris mob. And as time went on, and riots gave way to murder, and murder gave way to massacre, he still continued to keep his end up, assuring himself and his friends that all was for the best, and anyway anything was better than the Bourbons. But fifteen miles away at Beaconsfield, Burke was pursuing another and a deeper train of thought. Burke knew the faults of the French monarchy: but he saw something more in these disturbances than mere honest discontent. He saw atheism: he saw behind it the influence of Rousseau and of the propaganda that Rousseau had levelled against all law and all morals. He saw a people being led away from reality by a mere abstraction, away from their interests by a mere theory, away from their hopes and aspirations by a mere doctrine. And a doctrine that transcended the national boundaries of France. This movement could not end, as Fox conceived, in a constitution for France and peace and plenty all round. Burke foresaw that because the revolution went further back than mere hunger and injustice, it must go further forward than the satisfaction of material wants and constitutional demands. He foresaw, and he foretold at the very outset, that religion would be proscribed; that the King would be murdered; that there would be propaganda begun and disseminated in other countries; that there would be wars of aggression in the name of France. It all came true. Religion was proscribed; the King was murdered; seditious propaganda was set up in England; France invaded the Netherlands. Thanks largely to Burke, England rallied in good time; sympathy turned to fear, and fear to detestation. Fox was left babbling of toleration and fraternity, while the country steeled itself for war. Burke, after his *Reflections on the French Revolution*, became the admitted leader of the national opinion. When France at last declared war on England, Burke openly threw in his lot with Pitt, and carried with him all that was worth having of the old Whig party.

All this took place a century and a half ago. Many of the innovations of the French Revolution are now the accepted institutions of every free country, while its worst horrors have been forgotten, and the philosophies that inspired it have passed into the limbo of all crack-brained fancies. People tend to think that in this crisis of human history, Fox was the far-sighted and forgiving visionary; that Burke became all of a sudden, in his old age, a craven reactionary, who dragged us into a wanton and useless war with France. This is an inter-pretation that has been kept alive with strong doses of liberal didacticism: but it cannot stand on its own feet. There is nothing at all in Fox's utterances at this period but ignorant optimism eked out with spite. Burke's last works, on the other hand, though they have a touch of hysteria in them, are some of his noblest: and it was their influence more than anything else that saved England from a worse peril even than the Commonwealth.

Burke took no office under Pitt. He was old, and he was wretchedly unhappy: the death of his beloved son almost unhinged his mind. He accepted a small pension from the King: and when this was jeered at by Fox's new followers, he was roused to write the superb and devastating *Letter to a Noble Lord*. That work is at the same time his Apologia and his Nunc Dimittis. With infinite spirit and wit he defends the labours of his lifetime: but all the while he is praying for death. And two years later he died, having in his last seven years atoned for all the blunders of a long and stormy career. Almost his last act was a curt refusal to allow Fox to come and say farewell.

Fox by this time can hardly have expected that his presence would be very welcome at the deathbed of his old instructor.

His conduct at this time was such as no friendship could overlook. Supported by a body of about forty personal adherents, he was carrying on an opposition to Pitt which openly exulted in the defeat of British arms, and abetted an agitation among the working-classes which can have had no outcome but a French invasion: nor did he make a secret of the fact that he was actuated more by hatred of Pitt than by love of Napoleon. But by this time, Burke's prophecies had come true, and his warnings had done their work. Fox's attitude brought him into such execration with the public that he thought it best to retire from Parliament for five years. The resignation of Pitt and the conclusion of the Peace of Amiens enticed him forward again in 1802; and he was even foolish enough to pay a visit to Paris and to meet Napoleon. But war began again so soon as Napoleon's plans were ripe, and Pitt was soon once more in power. Fox's prospects seemed as hopeless as before: his spell seemed to be utterly broken. But he was still consumed with his old absorbing lust for power. There was one chance, and he took it. He knew that Pitt was a dying man. By a very shabby manoeuvre he contrived to form a squalid coalition with a body of dissentient Tories led by Addington: as in 1783, he stooped once more to gain numerical strength at the expense of all his principles. But this time the contrivance succeeded: for when Pitt died in January, 1806, there was simply no alternative to Fox. Addington was a pure nonentity, and Fox was in command of his supporters. With as good a grace as he could muster, the King was obliged to swallow Fox.

So it was that Fox took charge of the war that he had done his little best to lose. But the triumph was short-lived. After six months in office, during which he acquiesced in everything that he had been denouncing for the past twenty years, he was taken ill with dropsy, and in September he died.

Such was the evolution of Fox from a Tory to a Liberal,

and of Burke from a Whig to a Conservative. They began respectively where they began by the accidents of birth and necessity: they were drawn together by a common impulse to resist the folly and injustice of the American war: they ended as the founders of the two great parties of the nineteenth century. Burke was bound to react from the French Revolution, because what he hated above all things was the doctrinaire. In all his speeches or writings, whether about America or India or Ireland or France, the salient feature of his thought is this— that what is true of one nation, or one period, or one set of circumstances, will not hold good of another nation, or another period, or other circumstances. Fox's was a shallower mind, averse to the drudgery of particular investigations, and susceptible to a rather glib emotion—and not less so after he had been embittered by the failure of his political intrigues and the evaporation of his popularity. He disdained all trifling distinctions between one civilization or one century and another, but enveloped them all alike in a cloud of sanctimonious liberal aspiration. France and America—1688 and 1789— negro slave and English country gentleman—were all one to him: through oceans of innocent blood, deaf to the cries of elementary humanity, he was able to walk onwards with folded hands and upcast eyes. That was his legacy to Liberalism.

Both were men of extraordinary ability. Burke superadded his great industry and profundity of thought, Fox his unbounded personal charm. Few men have made more or closer friends than Fox: while Burke in his private life was a true saint. Both were intensely English: yet Burke was Irish, and Fox was, in my belief, a Jew. Among the richly varied heritage of all those who have lent their talents to the service of the State, Burke's is perhaps the most splendid legacy of all: but Fox's memory will always have an unspeakable fascination.

29

ROBERT BURNS

(1759-1796)

by Catherine Carswell

ROBERT BURNS, celebrated as the national bard of Scotland and as one of the world's most popular singers of love, social joys and the rights of a man to be a man, was born in poor circumstances in Ayrshire on January 25th, 1759. He died, famous, but still in poor circumstances, at Dumfries on July 21st, 1796. His life extended, that is to say, from the last year of the reign of George II not far into the second half of the reign of George III.

It was a time remarkable rather for its politics and its prose than for its poetry, a generation richer in ideas and in social ideals than in song. Men's minds were occupied with wars abroad and threats of invasion at home, while at the same time they seethed in welcome or in hostility to such intoxicating notions as the equality of man, the freeing of negro slaves and the return to nature—nature being conceived as a somewhat rococo-romantic goddess. But ideas and ideals, while they may inspire, do not make poets. Singers especially were few. England had grown accustomed to look rather for wit and intellectual beauties than for inspiration or emotional expression in her makers of verse, and no maker of verse since Pope had attained the stature of Pope in either respect. Poetic stature had indeed sadly declined in Charles Churchill and in William Shenstone. Poetic fire was smothered in sour satire when it was not cold or formal.

Looking back at Burns across the groups of great poets who stand only a little nearer to us in time, it is difficult to realize how his figure stood, and stands, out from them all in fact. We must remind ourselves that his best work was acclaimed before Coleridge had resigned from the Light Dragoons, that he was in his last decade before Wordsworth's "Evening Walk" and "Descriptive Sketches" were published, and that that decade was well on its way before, with a few years between them, Shelley was born in an English country house, Keats in a mean London room, and John Clare in a Northamptonshire hovel. Robert Bloomfield, though only seven years younger than Burns, did not emerge from his "wild obscurity" with "The Farmer's Boy" until after Burns's death. It may here be suggested that the conception of that poem, which has been dated in the very year (1786) in which Burns first challenged his world "in guid black prent", and the fact that it took literary London by storm, selling 26,000 copies right off, were neither of them unconnected with the impression made by the Kilmarnock volume.

The only two poets of eminence who were Burns's senior contemporaries were Cowper and Blake. But Cowper, though born in 1731, had, by 1781, produced nothing except the *Olney Hymns*; and his volume of heroics, published the following year, cannot be thought to have influenced the Ayrshire poet, however much enjoyment he may have derived from reading them.

Blake, who was two years older than Burns, published no poems before 1783, and his "Songs of Innocence" and of "Experience" did not respectively see print until six and eleven years later. If Blake, until after his death in 1827, had any readers in Scotland it is unlikely that Burns was one of them. Neither is there any indication that Blake ever read a line of Burns. Yet these two have certain traits in common which are not to be found in any other of their contemporaries. Severed as they were in their characters, their traditions, their gifts and their expression, they shared identical qualities of heart, fundamental convictions and conceptions regarding the functions of poetry, which set them apart from other eighteenth century writers and make of them blood brothers in retrospect. Both repudiate social restrictions of soul and body. Both add to this repudiation what Shelley lacks in his—a hard knowledge of the working-man's life. Unlike all who followed them, they are not gentlemanly nor romantic poets. Both are stoics as well as rebels. Blake and Burns were the only two men of their time who allowed themselves to be blithely instructed by the body. They gloried in the physical and the impulsive as against the ideal in living, and in the physical and the impulsive they perceived unending mystery. They were sweetly reasonable, but they suspected the dictatorship of the intellect to which all others bowed. They were not preachers but jocund partakers, not reformers but prophets in action. They dared pit the "light unanxious heart" against the sorry scheme of things as they found it, and if neither man saw his defeat with resignation he gave no quarter to despair. Without Utopian tincture, both of them—the one accepting his meed of neglect, the other never over-valuing his reward of unthinking praise—were consciously poets of a feasible future for humanity.

In any examination of Burns, however cursory, three aspects call for our attention. These are the literary, the human, and the legendary. Of the first, most that can be said shortly has been said by Burns himself in prose and in verse. We find his condensed account in the lovely, if unequal poem, "The Vision," in which he communes, first with himself and then

with his enchanting, green-clad country muse, in the nocturnal
solitude of the rat-infested farm of Mossgiel. Earlier, confronted with the multi-coloured drama of country life, he had
longed despairingly for the power of "a Shakespeare or an
Otway", and, in passing, it may be noted how eloquently this
indifferent juxtaposition of two names points to the limitations
of a lad who was equally abased before them both. But in "The
Vision", almost at the same moment that he decides to be
done with rhyming once and for all as a self-indulgent and
disastrous habit, he suddenly accepts the poet's garland. True,
it is a garland of holly, not of laurel, and in the very act of
assuming it he retires from competition with wearers of the
more exalted leaf. He is no more worthy to rank with Gray or
Shenstone than with Otway or Shakespeare.

> Yet all beneath the unrivall'd rose,
> The lowly daisy sweetly blows;
> Though large the forest's monarch throws
> His army shade,
> Yet green the juicy hawthorn grows
> Adown the glade.

> Then never murmur nor repine;
> Strive in thy humble sphere to shine:
> And, trust me, not Potosi's mine,
> Nor kings' regard,
> Can give a bliss o'ermatching thine,
> A rustic bard.

Thus his muse speaks. Earlier she has said to him by way of
encouragement—not be it remarked, by way of warning:

> I saw thy pulse's maddening play
> Wild, send thee Pleasure's devious way,

ROBERT BURNS

Misled by Fancy's meteor-ray,
        By passion driven.
But yet the light that led astray
        Was light from Heaven.

The thought in those last two lines might well have found
its expression in a dozen poems or drawings by Blake. So far
as Burns is concerned he was to take Nature's Self, and that
natural, if also meteoric, "light from heaven" as his guides
instead of relying upon daunting literary examples. And for
the rest he will:

Preserve the dignity of man
        With soul erect;
And trust, the universal plan
        Will all protect.

So much for his literary dedication. But the most rustic of
bards needs literary models for practical purposes, and "The
Vision" itself is written in a metre which had been handed
down and bandied about in Scotland for two centuries of
vernacular verse. Had the still earlier poetry of the *makars*,
such as Dunbar and Henryson, which was European as well
as Scottish, continued its line down to Burns's day, Burns might
have been, in a sense in which he is not now, a European poet.
The extraordinary thing is that, as things are, he ranks as a
world poet. For the classic line had long been broken and had
given place to a strictly local body of verse, which, with
Robert Sempill, Ramsay, Fergusson, Hamilton of Gilbertfield,
and many lesser men, had achieved homely expression and a
fair measure of success without, however, rising to any great
heights or over-running local limits. These poets, using stereo-
typed rhythms, some of which are said to have originated with
the Troubadours, found conversational expression in descriptive and narrative pieces, in rhymed addresses and epistles,

and in simple songs which at times achieved lyrical distinction. In his early youth Burns came in contact with none of them, but, being early a poet, he strove to copy the pure English models that reached him through his spasmodic education, and he tried his hand at country songs of the kind he heard sung by the women in his acquaintance. It was not until he had continued thus for some years with discouraging results, that he made discovery of his immediate Scottish predecessors and flung himself with zest into the conventions which he was destined to inform with his genius. His metres, his language, his subjects, even his stock of sentiments were there for him ready-made. But by his force of feeling and of fun, and by his natural and acquired art, he heightened, varied and transformed them in such a manner as to render them inimitable by after-comers because he was himself inimitable. An unequal, some times an atrociously poor poet, he outdistanced all his fore-runners in versatility, in flexibility and in abandon, and the exhilarating fling of his genius goes far to annul the efforts of the many who tried to follow him. In addition, he was born with a rich appreciation of his country's anonymous folk song, little of which was in print, and this he put into poetic practice by the highly original device of writing words to existing music. For the subtle and difficult dance rhythms of Scotland his ear was sharp as a newt's, and while he constrained professional musicians to help him in collecting and annotating these, he refused to yield to any of the prettifying musical fashions of the time. Thus he saved for his country numbers of melodies as well as verbal refrains, which would otherwise have been lost.

If, however, he is of all poets one of the most sung and quoted, he is also one of the least read and known. How many even of Scotsmen on New Year's Eve could recite drunk or sober all the words of "Auld Lang Syne" correctly? How many quoters of the address "To a Mountain Daisy" have read "Holy Willie's Prayer" even once through? How many lovers who have made their own the lines

> My luve is like a red, red rose,
> That's newly sprung in June:
> My luve is like the melodie
> That's sweetly played in tune.

are acquainted with that more intimate and uncommon song which deals with the results of love, and opens with the searching question put by a girl as to who will buy her "babie-clouts"?

How many persons, who are to be heard agreeing that

> The best laid schemes o' mice and men
> Gang aft agley.

would recognize as belonging to the same poem the stanza

> Still thou art blest compared wi' me!
> The present only toucheth thee:
> But, och! I backward cast my ee
> On prospect drear!
> And forwards, though I canna see,
> I guess and fear.

—with its well-founded envy of the fates of beasts? But perhaps it is one of the penalties of being a people's poet to exist chiefly as a patchwork in the common mind.

If Burns, however, had been a people's poet only, there would be less to say about his work. But he is also a poet's poet. He has commanded the eager homage of men as different as Wordsworth, Keats, Byron, Coventry Patmore and Aldous Huxley—to mention only a few high authorities who are neither his compatriots, his contemporaries, nor members of his class, while continental writers have not hesitated to give him a handsome place in the small hierarchy of supreme singers and satirists. "L'un des plus grands poétes, selon moi, qui aient paru dans ces derniers temps, c'est Robert Burns," says Stendhal. He has found exhaustive and enthusiastic biographers in France, Germany and America, and translators in Italy and Spain. He has the power of capturing readers in every generation and of re-capturing throughout their lives those readers who know him best and see his defects most clearly. As Patmore puts it: "Burns has done a certain amount of work so thoroughly and manifestly well that no sane critic has ever called it into question or ever will." "More has been written about Burns," says a recent commentator, "than about any other writer using the English Language, Shakespeare excepted. Only Shakespeare's works have been published in more numerous and more diverse editions. And not even Shakespeare has given rise to more controversies and more fury."*

Respectable critics as well as fatuous admirers have compared Burns with Shakespeare, and there are real points in the comparison, although these have not always emerged. Neither man was in a position to depend for his hearing upon the verdict of the literary. Each had to reckon upon impressing even the illiterate. Shakespeare wrote his plays with their songs for playgoers, which meant men and women of all sorts, including riverside groundlings. Burns was compelled to address himself—largely by words spoken or sung—to servants, hinds and local worthies. Shakespeare had the London rabble to cater for, Burns the population of Mauchline and Ayr. Not Clare nor Bloomfield, not Shelley nor Keats nor Wordsworth was bound by such considerations. Had they been so, their poetry would have been respectively less ethereal and less suggestive of black coats and views of mountains from leather-upholstered sofas. For, than the rustic circle and the patrons of a Southwark theatre no more forthright audiences exist. They are narrower yet wider, harsher yet freer from fashions

*Dr. Theodore Besterman. *The Times Literary Supplement*, March 7th, 1936.

than the literary world of any one period, and it is at all times the highest triumph of literature to penetrate with delight and wonder those who lack scholarship. Scarcely any English poets have attained it. And although in this respect Scotland has a different tradition, no other Scottish poet has here rivalled Burns, just as no other English poet has rivalled Shakespeare.

The difficulty of the task was large in Burns's mind when he said: "If any man thinks it is easy to write a song let him try it," which is not the same as saying: "if anybody thinks it is easy to write an epic let him do it"—no matter how hard it may be to write a good epic. Because a poem of the sort Burns had in mind must combine magic with homeliness in a manner so natural-seeming that the art with which it is done shall defy detection as absolutely as it woos the ear and wins the heart. If homeliness were enough, Scotland could show a galaxy of great singers: if magic were enough, a recitation from Keats or Shelley would hold a Bank Holiday tavern spellbound. But in this rare accomplishment Shakespeare is the English master, and he and Burns are unapproachable except by a few scattered, often anonymous, authors of folk song. That both were frequently constrained to borrow from folk songs before they could take flight should not be forgotten. They were driven to realize the value of immediacy.

Shakespearian examples to our purpose could be multiplied, but we need only recall the songs to "Spring" and to "Winter" which bring *Love's Labour's Lost* to its unforgettable close. While it must be allowed that those songs preserve throughout a level which Burns rarely keeps for half as many lines as either contains, this does not affect the finding that there is not a line in either which could not fairly be credited to Burns and to Burns alone among other poets. Further, if Burns might have written:

> When icicles hang by the wall,
> And Dick the shepherd blows his nail,

FROM ANNE TO VICTORIA

Shakespeare might equally as well have written

> To lie in kilns and barns at e'en,
> When banes are crazed, and bluid is thin.*

or:

> Thus resigned and quiet creep,
> To the bed of lasting sleep.†

or:

> When winds rave through the naked tree,‡

or:

> While briars and woodbines budding green,
> And Paitricks scraichin' loud at e'en,
> And morning poussie whiddin seen,§

or:

> When lintwhites chant amang the buds
> And jinkin' hares, in amorous whids,
>   Their loves enjoy,
> While through the braes the cushat croods
>   Wi' wailfu' cry!§

or even:

> When biting Boreas, fell and doure,
> Sharp shivers through the leafless bower;
> When Phoebus gies a short-lived glower
>   Far south the lift,
> Dim-darkening through the flaky shower,
>   Or whirling drift. ‖

—allowing, of course, for the Scottish form, and for the vernacular words as mere sound and sense, if not poetic fury. If the Scottish lines are more coarsely woven than the English, all are equally homespun stuff of Doonside or of Avonside. There exists, I think, more evidence than is generally allowed

*Epistle to Davie.
†Lines written in Friars' Carse Hermitage.
‡Epistle to William Simpson.
§Epistle to John Lapraik.
‖*A Winter Night.*

that Burns made a special study of Shakespeare's songs. And if many other poets have done the same, we know of none who has done it to such purpose that we can discover inherent likeness without a trace of mimicry.

Admittedly there is justice in the contention that no useful comparison can be drawn between a poet who can keep on a high level and another who reaches the same level only to lose it soon and often, while frequently he sinks to the devices of a mere rhymester. But it can be maintained that the reaching of the same level constitutes in itself a sort of equality, as does the ability to dive and to pierce, and to communicate successfully a prodigal enjoyment of the scenes created by "that various creature—*man*." Burns was himself quite as conscious of his falling short in artistry as he was of his power to do all these things. "I am nae poet in a sense," he says, and he explains how

> My spaviet Pegasus will limp,
> Till ance he's fairly het;
> And then he'll hilch, and stilt, and jimp,
> And rin an unco fit.*

—which needs no glossary to make itself clear to the most English of readers. But it is, after all, the capacity to soar and the fling of the flight that matters most. Burns also said that he "rhymed for fun". But he further issued the challenge, "let time mak' proof." And while he had, among other things, his fun, time has as certainly not betrayed him. He is that unusual phenomenon, a rustic bard whom the world has been forced to acknowledge.

In turning from a survey of the poetry to the man who wrote it, and to the legend, which, in a special degree, exists regarding him, we find that the three have already some-

*Epistle to Davie.

what overlapped. With Burns this is inevitable. In every line of his that is read or said or sung, his presence stands before the most ignorant as before those who have most studied his works. He leaps to eye and heart—a strong country figure in coarse, but neat and even dashing clothes, with gloom in his eyes but also with persuasive laughter in his boldly curving lips. Speak the name of almost any other poet, and to the ordinary man and woman nothing arises but a vague shape dressed in period costume. But we can all visualize Burns. Indeed, admire or belittle him as we may, we cannot help visualizing him. To a unique extent the man and his work are one. Acquaint yourself with a dozen lives of Wordsworth and with all his letters, and you can still read his "Lucy" poems or his "Prelude" without any intrusion of a real lover or a living schoolboy upon your field of vision. The difficulty is not to see a thin-legged, opinionative old gentleman in dark clothes—which is one of the weak points of "emotion recollected in tranquillity". Read even M. Maurois's realistic *Ariel*, or Mr. Middleton Murry's sympathetic *Keats*, and, later on, although you may be transported by the beauties of the odes to the West Wind and the Grecian Urn, you still experience not more than a whiff of emotion for the fascinating exile at Lerici or the unfortunate consumptive of Keats Grove. You sympathize with them and you pity their dead woes. But their ghosts are disembodied and their sorrows are a trifle staled by time. It is a reminiscent communion. But no life of Burns need ever have been opened for the merest quoter of Burns to partake, as if it were his own, in the warm experience from which Burns's expression gushed. For one thing he was a man of the people as no other poet of equal force has been. For another, there was in his character and his fate a mingling of the tragic and the typical which resides even in his feebler words and makes a perennial appeal to those who know in fact the barest outline of his life. Strange as it may seem, Burns here is again like Shakespeare, with whom we are profoundly obliged to identify ourselves when we read one of his sonnets or when we look on at one of his furthest-fetched plays. The barest outline is all we have of Shakespeare's life, and much has been said of his impersonality; whereas Burns is intensely autobiographical, and controversy has raged over his actions. None the less both elicit a similar passionate participation from their readers, for in both we feel "the life-blood streaming through the heart"* with the same compulsive force. The alleged portrait of Shakespeare, offering us a non-committal egg-shaped head set upon a ruff, interferes with our participation no more than does the peculiar dual "legend" of Burns, to which we shall presently come. Shakespeare is always the boy from Stratford-on-Avon who went up to London and came back again to Stratford. Burns is the "lad was born in Kyle", who went to Edinburgh and returned to the country, there, like Shakespeare, to breed beasts and to savour the fatuity of fame.

Of the Burns "legend", as distinct from his life, a longer essay than this might and ought to be written. Some years ago in America the *Philological Quarterly*† published an admirable outline by Professor J. DeLancey Ferguson, who is known to all students of the poet as the only definitive editor of his letters. But, as Dr. Theodore Besterman recently pointed out in *The Times Literary Supplement*‡, the new "acquisition by the National Library of Scotland, with the aid of the Friends of the National Libraries, of a practically complete set of original documents referring to the publication of the first (1800) and subsequent collected editions of the works of Robert Burns" furnishes for the first time all the information needed for a detailed account of the rise of the Burns cult during the century that followed his death.

*Epistle to Davie.
†*Vol. XI, No. 3, July,* 1932.
‡*The Times Literary Supplement, March 7th,* 1936.

Professor Ferguson in his amusing article points out that "the memory of Burns . . . lives in a dual role of fame and infamy", and he puts the question, "Was Burns really one man, or two?" Byron, in his journal, after reading Burns's "unpublished and never-to-be-published" letters to Robert Cleghorn, remarked that here was "an antithetical mind!— tenderness, roughness—delicacy, coarseness—sentiment, sensuality—soaring and grovelling, dirt and deity—all mixed up in that one compound of inspired clay!" And according to Matthew Arnold "Burns is a beast, with splendid gleams." The same man, as Professor Ferguson points out, to whose honoured memory "more and worse statues and monuments . . . have been dedicated than to any other individual except the late Albert, Prince Consort", is "the only poet of whom I have ever heard anedcotes related in American fraternity-houses and American smoking-cars". In fact "there are two Burns traditions: the public and the private; the written and the oral", and we all know which is which.

But when all will have been said by the scholars, the alleged cleavage goes far deeper than documents can reveal. It is as truly held that Burns was courageous, hard-working, a worthy citizen, a considerate and affectionate father and husband, and a generous and public-spirited man, as that he was a reckless and dangerous creature, that he ran "life's mad career, Wild as the wave", and that "thoughtless follies", quite as much as cardiac endocarditis, "laid him low."

> All devil as I am, a damned wretch,
> A harden'd, stubborn, unrepentant villain,

Not for nothing were those among the first words of verse he penned. His intelligence was of a high order and, no matter where he went or whom he addressed, he was regarded as a person of weight whose words were worth listening to for their sagacity. Charles James Fox, who was no mean judge of men, said of him that "he had a better understanding than Cowper", and was, indeed, "about as clever a man as ever lived." And Burns's own letters, though these were sometimes stilted or marred by affectations, fully endorse the testimony of contemporaries, who frequently found his conversation superior to his verses. Beneath even his poorer efforts as a correspondent we are aware of sound sense and of sympathies wider than common. Withstanding, as he did, the full brunt of Edinburgh snobbishness, and foreseeing the disastrous trend of the industrial revolution and machine age which had its beginnings in his lifetime, he understood far more profoundly than Wordsworth the true significance of the French Revolution, and no other poet who owed inspiration to the Revolution has written words that are comparable with Burns's for heart-felt employment by the modern man. We have only to contrast the phrase "A Man's a man for a' that" with:

> Bliss was it in that dawn to be alive,
> But to be young was very heaven.

to feel that here is all the difference between a call to arms and an arm-chair reflection; and the fact that the second comes from a more considerable poem than the first—which might fairly be reckoned as doggerel—makes no matter. The point is that in that dawn it was by no means bliss for Burns to be alive, while for him to be young was anything but heavenly.

At the same time the poet who wrote the tenth verse of "The Cotter's Saturday Night", counselling restraint to the cotter's young visitor, was at that moment glorying in the knowledge that his father's respectable servant, whom he had no intention of marrying, was with child by him—this being the first of his many proclaimable offences in that line, and, much nearer the end of his life, he announced that "the Kirk an' State may gang tae hell" but he would go to his Anna.

From beginning to end he made manifest that "Folly has rapture to give", and he held that rapture was highly desirable and easily obtainable. He was defiantly the father of at least seven illegitimate children by at least four different women. He failed—where admittedly others would have succeeded—in all his practical undertakings, poetry, Excise duties and ploughing apart. He repeatedly alienated the respectable and courted all manner of riff-raff. He merited the reproaches of those dearest to him. And he died under the shadow of failure, leaving behind him a "reputation of increasing disrepute among the influential Scots"* which called for the cloak of charity on account of his genius and of his penniless wife and children. Had he been an inferior or a bachelor poet, can anybody allege that this cloak would have been forthcoming? Can anybody disregard the grieved strictures of his first biographer, Heron, or the head-shaking, which, in spite of the careful whitewashing of his official biographer, Currie, persists in Dumfries to this day? It is an English writer who has called Burns "one of the lewdest, most drunken and most dissolute libertines who ever stained human records", and the judgment has not lacked support even in Scotland where the poet's moral praises are annually sounded by men who would certainly have felt unable to commend him in the flesh without severe reservations, while they would have positively hated him in his grandest moods. "To drink a toast to a man like Burns," our English writer continues, "ought properly to be considered as an affront to every decent thing in life. . . . In all the long erratic history of hero-worship there is probably not such another example where a reprobate, a deliberate, boasting defaulter from ordinary human decency, has carried his excesses to such repulsive extremes. No excuse can be made for Burns's calculated violation all through his life of human decency. He was a deliberate moral anarchist."

*Theodore Besterman.

If the picture does not carry entire conviction to the true reader of Burns it would yet be waste of time to argue against any one of the statements contained in it without challenging the conventions which made and make them possible. For there is chapter and verse for the worst of them in Burns's poetry and in his prose admissions.

Was Burns therefore either a schizophrenic, a hypocrite, or a weakling? Or was he, as his orthodox apologists are obliged to assert, a fine, gifted, strong and lovable poet, whose often expressed remorse for back-slidings, demands, as it merits, a charitable conspiracy of silence?

The world, without thinking, knows better. It divines that Burns continually challenged and condemned current notions of morality as he did current divisions of class, and that his reckless ways, his repeated joy in trespass, and his unconquerable belief that morals are made for man, not man for morals, are all and always deeper than his remorses. (The remorses were genuine, but they sprang less from conviction than from circumstances, which, though too strong for him, were not on that account necessarily admirable.) We are certain that Burns's so-called inconsistencies were needed to maintain his manly and consistent fullness of life. Times are changing, and rules. The figure of Burns remains firm, and he is justified by the changing times and by the reform of cruel and crippling rules. This is the real root of his legend, which it needs no documents to disclose. True, it was out of the clash between his blithely rebellious spirit and the folly of circumstances that his poetry accumulated its power. But the blitheness wins. There is in him no Shakespearian despair, no Wordsworthian resignation. And his legend, like his memory, is not dual, but exemplary in its human assertion. It follows that Burns, a poet of far narrower mental range than Shakespeare, was a more prophetic man, and that he remains, from the modern point of view, a far more potent influence.

30

ADAM SMITH

(1723–1790)

by HARTLEY WITHERS

KNOWN to fame as the founder of a dismal science which tells us to buy cheap and sell dear, Adam Smith was in fact a philosopher interested in every aspect of human life and well informed, as far as information went in his time, about most of them. Well versed in ancient and modern literature, in spite of having spent many years at Balliol at a time when Oxford was sunk in slothful slumber and Balliol was a nest of rowdy Jacobites, he had, long before he produced the *Wealth of Nations*, established a European reputation with a work known as the *Theory of Moral Sentiments*, to which was added, by way of appendix, a *Dissertation on the Origin of Languages*. He was no mere economist, peering through narrow blinkers at mankind as it is imagined to be when it is earning its living, but a versatile humanist who dealt with the wealth of nations as an important, but by no means all-important, element in human progress.

As a man, he was an amazing mixture of shrewdness, carelessness, generosity and practical sense. So absent-minded as sometimes to appear almost half-witted, he was at the same time gifted with a power of intelligent observation that has filled his works with apt and acute illustrations of man's behaviour in different fields of his activity. Eminently frugal in his personal habits, though always ready to give and enjoy the pleasures of hospitality and good fellowship, and having for many years earned an income which made him a rich man for a Scotsman of those days, he left behind him an estate which was found to be surprisingly small, owing to the many acts of private generosity which had been sedulously concealed; as we learn from Mr. F. W. Hirst's admirable portrait of him, in the English Men of Letters series.

Born on June 5th, 1723, at Kirkcaldy, he was son of another Adam Smith who died a few weeks before that date. The elder Adam had been a man of some note, having held the office, founded at the time of the union of the two kingdoms, of Judge Advocate for Scotland and having acted as private secretary to the Earl of Loudon, the Minister for Scotland; when on Loudon's retirement in 1713 he lost this post, he was appointed Comptroller of the Customs at Kirkcaldy. From a paper lately read before the Royal Economic Society by Professor Scott, we learn that his ancestors and relatives were very prosperous folk and one of them was Yeoman of the King's Wine Cellar.

On his mother's side Smith was a Douglas, descended from the gaoler of Mary Queen of Scots, and great-grandnephew of another Douglas who planned her escape. His mother, as we are told by John Rae, another of his biographers, was from first to last the heart of his life—"he being an only child and she an only parent, they had been all in all to one another during his infancy and boyhood, and after he was full of years and honours her presence was the same shelter to him as it was when a boy." Many of his friends have testified to the deep and beautiful affection with which he cherished her; and the Earl of Buchan, who knew him well during the last thirty years of his life, said that the principal avenue to his heart was through his mother.

As to his relations with other women, such hints as can be gleaned from the various accounts of his life, are mysterious and unsatisfactory. We shall see later that he was for a time a popular lion of the Paris salons, in spite of his awkward manners and halting French. Madame Riccoboni, who had forsaken the stage for letters and become the most popular novelist in France, is said to have been an "effusive admirer of Smith", and wrote of him, in a letter to Garrick, "*je l'aime beaucoup et je l'estime encore davantage.*"

Rae also tells us of a lady, not only a marquise but a woman of talents and wit, who met him in a hotel at Abbeville, where he was staying with his pupil, the Duke of Buccleuch, and several other British noblemen. "She had just come from Paris, where she found all the world talking about Hume, and having heard that Smith was Hume's particular friend and almost as great a philosopher as he, she was bent on making so famous a conquest, but after many persistent efforts was obliged eventually to abandon the attempt. Her philosopher could not endure her, nor could he—and this greatly amused his own party—conceal his embarrassment."

According to the tatler who records this incident—a certain Captain Lloyd, who was one of the English travellers— Smith's heart was steeled against the attacks of the marquise by being deeply captivated by an English lady who was also staying in Abbeville at the time. In fact, however, there appears to have been an early and mysterious romance which, for unknown reasons fruitless, had left Adam a confirmed bachelor. According to Rae, "Stewart" [Dugald Stewart, a contemporary of Smith's who left a memoir of him] "makes mention of an attachment which Smith was known to have cherished for several years in the early part of his life to a young lady of great beauty and accomplishment, whom Stewart had himself seen when she was past eighty, who still retained evident traces of her former beauty, while the powers of her under-

standing and the gaiety of her temper seemed to have suffered
nothing from the hand of time. Nobody ever knew what
prevented their union, nor how far Smith's addresses were
favourably received, but she never married any more than he.
Stewart says that after this disappointment he laid aside all
thoughts of marriage."

Professor Scott, however, in the above-mentioned paper,
which was entitled *New Light on Adam Smith*, tells us
more about this romance: "Soon after he came down from
Oxford, he fell violently in love. Years after, meeting his
former flame and having evidently quite forgotten her, he
waited expectantly to be introduced until his cousin, Miss
Douglas, exclaimed, 'Adam! don't you know it's your ain
Jeannie?'" And Professor Scott adds that before he went
to France there was another attachment, likewise unsuccessful.

Going back to the story of his early days, we find that
by the time he was ten years old he was at the Burgh School of
Kirkcaldy and had begun his Latin studies. A copy of
Eutropius, a class-book for beginners in Latin, is still extant
inscribed in a childish hand with the legend, "Adam Smith
his book May 4th, 1733." He is recorded to have made his
mark at school by his passion for books, extraordinary powers
of memory, a temper which though warm was uncommonly
friendly and generous, absent-mindedness and a trick of
talking aloud to himself.

In his fourteenth year he went on to the University of Glasgow, where he stayed three fruitful years; he had the good
fortune, says Mr. Hirst, "to study Greek under Dunlop;
mathematics under Simson, the editor of Euclid, and morals
under Hutcheson, perhaps the greatest philosopher of his
generation and certainly the most eloquent." From the lips
of Hutcheson he learnt to think of and for the "greatest
happiness of the greatest number"; and at the same time he
was taught by a study of Bacon and Locke and Grotius and

Newton to "discern through the obscuring mists of medieval philosophy the splendid dawn of science". Besides a wide course of reading in the literature and wisdom of the ancients, mathematics and natural philosophy are said to have been the favourite pursuits of this insatiable student, still not out of his 'teens.

At the age of seventeen he secured a Snell Exhibition at Balliol; and in June, 1740, he rode on horseback to Oxford, and was much struck, as he approached Carlisle, by the richness of England and the superiority of English agriculture. In later years he used to tell friends at his own table how, having fallen into one of his fits of meditation when dining for the first time in Balliol hall, he was roused by the attendant servitor who bade him fall to, for he had never seen such a piece of beef in Scotland.

But if the beef of Balliol was good, food for the mind was very much to seek in those days. At the beginning of the eighteenth century a visitor to Oxford found the dons as ignorant of the new philosophy as the South Sea savages. Twenty years later, Bishop Butler, then a student, found himself fobbed off with frivolous lectures and unintelligible disputations. Gibbon, who was "up" not long after Smith, relates that his tutor neither gave nor tried to give him more than one lesson; and a few years later Bentham found that it was impossible to learn anything at Oxford and that the time spent there was the most barren and unprofitable part of his life. Smith himself says in the *Wealth of Nations* that "in the university of Oxford the greater part of the public professors have, for these many years, given up altogether even the pretence of teaching". He even justifies the practice of sending lads abroad after leaving school, though he considers it makes a young man return home "more conceited, more unprincipled, more dissipated, and more incapable of any serious application either to study or business, than he could

well have become in so short a time, had he lived at home",
by the fact that this "very absurd" practice prevents their
being sent to the universities—"by sending his son abroad, a
father delivers himself, at least for some time, from so disagreeable an object as that of a son unemployed, neglected
and going to ruin before his eyes."

To a born glutton for learning like Smith, however, it
may be that the system of complete *laisser faire*, then adopted
by Oxford and afterwards so successfully applied to Sam
Weller by his father, may have been for the best. What
Balliol did for him was to confiscate, with a severe reprimand,
his copy—probably one given him by the author—of Hume's
Treatise of Human Nature. What he did for himself was to
devour the contents of Balliol's excellent library. He worked
to such purpose at the Greek and Latin classics that in the
later years of his life they were his constant companions; both
them and the Italian poets he could quote easily and extensively; he set himself to improve his own style of writing by
translating the French classics into English; and is said to
have had an extraordinary knowledge of English poetry. After
six years so spent at Oxford, and having taken his B.A., he
went back to Scotland and soon began his career as a public
lecturer by delivering a course at Edinburgh on English literature. In 1750 he was made Professor of Logic at Glasgow,
and so started the thirteen years of academic activity which he
afterwards describes as by far the most useful and therefore
by far the happiest and most honourable period of his life.
He certainly worked hard; for at one time he was acting not
only as Professor of Logic but also as Professor of Moral
Philosophy; and Rae tells us that by the traditional distribution
of subjects in the Scottish universities, the province of Logic
included rhetoric and *belles lettres*, and that of Moral Philosophy
included jurisprudence and politics. On the death of the Professor of Moral Philosophy, he was translated into the chair

of ethics, and his lectures therefrom laid the foundations, thanks to the wide sweep of the net of morality in those times, not only of his *Theory of Moral Sentiments* but also of the *Wealth of Nations*.

Living with his mother and a cousin (Miss Jane Douglas) in a good house in the Professors' Court, Smith was able to enjoy all the beauties of Glasgow, then, as Mr. Hirst tells us, famous for the clearness of its atmosphere and the loveliness of its surroundings. From the window of his study he could see "an immense landscape of woods and distant mountains". His income was about £170 a year, a very respectable one at a time when only twenty-nine ministers in all Scotland had as much as £100, and the highest stipend in the Church was £138. Stimulated by his lecture-room audience, which included preachers and advanced students in divinity and law, and, after the publication of the *Theory of Moral Sentiments*, learners from far countries such as Russia and Switzerland, Smith must also have got great benefit, on the business side of his subject, from the practical conversation of the canny merchants who were building up the prosperity of the Clyde. What he did for the College and the city may be recorded in Rae's words:

"Smith's teaching had taught the young people to think. His opinions became the subject of general discussion, the branches he lectured on became fashionable in the town, the sons of the wealthier citizens used to go to College to take his class though they had no intention of completing a university course, stucco busts of him appeared in the booksellers' windows, and the very peculiarities of his voice and pronunciation received the homage of imitation. One point alone caused a little—in certain quarters more than a little—shaking of heads . . . The distinguished professor was a friend of 'Hume the atheist'; he was himself ominously reticent on religious subjects; he did not conduct a Sunday class on

Christian evidences like Hutcheson; he would often, too, be seen openly smiling during divine service in his place in the College chapel (as in his absent way he might no doubt be prone to do). . . . In his lectures on jurisprudence and politics he had taught the doctrine of free trade from the first, and not the least remarkable result of his thirteen years' work in Glasgow was that before he left he had practically converted that city to his views. Dugald Stewart was explicitly informed by one of the most eminent Clyde merchants of that time, that Smith had, during his professorship in Glasgow, made many of the leading men of the place convinced proselytes of free trade principles."

This testimony clearly refutes the theory, which has on other grounds been shown to be unfounded, that the free trade doctrines taught by the *Wealth of Nations* were inspired by Quesnai and the French Physiocrats, whom he met when travelling on the Continent.

This Continental journey was a result of the publication in 1759 of the *Theory of Moral Sentiments*. Hume, in a letter to Smith from London in April of that year, tells him "the melancholy news that your book has been very unfortunate, for the public seem disposed to applaud it extremely. It was looked for by the foolish people with some impatience; and the mob of literati are already beginning to be very loud in its praises. Three bishops called yesterday at Millar's shop in order to buy copies, and to ask questions about the author . . . Charles Townshend, who passes for the cleverest fellow in England, is so much taken with the performance that he said to Oswald he would put the Duke of Buccleuch under the author's care, and would make it worth his while to accept of that charge."

Townshend, who had married the Duke's mother, succeeded in this scheme. Smith was offered a salary of £300 a year and travelling expenses and a pension of £300 a year for life, terms which look almost lavishly generous as compared with his academic income. Early in 1764 he resigned his professorship and started with his pupil, having first insisted on returning to his Glasgow students the fees that they had paid. The story of their refusal to take them back, and Smith's seizing the youngster who stood next to him, forcing the money into his pocket and pushing him away, is one more pleasant refutation of the common delusion about Scottish meanness.

After ten days in Paris, the travellers went to Toulouse, where owing to some hitch about introductions they were so severely bored that the tutor began "to write a book in order to pass away the time". Which book, after ten years of preparation, was the *Wealth of Nations*. Apart from this interlude of dulness, all went well. Hume, then secretary to the British Embassy in Paris, where Lord Hertford was ambassador, got them introductions to all the leading world of France, and they spent more than two years travelling in France, visiting Voltaire at Geneva, and enjoying the gay life of Paris, in the last brilliant flicker of the effulgence of the *ancien régime*. Here Smith's fame had already been established by a translation of the *Theory of Moral Sentiments*. He was a regular guest in almost all the famous literary salons, met Turgot, Necker, Quesnai and the other Physiocrats, Morellet, Helvetius, Horace Walpole, Necker, and everybody else who counted, poured oil on the anger of Hume against Rousseau, though admitting that Rousseau was "as great a rascal as you and as every man here believe him to be", was often seen at the opera and the play, and was handsomely petted by the literary ladies. He and the Duke returned to London in 1766, after having, as the latter said in a letter to Dugald Stewart, "spent near three years together without the slightest disagreement or coolness. . . . We continued to live in friendship till the hour of his death, and I shall always remain with the impression of having lost a friend whom I loved and respected, not only for his great talents, but for every private virtue."

After a short stay in London, Smith went to Kirkcaldy and lived there for eleven years. "My Business here," he wrote to Hume, "is study. My amusements are long solitary walks by the seaside. I feel myself extremely happy, comfortable and contented. I never was perhaps more so in all my life." The "study" was the *Wealth of Nations*, which at last appeared in 1776. By that time he had come to London and been made a member of the Literary Club of Johnson and Burke and Reynolds. Boswell thought that by Smith's admission the club had "lost its select merit", and Garrick found his talk "flabby", though Boswell thought that it evinced "a mind crowded with all manner of subjects". He was back in Kirkcaldy at the end of 1777, but being appointed Commissioner of Customs in Scotland he moved to Edinburgh, where he lived until his death in 1790.

Smith never sat for his picture, but from sketches of him by artists who knew him well it seems, as Rae tells us, that he had rather handsome features—full forehead, prominent eyeballs, slightly aquiline nose and firm mouth and chin, He was of middle height, full but not corpulent in figure. carried himself straight and his large grey eyes are said to have beamed with inexpressible benignity.

Among the many stories of his absent-mindedness, perhaps the most notable is that of his putting a piece of bread and butter into his teapot and pouring the water into it. He fell asleep at a meeting of the Royal Society, but perhaps that might happen to anybody. An eminently friendly and hospitable soul, he was happy in the society alike of the learned lights of Paris and London and of his humble neighbours at Kirkcaldy. Always ready to welcome visitors and show them the sights of his country, he once took a French geologist who was visiting Edinburgh to hear a bagpipe competition. "I confess," wrote the Frenchman afterwards, "that at first I could not distinguish either air or design in the music. I was only struck with a piper marching backward and forward with great rapidity, and still presenting the same warlike countenance. He made incredible efforts with his body and his fingers to bring into play the different reeds of his instrument, which emitted sounds that were to me almost unsupportable." When a number of performers played together, "the union of so many bagpipes produced a most hideous noise." The critic decided that some association of historical ideas was the real cause of the lively emotions of the persons around him.

Mild and gentle as Smith was, he was one of the few people who could stand up to Dr. Johnson and beat him at sheer Billingsgate. Scott tells the story on the authority of Professor Millar, who himself had heard from Smith how, when they met in Glasgow, "Johnson no sooner saw Smith than he attacked him on some point in his famous letter on the death of Hume. Smith vindicated the truth of his statement. 'What did Johnson say?' was the universal inquiry. 'Why, he said,' replied Smith, with the deepest impression of resentment, 'he said, you lie.' 'And what did you reply?' 'I said, you are a son of a ———!' On such terms," adds Sir Walter, "did these two great moralists meet and part, and such was the classical dialogue between the two great teachers of philosophy."

As to his works, the *Theory of Moral Sentiments* need not detain us long. Burke wrote of it that, "the author seeks for the foundation of the just, the fit, the proper, the decent, in our most common and allowed passions; and making approbation and disapprobation the tests of virtue and vice, and showing that those are founded on sympathy, he raises from this simple truth one of the most beautiful fabrics of moral theory that has perhaps ever appeared." And Mr. Hirst says, "there is plenty of warmth and colour. The argument is never bare;

you follow its thread through a wondrous maze, till your perplexities are all solved, and you finally congratulate your- self as well as the author on having rejected all the errors and collected all the wisdom of the ages". Such is the pleasant reward that awaits those who have time and patience enough to read through these once momentous volumes.

To most of us, the *Theory's* chief importance lies in the fact that it secured for Smith his Continental journey and so must have greatly increased the breadth of mind and knowledge of men and things that raises the *Wealth of Nations* so far above most works on economic subjects. As to it, Lecky in his *History of England in the Eighteenth Century* says that, "al- though it had little political influence for at least a generation after its appearance, its publication has ultimately proved one of the most important events in the economical, and indeed in the intellectual, history of modern Europe." And Buckle described it as "in its ultimate results probably the most important book that has ever been written". Already in 1796 a German Professor had pronounced that no book since the New Testament had produced more beneficial effects than this book would produce when it was better known. Translated into Italian in 1780, in Spain it was suppressed by the In- quisition on account of the "lowness of its style and the looseness of its morals"; but a Spanish translation was never- theless published in 1794. And Lecky must surely have under- estimated its immediate effect at home. In 1787 Smith met Pitt and other distinguished statesmen at Dundas's house, and when he came into the room all the company rose and remained standing. When he asked them to be seated Pitt said: "No, we will stand till you are first seated, for we are all your scholars."

Like all works that touch our political prejudices, it has been monstrously misunderstood and misrepresented, both by its eulogists and its critics. Professor Shield Nicholson, in a work called *A Project of Empire*, says that "the Adam Smith of popular tradition is supposed to be the apostle of selfishness —the creator and glorifier of the 'economic man'. The real Adam Smith, about twenty years before the publication of the *Wealth of Nations*, made a world-wide reputation by his *Essay on the Theory of Moral Sentiments*. The basis of the whole theory is not selfishness but sympathy. . . . In the whole range of the history of perversions there is no more curious error than the popular idea that Adam Smith treated the wealth of nations from the cosmopolitan standpoint"; and Nicholson quotes the *Wealth of Nations* as stating that "the great object of the political economy of every country is to increase the riches and the power of that country".

Thanks, perhaps, to his early association with the Glasgow merchants, Smith's teaching was always plain and practical. As he saw things before him, what was needed was freedom from restrictions and monopolies, and he preached this need with the effect that is well known. But he was by no means convinced that this freedom was an end in itself, admitting of no exception. He defends the Navigation Act on the ground that "defence is of much more importance than opulence", and that, in order to serve England's safety by diminishing the naval power of Holland, the Act "very properly endeavours to give the sailors and shipping of Great Britain the monopoly of the trade of their own country". He concludes by describing the Act as "perhaps the wisest of all the commercial regulations of England". Out of this passage an ingenious protectionist could easily dig arguments for protecting most of the chief industries of any country. And advocates of tariff wars can inscribe on their banner his saying that "it may sometimes be a matter of deliberation how far it is proper to continue the free importation of certain foreign goods, when some foreign nation restrains by high duties or prohibitions the importations of some of our manufactures into their country. Revenge in this case naturally dictates retaliation. . . There may be good policy in retaliations of this kind, when there is a probability that they will procure the repeal of the high duties or prohibitions complained of" —which, of course, the tariff warriors always maintain that they will.

Of the division of labour and its advantages his exposition is well known. His exposure of its disadvantages is one of his most eloquent passages: "In the progress of the division of labour, the employment of the far greater number of those who live by labour, that is, of the great body of the people, comes to be confined to a few very simple operations. . . . But the understandings of the greater part of men are necessarily formed by their ordinary employments. The man whose whole life is spent in performing a few simple operations . . . has no occasion to exert his understanding, or to exercise his invention. . . . He naturally loses, therefore, the habit of such exertion, and becomes as stupid and ignorant as it is possible for a human creature to become. The torpor of his mind renders him, not only incapable of relishing or bearing a part in any rational conversation, but of conceiving any generous, noble or tender sentiment, and consequently of forming any just judgment concerning many even of the ordinary duties of private life. Of the great and extensive interests of his country he is altogether incapable of judging; and unless very particular pains have been taken to render him otherwise, he is equally incapable of defending his country in war. The uniformity of his stationary life naturally corrupts the courage of his mind. . . It corrupts even the activity of his body and renders him incapable of exerting his strength with vigour and perseverance, in any other employment than that to which he has been bred. His dexterity at his own particular trade seems, in this manner, to be acquired at the expense of his intellectual, social and martial virtues. But in every improved and civilized society this is the state into which the labouring poor, that is, the great body of the people, must necessarily fall, unless government takes some pains to prevent it."

This is hardly the pure milk of *laisser faire*, still less of pacifism. And there are passages in the *Wealth of Nations* that even seem to claim that labour does all the work of production and distribution, and that those who organize business and provide capital contribute nothing. "No society can surely be flourishing and happy, of which the far greater part of the members are poor and miserable. It is but equity, besides, that they who feed, cloath and lodge the whole body of the people, should have such a share of the produce of their own labour as to be themselves tolerably well fed, cloathed, and lodged."

This compassion of Smith's for the lot of the workers comes out again when he says that "masters are always and everywhere in a sort of tacit, but constant and uniform combination, not to raise the wages of labour above their actual rate. . . . Masters too sometimes enter into particular combinations to sink the wages of labour even below this rate. These are always conducted with the utmost silence and secrecy, till the moment of execution, and when the workmen yield, as they sometimes do, without resistance, though severely felt by them, they are never heard of by other people."

Once more, "people of the same trade seldom meet together, even for merriment and diversion, but the conversation ends in a conspiracy against the public, or in some contrivance to raise prices."

"Gentlemen's agreements," as such arrangements are called nowadays, to keep wages down or "sink" them, and to fleece the public, are hardly consistent with Smith's famous theory of the "invisible hand" which, in his view, so often leads the individual employer to promote the public interest while intending only his own gain.

In fact, like all the great allegories, the *Wealth of Nations* provides powder and shot for the champions of a strange variety of doctrines. But Smith's main thesis, after falling into general discredit and neglect, has just been re-affirmed and put before the nations, now again sick of restrictions and the impoverishment that too much of them causes, by the Bank for International Settlements, in its report published in May 1936. "The world," says this authority, "has once more to learn the lesson that trade grows best when it is free from fetters." And thus, as the clown says in *Twelfth Night*, "the whirligig of time brings in his revenges."

31

ROBERT ADAM AND HIS BROTHERS

(1728-1792)

by GEOFFREY WEBB

ROBERT ADAM'S reputation is nowadays mainly concerned with his design of mantelpieces, door-cases and furniture, what a contemporary called the "decorative part of civil architecture", especially mantelpieces. In this posterity is in the main justified, except perhaps in regard to the mantelpieces which are given so much prominence because they are easily portable and saleable property for the antique dealers whereas ceilings and wall treatments are not. For it was, perhaps, Adam's greatest achievement to have given to eighteenth-century England its first consistent decorative style, which was sufficiently flexible to be used both for monumental and comparatively modest interiors. Before his time there had been tentative essays in that direction, such as that of Kent, but never with the success of Robert Adam. It is also true that the earlier architects had on occasion succeeded with the grand interiors, perhaps better than Adam had, but still the generalization will hold. In France, with the coming of rococo at the opening of the century, this consistency of style had been attained, and it seems as much a matter of individual personalities as of obvious social or economic forces that accounts for the discrepancy between the two countries. Adam's is essentially a drawing-room style as indeed was the rococo of Oppenord or Meissonier, but though drawing-rooms had been important quite as long in England as in France, we had to wait till the third quarter of the century before their proper architectural and decorative treatment was evolved.

Though Robert Adam's is a drawing-room style and especially suitable to town houses and country interiors of comparatively modest dimensions, his practice from the very outset was among the richest and most splendour-loving clients, and many of his most characteristic designs were done for interiors as monumental as anything the early eighteenth century had conceived. Adam arrived in London from Italy in the early part of 1758, and did not have long to await success. He is one of the earliest of those architects of whom it was bitterly said that "Mr. Trowell is just arrived from Rome! Bravissimo! He must undoubtedly be a great genius. Mr. Trowell's name is up and he may go to bed when he pleases." Moreover, Robert Adam was a Scotchman and a popular man in Scotch circles in London. It was through the dramatist Home that he obtained his introduction to Garrick, and his nationality probably helped him to obtain Court favour. He designed the Queen's Transparency, a garden *fête décor* in 1762, and some decorations for Buckingham Palace about the same time. It is amusing to recollect in this connection his indignation against Bute for his cold reception of him in 1758. Bute was afterwards a good friend to Adam, and through him came his employment at Lansdowne house and the designing of one of his greatest works, Bute's own house, Luton Hoo, which moved even Johnson to admiration.

Adam's stay in Italy from 1754 to 1758 was most profitably employed. He came of a family of architects; his father was a most successful practitioner, and Robert must have been brought up very much in an architectural atmosphere. He had also attended the University of Edinburgh. When he reached Rome he seems to have set about extracting the most from all that it could give, not only from the works of art, but from the personalities to be met there. It was the Rome of Winckelmann, filled with an archæological enthusiasm, more intense and wider in scope than in earlier times. In Rome he met Piranesi who dedicated a plate to him and engraved for him illustrations for his book on Spalatro, the fruit of his most important excursion into practical archæology. As a result Adam came back with his mind full, not so much of ancient precedent in the minutiæ of the handling of the Orders of Columns, though he knew enough of that, as of the romantic picturesque view of the remains of antiquity, both the sublimity of the piled up masses of the ancient ruins and the vast and varied space compositions suggested by their imaginative reconstruction. There are extant picturesque drawings and projections by Adam which date from this Roman visit. To this romantic enthusiasm for antiquity should be added an immensely rich and varied repertory of decorative forms derived from every antique and high Renaissance source, many of them of a kind that had hardly been exploited before in England.

With this romantic picturesque approach to even the ancients it is not surprising to find Adam prepared to design in the manner we most naturally associate with the romantic and picturesque, imitation Gothic. It is not indeed a manner we associate with Adam's name, yet there is in Spiers's Catalogue of his drawings evidence of over forty medieval designs, many of them involving numerous drawings. This is a large number, even in a practice as large as his. Moreover, these Gothic designs do not derive from any particular period or phase of his development, but are spread fairly evenly over his whole career. The earliest of them, the works at Alnwick,

Croome Church and Harewood Church, are the first works done for some of his most important clients and date from the very beginnings of his practice. These first Gothic designs are what may be called rococo Gothic and include elaborate Gothic interior decorations for Alnwick. And in 1766 Adam did some designs for Strawberry Hill for Horace Walpole, which also include interior decoration. Later his medieval buildings are so only in the character of their compositional grouping; the detail is mainly classic even externally, and entirely so inside, though Gothic interior designs continue at Alnwick into the 1780's. This later medievalizing manner is what we may call the castle style and most of the finest examples are to be found in Scotland. Culzean in Ayrshire may be taken as perhaps the best of them. Externally it is as grand and romantic a composition as could be desired. Inside the ingenuity of the space effects and the elegance of the detail are in Adam's most advanced late manner. Indeed the planning of the vestibule, the great elliptical staircase hall with its niches and the circular drawing-room is one of his greatest *tours de force*.

This medievalizing romantic architecture of Adam has been stressed here because not only is it often neglected, but because it helps to call attention to the similar qualities of romantic massing and picturesque grouping in his classical designs. These are too often regarded merely as over-refined and over-elegant versions of Georgian classic as practised by his predecessors. It is perhaps easier to recognize the romantic quality in his interior compositions, the elaborate vistas through rooms of nicely calculated variety of shape, the semi-domed apses screened by columns, as at Kenwood or Syon, and so forth. But such features as the grand portico which links the wings at Osterley and attains an effect more dramatic than that of any of the stock Palladian porticos, because one looks either through it to the landscape or up into it and into the court and sky beyond, shows how far the new picturesque feeling could make the dry bones of classicism to live, and the same can be said of the deep shadowed screens of columns at Luton Hoo and Compton Verney, and especially of the great group compositions such as Bowood extended behind its terraces, and the schemes for Cambridge, Bath and Edinburgh.

Robert Adam practised a classicism which had summoned up all its resources. Adam's predecessors had attained to richness of effect by the elaboration of a relatively few stock devices, except where they trusted to supplementing these by representational decoration of the freest kind. Adam immensely increased the number of stock devices and while reducing them all to the relative unimportance of details of an all-over scheme, took care that much of this detail should have literary overtones that would ensure its proving interesting and amusing on close inspection. "More elegant and more interesting" is his own phrase; the elegance consisting in the tactful social background he provided, the interest in the new variety of antiquarian flavour.

Robert Adam in the prefaces of his published volumes of "Works" which appeared in the course of the 1770's, defines his attitude to architecture with a completeness that we would welcome from every architect, and there can be no doubt that these books largely affected the work of his contemporaries. There can be equally little doubt that Adam was thoroughly conscious of the commercial value of such publications. It was customary for eighteenth century architects to produce these volumes of engraved plates of their building details, but Adam's Works contained more letterpress than usual, and are both more explanatory as well as more propagandist and more frankly self-advertizing than most. They are the more valuable to us, and we would give much to have such reflections on their art from such men as Wren, Vanbrugh and Kent. Perhaps the most illuminating passage in the Works is the following: "The parade, the convenience and social pleasures of life being better understood, are more strictly attended to in the arrangement and disposition of apartments. Greater variety of form, greater beauty of design, greater gaiety and elegance of ornament are introduced into interior decoration, while the outside composition is more simple, more grand, more varied in its contour and imposes on the mind from the superior movement and magnitude of its parts." Movement is explained by:

Movement is meant to express the rise and fall, the advance and recess, with other diversity of form, in the different parts of a building, so as to add greatly to the picturesque of the composition. For the rising and falling, advancing and receding, with the convexity and concavity, and other forms of the great parts, have the same effect in architecture, that hill and dale, foreground and distance, swelling and sinking, have in landscape; that is, they serve to produce an agreeable and diversified contour, that groups and contrasts like a picture, and creates a variety of light and shade, which gives great spirit, beauty and effect to the composition.

As to his typical handling of interior detail he says:

The mouldings in the remaining structures of ancient Rome are considerably less curvilineal than those of the ancient monuments of Greece. We have always given a preference to the latter, and have even thought it advisable to bend them still more in many cases, particularly in interior finishings, where objects are near, and ought to be softened to the eye: for circular mouldings are intended to relieve the sight from the acuteness of the square ones, of which too frequent a repetition would be infinitely harsh and tiresome: But . . . in the method we have always followed, as may be seen from our designs, they blend and mingle themselves more harmoniously with the square members, and attain more delicacy and elegance, than such as have been commonly used.

Many of Robert Adam's most important commissions for country houses, it would be fair to say most of them, did not allow of a new design from the beginning, but were adaptations of existing buildings. Syon, Bowood, Osterley, Nostell, Kedleston and Harewood are all of this character and many more of his finest works. In this kind of work it was his special gift as a planner and interior decorator that enabled him to excel, though occasionally, as at Osterley, he was able to achieve some bold stroke of exterior composition that makes the building his own both inside and out. In the period from 1758-70 when all these great works were undertaken, his manner was maturing very rapidly. The process of maturing was not however, completely and tidily consistent: the prefaces to the "Works" which began in the 70's, represent a retrospective view of his own tendencies and though we are right to interpret his development in the light of them, the work after the 60's does not show an even progress towards that ingenious recombination of highly stylised, low relief decorative forms that is a fair description of his fully developed style. Of the earlier works the Hatchlands ceilings with their big full mouldings and large scale low relief figures and bold pendants, are very clearly linked to the ornamental plaster work of the earlier part of George II's reign. Shardeloes has also some of this quality, and in some of the work at Kedleston there is a survival in doorway features of the "tabernacle frame" which he was later to claim to have abolished. The large size of the rooms at Syon also tended to perpetuate reminiscences of the bolder treatment of his predecessors as more suitable to their state and magnificence: but the long gallery there, perhaps because it is narrower, and partly perhaps because it was intended as a withdrawing-room, especially designed for ladies, is one of the most exaggerated if not the most successful earlier examples of his later type of treatment. On the other hand, the ceilings of two of the rooms at Osterley, considerably later than the Syon gallery, seem to hark back to his earliest manner, the dining-room in the freedom of the treatment of the foliage wreaths, and the drawing-room in the heaviness of the parts. It is impossible to say how far these things are to be explained as uncertainty on the part of Adam himself and how far to special circumstances in each example, such as the tastes of the client, or the abilities of his plasterer. After the 70's had set in it would be difficult to trace any throw-back to George II fashions in his decorations; the late rooms at Osterley and the work in such interiors as Home House, are completely free from anything of the kind. The great library for Lord Mansfield at Kenwood is as good an example as could be chosen of Adam's mature manner used on the grand scale.

The 70's (the Adelphi was begun in '69) are the great period of the Adam brothers in London. To that time belong the houses in Portman Square, Mansfield Street and Portland Place, as well as such works as 20 St. James's Square and Derby House, Grosvenor Square. In these works Adam's decorative manner was formed and established. Also the more cramped sites of the town houses brought out all that was best in Adam as a planner. It is astonishing the variety of effect that he can get out of the reception rooms in a London house, and in the less monumental space of London drawing-rooms his decoration shows to its greatest advantage compared with the saloons of great country seats. Lansdowne House is the most important predecessor of these London interiors and there the most important decorations were completed by 1768. The planning of No. 20 St. James's Square (1772) and old Derby House (1773) are veritable *tours de force* in the intricate variety that Adam has contrived to get in the arrangement of the suites. The staircase in the former is especially notable. Both these houses were designed for the deep, narrow-fronted sites that are usual in London, and in both he contrived to obtain effects that he could hardly surpass on the much broader and less hampering site of Home House in 1775. The decorations of this house (Derby House is now only known from drawings and engravings) are as fine examples of his fully matured style as could be found. Derby House seems to have been the most exaggerated of them and drew from Horace Walpole the crushing phrase "filigreed into puerility like l'Hotel de Derby". There and at Home House and in the later rooms at Osterley, Adam made his first excursions into the "Etruscan" style of decoration, basing his colour schemes of terra cotta, black and chocolate on the Greek vases that were becoming fashionable. This was a startling and self-conscious departure from the pale greens, pinks and buffs of his usual manner. Of these Etruscan rooms, only the Osterley example survives.

It is best to consider Adam's treatment of the exteriors of his town houses in connection with his large schemes of estate development of which the Adelphi is the first and most famous. In general his innovations consisted in a flattening down of the projections of such architectural features as the façade of the typical London house allowed of. In Mansfield Street the only external features are the cornice mouldings and the doorways recessed in the rusticated ground floor story. Even No. 20 St. James's Square, where there are "pilasters and what the Orders require" as well as the relics of the "tabernacle frame" Adam so despised, is no exception to the general rule and Home House, Portman Square, is an admirable example of it. At the back of both these houses he has a bolder treatment, presumably because there he had no need to consider the adjoining houses in the unity of the effect of the street. The Adelphi was Adam's most ambitious London scheme, and there the flatness of relief in the external features is most remarkable; the more so as the whole conception of the scheme in relation to the river was as bold and picturesquely massive as can be imagined. The consequence was a curious contrast between the boldness of the main massing and the over-refined elegance of the detail treatment that occasioned Horace Walpole's celebrated gibe "warehouses laced down the seams like a soldier's trull in a regimental old coat". Robert Adam's later large urban schemes, Fitzroy Square, London, and Charlotte Square, Edinburgh, both belong to the end of his life. Portland Place would seem to be mainly his brother James's work. These two late schemes are both stone-faced, and this would naturally suggest a rather bolder treatment, so that it is difficult to draw any conclusion from the strong contrast of their manner with that of the Adelphi, originally an entirely brick building, except that perhaps the very choice of stone for Fitzroy Square and its bolder relief treatment, may be an indication of a growing tendency to a more picturesque treatment for urban buildings as well as country ones.

The Adelphi proved a disastrous experiment for Adam and his brothers in many ways. The difficulty of the site with its steep slope to the river and the legal complications involved in relation particularly to the foreshore, proved so costly as to be almost finally ruinous from the financial point of view. Indeed the details of the complicated transactions the scheme involved, including a lottery to raise money, alienated some of Adam's former friends and one or two of his most important patrons. All this may have helped with, it is suggested, the effects of the American War, and perhaps most important of all, the appearance of rival architects, especially Wyatt who certainly helped to break Adam's monopoly of his now very fashionable style, to make Adam's career in the 70's and 80's less startlingly successful than in the ten years before. Towards the end of his life there are a number of works in Edinburgh attributed to Adam, but with the important exception of the Register House, none of them were carried to completion according to his intention. Edinburgh University and Charlotte Square are both the mutilated remains of the designs by him and Adam is best considered a London architect. Even in examples where the Scottish work was completed in his lifetime, as at No. 7 Queen Street, or the exterior of the Register House, Adam had to put much trust in the man on the spot, and the designs are hardly so personal as his London works.

Adam's conception of the internal finishing of the house as a unity included on occasion not only the major furnishings and hangings, but such details as door furniture, light fittings, clocks, inkstands, and even silver plate. William Kent, who had also designed all sorts of furnishings, even it is said, ladies' dresses of a strictly architectural character (involving the orders), is not known to have gone so far as the implications of this entry in Lady Shelburne's diary. "London 1766, Lord Shelburne consulted Mr. Adams about the chain of my watch." Broadly speaking Adam's furniture follows the development of his interior decoration with the same tendency to ever more lightening and over-refinement of form. Some of the furniture done for Sir Lawrance Dundas in the early 60's bears the same relation to the work of twenty years later that the Hatchlands ceilings do to those of Home House. In furniture proper, tables, chairs and so forth, the tendency shows itself in the partial abandonment of carving and relief moulding in favour of painting and inlay, but even in examples where this is not done, the same tendency to restraint of relief is noticeable. Adam attached great importance to his designs of these details, and published them very fully in his "Works". And though he worked so exclusively for the rich and great, and his style has been said to have had little immediate effect on the furnishings of the average house, these plates cannot have failed to exert an influence far beyond the circle of exclusive craftsmen who worked directly under him. Indeed Sir John Soane, lecturing to the Academy in 1812, goes so far as to say "To Mr. Adam's taste in the ornament of his buildings and furniture we stand indebted in as much as manufacturers of every kind felt as it were the electric power of this revolution in art". The revolution may be said to have consisted in a creative reaction against Venetian Baroque of the Kent School and the more imaginative aberrations of the rococo. There is however one curious exception to Adam's general reaction against the French rococo, his fondness for the Boucher-Nielson tapestries. It is not so surprising to find them at Croome in the early 60's, and a little later (1768 and 9) at Sir Lawrance Dundas's house, but the examples at Newby and Osterley date from well into the 70's. The robust opulence of their designs makes Adam's ceiling at the last house look strangely thin and skimpy, though it won the rare commendation from Horace Walpole, who says "enriched by Adam in his best taste" and only takes exception to the small scale of the marble mantelpiece enrichments.

Of Robert Adam's business associates his brothers naturally take first place. John, the eldest, inherited the property at Blair Adam, and only very rarely appears in connection with his brother's business. James, the brother next younger than Robert, was throughout the larger part of his career, a junior partner in the firm. James also travelled in Italy from 1760-63 and there is a diary extant of his visit. He was an accomplished draughtsman and designer and works of his own are recorded, as some of the ceilings at Bowood and the main share in the work at Portland Place. After Robert Adam's death in 1792, James continued the practice until he himself died two years later. Dr. Carlyle, an early friend of the Adams', has described

James as "though not so bold and superior an artist as his brother Robert, a well-informed and sensible man" and Mr. Bolton has aptly described him as Robert's "Chief of Staff". With William, the youngest of the brothers, James was largely responsible for the business part of the Adelphi scheme. William in Robert's lifetime seems to have been in the main the family man of business, though after the death of his brothers (John also died in 1792) it fell to him to wind up the practice, and some designs of his own have survived, notably a revised scheme for Edinburgh University. The unity of the family seems to have been remarkable.

Outside the family circle the most important of Robert's architectural collaborators was William Paine, a much older man than himself, who had formed his style under the influence of Burlington and Kent. Nostel in Yorkshire, where Adam was long after to follow him, was Paine's first work, and dates from 1735. The associations of the two architects comes at the very opening of Adam's career at Alnwick and Kedleston, which Paine says he handed over to Adam because of press of work. Adam also decorated the town house of Mr. Fitz-Maurice in Pall Mall for Paine. Paine was a bold and ingenious planner, and it may be that Adam learned something of this kind from their association; it is certain that Adam's decorative style affected that of Paine in such houses as Brocket, where the later rooms are markedly Adam in manner, and contrast strongly with the Kent style of the earlier ones, though there is no reason to connect Adam with the work directly. Robert Adam was also so closely associated with certain craftsmen artists as to justify them being called his collaborators. Of these the most important is Rose, the plasterer, who appears at Mersham le Hatch, Harewood, Syon, Kenwood and Nostel, and at the first is paid only through Adam, and not independently like the other craftsmen. Rose lived in one of Adam's houses in Mansfield Street. Other craftsmen are the Zucchi family, the one a painter who eventually married Angelica Kauffmann and took her off to Italy, and the other an engraver. Their names appear in connection with Adam quite as often as that of Rose. Of the sculptors to whom the marble mantel-pieces are due, Carter's is perhaps the most important name, and Chippendale among the woodworkers should be mentioned. Such men as Rose and Carter must be reckoned as perhaps the most important means whereby Adam's style became so widespread and accepted as to stand in men's general opinion for the whole decorative output of the late eighteenth century in England.

32

THE YOUNGER PITT

(1759–1806)

by P. H. M. BRYANT

AMONG the portraits of the Younger Pitt are two in striking contrast. There is the familiar Gainsborough portrait of which there are copies in many a country house to-day: it suggests brilliant youth and shrewd reserve in a rather smug and inexperienced harmony. And there is the less familiar painting by Hoppner of a gaunt figure and a fierce, care-worn, ageing face, suggestive of some noble animal grandly at bay. These two paintings tell the story of the Pitt who started his career as the inheritor of a great name and as the popular young Galahad in a world of corruption of which the champions had already been discredited; and of the Pitt whose last years were spent, little more than a decade later, fighting at the head of the great force of British conservatism what seemed a losing battle against the most powerful of adversaries without and the unknown and cunning force of revolution within. It was a life of only forty-six years. But it was a life which formed a link—which formed the link—between the early adventurous days of an expanding empire, the days when Chatham roused George the Second's England and "Hearts of Oak" was the song; and the days when the very civilization and freedom of the Island itself seemed threatened by a strange and terrible culture made almost irresistible by the strongest military domination Europe had ever known. And out of that struggle—the struggle which killed Pitt—was born the nineteenth century.

William Pitt the Younger, the second son of Chatham, began his life in the year of his father's *annus mirabilis*, 1759. He was one of those abnormally clever little boys whose infantile feats take the breath away. At the age of seven he wrote a letter to his father in Latin. He was not, however, robust: he inherited the same gout which had paralysed his father's latent energy so often and at such critical moments. It was a gout which poisoned the whole nervous system, and the object of the doctors was always to bring on a severe attack in the extremities in order to draw it away. The remedy they prescribed was port-wine, and little Pitt was given it in considerable quantities when still a mere child. They also made him ride.

Partly because of his delicacy he was not sent to a public school. His father had been a boy at Eton but had formed the conclusion that public schools drove the spirit out of a boy and quashed his individuality. One wonders, therefore, what Chatham would have been like if he had been spared this treatment! Young Pitt, however, was kept at home and educated by a tutor. There was only one type of education in vogue—construing from the great masters of Greece and Rome, and imitating their verses. But old Chatham directed these exercises to a special purpose: every evening he made the boy read over to him at sight, in carefully chosen English, the passages which he had been working at with his tutor during the day. The orator was deliberately fashioned.

The father died in 1778, at the crisis of the War of American Independence. The son entered Parliament in 1781, a representative of one of the old "Rotten Boroughs": had they not existed this young man would have had to fight his way up the political ladder by the same methods as our political young men have to fight to-day, and reach the sphere of power and usefulness with his youth and energy spent.

Like his father, forty-six years earlier, he joined the Opposition, the pack of lively and brilliant wits—Carteret, Pulteney, Windham in his father's early days; Fox, Burke, Sheridan in his own—who were hunting down the royal favourite—once Walpole, then North. Poor Lord North had nothing on his side but his own good humour and the mighty organization of royal patronage. Even his conscience had deserted him. Solely in deference to his master's desire he had prolonged the resistance to the American Colonies and remained himself in office. His colleagues were corrupt and inefficient men who had failed and failed again. The whole Government stank in the nostrils of the public. Yorktown was shortly to seal the fate of America, and with French, Spanish and Dutch navies in hostile coalition on all the seas of the world, there seemed little hope that much would remain of Chatham's empire.

In March, 1782, Lord North resigned and the Opposition came into its own, resolved to rescue Britain's prestige and clean up her house. The Marquis of Rockingham was Prime Minister, the noble head of the Whig Party. Pitt, who had sat in Parliament for two sessions of five and four months respectively, but whose speeches had already made him a leader, was offered a subordinate post in the Government without cabinet rank. He declined it. Perhaps he remembered tales of the power which his father had lost over the public during the ten years he served under the Pelhams, a supposed supporter of a Government whose policy he could not help to guide. Yet the father had then been in the late thirties: the son was twenty-two.

So the famous Rockingham administration—the administration which gave to England Burke's great Economic Reform Bill and enjoyed the credit of Rodney's victory over de Grasse—did not include the young William Pitt. It lasted only three months, and the breach between its two Secretaries of State, Shelburne and Fox, grew wider and wider. They represented the two wings of the Whig Party—Shelburne a faithful disciple of the late Lord Chatham, Fox once a Tory and now—after the manner of apostates—the most energetic champion of extreme causes. King George naturally preferred Shelburne as Rockingham's successor, and Fox resigned. Pitt accepted office under Shelburne as Chancellor of the Exchequer.

The Shelburne-Pitt ministry lasted nearly a year. Shelburne was an unpopular man and no one trusted him, but his was the ministry which concluded the Peace of Versailles with Britain's many enemies, and, all things considered, it was as favourable a settlement as could possibly be hoped for: the independence of America had for some time been a fact, and Minorca, Florida and Tobago were only a small fraction of Chatham's empire. The Opposition, however, found the Peace easy to assail. This was the time when Fox espoused the most hopeless of all his lost causes—the cause of Lord North and the "King's Friends" party. The two extremes overthrew the centre government and joined hands in a Coalition which outraged the scruples even of eighteenth-century political England. It had little chance of success, for the leader of the King's Friends was no longer a friend of the King, who after a few months caused its defeat in the House of Lords itself by an appeal to the very minions whom North had formerly commanded, and then instantly ordered his ministers to surrender their seals.

It had been a process of elimination. North had been discredited, Rockingham had died, Shelburne was disliked, Fox by joining with North had shared his opprobrium. Only the young man of twenty-four was left—brilliant, quiet, efficient, and the inheritor of the most revered name in England.

But he was a Prime Minister without a party: all the leading orators of the day—and they were some of the greatest that the House of Commons has ever produced—were opposed to him, and again and again he was defeated. He ignored it, for he did not at this moment regard the House of Commons as any measure of public opinion. The people admired his courage: the City trusted him as it had trusted his father. A sinecure fell vacant which it would have been customary for the Prime Minister to take for himself unless already provided with an income independent of the vicissitudes of office. Pitt, whose administration was known as the Mince-Pie administration because it was not expected to last beyond the Christmas holidays, and who was also very poor, scorned the usual practice, and by doing so made the gesture of a revolution in English public life.

When the time was ripe, he persuaded the King to dissolve Parliament. Lord Rosebery, in his little biography of Pitt, referred to the General Election of 1784 as "one of those great convulsions of feeling which in Great Britain express pent-up national sentiment and which in other nations provoke revolutions". England knew no Prime Minister but Pitt for the next momentous seventeen years.

The man as he appeared was the Pitt of the Gainsborough portrait. In place of the overbearing and thundering methods by which old Chatham had dominated his scared contemporaries, the young Pitt awed his seniors by a cold and haughty reserve. Only in his most intimate circle did he unbend.

The work which he did was to effect a reform in the public administration of Britain, far-reaching and abiding. His public life of a quarter of a century is the turning of eighteenth-century corruption and inefficiency into nineteenth-century conscientiousness and orderliness. His instruments were his personal spirit and example and a steady executive policy spread over many years.

Burke's Economic Reform Bill had done something, but Pitt carried its principle further. He found eighty-five more sinecures to abolish. He also insisted on the auditing of all government accounts; no longer could the Paymaster General make large personal profits from trading with public balances. When Pitt had occasion to raise loans, he did so publicly, securing by competition the lowest rate of interest, instead of allowing favoured private persons to lend their money at an unnecessarily high rate. He even tried to strike at the root of corruption by abolishing the rotten boroughs. Here, however, the vested interests in the House of Commons were too strong for him. But the scheme was an ingenious one: a million pounds were to be voted by Parliament with which to bribe the proprietors of thirty-six of the worst rotten boroughs to surrender their right to representation: if they refused, their share of the million pounds was to accumulate at compound interest until it proved a sufficient enticement. The seats of the disfranchised boroughs were to be transferred to London and the more populous counties. Unlike the framers of the first great Reform Bill of 1832, Pitt did not regard his own reform as final: after the first million pounds had been spent, another million was to be set aside for the disfranchisement of any other borough which decayed, in favour of any populous town which petitioned to be represented. It would have averted several crises.

His hardest work was the reform of the fiscal system. Many of the Customs duties were so heavy that smuggling had become the rule rather than the exception. Forty thousand persons were engaged in it, and, in the case of tea, out of thirteen million pounds annually imported, duty somehow was only paid on five and a half. Pitt passed various direct measures

to suppress smuggling, such as the Hovering Act which author-
ized the confiscation of all ships with dutiable articles found
hovering within twelve miles of the coast. But he also reduced
the temptation to smuggle. He carried out the plan which
Walpole had abandoned, of transferring the wine and tobacco
duties from customs to excise, and, calling himself a disciple
of Adam Smith, he began that work of removing or reducing
import duties which Huskisson, Peel and Gladstone continued
and completed in the nineteenth century. The duty on tea,
for instance, he reduced from 119 per cent to 12 per cent,
and in its place he substituted excise duties which could not be
evaded, such as the increased window-tax payable on all
windows in one house in excess of seven: he calculated that
the four million persons who would pay it would still be
paying less than their former tea duty, while the two million
persons living in houses of less than seven windows would
be relieved altogether. The collection of such customs as
remained Pitt drastically simplified, thereby eliminating much
waste. The Opposition accused him of "hunting in holes
and corners for abuses", but Pitt replied that he would not
be justified in omitting "any exertion that might tend, even
in the most minute particular, to promote the economy on
which the recovery of the state from its present depressed
situation so much depended."

Such was some of the work of the young administrator.
And his early wisdom was also applied to the diverse problems
of an Empire in the most critical stage of its development.
British India still belonged to the East India Company, and
only Warren Hastings had held in check its greed and narrow-
ness of vision. Canada was still one province of French
Catholics administered autocratically by a Governor, but in
accordance with French laws and customs. Australia was
uncolonized.

Pitt's India Act virtually transferred responsibility for the administration of India to the British Government without transferring to it also the resources of wealth and patronage which would have so aggravated political corruption at home. The system lasted till the Mutiny, seventy years later. Pitt's Canada Act created an English-speaking and English-practising province for the American loyalist emigrants, and the seeds of self-government were laid in both British and French provinces by the establishment of legislative assemblies. Finally, by sending to Botany Bay the convicts who could no longer be disposed of in America, Pitt began, in however sinister a fashion, the peopling of Australia.

A successful check to French pretensions in Holland and to Spanish in the Pacific made it clear that Britain and her fleet were once more factors that could not be brushed aside.

Perhaps most important of all was the tacit settlement of the constitutional problem at home. Pitt's position was a happy one: he was both the chosen servant of the King and the popular favourite. The friction, therefore, between the sovereign and a large section of the public, which had developed since George III's accession, came to an end in Pitt's person. For Pitt was no puppet. The King found in him a master as well as a servant; the Prime Minister was a Prime Minister once more.

All this might seem enough for the work of a great statesman. Yet Pitt's fame is not bound up with these halcyon years of steady and almost faultless handling of administrative problems. The Pitt whom Britain mourned in 1806, Scott's "watchman on the lonely tower", was the baffled but unbowed war-time Leader, sharing with his generation the responsibility for many blunders and mistaken prejudices, and dying in apparent failure.

The French Revolution broke upon the world before Pitt had completed his sixth year in office. Fox and his party hailed it with extravagant delight: so did enthusiasts for Parliamentary Reform: so did the enemies of the Established Church: so did avowed republicans like Tom Paine: so did poets. Tories in Church and State, on the other hand, with many friends among the victims across the Channel, could hardly be sympathetic, and when Burke sounded the trumpet of horror and alarm, they welcomed him as the prophet of law and property.

All these made the noise. But Pitt at first took what was the sensible view and what was also the quiet feeling of the people at large. They were glad that their neighbour, so long a formidable rival, was suddenly stricken powerless by internal combustion. Nor could they see any connection, either for good or evil, between the domestic affairs of a nation hitherto governed by a despot and peopled by nobles and serfs, and those of a nation of country squires, yeomen, craftsmen and apprentices, who had enjoyed freedom for centuries and who were separated from one another by no rigid barriers.

But events moved too swiftly. Goaded by intervention from without, the French revolutionary leaders became violent within: an aristocracy was massacred and a king guillotined. In the light of these events, revolutionary propaganda in England seemed increasingly odious. Meanwhile France, her army national and organized, took the offensive against her enemies. She would recognize no former international treaties which did not accord with the "law of nature", and she openly offered fraternity and assistance to all peoples desiring to overthrow their rulers. It was the former principle, as applied to the integrity of Holland and the navigation of the Scheldt, that forced a pacifically-inclined British Government to enter on the war which—though no one thought so—was to last so long. It was the other principle which made necessary the policy of repression.

The strategy which Pitt adopted was—naturally—the

strategy which had proved so successful a generation earlier—his father's. European armies were to be subsidized to engage the French in Europe, while British expeditionary forces, aided by the British Navy, were to seize what remained of the French Empire. But the right circumstances for Chatham's strategy had passed. There was no Canada to be won: only some West India islands (already once conquered and handed back), more costly to win than valuable to keep, for the British War Office had not yet learnt how to look after the health of its soldiers.

Moreover, there was no Frederick the Great to beat the French armies in the field. Pitt's subsidies were doled out to feeble princes of the *ancien régime*, who could effect nothing against these national armies, and who were more interested in the Partition of Poland and the problems of Eastern Europe. But until the French armies were beaten the cause could not be won. For the cause was not a colonial empire, as in 1756. It was the security and independence of the nations of Europe, as in 1702 and 1914. It was a case for Marlborough's methods rather than Chatham's. But Pitt's faith in the old policy never failed him: three times, in the course of over twelve years, he formed his European coalitions, and every time they broke. He died with the news of Austerlitz poisoning his life-blood. He appeared to understand at last: "Roll up that map." It was seven years later when the map became useful again, for Napoleon's mania had aroused a spirit of national resistance among the states of Europe. Then a coalition was worth the making, and Castlereagh used in the effective moment the machinery which Pitt had devised so painfully and patiently when it could be of no avail.

At home the struggle was a prolonged and bitter one against Jacobin propaganda. The Habeas Corpus Act was suspended so that suspected persons could be kept safe under lock and key pending investigations. The Seditious Mutiny Act for-

bade gatherings of more than fifty persons without consent
of a magistrate. The Treasonable Practices Act extended to
speeches and writings aimed against the Constitution the
category of offences—hitherto only overt acts—punishable
as Treason. And many prosecutions ensued.

Pitt has been censured for his policy, and contrasted un-
favourably with the ministers who piloted Britain through
the next Great War, 120 years later. But their war was against
a nation only. Pitt's was against a nation too, but it was also
against a creed which claimed to be of universal application,
and had adherents—none knew how many—in every country.
Mr. Fremantle shows in his *England in the Nineteenth Century*
how some of the persons prosecuted may have been half-
drunken men who in public houses used such expressions
as "Damn the King and Billy Pitt". But he shows also that
such would be the natural method of a man trying to spread
sedition: if the company were loyal, he would plead drunkenness: if there were ill-disposed persons among them, they
would know where they stood together.

There is a more serious indictment against Pitt, that he
abandoned his earlier principles. The three great causes
which were to remain the policy of the Whigs until their
fulfilment—Parliamentary Reform, the Abolition of the Slave
Trade, and Religious Equality—had once been Pitt's ideals too.
But Parliamentary Reform had already three times been deci-
sively rejected by the House of Commons. The charge that
Pitt should have made his proposal a question of confidence is
surely an anachronism. And once the nation was at war, he
may be condoned for refusing to alienate the majority to no
purpose and sacrifice unity. As for the Abolition of the Slave
Trade, that Pitt believed sincerely he was serving the cause
best in those dark years by avoiding precipitate action should
be proved by the faith in him which Wilberforce never lost.
His combat over the Catholic Emancipation question was

parallel. He recalled from Ireland the Viceroy Fitzwilliam who indiscreetly made known his intentions before the time was ripe; and, it cannot be denied, by so recalling him he made inevitable the Rebellion of 1798. But Catholic Emancipation remained his policy even after that tragedy, and he saw the best hopes for its realization in the Union of the two Parliaments. When the Union had been passed, and the King refused to agree to Catholic Emancipation, Pitt resigned. What more could he do? Whether or not he was glad to resign is neither here nor there. When, three years later, he again accepted office, pledged never again to raise the question during King George III's lifetime, England lived in hourly danger of Napoleonic invasion.

Pitt's war finance was contrary to the principles of modern economists, but so was that of twentieth century war Chancellors. Pitt's was based on the belief that the war could not last long, a Prime Minister's invariable illusion on such occasions. But when, after four years of reckless borrowing, he realized that Britain must fight on without allies, desperately and indefinitely, then his resources were boundless, and by his courage he inspired the whole nation to give and to endure. As well as an income tax (of two shillings in the pound), then for the first time imposed, voluntary contributions were asked for, and the response was a worthy one. The King gave a third of his income, the Ministers a fifth of theirs, and the Bank, City, gentry, artisans and labourers all showed their loyalty and patriotism in a similar way. Here was Pitt's real resemblance to his father, and in 1797, with Austria beaten, the fleet in mutiny, Ireland in rebellion, and the exchequer empty, his high fortitude was displayed in days darker and more critical for England than any which had been faced by Chatham.

He loved England and served her with the undivided devotion of his manhood. His dying words were of her. He served his generation faithfully, but not his alone. For a few years men used his name as a cloak for a policy which was stagnant. Then the better seed which he had sown blossomed again, in the spirit of his faithful disciple Canning. True Tories re-learnt their creed. Another of Pitt's most devoted supporters was the first Sir Robert Peel: he gave to England the first Factory Act and his more famous son. That son's disciple was Gladstone, while Canning fired the youthful imagination of Disraeli.

33

WILLIAM BLAKE

(1757-1827)

by Hugh Gordon Porteus

WILLIAM BLAKE, visionary by providence, and
by profession engraver, survives in his works as
one of the most extraordinary, and perhaps the
most fascinating, of all the figures of genius that enriched the
life of eighteenth-century England. He is justly, though not
widely, admired for certain precise achievements, as poet,
as painter, as mystic; for a handful of lyrics and frescoes; for
a few hundred small engravings and lines of verse. But these
components of Blake's genius can be properly appreciated
only in relation to one another and to his life. If this is true of
genius in general, it is still necessary to insist that there is
probably no personality in the history of English art for whom
a knowledge of the man is more important to an understanding
of the works. The biographical and expository literature that
has grown round Blake is in consequence considerable. The
list of his biographers alone is both long and impressive. And
it must be admitted that much of his work, such is its unity
with his life, could be made comprehensible only by a far
more detailed account than our space here will allow.

It is generally agreed that Blake's life falls conveniently into three periods. First comes the period of childhood and apprenticeship, the innocent and formative years between 1757 and 1782. Next comes the age of gathering experience, from the year of his marriage, through an existence of struggle and partial success, within the narrow circuit of his acquaintance, until the close of the century. Finally there is the darker period, from 1800 up to his death in 1827, which was responsible for his more profound works. Upon this framework let us erect, rather than the customary column inscribed with publication dates, a few tableaux designed to reveal the more significant crises in his spiritual life—which was all that mattered to Blake and is all that should matter, of course, to us.

A little after seven o'clock on the evening of November the 28th, 1757, the heavens were very appropriately set, it seems, for the dispatch to earth of the spirit of William Blake. It was the year of the Last Judgment in Heaven, according to the prophet Swedenborg. And the horoscope cast for this hour (it may be found in Mr. Arthur Symons's study of Blake) shows "the Moon in Cancer in the 12th house, both mystical, in trine to Herschell from the mystical sign Pisces, from the house of science and from the mundane trine to Saturn in the scientific sign Aquarius, in square to Mercury in Scorpio and in quintile to the Sun and Jupiter in the mystical sign Sagittarius. The square of Mars and Mercury has a remarkable tendency to sharpen intellects, and lay the foundation of extraordinary ideas . . . and the position and aspect of Uranus, the occult planet, indicates in the highest degree an inborn and supreme instinct for things occult, without showing the least tendency towards madness.". . . Who shall say that all this is not more relevant to our subject than the genealogical tree of the Blake family, which so many biographers have vainly sought to scale? For neither William's four brothers nor their sister shared his unique gifts; although all, by the humour and grace

of God, were born into the family of James, the Nonconformist hosier of Broad Street, Golden Square.

Young William began to manifest his peculiar gifts at a
very early age. Before he left the cradle, he had observed
God beckoning to him through the bedroom window. Romping as an infant in the fields of Westminster, he was surprised
by the prophet Ezekiel, staring from beneath a bush: and was
smacked by his mother for saying so. But William was not to
be thrashed out of his visions, as Mrs. Blake soon realized.
For when, at the age of nine, he described a tree at Peckham
Rye that was filled with angels, she stayed the angry hand of
his father. At ten, William began sketching such visions on
the fly-leaves of his father's books—Wesley, the Bible, and
Swedenborg—which he had learned to read. At eleven the
sketches, interspersed now with verses, had spread to the
backs of bills in the hosiery shop, and even to the inviting
surface of the counter, where they exhausted the patience of
his father but also attracted the attention of curious customers.
It was then that Mr. Blake was persuaded to send William, who
had had no schooling, to learn drawing. He was therefore
packed off to the classes of Mr. Pars, a romantic admirer of
classical marbles, there to copy "the noble antique in various
views". These Greco-Roman casts, miniatures of which his
father bought him, had a lasting influence on William's work;
but he soon learned to loathe them for their "smell of mortality". He spent his spare time and pennies in the auction
rooms, where he was known as "the little connoisseur",
knocking down reproductions of Dürer and Michelangelo
to supplement the Raphael prints at home. At fourteen William
was apprenticed to Basire, a cold and precise engraver; for it
was realized that to be a painter would mean an expensive
training followed by a precarious living, whereas a commercial engraver could always be sure of his hire. The discipline of engraving was exactly what dreamy William needed.

He worked hard, but he argued harder; and so heated and
endless were his quarrels with fellow apprentices that Basire
was obliged to pack him off to draw the ornaments and
monuments of London's churches. He took his arguments
with him to Westminster Abbey, from the scaffolding of
which he flung a blasphemous schoolboy (as a result of which
incident the Abbey precincts are still out-of-bounds for
Westminster School). It was in the Abbey, too, that William
first met Christ and the Apostles. But all this time he worked
prodigiously, engraving portraits real and imaginary, based on
the Abbey effigies; studying the form of stone drapery; and
soaking himself in the Gothic spirit that characterizes all his
work. Among the finest of his engraved portraits is a head of
Lavater done at this time. But Blake's interest in Lavater
was not confined to his *Physiognomy*, which he studied constantly: it stretched also to his *Aphorisms*; and these and many
other books—Milton, Swedenborg, Shakespeare and the
minor Elizabethan dramatists—Blake was in this period
mentally devouring and passionately annotating. At twenty,
after seven years of engraving, Blake was technically proficient; and he began to use his spare time earning with his
graver enough to pay his way during the next few years, which
he spent at the Royal Academy schools. At twenty-three he
exhibited at the first R.A. Summer Exhibition, side by side
with Reynolds, Gainsborough, and other big stars of the day.
He now had the opportunity to make new acquaintances.
He formed friendships with Flaxman (the illustrator of Homer),
Stothard (a fashionable painter) and Fuseli (a fellow engraver).

Towards a certain Miss Polly Woods he felt rather more
than friendly; but when she made it clear that he was wasting
his time, Blake at once changed his lodgings, taking a room
in the house of a Battersea market-gardener. When he told
his tale of woe to this market-gardener's dark-eyed daughter,
Kate, the atmosphere was so heavy with pity and sympathy

that an engagement was arranged upon the spot. Partly in order to subject this passion to the test of ordeal by absence, partly in order to earn the money necessary to keep it burning, Blake then withdrew from Battersea for the space of twelve months. In the August of 1782, when William was twenty-six and Catherine Boucher twenty, their marriage took place at Battersea Parish Church; with the very reluctant consent of Mr. Blake senior. Rather than return to Golden Square, therefore, they made their first home in Green Street, Leicester Fields; and William kept the pot boiling as a freelance engraver. No man of genius was ever blessed with a more suitable wife. They were perfectly complemented: for he was such a very positive young man, and she was such a very negative young woman. Blake taught her to draw and paint and read and write, and in return she helped to print and tint his designs. In these days he was a constant visitor to the literary house-parties of the Rev. Henry Mathew (who had found William in his teens reading Latin behind the hosiery counter), and his highbrow wife (who was so entranced by Blake's songs that she engineered their publication). *The Poetical sketches of W.B.* were published, through the help of this couple and of Flaxman, in 1783, three years before the advent of Burns. After the death of Mr. Blake senior, William's elder brother James took over the hosiery business; and William and Catherine thereupon decided to set up a printselling business next door, with a younger brother Robert as apprentice, and a financial partner called Parker. William was now twenty-seven, and had a fair name in the trade. But the partnership was a mistake, and the printshop a financial failure; so that when, three years later, poor Robert fell sick and died, "his soul rose up to heaven clapping its hands for joy"; and William, overcome, slept uninterruptedly for three days and three nights; after which he moved from the accursed Golden Square and established a workshop with Catherine in Lambeth.

During these years, Blake had seen something of the corruption of contemporary life; he had read diligently, and considered much; he had been fired with enthusiasm for the doctrines that were then making a new France and a new America. Towards his thirtieth year, he suddenly became an ardent revolutionary. At the house of his publisher, Johnson, behind St. Paul's Churchyard, Blake attended regular meetings of a small radical group which included among its members the great Dr. Priestley; Tom Paine (*The Rights of Man*); Mary Wollstonecraft (*The Rights of Woman*) and her fiancé Godwin. Of this group, Blake alone had the courage to sport in public the *bonnet rouge* of their political convictions. But only for a short time: for Blake soon learned to entertain as hearty a contempt for politics as he already had for Industrialism. He preferred to put his energies into his own designs, always, rather than into those of others. He continued to illustrate the works of other writers, but he spent more and more time, now, on the engraving and illuminating of his own poems, by a process of his own devising. *The Songs of Innocence* and *Experience* he had already issued in his Golden Square days. They were followed by the first group of his *Prophetic Books*, which chiefly occupied him from 1793 onwards; by a dozen colour prints, also made by an original process; and by a remarkable series of drawings, over five hundred in number, for Young's *Night Thoughts*. During his seven years in Lambeth, Blake made the fortunate acquaintance of Captain Butts, who bought several hundred pounds' worth of his works at a guinea or two apiece, and for several years kept him working at full pressure. It is worth noting that Blake's best work does not belong to this comparatively affluent period; for he became, in this time, a victim of a kind of patronage that encourages quantity at the expense of quality. It is not orders and payment that an artist needs, but leisure to work. Blake's next patron has not received what is due to him for providing just *that*. This patron was Hayley, whom Blake and his biographers alike appear to have treated with undue scorn.

Blake had been introduced by Flaxman to Hayley towards the end of the century. He was a rich, fussy, good-natured and well-meaning bore; and not more pompous than a man of his contemporary standing might justifiably be. He was an Etonian with a successful career at Trinity Hall and the Middle Temple behind him, and the offer of the poet laureate-ship (which he later chose to decline) before him, in his middle age. He was the owner of a "turretted marine cottage" near Bognor; he had a shrewd eye for spotting genius; and he gloried in the patron's rôle. In September, 1800, Blake and his wife readily accepted Hayley's cordial invitation to join him down at Felpham, on the Sussex coast. Blake needed the change of scene, Catherine needed the change of air, neither had hitherto travelled beyond the outskirts of London. Hayley needed a new specimen of genius to study; and wished Blake to illustrate his own poetical works. It seemed an admirable arrangement. But of course it was doomed to failure from the outset; for Blake and Hayley had the heartiest contempt for one another's verse, and each was embarrassed by a con-sciousness of the "patronage" that was about to be bestowed. Blake avoided Hayley as far as possible, and spent his time strolling along the shore, holding long conversations with Homer, Moses, Milton, and other uncommon visitors to English watering places, encountered *en route*. One day in the cottage garden he was disturbed, however, by a more corporeal visitant, in the shape of a Sergeant of Dragoons. This per-sonage, who had come in fresh from an hour at The Fox, stubbornly ignored both Blake's civil inquiry as to the purpose of his visit, and the polite request that he should go. Blake, with a most foolhardy courage, pinned this drunken trooper by the elbows and marched him down to the end of the road.

Sergeant Schofield immediately brought a charge against Blake of sedition and treason, a charge as serious at that time as it was false. It was well that the Duke of Richmond—an appreciative patron of Blake's, as well as a just and intelligent man—was on the bench; which indeed he did not leave for ten solid hours. Blake was acquitted; but the incident affected him considerably. He learned the pleasures of forgiveness: not only towards Schofield but towards Hayley, who had paid £100 for his defence and insisted, against doctor's orders, on attending the trial after being thrown by his horse. Blake returned at once, however, to London, and took a first-floor flat in South Molton Street.

The last period of Blake's life is in a double sense dark. It begins with the regrettable misfortune he suffered as a result of the piracy of his work by Cromek—the "nasty sneaking knave" of his well-known epigram. After commissioning a series of drawings, Cromek seized them before Blake could engrave them, and transferred the whole set to Schiavonetti, a popular engraver, who made of them elegant travesties. Cromek was guilty of an even more dastardly trick. He described some of Blake's unfinished works to the unwitting Stothard, so that they could be published in advance of the original designs and appear to convict Blake of plagiarism; with the result that Blake was alienated from one of his oldest friends. By the time Blake held his famous Exhibition he had many enemies. His "descriptive catalogue" to this, packed with pungent social- and art-criticism, was cruelly pilloried by Leigh Hunt in the *Examiner*. The general contempt and laughter which this venture of Blake's evoked seems to have driven him into retirement; for of his next ten years we know almost nothing.

His publisher had died in 1809, and he was obliged from that time onwards to print and publish his own works single-handed, or with the help of Catherine only. Nevertheless, by his sixtieth year, Blake had a small but staunch public. There ensued such a demand for his earlier works that he was able, in some cases, to more than quadruple his prices. Among his new friends were Cumberland, Linnell (his good angel), the amiable and credulous Varley (for whom he drew so many astonishing spooks), Tatham (his Judas, the iconoclast who destroyed his legacy of Blake's posthumous works, for mis-guided "religious" reasons), and Samuel Palmer (his only great disciple). In 1821 Mr. and Mrs. Blake moved to Fountain Court, Strand, to another first-floor flat. Here Crabbe Robin-son met them, as he has described in his diary.

It was in these final years that Linnell saved Blake from penury by commissioning the *Dante* drawings which engaged him until the end; and simultaneously Blake finished the engraving of his magnificent *Job* designs. And as an instance of his thoroughness, it is worth recording that, dissatisfied with Carey's translation, anxious to penetrate Dante for himself, Blake at the age of sixty-seven began to teach himself Italian. At sixty-nine, working in his back bedroom in the evening of Sunday the 12th August, 1827, he died quite quietly of gallstone colic. His mortal remains lie buried with those of seven paupers in Bunhill Fields.

Here we have the baldest summary, merely, of the main events of Blake's life. Every new contact, every fresh face or place, has added its quota to his experience, and etched some definite mark upon his work. It remains to relate the life to the man, and the man to the work.

Of William Blake himself we know something from con-temporary portraits. We can picture him in his prime as a well-proportioned figure, five-and-a-half feet in height, with an open countenance, large serene eyes, a stubby nose with clenched nostrils, a strong jaw, a fine domed forehead, and leonine hair. We see him rising at daylight, lighting the fire, before Mrs. Blake is awake, and boiling the breakfast kettle.

We see him at work, Dürer's *Melancholia* above his table, in the crowded bed-sitting-room-workshop-kitchen which he never left, at one period, for two years; except to go out at noon, in his tight black suit and wide-awake hat, to draw his daily pint of porter. We have it from witnesses as reliable as Crabbe Robinson and Lady Charlotte Bury that he was a pleasant sociable fellow, a picture in his eye, a joke up his sleeve, a song in his pocket; a witty and intelligent controversialist with unexceptionable manners, though too independent and outspoken to be a social success in any ordinary company for long. But always we see him working, incessantly, "like one possessed"—as of course he was.

So we have the narrow, humdrum, eighteenth century lower-middle-class life, and the sane, sober, orderly energetic man, on the one hand; and on the other hand we have his very odd and powerful work. The disparity between an artist and his art is often startling: how are we to account for it in the case of Blake?

Among the possible ways of approach to this kind of problem are two that have become in our time very fashionable. There is the psychological approach, which would seek to explain Blake as a victim of his own neuroses. And there is the sociological approach, which would seek to explain him as a victim of his environment. Each of these approaches, had we the space to pursue them, might tell us much that the other would not; and yet still leave something vital unexplained.

Probably it is in general doing a disservice to an artist to abstract him from his timeless achievement and restore him to his accidental environment. Yet his art is shaped and conditioned, necessarily, by the time-place, race-class machinery through which it passed. The further we push inquiry, indeed, the more plainly we see that almost everything in Blake's work is accounted for in his experience. We must realize, of course, that he was blessed from the outset with some queer visionary gift. He was born an exceptional individual, and that gives his art its exceptional quality. But if only to throw into relief this exceptional, timeless, visionary element in his work, it will be useful to form a picture of Blake in relation to his background. Blake does not strike one at first sight, it is true, as a characteristic flower of eighteenth century English culture. It is difficult to realize that he was contemporaneous with Coleridge and Wordsworth, with Gainsborough and Reynolds. Yet his work, we could show, springs direct from the same soil and climate. He is peculiarly English himself, notably in his humour and independence. A Spanish or Hindu Blake is inconceivable; and his gaiety has little in common with that of the Frenchman or the Japanese. His most mature art looks anything but English: such a work as "Death on the Pale Horse" might be Sassanian; and some of his verse might easily have arrived from "an island in the Moon". But if we trace the evolution of these works from their early origins, we see their inevitability. Blake saw little, absorbed it all, and transmuted it with his strong personality. Paul Berger has shown how he borrowed and transformed his early literary models: a similar evolution may be traced in his pictorial designs. We see clusters of pale female nudes emerging, like forced celery, from the Medici Venus he courted so assiduously in his youth. His early drawings are like Flaxman's, as his early poems resemble Collins's; and the "classical features" persist. We see him dreaming into fresh and personal shapes images derived from his limited but intensive reading; stealing the majestic glooms of Milton or the electrical thunders of Michelangelo, and making of them a strange mythology of his own.

"I must create my own system," he said, "or else be enslaved to another man's." And he insisted on being independent. His system he improvised, like his techniques, out of material to hand. He is always too personal to be content to imitate; so that he is no use at copying, at burlesque or parody; though as a satirist, when he is actuated by strong passion, he can be brilliant. The slight paranoia resulting from his realization that he was not quite as other men ("O why was I born with a different face?") gave him that curious clairvoyant detachment that, when associated with a powerful intellect, often turns the persecuted man into a penetrating critic of his contemporaries. And the social criticism of Blake, which space does not permit us to examine here, must take rank among his most useful achievements. He seems not to have been distressed by his own economic limitations, but he was angry that others should be subject to artificial restraint in his time, the beginning of the age of plenty. His own life was not, as it happened, one of grinding poverty. He was not obscure and seldom in serious want. He might have chosen fame and wealth, but he preferred to keep his individuality and integrity intact. His life might have been different if he had agreed to lend his talents to the decoration of the Court. But he refused a handsome retaining fee offered by the Duke of Richmond for a "painter in ordinary", or society miniaturist. And in order to evade tactfully a proposal that he should teach drawing to the Royal children, he diplomatically dismissed all his own pupils. (This, perhaps, was as well, for when George III was shown some of Blake's work later on: "Take 'em away! take 'em away!" cried he, in horror.) Blake refused to kowtow to any man. "My business is not to gather gold," he said, "but to make glorious shapes." It seems possible, however, that Blake was here rationalizing the inevitable, for we know that he did in fact try to justify many of his characteristics—defects (technical incapacity, e.g.,) as well as qualities. He realized that he must live with his deficiencies, and so erected them into proud virtues. The economic necessity that denied him a liberal education, and forced him to improvise his own system while making a bare living, certainly mothered his most interesting inventions. In some respects he resembles the type of the crank inventor rather than the typical poet or mystic. There was nothing of the fool, or prig, or dilettante, or milksop or masochist or madman about Blake. Only his imagination was abnormal. He was essentially an artist and a moralist, divorced by uneducation from the traditions—religious, literary and plastic—which he in consequence treated with open derision and a good deal of secret respect. He despised the priesthood, but insisted at the last on a Church of England burial. He poured scorn on asceticism ("the vilest blasphemy against the whole human race"), on chastity and, equally, on marriage; yet himself led a temperate, frugal and exemplary married life. He found his "spiritual life" quite rich enough without dunning his physical existence for its debts: he could afford to be charitable to the flesh.

This full-blooded belief in the *body*—as exemplified by his anthropomorphism, his partiality for "the human form divine", vivid personification of all abstractions, in his poems and designs—distinguishes Blake from the oriental artist-mystic type, from the far-eastern Zen or Taoist monks, and equally from unstable semi-oriental "visionaries" like the epileptic Dostoievski or the flesh-mortifying ex-*roué* Tolstoy. Blake's oft-reiterated moral exhortations (e.g., "the road of excess leads to the palace of wisdom") actually represent little more than an extension of the "hard wiry bounding-line" and "minute particulars" of his busy burin: he preached chiefly what he had learned, as an engraver, to practise. Much ingenuity has been expended in attempts to decipher the supposed "system" and "message" of the Prophetic Books which, with all the vivid objectification and meaningless incoherence of a serial dream, appear to dramatise in epic form the conflict within himself between imaginative freedom and repressive convention. Blake's confused and obscure metaphysic, derived mainly from his mixed reading but made to inform a mythology largely his own, would be of little value had it not crystallized out into magnificent visual images. Blake believed in an English race-myth: that our *paideuma*, which we should one day realize and erect into a new Jerusalem, was a heritage of the days of Albion, when the heroes of the Old Testament were Druids, a race of Stonehenge-makers.

But the *Prophetic Books* were a bag into which Blake stuffed any phantom that happened to come along. For Blake's "visions" of course sprang directly from his experience. It was his mother who put the angels and prophets in his head, before he could toddle. Hearsay and reading peopled his brain with the innumerable spooks he came to live with on such familiar terms. The practice of drawing enabled him to invest them with a peculiarly precise formal definition, so that it is quite likely that on occasion he confused the vision of his mind's eye with that of his corporeal eye. He had the gift of dreaming, with a nightmarish intensity, by broad daylight: and when, as sometimes happened, this faculty failed, so too did his work. But he was never haunted by ghosts alien to his own quotidian experience. He hob-nobbed with Welsh bards and Surrey fairies, respectable classical poets and biblical personalities; it is noteworthy that he never became acquainted with the immortals of China or Peru. Yet it would be unwise to take too materialistic a view of Blake's visions; for that he had some occult faculty is evident from his substantiated prophecies—as for example when he correctly foretold the death by hanging of Ryland, a young painter years afterwards so sentenced for forgery. Blake's visions, however, whatever their source, were invariably worked up by conscious art and given a formal validity. Even in its most turgid strata, his work is never vague, or suggestive of "automatic" scribbling. There is no pretence of snapshotting (like Dali and other *surréalistes* to-day) an affected "unconscious" vision. His images are manipulated into *designs*; and his best verse is that on which he quite evidently spent some technical care. And although he realized that conscious care might at any moment kill the visionary cat—that "the tigers of wrath are stronger than the horses of instruction", that "Prudence is a rich ugly old maid courted by Incapacity" etc.—his writing is always primed with the dynamic verb, the plastic image.

Perhaps the very precision of his dreaming guaranteed that. It is in these triumphant fragmentary statements of his vision that the "eternal" values in Blake's achievement are to be sought: statements too intensely personal ever to tempt the vulgarizer and traducer. As artist Blake has probably been without imitators, unless we count his contemporary disciples Calvert and Samuel Palmer. Yet it is perhaps a measure of its durability that the weakest point of his work—his "mysticism"—has exerted the greatest influence. Romantic, parasitic and propagandist minds thrive on the undecipherable bulk of his work, finding in it a reflection of whatever they seek. But William Blake was not only a great visionary: he was a great wag. So that he may well have had a vision of Posterity in his eye when, with a chuckle, he described himself, once, as a Book "published elsewhere—and beautifully bound. . . ."

34

JOHN HUNTER

(1728-1793)

by CHARLES SINGER

JOHN HUNTER was, beyond all cavil, the greatest British figure of the eighteenth century in the medical and biological sciences. As with most men of distinction in these departments, his life was not very eventful, so far as worldly relations are concerned. From early years his entire energies were, to the limit of his powers, uninterruptedly directed towards scientific ends. His life was his science and his science was his life. Nevertheless his achievement can by no means be appreciated unless the general outline of his career, the background of the contemporary practice of medicine, the conditions of the advancement of science in his day, and, perhaps above all, the limitations and handicaps of the man be in some measure understood.

§ 1. *His Life*

John Hunter was born near Glasgow in the year 1728. He was youngest of the ten children of a small landed proprietor with intellectual interests and wise ambitions for his family. As child and youth, John was backward, unruly, unteachable

and rough, but fond of country pursuits, observant of nature
and never accounted dull. At eighteen he was sent to assist
a relative who dealt in timber at Glasgow. Soon however he
persuaded his brother William to take him as his anatomical
assistant in London (1748).

William Hunter (1718-83) was a highly accomplished,
courtly and successful physician—in character the very
antithesis of his abrupt, passionate, ill-educated brother. He
had opened a private medical school where he lectured on
anatomy and other departments of medicine. Here John
immediately exhibited the highest order of skill as a dissector
and rapidly became a most proficient anatomist. He "walked"
various hospitals, had some foreign experience as a surgeon
in the army, and in 1763, at the age of thirty-five, settled in
London and began the career of a surgeon there.

John Hunter's immense application, his genius for experiment and observation, his open-mindedness, his boundless
curiosity, rapidly led his scientific interests far beyond the
practice of anatomy or even its application to surgery. The
whole range of living phenomena became his field of investigation. He realized that he was ahead of his time and he was
under no illusion as to the importance and significance of his
task. He slept habitually only four or five hours, and all his
leisure and all his spare funds were, till the end, devoted to
scientific studies. No trouble was too great for him if he
wished to obtain a rare animal or to perform a difficult experiment. Hasty and even overbearing in personal relations, in
all that related to research he was patient and persistent in the
extreme.

In 1767 he was elected a Fellow of the Royal Society.
About the same time he was elected surgeon to St. George's
Hospital, a position of profit and distinction. He became
known as a distinguished exponent of surgery and his lectures
on the subject, given in his own house, were attended by a

small band which included most of the abler young men working on his line.

In 1770 John Hunter married a beautiful, gay and very
gifted woman with whom he always lived happily, though it
is difficult to see what the two can have had in common. Soon
after, he built a house at Earl's Court—then quite in the
country though now absorbed into London—where he
arranged menageries for his animals and laboratories for his
experiments. From now on most of his time and all his means
were employed in amassing and arranging his museum, which
remains his chief memorial.

Hunter became very successful in practice which took far
more of his time than he would have wished. Nevertheless he
showed no abatement of his scientific zeal. For money and
honours he cared nothing at all, except in so far as they
aided his scientific ends. From 1773 his health began to fail.
In general a man's medical record is neither a significant nor
an attractive part of his biography but the long, painful and
final illness of John Hunter is important as revealing the
character of the man and as affecting his work.

Hunter had always taken a deep interest in the venereal
diseases. He believed, quite wrongly, that they were all merely
varieties of infection by the same virus. In 1767 he inoculated
himself with some discharge from a venereal lesion which
he believed not to be of the 'variety' known as syphilis. Nevertheless he developed syphilis and was treated for it—inadequately as the event showed. He concluded, wrongly
as we now know, that his experiment proved the essential
identity of syphilis with other venereal diseases.

Twenty years of ill health followed. His sufferings were the
sequelae of this inoculation with syphilis, though the state of
knowledge in his day did not enable him to recognize the fact.
The same disease was the cause of his death in 1793. As a
crowning tragedy his children were recipients of this *damnosa*

hereditas. Only two survived childhood; both were inadequate and both died young and childless. Hunter and his children are truly among the martyrs of science.

But this is not the end of the tragedy. Hunter had a brother-in-law, one Everard Home (1756-1832), who was in turn his pupil, his assistant, his successor and his executor. Home was an extremely successful practitioner who received the honour of a baronetcy and became surgeon to the King. After Hunter's death, this Home appropriated much of his work, publishing it in his own name and earning thereby great distinction. The charge against the wretched man is now abundantly proved, but yet worse was to follow. In 1800, just before Hunter's collection was delivered to the College of Surgeons, Home had many of Hunter's manuscripts conveyed to his own house, and there, after having long refused to give them up, he ultimately burned them, falsely alleging that Hunter requested him to do this on his death-bed. For this wicked act—the motive of which was to cover his robbery of a dead man's work—the memory of Home will be execrated as long as that of Hunter remains upon men's tongues.

Perhaps no great man of science is quite so refractory to literary treatment as Hunter. His education was defective and he was confessedly ignorant of much of the work of his contemporaries in his own chosen fields. He was completely lacking in oratorical graces and could not put outside himself the thoughts surging in his mind. Nor could he even use with facility a plain or blunt style for, while devoid of literary taste and skill, he was at the same time often at the mercy of words and phrases the meaning of which he but half divined. On many important points we can reach his meaning only by piecing together hints and notes and sometimes we can get no clear meaning from him at all. While the most systematic of men in his work, in his writings he was disorderly and devoid of any obvious method.

These were his limitations. They are very great limitations—and they must ever be in mind in considering him. But the greatness of Hunter lies in his work and not in what he says about it. By his work, and by his work alone, should after ages judge him.

§ 2. *His Setting*

The intellectual setting of Hunter is, on the whole, depressing. The eighteenth century had dawned with the refreshing breeze of the Newtonian philosophy blowing through it. During the previous two hundred years an immense amount of fruitful knowledge had been garnered in diverse fields. Human anatomy had been put on an exact basis. Chemistry and Mechanics, Botany and Comparative Anatomy, Experimental Physiology, Epidemiology, and Microscopic Analysis had all yielded startling results. But men were bewildered with the very mass and novelty of the material. The biologists of the time, contemplating with envy the beauty and symmetry of the mathematical relations that Newton and his followers had introduced into cosmic conceptions, lost all hope of reducing their own vast accumulations to order. There was thus a halt in the advance of the biological sciences, though this was hidden from contemporaries by the endless mechanical systematization of species of living things carried on under the name of Linnæus.

Nor was the teaching of science in better case than its advancement. Of the institutions of the eighteenth century few can present a spectacle less edifying than the ancient English universities. Their great endowments were expended by their professors and fellows either in bombastic celebration of the rites of their order or were sheerly misappropriated. Cambridge, where Newton had been reared, Oxford, the nurse of the Royal Society, provided no longer any scientific teaching worthy of the name. At both seats of learning mere place-hunters masqueraded as professors of medicine. Nearly all the scientific physicians and surgeons of the day came from across the border, trained at Edinburgh or Glasgow. The only great English physiologist fit to name after the great Harvey (1578-1657), discoverer of the circulation of the blood, was parson Hales (1677-1761) who left Cambridge and became for fifty-three years "perpetual curate" of Teddington, where his experiments were performed in the intervals of his pastoral duties.

Medical teaching, almost entirely neglected at the universities, was inadequately carried on in London. Surgical lectures were given at several of the London hospitals and notably at St. George's where John Hunter was attached. The practice of these hospitals was especially open to apprentices or pupils articled, for a sum of money, to members of the staff. These young men occupied a position somewhat analogous to that of house-surgeons in our own day. Hunter, like other surgeons of his time, had a number of articled pupils who resided in his house. Of these, the most famous was Edward Jenner (1749-1823) the introducer of vaccination.

So far as the advancement of knowledge was concerned, the London hospitals were almost as supine and indifferent as the universities. As a rule the ancillary sciences, Materia Medica or the study of the nature and action of drugs, Chemistry and Anatomy were left to private effort. They were taught by lectures and demonstrations at schools supported by the private enterprise of a small band of far-sighted medical men.

The neglect of science by the English universities and hospitals was in part made good by the meetings of the Royal Society. In its *Philosophical Transactions* appeared more than a dozen of contributions by Hunter—some of them of great importance. But, so far as Natural History was concerned, the Royal Society was under the blighting influence of the Linnæan systematists and its meetings were far too formal to be suited for the conveyance of the type of idea and of experience that made the greatest appeal to Hunter. In 1762 he joined a few colleagues in founding a "Society for the Improvement of Medical Knowledge" which met in a coffee-house and provided him with a suitable exchange for information on medical topics. In later years, when he had risen to affluence, his own museum and country house provided a centre for men of science.

Many medical men in eighteenth century England lived in great state but such things, of themselves, made no appeal to Hunter's nature. Science was his sole aim. Some idea of the spacious scale of his scientific methods may, however, be gained by an enumeration of his household. This in his later years never fell below fifty persons. The list was made up somewhat as follows:—

Family 5.
Articled pupils 5.
Personal servants 11.
Museum and scientific assistants 4.
Gardeners and attendants at Earl's Court 6.
Female servants at Earl's Court 4.
Scientific assistants at Earl's Court 3.
Mechanics 9.
Printers 3.

This community appears to have worked amicably and smoothly, its activities being directed to one constant end, the advancement of science. The even functioning of such a body itself speaks for its head's capacity. Its support naturally demanded the entire income of a successful surgeon.

JOHN HUNTER

§ 3. *His Achievement*

Hunter's greatest achievement is undoubtedly his wonderful museum. For this he maintained his assistants and draftsmen, his mechanics and secretaries, his gardeners and animal keepers. He even set up his own printing-press and acted as his own publisher. He performed an enormous number of physiological experiments, kept his own menagerie, and never missed an opportunity of securing the body of a rare beast for dissection. He was interested in fossil no less than living forms, in physiology as much as in anatomy. His energy in the pursuit of science became at times feverish, for he was ever fearful that he would die with his museum and his papers in disorder—a presage which was, in fact, justified by the event.

A spirit informs the Hunterian Museum which is as different as can be from the "magpie instinct" which has been the motive of many great collections. His aim was not to accumulate and complete but to illustrate and illuminate. Every object in the Hunterian collection had its place and there was a reason for its inclusion. Hunter had anatomized over 500 species of animals—many a great number of times—as well as numerous species of plants. He designed to trace systematically the different phases of life as exhibited by the organs, the structure, and the activities both of animals and of plants.

Many of the biological observations which occupied Hunter appeared in the *Philosophical Transactions* or in the four volumes which he produced, but far more were buried in his written notebooks. Of these some survive, though cart loads were burned by the accursed Home. It is difficult to set any limits to the range of Hunter's studies. Some, as we have seen, were published by Home. Hunter was interested in monstrosities, and was the founder of their experimental investigation. He

487

was a pioneer in the investigation of the early development of animals or "Embryology" as it is now called. Animal behaviour attracted him, and he investigated, for example, that of bees with much care. He made experiments on the temperature both of plants and of animals. Anything related to animal mechanism particularly appealed to him, and his researches on the air-spaces of birds—a condition of their power of flight —on the electric organs of fish, and on the structure of whales and sea-cows added greatly to knowledge.

But Hunter did more than found the modern conception of a museum and more than contribute to the knowledge of the phenomena of life. He modified our way of thinking about life, and to this extent he was a philosopher, though he was as far from being a philosopher in any formal sense of that word as it is possible for any man to be.

Hunter's older contemporary, Linnæus (1707-78) and his younger contemporary, Cuvier (1769-1832), who between them set the biological tone for over a century, used their knowledge of comparative anatomy as a guide to the classification and arrangement of living things. These were not Hunter's ways. He was ever seeking the more general principles that underlie similarities or dissimilarities of structure. The most general principle of all, the principle from which the science of *Biology* takes its name, is that mysterious thing called life. Hunter came no nearer to answering the question "What is life?" than later biologists. In the course of his search, however, he reached some important conclusions.

Hunter considered that, whatever life may be, it is something held most tenaciously by the least organized beings, and is something that is independent of structure. These ideas lead to the conception of *protoplasm*, the substance, simple in appearance, inconceivably complex in fact, which seems the inseparable material factor without which life is never found. Hunter did not use the word protoplasm, which was invented fifty years after his death, but he was reaching out to this conception.

Life is normally exhibited, according to Hunter, in the various activities of living things, and notably in the power of healing, repair and renovation—a matter in which his surgical experience was of special value. This power of repair is quite peculiar to living things and cannot be paralleled in the non-living world. Nevertheless Hunter thought that vital activity can be suspended—as for instance, in the seed or in the egg. He was thus led to investigate what he considered the simplest forms of life. In doing so, he discovered what was from his point of view "a latent heat of life," set free at death. Thus he found that sap removed from a tree congeals at freezing-point, but that the living tree itself may be reduced far below freezing-point before the sap loses viscous or liquid quality.

The suggestion was interesting, though the phenomena, as we now know, are susceptible of other explanations. He made similar experiments on other forms of life to illustrate the same point. He also came to regard the heat given off by germinating seeds as evidence of something of the nature of a "latent heat of life."

Hunter's work as a surgeon is of the very highest importance but peculiarly difficult to summarize for those untrained in medical matters. He cannot be said to have introduced any great new principle into surgery, but there can be no doubt that he did introduce a new spirit. With him surgery became, at last, a real science based on certain general principles drawn from his own wealth of biological knowledge. It ceased to be a mere applied art or craft. Hunter constantly brought to bear on the theme of operative surgery a host of ideas derived from comparative studies of anatomy, pathology and physiology in a large variety of living forms. In all such comparisons he was quick to detect analogy, shrewd in his scientific judgments, tireless and unsparing of himself.

So far as actual surgical advances are concerned, that most commonly connected with Hunter's name is in the treatment of the deadly condition known as "Aneurysm", for which he introduced a method of operation which is still in vogue. It depends for its efficacy on a series of observations which he made on the effects of the ligature of arteries. When certain major vessels are tied, the circulation of the parts which they supply can be maintained by the enlargement of smaller vessels, the so-called "collateral circulation". In connection with the establishment of collateral circulation, the surgeons of our day still speak of him and they also attach his name to certain anatomical structures, but for most of them his real monument is the Hunterian Museum in London, based on his specimens, many of which may still be seen there. The museums of Natural History as well as Medical museums, as now constituted in all civilized countries, have been influenced by, if they have not been derived from, that which he literally gave his life's blood to found. He was right when he said musingly in his illness: "You will not easily find another John Hunter."

The history of Hunter's museum is something of a romance. He willed that on his death his collections should be offered to the British Government for purchase at a low price. The Prime Minister, the younger Pitt, on being approached, answered: "What! buy preparations! Why, I have not money enough to buy gunpowder!" Fortunately an old servant was more generous. He devoted himself to these despised preparations, though he had only seven shillings a week on which to live and to buy spirit to keep the specimens in condition. It was not the specimens which suffered! The price of bread rose enormously owing to the war, but this zealous man never relaxed his ward. Hunter died in 1793. In 1795 the Government decided to reconsider the matter. The guardian of the collection was almost starving, but he still held on.

In 1799, having taken six years to make up its mind, the Government bought the collection and handed it over to the Royal College of Surgeons of London. Hunter's old servant was appointed curator. At the end of his long and hungry vigil, the specimens were in a better state than on his master's death. His name was William Clift (1775-1849). This admirable man made no important discovery but he has an honoured place in the history of science.

The daughter of the faithful Clift married Richard Owen (1804-92), the first director of the Natural History Museum in London which was designed by him, and was opened to the public in 1881 after thirty years of effort and agitation. Owen was a devoted admirer of Hunter whose tradition he received from Clift and whose spirit still lives in our great national foundation for the study of Natural History as well as in the Hunterian Museum itself.

35

JAMES WYATT

(1746-1813)

by JOHN SUMMERSON

"IF Wyatt can get near a large fire and have a bottle by him, he cares for nothing else". This was William Beckford's comment when his architect had been more than usually exasperating. It was not altogether unjust; fondness for wine, still more for women, and a fatal inability to consult anyone's inclinations but his own, seriously interfered with James Wyatt's professional competence. Yet he was supremely successful; and, in his flighty, spasmodic, off-hand way, a brilliant designer.

But brilliant as he was, he came very near to being spoiled by the stupidities of his age and a corresponding streak of stupidity in himself. At twenty he won success of a kind which men three times his age might envy and for the rest of his life he was the victim of this precocious triumph. His later career is a curious study in the cumulative effects of flattery. Men told him he was a genius, and if he had the intelligence to know this was untrue, he lacked the self-respect or the courage to undeceive them. By indulging every erratic and irresponsible trait in his character he merely established the legend of genius more firmly; he deceived his age and almost deceived himself.

JAMES WYATT

The building which carried young Wyatt headlong to fame was the Pantheon, in Oxford Street, an expensive setting for the routs and masquerades of London society at its most brilliant. The building was begun in 1770, which was four years after the return of its architect from Venice, where a pupil of Canaletto's had been training him to paint and design. Humbly born, Wyatt owed this Venetian background to noble patronage, while friendship with the King's librarian helped him still further to opportunity and recognition.

Wyatt's drawings triumphed easily in the Pantheon contest and when the building was finished, two years later, it took the town by storm. Few buildings before or since have so captivated the intelligentsia of their time, and it is a sad pity that although the façade towards Oxford Street survives, as part of a famous distiller's head offices, even this last shred of splendour is soon to depart.

The Pantheon was designed as "a winter Ranelagh". There were several different rooms but its principal glory was a domed church-like hall with double-storied aisles and rounded ends. The shape was so very like a compressed version of Santa Sophia, Constantinople that it is hard to believe that Wyatt did not consciously imitate it, although Justinian's church was neither well-known nor admired in his time. No interior so gorgeous had been built in London since Wren finished St. Paul's, and Wyatt, whose timber-framed dome involved no statical difficulties, avoided Wren's mistakes and produced what Walpole enthusiastically called "the most beautiful edifice in England".

The Byzantine body, mantled in rich but not too sugary Adam detail, must have been superbly glamorous, and the artificial lighting played up well to the architecture. There were figure paintings in chiaroscuro which the flicker of candle-light quickened into glimpses of Valhalla; friezes and niches were accented with green and purple lamps and the dome floated in a seductive heathen twilight, reflected from gilt vases. To a Georgian mind here was the Roman Pantheon vividly recreated, with all its pagan glamour still about it.

No wonder that after this triumphant beginning Wyatt's house was besieged by those of the nobility who found patronage of the arts an effective and agreeable passport to social esteem. Catherine of Russia, always ready to fortify the prestige of St. Petersburg with foreign talent, put forward a generous offer of employment, which might have been accepted had not a group of English noblemen defeated her by tactful warnings backed with a joint retaining fee of £1,200 a year. Wyatt was soon the first country-house architect in the land. Even the Adam brothers, to their considerable mortification, were put in the shade.

It is difficult to say how soon after this Wyatt became afflicted with the chronic boredom and impatience which lends such a sensational air to his later activities. No doubt he was always prone to it, but it seems to have been after his capitulation to the charms of Gothic that it really took hold of him. There is a vast difference between the practice of an art which has a technical code of acknowledged universality, and one in which the only criterion is the taste of a literary clique; especially when the artist is as dependent upon current ideas and accepted values as was James Wyatt. Had he been obliged to develop along the lines laid down in the Pantheon his interests would have been disciplined. Careless composition and insensitive modelling can never be mistaken for originality in classical design. But in romantic improvisations on literary themes they can, and it was this sort of thing which occupied Wyatt, making him fashionable and admired in his life and despised and ridiculed almost ever since.

The first Gothic venture was Lee Priory in Kent (now rebuilt in Victorian brick). The client was a friend of Walpole's and the creator of Strawberry Hill had a finger in the business from the start. Gothic ruins and castellated houses were, of course, nothing new. It was already thirty years since Strawberry had suffered its first metamorphosis and there was plenty of Gothic-Rococo decoration up and down the country. But at Lee, Wyatt went one better than any previous Gothic designer by combining a really substantial and alluring deception which was at the same time no mere landscape feature, but a habitable house. Instead of being an obviously modern building with Gothic enrichments, Lee posed successfully as an Abbatial relic converted for the purposes of the eighteenth century. "The three fronts of the house," wrote a contemporary topographer, "convey an idea of a small convent never attempted to be demolished, but partly modernized and adapted to the habitation of a gentleman's family." Walpole was delighted, thought Lee prettier even than Strawberry and considered Wyatt to have more taste than anybody in the whole world.

Judged by any other standards than those vaguely antiquarian ones affected by the Walpole set, Lee was a stupid house. It consisted mainly of a symmetrical block with a square tower in the middle, rather like part of an Oxford College, while by the side of this was a sort of church with a central tower and lead spire. As a composition it was clumsy. As an archæological essay it was ignorant, even for its time. But it did impinge deliciously on the sensibilities of an age to which Gothic architecture was mysterious and irrational.

The success of Lee and the applause of Walpole established Wyatt as the captain of the Gothic movement, the master whose genius had recreated medievalism and raised it to an academic level. Commissions poured in and there is scarcely a diary or memoir of the period in which his name is not to be found. As each successive work brought its meed of adulation his confidence mounted till the ultimate personal triumph

495

came with the patronage and friendship of the King and his family.

King George III liked professional men so long as they were neither servile nor facetious and Wyatt knew exactly how to please. He was a good-humoured, gregarious person, at ease in any company which did not bore him and never short of small-talk. He was probably the kind of artist who in these days finds it easy to cultivate the airs of a stock-broker or a retired major, and the heavy countenance and slightly prominent brown eyes shown in his portrait suggest a not unattractive mixture of wisdom and sensuality. Long before the King took him up he was a great favourite with the Queen and her two bustling daughters. He built them a set of ruins at Frogmore, decorated the Queen's parties and helped Princess Elizabeth with her hand-painted hermitage.

The King, who was rather frightened of his old architect, Sir William Chambers, found Wyatt's geniality a relief, so that in spite of ugly stories put about, quite unscrupulously, by a noble partisan of the Adams, the Queen's architect soon became the King's friend and had been promised the reversion of Chambers's appointment as Surveyor General. Indeed, the King went so far as to put off some rebuilding at Windsor till Wyatt should have stepped into Chambers's office, which he did on the latter's death in 1796.

In this year Wyatt was fifty. The stimulus of unreaped honours was spent and side by side with his reputation as a man of infinite taste and Gothic genius, there were devastating rumours of his inordinate pride, his high-handedness, and his laziness. His gauche handling of the cathedrals which came under his control embroiled him in bitter contests with the antiquaries. They gasped with horror at his proposed demolition of the Galilee at Durham, while even Walpole was shocked at his merciless destruction of the chantries at Salisbury. When he was proposed as a member of the Society of

Antiquaries, eleven members black-balled him. Nevertheless, a genius the world at large still thought him and so when William Beckford, wealthiest and most fastidious of amateurs, decided to turn into actuality the architecture which haunted his turgid, reminiscent day-dreams it was natural enough that he should employ Wyatt as his executive.

Beckford had known Wyatt for some years, but it would be hard to imagine two men less suited to fill the complementary rolls of client and architect. Both, in different ways, were eccentric and resentful of discipline and responsibility; Wyatt out of boredom and the indifference bred of too facile success, Beckford out of a delicate and self-torturing pride.

Beckford's personality was complex. An only son, he was brought up by a too devoted mother amid the grandiose but fading regalia of his dead father. At an early age architecture entered into his imaginative life. The horror and mystery of long-neglected structures, the fascination of gigantic height and extent were aspects of architecture which became absorbing to him and he invested the domain of Fonthill with a dream world, haunted by the giaours and goblins of oriental romance. Along with his partiality for the grotesque, Beckford had a keen sense of the position in which his immense inherited fortune placed him. He was aware of the loneliness as well as the opportunities which wealth affords. When he was twenty-two, he wrote *Vathek*; in it is displayed the futility of auto-cratic self-indulgence and in the person of the Caliph Beckford crucifies a reflection of himself. In *Vathek*, too, we find his romantic preoccupation with colossal architecture and he tells us himself that the "Halls of Eblis" are the Halls of Fonthill House transposed into an oriental key.

Beckford belonged to a type not unfamiliar to the student of biography. His self-indulgence, his pride, his love of scholarship, his self-criticism and his anxiety to separate himself from his fellow-creatures and their mode of life, belong to a configuration which is recognizable and consistent. His sexual proclivities, too, which made him something of a monster in the eyes of his contemporaries, fall into place in the psychological picture. Beckford was one of those people to whom unhappiness is essential; wealth was his enemy because it beckoned him to worldly honours, easy success and the dreamless routine life of the man of affairs. He revenged himself upon his fortune by extravagant intellectual self-indulgence and soothed a smarting conscience with the balm of a deepening unhappiness.

It was in 1796, the year of Wyatt's accession to the Surveyorship, that Beckford decided to rebuild Fonthill. He had just come back from his second long sojourn in Portugal, and had already been in correspondence with his architect about a ruined chapel he wanted to build on an eminence within sight of the old house. Returned to England his ideas broadened; his mind was full of the extravagance of Portuguese Gothic and of the baroque-medieval life of eighteenth century Lisbon. He would build in Wiltshire something as proud as Batalha; as richly appointed as Alcobaça; there he would live, half anchorite, half caliph, in defiance of the society which envied and loathed him and which he in turn despised.

So Fonthill "Abbey" was begun. Wyatt's design was for a ruined monastery, with a habitable suite of rooms intact among the "debris", and this he started to build rapidly in wood and plaster. But Beckford's ideas were still fluid; the models and drawings grew in size and number till nothing would satisfy him but a complete masonry structure of such magnitude and splendour as to render the old, Palladian Fonthill, in its dank valley, a redundant hulk.

Wyatt followed every stage of his client's ambition with enthusiasm, for even he, the prince of English architects, had never been offered an opportunity so vast. The conception of this monstrous fantasy really absorbed him and the designs he produced were elaborately worked out and in their way as fully equal to the occasion as the glorious Pantheon of twenty-six years before.

But alas! Hard as it was to raise Wyatt's enthusiasm, it was even harder to maintain it, as Beckford soon learnt. In the first winter, the tower, too hastily constructed, fell. Beckford, calmly regretting that he had not witnessed the crash, gave orders for its rebuilding. Two years later the new tower collapsed in ruins. This time Beckford, smarting under the sneers of the press and the humiliating bathos of the situation, was roused. He demanded his architect's immediate presence, but Wyatt, who regarded an angry client as even more tiresome than a friendly one, would not come. Time after time he excused himself, pleading business at the Board of Works, and his obligations to the King. Finally, a really furious letter, in which Beckford threatened not merely to call off the workmen but to conduct a press campaign against his architect, brought Wyatt to his senses. A reconciliation was patched up and work at Fonthill proceeded at break-neck speed. Soon five hundred workmen were on the job and building never stopped. All night the masons worked by the light of lamps and torches.

This haste, with its Arabian Nights extravagance, had an object more immediate than to assuage the Caliph's thirst for realization. This was to provide a setting for the reception of Lord Nelson, Victor of the Nile, whose recent return to England had produced a wave of hero-worship. Nelson's visit to Fonthill was a great occasion. The medieval effects, the monkish attendants, the hidden choirs and the glamour of the final banquet fell nothing short of Beckford's sublime intentions. Among the many celebrities assembled was James Wyatt. But it would have been better had he stayed away for boredom overtook him and in the midst of the banquet he fell asleep.

In fits and starts, Wyatt drew Fonthill Abbey to something like completion. When he was in the mood everything went smoothly; when he was not, everything was held up by his prolonged neglect. At one period he was constantly being arrested for debt and Beckford, in order to keep things going, was obliged to bail him out. Even more wounding to Beckford's pride was the occasion when he found that in his absence from Fonthill, Wyatt, who was supposed to be in London, had been exploiting his hospitality on the sly for three days.

As long as it stood, Fonthill Abbey was the supreme monument not only of its architect but of the school of architectural medievalism which he initiated. But if it were standing to-day it would not be much admired, for few people can relish Gothic forms in the way that Beckford's generation did; to do so requires the same effort of sympathy as the enjoyment of the antiquarian prolusions in the *Waverley Novels*. In pictures and engravings, on the other hand, the romantic state of mind which Fonthill was designed to capture is far more easily accessible, for the artist side-tracks us from objective criticism, chooses our view points and manages the lighting. If we forget the sprawling gaucherie of the plan we can let ourselves be amused by the gigantic pile of thin gables and improbable turrets. We can be surprised by the sudden contrasts: the modest cloister, the jagged escarpment of roofs and battlements rising to the steeple, and the monstrous transept suggesting the forsaken beginnings of a too-ambitious cathedral.

It is amusing, but unimpressive; and if we feel emotion at the passing of this bogus masterpiece it has more to do with the tragedy of Beckford as a person than with the building as a work of imagination or as the fruit of Wyatt's wisdom and labours. That the building's ruin was brought about as the result of its architect's preposterous inattention is not surprising. Some years after Beckford had sold the place a dying clerk of works confessed that proper foundations had never been provided for the tower and it was not long before the truth of his statement was disastrously confirmed.

At the turn of the century, Wyatt's career had already passed its meridian. Indolent, spendthrift, autocratic and intolerant, the chief architect of Great Britain journeyed restlessly from house to house, never appearing where he was most needed or producing drawings of immediate urgency. His perversity knew no bounds. He would abruptly leave a dinner party to join his draughtsman, Dixon, in an all-night session of drawing and designing; but he would forget a whole calendar of pressing state appointments to immerse himself in the detailing of some lordly Gothic project which happened to have set his imagination alight.

Yet peers, bishops, statesmen, even the King himself, submitted to Wyatt's autocracy more humbly than Pope Innocent V to the sovereign genius of Bernini. The Bishop of Salisbury postponed a visit to the fleet for fear of missing him. William Windham waited ten years before the accumulated annoyance of unanswered letters and unfulfilled engagements drove him to calm, dignified retaliation and the rebuke that "the plea of this being your way and that you treat everyone else so, is really not sufficient to justify a mode of proceeding so remote from all that is expected and all that is observed by the rest of the world".

But Windham, like everyone else, believed in the Wyatt legend and was reluctant to suppose that Porden or Hopper or Nash or a dozen other practitioners of the younger school could design as well while serving their clients better.

In London the effects of Wyatt's irregularities were as far reaching. The Board of Works had to muddle along as best it could since its official head was never to be relied upon to attend a meeting and would be out of town for months on end.

At the Royal Academy, where he was elected President during a crisis which temporarily unseated West, they complained that he dozed during meetings and squandered the funds on entertaining.

When the buildings under his care did go forward they came near to ruining their owners. The works at Windsor and Frogmore and the cast iron palace at Kew were a constant drain on the Royal purse; yet their architect, who dined at the equerries' table whenever he came to court, was unassailable. Inefficiency, nepotism, outrageous rudeness, neglect of the King's personal commands, all were patiently borne as the eccentricities, the stigmata, as it were, of transcendent genius.

Had he lived ten years longer, the Wyatt legend must surely have collapsed. But just at the proper moment death intervened; suddenly, as he had always hoped it would. He was travelling with one of his clients; their carriage, going at a furious pace, clashed with a horseman and a standing vehicle; in the ghastly mêlée, Wyatt's neck was broken.

He had made confusion all his life and he left confusion behind him. His own splendid palace in Foley Place (where Broadcasting House stands to-day) was mortgaged to the utmost, and his unhappy wife was at her wits' end to find money to live. The faithful Dixon, who had served Wyatt since the Pantheon days, was £900 to the bad, Beckford and others a great deal more. His academic colleagues shook their heads; they had been jealous of his success and they were reluctant to honour his memory. Soane generously helped the widow. Farington noted dryly that Wyatt's love of women "led him away from other pursuits" and added that at his death one of his maids was within three weeks of her confinement. There was a general scramble for the salaries and sinecures suddenly vacated and Wyatt's innumerable architect sons and nephews came off with some of the spoils.

Wyatt was soon forgotten. The Prince Regent, who had

wept a little when he heard of the accident, hastened to set up John Nash in his stead. Soane, with his abstract vision and Smirke with his ponderous Ionic formula, soon outmoded Wyatt's classicism, which was seen to have been nothing but a genteel version of the Adam manner. As for his Gothic, its reputation sank lower and lower, till Pugin buried it securely under a heap of perfervid abuse.

Wyatt has never been restored to popularity or even respect. Yet he does not deserve this neglect; for if biographers can find little to interest them in this exemplar of irresponsibility, critics of Georgian architecture cannot afford to forget such fine designs as Heaton, Dodington and Castle Coole. Even some of the Gothic houses can still stir enthusiasm. The library and staircase at Ashridge are genuinely impressive, and Norris Castle, on the Solent, is impeccable in its simple massing and subtle irregularity.

But when Wyatt is remembered by the amateur of architecture it is still as "the destroyer" (Pugin's phrase) who ravaged the fabrics of Salisbury, Durham, Hereford and Lichfield, or as the architect who gave more trouble to his clients than any in the annals of the art.

He was an opportunist through and through. On his own admission, he despised the style in which his early success was won, but he never sought to set up a new standard. That his age accepted him as a man of genius was not his fault but that of his contemporaries. He was forced, not unwillingly, into the roll of society racketeer; with his charm, his ability, and his ambition he was well suited to it, but the spark of fine imagination which he undoubtedly possessed was very nearly smothered.

36

TOM PAINE

(1737-1809)

by Leonard Woolf

THOMAS PAINE, whom all the world knows as Tom Paine, was a very remarkable man and his life is of great significance in the history of mankind and of civilization. The subjects which I propose to deal with here are the individuality of the man and his significance in history, but in order to do this briefly and intelligently it is necessary first to set down certain bare facts with regard to his life which the reader must have in mind in order to understand what follows.

Tom Paine was born at Thetford in Norfolk on January 29th, 1737. His father was a poor man, a stay-maker and a Quaker; his mother, Frances Cocke, was the daughter of an attorney and was reputed to be a woman "of sour temper and an eccentric character". Tom Paine, therefore, came from a family hovering on the border-line between the lower middle class and the working class in a small country town in the first half of the eighteenth century. He was educated at the Thetford Grammar School until the age of thirteen. For the next five years he worked at stay-making with his father. Two incidents in his early youth already showed that he might not be content to live and die in the obscurity of stay-making and Thetford. At the age of seventeen he tried to sail under Captain Death in a privateer, the *Terrible*, but was brought back by his father. Two years later he made a second attempt to escape and this time succeeded, for he joined the privateer *King of Prussia*. His service at sea was short, for in 1757 he was working for a stay-maker in Long Acre, London. From 1757 to 1761 he pursued his trade at various places in Kent, and during those years he married and became a widower.

After his wife's death he became an exciseman and exercised that calling at various places until 1765, when he was dismissed by the Board of Excise, apparently for a not very serious irregularity. For the next two years he lived in the greatest poverty, and was at one time existing on a salary of £25 a year, which he earned by teaching English in a school. Early in 1768, however, he was taken back into the excise service and appointed to Lewes, in Sussex. He remained there for six years, and it was during this time that he first began to take an active part in politics: he became the leader of a movement among the excisemen to petition Parliament to raise their salaries and improve the conditions of service. It was probably this activity which was the indirect cause of his second dismissal for "having quitted his Business without obtaining the Board's Leave for so doing, and being gone off on Account of the Debts which he hath contracted".

The significance of these facts lies in this, that at the age of thirty-seven Tom Paine was unemployed, penniless, and completely obscure; he had probably never earned more than £50 a year at manual labour or the mean duties of an exciseman; and after thirty-seven years he was a complete failure. Yet he was undoubtedly a man of genius, of extraordinary intellectual power, energy, and practical ability. His education and his life so far had been those of the lower orders during the first half of the eighteenth century, and his experiences show how difficult it was for a child of those orders, whatever his powers and abilities, not to be defeated and submerged by his environment. There was nothing rare or strange in such experiences; for the last five hundred years of European history—to go back no further—the task of breaking out of the prison of class and environment has always been for the poverty-stricken, uneducated, manual worker all but impossible. The significant thing is that Paine did it, that he did it in a peculiar way, and that he was not alone in doing it in that way in the middle of the eighteenth century. When the Board of Excise dismissed the Lewes exciseman—thereby unwittingly helping to make the American revolution and the democratic movement of the nineteenth century—there was still living in Paris, supporting himself in poverty and loneliness by copying music, one of the most famous men of his time. Like Paine, Rousseau had begun life as an artisan; he was apprenticed to an engraver where Paine was apprenticed to a stay-maker. At the age of thirty-seven Rousseau had also been a failure; he had known the depths of poverty, had lived the life of a vagabond, had been a valet, a teacher, a musician. He wrote nothing at all until he was thirty-eight, he was forty-six before he wrote the book which made him famous. Between the ages of forty-six and fifty he wrote three books, the *Nouvelle Hèloïse*, the *Contrat Social*, and *Emile*, which had a profound, revolutionary effect upon social and political life and thought of his time and the century which followed.

Allowing for the natural differences in temperament, genius, and nationality, there is a remarkable similarity between the careers, achievements, and influence of Rousseau and Paine. They came from the same class; they came of the common people, and, when they found their voices at last, they both spoke for the common people. In 1774 Paine went to America, on the advice of Benjamin Franklin whom he had known in London. Franklin gave him a letter to his son-in-law at Philadelphia and the letter asks Mr. Bache to find Paine some job as a clerk, assistant tutor, or assistant surveyor, in order that he might earn a living. In 1775, at the age of thirty-eight, like Rousseau, Paine began to write, in the *Pennsylvania Magazine*, of which he soon became the editor. A year later he wrote his first book, *Common Sense*, and immediately became famous, because it played a large part in determining the course and manner of the American Revolution. He was the author of only two other books, *The Rights of Man*, published in 1791, when he was fifty-four, and *The Age of Reason*, published in 1794, when he was fifty-seven. Those books had an enormous effect upon democracy and free thought during the nineteenth century.

The process which changed Paine from a penniless failure into a famous man in the course of a few months is worth study. It is obvious that the remarkable ability, the knowledge, energy, the power and passion with which he thought things out for himself, the infinite curiosity of mind, the gift of words, must all have been in him already fully developed when he arrived in Philadelphia in 1775. For thirty-eight years the English environment had been too strong for him; suppressed and repressed he had failed to find any outlet for his powers. The moment that he arrived in America he felt that he was in a different atmosphere, an atmosphere of freedom. Within five months of his arrival he had written a remarkable essay against slavery; it was followed by one of the earliest statements of the facts and arguments which a century later were to become the commonplaces of feminism, by an attack upon the practice of duelling, by the advocacy of international arbitration, by proposals which anticipated by many years the existing system of copyright, by an article anticipating many of the modern views on marriage and divorce, and by another advocating a more humane treatment of animals.

Paine once said that it was the cause of America which made

him an author. He was mistaken in this. He became an author as soon as he landed in America, and several months before the American Revolution induced him to write *Common Sense*. He had already in his very bones the genius of a writer and it is significant that only four years after leaving England he could write to Laurens in a letter: "I know but one kind of life I am fit for, and that is a thinking one, and, of course, a writing one." What these first articles in the *Pennsylvania Magazine* prove is that the mind and style of Tom Paine, the author of *The Rights of Man*, had already been formed—though silent and suppressed—in England. The editor of the *Pennsylvania Magazine* was a hundred years ahead of his time—he was what came to be known as a democrat, a rationalist, a humanitarian, a pacifist, a feminist. And Tom Paine's fame and achievement, like Rousseau's, rest upon the fact that he was among the most powerful influences which spread broadcast through the world the ideas and ideals which those labels conceal.

On April 19th, 1775, the "massacre of Lexington" took place and the American Revolution had begun. On January 10th, 1776, Paine's pamphlet *Common Sense* was published in Philadelphia, "turned upon the world like an orphan to shift for itself," as its author said of it. The orphan proved a lusty infant; 120,000 copies were sold in under three months. There is ample contemporary evidence, from George Washington downwards and from Paine's enemies as well as from his friends, to prove that *Common Sense* had a more immediate and decisive effect upon public opinion and upon world history than perhaps any other similar piece of controversial writing. Its importance lay in the fact that it determined irrevocably at the very outset of the Revolution, when public opinion was still fluid and vacillating, exactly what political form that Revolution, if it should be militarily successful, would take. In January, 1776, the inhabitants of the American colonies were exasperated with the British Government, but the majority had no clear notion of what they wanted; Tom Paine in the course of a few months made up their minds for them; he convinced them that they wanted to be not colonists, but Americans; he made separation and republicanism inevitable. Any one who wishes to know how he achieved this can learn by reading *Common Sense*; its power is still in it to-day. The title is an honest title. Tom Paine is a common man talking common sense to common men; he had a genius for doing so and the genius is astonishingly rare. In the eighteenth century no one talked common sense about the subjects which Paine dealt with, politics, society, kings, classes, and religion; indeed very few people do so in the twentieth or have done so in any century. When they do so and have the gift of speaking or writing, whether it be a Socrates, a Christ, a Voltaire, a Rousseau, or a Tom Paine, the effect upon large numbers of people is explosive. The simple and supple style in which Paine talked his common sense is already fully formed in this pamphlet; its power and effectiveness can be shown by the following quotation:

In England a king hath little more to do than to make war and give away places; which, in plain terms, is to impoverish the nation and set it together by the ears. A pretty business, indeed, for a man to be allowed eight hundred thousand sterling a year for, and worshipped into the bargain! Of more worth is one honest man to society, and in the sight of God, than all the crowned ruffians that ever lived.

Common sense is reason applied by ordinary men to ordinary things. Paine was a rationalist; he belonged to the same school of thought as Godwin. But unlike Godwin, he was a man of great practical ability. He was, therefore, never, like

Godwin, silly and pedantic in his rationalism, for he never allowed his reason to detach itself from the realities of life and spin cobwebs in a vacuum. When he had written *Common Sense* he joined the American army and fought in its ranks throughout the war. At the same time he was employed by the American Government to write for them a series of pamphlets, *The American Crisis*, which had almost as great an effect upon public opinion as *Common Sense*. He soon became well known to Washington and the other American leaders, and his advice or opinion was given and valued on almost every department of administration from finance to foreign affairs. In 1777 he was made secretary to the Committee of Foreign Affairs by Congress, though he continued to serve in the American army. In 1779 he was elected Clerk to the Pennsylvania Assembly. In 1781 he went with Colonel Laurens on a diplomatic mission to France, the object of which, the raising of a loan, was successfully accomplished. The success was very largely due to Paine.

When the American war ended, in 1783, the State of New York recognized Paine's services by presenting him with a house and an estate of nearly 300 acres. In 1787 he returned to England on what he intended to be a short visit. The object of his visit was characteristic. Even in his stay-making days in London he had developed an intense interest in science and mathematics, and if his opportunities and education had been different, he might well have attained eminence as a scientist. Throughout his life he was occupied from time to time with experiments and inventions. In 1787 he was absorbed in the design of a new kind of bridge, a suspension bridge. He carried it to England and with his usual energy set to work in order to get models made and people interested. He was now a well-known man and was accepted as such by people of importance. He might have made a success of bridge-building if it had not been for the French Revolution. The importance

of that event was that it opened a chasm between the old
world and the new; it forced a choice upon every man, a
choice between the ideals of the ancient regime of privilege
and the new world of freedom and equality, a choice between
the politics of emotion and the politics of reason. Tom Paine
had already made his choice and so had Edmund Burke.
Burke's passionate defence of the ancient regime and attack
upon the Revolution appeared at the end of 1790. Paine sat
down and wrote an answer to this attack and *The Rights of
Man* was published on March 13th, 1791. It was a great success
and next year he published Part II. In the interval between the
publication of the two parts, a change had come over the face
of Europe and England. Every one could now see the chasm
opened by the Revolution, and governments and governing
classes were afraid. The publisher and author of *The Rights
of Man* were prosecuted for publishing "a false, scandalous,
malicious, and seditious libel", the gist of the sedition being
contained in Paine's argument that "all hereditary government
is in its nature tyranny". The persecution of Tom Paine and
his writings had begun.

I must say something more about that persecution, but I
will first finish this brief account of Paine's life. He escaped
imprisonment by crossing to France. There his fame was
great and he was elected Deputy for Calais in the Convention.
He lived in Paris throughout the Revolution taking an active
part in it, so far as his ignorance of the French language permitted. He was one of those rare people who carry over their
political principles into their political practice even though
such consistency jeopardize their interests or safety. All
through those dangerous days he stood firm for democracy,
republicanism, liberty, and humanity. On January 19th, 1793,
he faced Marat and the Mountain boldly in the Convention
by speaking and voting against the execution of the King.
The Jacobins never forgave him and, when the Terror was

at its height, he was arrested and imprisoned. It was mere chance that he escaped the guillotine. He was kept in prison for ten months and during that time he wrote or finished writing his last book, *The Age of Reason*, a destructive criticism of the Bible and orthodox Christianity, which was published in 1794 and 1795. In 1802 he returned to America. *The Rights of Man* had made him anathema to all political conservatives; his criticism of religion now made him an outcast for all respectable people. The position assigned to him in society by his respectable contemporaries is indicated by the words of an old hymn which sings of "The World, the Devil and Tom Paine". During the last seven years of his life he was cold-shouldered by nearly all his old friends who were now distinguished, and ceaselessly pursued by the upholders of morality and religion with fantastic slanders and ingenious lies. Paine was not one of those who meekly turn the other cheek or are much upset by the vindictiveness of the righteous, and he bore this unjust persecution and considerable poverty with equanimity. His death-bed was made unnecessarily painful to him by the intrusion of strangers who wished to prove that such a wicked atheist had died either repentant or in agony. He disappointed them, but even the dead bones of Tom Paine were not left in peace. No Christian sect, not even the Friends, would give them burial, and they were buried in the grounds of his house at New Rochelle, in the presence of a French-woman, her two sons, two negroes, and one Quaker. Ten years later, William Cobbett was suddenly converted to the view that Paine was a great man, because he found him to have been against paper money. He determined to bring Paine's bones back to England and give them honourable interment. The bones were dug up and landed in Liverpool on November 21st, 1819. Tom Paine's reputation with the governing classes was such that a town-crier in Bolton who announced the arrival of his bones was sentenced to nine weeks imprisonment. Cobbett seems immediately to have lost all interest in the matter, for at his death the bones passed, unburied, to his son. In 1836 the son became a bankrupt, but when it was proposed to put them up for auction, the Lord Chancellor held that the bones of Tom Paine were not an asset. In 1844 they were in the hands of a furniture dealer in Bedford Square, and in 1854 the skull and right hand of Thomas Paine were said to be in the possession of a Unitarian clergyman, who, however, "evaded subsequent enquiries." After that the body of Tom Paine passes into complete oblivion.

His mind has gone marching on. The persecution of thought is a subject of which little is really known. It is often said that persecution never succeeds and that truth in the end always prevails. There is no reason to believe anything of the sort. But there is no doubt that the persecution of Tom Paine's mind failed. In *The Rights of Man* and in *The Age of Reason* he wrote, as I have said, common sense for common people about government, society and religion. He wrote it in language which ranks only just below that of the greatest English prose writers. He asked men to use their reason and to observe the evil results of passion and privilege, of violence and superstition. He preached the doctrine that society should be ordered by liberty, equality, justice, and humanity, and by so doing he was a democrat long before the days of democracy. As regards religion, he was a deist, an eminently religious man who yet held that religion was a subject on which men should exercise their reason and common sense freely. Rousseau and Paine were new phenomena in the world; the horror that they inspired in their contemporaries was the horror of novelty, the terror at seeing something new and alive breaking from the future into a dead or dying society. Nothing like these two men had been seen before the eighteenth century. They were the voice of the underworld demanding a share in civilization; they spoke for civilization, for reason, liberty, equality, and humanity, in a world of chains and barbarism. No doubt Burke too was a civilized man, but he stood for vested interests in civilization, he hated the idea of civilization unless it were broad based upon the barbarism of the masses. The answer of Burke's world to Paine was the same as it had been to Rousseau, to persecute and suppress his books and opinions by means of the law. The prosecution of *The Rights of Man* in 1792 was the beginning of an attempt, lasting for thirty-three years, of the British governing classes to prevent what they considered dangerous thoughts being written, expressed or heard by the lower orders of society. The works of Tom Paine became the centre of this struggle for the Freedom of the Press, as it has been called. Hundreds of humble people were prosecuted and imprisoned for publishing or selling *The Rights of Man* and *The Age of Reason*. The struggle ended in the defeat of the government and governing classes when in November, 1825, Richard Carlile, the bookseller, was released from Dorchester Prison after five years imprisonment. This long process of persecuting opinion unsuccessfully ensured for Tom Paine a very great influence upon the political and social thought of the lower orders. It was pre-eminently from him that the working classes and working class movements of the nineteenth century first learnt to think, and what they learnt was common sense, toleration, reason, humanity, a hatred of privilege and the abuse of power, a love of liberty in life, speech, and thought. It was in fact from Tom Paine that they learnt to lisp the language of democracy.

37

NELSON

(1758-1805)

by BRIAN TUNSTALL

"If I had died upon the throne amid the clouds of my omnipotence, I should have remained a problem to many: to-day, thanks to my misfortune, they can judge of me naked as I am."

Napoleon at St. Helena.

FROM a purely dramatic standpoint no great career can be made completely satisfying unless it closes with an effective curtain, and in this respect Nelson's career was perfect of its kind. Though less important than Napoleon's and even than Wellington's, it possessed just those elements necessary to achieve secular canonization amongst English-speaking peoples.

For Nelson there could be no Moscow, no Waterloo, no St. Helena, and no Reform Bill. The perfect finality of Trafalgar stifles censure and rings down the curtain of patriotic mysticism. Trafalgar was a formidable achievement. It still stands as the greatest naval victory ever obtained by the British. It was the last great battle under sail, and it provides the only case since the death of Sir Edward Howard in 1513 of the Commander-in-Chief of a British fleet being killed in battle. In fact, the only thing which Trafalgar failed to do was to bring the Napoleonic Wars immediately to an end, but this slight defect has been easily remedied by those writers on naval history who ignore the remaining ten years altogether.

The interpretation of Nelson's career is by no means easy, and in some respects he is still "a problem to many", partly owing to the technical nature of his triumphs, and partly owing to the issues raised by his private life and the reactions of his countrymen to them. Nelson's career is the kind of one which has to have a book written about it every few years in order to give it a new setting in contemporary thought. During the mid-nineteenth century, for instance, lives of Nelson were either ponderous and official in tone or else full of light and dark shading, provided by the Romantic Movement (see Southey), with Emma Hamilton as a kind of bad fairy flapping balefully at dramatic moments. From about 1890 onwards increasing interest was shown in Nelson's purely technical achievements, and Admiral Mahan published his life of Nelson designated with the sub-title *The Embodiment of the Sea Power of Great Britain*. Yet even to Mahan, Emma Hamilton was a sinister figure lurking in the background, while to other writers she ceased to be any longer "romantic", and degenerated into being merely a "vulgar adventuress", though this view was ably refuted by the publication of Walter Sichel's life of her in 1905. In this same year, the centenary of Trafalgar, considerable controversy was aroused in the press as to the tactics employed in the battle, and in order to settle the matter the Admiralty set up a technical committee of inquiry. On the eve of the Great War Sir Julian Corbett published his large scale "staff history", *The Campaign of Trafalgar*, a work of some 150,000 words in which Emma Hamilton is not mentioned. Meanwhile several thousand of

Nelson's letters and despatches had been edited by Sir Harris Nicolas in the 1840's, but this collection is by no means exhaustive and those who wish to know something more about Nelson's feelings for Emma should consult *The Nelson and Hamilton Papers*, in the collection formed by Alfred Morrison, and privately published in 1893-4. Since the Great War people have tended to be less shocked or excited about Nelson's private life and the late Clennell Wilkinson's biography, though somewhat vague as regards naval matters, has at any rate contrived to present a balanced account of his life free alike from prudery and sentimentalism.

Nelson's early career is dominated by one outstanding event, his promotion to the rank of Post-Captain at the age of twenty, the importance of which it is impossible to overestimate. In those days promotion to post-rank was by selection, but from post-rank to flag-rank it was by seniority alone. This meant that an officer who reached the post list early was guaranteed lengthy employment as an admiral, provided that he avoided official censure and that his life and health were spared. Captains promoted late in their careers often died before they became due to receive their flags or else were too enfeebled to accept employment. Edmund Dod, for instance, whose name stood immediately above Nelson's on the list of post-captains promoted in 1779, was aged forty-five at the time. Thus when they both received their flags eighteen years later Dod was sixty-two while Nelson was only thirty-eight.

Nelson's promotion was due, of course, to the influence of his uncle, Captain Maurice Suckling, who was Comptroller of the Navy, and under whose patronage he had entered the service as a boy of twelve. His promotion, however, actually came from Sir Peter Parker, Commander-in-Chief in the West Indies who, though doubtless anxious to "oblige" the Comptroller, was not likely to have acted thus unless Nelson had given proof of exceptional merit. No man, moreover, elevated to senior rank in the service before he was twenty-one could have exercised command in that rank, with any success, unless possessed of outstanding ability.

After the American War of Independence Nelson had command of a frigate in the West Indies. It was peace-time service and somewhat uncongenial to his tastes, but he managed to obtain from it the maximum amount of excitement. By nature he was not contentious. He would never have undertaken a crusade against the Malta Prize Court in the light-hearted manner of Dundonald, nor did he ever act in a manner contrary to the considered opinion of the Cabinet, as Sir Sidney Smith did after the defence of Acre. On the other hand he interpreted the word "duty" in a manner which often brought him into direct collision with senior public servants. In the West Indies he set himself the dual task of putting a stop to breaches of the Navigation Laws by American traders and of exposing the large scale frauds then rife in the naval dockyards. In both cases his action was justified by the nature of his official instructions, but in both cases the existing state of affairs was connived at by the majority of the Governors, Presidents, Judges, and Naval and Military officers stationed in the Islands. Nevertheless Nelson triumphed. The American ships were condemned, the Governor-General was "soon trimmed up and silenced" and the home authorities were given ample evidence for dealing with the dockyards, while Nelson returned to England with the daughter of a local notable as his bride and with the assured friendship of England's future King. His bride was Frances Nisbet, daughter of William Woodward, late senior Judge of Nevis, and niece of John Richardson Herbert, President of the Island. Her first husband, Dr. Josiah Nisbet, had died insane, leaving her with an infant son, also Josiah, whom Nelson undertook to provide for in the service.

After six tedious and bitter years of unemployment Nelson

found active service again at the outbreak of the Revolutionary War. He played a prominent part in the operations of the Mediterranean Fleet, under Lord Hood, and commanded the naval landing parties at the capture of Bastia and Calvi, in Corsica, where he lost his right eye. Hood's successor, Sir William Hotham, was of a more cautious disposition and Nelson fiercely criticized his lack of initiative in two partial fleet actions with the French. In the first of these actions, fought in the Gulf of Genoa, Nelson succeeded in capturing two French ships of the line single-handed, these being the only captures made.

The arrival of Sir John Jervis as Commander-in-Chief entirely altered the character of the campaign, but unfortunately the successes of Napoleon in Northern Italy and the alliance between France and Spain altered it still further, and in the winter of 1796 the British Cabinet reluctantly gave Jervis discretionary orders to abandon the Mediterranean. He, therefore, retired his base from Corsica to Gibraltar and concentrated on the blockade of Cadiz. As part of this plan Nelson was sent to arrange for the evacuation of Elba which had been temporarily occupied and he only rejoined Jervis just in time to take part in the Battle of St. Vincent. This was Nelson's first experience of a major action between two fleets and in it he showed remarkable initiative by quitting the "line of battle" without orders and steering on the opposite course to the British ships immediately ahead of him in order to cut off part of the Spanish Fleet which would otherwise have escaped untouched. Jervis instantly divined the brilliance of this manœuvre and signalled Captain Collingwood to go to his support. As a result of the battle the Spaniards were completely defeated and four of their ships of the line taken, two of them by Nelson.

After the battle Jervis, now Earl St. Vincent, gave Nelson command of the famous "inshore squadron" blockading

Cadiz, which resulted in an almost nightly succession of cutting-out raids and boat actions with the Spanish flotilla. "It was during this period," as Nelson himself said, "that perhaps my personal courage was more conspicuous than at any other period of my life." In July, 1797, St. Vincent sent him with a tiny squadron to attack the strongly garrisoned island of Teneriffe. After failing to make a surprise landing at Santa Cruz, owing to contrary currents and winds, Nelson insisted on making a night attack in boats and leading it in person. Naturally enough the Spaniards were well prepared and the attack was repulsed with heavy loss, Nelson losing his right arm.

On rejoining the fleet off Cadiz in the summer of 1798, after sick leave in England, he was sent into the Mediterranean with a minute squadron to watch Toulon. Great activity was taking place but for an unknown purpose, and while Nelson was blown off his station by a north-westerly gale the French armament put to sea and sailed for Egypt, capturing Malta on their way. Nelson, meanwhile, had been reinforced by St. Vincent, but he had completely lost touch with the enemy and could only act on information and surmise. Moreover, he had no frigates. Nevertheless he managed to penetrate the French design and sailing for Egypt arrived there first. Fearing a mistake, he returned to Syracuse for fresh water and provisions and then, on more definite information, set off again. This time he found the French battle fleet and four frigates at anchor in Aboukir Bay, Napoleon having landed his troops some days previously.

Although the bay was practically uncharted and the French were lying in shoal water close to sandbanks, Nelson decided to attack at once, risking, in addition, the exceptional difficulties of a night action. The British fleet sailed straight into the bay without any preliminary signalling as to the tactics to be employed. Plans for every eventuality had already been worked out with his captains, the "Band of Brothers", all picked men trained at the "inshore station". By next morning ten out of the twelve French ships of the line were taken or destroyed, including the flagship ·*Orient*, mounting 120 guns.

After the Nile Nelson's life became more complicated. He reached Naples, where he went to refit, suffering from a head wound received in the battle and from a subsequent attack of fever, which in his own words "had very near done my business". His appearance there, ably stage-managed by Lady Hamilton, wife of the British Ambassador, aroused such enthusiasm that in a few weeks he was installed as guardian deity of the whole Kingdom of the Two Sicilies. Urged on by the King and Queen and the Hamiltons to do something to save Naples from the southward drive of the French Republicans, he urged the Neapolitans to help themselves by marching on Rome. The result, however, was disastrous: the Neapolitan army bolted, and the Royal Family, plus the Hamiltons, had to be taken to Palermo in Nelson's flagship. The French then seized Naples and overran the whole of Calabria.

In the summer of next year (1800) Nelson was able to ensure King Ferdinand's restoration at Naples by naval action, but his movements were hampered by the sudden appearance in the Mediterranean of Admiral Bruix's fleet from Brest. Nelson was still only commanding a detachment of the Mediterranean Fleet and officially, therefore, was under the orders of Lord Keith, St. Vincent's successor. Keith, in order to check Bruix, ordered Nelson to concentrate his whole squadron at Minorca. Nelson refused to obey, firstly because he thought the safety of Naples to be more important than that of Minorca, and secondly because he had landed 1,000 seamen and marines to help the Neapolitans recover Capua, and would have been too weak to put to sea without them. In the end he sent part of his squadron to Minorca, and in writing to the Admiralty vehemently defended his disobedience to Keith's orders.

Luckily his opinion as to the strategic importance of Naples and Sicily was shared in general terms by the Cabinet, though for somewhat different reasons, and he was thus lucky to avoid what for other men might have meant court-martial and disgrace. Meanwhile his English Barony (which incidentally he considered a poor reward for the Nile) had been supplemented in magnificent style by King Ferdinand, who made him Duke of Bronte in Sicily, with estates said to be worth £3,000 a year. Keith now urged on him the necessity of reducing Malta, still in the hands of the French garrison left by Napoleon in 1798, a task which Nelson had so far delegated to his subordinates. Stung by Keith's very reasonable demands, with their implied censure on his previous conduct, and angry that he himself had not succeeded St. Vincent as Commander-in-Chief, Nelson pleaded ill-health and soon after received Admiralty permission to come home.

Hamilton, meanwhile, had also been superseded, and he, Emma, and Nelson travelled home across Europe together. The "*Tria juncta in uno*", as they called themselves, caused a remarkable stir wherever they appeared, and their journey through Germany became a triumphal progress. Their arrival in London brought the whole question of their personal relationships to a head. Nelson and Emma were already lovers, with Hamilton in the background, ambiguously complaisant and slightly senile. Nelson attempted to explain the position by intimating that the "*Tria juncta in uno*" were the essential combination of patriotism and friendship through whose energies British interests in the Mediterranean had triumphed at the expense of the French. To Fanny Nelson, however, and to many other people besides, this was nonsense. The shifts, exigencies, and lack of convention which had characterized their relations in the exotic world of Naples could hardly be given social permanence in London. Nelson's boastful letters when he first reached Naples, filled with extravagant and tactless laudations of Emma, and succeeded by long silences and curt notes, had already prepared his wife for the worst. Emma, moreover, refused to give way, went everywhere with Nelson in London and openly exulted in the humiliation of her helpless rival. Nelson, who had been practically living with the Hamiltons for the last two years, found it impossible to banish them from his conversation, especially as those two years included the most triumphant moments of his life. Fanny, in consequence, was soon so "sick" of hearing about "dear Lady Hamilton" that she left Nelson for good. That she knew, or at least suspected, the relations between Nelson and Emma is certain, but even so she was only driven to extremities by their extraordinary lack of tact.

In January, 1801, Emma gave birth to Nelson's child, Horatia, the whole event taking place with the utmost secrecy and the child being removed to the care of a nurse within a week. Nelson was at Plymouth, awaiting orders for the expedition to the Baltic in which he was to be second-in-command to Admiral Sir Hyde Parker, and worry about Emma drove him to the verge of a nervous breakdown. "God strike him blind if he looks at you," he wrote, fearing the attentions of the Prince Regent: "Never, if I can help it, will I dine out of my ship, or go on shore, except duty calls me . . . I love, I never did love anyone else." Referring to Charles Greville, Hamilton's nephew, Nelson wrote, "That other chap did throw away the most precious jewel that God Almighty sent on this earth." Greville had kept Emma as a mistress and had then sold her to Hamilton hoping to prevent his marriage and so inherit his fortune.

The British Fleet reached the Baltic at the end of March, charged with the duty of forcing the Danish Government to abandon the armed neutrality, recently formed by the Northern Powers to dispute the restrictions placed by England on neutral trade with France and her subsidiary allies. The Danes, however, refused to desert Russia and Sweden, and Nelson with a special squadron undertook to attack their fleet, moored in shoal water before Copenhagen, and only approachable by the most difficult passages. Nelson boldly ran past their position, and then, by expert navigation and the use of favourable winds, attacked their fleet from the far end. The resulting battle was very severe for both sides, but Nelson managed to persuade the Danes to accept an armistice which saved many lives on their side and enabled him to withdraw his ships past the still active island batteries. He then negotiated an extension of the armistice to cover Denmark's complete withdrawal from the Armed Neutrality.

On returning to England Nelson was made a Viscount, and after the Peace of Amiens he lived with the Hamiltons for nearly a year and a half, chiefly at Merton (now Wimbledon) where they bought a house. A visit to Greville at Milford Haven became a grand tour through the West and Midlands with their progress attended by huge and enthusiastic crowds. It proved too much for Sir William Hamilton, however, who died soon after, without ever making the slightest admission of the deception practised upon him.

Thereafter Nelson and Emma continued to live together at Merton, happily enough, with the house a crowded museum of naval achievements. Yet circumstances were not altogether favourable; Emma was left badly off and Nelson was paying over two thousand a year to Fanny and his own relations out of his unemployed pay. Fanny, moreover, was either unwilling, or unable, to institute proceedings for divorce.

In the summer of 1803 the War began again; Nelson hoisted his flag in the *Victory* and sailed to blockade Toulon. He kept up the blockade for nearly two years, never once going ashore, and then in March, 1805, Villeneuve left Toulon with the French Mediterranean Fleet. Discovering Nelson's whereabouts by a chance meeting with a neutral merchantman, he turned west along the Spanish coast, passed the Straits, and sailed to the West Indies, collecting the Spanish Cadiz squadron on his way. This move was part of Napoleon's scheme for a general concentration of battle squadrons in the West Indies, as a preliminary to the invasion of England. Nelson lost valuable time in waiting for a supposed attack on Sicily or Egypt, and when at last he discovered the truth was opposed by contrary winds. Villeneuve's destination after leaving Europe was a secret but Nelson obtained enough evidence to warrant him following to the West Indies. Arriving at Barbados he was informed that Villeneuve had gone south to attack Trinidad. Villeneuve in reality had gone north to attack Barbuda, but, hearing that Nelson was already in the Caribbean, he disembarked his troops and sailed for Europe with Nelson in pursuit only four days astern. Their return courses eastward, however, soon diverged, Nelson racing for Cape St. Vincent to cut off Villeneuve from Cadiz, while Villeneuve himself headed north-east towards Ferrol. Nelson had sent a brig direct to England with despatches, and the captain, passing Villeneuve's fleet on the way, luckily reached England quick enough to enable the Admiralty to arrange for Villeneuve's interception off Ferrol by a fleet under Sir Robert Calder. Nevertheless Villeneuve forced his way into Vigo and from thence to Ferrol and finally, in Calder's temporary absence, ran down the coast to Cadiz. Meanwhile Nelson reached Gibraltar without incident and went ashore there for the first time in 721 days. On joining Cornwallis off Ushant immediately afterwards, he was sent straight home on leave and joined Emma and his family at "Paradise Merton".

Villeneuve's move to Cadiz had seriously disturbed the British Cabinet, as it suggested a further move through the Straits and a threat to Naples and Sicily where British troops were now established. The British blockading forces were

again reorganized, Calder was recalled and Nelson was sent
out to take command of the fleet before Cadiz. He was faced
by two main problems, how to force the enemy out of port
and how to defeat them in battle. Luckily the first was solved
for him by Napoleon ordering Villeneuve into the Mediterranean in the mistaken belief that an expedition of British
troops preparing to sail for the Cape of Good Hope was really·
intended for Italy. Villeneuve, unaware of Nelson's numbers,
but hearing that he had sent six of the line to Gibraltar for
water and provisions, put to sea on 19th October, 1805.
Nelson was well out to sea with his battle fleet at the time, but
he was informed of the enemy's movements by frigates and
steered south-east to cut them off from the Straits. Villeneuve,
however, turned back towards Cadiz while Nelson closed in,
and on the morning of 21st October both fleets were visible
to each other for the first time since the opening of the campaign in 1803.

Nelson had only twenty-seven of the line against thirty-
three, but he had a poor opinion of the enemy's fighting
efficiency and general organization, and was prepared to take
risks. He, therefore, directed Collingwood to attack the rear
of the enemy's line with fifteen ships, while he himself attacked
their centre with twelve. Despite the fact that the enemy were
able to bring broadside fire to bear against Collingwood's
"line of bearing" (advance in echelon) and also against
Nelson's "line ahead" (advance in single file), they were
unable to prevent the British from forcing a close action.
With ships actually touching they repeatedly attempted to
board the British ships under cover of musket and grenade
fire, but in every case were beaten back. Their van, moreover,
which was disengaged at the start was very slow at coming
to their aid and when it did so proved completely ineffective.
All these points had been accurately foreseen by Nelson in his
tactical "Memorandum" issued some days prior to the battle.

The British fleet was superior in gunnery and seamanship and unlike the combined fleet of French and Spaniards, its morale was extremely high.

Nelson realized that the conditions of the battle would expose him personally to great danger, but he refused all suggestions that he should remove or cover the bullion replicas of his decorations and orders. It is a mistake, however, to imagine that he wished to die.

"My dearest, beloved Emma," he wrote, ". . . the signal has been made that the Enemy's combined Fleet is coming out of port . . . and as my last writing before the battle will be to you, so I hope in God that I shall live to finish my letter after the Battle."

Firing began at 11.30 in the morning against Collingwood's flagship, the *Royal Sovereign*: at 12.30 the *Victory* broke into the enemy's reduplicated line: three quarters of an hour later Nelson was wounded. Every saying of his dying moments is recorded in Sir William Beatty's *Authentic Narrative*.

"Partial firing continued until 4.30," records the Master's Log of the *Victory*, "when a victory having been reported to the Right Honourable Lord Viscount Nelson, K.B., and Commander-in-Chief, he then died of his wound."

Thus ended the Englishman's perfect type career as defined in terms of action. But to the men of his own age Nelson himself had a special appeal. To them he personified the spirit of resistance to Napoleonic dictatorship, a feeling which in our own times is only dimly appreciated. To the officers and seamen of the Navy Nelson was the humane commander, the man who spent his leave agitating for the seamen to be given their hard-earned pay, who tempted nervous midshipmen up the rigging by gentle example, and who in every possible manner made the health and welfare of his own subordinates his chief means of beating the enemy.

38

WALTER SCOTT

(1771-1832)

by Edwin Muir

LOOKING at Scott's life as a whole, one cannot but be struck by a deep cleft in it. This was shown early and may have been implicit in his parentage. His father was a lawyer, strict, conforming, respectable. His mother was impulsive and affectionate, a lover of poetry with a head stuffed with lawless tales. Scott inherited her love of poetry and her memory for stories; but in practical life he followed the example of his father. This antithesis clung to him permanently, making him pay in his novels a lip-service to lawlessness, while at the same time expressing a respectable man's reprobation of it. The division had another aspect as well. His mother's stories were about the past, and mainly about the past of the wild Border from which she came. His father was a faithful adherent of the Hanoverian House, who lived in the present and had no use for romantic legends. Scott set himself to live in the present; but he found himself pulled back into the past again and again, harmlessly in imagination and fatally in practice. Abbotsford is only understandable as the realization of an early dream which he had perhaps forgotten in the busy turmoil of his life, but which still determined his actions. The money which he made by his legal business and literary work gave him the means to realize this dream; yet of the last he wrote in words which would have pleased his father: "No man shall find me rowing against the stream." In his writing he never rowed against the stream; but in building a replica of an ancient Border community at Abbotsford he rowed against it systematically. The situation was roughly similar to a dozen or so in the Waverley Novels, where the young hero gets himself involved in a romantic adventure by some explained or unexplained necessity, without denying that the opposite side is right. In the novels the hero always returns at the end unscathed. Scott himself was never able to return; the necessity that drove him to create the extravagance of Abbotsford was a deeper one, and it finally destroyed him.

This conflict and its consequences he concealed from himself in his novels in the wish-fulfilment of the happy ending and in anonymity. It was his respectable paternal side that made him refuse to put his name to the Waverley Novels. He gave a number of reasons for this, but the only convincing one was: "In truth, I am not sure it would be considered quite decorous of me, as a Clerk of Session, to write novels." It was his father's side too that made him conceal his extravagantly fanciful business dealings with James Ballantyne, and perhaps his mother's side that drove him into them. Yet these two parts of his nature, the lawless and the conforming, the imaginative and the practical, never appeared in direct conflict; it would be more true to say that they played a complicated game of hide-and-seek with each other. In the novels this game is seen in an accommodating arrangement of experience whereby the blameless hero is able to indulge all the joys of lawlessness without coming to harm. In Scott's life the form it took was much more ingenious; it let him be a romancer and an anonymous gentleman of means at the same time, for his stories provided him with a very good income; but that income in turn paid for his most fatal romantic exploit, that is Abbotsford; so that it might be said that one side of him grew by a sort of blackmail on the other. The respectable side had finally to pay for all the excesses of the fanciful; for in life such opposites have to meet sometime. But in the novels they never meet, and the result is that Scott's picture of life is always partly true and partly untrue in a very defined way; we can separate the one from the other as we cannot separate them in any other fiction of the first rank. There are dozens of characters in his novels whom one feels he does not even wish to make real; almost all his women except the old ones, almost all his young men except those of the lower classes. His imagination was hampered by practical considerations. His love for Scotland was equally hampered by his adherence to the established order of the Union. This rendered his novels and his patriotism romantic in the bad sense, and made him get out of his two worlds, the past and the present, the cheapest they could give him; that is romantic illusion and worldly advantage.

Scott was born in Edinburgh, in August, 1771. He was a robust child, but at the age of eighteen months he had a teething fever during which he lost the use of his right leg through a form of infantile paralysis. The doctor advised country air, and he was sent to his grandfather's farm of Sandy Knowe in Tweeddale. There he received his first impressions of the world, which were to determine the shape of his imagination.

In his fourth year he was taken to Bath by his Aunt Janet, where it was hoped that the waters would do him good. He saw his first play, *As You Like It*, and the impression was so vivid that he could remember it distinctly thirty years later. From Bath he returned to Edinburgh for a few weeks, after which he was sent to Sandy Knowe again. A letter of Mrs. Cockburn, the author of the modern version of *The Flowers of the Forest*, gives a delightful picture of him at this time:

WALTER SCOTT

I last night supped at Mr. Walter Scott's. He has the most extraordinary genius of a boy I ever saw. He was reading a poem to his mothèr when I went in. I made him read on; it was the description of a shipwreck. His passion rose with the storm. "There's the mast gone," says he. "Crash it goes! They will all perish!" After his agitation he turns to me. "That is too melancholy," says he. "I had better read you something more amusing." I proposed a little chat and asked his opinion of Milton and other books he was reading, which he gave me wonderfully. One of his observations was, "How strange it is that Adam, just new come into the world, should know everything—that must be the poet's fancy," says he. But when he was told that he was created perfect by God, he instantly yielded. When taken to bed last night, he told his aunt he liked that lady. "What lady?" says she. "Why, Mrs. Cockburn, for I think she is a virtuoso, like myself." "Dear Walter," says Aunt Jenny, "what is a virtuoso?" "Don't you know? Why, it's one that wishes and will know everything." Now, sir, you will think this is a very silly story. Pray, what age do you suppose that boy to be? Name it now, before I tell you. Why, twelve or fourteen. No such thing; he is not quite six years old. He has a lame leg, for which he was a year at Bath, and has acquired the perfect English accent, which he has not lost since he came, and he reads like a Garrick. You will allow this an uncommon exotic.

When he was seven he returned to his home in Edinburgh. He had spent most of his life in the society of grown people, and he was not used to dealing with rough children. He took it hard at first, but in spite of his lame leg soon became a great fighter. Until he was a young man he continued with great readiness to get into broils. His boyhood had been sickly, and at sixteen he burst a blood vessel in his bowels and had to keep to his bed for several weeks. But after that he grew strong. James Hogg the poet considered him later the strongest man he had met. And a naval officer said of him: "Though you may think him a poor lamiter, he's the first to begin a row, and the last to end it." This love of fighting was harmlessly sublimated later in his novels.

He was at the same time the story-teller of his class at school, and he read enormously, chiefly poetry. He knew all Shakespeare, and could recite whole passages from Spenser. He was carried away by *Ossian* for a time, but the fascination soon palled. Later he discovered Percy's *Reliques* during a visit to Kelso, and the book had a lasting effect on him.

In 1786 his father took him into his office as an apprentice, on an indenture that was intended to last for five years, but it was mercifully cut short by the bursting of the blood vessel. When he recovered it was decided that he should go in for the higher branch of the legal profession. He threw himself into his studies and passed his final trials in 1792. He seems at this time to have lived the life of a young man about town, drinking a good deal, as was the custom. It was the years of the French Revolution; respectable opinion in Scotland was alarmed, and Scott joined the loyal Volunteers and sent to Kelso for "a strong gelding such as would suit a stalwart dragoon". Revolution was distasteful to both sides of him, the side that glorified the past, and the side that respected the established order. His holidays he spent chiefly in exploring the Border, and Liddesdale in particular, where he returned for seven successive years, and where he began to collect old tales and ballads. These explorations were really explorations into the past of Scotland.

A little before he was twenty an event occurred which affected his whole life. He fell in love with Williamina, the daughter of Sir John Stuart-Belsches of Fettercairn. Very little is known about this affair, but Scott himself said that he had three years of dreaming and two of wakening. He proposed in 1795 and by the end of the year began to doubt his chances. His hopes woke again in 1796, but in the autumn of that year he was definitely rejected. Williamina married another man, a friend of his own, in the beginning of the next year.

We do not know much of this affair except that his friends were concerned for his life after his rejection, and that on the eve of unlucky events Williamina is said to have appeared to him in his sleep. Seventeen years after her death he met her mother in Edinburgh and wrote in his Journal:

> I fairly softened myself, like an old fool, with recalling stories, till I was fit for nothing but shedding tears and repeating verses for the whole night. This is sad work. The very grave gives up its dead, and time rolls back thirty years to add to my perplexities.

He resolutely buried his love for Williamina, and on the summer after her marriage his heart was "handsomely pierced", as he put it, by a young lady whom he met during a visit to the English lakes. This was Charlotte Margaret Carpenter, daughter of Jean Charpentier, a French refugee, and ward of Lord Downshire. She was twenty-one, a lively and sensible girl with black hair and brown eyes, not beautiful. Scott proposed at once and was in wild spirits during the engagement. They were married before the end of the year.

A great deal has been written about Scott's marriage, but the best comment on it is a letter which he wrote twelve years later to Lady Abercorn:

> Mrs. Scott's match and mine was of our own making, and proceeded from the most sincere affection on both sides, which has rather increased than diminished during

twelve years' marriage. But it was something short of love in all its forms, which I suspect people only feel once in all their lives; folk who have been nearly drowned in bathing rarely venturing a second time out of their depth.

There seems little doubt from this that it was his mother's son who fell in love with Williamina, and his father's who married Charlotte. Whether Scott's heart was "handsomely pierced" or not we cannot say; his letter to Lady Abercorn seems to deny it. But the sudden substitution and his resolute burial of Williamina probably crippled his imagination on one side and made him incapable of portraying love in his novels. Certain of his women were drawn from Williamina, but they are remote and bloodless versions. It may be that he could not afford to resurrect her, or perhaps the ghost of his father forbade him.

The young couple settled down in Edinburgh at 39 North Castle Street. Scott was making about £150 a year at his law work; his father was giving him an allowance; and Charlotte had a few hundred pounds of her own. They lived quite comfortably, but when, in 1799, the Sheriff-deputy of Selkirkshire died, Scott succeeded in being appointed his successor. His father died in the same year; and with the Sheriffdom and the paternal estate Scott now enjoyed an income of about £1,000 a year, a sum which at that time was worth about three times what it would be now. These figures must be given, for no account of Scott's life would be comprehensible without a rough summary of his money affairs.

His first important work, the *Minstrelsy of the Scottish Border*, on which he had been engaged for several years, appeared in 1802. The *Minstrelsy* is still a work of value, and the preface contains a passage which describes better than any other his attitude to Scotland. Speaking of the ballads he had assembled, he said:

By such efforts, feeble as they are, I may contribute something to the history of my native country; the peculiar features
of whose manners and character are daily melting and dissolving into those of her sister and ally. And, trivial as may
appear such an offering to the Manes of a kingdom, once
proud and independent, I hang it upon her altar with a
mixture of feelings which I shall not attempt to describe.

There is no mistaking the emotion in these words. Scott
saw with keen regret the manners and character of Scotland
dissolving; yet at the same time he remained a steadfast supporter of the Union which caused that dissolution. From this
contradiction he never found a way of escape. His attachment
to Scotland was romantic, his attachment to the Union a
matter of practical conviction, and that made both of them
false. The final phrase, "the mixture of feelings which I shall
not attempt to describe," shows an inner confusion which he
probably did not wish to clear up. This conflict of allegiances
returns again and again in his novels. It was not so much a
conflict of allegiances to Scotland and England, as a symptom
of the division in his own nature.

As his Sheriffship of Selkirkshire demanded that he should
live there for part of the year, he cast his eye round for a
house and found it at Ashestiel on the upper Tweed. There
he finished the *Lay of the Last Minstrel*, a long poem which,
like the *Minstrelsy*, was an immediate success. From that
moment he was an almost disastrously successful writer.

More important than the *Lay* was a business connection
which he entered into about this time. While on an early
visit to Kelso he had met James Ballantyne, a boy of his own
age, whom he had liked. Ballantyne had since tried the law
but made little of it; he was now editor of a local paper, and
had shown himself a good printer. He was an engaging,
enthusiastic, likeable man, honest but muddled, and devoted to

Scott. Publishing was booming, largely because of the enter-
prize of Archibald Constable. Scott thought that Ballantyne
would have a better chance of exercising his talents in Edinburgh. By the end of 1802 Ballantyne was established in a
dingy press near Holyrood with the help of several hundred
pounds which Scott had lent him. The press went well and
was moved to larger premises in the Canongate. But the
new place required more capital. Scott had prospects of being
appointed a Clerk of Session, a well-paid post; and the *Lay*
had been doing well. He therefore decided to buy a third share
in the business.

This step cost him untold trouble, partly because it linked
him with Ballantyne, who was a hopelessly inefficient man of
business, and partly because he had to keep the association secret.
There was perhaps nothing ambiguous or even unusual in this
secrecy: people at that time did not go about proclaiming their
investments. The real charge against Scott is that he exploited
his secret in a way that was not fair to others. That he did this
deliberately is unbelievable; all we know about his life refutes
such an idea. But he found himself in a position which was
both compromising and advantageous. He had an interest in
Ballantyne's printing firm; he naturally wished to secure work
for it; and he did this by recommending ventures to publishers
who did not know that he would derive any advantage from
them. There was in the situation itself an indirect dishonesty,
and in the end it brought more inconvenience to Scott than to
his victims. It made him embark on nine years of literary
drudgery, for the press had to be kept going. He began by
producing a fine edition of *Dryden* in eighteen volumes, an
admirable piece of work. It was followed by a *Swift*, which
occupied him for six years, but was not a success. There were
other volumes which gave work to Ballantyne but were a
loss to the publishers. Scott was also writing during this time
for the *Edinburgh Review*, and after a difference with the editorial

policy, for the *Quarterly*. All this was to lead him towards that morass of work into which he finally sank.

We have a picture of him at Ashestiel. He was always up at five or six and at his desk in breeches and shooting jacket, a dog at his feet. By breakfast time he had got the main part of the day's work over, and another two hours finished it, after which he was free. At this time he liked to be ten hours a day outdoors, shooting, fishing or riding.

In 1808 appeared *Marmion*, which was a great success. Next year he visited the Highlands to find a pendant theme. *The Lady of the Lake* followed; also a great success. Meanwhile he had been getting on bad terms with Constable, his publisher, and was thinking of going over to Murray. Hunter, Constable's partner, a man whom he did not like, bluntly demanded that he should first finish the *Swift*, on which a large advance had been paid. Scott was offended, and resolved to be his own publisher.

James Ballantyne had a brother John, who had been various things and was now chief clerk in the printing firm. He was frail, volatile, with a smattering of miscellaneous knowledge, a hopeful mind, and an amusing tongue. The publishing firm of John Ballantyne and Company was launched in July, 1809. Scott advanced half the capital, as well as another fourth in John's name. The brothers had no idea of business, and by the end of 1810 the firm was in difficulties. Scott became discouraged, but next year took heart again, for his income was increased by £1,300 through his salary as Clerk of Session. This, his Sheriffship and his wife's income now assured him of £2,000 a year, with every likelihood of another thousand from his writings. He decided that the position was by no means hopeless; he decided at the same time to buy an estate.

He chose a plot of ground sloping down to the Tweed. The land was poor, the situation not particularly pretty; but it had been the scene of the last battle in Border history, and

that was enough. Scott paid the unreasonable sum of £4,000
for the place, half of which he borrowed from his brother
John, and half from the firm of Ballantyne on the security of
a poem which he had not yet written. Building was begun at
once, and in May, 1812, Scott left Ashestiel to superintend it.
There in the midst of enormous confusion he finished his
poem, *Rokeby*. It was not so great a success as he had hoped.
About the same time appeared the first two cantos of *Childe
Harold*, and Scott immediately saw that he could not compete
with such an entirely popular product. He began to look round
for some other way of exercising his literary abilities.

Meanwhile he was seriously worried, for the firm of Ballantyne was heading for failure. Scott at last recognized that it
would have to be wound up. But this would mean bankruptcy
and a betrayal of his connection with it. Another publisher
would have to step in and save it; the only choice was Constable; and to Constable Scott went, pocketing his pride.
£6,000 was needed to save the firm; Constable could only
advance £2,000; the young Duke of Buccleuch guaranteed
the other £4,000. This temporarily saved the publishing firm
of Ballantyne; the printing firm still remained, and Scott considered severing his connection with it too; but his liking for
James Ballantyne and a reluctance to lose the money he had
invested prevented him. At the same time he was contemplating an extension of Abbotsford.

In 1805 he had begun a prose romance entitled *Waverley*:
'Tis Fifty Years Since, which he had shown to his friend
Erskine, who had thought it dull. Seven years later he returned
to it and wrote a few more chapters, but again was discouraged
by his friends. The manuscript was mislaid when he moved
from Ashestiel to Abbotsford. One day it turned up as he was
searching for fishing tackle. He looked it over and resolved to
finish it. In a few months he had done so, and it appeared in
July, 1814, under Constable's imprint, but without the name of

the author. It was the beginning of his major success as a writer. He sat down at once to another novel, *Guy Mannering*, which he claimed to have written in six weeks, though this has since been disputed. Thereafter he expanded the original 130 acres of his estate to 1,000, and James Ballantyne appeared with a new sheaf of unpaid bills. Scott had immediately to start on another novel, *The Antiquary*, which was once more a success.

From now on it is almost impossible to dissociate Scott's business from his literary activities, for they fall into the position of cause and effect, the income for his novels paying his debts and encouraging him to get more deeply into debt. But in spite of his successes the Ballantyne publishing firm had at last to go. On its final liquidation in 1817 its debts were estimated at £10,000. These were accordingly transferred to the printing firm, though nobody could determine at the time whether it was solvent. The two firms had been lavishly exchanging with each other bills without any real backing, and the position had been complicated still further by a similar exchange of bills between them and Constable. All this time the Ballantynes and Scott had been living expensively. Scott now decided to assume full ownership of the printing firm, a step which was to be still more disastrous, for he thereupon proceeded to use it as his bank and draw upon it whenever he needed money for his private uses. But his novels continued to be successful.

During these years he had been working very hard, and he now began to suffer from pains in his intestines. In March, 1817, he had to take to bed in great pain with gall-stones. All that year he remained in pain, but he wrote on and expanded Abbotsford until it included all the haunts of Thomas the Rhymer: a luxury which cost him £10,000. He recovered somewhat during 1818, but in 1819 he grew worse again. He wrote to the Duke of Buccleuch:

I have been ill—very—very ill . . . I did not lose my senses, because I resolved to keep them, but I thought once or twice they would have gone overboard, top and top-gallants. I should be a great fool, and a most ungrateful wretch to complain of such afflictions as these. My life has been, in all its private and public relations, as fortunate perhaps as was ever lived, up to this period; and whether pain or misfortune may lie behind the dark curtain of futurity, I am already a sufficient debtor to the bounty of Providence to be resigned to it. Fear is an evil that has never been mixed with my nature, nor has even unwonted good fortune rendered my love of life tenacious.

He recovered somewhat, riding out on Sybil Grey "the very image of death on the pale horse, lanthorn-jawed, decayed in flesh, stooping as if I intended to eat the poney's ears, and unable to go above a foot-pace." Then he grew worse again, and one night in June thought that he was going to die, and called his family to his bedside. But it was the turn of his illness, and after that he gradually recovered.

To these years of illness belong the best of his novels, except for *Old Mortality*, which he wrote before them, and *Redgauntlet*, which came later. They include *Rob Roy*, *The Heart of Midlothian*, perhaps the greatest of all his novels, and *The Bride of Lammermoor*, the most tragic. He wrote the last in a delirium of pain, so that he could not remember a single scene when the book was presented to him. It seemed to him "monstrous, gross and grotesque", and certainly his respectable side exercised less supervision over it than over his other novels. Perhaps because of this it is the most perfectly constructed of his works. To this period also belongs the romance of *Ivanhoe*, the first of his stories in the inferior historical mode.

Though he had recovered, Scott was now a changed man, and he was no longer capable of the intellectual or the bodily feats of his former life. Ballantyne's debts continued to pile up. Novels continued to appear: *The Monastery* and *The Abbot* in 1820, both inferior works; *Kenilworth* in 1821, *The Fortunes of Nigel* and *The Pirate* (about his worst novel) in 1822. In the same year he managed a historical pageant for George IV on his visit to Edinburgh, and re-admitted James Ballantyne as a partner. The firm's debts now came to £27,000. Scott had overdrafts on Constable as well. Yet for some time he had been making about £10,000 a year by his novels.

In 1823 appeared *Peveril of the Peak*, his first serious failure; but it was followed by *Quentin Durward* and *St. Ronan's Well*, the first a popular and the other an artistic success. Only one novel, *Redgauntlet*, appeared in 1824, and it was indifferently received; yet it is one of his finest works and contains probably the greatest scene in the heroic style that he ever wrote. By next year Ballantyne's debts had mounted to about £40,000; and Scott began to toy with the idea of buying the neighbouring estate of Faldonsyde at an almost equal figure. He quickly wrote two more novels, *The Betrothed* and *The Talisman*, both of them inferior works. He was deeply depressed about this time; he saw the aristocratic society of England threatened by Democracy and his own fortunes endangered by the financial crisis in London. Rumours persisted throughout most of the year that Constable was going bankrupt, but Scott refused to credit them. On the 18th of December he realized that he was ruined. He received the announcement with courage. "This news will bring sad hearts at Darnick and the cottages of Abbotsford," he wrote. He thought of his dogs: "Poor things, I must get them kind masters." When everything was reckoned up, it was found that Ballantyne's liabilities amounted to £130,000. Scott, now a man of fifty-four, set himself to pay what he owed, and started at once on another novel, *Woodstock*. "I feel neither dishonoured nor broken," he wrote in his Journal . . . "I will not yield without a fight for it. It is odd, when I set myself to write *doggedly*, as Dr. Johnson would say, I am exactly the same man that I ever was, neither low-spirited nor *distrait*. In prosperous times I have sometimes felt my fancy and my power of language flag, but adversity is to me at least a tonic and a bracer; the fountain is awakened from its inward recesses, as if the spirit of affliction had troubled it in his passing." *Woodstock* showed no diminution of his cheerfulness and vigour; but the last chapter sounded a note which had never been heard in his published work before, though it recurred often enough in the Journal. "Years rush by us like the wind. We see not whence the eddy comes, nor whitherward it is tending, and we seem ourselves to witness their flight without a sense that we are changed; and yet Time is beguiling man of his strength, as the wind robs the woods of their foliage." His wife died the same year, while he was away in Edinburgh. "I wonder," he wrote in the Journal, "what I shall do with the larger portion of thoughts which were hers for thirty years. I expect they will be hers yet for a long time at least. . . . They are arranging the chamber of death; that which was long the apartment of connubial happiness, and of whose arrangements (better than in richer houses) she was so proud. They are treading thick and fast. For weeks you could have heard a footfall. Oh, my God!" During that year he was haunted by the thought of the vanity of life and the ravages of Time. "There is some new subject of complaint every moment; your sicknesses come thicker and thicker; your comforting or sympathizing friends fewer and fewer; for why should they sorrow for the course of nature?"

During the next year he picked up heart again; his *Life of Napoleon*, on which he had been working for several years, was well received. But that relief was temporary. In 1830 he collapsed with a paralytic stroke, recovered again and went on working. After the stroke his mouth had a nervous twist, and his tongue a slight stammer. Next year he had a worse stroke, but went on working on a new novel, *Count Robert of Paris*, on which he could make no progress. He turned from it at last to *Castle Dangerous*, but without enthusiasm. He felt his powers visibly going. "I have suffered terribly, that is the truth, rather in body than in mind, and I often wish I could lie down and sleep without waking. . . . My bodily strength is terribly gone, perhaps my mental too." He had by now succeeded in paying off a considerable part of his liabilities, and at last yielded to his doctors and sailed for Italy. At Naples in March, 1832, he read of Goethe's death and exclaimed: "He at least died at home! Let us to Abbotsford." On the road back Rome roused no interest in him. He still dreamt of buying Faldonsyde. Passing Venice, Tyrol, Munich, Heidelberg and the Rhine, the party at last reached Nimeguen, where he had another stroke. He lay for three weeks in London, sunk in a coma. On July 5th he was carried on board ship, with a great crowd watching. He reached Newhaven on the ninth, and on the eleventh set out for Abbotsford. As the carriage was descending the valley of the Gala water he woke from his stupor and muttered familiar names, and when the Eildons came in view he exclaimed in delight.

After reaching Abbotsford he relapsed again. A few days before his death he sent for Lockhart and delivered his last message. "My dear, be a good man—be virtuous—be religious —be a good man. Nothing else will give you any comfort when you come to lie here." He died on the afternoon of September 21st, 1832.

To generalize on a man so great in outline and so complex in nature as Scott must seem useless; but a short sketch such as this cannot avoid it. Perhaps his main quality was a splendid largeness and generosity. He was incapable of jealousy. He was continually helping other people, and even after his ruin he could not rid himself of the habit. His novels show that he was incapable of hatred. He was what is called a quick judge of character, but he never judged people in the ordinary sense, except in two known instances; for he was harsh to one of his brothers and unfair to Constable. His Abbotsford experiment cannot be set down to snobbish love of display; it was the fatal realization of a dream which he had dreamt in childhood. His powers were probably crippled by his parental heritage, by his romantic attachment to the past and his prosaic respect for the establishment. If he had thrown himself into the real life of his time and looked forward to the future instead of clinging to the past, one feels that both his life and his writings would have been greater. "What a life mine has been!" he wrote towards the end, "half educated, almost wholly neglected or left to myself, stuffing my head with most nonsensical trash." This was his epitaph on his life, written in a moment of dejection. The "most nonsensical trash" must have been the mementoes of Scotland's past with which he filled his imagination and his rooms. The question is whether he had any choice; for there did not exist round him in Scotland a life as whole as the life represented by these mementoes and relics. Scotland in his time was neither a nation nor a province; it was a part of England and yet not a part of England; and this No Man's Land gave the final impress to his imagination and his life.

His novels show the same largeness and generosity. He is probably the greatest creator of character and situation in English literature except Shakespeare. His work, it is true, is consistently spoilt by the disparity in it between the man of imagination and the man who wanted to have the approval of the Edinburgh upper classes. Yet he was not merely a great writer spoilt, but a very great writer spoilt. Certain scenes in his novels are on the highest plane of poetic imagination: the scene in *Redgauntlet* where the Jacobites realize that all is lost because of an act of magnanimity by the English

Government; the scene where Jeanie Deans pleads her case in London; and countless scenes in the pathetic style which have never been surpassed. His Scottish dialogue is an instrument for expressing all the varieties of human feeling, and his mastery over it was absolute. His Journal will be read as long as his novels, as one of the most moving autobiographical documents in the English language. His long poems are second-rate; but he wrote several lyrics which, like parts of his novels, belong to the highest world of imagination. These expressed a sense of the vanity of action which ran completely counter to the glorification of action in his stories, and in them the tumultuous world of romance seems to die beyond resurrection. These lyrics belong to a private but very profound stratum in Scott's nature; his novels, with their splendid variety and richness, rather to his public character. The public and the private character never came together. If they had, one feels he would have been one of the greatest writers in English literature. As it is, he is very great on the level of obvious greatness, and perhaps the most remarkable man that his country ever produced.

39

WORDSWORTH AND COLERIDGE

(1770-1850 : 1772-1834)

by F. W. BATESON

IT is no longer possible to take Wordsworth and Coleridge with complete seriousness. Their names have lost the halo of almost religious awe with which they were once encircled, and they now provoke something that often approaches a sympathetic snigger. We pay our tribute, indeed, but accompanying it with a friendly raising of the eyebrows. Admittedly they are very great poets—but their poetry is like the little girl in the song: when it is good it is very, very good, when it is not (which is three lines in four) it is *horrid*. And there is the same contradiction in their lives. Can the elderly gentleman in the Jim Crow hat and the old blue cloak, who astonished the Westmorland yokels by his fondness for "goin' out wi' his family, and sayin' nowt to noan of 'em", ever have been, in any but a historical sense, the revolutionary of Blois who was the lover of Annette Vallon? Who, again, would recognize the "inspired charity boy" of Lamb's reminiscences in the young Coleridge who broke into his indignant headmaster's study demanding to be apprenticed to a cobbler? And

> The rapt One, of the godlike forehead,
> The heaven-eyed creature,

was surely but faintly prefigured in the despondent undergraduate who ran away from Cambridge to be metamorphosed,
for four uncomfortable months, into Trooper Silas Tomkyn
Comberbacke, of the 15th Light Dragoons.

But the significant fact in these episodes is that the
dramatis personæ do not include Wordsworth *and* Coleridge.
The figure of fun is either Wordsworth alone or Coleridge
alone. When the two poets were together they succeeded in
retaining a sufficiency of dignity and common sense; it was
only when separate that they were liable to degenerate into
their own caricatures. The case is the same with their poetry.
It is a notorious fact that Wordsworth's and Coleridge's
claims to poetic greatness rest almost exclusively upon their
achievements in the seven years from 1797 to 1804. The earlier
and the later poems, though occasionally interesting and
attractive, are, comparatively, feeble in the extreme. Something *happened* to both poets in 1797 that ceased to continue
to happen after 1804. What was it? I suggest that it cannot be
altogether an accident that 1797, the year of *The Ancient
Mariner* and *The Old Cumberland Beggar*, was the year in which
Wordsworth and Coleridge first became intimate, and that
1804, in which the last of their greater poems was written, was
the year when that intimacy was interrupted, to be only
partially renewed later, by Coleridge's departure for Malta.
The thesis of this essay, in so far as it has a thesis, is that
Wordsworth and Coleridge, as personalities and as poets,
were incomplete without each other, that each supplied something the other lacked, and that the history of their friendship
is the best key to understanding both them and their poems.

The time and the place of the first meeting of William
Wordsworth and Samuel Taylor Coleridge are not known for
certain. They had both been undergraduates at Cambridge,
Wordsworth at St. John's and Coleridge at Jesus; but Words-

worth, who was the elder by two and a half years, had taken his degree before Coleridge came up. The probability is that they did not meet until 1795, at Bristol. Coleridge, who was just twenty-three, was then on the point of making his rash, loveless and ultimately disastrous marriage to Sara Fricker. They seem also to have met once or twice in 1796. Their intimacy, however, dates from early in June the following year, when Coleridge, recently installed with his wife and the baby Hartley at Stowey, in the Quantocks, paid a short visit to Wordsworth, who was living with his sister Dorothy at Racedown, in the north-west corner of Dorset.

The visit was a memorable one. Coleridge never forgot the warmth of his welcome "when first I visited you at Race-down", and half a century later the Wordsworths still had "a distinct remembrance of his arrival. He did not keep to the high road, but leapt over a gate and bounded down the pathless field, by which he cut off an angle". The two poets had both already published collections of immature verse and, as was natural, the first day of Coleridge's visit was passed in showing each other their more recent work. Wordsworth read Coleridge *The Ruined Cottage* (a fragment of some power later to be absorbed in *The Excursion*), and after tea Coleridge recited two and a half acts, all that were then in existence, of his tragedy *Osorio*. (The tragedy had been commissioned by Sheridan and was ultimately acted at Drury Lane Theatre, in 1813, with some success, as *Remorse*.) The following morning Wordsworth retaliated by reading the whole of *his* tragedy *The Borderers*. And, as was also natural, the cups of mutual admiration brimmed over. Coleridge reported to a friend that "Wordsworth admires my tragedy, which gives me great hopes". His own opinion of *The Borderers* was that "There are in the piece those *profound* touches of the human heart which I find three or four times in *The Robbers* of Schiller, and often in Shakespeare, but in Wordsworth there are no *inequalities*".

WORDSWORTH AND COLERIDGE

(Posterity has not shared these enthusiasms. *The Borderers* and *Remorse*, as a matter of sober fact, are two of the feeblest would-be-Shakespeare tragedies of the period.)

An intimate record of Coleridge's ten days at Racedown survives in a letter written by Dorothy Wordsworth to a friend who had left earlier in the year:

> You had a great loss in not seeing Coleridge. He is a wonderful man. His conversation teems with soul, mind, and spirit. Then he is so benevolent, so good-tempered and cheerful, and, like William, interests himself so much about every little trifle. At first I thought him very plain, that is, for about three minutes. He is pale, thin, has a wide mouth, thick lips, and not very good teeth, longish, loose-growing, half-curling, rough, black hair. But if you hear him speak for five minutes you think no more of them. His eye is large and full, and not very dark, but grey, such an eye as would receive from a heavy soul the dullest expression; but it speaks every emotion of his animated mind: it has more of "the poet's eye in a fine frenzy rolling" than I ever witnessed.

The interest of this letter is not only in the picture it gives of Coleridge in the first flush of his genius but even more in the reactions of the letter-writer. The Wordsworths, evidently, had fallen completely under Coleridge's spell. That glittering eye, not less compelling than his own Mariner's, had already worked its potent charm, and they "could not choose but hear". And no wonder. Coleridge was the most brilliant conversationalist of his time. His *Table Talk*, though entirely selected from notes taken in his semi-invalid old age, is still a fascinating bedside book. Heightened by the music of a voice of great power and sweetness and a manner almost prophetic, his talk may well have been irresistible.

Coleridge's visit was returned early in July when Wordsworth and his sister were the Coleridges' guests at Stowey.
Charles Lamb, Coleridge's old schoolfellow at Christ's Hospital, was also one of the party, and it was to Lamb that Coleridge addressed, as a memento of the occasion, the charming
lines beginning:

> Well, they are gone, and here I must remain,
> Lam'd by the scathe of fire, lonely and faint,
> This lime-tree bower my prison!

(The others had gone for a walk and Coleridge had had to be
left behind, as his "dear Sara" had emptied "a skillet of
boiling milk" on his foot!) The immediate result of the Wordsworths' stay at Stowey was a decision to give up their Race-
down house, and they were lucky enough to secure for the
modest sum of £23 a year's lease of Alfoxden, "a gentleman's
seat, with a park and woods, elegantly and completely furnished, with nine lodging rooms, three parlours, and a hall,"
only three miles from Stowey. "Our principal inducement,"
Dorothy Wordsworth explained to her friends, "was Coleridge's society." But Alfoxden itself must have been a powerful secondary inducement. It was a house that might have been
built specially for poets. On the south side a little court,
flaming with roses, provided the foreground. Beyond was the
park, with its sheep and deer, and beyond that there were
smiling hills, dotted with oaks and topped with fern. Between
the hills the sparkling waves of the Bristol Channel could just
be seen. There was a waterfall a quarter of a mile away and
behind the house the Tor of Glastonbury reared its head.
William Hazlitt, then a raw youth of twenty, spent a night at
Alfoxden in 1798, "in an old room," as he described it twenty-
five years later, "with blue hangings, and covered with the
round-faced family-portraits of the age of George I and II,

and from the wooded declivity of the adjoining park that overlooked my window, at the dawn of day, could

—'hear the loud stag speak'."

Jane Austen would have been at home in Alfoxden. Indeed, the Sir Walter Elliot of her *Persuasion* cannot have lived many miles away. But Sir Walter, had he called, would have been sadly puzzled by the new tenants. Wordsworth was a gaunt Don Quixote of a man at this time, eccentrically dressed in a brown fustian jacket and striped pantaloons, and still speaking with a deep Westmorland burr. His "exquisite sister", though by all accounts no housekeeper, was, at any rate as described by Coleridge, more presentable. "She is a woman indeed!" he wrote, "in mind I mean and heart; for her person is such that if you expected to see a pretty woman, you would think her rather ordinary; if you expected to see an ordinary woman, you would think her pretty! but her manners are simple, ardent, impressive. In every motion her most innocent soul outbeams so brightly, that who saw would say:

'Guilt was a thing impossible with her.'

Her information various. Her eye watchful in minutest observation of Nature; and her taste a perfect electrometer. It bends, protrudes, and draws in at subtlest beauties and most recondite faults." Dorothy Wordsworth was twenty-five in 1797—almost two years younger than her brother and rather less than a year older than Coleridge.

The Wordsworths spent at Alfoxden the twelve months from July, 1797, to June, 1798, when they were refused a renewal of the lease because they were suspected locally of Jacobinism. The day-to-day record of those months is to be read in Dorothy's Journal. The Journal is a fascinating document—though its fascination at this period lies almost as much in what it does not say as in what it does. Were Dorothy and Coleridge beginning to fall in love? If they were, and the *a priori* probability of it is considerable, the fact has to be read *between* the lines. The Journal itself is strictly non-committal. Coleridge, indeed, is a far less important figure in its pages than "William", and even "William's" doings receive none of the intimate attention that is given to the changing aspects of the trees and the weather: "A pleasant morning, the sea white and bright, and full to the brim. I walked to see Coleridge in the evening. William went with me to the wood. Coleridge very ill. It was a mild, pleasant afternoon, but the evening became very foggy; when I was near Woodlands, the fog overhead became thin, and I saw the shapes of the Central Stars. Again it closed, and the whole sky was the same." Before a reserve so impenetrable the most determined scandalmonger is helpless. Later Dorothy was to wear her heart more openly in her diaries. All that we can be said to *know* of the Alfoxden months is that Coleridge used to walk over from Stowey almost daily and that his "dear Sara" was a very much rarer visitor.

But Dorothy's Journal, for all its minute felicity of observation, is not the most important literary record of the Alfoxden period. Those twelve months were also the months of the *Lyrical Ballads*. It is true, that landmark in the history of English poetry was not published until the beginning of September, 1798, but the poems included in it were almost all written either at Alfoxden or Stowey. They were the immediate product of the intimacy that sprang up between Wordsworth and Coleridge there, and they express, indirectly indeed but not less clearly than the Journal, the ardours and ecstasies of those intoxicating months. The first of the ballads to be written, the "Rime of the Ancyent Marinere", was begun by the two poets in collaboration. On the 13th November, 1797, the two Wordsworths and Coleridge had set off at half past four in the afternoon for a walking tour that was to take them to Devonshire, and the poem was intended to defray the cost of the expedition. But before the first eight miles had been covered the attempt at joint composition had broken down— Wordsworth found he was "a clog" on his friend's imagination —and the £5 which it was hoped to extract from the editor of the *Monthly Magazine* never materialized. On returning to Alfoxden, however, a joint volume of poems was planned. Wordsworth was to write on subjects "chosen from ordinary life" and Coleridge on those in which "the incidents and agents were to be, in part at least, supernatural". Both series of ballads were to conform to "the two cardinal points of poetry, the power of exciting the sympathy of the reader by a faithful adherence to the truth of nature, and the power of giving the interest of novelty by the modifying colours of imagination". The months that followed were spent in filling in this scheme. Wordsworth wrote *The Idiot Boy, The Thorn, We are Seven* and similar pieces, and Coleridge, in addition to completing *The Ancient Mariner,* began *Christabel* and *The Dark Ladie.* But Wordsworth was much the more industrious of the two and when the book eventually appeared the greater part of it was his.

Lyrical Ballads is often described as though it was simply a collection of Wordsworth's poems to which Coleridge had contributed "The Ancient Mariner". But that is a superficial view. *Lyrical Ballads* was essentially a collaboration, but a psychological rather than a literary collaboration. With the exception of a line or two here and there, like the opening of "We are Seven", every word of Wordsworth's poems was written by Wordsworth and every word of Coleridge's by Coleridge. But neither Wordsworth's nor Coleridge's poems would have been what they are if it had not been for each other's influences. The two poets benefited and profited by each other almost equally. The more philosophic cast that Wordsworth's poems assume at this period was clearly Coleridge's doing; the pantheism, the

> sense sublime
> Of something far more deeply interfused,
> Whose dwelling is the light of setting suns,
> And the round ocean and the living air,
> And the blue sky, and in the mind of man,

which was henceforth to colour all his more ambitious poetry, was a sense that he had learned from Coleridge. And, not less clearly, the new vigour and realism that Coleridge's poems suddenly acquire were the gifts of Wordsworth. The latter's sole surviving contribution to *The Ancient Mariner* is the two lines:

> And thou art long, and lank, and brown,
> As is the ribbed sea-sand.

It was precisely the absence of images of this quality that had prevented Coleridge's earlier poems from being more than minor poetry; it is their constant presence that is, in great part, the making of *Christabel*, *Kubla Khan*, and *The Ancient Mariner*. If Wordsworth learned from Coleridge how to *think*, Coleridge learned from Wordsworth how to *see*.

A third influence, the influence of Dorothy Wordsworth, also went to the making of *Lyrical Ballads*. Wordsworth has recorded how

> She gave me eyes, she gave me ears,

and it is notorious that many of his most familiar poems and most striking images derive from incidents and observations reported to him by Dorothy. It is more than possible that she performed something of the same office for Coleridge too. It is difficult at any rate not to connect an entry in her Journal for March 1798 ("One only leaf upon the top of a tree—the sole remaining leaf—danced round and round like a rag blown by the wind") with the lines in *Christabel*:

> The one red leaf, the last of its clan,
> That dances as often as dance it can,
> Hanging so light, and hanging so high,
> On the topmost twig that looks up at the sky.

But the most important service that the two poets, and Dorothy, did for each other was that of a stimulus. Before Alfoxden, Wordsworth and Coleridge wrote only occasionally and with difficulty. In 1797 and 1798, in the contagion of their proximity, poems of the finest quality came tumbling out almost effortlessly. Measured simply by the mechanical criterion of lines and pages Coleridge's output for the two years represents nearly a *third* of the whole of his poetic works; and the proportion in Wordsworth's case is probably almost as high. In point of quality the contrast, it is hardly necessary to say, is even more marked. Wordsworth and Coleridge had found themselves for the first time; or rather, they had *helped each other to find themselves*. For the point of real interest is that their mutual influences, instead of compromising their originality, emphasized and fostered it. The intimate and daily communion, which Coleridge expressed by saying that they were "three people but one soul", only made Wordsworth more Wordsworthian and Coleridge more impenitently Coleridge. No two poems could well be more different than *The Old Cumberland Beggar* and *Kubla Khan*, the one as solid and sober as rock, the other all air and fire. That is their triumphant justification. But indirectly and by the subterranean channels through which poetic genius flows they emerged from a common source of experience.

Immediately after the publication of *Lyrical Ballads* the Wordsworths and Coleridge went to Germany together to learn the language. After some days in Hamburg, where they paid their respects to Klopstock "the German Milton" ("a very German Milton" was Coleridge's comment), they separated, the Wordsworths settling at Goslar, where Wordsworth wrote some of his best poems (including the "Lucy" series), and Coleridge at Ratzeburg and Göttingen where he drank deep of the heady liquors of the Transcendental philosophy. Coleridge stayed behind after the Wordsworths, but by the summer of 1799 they were all back in England and in October the two poets were touring the Lake Country together. They were both much attracted by Grasmere and before the end of the year the Wordsworths had installed themselves there in Dove Cottage. The Coleridges settled at Greta Hall, twelve miles away, the following July.

A period of almost daily intercourse then began, similar to that in Somerset. The entries in Dorothy's Journal now become more susceptible of a sentimental interpretation. For the 29th August, 1800, we have: "At eleven o'clock Coleridge came when I was walking in the still clear moonshine in the garden. He came over Helvellyn. William was gone to bed. . . . We sate and chatted till half-past three." And there is a similar entry for the 2nd September: "The moonlight shone only upon the village. It did not eclipse the village lights, and the sound of dancing and merriment came along the still air. I walked with Coleridge and William up the lane and by the church, and then lingered with Coleridge in the garden. John [the sailor brother commemorated in 'Character of the Happy Warrior'] and William were both gone to bed and all the lights out." The entry for the 12th December, 1801, is still more explicit: "The snow hid all the grass . . . The ashes glittering spears with their upright stems. The hips very beautiful, and so good!! and, dear Coleridge!

I ate twenty for thee, when I was by myself." But by the end of 1801 the emotion of love, if it was love, was being complicated by that of pity. Coleridge had had a bad bout of rheumatic fever at the beginning of the year, which left behind it the seeds of further illness. To relieve his pains he began to take opium—not apparently for the first time—in increasing doses. He was also suffering from the recurrent nightmares that are depicted in *The Pains of Sleep*, and his debts and unfulfilled literary promises were a continual worry. The growing estrangement, too, between himself and his wife, who was a good *bourgeoise* but a very bad Bohemian, added to his troubles. It was only gradually that Coleridge's friends learned the whole truth; but Dorothy, if we may judge by the Journal's entry for the 10th November, 1801, seems to have known almost from the first: "Every sight and every sound reminded me of Coleridge—dear, dear fellow, of his many talks to us, by day and by night, of all dear things. I was melancholy and could not talk, but at last I eased my heart by weeping . . . O! how many, many reasons have I to be anxious for him." A marriage between Coleridge and Dorothy Wordsworth is one of the intriguing might-have-beens of history. If he had been happily married it is more than possible that the gradual demoralization of which the remainder of his life was the tragic progress might have been averted.

The first years at Grasmere were for Wordsworth almost as productive as the Alfoxden period. "Resolution and Independence," many of the finest sonnets, and portions of his great *Ode* and *The Prelude* were all written in 1802. Coleridge, however, had lost his facility. The only great poem he composed at this period, but in some ways his greatest poem of all, is characteristically *Dejection: An Ode*. In its first form the poem was addressed to Wordsworth.

Dejection is dated 1802, and the entries for that year in Dorothy's Journal concerning Coleridge make pathetic reading. One day they have had, "A heart-rending letter from Coleridge. We were sad as we could be." On another occasion it is: "Two very affecting letters from Coleridge; resolved to try another climate. I was stopped in my writing, and made ill by the letters." Or again: "Coleridge came in. His eyes were a little swollen with the wind. I was much affected by the sight of him, he seemed half-stupefied." The resolution to try another climate was not put into effect until 1804. In the April of that year he sailed for Malta, and there and in Italy he remained until the summer of 1806. When he returned the old intimacy appeared to revive once again, and when Wordsworth read him *The Prelude*, the last great poem that either of them was to write and the greater part of which had been written in Coleridge's absence, the infection of his friend's voice inspired a final flicker of poetic genius. The lines "To William Wordsworth composed on the Night after his Recitation of a Poem on the Growth of an Individual Mind", though inferior to *Dejection*, have a more than merely autobiographical interest:

> Sense of past Youth, and Manhood come in vain,
> And Genius given, and Knowledge won in vain;
> And all which I had culled in wood-walks wild,
> And all which patient toil had reared, and all,
> Commune with thee had opened out—but flowers
> Strewed on my corse, and borne upon my bier
> In the same coffin, for the self-same grave!

In the years that followed, the friendship was outwardly maintained, but a gradual widening of the gap is all the time apparent. There was a growing harshness on Wordsworth's side and a growing touchiness on Coleridge's, and the explosion of 1810, though it might have been postponed, was inevitable sooner or later. Its immediate cause was a mutual friend, a certain Basil Montagu, who "told Coleridge that Wordsworth had *commissioned* him to say that 'he had no hope' of Coleridge, that he had been a nuisance in the Wordsworth family, and had contracted debts for gin in the public houses of Grasmere village". Coleridge not unnaturally was stunned, not the less, perhaps, because there were several grains of truth in the charges; and though Wordsworth denied the "commission" and a reconciliation was patched up later, things were never the same. In a curious letter, written many years after to a young admirer, Coleridge described the breach with Wordsworth as one of the "four griping and grasping sorrows, each of which seemed to have my very heart in its hands", that had embittered his life. It is not certain that he ever saw Dorothy Wordsworth again. Wordsworth, however, he met occasionally in other people's houses, and in 1834, shortly before his death, Wordsworth paid him a short visit at Highgate. A single anecdote survives of that visit. It is told by Coleridge's daughter Sara:

How well do I remember Mr. Wordsworth, with one leg upon the stair, delaying his ascent, till he had uttered, with an emphasis which seemed to proceed from the very profoundest recesses of his soul: "I would lay down my *life* for the Church."

Ironically, in the very first reference to Wordsworth in Coleridge's letters, thirty-eight years before, Coleridge had described him as "at least a *semi*-atheist". But the irony was not noticed in 1834. In 1834 Coleridge was the Sage of Highgate and Wordsworth the Bard of Grasmere. The poets in them had been dead for a quarter of a century.

40

MARY WOLLSTONECRAFT

(1759-1797)

by MONA WILSON

MARY WOLLSTONECRAFT was a new sort of woman, the first of the moderns: she is still a modern woman: at moments I echo her impatient cry, "Women are certainly great fools: but nature made them so," and say that she is the woman of the future. Hannah More, Elizabeth Fry, Mrs. Barbauld, Harriet Martineau all carry their dates and belong to their period: we admire and sometimes smile: Mary Wollstonecraft insists upon a more intimate reception.

She was born in 1759. The Wollstonecrafts were of Irish extraction, and her mother was pure Irish. Wollstonecraft was a wastrel and a wanderer, a bad husband and a bad father, and Mary early assumed a thankless burden of family cares and claims. Constant changes of abode—a real home she never had—made any regular education impossible. Her first gleam of intellectual day came from a hunch-backed clergyman at Hoxton, somewhat like Mr. Pope in appearance, a scholar and a lover of poetry. More potent still was her worship of Fanny Blood, a girl two years older than herself, artist and musician, with a delicate taste in both reading and writing.

It was Fanny who inspired her with a wish to write. She determined to break away and lead an independent life, but her attempts were hampered by her mother's long illness, and by responsibility for her sisters when Wollstonecraft married again and they lost any semblance of a home. The younger made a miserable marriage, and Mary, with a courage in advance of her years and her time, took the half-maddened creature away—she bit her wedding ring to pieces in the coach —and hid her in lodgings till a separation was arranged. After this, Mary and Fanny Blood settled to live together and make a home for the unfortunate Eliza Bishop. Fanny supported herself as an artist, while Mary and Eliza started a little school at Newington Green with, at its most prosperous moment, twenty day scholars and some boarders. Mary's passionate friendship for Fanny Blood remained, but their relation had changed. Fanny's was the weaker character: combining ill-health with a dragging love-affair, instead of a support she became one of Mary's cares. She married and sent for Mary to Lisbon. Ignoring the protests of her friends, Mary borrowed money for her journey and set off at once: a child was born, and the mother died. On the voyage back a French vessel in distress hailed the captain: he refused help lest his store of provisions should run short. But he reckoned without one of his passengers: Mary Wollstonecraft threatened to ruin his career unless he took the crew on board.

The school had lingered on for over two years: Mary's absence was the final blow. Godwin mentions the one stirring event of her life at Newington Green, a visit to Dr. Johnson: "The doctor treated her with particular kindness and attention, had a long conversation with her, and desired her to repeat her visit often." Then came his last illness. Neither Boswell nor Mary tells us more: only a picture remains of the old man charmed by an impetuous girl with auburn hair and amber-coloured eyes, perceiving that both in character and intelligence she belonged to a different order from his former pets.

Mary, as though her own family were not anxiety enough, now felt herself responsible for Fanny Blood's parents: she dedicated to their use ten guineas which Joseph Johnson, the publisher, gave her for a pamphlet, *Thoughts on the Education of Daughters*. Not yet daring to face the precarious struggle of a literary life, she took a post as governess in Ireland from which she was dismissed within a year: the children loved her too well. But her chance had come at last: Joseph Johnson had recognized her gifts: he persuaded her to rely on her pen. Still diffident, she concealed at first her design and her address: "I am then going to be the first of a new genus; I tremble at the attempt."

Johnson settled her in a little house near Blackfriars Bridge, supplied her with work—translations and articles for his *Analytical Review*—published her *Original Stories from Real Life*, illustrated later by William Blake, and *Mary*, a short novel reminiscent of her friendship with Fanny Blood, and proved himself a heaven-sent adviser and friend. "You are my only friend"—she writes—"the only person I am intimate with. I never had a father, or a brother—you have been both to me, ever since I knew you." His own dry note reads: "During her stay in George Street she spent many of her afternoons and most of her evenings with me. She was incapable of disguise. Whatever was the state of her mind, it appeared when she entered, and the tone of conversation might easily be guessed. When harassed, which was very often the case, she was relieved by unbosoming herself, and generally returned home calm, frequently in spirits." Her family were now, and later, a constant drain on her resources, both nervous and financial, and from time to time Joseph Johnson and other friends rescued her from debt.

It was not till 1790, when she was thirty-one, that Mary

Wollstonecraft was ready to make her mark. Her friend, Dr. Price, had provoked Burke's *Reflections on the French Revolution*, and she dashed off a reply, *A Vindication of the Rights of Men*. She makes an audacious attack on the existing state of society, mocking at the "rhetorical flourishes and infantile sensibility" exhibited by the complacent Burke. Her indignation is often witty: "Full of yourself, you make as much noise to convince the world that you despise the revolution, as Rousseau did to persuade his contemporaries to let him live in obscurity". But she was dealing with an opponent whose inconsistencies made him as vulnerable as his extravagance: it was useless to ask, even rhetorically, how Burke could reconcile his attitudes to the French and American revolutions, or why he had so much sympathy with the King of France in 1789, and so little for his own sovereign in 1788. That was Burke.

Some other radical journalist might have dealt effectively with him: Mary Wollstonecraft alone could write her greater vindication, *A Vindication of the Rights of Women: with Strictures on Political and Moral Subjects*. The book which, whether they have read it or not, has earned her the gratitude of all women whom she would have thought worth the winning, was published early in 1792, and reprinted sixteen times within a century: to it I shall return.

In Joseph Johnson's office, and at his weekly dinners, Mary met his friends and clients, many of them men of note, Price and Priestley, Holcroft and William Blake. Godwin disliked her: she talked too much and spoilt his duet with Tom Paine. Hitherto the needs and misfortunes of others had absorbed her, but she was too complex a creature not to long for personal happiness. She fell in love. Her choice was unfortunate: Fuseli was a flirt and married. Rumour credits her, as it credits Blake, with the wish for a household *à trois*, probably based in both cases on some wild saying. A few years later she asked Fuseli in vain to return her letters. They are now lost: I do

not wish to find them: later letters of hers have given me pain
enough. At bottom she was always a reasonable woman: in
December, 1792, she went off to Paris that she might free herself from this emotional disturbance. A long stay was no part
of her plan, but she was trapped by the Terror, and unable to
leave France or communicate with her friends in England. Her
history during the next three years may be read in those
poignant letters to Imlay, an American with gifts and superficial graces, whom she believed capable of giving her the love
and intellectual sympathy which alone could fulfil her nature.

> I like the word affection, because it signifies something
> habitual; and we are soon to meet, to try whether we have
> mind enough to keep our hearts warm. . . . I look forward
> to a rational prospect of as much felicity as the earth affords
> —with a little dash of rapture into the bargain. . . . I do
> not want to be loved like a goddess; but I do wish to be
> necessary to you.

Women were necessary to Imlay, but no one woman—
much less such an one as Mary Wollstonecraft. She was
ardently in love with Imlay, and her *Letters*, generous and
courageous, reflect all the ups and downs of their relationship.
At first her misery came from his absorption in commercial
speculations: she reproaches him for preferring money-making
to the quiet life of equal companionship for which she longed
so passionately. She bore his name and was generally recognized as his wife, although there was in fact no marriage
ceremony—in the circumstances it was impracticable in
France—but he was constantly absent from her both during
her pregnancy and after the birth of little Fanny. When she
realized at last that she had lost her hold on him she tried to
drown herself in the Thames, but was rescued and had to
face life again. During this time she had written two books.

An Historical and Moral View of the Origin and Progress of the French Revolution and the Effect it has Produced in Europe, intended as the first instalment of a long history, was published towards the end of 1794, and went at once into a second edition. It is less readable nowadays than the *Letter to Burke*, and does not bear to the same extent the stamp of the writer's personality, but it is a competent piece of dated journalism, showing a careful study of French psychology.

Her *Letters Written during a Short Residence in Sweden, Norway, and Denmark* appeared in 1796. Imlay had asked her to look after his business affairs, and her account of the journey, taken from her letters to him purged of private matter, charmed her contemporaries, among them William Godwin.

Their acquaintance had been renewed early in 1796, and after her final breach with Imlay in the spring she called upon him: "a deviation from etiquette," remarks Godwin, "but she had trampled on those rules which are built on the assumption of the imbecility of her sex." The gradual intimacy which followed was, as he says, "friendship melting into love." They did not marry till March, 1797. Old Mrs. Godwin's reception of the news is delightful.

> Your broken resolution in regard to mattrimony incourages me to hope that you will ere long embrace the Gospel, that sure word of promise to all believers, and not only you, but your other half, whose souls should be both one, as Watts says of his friend Gunston, the sooner the better. . . . You might have been so good as told me a few more particulars about your conjugal state, as when you were married, as being a father as well as a husband; hope you will fill up your place with propriety in both relations.

Fuseli wrote to a friend: "You have not, perhaps, heard that the assertrix of female rights has given her hand to the *balancier* of political justice." Holcroft was more sympathetic: "I think you the most extraordinary married pair in existence. May your happiness be as pure as I firmly persuade myself it must be."

Godwin had a study a few doors from their house in the Polygon, Somers Town, that they might not encroach on each other's independence. Their ideal was

> Companionship in those mysterious things
> That makes a man's soul or a woman's soul
> Itself and not some other soul.

Mary was finding peace at last. "A husband is a convenient part of the furniture of a house," she writes when he was away from her, "unless he be a clumsy fixture. I wish you, from my soul, to be rivetted in my heart; but I do not desire to have you always at my elbow, although at this moment I should not care if you were." She might reproach him sometimes for his aloofness and lack of consideration, but these were mere echoes from her past sufferings: she was learning the wisdom which only comes from established happiness. Godwin was, as she says herself, the best and kindest man she had ever known. But some measure of egotism must be allowed among the Rights of Men. When relieved by an anodyne during the agony of her last illness, she exclaimed: "Oh, Godwin, I am in heaven," he corrected her with: "You mean, my dear, that your physical sensations are somewhat easier". I can see her smile.

Mary Wollstonecraft—so we must always think of her for she had borne Godwin's name only a few months—died on September 10th, 1797, a few days after the birth of the child who was to become Mary Shelley.

Mary Wollstonecraft was a religious woman, who believed that life was a preparation for eternity and that marriage was a fundamental institution of society. To the modern reader *A Vindication of the Rights of Woman* will appear singularly unsubversive. Its thesis is the right of woman to develop and preserve a complete, mature and separate personality. From this position certain corollaries, never drawn out into a system —perhaps because the book was unfinished—necessarily follow: the natural companionship of boys and girls, the economic independence of women after marriage, access to the professions, specifically medicine, and ultimately direct representation in Parliament. In outline, it will be seen, she had sketched the women's programme of the later nineteenth century, but an initial obstacle had to be carried first, the dominant conception of the Attractive Girl, a conception which rested on a coarse and sentimental exaggeration of certain secondary sexual qualities, sensibility, fragility and reserve, qualities which doubtless always have been and always will be alluring to men, but which the current teaching of the day had systematized and inculcated as arts of capture. It is the "delicate female", the "lovely trembler", and the "Philosophy of lasciviousness" that rouse her anger and contempt. Her strongest invective is directed against the Sophie of Rousseau, and, after Rousseau, Dr. Gregory's *Legacy to his Daughters*, and the *Sermons* of Dr. Fordyce, which Lydia Languish found so useful: nor does Milton's Eve escape her mockery. "'Educate women like men,' says Rousseau, 'and the more they resemble our sex the less power will they have over us.' This is the very point I aim at. I do not want them to have power over men, but over ourselves." And, after quoting Rousseau's description of the dress which his sophisticated savage should affect, "only put in its proper order to be taken to pieces by imagination," she asks, "Is this modesty? Is this a preparation for immortality?" Dr. Gregory had recommended his daughters to conceal any intelligence they might happen to possess:

567

Be ever cautious in displaying your good sense. It will be thought you assume a superiority over the rest of the company. But if you happen to have any learning, keep it a profound secret, especially from the men, who generally look with a jealous and malignant eye on a woman of great parts and a cultivated understanding.

To Mary Wollstonecraft "ripeness is all".

In the countenance of girls we only look for vivacity and bashful modesty; but, the spring-tide over, we look for soberer sense in the face, and for traces of passion, instead of the dimples of animal spirits; expecting to see individuality of character, the only fastener of the affections. We then wish to converse, not to fondle, to give scope to our imaginations as well as to the sensations of our hearts.

She insisted not only that every woman should have a Room of her Own—and it was in quite a handsome room in Store Street, Bedford Square, that she entertained M. Talleyrand, the unworthy recipient of her Dedication—she must have a face of her own. Like Balzac she maintained that no woman can have a physiognomy before she is thirty.

The French, who admit more of mind into their notions of beauty, give the preference to women of thirty. I mean to say that they allow women to be in their most perfect state, when vivacity gives place to reason, and to that majestic seriousness of character, which marks maturity.

The beautiful and expressive face in the National Portrait Gallery, painted by Opie, proves that at thirty-five she had no reason to envy the charms of twenty: Amelia Alderson, who became later the artist's wife, wrote that all first sights to which she looked forward had disappointed her "except those of Mrs. Imlay and the Cumberland Lakes". It is a face, too, without any trace of what George Eliot calls "that most disagreeable of all monsters, a blue stocking—a monster that can only exist in a miserably false state of society, in which a woman with but a smattering of learning or philosophy is classed along with singing mice or card-playing pigs". She can pay a warm tribute to Mrs. Macaulay's learning, but her concern is for the ordinary woman: the exceptional woman can look after herself. Madame de Stael was quite content that the bulk of her sex should conform to the canons of Rousseau; Hannah More, who had made up her mind not to read the *Vindication,* expressed her opinion that "there is perhaps no animal so much indebted to subordination for its good behaviour, as woman". Mary Wollstonecraft belonged to the aristocratic tradition of reformers who "love the people well", and descend from their eminence to champion their inferiors.

To minimize the place of sexual passion in married life is no part of her philosophy. She felt the disgust of the natural healthy woman for Dr. Gregory's advice that a wife should stimulate her husband's appetite and prolong his pursuit by an assumed frigidity. There is much psychological astuteness in her remark: "A man, or woman, of any feeling, must always wish to convince a beloved object that it is the caresses of the individual, not the sex, that are received and returned with pleasure; and, that the heart, rather than the senses, is moved. Without this natural delicacy, love becomes a selfish personal gratification that soon degrades the character." But passion will not last, and the woman must keep her husband's affections not by lascivious cunning, but by friendship and companionship.

The security of marriage allowing the fever of love to subside, a healthy temperature is thought insipid, only by those who have not sufficient intellect to substitute the calm tenderness of friendship, the confidence of respect, instead of blind admiration, and the sensual emotions of fondness.

But if a woman is to be a good wife, a good mother, or indeed a good widow, competent to fulfil her responsibilities towards her husband's children, her education as a girl must be directed to reason and not to sensibility. Blind obedience to parents, engendering a selfish prudence, is the worst preparation for life; experience and independence, even though likely enough to be attended by error and sorrow, can alone build up character: "most of the women," she says, "in the circle of my observation, who have acted like rational creatures, or shown any vigour of intellect, have accidentally been allowed to run wild." Her own experience, both as governess and as schoolmistress, had convinced her that drastic reform of educational methods was essential both for boys and girls. During a short visit to some friends at Eton she had been scandalized by the moral tone of the school, especially by the half-guinea fine which ensured the boys' attendance at the Communion service. She emphasizes the advantages of close association between the sexes in youth as conducive to early marriage, of which she is a strong advocate, and marriage likely to be based on intimacy and affection. Her ideas are as ever democratic, and might well startle an age whose high priestess, Hannah More, thought that every one should read the Bible and her own tracts to learn contentment and duty, but reassured her anxious bishop with the words: "I allow of no writing for the poor." "Day schools, for particular ages, should be established by government, in which boys and girls might be educated together. The school for the younger children, from five to nine years of age, ought to be absolutely free and open to all classes." They were to be taught botany, mechanics, astronomy, reading, writing, arithmetic, natural

history and simple experiments in natural philosophy, varied
by open air gymnastics. "The elements of religion, history,
the history of man, and politics, might also be taught by
conversations, in the Socratic form." At nine those intended
for domestic employment and trades should be removed to
other schools, working together in the mornings, but receiving
the necessary special instruction separately in the afternoons.
Children, cleverer or better off, should attend other schools,
boys and girls still together, where they could learn languages,
classical and modern, science, literature, history and politics.
She would have no more *coming out* for girls, "which, in other
words, is to bring to market a marriageable miss, whose
person is taken from one public place to another, richly
caparisoned." The universities she ignores: "young people
of fortune" should remain, more or less, at school until they
are of age, but in the later years they are to be allowed dancing,
music, and drawing, together with attendance three or four
mornings a week at schools which will fit them for their
chosen professions.

Perhaps Mary Wollstonecraft, happy in her equal intercourse
with Joseph Johnson and his friends, and shocked by the
folly and ignorance of most women she met, underrated the
male objections to advanced education for women, though
she quotes with indignation a writer who denied that women
could be taught botany "consistently with female delicacy".
Well, we remember a much later story of a professor who
continued his lecture "Now the *ladies* have left the room",
some *women* having persisted in their intention to learn about
the sexual habits of butterflies. We remember the long struggle
before the medical profession was opened to women—and
even now, from time to time a woman may be heard murmur-
ing from the *Pilgrim's Scrip*, without apologies to Sir Austin
Feverel, "I expect that Man will be the last thing civilized by
Woman."

Among Mary Wollstonecraft's *Posthumous Works* is an unfinished novel, *The Wrongs of Women*, showing the conditions of society from which the *Vindication* was intended to deliver them. It is a gloomy fragment, unreadable now save for a measure of autobiographic significance. But her cause was safe in the hands of the greatest of women novelists. No thought of woman's rights or wrongs ever ruffled the serene surface of Jane Austen's mind, but the artist is usually on the side of the gods, especially when unaware that there is any controversy, and of Mary Wollstonecraft's main thesis she has been the most effective exponent. Elizabeth Darcy, who teased her husband, Elinor, Emma and Jane Fairfax are all complete and rational personalities: the mature individuality of Anne Elliot has been a "fastener of the affections" for over a century, and the world will be the poorer if it loses its hold.

The *Vindication* was widely read, but the time was hardly favourable for the judicial consideration of new ideas. Horace Walpole promptly dubbed the author a "hyena in petticoats". He had not read the book, he told Hannah More: the fact that she had borrowed her title from the demon, Tom Paine, was enough to excommunicate her from the pale of his library. And Mrs. West in her *Letters addressed to a Young Man on his first entrance into Life and adapted to the peculiar circumstances of the present Times* warns her dear Thomas that:

Among the writers whose extravagant doctrines have not only been published in this country, but circulated with uncommon avidity, loaded with extravagant praise, transfused into a thousand shapes, and insinuated into every recess, the name of Mary Wollstonecraft has obtained a *lamentable* distinction. . . . From those writings I extract the following sentiments: "Who would dare coolly to maintain, that it is just to deprive a woman of her rights of citizenship, and to treat her as an outcast of society, because her revolting soul spurns the tyrannical power of a husband whom she can neither love nor respect, and flies to the protection of a kindred mind? This is one of those prejudices in the present state of society which blast the promise of life." I will make no other comment on this passage than an earnest prayer, that neither you nor I may ever live to see this *prejudice* removed.

"Who can tell," wrote Mary Wollstonecraft, "how many generations may be necessary to give vigour to the virtue and talents of the freed posterity of abject slaves?" And again —"Men of genius and talent have started out of a class, in which women have never yet been placed." What would her verdict be could she return to earth for a space? Would she feel assured that woman's individuality was really developing? A uniform mask of emancipation and efficiency would please her as little as a fluttering diversity of vapid faces. But hopefulness would prevail when she considered how much of her ideal had been realized, and we may think of her in the words of William Blake, as one who kept the Divine Vision in time of trouble.

41

KEATS AND SHELLEY
(1795-1821 : 1792-1822)

by STEPHEN SPENDER

THESE names have been bracketed together for over a century: too late now to protest that it is difficult to imagine two writers, contemporaries acquainted with each other, who were more different. Whilst there were no resemblances, yet their lives, as also their deaths, ran strangely parallel. Public imagination is struck by these facts: that both enjoyed a posthumous fame, being neglected while they were living, by the literary world; both died young; both were wanderers, Keats taking England, Scotland and Ireland, with the last sad pilgrimage to Rome, as the theatre of his travels, Shelley, Italy: each was unfortunate in his relations with women, though Shelley, whose femininity was pathological, spent much time in women's company, whereas Keats, who was sexually normal but afraid of women, chose the society of men. In the neglect they endured, in the restrictedness of their personal lives over-shadowed by certain financial anxieties, they seem like two angles at the base of an isosceles triangle whose dazzling apex is Lord Byron.

On the few occasions when they met, they did not like or understand each other. Before Keats had published any

574

book, they walked across Hampstead Heath, Shelley earnestly recommending him not to publish his "first blights". Keats did not forget this. Did he resent it? At all events, to use his own words, he returned the advice on Shelley's hands. Writing of *Prometheus Unbound,* before it appeared, he said: "Could I have my own wish effected, you would have it still in manuscript, or be now putting an end to the second act." "Poor Shelley," he cracks to his brother George, "I think he has his Quota of good qualities, in sooth la!" Shelley was critical of *Endymion:* Keats seems to have associated his captiousness with that of Leigh Hunt, the friend about whom, in his letters, he is most consistently spiteful: "he and Shelley are hurt, and perhaps justly, at my not having showed them the affair officiously and from several hints I have had they appear much disposed to dissect and anatomize any trip or slip I may have made." Shelley's judgment was more generous. When Keats was ill, he warmly invited him to stay at Pisa. After his death he wrote *Adonais,* a poem which, while showing no understanding of Keats as a man, is a tribute to genius; and the appearance of Chatterton among the mourners would have pleased Keats.

A comparison of the characters of these two men would be pointless, simply because there is nothing to compare. They are opposites; where Keats had virtues, Shelley had faults; where Shelley has the generosity, the unselfish egotism, the spiritual eloquence and the political vision of the prophet, Keats seems unconfident and small. One was tall and shrieked with a gaiety that showed no humour: the other was small, modest, observant, courageous, humorous, a cockney who knew he had the power to converse with genius in its own language. Shelley's Hellenism, his love of Italy, of boats, of the sea, of writing in woods, are carried to a point of enthusiasm which seems German rather than English; equally, Keats's desire to escape to green fields from the "city din", to "sit upon an alp as on a throne", to hear the nightingale in a Hampstead garden, have the moving but slightly absurd romanticism of the born Londoner. It is no wonder they did not get on; in writing about them one cannot compare, one can only set the brilliant patches of the one against the darkness of the other, using each as a foil in turn.

Apart from all differences of character, they were divided, as by a wall, by irreconcilable theories of the function and nature of poetry. Shelley's poetry tends towards an art which is in the widest sense political: that is to say it is concerned with the beliefs of those members of society who genuinely desire justice and liberty for the whole of society, hating superstition. His mind was set on a path where politics becomes morals.

Shelley believed that poetry was about a world outside the poetry itself, whereas to Keats poetry was simply about poetry, so that his poetry refers one back not to an observed world but to a trance-like state of mind, a classical mythology, Shakespeare, Boccaccio, or, in *Hyperion*, Milton. Immersed in Greek as Shelley was, and although he achieved effects of "pure" poetry as striking as those of Keats, he endeavoured to refer his readers to moral impulses of their own natures and to palpable examples of tyranny and injustice in the contemporary world. His aims were stated frequently and clearly: "Poets are the unacknowledged legislators of the world;" thus, for moral ideas. "We want the creative faculty to imagine that which we know; we want the generous impulse to act that which we imagine; we want the poetry of life: our calculations have outrun conception; we have eaten more than we can digest"; thus for his own age and the sense in which we should observe and understand the contemporary world. In the preface to *Prometheus Unbound*, the problems of the kind of poetry which he wrote are stated, as though for the poets of the future, with clarity: "Let this opportunity be conceded to me of acknowledging that I have, what a Scotch philosopher

characteristically terms, 'a passion for reforming the world.' . . .
But it is a mistake to suppose that I dedicate my poetical compositions solely to the direct enforcement of reform, or that I
consider them in any degree as containing a reasoned system on
the theory of human life. Didactic poetry is my abhorrence;
nothing can be equally well expressed in prose that is not
tedious and supererogatory in verse. My purpose has hitherto
been simply to familiarize the highly refined imagination of
the more select classes of poetical readers with beautiful
idealisms of moral excellence; aware that until the mind can
love, and admire, and trust, and hope, and endure, reasoned
principles of conduct are seeds cast upon the highway of life
which the unconscious passenger tramples into dust, although
they would bear the harvest of his happiness."

Because Shelley wished the world to be changed, his
contemporaries accused him of writing propaganda. His
defence is, in effect, that he endeavours to re-create in his
poetry moral-political impulses that are already latent in the
human mind: it is true, of course, that these passions, if they
are made to glow by the poetry, may transform the lives of
his readers, making them desire to change the world. The
passion for justice is not negative; it has a positive effect on
the mind which reaches outside itself to other minds and
towards the future. When Aristotle claimed that tragedy
purged the mind with pity and terror, did he mean anything
so very different from this? Did he not imply that pity and
terror would effect the future life and will of the spectator?

So that Shelley's theory of poetry was positive; one can
see how it led him to repent of the crudities of political expression in *Queen Mab* (much of which could be expressed
better in prose); how it fixed the symbolism of his imagery;
how in *Prometheus Unbound* he attempted a synthesis of the
ancient with the modern world; how in *The Triumph of Life*,
the stage to which all this was leading would have been

achieved in a vision at once contemporary and applicable to any time. This is only one aspect of Shelley, but it is that in which one can trace the clearest development.

Keats had need to write no *Defence of Poetry*. For poetry existed in its own right and came to the poet as naturally as leaves to a tree. "I never wrote one single Line of Poetry with the least Shadow of public thought." "I have not the slightest feeling of humility towards the public—or to anything in existence—but the eternal Being, the principle of Beauty, and the Memory of great Men." One morning when he had composed, he wrote to Reynolds of relapsing into "those abstractions which are my only life".

Poetry, then, was the element from which Keats's spiritual being breathed. Impossible here to distinguish between the poetry which he read and that which he wrote, for his reading in Shakespeare, Chatterton and Milton was part of the same creative process as his own writing. What follows though, is that if he breathed poetry, he did not breathe the same air as his fellow men. He shared their world not in his verse but in his letters, which give one a vivid enough picture of literary gossip in Hampstead, that depressing suburb dominated by the puns and critical pronouncements of Leigh Hunt. Keats was left-wing in his politics, and his poet's intuition helped him in life; the more so, perhaps, because his opinions were so dissociated from his poetry. He was an acute observer, remarking in 1818: "Notwithstanding the part which the liberals take in the Cause of Napoleon, I cannot but think he has done more harm to the Life of Liberty than anyone else could have done." As one reads on in these letters, one is struck by a growing sense of the writer's disillusion. We realize that Keats was disappointed in his circle of friends: Hunt, Dilke, Reynolds, Haydon; one by one they prove to be ordinary men. They do not betray him: they simply fail to be part of the "eternal Being".

When one has absorbed Keats's factual life—with all its brightness and courageous smallness—from his letters, one cannot then transfer one's attention to his poetry and find that reading of life again, illuminated and better proportioned. For Keats does not *say* anything in his poetry: since when we speak of a poet saying something in poetry we mean that he translates and re-lives life in terms of poetry: thus everything is said by Shelley in his poetry, whose letters have little or nothing more to tell us. Keats, in his poetry, shed his factual life and lived another life in which he was companioned by Shakespeare and the memories of great men.

Middleton Murry, in that intuitive book *Keats and Shakespeare*, has shown how completely absorbed Keats was in the world of Shakespeare. Even in his letters the Shakespearian theme is constantly appearing: when he is emotionally wrought up or "in a rant", a spasmodic, intense utterance broken only by dashes of the pen, replaces his usual twinkling quietness and recalls the irony underlying tragedy of the prose passages in *Hamlet*. His courage, his fantasy, his out-bursts of self-regarding heroic humour, his impulses of dramatic self-pity, are all Shakespearian.

The theme culminates in a famous passage of a letter to Richard Woodhouse: "As to the poetical character itself (I mean that sort, of which, if I am anything, I am a member; that sort distinguished from the Wordsworthian, or egoistical Sublime; which is a thing per se, and stands alone), it is not itself—it has no self—it is everything and nothing—it has no character—it enjoys light and shade; it lives in gusto, be it foul or fair, high or low, rich or poor, mean or elevated—it has as much delight in conceiving an Iago as an Imogen. What shocks the virtuous philosopher delights the chameleon poet . . . A poet . . . is certainly the most unpoetical of all God's creatures." Add to this the earlier passage in which he discusses that quality which "Shakespeare possessed so enormously—I mean *Negative Capability*, that is when a man is capable of being in uncertainties, mysteries, doubts, without an irritable reaching after fact and reason"; then one sees that in these two passages Keats has outlined the peculiar poetic territory on which he meets Shakespeare.

Keats's intuition of the nature of the poetic temperament is profoundly true and even throws light into the mind of Shakespeare: he is expressing in heightened language what Shelley also meant when he wrote "one great poet is a master-piece of nature which another not only ought to study but must study". Yet Shelley, with a twist that should please Marxists, gave the poet an historical setting, whilst refusing to isolate him from other artists and thinkers: "Poets, not other-wise than philosophers, painters, sculptors and musicians, are in one sense, the creators, and in another, the creations of their age." To Keats, the poet is the creation of objects and sensations: to Shelley he is the creation of his age. Thus the isolation of Keats is romantic; the isolation of Shelley is an accident of history, which foreshadows another age in which Shelley might find his classical historic setting.

The fact that Keats did not see himself as a contemporary, while it may seem to many his timeless asset, seems to me the central defect of his poetry. At a first glance, it may appear absurd to suggest that a poet who had so much self-knowledge may not have been, to the last degree of analysis in his work, self-critical. But was he? His awareness of the failures in *Endymion*, his despair at the Miltonics of *Hyperion*, go to prove he was. Yet did he not allow himself to become absorbed, to the point of losing his poetical identity, in the world of poetic experience created by Shakespeare? Is there not, even in the letters, a slight blur over his remarks about poetry, so that when he discusses Shakespeare, he is, more deeply than he knows, thinking about himself? When he writes of himself, does he not sometimes assume the attributes of Shakespeare?

On occasions he is in that state of mind which Proust describes of the artist who, in order to encourage himself, con-
fuses in his mind some passage of his own with a page of some
great writer. A writer as great as Keats does this, not to flatter
himself, but to sacrifice at some greater altar his artistic
independence.

In his poetry Keats escaped from the world of his contemporaries and became the contemporary of Shakespeare:
not in the sense that he was (like Beddoes) an Elizabethan,
but in the sense that, spiritually, he existed on Shakespeare's
poetry. His own idea of what he was doing is expressed in the
passages which I have quoted: he was exercising Negative
Capability. Yet here one has to protest that in choosing thus
to live in Shakespeare's poetry, he was behaving in a very
un-Shakespearian way; because although Shakespeare projected that world of invention which is timeless in so far as
it is available to us and has not been ruined or moss-grown in
the gulf of time between Shakespeare and us, yet, in a sense
that Keats certainly was not, Shakespeare himself was a
contemporary. To imply that because Shakespeare expresses
none, or few, moral, religious, political or philosophical
opinions, he therefore only reflects a constantly transforming
identity, is to admit too much; for what his poetry undeniably
states is his own extraordinary development and the life of his
time. In short, Shakespeare used as material for his poetry
the stuff of life as he knew and experienced it, which was precisely what, in his own environment, Keats, for the purposes of
making poetry, rejected. Shakespeare's spiritual home was not
Chaucer, nor Plutarch; if Keats had been in the profoundest
sense Shakespearian, the stuff of his letters, which certainly is
very living material, the suburban life of Wentworth Place
(now Keats Grove), the entertainments provided by Hunt,
would have been material for his epics and poetic drama.

The result of Keats's absorption by Shakespeare combined

with his aversion from contemporary or public matters, his determination always to aim at the most universal subject, is that his fame, great as it is, rests not on the broad outlines, but on the minutiæ of the poetry which he planned. His two long poems, the foundations of his life-work, are admittedly failures; the later and greater of the poems, is also the greater failure, which gives one some idea that when he chose the subjects of *Endymion* and *Hyperion,* he was proceeding in a very wrong direction. In all literature there can be few landscapes where it is so difficult to see the wood for the trees as in *Endymion*; yet the trees, the undergrowth, the pavilions, the strange excitements and encounters in that aimless forest finally make the very confusion an end in itself and there is a peculiar charm in wandering down these paths that may lead anywhere or nowhere. The confusion of *Endymion* does not make it "bad art", for since one's expectations of a consistent structure are never raised, one is never disappointed. The poem too has consistency of texture: it is all equally bosky. As a whole it is unreadable, but that does not matter much, because one can sample it at any point with equal enjoyment.

Endymion with its burrs and shrubs has an innocence that never cloys. *Lamia, Isabella* and the *Eve of St. Agnes* are not innocent and they do cloy. Here again, in our admiration we miss the effects Keats aimed at. We admire instead the detail, the lines of pure poetry, the pre-Raphaelite atmosphere, a narrative skill curiously like an exquisite performance of a sonata, and, above all, not a deep animal or tragic sensuality, as in Shakespeare or Donne, but a pervading light lasciviousness, as though Keats saw everything through his lips. The opening of *Hyperion* is magnificent, but the interest of the poem dies away almost immediately. "I have given up *Hyperion*— there were too many Miltonic inversions in it." The Miltonic inversions do not explain the contrast between the magnificence of the opening, and the rest: the lack of interest does. Keats's passion for a really poetic and unephemeral subject had once more betrayed him: his fund of classical allusions is soon exhausted, and the poetry, through being too much insisted on, would not come.

So that, with almost every other reader of Keats, I have to fall back on half a dozen sonnets and the odes, to find complete satisfaction. Here Keats is recording a mood, re-creating the experience of a few moments: he writes from the deepest centre of what interests him and for a few lines the hermetically sealed wall which divides the life he lived in his poetry from the life described in his letters, is penetrated, when the two lives become fused into one. Without the letters and without the odes Keats's poetry would still reveal genius: but it would seem the genius of an automatic prodigy like Chatterton.

The most superstitious, and I think silly, of Goethe's remarks was his saying that no great genius dies until his life's work has been fulfilled. To me it seems obvious that Keats and Shelley died before either had fully solved the central problem of his art. Keats's problem was to break down the barrier that divided his life into two streams: to find the subject for a long poem which he was able to refresh with the stream of his life as a contemporary.

Shelley's problem was different. It was, primarily, to imagine, to re-create, in poetry, that which he knew. His knowledge rejected the time in which he lived and accepted the poetry and philosophy of Greece. Therefore in order to imagine, to invent images of this knowledge, he projected in the future "a brighter Hellas".

The classical poet derives fundamental moral values from the accepted precepts of his own age. He is the very kernel of his time, reflecting the principles which support the court or the republic. The romantic poet, who rejects these principles, is either completely isolated in a world of his own which

becomes progressively more incomprehensible to his contemporaries (when poetry becomes entirely "pure" or when
all jokes are private); or he is faced with the prodigious task
of imagining a new order, a new world-background embody-
ing values which he accepts. Shelley chose this latter alternative. I may add that whichever path the poet sets out on,
as his imagination strengthens, his isolation becomes exaggerated, so that this isolation may finally merge him in
depressive mania or death; consider the madness of Hölderlin;
and that despair of all the values of existence which obsessed
both Shelley and Keats in the last weeks of their lives.

Naturally a poet cannot invent in his poetry a factual world
outside, which conditions that poetry. So that Shelley's
failures are inevitable. The world in which he lives he treats
as past history: he imagines himself in the future where men
are free, where there is equality between the sexes, where
there are no slaves nor tyrants. This habit of looking back
on his present existence resulted in personal tragedy. Unfortunately, at different times, he persuaded two women to
share with him the domestic freedom of the future: the present
asserted itself so that after the first marriage Harriet committed
suicide, after the second, Shelley himself lost all desire to go
on living.

In his poetry one notices that the symbols which refer to
tyranny and injustice are over-simplified, because they are
seen in the light of a historic perspective which Shelley invented for himself. "Fear, hatred, faith and tyranny"; when
these names are uttered in his poetry, we seem to have reached
a blank wall beyond which we cannot penetrate: opposite
that blank wall of evil is one equally blank of good:

> And behold, thrones were kingless, and men walked
> One with the other, even as spirits do.
> None fawned, none trampled; hate, disdain or fear,

KEATS AND SHELLEY

Self-love or self-contempt, on human brows
No more inscribed, as o'er the gate of hell
"Abandon hope, ye who enter here".

In such lines reality withers because certain types of human behaviour are asserted as absolute: the tyrant is absolutely bad, the free man is absolutely good.

Since Shelley's work has, particularly in its weaknesses, a social bearing, his critics have attacked him on the grounds that these passages prove him to have been an adolescent visionary whose ideas for "saving humanity" can only appeal to adolescents: so that whilst his ideas are used to discredit Shelley, Shelley's name is also used to discredit socialist ideas. This is a confused view which would never have been offered had not Shelley been interested in improving humanity.

The German romantic poet, Hölderlin, provides an interesting parallel to Shelley: in Hölderlin's poetry, directly Greece or the gods are mentioned, a blank wall seems to have been reached, beyond which it is impossible to go. However beautiful it may be, we are forced to recognize this language as that of dead, flat assertion: to Hölderlin ancient Greece is absolutely good and the modern world absolutely evil:

Aber Freund! wir kommen zu spät. Zwar leben die Götter,
Aber über dem Haupt droben in anderer Welt.
Endlos wirken sie da und scheinens wenig zu achten,
Ob wir leben, so sehr schonen die Himmlischen uns.

Yet Hölderlin, because he did not believe in liberating contemporary humanity, is not open to the same sneers as Shelley: nor to the silence with which even Shelley's admirers are able to dismiss his "ineffectual" ideas.

No one who has read Shelley's prefaces, nor his lyrical

poems, nor the biographical sketches of Peacock, Trelawney and Mary Shelley, nor the lyrical poems, is justified in dismissing his mind as that of an adolescent. It seems to me that the explanation of failures in Shelley and Hölderlin is the same. It is that in these flat passages in which they assert absolute values they are exploring boundaries of their isolation beyond which they have not the knowledge to penetrate. Unlike Keats, who rejoiced in his isolation, they are both unwilling romantics; possibly they are classical poets born in an age whose values they reject. The implication of Hölderlin's work is that if he had been born in classical Greece his poetry would be complete; of Shelley's, that if he had been born after the change that will eventually transform society, the outlines of his characterization would be filled in. The premises on which both their lives are founded are fragmentary, so their work too is necessarily incomplete.

Thus Hölderlin cannot explore the defects of the Greek gods; he can only project an absolute belief in the gods and an acceptance of beauty as the conditions in which he could have released, in its completeness, his poetic energy. Shelley does not probe into the faults of the inhabitants of this transformed society: since these men do not exist, he is not concerned in pointing out that human nature is, and will always remain, human nature; he is creating a mythology to outline the social conditions in which he could, as a part of the whole movement of society, create. It is absurd to pretend that Shelley imagined that men when free would have no faults; but he did think that when they were free they would be able to enjoy the "poetry of life"; his poems were not an account of ordinary men, but of that poetry which all men might one day live. Since the society he envisaged did not exist, he was frustrated; instead of being a poet within that society, he saw it as something he could not reach, a condition of being that was not his environment but his postulate. Since he did not believe in gods, kings, or wealth, a changed society became to him the primary good.

In the light of what has happened since, it is easy to dismiss the romantic poets with scorn or surface admiration, or ecstasies that have no understanding. To do so is to deny their historic role. They lived and wrote *before* the cataclysms which have taken place since. Because the material disaster which followed on the industrial revolution had not taken place, their protest is an emotional and idealist one against the ideas of their time. They appeal against material values to values of the mind, to the creative imagination, to the "eternal Being" and to the "memory of great men". Different as their approaches were, that appeal, where it is explicit in Shelley, is implicit in Keats, in many of whose letters it even attains expression. The romantics failed. But the ideas which Shelley stated are as living now as they were when he died. The difference is that we live after, instead of before, the disasters of the century that divides us from Keats and Shelley: the weapons of our poetry must be different from theirs.

42

THE DUKE OF WELLINGTON

(1769-1852)

by Major-General J. F. C. Fuller

IN so brief a memoir as this, it is not easy to do justice to so great a man as Arthur Wellesley, Duke of Wellington, for his was a long life and a full one. Not only did it cover the whole of those tremendous years 1789-1848 (the greatest war in history until 1914 and the greatest revolution until the present age emerged) but for nearly fifty years his personality was a dominant factor in Europe. This being so, I think it will be both more just to him and more profitable to the reader if I avoid encyclopædic methods, and, instead, examine him in such a way that we may discover what manner of man he was.

Fourth son of the first Earl of Mornington, he was born in 1769, the same year as Napoleon, probably on May 1st,* yet the date is uncertain, as it was also in the case of his great opponent. Of his boyhood not much is known outside that he had a liking for music and that his mother thought so little of him that to her he was "food for powder and nothing more". Partly educated in France he was gazetted to the 73rd Foot in 1787; became a Lieut.-Colonel in 1793, a Major-General in 1802,

---

*Wellington claims this date as his birthday, and on May 1st, 1850, he stood sponsor to H.R.H. the Duke of Connaught.

a Lieut.-General in 1808, a General in 1811, and Field Marshal in 1813. This rapid rise in rank was due as much to his parentage as to his abilities; for, without the first, the second would have been of little avail in a man of humbler birth.

In stature he was of middle height, slight and wiry; his face was rather long, his eyes a cold grey and his nose aquiline: "the sight of it among us," wrote Sir John Kincaid during the Peninsular War, "was worth ten thousand men any day of the week"; also his soldiers used to say: "Arty, that long-nosed——that licks the Parleyvoos!" Physically his endurance was amazing, and this was no doubt in part due to his simple way of living. He ate and drank little. . . . "We dined on rations; no wine and no money!" wrote one of his officers in 1812. He slept on a twenty-inch camp-bed, and could sleep at any time and in any place. At the battle of Salamanca he said to his A.D.C.: "Watch the French, Fitzroy, I am going to take a rest; when they reach that gap in the hills wake me," and a minute later he was asleep. He was practical in his dress and simple in his requirements; one of his officers says: "I suppose no army ever had less baggage," and another: "We had no unnecessary drilling, nor were we tormented by that greatest of all bores . . . uniformity of dress." So little did he worry over it, that he saw nothing peculiar in General Picton riding at the head of his troops carrying "a huge white umbrella lined with green".

Inwardly he was even more remarkable: first and foremost, and this is the key to his character, to his successes and his failures, his virtues and his vices—he was a believer in the divine right of blue blood. In short, he was an aristocrat to his finger tips; nevertheless he loathed ostentation and outward show. Possessed of a profound sense of duty, he was autocratic and dictatorial and was never able to suffer fools gladly. Outspoken to a degree, he made many enemies and few friends, except among women, and even then, should they show a lack of breeding, he could freeze them up with such remarks as: "Publish, and be damned!" A voluminous writer and a profound student of war, he cultivated an unshakable self-confidence and control. He was never elated by success or depressed by failure, yet I feel that his chief assets lay in his power of bearing responsibility, in his integrity, moral courage and his profound common sense. Humbug and sycophancy he simply could not tolerate. When quite an old man, once a gentleman assisted him across Piccadilly, and whilst with hat in hand he expressed in fulsome words the honour done to him, in reply all the thanks he received was: "Don't be a damned fool, Sir!" This realism was reinforced by an acute sense of humour. Thus, when he fought his famous duel in Battersea Fields with Lord Winchilsea, directly that gentleman arrived he turned round to his second, Sir Henry Hardinge, and said: "Look sharp and step out the ground. I have no time to waste. Damn it!" he continued, "don't stick him up so near the ditch. If I hit him he will tumble in." Yet I like best his reply, when he was told that General Cambronne had exclaimed: "La garde meurt, mais ne se rend pas!" Looking at a group of elderly Brussels cocottes, known as "la vieille garde", he replied: "Elles ne meurent pas et se rendent toujours!" But sometimes he could be bitingly sarcastic. For instance, in 1815, when at the Court of the Tuileries some of Napoleon's generals, who had become Royalists, turned their backs upon him, and Louis XVIII attempted to excuse their rudeness, his Majesty received the following reply: "Sire, ils sont si accoutumés à me tourner le dos, qu'ils n'en ont pas encore perdu l'habitude!"

Such was Wellington, a man of outstanding personality who saw his first active service in the Netherlands in 1794; a poor beginning, for there, as he said some time afterwards, "I learnt what one ought *not* to do, and that is always something." Three years later he went to India, where his brother, the second Earl of Mornington, was Governor-General. It was to him that Pitt once said concerning his brother Arthur: "I never met any military officer with whom it is so satisfactory to converse. He states every difficulty before he undertakes any service, but none after he has undertaken it." There he remained eight years and saw much active service. During the invasion of Mysore he was repulsed in a night attack, after which he resolved "never to attack by night a post which had not been reconnoitred by day". In 1803, he won the battles of Assaye and Argaum and, in 1805, returned to England putting into St. Helena on the way; of which he wrote: "The island is beautiful, and the climate apparently the most healthy I have ever lived in." Perhaps ten years later, when Napoleon was a prisoner, he remembered that visit.

In 1807, he commanded a division in the Copenhagen campaign and the following year was placed in command of an expedition to Portugal. Landing at Mondego Bay, in August, he at once assumed the offensive, won the combat of Roliça on the seventeenth and the battle of Vimeiro on the twenty-first, during which he was superseded by two incompetent generals—Sir Harry Burrard and Sir Hew Dalrymple. This led to the Convention of Cintra and, on account of the storm it raised in England, in all probability, had it not been for the good services of Castlereagh, Wellington's career as a soldier would have come to an end.

Urging upon the Government to continue operations in Portugal and Spain, in 1809 he was appointed to lead a new expedition, and before taking over his command he placed before Castlereagh an appreciation entitled "Memorandum on the Defence of Portugal", which Sir Charles Oman, the historian of the Peninsular War, rightly acclaims to be "a marvel of prophetic genius", for in it he predicted the whole course of the six years' campaign. He stated that the war would be a long one and that his task was to keep it going as long as possible, and that ambitious schemes should be set aside. Further, that by using Portugal as a fortress supplied by the sea, with no more than 30,000 men backed by Portuguese levies he would be able to operate against the flank of the French armies in Spain, and by paralysing them gain time for the Spaniards to develop a formidable guerilla war on their communications.

Such was his plan, yet what were the means at his disposal? When, on April 27th, he took over command of the British military fragments in Portugal, in all some 22,000 strong, the situation which faced him was as follows: Of commissariat there was practically none; there was no siege train, no ammunition columns, no ambulances and no pontoons. The men were in a bad state of discipline; many of his officers disloyal; the staff inexperienced; the cavalry very weak and the artillery totally inadequate and drawn by oxen. What did he do? By sheer force of will he shook these fragments into an army, concentrated at Coimbra and, on May 12th, crossed the Douro, occupied Oporto and pushing deep into Spain, on July 27th and 28th won the battle of Talavera.

That he was able to carry out such a campaign, as brilliant as Napoleon's of 1796, as well as the many others which were to follow it, was due to his long-sighted calculations and his faculty for judging the characters of his opponents. He was always observing them, and at Talavera was nearly captured whilst doing so. On another occasion, when on a reconnaissance, seeing Soult in the distance he said: "I had an excellent glass: I saw him spying at us—then write and send off a letter: I knew what he would be writing, and gave my orders accordingly."

As a strategist, few generals have possessed so clear and calculating a brain as Wellington's. Not only could he weigh up space and time factors with extreme accuracy, but above all he realized how Nelson's victory at Trafalgar could be exploited on land. Once he said: "All the business of war, and indeed all the business of life, is to endeavour to find out what you don't know by what you do!" And it was because he was so careful a student of men and of events, that he saw that the main problem of this war was one of lines of communication and supplies, not of numbers of fighting men, and that here England held the trump card—command of the sea. Of his strategical undertakings, it has always seemed to me that his masterpiece was his planning of the Torres Vedras campaign. This he thought out a full year in advance, as he did his move on Badajoz in 1812. Though Masséna did not appear before the famous lines which protected Lisbon until October 14th, 1810, he had ordered their construction on October 26th, 1809. Foreseeing that Napoleon would reinforce his armies in Spain, and that, when this happened, the British army would be compelled to retire, he built the lines of Torres Vedras, and ordered that the neighbouring country should be devastated, so that, whilst the fortifications protected his men, Masséna would be "attacked" by starvation. This is what actually happened, the French were starved out of Portugal and the road to Spain was opened. Then, in 1811, the battles of Fuentes de Onoro and Albuera were fought, in 1812 Ciudad Rodrigo and Badajoz stormed and the battle of Salamanca won. Lastly, during 1813 and 1814 the campaigns of Vitoria and the Pyrenees successfully ended by carrying the war out of Spain into France.

Though throughout this most difficult of wars Wellington's foresight never failed him, it is strange that in his last campaign, the most decisive he ever fought, namely that of Waterloo, he was caught napping. Undoubtedly he misjudged the Royalist strength in France, and was deceived as to the nature of Napoleon's movements. Yet, also, I think that there were too many attractive women in Brussels at the time, for on June 13th, 1815, we learn that, when Napoleon was but thirty or forty miles away "he took Lady Jane Lennox to Enghien for the cricket match . . . apparently having gone for no other object but to amuse her". And it is somewhat instructive to find him at 3 a.m. on the nineteenth, that is on the morning immediately following the battle, writing to Lady Frances Webster, "a very pretty woman," to tell her she might remain in Brussels "in perfect safety". Anyhow, according to the Duke of Richmond, late on the fifteenth, during the famous ball given by his wife, Wellington said to him: "Napoleon has *humbugged* me, by G——! he has gained twenty-four hours' march on me," which he certainly had done; but was it he who had done the humbugging?

As a strategist Wellington was a truly great artist, because he possessed the faculty of being able to combine foresight with common sense, consequently he never allowed his imagination to run away with his reason. Upon this foundation he built his tactics, and here again the same mental process is to be seen at work, for, unlike most Generals, he did not merely accept his army as a fighting instrument, but instead he measured up its powers and limitations and devised his tactics accordingly. As an aristocrat he stood apart from his men. He disdainfully looked upon them as a potential rabble and called them "the scum of the earth". Nor was he altogether wrong. For instance, when, in the winter of 1813-1814, the French peasants refused to accept Spanish dollars and English guineas, deciding to set up a mint, Wellington appealed to his colonels to find him professional coiners, whereupon forty were produced! Often has he been blamed for his cynical outlook; yet, in my opinion, he was justified, because whenever his men got out of hand, as they did at Ciudad Rodrigo and Badajoz, they behaved like fiends.

Though at times he could deal leniently with desertion, plundering he would never tolerate, not only because, as an aristocrat, it offended his dignity to allow hardships to be inflicted upon the common people, but also because it led to a relaxation of discipline and so impaired the fighting power of his army. It was for these reasons that his discipline was so severe and at times brutal. There are ten recorded cases of 1,200 lashes and fifty of 1,000 being given, and up to 500 was a common punishment. Yet, whatever we may think to-day of such brutality, it must not be overlooked that the age was a brutal one, also that, tactically speaking, brutality paid. It was not the kindly generals, such as Sir John Moore, who succeeded, but men like Wellington and Craufurd. Once, when a Commissary of the Light Division complained that Craufurd had threatened to hang him if supplies were not punctually delivered, Wellington replied: "Then I advise you to have them up in time. For Craufurd is just the man to keep his word." Further, it should be remembered that Wellington's system did succeed in fashioning an army which, in 1813 he said: "could go anywhere and do anything." Also he said: "There is but one way—to do as I did—to have a hand of iron."

With his officers he was the same, for he realized that most of them were grossly ignorant. In consequence he demanded of them implicit and blind obedience. Yet it is interesting to note that, when he dealt with men like Hill and Graham, he gave direct orders; nevertheless with those like Craufurd and Picton, intelligent and independent characters, he generally added the reason why a certain course was to be adopted.

In spite of the fact that until near the close of the Peninsular War his army was almost always outnumbered by the French, as I have mentioned, he was not one of those generals who saw strength numerically, but instead in relationship to bread and beef. That is to say, he realized that a small army which could be adequately fed was tactically superior to a larger army which was reduced to foraging. As Sir Charles Oman says: "Wellington's salvation lay in the fact that he could

hold his entire army together, while his adversaries could not."
Even more clearly than Napoleon did he realize that "an
army marches upon its belly"; in other words, that there is
a definite relationship between bread and bullets.

His army being small, he was compelled to be prudent;
yet it is a great mistake to consider, as many have done, that
he was no more than a cautious general. Though a master in
defensive war, he could, when conditions were favourable,
be audacious in the extreme, as he was at Assaye and Argaum
in 1803, in the Vimiero and Talavera campaigns, and in his
stormings of Ciudad Rodrigo and Badajoz. His Fabian tactics
were sheer common sense: when conditions demanded prudence, he was prudent, and when they did not he could strike
like a thunderbolt.

Besides adequacy of supply, few generals have understood
the ingredients of tactics so thoroughly as he did. He grasped
the limitations of the musket of his day, that it was a deadly
weapon at point-blank range, yet next to useless at a distance;
he realized that the dominant characteristics of the English
soldier were steadiness and stolidity, and that the French
soldiers did not possess them, therefore he could risk meeting
column by two-deep line, which meant that he could multiply
his fire power at least fourfold. In order to protect his men
and also to mystify his enemy, he seldom failed to make the
fullest use of cover by ground. Because of this, at Vimiero,
Junot was completely deceived, and, at Busaco, Masséna
mistook the British centre for its right. At Salamanca it was
the same, so also was it at Waterloo. At Quatre Bras, General
Reille, a veteran of the Spanish Wars, needlessly halted before
a position held by a single Dutch-Belgian division, because
as he thought and said: "Ce pourrait bien être une bataille
d'Espagne—les troupes Anglaises se montreraient quand il
en serait temps."

Though I should like to enter more fully into the detail

of his tactics, it is not possible to do so here; in the main they were of a defensive-offensive order, that is to say, Wellington encouraged the enemy to attack, and, when in confusion, under cover of the smoke cloud of his muskets, he attacked him in turn. He seldom massed his guns, not only because he seldom had a sufficiency of them, but because his line tactics demanded artillery dispersion and not concentration. Also, he seldom pursued a defeated foe, because his cavalry was weak and indifferent; he said himself: "They could gallop, but could not preserve their order." One remaining fact must, however, be mentioned, for, combined with his use of ground, it raised him to the position of a supreme tactical artist. It was that he saw everything for himself, relying only upon secondhand information when it was impossible for him to do otherwise. As he said: "The real reason why I succeeded . . . is because I was always on the spot—I saw everything, and did everything for myself." Probably the most noted instance of this was at Salamanca. He was "stumping about munching" his breakfast, when an A.D.C. came hurrying in and said: "The enemy are in motion, my lord" . . . "Very well—Observe what they are doing," he replied. In came the A.D.C. again: "I think they are extending to the left!" . . . "The devil they are!" remarked Wellington. "Give me the glass." Taking it he scanned the moving French columns for about a minute and then exclaimed: "Come! I think that'll do! Ride off and tell Clinton and Leith to return to their former ground." Next, ordering up his horse and closing his telescope with a snap, he turned to his Spanish A.D.C. and said: "Mon cher Alava, Marmont est perdu!" . . . and he was. At Waterloo his tactics made good his strategical lapse, not forgetting the rain, "it seemed as if the water were tumbled out of tubs"—a greater assistance to him even than Blücher.

After the war he remained the same as he always had been

—an exalted individualist, and because his aristocratic outlook ran counter to the rising democratic spirit of the age, it has been customary, as a statesman, to write him down as a failure. Instead, was not it his amazing foresight, his vision almost prophetic in its clearness, which showed him whither this spirit would lead? And now, to-day, are not events justifying it? A failure he may have been during his short premiership of 1827-1830; yet a failure from which to-day much wisdom may be learned.

As a statesman his limiting factor was his contempt for the common people. Once he said: "I always had a horror of revolutionizing any country for a political object. I always said—if they rise of themselves, well and good, but do not stir them up; it is a fearful responsibility". Therefore he was fervently anti-democratic. He did not believe in "the collective wisdom of individual ignorances", as Carlyle put it. He had no faith in the theory that Members of Parliament should be elected, as he said, "to obey the daily instructions of their constituents, and be cashiered if they should disobey them"; because he considered that such a system of government would kill "the race of English gentlemen".

Long before this, when in India, he had urged his brother, the Governor General, to re-establish the native princes after they had been defeated, and why? Because he realized that, in India, bureaucracy or democracy spelt ruin. In 1815, he prevented the dismemberment of France, so that, as he said: "We do not leave the world in the same unfortunate situation respecting France that it would have been in if Bonaparte had continued in possession of his power". His object was "to put an end to the French Revolution" and not to humiliate a great nation. It was he who, in 1820, put forward a memorandum which led to the foundation of the London Police, because he was insistent upon the maintenance of law and order. It was he, and almost he alone, who forced Catholic Emancipation through the Commons and the Lords, in spite of the fact that he was a Tory of the Tories. He did it because he realized that, unless it were done, civil war would break out in Ireland. He opposed Parliamentary Reform, because he considered it would lead to a slackening of authority and the strengthening of mob opinion. He believed that the best of all systems was what he called "la Democratie Royale"—as much autocracy and as little democracy as possible. Once he exclaimed to Lady Salisbury, when she expressed her apprehension of a split in the party: "The party! what is the meaning of a party if they don't follow their leaders? Damn 'em! let 'em go!" And Lord Clarendon once said of him: "Oh, that will be simple enough. He'll say, 'My lords! Attention! Right about face! Quick march!' and the thing will be done."

It is true that he was an indifferent politician, because he was a great leader of men, and not a follower of public opinion. He cared nothing for popularity. Again, he was never a Parliamentarian. As leader of the Lords, in 1834, he wrote to Lord Londonderry: "I do not choose to be the Person to excite a quarrel between the two House of Parlt. This quarrel will occur in its time; and the House of Lords will probably be overwhelmed." He wrote thus, because he never held the opinion that the chief duty of the Opposition was to oppose. In 1838, to Lord Redesdale he wrote: "There is nobody who dislikes, so much as I do, and who knows so little of Party Management. . . . That which I cannot and will not do is to become Party to any vote which is to involve the Honor of the Country or that of the House of which I am a Member . . . if I am to act it must be according to my own opinions."

He lived long enough to witness the democratic revolution of 1848 and to discern therein a menace to honesty and efficiency in government. He died peacefully on September 14th, 1852, and though Disraeli described him as "the sovereign

master of duty", I would prefer to call him "the last of the
great aristocrats"; a man who, it seems to me, will be better
understood and appreciated by his countrymen a generation
hence, than he was in his day or still is in ours.

43

BYRON

(1788-1824)

by T. S. Eliot

THE facts of a large part of Byron's life have been well set forth, in the last few years, by Mr. Nicolson and Mr. Quennell; who have also provided interpretations which accord with each other and which make the character of Byron more intelligible to the present generation. No such interpretation has yet been offered in our time for Byron's verse. In and out of universities, Wordsworth, Coleridge, Shelley and Keats have been discussed from various points of view: Byron and Scott have been left in peace. Yet Byron, at least, would seem the most nearly equally remote from the sympathies of every living critic: it would be interesting, therefore, if we could have half a dozen essays about him, to see what agreement could be reached. The present article is an attempt to start that ball rolling.

There are several initial difficulties. It is difficult to return critically to a poet whose poetry was—I suppose it was for many of our contemporaries, except those who are too young to have read any of the poetry of that period—the first boyhood enthusiasm. To be told anecdotes of one's childhood by an elderly relative is usually tedious; and a return, after many years, to the poetry of Byron is accompanied by a similar gloom: images come before the mind, and the recollection of some verses in the manner of *Don Juan*, tinged with that disillusion and cynicism only possible at the age of sixteen, which appeared in a school periodical. There are more impersonal obstacles to overcome. The bulk of Byron's poetry is distressing, in proportion to its quality; one would suppose that he never destroyed anything. Yet bulk is inevitable in a poet of Byron's type; and the absence of the destructive element in his composition indicates the kind of interest, and the kind of lack of interest, that he took in poetry. We have come to expect poetry to be something very concentrated, something distilled; but if Byron had distilled his verse, there would have been nothing whatever left. When we see exactly what he was doing, we can see that he did it as well as it can be done. With most of his shorter poems, one feels that he was doing something that Tom Moore could do as well or better; in his longer poems, he did something that no one else has ever equalled.

It is sometimes desirable to approach the work of a poet completely out of favour, by an unfamiliar avenue. If my avenue to Byron is a road that exists only for my own mind, I shall be corrected by other critics: it may at all events upset prejudice and encourage opinion to form itself anew. I therefore suggest considering Byron as a Scottish poet—I say "Scottish", not "Scots", as a reminder that he wrote in English. The one poet of his time with whom he could be considered to be in competition, and one of whom he spoke invariably with the highest respect, was Sir Walter Scott. Possibly Byron, who must have thought of himself as an English poet, was the more Scotch of the two because of being unconscious of his true nationality. I have always seen, or imagined that I saw, in busts of the two poets, a certain resemblance in the shape of the head. The comparison does honour to Byron, and when you examine the two faces, there is no further resemblance. Were one a person who liked to have busts about, a bust of Scott would be something one could live with. There is an air of nobility about that head, an air of magnanimity, and of that inner and perhaps unconscious serenity that belongs to great writers who are also great men. But Byron—that pudgy face suggesting a tendency to corpulence, that weakly sensual mouth, that restless triviality of expression, and worst of all that blind look of the self-conscious beauty; the bust of Byron is that of a man who was every inch the touring tragedian. Yet it was by being so thorough-going an actor that Byron arrived at a kind of knowledge: of the world outside, which he had to learn something about in order to play his rôle in it, and of that part of himself which was his rôle. Superficial knowledge, of course: but accurate so far as it went.

Of a Scottish quality in Byron's poetry, I shall speak when I come to *Don Juan*. But there is a very important part of the Byronic make-up which may appropriately be mentioned before considering his poetry, for which I think his Scottish antecedence provided the material. That is his peculiar diabolism, his delight in posing as a damned creature—and in providing evidence for his damnation in a rather horrifying way. Now, the diabolism of Byron is very different from anything that the Romantic Agony (as Mr. Praz calls it) produced in Catholic countries. And I do not think it is easily derived from the comfortable compromise between Christianity and paganism current in England and characteristically English. It could come only from the religious background provided by a nation which had been ruined by religion. It was a monstrosity, of course, for Scotland to bring forth; but it could come only from a people who took religion more seriously than the English.

Byron's diabolism, if indeed it deserves the name, was of

a mixed type. He shared, to some extent, Shelley's Promethean attitude, and the Romantic passion for Liberty; and this passion, which inspired his more political outbursts, combined with the image of himself as a man of action to bring about the Greek adventure, in which he could not be said to be wholly insincere. And his Promethean attitude merges into a Satanic (Miltonic) attitude. The romantic conception of Milton's Satan is semi-Promethean, and also contemplates Pride as a *virtue*. It would be difficult to say whether Byron was a proud man, or a man who liked to pose as a proud man—the possibility of the two attitudes being combined in the same person does not make them any less dissimilar in the abstract. Byron was certainly a vain man, in quite simple ways:

> I can't complain, whose ancestors are there,
>   Erneis, Radulphus—eight-and-forty manors
> (If that my memory doth not greatly err)
>   Were their reward for following Billy's banners . . .

His sense of damnation was also mitigated by a touch of unreality: to a man so occupied with himself and with the figure he was cutting nothing outside could be altogether real. It is therefore impossible to make out of his diabolism anything coherent or rational. He was able to have it both ways, it seems; and to think of himself both as an individual isolated and superior to other men because of his innate daring evil, and as a naturally good and generous nature distorted by the crimes committed against it by others. It is this inconsistent creature that turns up as the Giaour, the Corsair, Lara, Manfred and Cain; only as Don Juan does he get nearer to the truth about himself. But in this strange composition of attitudes and beliefs the element that seems to me most real and deep is that of a perversion of the Calvinist faith of his Scottish ancestors.

BYRON

One reason for the neglect of Byron is, I think, that he has been admired for what are his most ambitious attempts to be poetic; and these attempts turn out, on examination, to be fake: nothing but sonorous affirmations of the commonplace with no depth of significance. A good specimen of such imposture is the well-known stanza at the end of Canto XV of *Don Juan*:

> Between two worlds life hovers like a star,
>   'Twixt night and morn, upon the horizon's verge.
> How little do we know that which we are!
>   How less what we may be! The eternal surge
> Of time and tide rolls on, and bears afar
>   Our bubbles; as the old burst, new emerge,
> Lashed from the foam of ages; while the graves
> Of empire heave but like some passing waves.

verses which are not too good for the school magazine. Byron's real excellence is on a different level from this.

The qualities of narrative verse which are found in *Don Juan* are no less remarkable in the earlier tales. Before undertaking this essay I had not read these tales since the days of my schoolboy infatuation, and I approached them with apprehension. They are, however, extremely readable. However absurd we find their view of life, they are, as tales, extremely well told. As a *tale-teller* we must rate Byron very high indeed: I can think of none other since Chaucer who has an equal readability, with the exception of Coleridge whom Byron abused and from whom Byron learned a great deal. And Coleridge never attempted narratives of such length. Byron's plots, if they deserve that name, are extremely simple. What makes the tales interesting is first a torrential fluency of verse and a skill in varying it from time to time to avoid monotony; and second a genius for divagation. Digression, indeed, is one of the valuable arts of the story-teller. The effect of Byron's digressions is to keep us interested in the story-teller himself, and through this interest to interest us more in the story. On contemporary readers this interest must have been strong to the point of enchantment; for even still, once we submit ourselves to the point of reading a poem through, the attraction of the personality is powerful. Any few lines, if quoted in almost any company, will probably provide a momentary twitch of merriment:

> Her eye's dark charm 'twere vain to tell,
> But gaze on that of the Gazelle,
> It will assist thy fancy well;
> As large, as languishingly dark,
> But Soul beam'd forth in every spark. . . .

but the poem as a whole can keep one's attention. *The Giaour* is a long poem, and the plot is very simple, though not always easy to follow. A Christian, presumably a Greek, has managed, by some means of which we are not told, to scrape acquaintance with a young woman who belonged to the harem, or was perhaps the favourite wife, of a Moslem named Hassan. In the endeavour to escape with her Christian lover Leila is recaptured and killed; in due course the Christian with some of his friends ambushes and kills Hassan. We subsequently discover that the story of this vendetta—or part of it— is being told by the Giaour himself to an elderly priest, by way of making his confession. It is a singular kind of confession, because the Giaour seems anything but penitent, and makes quite clear that although he has sinned, it is not really by his own fault. He seems impelled rather by the same motive as the Ancient Mariner, than by any desire for absolution—which could hardly have been given: but the device has its use in providing a small complication to the story.

As I have said, it is not altogether easy to discover what happened. The beginning is a long apostrophe to the vanished
glory of Greece, a theme which Byron could vary with great
skill. The Giaour makes a dramatic entrance:

> Who thundering comes on blackest steed,
> With slackened bit and hoof of speed?

and we are given a glimpse of him through a Moslem eye:

> Though young and pale, that sallow front
> Is scathed by fiery passion's brunt. . . .

which is enough to tell us, that the Giaour is an interesting
person, because he is Lord Byron himself, perhaps. Then there
is a long passage about the desolation of Hassan's house,
inhabited only by the spider, the bat, the owl, the wild-dog
and weeds; we infer that the poet has skipped on to the conclusion of the tale, and that we are to expect the Giaour to kill
Hassan—which is of course what happens. Not Joseph
Conrad could be more roundabout. Then a bundle is privily
dropped into the water, and we suspect it to be the body of
Leila. Then follows a reflective passage meditating in succession on Beauty, the Mind, and Remorse. Leila turns up again,
alive, for a moment; but this is another dislocation of the
order of events. Then we witness the surprise of Hassan and
his train—this may have been months or even years after
Leila's death—by the Giaour and his banditti, and there is no
doubt but that Hassan is killed.

> Fall'n Hassan lies—his unclosed eye
> Yet lowering on his enemy. . . .

Then comes a delightful change of metre, as well as a sudden
transition, just at the moment when it is needed.

The browsing camels' bells are tinkling:
His mother look'd from her lattice high—
She saw the dews of eve besprinkling
The pasture green beneath her eye,
She saw the planets faintly twinkling:
" 'Tis twilight—sure his train is nigh."

Then follows a sort of exequy for Hassan, evidently spoken
by another Moslem. Now the Giaour reappears, nine years
later, in a monastery, as we hear one of the monks answering
an inquiry about the visitor's identity. In what capacity the
Giaour has attached himself to the monastery is not clear; the
monks seem to have accepted him without investigation, and
his behaviour among them is very odd; but we are told that
he has given the monastery a considerable sum of money for
the privilege of staying there. The conclusion of the poem
consists of the Giaour's confession to one of the monks. Why
a Greek of that period should have been so oppressed with
remorse (although wholly impenitent) for killing a Moslem
in what he would have considered a fair fight, or why Leila
should have been guilty in leaving a husband or master to
whom she was presumably united without her consent, are
questions that we cannot answer.

I have considered *The Giaour* in some detail in order to
exhibit Byron's extraordinary native ingenuity in story-telling.
There is nothing straightforward about the telling of the
simple tale; we are not told everything that we should like to
know; and the behaviour of the protagonists is sometimes as
unaccountable as their motives and feelings are confused.
Yet the author not only gets away with it, but gets away with
it *as narrative*. It is the same gift that Byron was to turn to
better account in *Don Juan*; and the first reason why *Don
Juan* is still readable is that it has the same narrative quality
as the earlier tales.

BYRON

It is, I think, worth noting, that Byron developed the verse *conte* considerably beyond Moore and Scott, if we are to see his popularity as anything more than public caprice or the attraction of a cleverly exploited personality. These elements enter into it, certainly. But first of all, Byron's verse tales represent a more mature stage of this transient form than Scott's, as Scott's represent a more mature stage than Moore's. Moore's *Lalla Rookh* is a mere sequence of tales joined together by a ponderous prose account of the circumstances of their narration (modelled upon the *Arabian Nights*). Scott perfected a straightforward story with the type of plot which he was to employ in his novels. Byron combined exoticism with actuality, and developed most effectively the use of *suspense*. I think also that the versification of Byron is the ablest: but in this kind of verse it is necessary to read at length if one is to form an impression, and relative merit cannot be shown by quotation. To identify any passage at random as being by Byron or by Moore would be connoisseurship beyond my powers; but I think that anyone who had recently read Byron's tales would agree that the following passage could not be by him:

> And oh! to see the unburied heaps
> On which the lonely moonlight sleeps—
> The very vultures turn away,
> And sicken at so foul a prey!
> Only the fierce hyaena stalks
> Throughout the city's desolate walks
> At midnight, and his carnage plies—
> Woe to the half-dead wretch, who meets
> The glaring of those large blue eyes
> Amid the darkness of the streets!

This is from *Lalla Rookh*, and was marked as if with approval by some reader of the London Library.

Childe Harold seems to me inferior to this group of poems (*The Giaour*, *The Bride of Abydos*, *The Corsair*, *Lara*, etc.) because of the slightness of the narrative. Time and time again, to be sure, Byron awakens fading interest by a purple passage, but Byron's purple passages are never good enough to do the work that is expected of them in *Childe Harold*.

Stop! for thy tread is on an Empire's dust

is just what is wanted to revive interest, at that point; but the stanza that follows, on the Battle of Waterloo, seems to me quite false; and quite representative of the falsity in which Byron takes refuge whenever he *tries* to write poetry.

Stop! for thy tread is on an Empire's dust!
An Earthquake's spoil is sepulchred below!
Is the spot mark'd with no colossal bust?
Nor column trophied for triumphal show?
None; but the moral's truth tells simpler so,
As the ground was before, so let it be;—
How that red rain hath made the harvest grow!
And is this all the world has gained by thee,
Thou first and last of fields! king-making victory?

It is all the more difficult, in a period which has rather lost the appreciation of the kind of virtues to be found in Byron's poetry, to analyse accurately his faults and vices. We abominate the commonplace, we expect profundity—though often satisfied by the appearance without the reality—we are suspicious of anything immediately intelligible, we demand an insurgence of the unconscious, and we are patiently prepared to be bored. Hence we fail to give credit to Byron for the instinctive art by which, in a poem like *Childe Harold*, and still more efficiently in *Beppo* or *Don Juan*, he avoids monotony by a dexterous turn from one subject to another. He has the cardinal virtue of being never dull. But, when we have admitted the existence of forgotten virtues, we still recognize a falsity in most of those passages which were formerly most admired. To what is this falsity due?

Whatever it is, in Byron's poetry, that is "wrong", we should be mistaken in calling it *rhetoric*. Too many things have been collected under that name; and if we are going to think that we have accounted for Byron's verse by calling it "rhetorical", then we are bound to avoid using that adjective about Milton and Dryden, about both of whom (in their very different kinds) we seem to be saying something that has meaning, when we speak of their "rhetoric". Their failures, when they fail, are of a higher kind than Byron's success, when he succeeds. Each had a strongly individual idiom, and a sense of language; at their worst, they have an interest in the *word*. You can recognize them in the single line, and can say: here is a particular way of using the language. There is no such individuality in the line of Byron. If one looks at the few single lines, from the Waterloo passage in *Childe Harold*, which may pass for "familiar quotations", you cannot say that any of them is great poetry:

> And all went merry as a marriage bell. . . .
> On with the dance! let joy be unconfined. . . .

Of Byron one can say, as of no other English poet of his eminence, that he added nothing to the language, that he discovered nothing in the sounds, and developed nothing in the meaning, of individual words. I cannot think of any other poet of his distinction who might so easily have been an accomplished foreigner writing English. The ordinary person *talks* English, but only a few people in every generation can write it; and upon this undeliberate collaboration between a great many people talking a living language and a very few people writing it, the continuance and maintenance of a language depends. Just as an artisan who can talk English beautifully while about his work or in a public bar, may compose a letter painfully written in a dead language bearing some resemblance to a newspaper leader, and decorated with words like "maelstrom" and "pandemonium": so does Byron write a dead or dying language.

This imperceptiveness of Byron to the English word—so that he has to use a great many words before we become aware of him—indicates for practical purposes a defective sensibility. I say "for practical purposes" because I am concerned with the sensibility in his poetry, not with his private life; for if a writer has not the language in which to express feelings they might as well not exist. We do not even need to compare his account of Waterloo with that of Stendhal to feel the lack of minute particulars; but it is worth remarking that the prose sensibility of Stendhal, being sensibility, has some value of poetry that Byron completely misses. Byron did for the language very much what the leader writers of our journals are doing day by day. I think that this failure is much more important than the platitude of his intermittent philosophizing. Every poet has uttered platitudes, every poet has said things that have been said before. It is not the weakness of the ideas, but the schoolboy command of the language, that makes his lines seem trite and his thought shallow:

Mais que Hugo aussi était dans tout ce peuple. The words of Péguy have kept drifting through my mind while I have been thinking of Byron:

Non pas vers qui chantent dans la mémoire, mais vers qui dans la mémoire sonnent et retentissent comme une fanfare, vibrants, trépidants, sonnant comme une fanfare, sonnant comme une charge, tambour éternel, et qui battra dans les mémoires françaises longtemps après que les réglementaires tambours auront cessé de battre au front des régiments.

But Byron was not "in this people", either of London or of England, and the most stirring stanza of his Waterloo is this:

> And wild and high the "Cameron's gathering" rose!
> The war-note of Lochiel, which Albyn's hills
> Have heard, and heard, too, have her Saxon foes;—
> How in the noon of night that pibroch thrills,
> Savage and shrill! But with the breath which fills
> Their mountain-pipe, so fill the mountaineers
> With the fierce native daring which instils
> The stirring memory of a thousand years,
> And Evan's, Donald's fame rings in each clansman's ears!

All things worked together to make *Don Juan* the greatest of Byron's poems. The stanza that he borrowed from the Italian was admirably suited to enhance his merits and conceal his defects, just as on a horse or in the water he was more at ease than on foot. His ear was imperfect, and capable only of crude effects; and in this easy-going stanza, with its habitually feminine and occasionally triple endings, he seems always to be reminding us that he is not really trying very hard, and yet producing something as good or better than that of the solemn poets who take their verse-making more seriously. And Byron really is at his best when he is not trying too hard to be poetic; when he tries to be poetic in a few lines he produces things like the stanza I have already quoted, beginning:

> Between two worlds life hovers like a star.

But at a lower intensity, he gets a surprising range of effect. His genius for digression, for wandering away from his subject (usually to talk about himself) and suddenly returning to it, is, in *Don Juan*, at the height of its power. The continual banter and mockery, which his stanza and his Italian model serve to keep constantly in his mind, serve as an admirable antacid to the highfalutin which in the earlier romances tends to upset the reader's stomach; and his social satire helps to keep him to the objective and has a sincerity that is at least plausible if not profound. The portrait of himself comes much nearer to honesty than any that appears in his earlier work. This is worth examining in some detail.

Charles Du Bos, in his admirable *Byron et le besoin de la fatalité*, quotes a long passage of self-portraiture from *Lara*. Du Bos deserves full credit for recognizing its importance; and Byron deserves all the credit that Du Bos gives him for having written it. This passage strikes me also as a masterpiece of self-analysis, but of a self that is largely a deliberate fabrication—a fabrication that is only completed in the actual writing of the lines. The reason why Byron understood this self so well, is that it is largely his own invention; and it is only the self that he invented that he understood perfectly. If I am correct, one cannot help feeling pity and horror at the spectacle of a man devoting such gigantic energy and persistence to such a useless and petty purpose: though at the same time we must feel sympathy and humility in reflecting that it is a vice that we most of us are addicted to in a fitful and less persevering way; that is to say, Byron made a vocation out of what for most of us is an irregular weakness, and deserves a certain sad admiration for his degree of success. But in *Don Juan*, we get something much nearer to genuine self-revelation. For Juan, in spite of the brilliant qualities with which Byron invests him—so that he may hold his own among the English aristocracy—is not an heroic figure. There is nothing absurd about his presence of mind and courage during the shipwreck, or about his prowess in the Turkish wars: he exhibits a kind of physical courage and capacity for heroism which we are quite willing to attribute to Byron himself. But in the accounts of his relations with women, he is not made to appear heroic or even dignified; and these impress us as having an ingredient of the genuine as well as of the make-believe.

It is noticeable—and this confirms, I think, the view of Byron held by Mr. Peter Quennell—that in these love-episodes Juan always takes the passive rôle. Even Haidee, in spite of the innocence and ignorance of that child of nature, appears rather as the seducer than the seduced. This episode is the longest and most carefully elaborate of all the amorous passages, and I think it deserves pretty high marks. It is true that after Juan's earlier initiation by Donna Julia, we are hardly so credulous as to believe in the innocence attributed to him with Haidee; but this should not lead us to dismiss the description as false. The *innocence* of Juan is merely a substitute for the *passivity* of Byron; and if we restore the latter we can recognize in the account some authentic understanding of the human heart, and accept such lines as

> Alas! They were so young, so beautiful,
> So lonely, loving, helpless, and the hour
> Was that in which the heart is always full,
> And having o'er itself no further power,
> Prompts deeds eternity cannot annul. . . .

The lover of Donna Julia and of Haidee is just the man, we feel, to become subsequently the favourite of Catherine the Great—to introduce whom, one suspects, Byron had prepared himself by his eight months with the Countess of Oxford. And there remains, if not innocence, that strange passivity that has a curious resemblance to innocence.

Between the first and the second part of the poem, between Juan's adventures abroad and his adventures in England, there is a noticeable difference. In the first part the satire is

40

incidental; the action is picaresque, and of the best kind. Byron's invention never fails. The shipwreck, an episode too well known to quote, is something quite new and quite successful, even if it be somewhat overdone by the act of cannibalism in which it culminates. The last wild adventure occurs directly after Juan's arrival in England, when he is held up by footpads on the way to London; and here again, I think, in the obituary of the dead highwayman, is something new in English verse:

> He from the world had cut off a great man,
> Who in his time had made heroic bustle.
> Who in a row like Tom could lead the van,
> Booze in the ken, or at the spellken hustle?
> Who queer a flat? Who (spite of Bow-street's ban)
> On the high toby-spice so flash the muzzle?
> Who on a lark, with black-eyed Sal (his blowing),
> So prime, so swell, so nutty, and so knowing?

That is first-rate. It is not a bit like Crabbe, but it is rather suggestive of Burns.

The last four cantos are, unless I am greatly mistaken, the most substantial of the poem. To satirize humanity in general requires either a more genial talent than Byron's, such as that of Rabelais, or else a more profoundly tortured one, such as Swift's. But in the latter part of *Don Juan* Byron is concerned with an English scene, in which there was for him nothing romantic left; he is concerned with a restricted field that he had known well, and for the satirizing of which an acute personal animosity sharpened his powers of observation. His understanding may remain superficial, but it is precise. Quite possibly he undertook something that he would have been unable to carry to a successful conclusion; possibly there was needed, to complete the story of that monstrous house-party, some high spirits, some capacity for laughter, with which Byron was not endowed. He might have found it impossible to deal with that remarkable personage Aurora Raby, the most serious character of his invention, within the frame of his satire. Having invented a character too serious, in a way too real for the world he knew, he might have been compelled to reduce her to the size of one of his ordinary romantic heroines. But Lord Henry and Lady Adeline Amundeville are persons exactly on the level of Byron's capacity for understanding; and they have a reality for which their author has perhaps not received due credit.

What puts the last cantos of *Don Juan* at the head of Byron's works is, I think, that the subject matter gave him at last an adequate object for a genuine emotion. The emotion is hatred of hypocrisy; and if it was reinforced by more personal and petty feelings, the feelings of the man who as a boy had known the humiliation of shabby lodgings with an eccentric mother, who at fifteen had been clumsy and unattractive and unable to dance with Mary Chaworth, who remained oddly alien among the society that he knew so well—this mixture at the origin of his attitude towards English society only gives it greater intensity. And the hypocrisy of the world that he satirized was at the opposite extreme from his own. Hypocrite, indeed, except in the original sense of the word, is hardly the term for Byron. He was an actor who devoted immense trouble to *becoming* a rôle that he adopted; his superficiality was something that he created for himself. It is difficult, in considering Byron's poetry, not to be drawn into an analysis of the man: but much more attention has already been devoted to the man than to the poetry, and I prefer, within the limits of such an essay as this, to keep the latter in the foreground. My point is that Byron's satire upon English society, in the latter part of *Don Juan*, is something for which I can find no parallel in English literature. He was right in making the hero of his house-party a Spaniard, for what he understands and dislikes about English society is very much what an intelligent foreigner in the same position would understand and dislike.

One cannot leave *Don Juan* without calling attention to another part of it which emphasizes the difference between this poem and any other satire in English: the Dedicatory Verses. The Dedication to Southey seems to me one of the most exhilarating pieces of abuse in the language.

> Bob Southey! You're a poet—Poet Laureate,
> And representative of all the race;
> Although 'tis true that you turn'd out a Tory at
> Last, yours has lately been a common case;
> And now, my Epic Renegade! what are ye at? . . .

kept up without remission to the end of the seventeen stanzas. This is not the satire of Dryden, still less of Pope; it is perhaps more like Hall or Marston, but they are bunglers in comparison. This is not indeed English satire at all; it is really a *flyting*, and closer in feeling and intention to the satire of Dunbar:

> Lene larbar, loungeour, baith lowsy in lisk and lonye;
> Fy! skolderit skyn, thow art both skyre and skrumple;
> For he that rostit Lawrance had thy grunye,
> And he that hid Sanct Johnis ene with ane womple,
> And he that dang Sanct Augustine with ane rumple,
> Thy fowll front had, and he that Bartilmo flaid;
> The gallowis gaipis eftit thy graceles gruntill,
> As thow wald for ane haggeis, hungry gled.

To some this parallel may seem questionable, but to me it has brought a keener enjoyment, and I think a juster appreciation of Byron than I had before. I do not pretend that Byron is Villon (nor, for other reasons, do Dunbar or Burns equal the French poet), but I have come to find in him certain qualities, besides his abundance, that are too uncommon in

English poetry, as well as the absence of some vices that are too common. And his own vices seem to have twin virtues that closely resemble them. With his charlatanism, he has also an unusual frankness; with his pose, he is also a *poète contumace* in a solemn century; with his humbug and self-deception he has also a reckless raffish honesty; he is at once a vulgar patrician and a dignified toss-pot; with all his bogus diabolism and his vanity of pretending to disreputability, he is genuinely superstitious and disreputable. I am speaking of the qualities and defects visible in his work, and important in estimating his work: not of the private life, with which I am not concerned.

INDEX

INDEX

INDEX

INDEX

INDEX

INDEX

INDEX

INDEX